Economy and Interest

Economy and Interest

A New Presentation of the Fundamental Problems Related to the Economic Role of the Rate of Interest and Their Solutions

MAURICE ALLAIS

TRANSLATED BY
JOHN STEPHEN DALY
PREFACE TO THE AMERICAN
EDITION BY BERTRAND MUNIER

THE UNIVERSITY OF CHICAGO PRESS   CHICAGO AND LONDON

The University of Chicago Press, Chicago 60637
The University of Chicago Press, Ltd., London
Translation © 2024 by Christine Allais
Preface © 2024 by Bertrand Munier
Published 2024
Printed in the United States of America

33 32 31 30 29 28 27 26 25 24   1 2 3 4 5

ISBN-13: 978-0-226-82620-2 (cloth)
ISBN-13: 978-0-226-82621-9 (e-book)
DOI: https://doi.org/10.7208/chicago/9780226826219.001.0001

Originally published in French as *Economie et Intérêt* by Imprimerie Nationale, 1947. © The Estate of Maurice Allais.

This new edition of Maurice Allais's work *Economy and Interest*, translated into English for the first time, has been published with the support of the Maurice Allais Foundation under the aegis of the Mines Paris Foundation and the French Institute of International Relations (IFRI), as well as numerous individual contributors. Grateful thanks are extended to them all.

Library of Congress Cataloging-in-Publication Data

Names: Allais, Maurice, author. | Daly, John Stephen, translator. |
    Munier, Bertrand, writer of preface.
Title: Economy and interest : a new presentation of the fundamental
    problems related to the economic role of the rate of interest and their
    solutions / Maurice Allais ; translated by John Stephen Daly ; preface to
    the American edition by Bertrand Munier.
Other titles: Économie & intérêt. English
Description: Chicago ; London : The University of Chicago Press, 2024. |
    Includes bibliographical references and index.
Identifiers: LCCN 2023021451 | ISBN 9780226826202 (cloth) |
    ISBN 9780226826219 (ebook)
Subjects: LCSH: Interest. | Economics.
Classification: LCC HB539 .A413 2024 | DDC 332.8—dc23/eng/20230601
LC record available at https://lccn.loc.gov/2023021451

♾ This paper meets the requirements of ANSI/NISO Z39.48-1992 (Permanence of Paper).

This study is dedicated to IRVING FISHER,
to whom the theory of capital, income,
and the rate of interest is indebted for so much progress,
as a mark of my deep and respectful admiration.

Contents

Preface to the American Edition

Maurice Allais is a fountain of original and independent discoveries. . . . Had Allais' earliest writings been in English, a generation of economic theory would have taken a different course. — Paul Samuelson (1982, 164–65)

The book here presented for the first time in English is one of those that Paul Samuelson highlights in the above epigraph. It deserves to be counted as one of the landmarks of 20th-century economics, in the same way as Keynes's *The General Theory of Employment, Interest, and Money* or von Neumann and Morgenstern's *The Theory of Games and Economic Behavior*. It was originally published in 1947, the same year as Samuelson's *Foundations of Economic Theory*, but under very different conditions. In postwar France, paper was almost unobtainable, even for publishers, and the quest for theoretical foundations, even in the field of economics, was overshadowed by concerns more fundamental still. In fact, an 800-page work on economics and interest was hardly marketable at all. It could only be published by subscription as a sort of Wicksellian public good: interested parties were invited to make a modest contribution toward costs. Yet its pages channel a hard-to-rival array of startling ideas, identified only half a century later as major economic breakthroughs — some of which had meanwhile been inadvertently credited to other well-known authors. This translation thus makes available a goldmine to English-speaking readers interested in economics.

Beyond this immediate goal, it also aims to fill wider needs. In fact, even today the ideas presented in the first ten chapters have not all been taken advantage of, mainly because hitherto they have only been available to a readership at home with French. Former Nobel Committee member Ingemar Ståhl correctly assessed the situation when he wrote that Allais "offered a wealth of ideas, whose full exploitation could happen only long after their original publication in French," adding more specifically: "It may well be in the interests of young researchers to glean fruitful ideas, still unexploited, within the sheer goldmine of original views which Allais' work represents" (Ståhl 1988). And Edmond Malinvaud, one of the most distinguished French economists of the last century, echoes this insight, writing: "The work of a great scientist teems with far more rich resources than any one inquirer could ever turn to account. No doubt within [Allais's] work there remain treasures that have escaped my attention waiting for the day when others will discover them" (Malinvaud 1989). This volume opens a path for such new discoveries to be made by English-language readers.

Yet in one important sense, this book originated in the United States. Born into a very modest family, Maurice Allais won entrance to France's most prestigious establishments of higher education (first the École Polytechnique, then the École des Mines). As a graduate of the former, he accompanied his class to the United States in the early 1930s. The sight of queues at soup kitchens shocked young Maurice and branded itself on his memory. This gave rise to a deep-seated conviction that the economics of the day needed to be strongly questioned, and, though his formal training so far had been in high-level engineering, Allais decided to dedicate such time as he could spare to proposing potential improvements to this "dismal science." Just a few years later, having devoured a broad selection of the great authors then available, he conceived the gargantuan project of reconstructing economic theory on a more rigorous footing than anything he had read, while at the same time setting forth optimal policies for the avoidance of unemployment crises and the alleviation of poverty (Munier 1991, 1995). Allais was never a man for shortcuts or shirking any of the means imposed by scientific rigor. In his view, such a project would have to encompass embedded analyses of

1. pure economics, first of economies having simply a *unit of account*, then of economies having circulating money, in various environments of increasing complexity (initially in stationary and later in growing environments, under closed and then open situations), and would analyze every case, first using static, and later dynamic modeling;
2. institutional organizations at the root of real-world economies, simultaneously supporting and constraining "pure" behavior; and
3. "pure" normative economics as a basis for optimal economic policy in real-world economies.

As a start toward (1) above, 1943 saw the "publication"[1] of a 930-page book (*À la recherche d'une discipline économique* [In quest of an economic discipline])[2] reconstructing microeconomics from scratch in a highly rigorous and technically innovative way. But it soon became apparent that the abovementioned all-embracing project was unfeasible within a single lifetime: Allais would have to curtail somewhat the scope of his initial program. With this 1947 work, he endeavored to extend results from the previous book to an intertemporal framework—enriched with some institutional details to partially fulfill phase (2) of the initial project. The new book was also to offer a short summary of what might have emerged from phase (3). This background explains why the work translated here displays an unusual blend of genres, ranging from pedagogical explanations to groundbreaking research, from the simplest to the most sophisticated models, and finally to several aspects of policy recommendations intended for postwar Europe. As Boulding (1951) put it in an early review of the book, "Reading M. Allais is rather like going for a walk with a highly intelligent and active fox terrier. No alley is left unexplored and no rabbit unchased, even through several pages of footnotes. . . . However, there is such 'joie de vivre' in the performance that one can forgive a good deal of long-windedness. . . . Allais is a provocative and original thinker."

Readers approaching Allais's book in the spirit encouraged by Malinvaud and Ståhl rather than of Boulding's fox terrier may appreciate a few hints as to the topics Samuelson probably had in mind when evoking a possible "different course" for "an entire generation of economic theory" and even one or two tentative ideas as to what that course might have been.

With this in mind, before offering a short overview of the Allaisian vision of economics, we shall first briefly examine the book under four main headings:

1. Multi-agent modeling and interest rate equilibria
2. From welfare theory to behavioral economics
3. Monetary theory and general equilibrium
4. Economic policy

1. In fact, the text was mimeographed using a hand-operated stencil machine—a happy outcome in World War II France. A mere Xerox of the original mimeo appeared with a printed introduction in 1952 under the title *Traité d'économie pure* (A treatise on pure economics). Publication in our sense of the word took place only in 1998, with an additional preface and new appendixes, under the same title (Paris, Clément Juglar Press).

2. "A monumental volume into which, I confess, I have only dipped" (Boulding 1951).

Multi-agent modeling and interest rate equilibria

Economy and Interest departs sharply from the usual path macroeconomics had taken for decades—still often followed today. Allais was the first to discard the more or less implicit hypothesis of a "representative" agent, whether on the consumption or on the production side. He argues from the outset that macroeconomic models must take into account multiple agent types on each side, even though, for pedagogical reasons, he starts with stationary models comprising only consumers. His "fable of the fishermen" deserves close attention. It provides grounds for departing from the deeply rooted idea that the real interest rate is necessarily positive. Multiple agents with different preference types and the intricate network of their interactions lie at the heart of his astonishingly modern conclusions. Thus, in a barter economy, in which fishermen in different personal situations can only lend or borrow perishable fish and own no natural resource, the ex ante rate of interest depends on preferences that are discretionary, and a negative real rate of interest is perfectly conceivable. In the book's pages, the reader will find further reflections on possible lower limits to the interest rate, above or below zero. Allais submits that only specific historical reasons explain the common observation of a strictly positive real rate of interest. Recent experience shows how relevant these views turn out to be.

Further to this conclusion, the book also draws attention to the multiplicity of equilibria to be considered, even when multiple income distributions are disregarded (Grandmont 1989). Indeed, one of the text's major innovations is the idea of *overlapping generations* (OLG hereafter) within an economy. It can be subsumed under the generic idea of multiple agents. The rigorous analysis of OLG general equilibrium under various institutional assumptions is deferred to the lengthy appendix II (nos. 175–217),[3] though a very simple exposition of the idea is found in section number 175. Yet elsewhere models using different agent types, as opposed to models entailing only "representative" agents, were addressed only much later in the literature (Ramrattan and Szenberg 2011). Even in the limited case of "young" and "old" agents, modeling of this kind was so revolutionary in the late forties that nobody spotted its importance. OLG models were for a long time attributed to Paul Samuelson (1958), whereas Allais had in fact developed them eleven years earlier. The contributions of Allais and

---

3. Section numbers.

Samuelson simply bring to light different effects of the overlapping generation's structure, as Malinvaud (1987, 1995) has shown.

One can reflect on the very different path that economic analysis might have taken if these ideas and analyses had been available in English and widely disseminated in the late forties, from capital theory to optimal utility pricing or regarding monetary intervention and welfare economics. One can imagine the impact they would have had—much earlier than actually experienced—in the domains of retirement schemes and social security, in environmental sustainability, and more generally in general equilibrium analysis, beyond the account given 25 years after *Économie et intérêt* by Arrow and Hahn in their neoclassical *General Competitive Analysis* (1971). Recent examples in the first domain can be found in Tirole (1985), Drouhin (1997), Tosun (2003), Song (2008), and Nishimura (2011). What environmental studies might have become is convincingly argued by Pecchenino (1994). As for general equilibrium analysis, the highly insightful bridges built only in recent years (Geanakoplos 2008) between the Allais-Samuelson modeling and the Arrow-Debreu neoclassical vision could have blossomed much earlier. One can easily realize Peter Diamond's and Jean Tirole's amazement when they discovered in the mid-eighties that appendix II to *Économie et intérêt* contained proofs of the non-Ricardian equivalence of the public debt, the impact of the land rent on the increase of the interest rate, as well as the possible indetermination of the value of money (Tirole 2012).

From welfare theory to behavioral economics

There may be additional aspects to multiplicity of equilibria. In particular, standard theory considers that individuals maximize their utility S_0 as perceived *today*. But Allais stresses that even the usual meaning of perfect foresight by young individuals would not encompass the evolution of their preferences once they have become old and their utility has changed to S_1:

> In fact there is as much difference between satisfactions S_0 and S_1 of the same individual considered at two different times as between the satisfactions of two distinct individuals considered at the same time. They are magnitudes of a different nature, and they cannot be compared except by adopting an absolutely arbitrary convention. (no. 60)

Many economists would nowadays agree with such claims, as very recent contributions (e.g., Farhi and Gabaix 2020) demonstrate. This type of mathematical behavioral economics might have developed much earlier had Allais's contribution been more widely read. Meanwhile Allais took the view that Pareto's definition of optimality should be extended to take account of such evolutionary aspects of economic analysis. Equilibrium cannot be exclusively defined from the first period on, owing to the cognitive factors mentioned. Again, the same holds for the efficient interest rate. This is what Allais calls the *generalized* theory of social efficiency. Usual competition yields equilibria that are socially efficient only in the usual welfare sense, not in the generalized sense. The latter increases the number of optimal states of the economy. And it may be the responsibility of government to open the way, for ethical or political reasons, to optimal states of the economy that could not have been attained otherwise, in particular by adjusting the intertemporal distribution of income. Such specific government intervention, which may take place through institutions such as social security retirement schemes (e.g., compulsory pension plans for the young), works like "a simple catalyst in chemistry" (no. 65). This role of government amounts to opening people's minds to a better appraisal of what their future might be, based on past experience and on what their future preferences are most likely to be. This is part of Allais's view of what would today be subsumed under behavioral economics. This specific type of policy might be termed *tutelary intervention*. Its potential role extends to a number of very different situations, such as vaccination policies when confronting community health issues or, for instance, issues arising in certain pandemic scenarios. Without interventions of this type, Allais argues that a subset of competitive allocations can be shown to be inefficient. Malinvaud (1986, 1987) has provided a highly instructive exposition that the reader might want to look at before reading Allais's appendix II to this book.

Another gem can be found in chapter 7, which might have enabled economic theory to leap many years ahead in two different respects. The first has to do with capital accumulation in growth theory. While standard theory assumes that capital is a one-dimensional quantity, Allais argues that it should be viewed as subsets of factors introduced into the production process in a given sequence and that choosing the optimal sequence impacts interest rate equilibrium. Within the world of stationary economies, it turns out that the welfare-maximizing interest rate must be zero. This conclusion was misunderstood at the time, and several reviewers mocked it outright. Yet, it is the first rigorous proof—in the specific case of stationary economies—of what 15 years later came to be known in economics as the *golden rule of capital accumulation*,[4] very often credited to Phelps (1961).

The other aspect of the issue deals with the fundamentals of capital theory, more specifically with the idea that capital should not be viewed as a one-dimensional index. Had Allais's criticism been more closely considered, controversies such as the "two Cambridges debate" could have taken place much earlier than they actually did. One might conjecture that it would have led to similar conclusions, along the lines remarkably elaborated by Baqaee and Farhi (2018), but it would nevertheless have amounted to another gigantic stride forward for economic theory.

Monetary theory and general equilibrium

Monetary economies are considered in chapter 8, by far the longest chapter of the book. It should be regarded as an effort toward integrating a theory of money into equilibrium and disequilibrium theory. Hence its scope and size make it almost a book in itself. It starts rather classically with considerations about the two motives the author sees for holding money balances: the transaction motive is essential in Allais's view, while the speculative motive plays a secondary role. In section number 82 the reader may observe that the celebrated model attributed to Baumol (1952) is fully developed in note 12 and pursued somewhat further than had been done elsewhere in note 13. The model of the transaction demand for money is thus established in two footnotes of the book five years before Baumol, and the derived interest elasticity nearly ten years before Tobin (1956). Baumol and Tobin, when made aware of this, very graciously acknowledged it: "Maurice Allais' well-deserved Nobel Prize fortuitously brought to our attention an injustice inadvertently done him, to which we were unknowing accessories. For years the literature has ascribed to us the parentage of the transactions-cost model of optimal cash balances, with its notorious square-root formula derived from inventory theory. Recently, we found that its essence is contained in Allais' 1947 *Economie et Intérêt* (pp. 238–41)" (Baumol and Tobin 1989). A similar remark could be made

---

4. Fifteen years later, Allais (1962) was to generalize his theorem to the case of a growing economy, yielding at that point the standard version of the golden rule, whereby the interest rate has to match the growth rate. The initial case of stationary economies then turned out to be only the application of the rule to the specific situation of a zero rate of growth.

regarding a rather more detailed derivation of what later became known as the Gordon-Shapiro formula, credited to the latter authors in view of their 1956 paper (Gordon and Shapiro 1956).

A large part of chapter 8 is devoted to various macroeconomic aspects of monetary equilibrium and—even more interestingly—of the monetary dynamics of disequilibrium. The banking system is drawn to the reader's attention, and the chapter concludes that this system, which consists in leaving to private commercial banks (and to their clients) the capacity to create money, while endeavoring to regulate[5] their behavior via the central bank, is ineffective.[6] It should be stressed that several authors have come to similar conclusions, using various approaches, over the last 30 years. The different versions of such a system cannot prevent instability and give rise to boom-and-bust sequences. After reviewing so many cases as to strikingly recall Boulding's fox-terrier simile, Allais concludes in favor of a 100% money system (sometimes called "full reserve banking"), calling for a reorganization of the banking sector. It is well known that Allais does not have precedence in this respect, for several authors, notably Silvio Gesell (1906, 1958) and Irving Fisher (1935), had already reached similar conclusions.[7] Later on, Allais realized that, notwithstanding its length, chapter 8 was not really sufficient to make his points convincingly enough. Hence, he undertook—another part of the huge initial project!—to ground his views on disequilibrium in other writings of the 1950s and, moreover, to develop a detailed monetary theory on new psy-

5. In postwar France, this regulation resulted from the discount rate practiced by the central bank rather than from open market techniques as it does today, but the arguments presented are unaffected by that change in techniques, as Allais points out in note 19 to no. 108 and in the following pages.

6. Allais always stressed that in such systems, money creation essentially depends on both the commercial banks' willingness to lend and their clients' willingness to borrow, these propensities being in turn the expression of their respective expectations. The concept of psychological time yields behavioral grounds for what may be regarded as expectation formation.

7. It is, however, very interesting to note that Allais had only heard of the relevant paper by Fisher as well as of the translation into English of Gesell's book (note 6 to no. 161). This is simply explained by the post–World War II situation in Europe. The existence and importance of the latter book had been made known to him only through Keynes's *General Theory*. Allais realized that, though his conclusions were close to Gesell's, the latter's argumentation was likely to be very different. But he had been impressed by Keynes's statement that "the future will learn more from the spirit of Gesell than from that of Marx" (see note 34 to no. 164). After Allais's death and thanks to his daughter Christine, I was granted from Allais's personal library a copy of Gesell's book (a translation into French dated 1948, which Allais could not have known of when writing *Économie et intérêt*).

chological grounds (*memory decay, psychological time*, etc.) in the 1960s and 1970s.[8] Here again, Allais's work clearly offers a basis for behavioral economics arguments, albeit within a more mathematical framework than is commonly found in that branch of economics.

Economic policy

Chapter 10 contains the elements that would have formed the subject of the policy volume[9] within the initial gigantic project of the author. It is heavily permeated by the postwar atmosphere. Samuelson has written of the adventure experienced in the Paris of those years by Ursula and John Hicks, who had been told of an interesting meeting in Paris, which they decided to observe. They saw workers, clerks, curious bystanders, shop-keepers, army officers, and soldiers back from the front gathered to listen to a young lecturer who was explaining, enthusiastically and volubly, that the economy would henceforth have to be run in accordance with the lessons to be learned from general economic equilibrium, beginning with the issue of why the rate of interest should be zero in a stationary economy. The speaker was Maurice Allais. What he must have been saying on that occasion can easily be established from chapter 10 of the book. He took the view that the general equilibrium theory and the theory of interest would have to be implemented under a regime of specific institutions that must combine planning and free-market competition. The idea was to avoid both crises like the 1929 Great Depression—which free markets had failed, and still fail, to avoid—and dramatic failures of the Soviet type. It amounted in essence to firmly controlling the money supply by switching to a 100% money system, to ensuring fairness in the distribution of income by eliminating private appropriation of all possible rents, and to encouraging, within these bounds, private initiative as the essential driving force of innovation and growth. Some softer variants of these ideas found application in the 1950s and 1960s, until the French economy became so extensively connected to the European markets, and then to world markets, that any kind of "planning" became unsustainable. But as envisaged by Allais and as actually carried out over the next 20 years in France, this

8. See Allais 1966, 1974, and Barthalon 2014.

9. Announced in note 8 to no. 158 as *The Philosophy of the Economy of Tomorrow: Competitive Socialism*, which evokes the school of thought developed by Oskar Lange and others and which Allais had not yet heard of for the reasons already mentioned.

"planning" never had anything to do with the type of institutions that
Eastern European countries came to be burdened with. Indeed, Allais's
main preoccupation was that incomes should be genuinely earned in order to maintain individual motivation and distribution kept sufficiently
fair to avoid discouraging individual work, investment, and enterprise on
the part of entrepreneurs (Diemer, Lallement, and Munier 2010).

The main challenge here, however, was—and to a large extent still remains in today's capitalist economies—how to avoid private appropriation of rents. The main rent sources Allais had in mind in the aftermath
of World War II were land and money. As to the latter, 100% money institutions would avoid private appropriation of "seigniorage" by private
commercial banks (no. 162). As for rents derived from land, nationalization of land was the solution that—following Walras and others—Allais
advocated for a brief period of time (no. 163).

While he was never to change his point of view on money, Allais very
quickly changed his view on land. He realized that land nationalization
would give far too much power to the state and that democracy could perhaps not survive such a radical step. As an alternative, he suggested, besides
monetary reform, levying a tax on all existing *physical* capital (and consequently alleviating other taxes, notably on income), alongside a general
indexation of financial claims so as to exclude any transfer of wealth from
claimants to debtors.[10] One can only try to imagine what Jackson Hole
discussions and optimal taxation theory might have become along such
lines—the very topic Samuelson dealt with when he wrote the sentence
quoted in the epigraph above.

Maurice Allais's vision of economics

It is natural to wonder why, even aside from the relative inaccessibility of
its French language and the dark period in which it was published, such a
remarkable book should for so long a period have met only limited acclaim.
At least three factors were at work here. First, the book's postwar publisher
was in fact an administrative service (the Imprimerie Nationale, a government printing office)—that is, not a real publisher in the modern sense of
the word, one that superbly ignored any form of advertising and for which
the very idea of marketing was at that time simply nonexistent (de Mont-

---

10. More details can be found on the website of the Maurice Allais Foundation, English
version, http://www.fondationmauriceallais.org.

brial 1995). A new edition came out only in 1998, boasting a new preface and new appendixes, under the auspices of a recognized publishing house: this time it attracted considerable renewed attention, albeit essentially among the French-speaking community.[11] Second, the book was in a sense too advanced with respect to the state-of-the-art economics of its day, and some of its groundbreaking contributions were left aside if not mocked (Belloc and Moreaux 2018). Third, Allais's presentation often fails to highlight his key findings, while he devotes lengthy explanations to secondary issues. This tendency made it unlikely to win over most researchers, whether in France or abroad—not unlike what happened to the "Allais paradox" in the 1950s and 1960s.[12] Some of the early reviews thus misunderstood the text, failing to identify even the most important contributions it contained, and expressed negative judgments, which appear today to have been based on mere errors (Papandreou 1949, Boulding 1951) or on misplaced aversion to—or failure to understand—the approach of mathematical economics. Some other early reviews cautiously did not go beyond very general remarks, praising the methodology (Guitton 1952, Shackle 1949) without coming to grips with the contents in detail. Such reviews were obviously no incentive to potential readers. Finally, even French academic economists had a hard time getting hold of the book, as the author of this preface can testify.[13] Thus the present edition will considerably enlarge the potential readership.

As an economist Maurice Allais defies any attempt at facile labeling. Is he a free-market economist? Yes, but he thinks that markets far from always perform satisfactorily due to limitations often linked with the

11. Yet, this 1998 second edition (Paris, Clément Juglar Press) multiplied by a factor of 13 the average annual number of academic references to the book (Google Scholar).

12. The paper containing the "Allais paradox" was published with great difficulty "on the author's responsibility" ([sic], see the "Editor's Note" in *Econometrica* 21 [1953]: 503).

13. In the late 1960s, having accidentally seen a reference to *Économie et intérêt*, I thought that I should read the relevant part. But the book was not available in the library of my university, so, taking advantage of a trip to Paris, I was able to find it in another university library. The librarian, however, would not let me borrow the book, so I decided to make (by then illegal) copies of the text. However, no card copying machines were available at the time—only coin machines existed—so I had no choice but to collect enough of the type of coins accepted by the machine to enable me to copy the book page by page. I spent more than half a day hunting for them, but never succeeded in collecting the 800 that would have been necessary to copy all the book's pages! Some years later, having been elected to the Comité National de la Recherche Scientifique (National Committee for Scientific Research), of which Maurice Allais was a member, I met Maurice and told him the story, making him laugh to tears. Two weeks thereafter, I received as a present from the author the two volumes of the original edition of this book. It had taken me over seven years to access it!

psychological traits of economic agents. Government intervention is therefore by no means to be discarded and should be considered when appropriate in order to ensure social efficiency—especially in the generalized sense touched on above. Public policy should in particular ensure a fair distribution of income, as has already been mentioned. But is Maurice Allais a socialist? Certainly not, in view of his constant criticisms of government-owned centralized economies and his firm conviction that individual entrepreneurship in decentralized economies should be the *primum movens* of social progress. Allais was one of the very few European intellectuals who consistently refuted the widespread positive claims of the time regarding Soviet achievements in terms of living standards.[14] Throughout his life, he argued in favor of opening national borders progressively toward a European common market and to some kind of federal—or confederal—European Union. He nevertheless considered—as the usual theory of economic integration teaches—that a common currency within such regional unions could only be the crowning stage of such an integration (as is proved by several papers and books from different periods of his life). These considerations taken together explain the hostility he expressed to the hasty construction and premature launch of the Euro in the early 2000s but also to the kind of excessive, breathless globalization and deregulation experienced after the end of the 1980s. More generally, he viewed the world economy as made out of large regional competitive markets, embracing countries of similar levels of development. It is little known that he was one of the very few economists perceptive enough to have argued in the late 1950s in favor of an American-European common market. He later abandoned that idea, however, because of his perception of the oligopolistic path taken by American competition, a step Philippon (2019) has called "the great reversal." Obviously, none of these stances could ever make Allais a protectionist, though his criticisms of globalization led him to label his own views as a sort of "reasonable protectionism," an expression in which the adjective should be stressed rather than the noun. Maurice Allais was indeed a special kind of *both* a socialist *and* a free-market economist (Munier 2011)—holding a rather unusual, idiosyncratic view that could be called

---

14. Few economists know that Jean-Paul Sartre wrote in 1956 that Soviet economies would bridge the gap separating them from the American standard of living "before 1960." Ridiculous as that statement may appear today, at the time it represented mainstream European intellectual opinion, in France and in the United Kingdom as well as in other European countries.

"competition-based planning" or *planisme concurrentiel*. In a word, he was the epitome of a *really free* thinker, both in the sciences and in philosophy. This may well be the key factor Samuelson wished to draw attention to.

Bertrand Munier

References

Allais, M. 1943. *À la recherche d'une discipline économique*. 1st ed., Paris: Ateliers Industria. 2nd ed., 1952, *Traité d'économie pure*, Paris: Imprimerie Nationale. 3rd ed., 1994, Paris: Clément Juglar.

——. 1947. *Économie et intérêt*. Paris: Imprimerie Nationale. 2nd ed., 1998, Paris: Clément Juglar. The second edition includes a 250-page "Introduction to the Second Edition," which is not reproduced in the present edition.

——. 1953. "Le comportement de l'Homme rationnel devant le risque: critique des postulats et axiomes de l'école américaine." *Econometrica* 21:503–46.

——. 1962. "The Influence of the Capital-Output Ratio on Real National Income." *Econometrica* 30:700–728.

——. 1966. "A Restatement of the Quantity Theory of Money." *American Economic Review* 56:1123–56.

——. 1974. "The Psychological Rate of Interest." *Journal of Money, Credit and Banking* 6:285–331.

Arrow, K. J., and F. Hahn. 1971. *General Competitive Analysis*. San Francisco: Holden-Day.

Baqaee, D., and E. Farhi. 2018. "The Microeconomic Foundations of Aggregate Production Functions." NBER Work. Pap. 25293.

Barthalon, E. 2014. *Uncertainty, Expectations and Financial Instability: Reviving Allais's Lost Theory of Psychological Time*. New York: Columbia University Press.

Baumol, W. 1952. "The Transactions Demand for Cash: An Inventory Theoretic Approach." *Quarterly Journal of Economics* 66:545–56.

Baumol, W., and J. Tobin. 1989. "The Optimal Cash Balance Proposition: Maurice Allais' Priority." *Journal of Economic Literature* 27:1160–62.

The author of the preface is Emeritus Professor at the Sorbonne's IAE Business School and former head of the economics department at the École Normale Supérieure de Paris-Saclay. He is very thankful to Christine Allais, Eric Barthalon, Xavier Botteri, John Daly, Xavier Gabaix, Christian Gomez, Jacques Lesourne, Mark Machina, Jean Tirole, and to the Scientific Committee of the Maurice Allais Foundation (http://www.fondationmauriceallais .org), as well as to an anonymous referee for numerous suggestions on earlier versions of this text. Possible errors remain obviously his own.

Belloc, B., and M. Moreaux. 2018. "Allais, Maurice (Born 1911)." In *The New Pal-grave Dictionary of Economics*. London: Palgrave Macmillan.

Boulding, K. 1951. "M. Allais' Theory of Interest." *Journal of Political Economy* 59:69–73.

Diemer, A., J. Lallement, and B. Munier, eds. 2010. *Maurice Allais et la science économique*. Paris: Oeconomia.

Drouhin, N. 1997. "Systèmes de retraite et accumulation du capital: Un modèle à générations imbriquées avec durée de vie incertaine." *Recherches économiques de Louvain* 63:133–51.

Farhi, E., and X. Gabaix. 2020. "Optimal Taxation with Behavioral Agents." *American Economic Review* 110:298–336.

Fisher, I. 1935. *100% Money*. Binghamton, NY: Vail-Ballou Press.

Geanakoplos, J. 2008. "Overlapping Generations Models of General Equilibrium." Cowles Foundation DP 1663. New Haven, CT: Yale University.

Gesell, S. 1958. *The Natural Economic Order*. London: Owen. Original in German (1906).

Gordon, M. J., and E. Shapiro. 1956. "Capital Equipment Analysis: The Required Rate of Profit." *Management Science* 3:102–10.

Grandmont, J.-M. 1989. "Report on Maurice Allais' Scientific Work." *Scandinavian Journal of Economics* 91:17–28.

Guitton, H. 1952. "Allais, Maurice: Économie et intérêt. Présentation nouvelle des problèmes fondamentaux relatifs au rôle économique du taux de l'intérêt et de leurs solutions." *Revue économique* 3:892–95.

Keynes, J. M. 1936. *The General Theory of Employment, Interest, and Money*. New York: Harcourt Brace.

Malinvaud, E. 1986. "Maurice Allais, précurseur méconnu des modèles à généra-tions renouvelées." In *Marchés, capital et incertitude: Essais en l'honneur de Maurice Allais*, edited by M. Boiteux, Th. de Montbrial, and B. Munier, 91–104. Paris: Economica.

———. 1987. "The Overlapping Generations Model in 1947." *Journal of Economic Literature* 25:103–5.

———. 1989. "Hommage à Maurice Allais, Prix Nobel d'Économie 1988." *Annales des mines, No. spécial* (March): 28–29.

———. 1995. "Maurice Allais, Unrecognized Pioneer of Overlapping Generations Models." In *Markets, Risk, and Money: Essays in Honor of Maurice Allais*, ed-ited by B. Munier. Dordrecht: Kluwer Academic Publishers.

Montbrial, Th. de. 1995. "Maurice Allais, a Belatedly Recognized Genius." In *Mar-kets, Risk, and Money: Essays in Honor of Maurice Allais*, edited by B. R. Mu-nier. Dordrecht: Kluwer Academic Publishers.

Munier, B. 1991. "Nobel Laureate: The Many Other Allais' Paradoxes." *Journal of Economic Perspectives* 5:179–99.

———. 1995. "Fifty Years of Maurice Allais's Economic Writings: Seeds for Re-newal in Contemporary Economic Thought." In *Markets, Risk, and Money:*

Essays in Honor of Maurice Allais, edited by B. R. Munier. Dordrecht: Kluwer Academic Publishers.

———, ed. 1995. *Markets, Risk, and Money: Essays in Honor of Maurice Allais*. Dordrecht: Kluwer Academic Publishers.

———. 2011. "Maurice Allais, libéral ou socialiste? Libéral et socialiste?" *Commentaire* 133:107–14.

Nishimura, K. G. 2011. "Population Ageing, Macroeconomic Crisis and Policy Challenges." Bank of Japan DP, *Proceedings of the General Theory and The Policy Responses to Macroeconomic Crisis (June 19–21)*. Cambridge: Cambridge University Press.

Papandreou, A. G. 1949. "Review of *Économie et intérêt*, by M. Allais." *American Economic Review* 39:751–54.

Pecchenino, J. R. 1994. "An Overlapping Generations Model of Growth and the Environment." *Economic Journal* 104:1393–410.

Phelps, E. 1961. "The Golden Rule of Accumulation: A Fable for Growthmen." *American Economic Review* 51:638–43.

Philippon, Th. 2019. *The Great Reversal: How America Gave Up on Free Markets*. Cambridge, MA: Harvard University Press.

Ramrattan, L., and M. Szenberg. 2011. "Maurice Allais: A Review of His Major Works, a Memoriam, 1911–2010." *American Economist* 56:104–22.

Samuelson, P. A. 1947. *Foundations of Economic Analysis*. Cambridge, MA: Harvard University Press.

———. 1958. "An Exact Consumption-Loan Model of Interest with or without the Social Contrivance of Money." *Journal of Political Economy* 66:467–82.

———. 1982. "A Chapter in the History of Ramsey's Optimal Feasible Taxation and Optimal Public Utilities Prices." In *Economic Essays in Honor of Jorgen Gelting*, edited by Sven Andersen et al., 157–81. Copenhagen: Danish Economic Association.

Shackle, G. L. S. 1949. "Review of *Économie et intérêt*, by M. Allais." *Economic Journal* 59:86–88.

Song, Z. 2008. "The Dynamics of Inequality and Social Security in General Equilibrium." *MPRA Paper No. 10365*, Munich Personal RePec Archive.

Ståhl, I. 1988. "The Prize in Economic Sciences in Memory of Alfred Nobel." Speech presenting Maurice Allais's work at the Nobel Award Ceremony in Nobel Foundation, *Les Prix Nobel (The Nobel Prizes) 1988*, 339–41. Stockholm: Almqvist & Wiksell.

Tirole, J. 1985. "Asset Bubbles and Overlapping Generations." *Econometrica* 53:1071–100.

———. 2012. "La vie et les travaux de Maurice Allais." Académie des Sciences Morales et Politiques, November 26. https://academiesciencesmoralesetpolitiques.fr/2012/11/26/.

Tobin, J. 1956. "The Interest Elasticity of Transactions Demand for Cash." *Review of Economics and Statistics* 38:241–47.

Tosun, M. S. 2003. "Population Ageing and Economic Growth: Political Economy and Open Economy Effects." *Economics Letters* 81:291–96.

Von Neumann, J., and O. Morgenstern. 1944. *Theory of Games and Economic Behavior.* Princeton, NJ: Princeton University Press. 2nd ed., 1947. 3rd ed., 1953.

A Note on the Translation

In writing this groundbreaking work in French over seventy years ago, Professor Allais was obliged to forge part of the vocabulary he needed to express his new concepts. With the progress of economics in the intervening period, many of these concepts have now become commonplace but are often expressed in different terminology. In this translation I have given preference to more modern terms when they undoubtedly express the identical meaning, but rather than risk distorting the author's thought I have at times maintained expressions that may surprise the contemporary reader. The main examples of this are as follows:

1. For Allais, the unqualified word "capital" designates the value of the entire set of tangible assets *including land*, so when land is *excluded*, he uses the term *capital mobilier*, which I have simply rendered by "capital" when there is no ambiguity but otherwise by "reproducible capital."
2. The unqualified term "money" denotes in Allais's system the medium of exchange, whether it circulates or is merely used for accounting purposes (as, for example, applied to the Euro prior to 2002). Hence Allais refers to "*circulating money*" to denote what is ordinarily understood by the simple word "money."
3. Allais uses "premium" for factors that either increase *or decrease* the value of a security or investment: liquidity premium, storage premium, risk premium, depreciation premium—all to be added or deducted depending on whether their value is positive or negative.

Readers should further note that in this translation "rent" designates the income of the rentier; "false claims" (translating Rueff's *faux droits*) express any title to withdraw *from* the economy without having contributed *to* it; and "social," in expressions such as "social efficiency" and "social productivity," simply means *of society* or *national.*

The translation is completely faithful to the text as published in 1947 except that the obvious typographical errors have been corrected and a single extraneous illustration has been omitted.

I must thank the Maurice Allais Foundation under the aegis of the Mines Paris Foundation, under whose auspices this translation was commissioned and accomplished. I am very deeply indebted for their more than generous help to Professor Bertrand Munier, chairman of the Scientific Committee of the Maurice Allais Foundation; Christian Gomez, a former student of Maurice Allais; as well as to the late Professor Edmond Lisle, who not only placed his exhaustive knowledge of economics vocabulary in both French and English at my disposal but also subjected my manuscript to more painstaking positive criticism than I had any right to expect; and finally to Eric Barthalon for checking formulas and equations. I also warmly thank Madame Christine Allais for her conscientious proofreading, which saved me from several inadvertent departures from her father's exact thought and countless sausage-fingered mistranscriptions of his equations.

There are so many variables, parameters, and formulas in *Economy and Interest* that even now some mistakes have probably slipped through. Readers finding any such are invited to notify contact@fondationmaurice allais.org. They will receive a then-current complete errata sheet and many thanks.

Needless to say, no one but myself is responsible for whatever defects remain.

John Daly

To the Reader

This work draws on the most up-to-date methods of economics to tackle one of the most important and most difficult problems falling within the scope of this science: the problem of interest.

After recalling the basics of interest theory and introducing substantial new contributions to that theory (chapters 1–5), it shows what the role of the interest rate in economic management is and what it ought to be; it introduces major corrections to the classical theory according to which optimal satisfaction and competitive equilibrium coincide; in particular it shows that zero interest rates would make it possible to optimize the stock of capital equipment, thanks to which the factors of production (land and labor) would achieve maximum productivity (chapters 6 and 7).

By studying the mechanism that links the variation of interest rates and economic development, it presents a comprehensive theory of interest, prices, and money that gives order and coherence to the results obtained both by classical economists and by those of the modern schools: there emerges the broad outline of a new theory of economic cycles (chapter 8).

After this general presentation, the book shows why interest on capital exists and discusses to what extent it is justified. In particular it focuses on the changes that would have to be made to existing structural conditions in order to attain the optimal capital stock analyzed in chapter 7 (chapter 9).

The final chapter presents an overview of the results obtained and shows how they ought to be interpreted and their practical bearing on our economic action (chapter 10).

*　*　*

Taken as a whole, this book presents a *comprehensive synthesis of modern economics*, chiefly focused on analyzing the phenomenon of interest and the essential but complex role it plays, as well as *an introduction to an economic policy capable of uniting mankind in a common faith overshadowing all ephemeral private interests.*

Economy and Interest is a new submission relative to the tragic conflict, fraught with dire consequences, between the proponents of "laissez-faire" and those of "authoritarian planning." My aim is to open up *hitherto unperceived paths*, far from the extreme and simplistic solutions advocated on either side and *capable of completely changing the current appearance of economic and social problems through a fairer distribution of incomes combined with a greater efficiency of production.*

I therefore fervently hope that it will attract the attention not only of the many economics specialists but also of all those who must on a daily basis take decisions of an economic nature that will affect our future (politicians of all parties, leaders of trade unions and of employers' federations, businessmen, engineers, etc.).

* * *

In pursuit of logical rigor I have applied, in the earlier chapters, the methods of demonstration currently used in the physical sciences, and I have not shrunk from advanced mathematical reasoning. Although none of the concepts involved calls on highly sophisticated mathematics, and any explanations that are genuinely difficult have been relegated to appendixes at the end of the volume, nonetheless this first part is chiefly addressed to engineers.

However, the last chapter of the book, in which the findings reached are summarized and the economic and social consequences of the theory of interest are set out, *is entirely free of calculus and expressed throughout in everyday language. Thus the work's underlying philosophy, though highly scientific, is put within reach of every reader, even those unfamiliar with calculus.*

* * *

There is no denying that the book is not an easy one to read, calling, as it does, for sustained attention—the unavoidable price to be paid for my decision to keep my analysis on the level of unassailable scientific rigor. For this reason, I think it may prove useful to offer readers some advice.

I suggest you should begin by skimming through the work, sticking to the headings and ends of chapters and statements of theorems, paying attention only to the solution of problems that have already occurred to you.

Having thus obtained a bird's eye view, *you will find in the last chapter (chapter 10) an overview of the main theses of this work and their practical applications. You should then proceed to an attentive perusal.* This would certainly be the best introduction to the book, and I think the only way for the reader to convince himself to make the considerable effort—in terms both of time and of thought—required for a full and attentive study: *the only way*, I believe, for him to grasp all the difficulties and all the nuances of the problems studied and be convinced of the validity of the solutions proposed.

This is the sort of book that needs to be read *several times* if it is to be fully understood. In light of the experience of those who have been kind enough to read the review copies, readers may be assured that this effort will not be in vain and that they will have no cause to regret it.

*   *   *

I have *streamlined the text* by relegating to *footnotes* such explanations as I have found necessary in order to avoid ambiguity, as well as any considerations that, though interesting, were less directly attached to the subject or less solidly established.

I have likewise relegated to *appendixes* those considerations that only need to be understood by readers for whom the strictest analysis is an indispensable precondition of the assent of the mind. These appendixes are specifically addressed to specialists.

Any reader wishing only to acquire an exact idea of the broad outline of this work may content himself with reading chapter 10, the first part of which (§ A to E) was drafted especially for him.

Readers wishing to study the subject more deeply must become acquainted with chapters 1–10 but may safely omit the footnotes and appendixes. They will draw greater profit from their reading if they *begin* with a rapid perusal of chapter 10.

Finally those who wish to make the utmost progress in mastering the difficulties the book addresses must embark on a complete reading. Yet they need not linger over the footnotes and appendixes on their first reading, and they too will find great value in a *preliminary* acquaintance with the contents of chapter 10.

xl TO THE READER

*   *   *

Finally, to enable the reader to consult the text more easily I have inserted a general order number after the title of each numbered section.[1]

1. At the beginning of this book, I particularly wish to thank Messrs. Boiteux and Debreu, both holders of the *agrégation* in mathematics, who have been kind enough to lend their efficient help in correcting the proofs.

CHAPTER ONE

Introduction

1. Importance and difficulty of the theory of interest (1)

The most penetrating and subtle thinkers in the field of economics, foremost among whom must be mentioned Eugen von Böhm-Bawerk, Irving Fisher, and John Maynard Keynes, have striven for more than two centuries to resolve the problem of interest, but despite the diversity of methods used, there is no denying that minds remain troubled and that no theory has hitherto definitively prevailed. Indeed the more deeply the problem of interest has been analyzed, the greater the difficulties it presents have seemed to grow.[1] Yet the expenditure of such great efforts in such different directions in order to grasp an ever-elusive truth clearly attests to how important yet how difficult it is to shed real light on the subject.

In fact, the problem of interest certainly constitutes the most difficult problem in economics,[2] and the usefulness of studying it is fundamental:

---

1. Here perhaps more than anywhere else the present insufficiency of economic theory is made manifest and with it the falsity of John Stuart Mill's somewhat imprudent assertion in his *Principles of Political Economy* (1848), "Happily there is nothing in the laws of value which remains for the present or any future writer to clear up; the theory of the subject is complete" (bk. 3, ch. 1, § 1).

2. The subject is mathematically less complex than that of social efficiency, already studied in my *À la recherche d'une discipline économique* [In quest of an economic discipline] (published by the author, 1943) and summarized in my booklet *Économie pure et rendement social* [Pure economics and social efficiency] (Paris: Sirey, 1945), but it is certainly much more difficult to set out logically owing to the very fact of the general interdependence of economic parameters.

N.B. Each section is identified by two distinct numbers, the one specific to the chapter and the other general. They appear respectively before and after the title. To refer from one numbered section to another the general number will be used.

Moreover, footnote numbering is by section and not sequentially throughout the book.

upon its complete resolution depend our understanding of the economy as a whole and the practical measures to be adopted by any rational policy.

Anyone hoping to comprehend the role played by interest in the real economy must first master the theoretical mechanism of interest both in an account-based (moneyless) economy and in a monetary economy and bear it constantly in mind, for to the subtle functioning of the theoretical economic model the real world adds highly complex disturbances of its own, particular of a monetary nature.

The subject of the rationale of interest was passionately discussed throughout the 19th century but today seems somewhat abandoned; yet it is one of the most fundamental questions in economics, and its importance cannot be over-emphasized.

2. Aim of the present study (2)

The present study aims to present the reader with a compact and in many respects original presentation of the theory of interest—one that, it is hoped, will enable him swiftly to reach a comprehensive view that is both clear and coherent.

There is no question at present of a rigorous and complete scientific presentation of the entire problem of interest. Such a task would call for a huge volume in itself, and the sheer time involved, measured against my other occupations, rules out any such undertaking for at least two years.

So the present study will be limited to the essentials[1] and, in my view, will have fully achieved its objective if it elucidates certain particularly subtle features of the theory of interest and if it stimulates remarks and suggestions in the short term that cannot fail to prove of great value for the finalization of my general study.[2]

In its present state the presentation that follows already takes account of remarks and suggestions from key figures who unite deep scientific and economic culture with business experience, among whom I must especially express my thanks to Messrs.

Angoustures, graduate of the École Polytechnique, senior executive with the Société Générale;

Caquot, consultant engineer, member of the Institut de France;

Dayre, chief engineer of the Génie Rural;

Demousseaux, graduate of the École Polytechnique, barrister of the French courts;

Denis, professor at the Rennes Faculty of Law;

1. Indeed all the explanations that follow will be very brief and concise, as I have been reluctantly obliged to eliminate many details that would have helped to clarify some exceptionally demanding or significant aspects of the theory of interest. If this leads to some inconvenience for the reader, he is invited to bear in mind that it is the inescapable price to be paid for the advantage of having at his disposal a short but complete presentation of the general theory of interest—a theory whose complexity makes it one of the most fundamental obstacles yet to be overcome by the science of economics.

2. This is intended to be the main subject of the second volume of my general work *À la recherche d'une discipline économique.*

Deschamps, former engineer with the Génie Maritime;

Detoeuf, former chief engineer of the Ponts et Chaussées, president of the Syndicat Général de la Construction Électrique;

Divisia, inspector general of the Ponts et Chaussées, professor of economics at the École Polytechnique;

Dubourdieu, professor at the Conservatoire des Arts et Métiers, consulting actuary at the Banque de Paris et des Pays-Bas;

Dupont-Ferrier, secretary-general of the Entreprises Campenon-Bernard;

Lavaille, engineer of the Ponts et Chaussées;

Lochard, vice-president of the Conseil Général des Mines;

Lutfalla, secretary-general of the École Nationale d'Organisation Économique et Sociale, chairman and managing director of La Nationale insurance company;

Refregier, graduate of the École Polytechnique;

Robin, engineering graduate of the École Centrale de Paris, of the Société Citroën;

Roy, inspector general of the Ponts et Chaussées, professor of economics at the Institut de Statistique.

Throughout this study the context chosen will be that of a competitive economy, although, needless to say, the basic hypotheses underlying such an economy are far from being confirmed in real economic life.

However, although imperfectly verified, they are often found in the real economy in the form of tendencies, and in any event, they correspond to a reference economy characterized by optimal management, the study of which is indispensable.[3]

---

3. It can in fact be shown that for any given distribution of consumer services there exists an inherent optimum of the economy and that this optimum corresponds to a competitive management. (See my study *Économie pure et rendement social*.)

3. The plan followed (3)

After setting out some general notions about the theory of interest and a short fable to illustrate some of its fundamental characteristics by way of a simple example, I shall set out the role played by the rate of interest in capitalization and in determining the supply and demand of capital, and we shall see how it is itself determined.

Then I shall examine in particular the function of the rate of interest in the general operation of the economy from the twofold viewpoint of the quest for optimal management[1] and optimal structure,[2] and I shall endeavor to draw out the links that connect the interest rate with monetary phenomena.[3]

Next, I shall endeavor to show why, in the various known economies, the interest rate has always, in every time and place, had a positive value, and I shall close this study with a few remarks about the scope of the theory here presented, from the threefold viewpoint of the management of the economy, its capital stock, and its monetary policy.

Taken as a whole, the presentation that follows is but the logical culmination of the labors of the eminent economists who have gone before, in the first rank of whom must be placed Irving Fisher, Eugen von Böhm-Bawerk, John Maynard Keynes, and James Meade. However, on four points I believe I have significantly advanced the theory of interest.

The first of these concerns the existence of an *optimal stock of capital equipment* for the economy and is the subject of what I shall call the *social productivity* theory. In December 1940 I believed I was the first to have observed its principles, but since then I have twice found them formally mentioned in English-language literature. The first case is a brief allusion by Keynes in his *General Theory of Employment, Interest, and Money* published in 1936,[4] and the other comprises the extensive and detailed analysis presented by Meade in his *Economic Analysis and Policy*, also published in 1936.[5] In each case the context seems to indicate that the results in question are generally recognized, but I have been unable to find

1. Interest and social efficiency.
2. Interest and social productivity.
3. Interest and money.
4. French translation, Payot, 1942, 232, lines 11–16.
5. Pages 394–403 of the French translation published by Payot in 1939 under the title *Économie politique et politique économique.*

the slightest trace of them in the whole of the French literature, and direct contacts with English-language economists incline me to think that even in England the theory is not yet widespread. In any event, the reader has at his disposal in what follows a presentation that differs fundamentally from Meade's, though reaching substantially the same conclusions.

Secondly, I believe I have shown that, with regard to the role of the rate of interest, *some major reservations are needed as to the classical doctrine according to which the inherent optimum coincides with the spontaneous competitive equilibrium* since the use of a single interest rate and free savings in the context of a competitive economy necessarily leads to an inherent optimum.

Though somewhat intricate, the explanations I shall set out and that I believe to be original will certainly strike the reader by their fundamental importance[6] for any practical investment policy.

Thirdly, concerning *the connection between the classical theory of interest rates and the general theory of prices and money*, I believe I have presented some new elements that are capable of shedding much welcome light on some subtle issues still under discussion.[7]

Finally, regarding the theory of the rationale of interest, I think that the existence of a nominal interest rate that is always positive depends essentially on two facts: (a) in a world in which land is privately owned, the rate of interest cannot fall below the point at which the value of the land becomes greater than the total capital demand, and (b) in our economies in which circulating money also serves as unit of account, the hoarding of money would be preferred, at low interest rates, to any other investment; and although my starting point is fairly close to those of Turgot in his fructification theory and of Cassel in his annuity theory with regard to the private ownership of land, and to those of Rist, Fisher, and above all Keynes with regard to the liquidity advantages of money, I believe that in both form and content my contribution is substantially original.

6. These explanations are the fruit of lengthy research whose starting point for me was the apparent theoretical anomalies presented by rival systems using negative interest rates, which I have been pursuing since 1942.

7. This contribution is directly connected with the main preoccupations of the contemporary schools of economics, in the first rank of which figures the Anglo-Saxon school, and it relies essentially on the distinction between the development of the economy in and out of equilibrium.

As to method, I have once again[8] appended, by way of support for my general theory, simplified outlines thanks to which it is possible to examine with precision the economic states corresponding to given structural conditions (satisfaction and output functions). By choosing suitable data, we will see that the general system of equilibrium conditions can be resolved and the unknowns (the prices and quantities characterizing the equilibrium) can be determined *as a function of the structural conditions.*[9]

Such applications have the twofold advantage of embodying in the shape of concrete examples the interdependence of the economic parameters and enabling the results obtained by deductive reasoning to be verified.[10]

Owing to their abstract character I have thought it best to relegate these applications en bloc to an appendix. However, thanks to the assurance they provide, it remains vital to consider them, and in studying different economic problems I shall often refer the reader to these theoretical models, study of which is apt to be of the greatest help toward understanding the economic mechanism more thoroughly.[11]

---

8. I have already made a first application of this method in my *Économie pure et rendement social.*

9. So far as I am aware, at least, no work of this kind has yet been carried out.

10. This does not mean empirical verification, of course, but the comparison of the results obtained by ordinary logic against those yielded *from identical hypotheses* by mathematical logic.

I fear that this method will receive a less than warm welcome from those economists who undertake to discuss the philosophical and methodological impact of the use of mathematics without even knowing what differential calculus is; but in my opinion a new path has here been opened to progress in the field of abstract research.

11. For my own part, I owe the bulk of the results I have reached to the study of such models.

The reason for this, I think, is that constructing such simplified models *demands* reflection, precision of mind, and concentration, both in working out simplifying hypotheses and in interpreting the results obtained. They leave no room for eluding genuine difficulties by verbal acrobatics that belong rather to the world of conjuring tricks than to that of science. The need for rigor is constantly stressed, approximate thinking is absolutely excluded, and the main difficulties are fully identified.

In themselves the calculations called for to work out such models—through countless trials and hundreds of hours of work—are sometimes useless, often repellent, and always laborious. Their abstractness and artificiality call for considerable effort of thought, and the results they yield never have more than relative value. But, I stress, these calculations are a means, not an end, and in so far as they force one to reflect on unsuspected difficulties or new problems, they are exceedingly beneficial. It is a tough school, but a highly *rewarding* one!

Some will claim that all this is inadmissibly abstract and that such studies are no more than intellectual gymnastics. Yet no one would query the fact that rational mechanics can only be completely understood after applying its principles to specific examples, even if they bear no relation to practical reality. The same applies to theoretical economics. For my part I am convinced that *it would greatly benefit the progress of economic understanding for pure economics to set itself, and resolve, theoretical problems corresponding to such and such ideal conditions*. The theoretical models I shall be presenting aim to satisfy this need.

Overview

1. Capital and the availability of capital (4)

The term *capital* can denote the value of any set of tangible goods,[1] while *nominal capital* denotes the amount of the capital expressed in units of account. Capital so defined represents an abstract magnitude, the expression of which, in units of account, is nominal capital.[2]

Experience shows that the availability of any capital over a given period of time enables it to render services that have value. It also shows that these services vary according to when they are rendered. This invites us to devise a new abstract magnitude that could be called "availability of capital" to represent the services rendered by the capital per unit of time at a given point during the relevant period.

Thus capital and the availability of capital are in fact two abstract magnitudes closely analogous to those constituted by the quantity of a physical good and the quantity of its services. For this reason it is convenient to consider capital as an abstract good and the availability of the capital as the abstract service rendered by this abstract good.

---

1. The concept of capital will be clarified in what follows (see in particular nos. 36 and 47).

2. The concept of capital is not made redundant by that of value. Value is a magnitude associated with every group of goods and services, whereas capital—a magnitude of the same species as value—is a magnitude that relates *only* to goods. Thus capital is one particular instance of value.

2. Definition of interest (5)

The value of the availability of any given capital, i.e., of the service rendered by the capital over a given period of time, bears the general name of *interest*, as well as specific names (arrearage, discount, contango) in specific cases.

The term *rate of interest* denotes the price of the availability of capital, i.e., the value of the unit of availability of capital. It follows that the rate of interest is the value of the services rendered by a unit of capital during a unit of time.[1,2]

The interest rate commonly used is the annual rate payable annually; i.e., it is the price of the services rendered by the unit of capital over a year, this price being paid at the end of the year in question.

I shall call the level of the interest rate the *nominal interest rate*, the *monetary interest rate*, the *wage interest rate*, the *real interest rate*, the *gold interest rate*, or, in a general sense, the *true interest rate*, according to whether the standard of value used in each case is the unit of account, the unit of circulating money, the hourly wage of unskilled labor, the value nominally equal to the price index P, the gold standard unit, or the unit value of any good or service.

---

1. Note that the rate of interest so defined is a concept entirely distinct from the rate of return of a business, which is the ratio of its profits to the capital committed. When the books are correctly kept, the interest on the capital committed should in fact be entered as expenditure, so that the book profit emerges, at least in theory, as the net income of the business minus the interest on its capital.

The confusion between the rate of interest and the rate of return that disfigured the writings of the early economists now seems to have been entirely cleared up. (On the concept of profit the reader may usefully consult my general work *À la recherche d'une discipline économique*, nos. 157–59.)

2. Thus the rate of interest is seen to be the ratio of the value of the income provided by a capital sum to the value of this capital. Consequently the interest rate relative to time is given by θ^{-1}.

3. The case of conventional monetary economies (6)

In conventional monetary economies in which the unit of account is defined as the value of the unit of circulating money,[1] the monetary interest rate is equal to the nominal interest rate, and the value of the service rendered by the unit of money[2] is necessarily identical to the value of the service rendered by the unit of capital, i.e., the rate of interest. Hence, in such economies *the rate of interest is simply the price paid for the use of the unit of money per unit of time.*

In equilibrium, the market for the services of money is indistinguishable from the capital services market, a fact that it is vital to grasp for anyone wishing to understand the general theory of interest.[3]

1. Note that in the commonest monetary system, however, the unit of account is distinct from the value of the unit of circulating money.

For instance, in the Middle Ages the unit of circulating money, represented by the *écu*, was distinct from the unit of account, represented by the *livre tournois*. Prices were expressed in *livres tournois*, while transactions were settled in *écus*; royal edicts periodically fixed the value of *écus* in terms of *livres tournois*, i.e., the price of the *écu*.

2. Bear in mind that circulating money is a particular sort of intermediate good that provides, on the one hand, the float ("working capital") needed to balance income and expenditure over time, and, on the other hand, the store of value needed to deal with unforeseen needs or to take advantage of price differences over time. Money therefore renders two valuable services, which naturally have their price. This price in fact corresponds to the opportunity cost incurred when capital that could have been invested is instead held in monetary form (see nos. 79–82 below).

Circulating money takes the form either of cash (coins or notes) or of bank deposits available on demand. The total amount of circulating money is equal to the sum of the money balances held by economic agents other than banks. Thus it is also equal to the sum of the total cash in circulation (in the shape of the various cash holdings, including bank liquidities) plus the total unbacked deposits made available on demand by the banks.

3. See below chapter 8, "Interest and Money." It should be stressed that circulating money is simply one particular form of capital (see no. 90).

4. The rate of interest as price of use and as exchange premium (7)

When the annual interest to be paid annually is, for example, 5%, the lender of 100 francs is simply giving up this capital in exchange for another capital of 105 francs receivable a year later. In this case *the rate of interest can be defined as the difference between the valuation at the same moment of a capital sum immediately available and the same capital sum to be received later.* From this point of view, it is basically an *exchange premium* that must be added to future capital to make it equal in worth to a present capital of the same amount.

Thus the rate of interest may be considered either as the *price paid for the use* of capital when capital is loaned or as a *premium* representing the difference in the valuation of two equal quantities of capital available at different points in time, and applicable in *the exchange of capital over time.*[1]

And similarly in conventional monetary economies, the rate of interest may equally well be considered either as the price paid for the use of money or as a premium representing the difference in valuation between two sums of money available at two different points in time.

---

1. In reality, these two aspects of interest amount to equivalent definitions of a single notion. Notwithstanding the contrary claims of certain authors, they are by no means mutually exclusive; indeed the failure to note their identity is liable to give rise to grave errors.

5. Quadruple aspect of the rate of interest in conventional monetary economies (8)

These explanations bring out all the complexity, in the real economy, of the phenomenon of interest, which in fact takes on four different aspects depending on whether the abstract capital market or the money market is involved and on whether interest is being studied as a premium or as a price of use; they also explain the obstacles encountered by all the simplistic theories that considered only one aspect of the subject.

Theories that study the rate of interest in relation to issues pertaining to capital may be called *capital-based theories of interest*,[1] while those that study it in relation to money are termed *monetary theories of interest*.[2]

---

1. Such are the theories of von Böhm-Bawerk and Keynes.
2. Such are the theories of the medieval canonists and Keynes.

6. Capital-based and monetary theories of interest (9)

The duality of interest theory constitutes one of the most demanding topics in the whole field of economics, and its study has given rise to much confusion.

When the science of economics was in its early days, it was the monetary aspect—the more obvious aspect, that dominated. Later, further study led economists to realize that this obvious aspect concealed a deeper reality, and they focused their attention on interest from the standpoint of capital. Finally, in recent years, the observation of economic worlds far removed from equilibrium has brought the attention of economists back to the monetary aspect of interest, and monetary theories have enjoyed a major revival.

In reality, as we shall see, these different theories, however opposed they may appear at first sight, are but two different facets *of the same reality*, and, far from being mutually exclusive, they are perfectly reconcilable.

Monetary theories are essentially primary, while capital-based theories are secondary.[1] The former cover the dynamic development of the economy

1. When structural changes occur in the economy, each parameter adapts, taking on the new value corresponding to equilibrium.

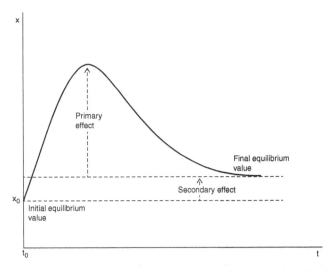

FIGURE 2.1 FOOTNOTE The variations of a parameter *x* following structural modifications

out of equilibrium, while the latter examine the basic characteristics of an economy assumed to be in equilibrium and hence identify the underlying tendencies of the economy.

In fact it is perhaps in the context of the theory of interest that careful distinction is most needed between what is valid for dynamic disequilibrium and what is valid only for dynamic equilibrium.[2] In the former case, only the superficial effects usually observed are attended to, whereas in the latter the fundamental tendencies of the economy are addressed.

As will be seen, the distinction between the causal agency at work in disequilibrium and the interdependence involved in equilibrium[3] makes it possible to discern—beyond the real determination of interest in instantaneous

---

In the real economy certain alterations can immediately be observed. These may be called *primary* or *transient effects*. These alterations correspond to the evolution of the out-of-equilibrium system, under the influence of structural variations (alterations of taste, technology, or monetary structure). They are distinct from those that would correspond to *direct* transition to equilibrium and that may be called *secondary* or *durable effects*.

These different effects are very similar to those commonly observed in the physical sciences. For instance, when a pebble is thrown into a tank, a series of waves are observed, spreading out from the point of impact and gradually dying away (primary effects). When equilibrium is reestablished, the surface of the water is smooth once again and the water level has simply risen to a height corresponding to the volume of the stone (secondary effect).

The term *primary theories* may usually be used to denote theories that are concerned only with primary effects, while those involving secondary effects are called *secondary theories*.

Primary theories are incomplete theories, which take into account only part of the phenomena. Generally speaking, the laws they enunciate are derived from everyday observation and are often intuitive. The parameters they assume to be constant are those that are the most inert and that as a first approximation may indeed be considered invariable.

2. An economic system may be termed *static* when its elements, outputs, consumptions, prices, etc., do not involve time. Otherwise it is called *dynamic*.

Notwithstanding a widely held opinion, equilibrium theories are not necessarily static theories: if the equilibrium being studied involves time, the theory in question is a dynamic theory.

Equilibrium dynamics concern the development over time of a system in equilibrium; quite distinct are *disequilibrium dynamics*, which refers to the development over time of a system in disequilibrium.

These two kinds of dynamic processes relate to very different phenomena. Thus the correlative variations, in equilibrium, in savings and in the interest rate, belong to the former, while studies bearing on how equilibrium becomes established in a market belong to the latter (see note 12 to no. 40 and note 46 to no. 47).

Primary effects correspond to the disequilibrium process and secondary effects to the equilibrium process.

3. See in particular nos. 96–100 below. Also relevant here is my general work *À la recherche d'une discipline économique*, nos. 225–27.

monetary equilibria, where causality is to the fore—the fundamental role played by interest in the phenomena of capital accumulation in a sustainable equilibrium and thus to arrive at a complete explanation based on the general interdependence of the economic parameters. By thus carefully distinguishing primary from secondary effects it will be possible to identify, among the theories of interest, those that are secondary and that alone provide a genuine explanation, unlike primary theories, which enable us to understand only differential variations around an average level that remains undetermined.[4]

4. These unavoidably cursory remarks will become clearer as the reader advances in the perusal of this study (see in particular chapters 8 and 9, "Interest and Money" and "The Problem of Interest").

7. Diversity of interest rates (10)

In point of fact there is not just a single rate of interest in a country; there are many: to every investment whose terms differentiate it from others, there corresponds a specific rate of interest.

The diversity of interest rates may depend on the nature of the loans or on their terms.

(i) Nature of loans

The main differences in the nature of loans liable to impinge on the level of interest rates are different risk levels, different administrative costs, and different loan periods.

DIVERSITY OF RISK.   Risk is always present, even in the case of loans that are theoretically assumed to be safe. So it is natural that lenders should obtain an interest rate that takes account of the degree of the risks they run.

DIVERSITY OF ADMINISTRATIVE COSTS.   Scarcely any loan fails to cost the lender some labor, whether in the shape of precautions to be taken before the loan, supervising the capital loaned, holding any security pledged, procedures to be followed to obtain repayment, etc. Thus a certain part of the sum paid by the borrower, which appears to him to be interest, in the eyes of the lender is simply compensation for the different tasks to which the loan has given rise. This compensation is what is meant by administrative costs.

DIVERSITY OF LOAN PERIOD.   In addition to the risk, the loan period is a key factor in determining the level of the interest rate. For as a matter of fact it is by no means the same thing to give up the use of the sum of 100 francs for a year in return for the payment of interest of 5 francs, as to give up the use of the same sum for ten years in return for an annual payment of the same interest. In the first case, the lender has the option, after one year, of either consuming the sum in question or reinvesting it, whereas in the second case this choice is available only after ten years.

So theoretically as many interest rates can be imagined as there are possible loan periods.

(ii) Loan terms

For loans that are identical in nature, interest rates may differ according to the terms applied. I have defined the rate of interest as the use-value of the unit of capital during the unit of time, and following this definition, the rate of interest depends both on the unit of time chosen and on the interval between the dates when interest is to be paid, which I shall call the *specified period*.

By shortening the payment intervals it is possible to move from income paid at regular intervals to a continuous income flow; hence the notion of a rate of interest that is continuously payable is attained. If, for instance, the interest rate is j% per unit of time, continuously payable, this means that at the end of each infinitesimal period dt, the borrower pays an interest $j\,dt$.

I shall call rates of interest that are continuously payable *continuous rates* as opposed to rates of interest to be paid discontinuously, which I shall call *discontinuous rates*.

As a matter of fact, there are so many different ways of determining the interest yielded by loans of the same nature that depend on two parameters—the unit of time employed and the specified period—that it may at first be perplexing, but it can be shown that the different corresponding rates can all be reduced to a single one, which may be taken as the typical interest rate and to which all the others are deemed to be *equivalent*.

In what follows, the year will be taken as the unit of time and the only specified periods considered will be the year and zero. Thus the only rates of interest to be considered will be the annual rate of interest payable annually and the annual continuous rate of interest.

8. Pure interest (11)

On the basis of this analysis, the classical theory breaks down gross interest — mentally at least — into three elements: *pure interest*, which is the price of the services of the capital not counting any risk or administrative factors, a *risk premium*, specific to each loan and corresponding to the uncertainty of the transaction, and finally a *management premium*, once again specific to each loan and corresponding to the administrative labor.[1]

In practice there can be scarcely any investment that does not involve some risk on the part of the lender, and it is hard to see a means of calculating the premium that would enable a pure interest, entirely risk free, to be isolated when the statisticians know of no such thing.[2] Pure interest in the meaning of the classical analysis is in reality an elusive concept devoid of practical application.

So I will not retain this definition and instead I shall call *pure interest* the interest yielded by a loan needing no administrative input and whose total reimbursement, value for value, is *certain*, apart from any possible changes in the value of the different goods.

By such a definition, the pure *nominal* interest will be the nominal interest yielded by a loan that attracts no administrative costs and the full repayment of which as to nominal value is certain, abstracting from possible changes in the nominal value of the different goods.[3]

Doubtless the fear of depreciation of the money of account involves an undeniable risk bearing on the nominal rate of interest, but I shall treat this risk premium as included in the pure nominal interest.[4]

---

1. This analysis will be completed and clarified later (nos. 33 and 84).

2. If it were possible to discover the actual interest, taking into account losses really incurred, yielded on average by different investments, this could be taken as an approximate measure of pure interest, subject to the assumption — which seems to be generally the case — that management premiums are negligible compared to risk premiums. It may be admitted on this assumption, as a first approximation and by the interplay of averages, that the portion of interest payable as a risk premium is entirely offset by losses incurred and therefore that the average interest actually yielded by the different investments is equal to the pure interest.

3. It will be seen later (no. 84) that this definition must be completed to take account of the liquidity advantages presented by such loans.

4. These unavoidably cursory indications will be made clearer in what follows (no. 84).

When the pure interest rate is thus defined, it is clear that the risk premium covers all risks other than that of depreciation of money.

In what follows, to simplify the theory, the management premium will usually be disregarded in first-order approximations.

9. The assumption of perfect foresight (12)

In order to simplify this study, I will assume in general, as a first approximation, that foresight of the future development of the market both from the psychological and from the technical point of view is perfect.

This assumption implies that any economic decision taken in the present and involving the future will be verified in practice. There will therefore be *no error*, and risk will be entirely absent; every loan will be reimbursed in full on the terms specified, all industrial equipment will be fully used, depreciations will be apportioned exactly, and production will be rigorously balanced by consumption.

In the absence of risk, *the only limit on transactions involving the future will be the limit imposed by the prices themselves.* Thus in the exchange of future goods against present goods, the borrower will be able to obtain a loan as small or as great as he may wish at the market price. A request for 100,000 francs will not be reduced to 5,000 simply on the grounds that he lacks sufficient security, for by definition there will be no risk.

> In the actual world, of course, no such perfect market exists. While many people in New York City can obtain as large loans as they wish, there are thousands who are unable to obtain any at all. The price of a loan is paid not in the present, as the price of sugar is paid, but in the future. What the lender gets when he makes the loan is not payment but a promise of payment, and the future being always uncertain he needs some sort of assurance that this promise will be kept. We are assuming . . . that there will never be a lack of such assurance. . . . *The element of risk is assumed to be entirely lacking.*[1]

Granted such a hypothesis is highly abstract and may at first seem far removed from reality. But although reality does not exclude economic errors, its predictions nevertheless typically display a significant measure of exactitude. The baker calculates without appreciable error the quantity of bread he needs to bake. The trader who orders a load of bananas to be delivered to Marseille generally receives them within the allotted time and sells them at the price intended. This being so, the *simplest approximation* to reality that can be made is in fact perfect foresight.

1. Irving Fisher, *The Theory of Interest* (New York: Kelley & Millman, 1954), pt. 2, ch. 5, § 1. Emphasis mine.

This approximation makes every economic calculation bearing on the future exactly right; it eliminates risk and hence also eliminates arbitrary factors that would be difficult to represent; thus it enables us to give a simple representation of the key economic mechanisms involving *time* and ultimately to determine the rate of interest with precision.

Naturally, whenever needed, I shall indicate in the course of the ensuing explanations what modifications should be made to the results obtained in order to take account of risk.

10. Stationary models (13)

Of the different sets of economic conditions involving time, the simplest that can be conceived are certainly those for which the different prices and overall parameters of quantity remain constant over time. I shall call them *stationary models* or *stationary processes*.

In a stationary model, the psychological and technical structures are assumed to remain identical over time. The number of individuals in each category is assumed not to vary, and the tastes and needs corresponding to each category are invariable. Production techniques also remain unchanged and there is no technical progress.

Over a given period, let us say a year, the same goods follow the same route. Of the total output, the fraction just necessary to make good the wear and tear of capital as and when necessary is retained, while the rest is consumed.

"From period to period, the life of this economy continues, 'today' reproducing 'yesterday' and 'tomorrow' reproducing 'today.' This life from which economic risk is excluded is a circuit whose unchanging course repeats itself, never being modified by any development."[1,2] If the equilibrium is competitive, it corresponds, as we shall see,[3] to optimal use, for given psychological and technical structures, of final and intermediate goods, obtained after initial trial and error.

The stationary model can be taken as a first approximation to the real economy, at least in periods of economic stability. In point of fact, in most sectors, and for periods that may cover several years,[4] consumption and production remain more or less constant and of the same nature. This is

---

1. François Perroux, *Cours d'économie politique*, vol. 4 (Paris: Domat-Montchrestien, 1941), 169.

2. It must be clearly understood that a stationary economy is by no means one in which no change is *possible*. A stationary economy *could* in fact undergo modifications, for its development depends at every point in time on the decisions of different economic agents (individuals and firms). That it does *not* change is due to the fact that the *data* remain unchanged. In reality, the decisions of individual economies are *continually being reviewed, but they remain the same* simply because a change in these decisions would lead to no improvement.

3. No. 55.

4. And in some cases even for several centuries (Chinese or Arab economies).

the case, for example, for the production of coal and electricity, and for the consumption of bread, wine, etc., in a given country.

And, as we shall see, the consideration of stationary processes is particularly useful in the study of interest.[5,6]

5. See in particular the study of social productivity in chapter 7.

6. Some authors have maintained that interest could not exist under stationary economic conditions. As may be verified by simple examples, this is a gross delusion. (See appendix II.)

11. Representation of the rate of interest (14)

Bearing in mind the law of uniqueness of prices in a competitive equilibrium and assuming no administrative fees and perfect foresight, it follows that *between any two points of time, for any given terms of payment, there can be only a single interest rate in the market*: the pure interest rate.

This is the reason behind the assumptions made, particularly that of perfect foresight. The single rate facilitates mathematical representation and discussion.

I shall denote by I_q the rate of annual interest payable annually for the year T_q, and by J_q the rate of annual interest payable annually for the period (t_0, t_q).

And I shall denote by the symbol i the continuous interest rate relative to the infinitesimal period $(t, t + dt)$ and by j the continuous interest rate relative to the period (t_0, t).

The rate i represents the continuous rate of interest at a given point in time; I shall call this the *continuous instantaneous rate*. The rate j represents the continuous interest rate between any two given instants; I shall call it the *continuous average rate*.

Generally speaking the discontinuous rates I and J are average rates[1] between two specific points in time. When these points constitute the limits of a single period of time T, I shall term the corresponding rates *instantaneous rates*.

Thus the notation I_q denotes the discontinuous instantaneous rate relative to time t_q; this is the interest yielded during the year T_q and paid at the end of this period.[2]

---

1. This notion will be clarified further on (no. 17).

2. The use of the different letters i, j, I, and J depending on the modalities considered can be summarized in the following double entry table:

TABLE 2.1 FOOTNOTE

Rates ⇒ Characteristic Period ↓	Instantaneous	Average
0	i	j
1	I	J

Range of variation of interest rates

It is clear that the annual rate of interest payable annually cannot be lower than –1, whereas the continuous interest rate may have any value.

These results are self-evident. Plainly within the period of a year no capital can lose more than 100% of its value; so the annual rate of interest payable annually must be greater than –1. On the other hand, it is clear that continuous interest rates can have any value and display no lower limit as discontinuous rates do. This is because a continuous rate obtains only for an infinitesimal period of time *dt*, so that a very high negative continuous rate, if in force only for very short period, might in fact lead to a final depreciation of less than 100%. For instance, a continuous interest rate of –500% applied for a period equal to only 1/100 of the unit of time yields a net depreciation of only 5%.[3]

No doubt some readers will initially be surprised to find *negative interest rates* under consideration, since experience shows that nominal interest rates[4] are always positive. But this is one of the very points that call for explanation;[5] indeed it constitutes one of the fundamental problems posed by the theory of interest, and, as we shall see, it is necessarily verified only under certain structural conditions.[6]

In any event, while experience only ever presents us with positive *nominal* interest rates, we often encounter negative[7] *real*[8] interest rates during periods of high inflation.

So in order to be comprehensive I shall be taking into account the possibility of negative interest rates in what follows.

3. The lower limit of the range of variation of the interest rate naturally varies according to how it is defined (no. 10). Readers wishing to study this question more closely are recommended to consult my general work *À la recherche d'une discipline économique*, no. 49.

4. I.e., expressed in units of account (no. 5).

5. See what was said above in no. 3.

6. It will be shown later that in an economy in which land was publicly owned and money depreciated in nominal value over time, negative nominal interest rates would be perfectly possible (chapter 9, "The Problem of Interest").

7. Thus in 1937, while the compound interest rate on fixed-income securities in France was 5.6%, the real interest rate for these same securities, taking price rises into account, had fallen to –15.2% (Institut de Conjoncture français, *L'intérêt réel du capital* [Real interest on capital], 1942, 7).

8. I.e., expressed in terms of goods (see nos. 5 and 19 below).

12. Continuous capitalization and discounting (15)

Capitalization

Capitalization is the process of finding out what capital C_1 invested at time t_1 has become at time t if its successive interest yields have been reinvested as soon as they accrue.

Let C be the value at time t of capital C_1, and let dC be the differential growth of this capital over period dt. From the definition given of the continuous instantaneous interest rate $i(t)$, these notations give us

(1) $$dC = iC\, dt.$$

This equation simply translates into mathematical terms the definition given[1] of the continuous instantaneous rate; it can therefore be regarded as the equation defining this rate. From this viewpoint the interest rate is seen to be a quantity characterizing the growth of any capital yielding interest that is continuously compounded.

In the accepted terminology, capital is said to be productive of value and the rate of interest represents the rate at which it produces value.

Equation (1) gives

(2) $$C = C_1 e^{\int_{t_1}^{t} i\, dt}.$$

For the difference $(C - C_1)$ I shall use the term *value acquired* by capital C_1 between time t_1 and time t.

It is easy to see that for given values of the function $i(t)$, equation (1) in the (t, C) plane, represents a cluster of curves (fig. 2.2) depending on a single parameter. In fact we may write

(3) $$C = \frac{C_1}{e^{\int_{0}^{t_1} i\, dt}} e^{\int_{0}^{t} i\, dt},$$

C_1 being the value of C at time t_1. These curves, which I shall call capitalization curves, are all homologous to the curve

1. Nos. 10 and 14.

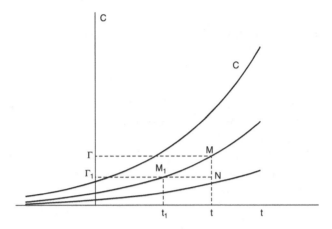

FIGURE 2.2 Variations in capital as a function of time for given levels of interest

(4)
$$C = e^{\int_0^t i\,dt}$$

in relation to the t-axis.[2]

If the continuous instantaneous rate i is *constant*, we have

(5)
$$C = C_1 e^{i(t-t_1)}.$$

In this case the compounding curves are exponential, and it is immediately verified that they are all deduced from the curve

(6)
$$C = e^{it}$$

by a translation parallel to the t-axis.[3]

Discount

If capital C is stipulated to be payable at a certain time, its value C_1 at every time t_1 earlier than maturity time t, i.e., its *present* value at time t_1, is generally less than C; the process of calculating this present value is termed *discounting* the capital C. The discount is defined as the difference between the stipulated value and the present value.

---

2. The curves of figure 2.2 have been drawn on the assumption that rate i is constant.
3. In fact it suffices to note that we have $C_1 e^{i(t-t_1)} = e^{i[t-(t_1-\frac{LC_1}{i})]}$.

Since the present value C_1, at time t_1, capitalized from t_1 to t, must give the stipulated value C, it follows that the discount process is the inverse of the capitalization process, and the results obtained in the preceding paragraph can be transposed without difficulty.

Thus as the expression of the present value we find

(7)
$$C_1 = Ce^{-\int_{t_1}^{t} i\,dt}.$$

13. Discontinuous capitalization and discounting (16)

It is easy to see what happens to the preceding formulae when the rates of interest studied are discontinuous rates. Let J_q be the average discontinuous interest rate between t_0 and t_q. The interest paid at the end of each year is equal to the product of the capital sum by J_q, so that if the accruing interest is continuously compounded, the capital is multiplied at the end of the year by the binomial $(1 + J_q)$. Hence, we have

(1) $$C_q = C_0(1+J_q)^{(t_q-t_0)}.$$

This equation simply translates into mathematical language the definition given of the discontinuous rate of interest; it can therefore be regarded as the equation defining this rate.

Conversely, the present value C_0 at time t_0 of capital C_q is given by the equation

(2) $$C_0 = C_q(1+J_q)^{-(t_q-t_0)}.$$ [1]

1. The situation can be more directly expressed as follows. If a sum of money is loaned between times t_0 and t_q at rate J_q its owner receives at time t_q a sum $(1 + J_q)^q$. So the statement that the interest rate is J_q means that the sum of money available at time t_0 is exchanged against a sum $(1 + J_q)^q$ to be received at time t_q; in other words, the *present value* at time t_0 of a sum of money to be received at time t_q is $\frac{1}{(1+J_q)^q}$.

14. Equivalent rates (17)

Definition

Two investments are said to be equivalent between two instants t_0 and t if they enjoy the same relative growth of capital reinvested between these two instants. The corresponding rates of interest are said to be equivalent.

It is of course easy to see that in a competitive system in equilibrium all financial investments must be equivalent.

(i) The average continuous rate of interest

Let there be an investment for which the continuous instantaneous rate of interest is defined by the function $i(t)$. By definition, the average continuous rate $j(t)$ between the instants t_0 and t must satisfy the equation

(1)
$$e^{jt} = e^{\int_0^t i \, dt},$$

i.e.,

(2)
$$j(t) = \frac{\int_0^t i(t) \, dt}{t},$$

Hence the average continuous rate of interest is seen to be the arithmetic mean of the continuous instantaneous rates over the period in question.

(ii) The discontinuous rate of interest

Let J be the average discontinuous rate of interest between t_0 and t. We must have

(3)
$$(1 + J)^t = e^{jt},$$

i.e.,

(4)
$$(1 + J) = e^j. \qquad\qquad\qquad 1$$

1. This equation shows that the discontinuous rate and the continuous rate are of the

As a first approximation, if j is low, we therefore have

(5) $$J = j.$$

For values of j on the order of 1% to 10%, the relative error thus committed is on the order of 1/1000.

Moreover, in light of the definition given of the different discontinuous rates and taking account of the condition of equivalence, we must have

(6) $$(1 + J_p)^p = (1 + I_1)(1 + I_2) \ldots (1 + I_p),$$

(7) $$1 + I_p = \frac{(1 + J_p)^P}{(1 + J_{p-1})^{P-1}}.$$

Such are the equations that link the different annual interest rates payable annually.

The case of stationary conditions

If the economy under consideration is stationary,[2] we have

(8) $$I_1 = I_2 = \ldots = I_p = I$$ $i = \text{constant},$

and consequently

(9) $$J_1 = J_2 = \ldots = J_p = J = I$$ $j = i.$

It follows from these equations that in a stationary equilibrium, the level of the annual rate of interest payable annually is independent of the loan period. Hence there is no difference between the rates of pure interest corresponding to short- and long-term financial assets.

Moreover, it follows from equation (4) that we have

(10) $$1 + I = e^i$$

---

same sign. Indeed it can be shown that this is universally applicable and that the sign of the
rate of interest relative to a given period is independent of how it is defined.
    2. No. 13.

or, for low rate levels,

(11) $I \sim i.$

Variation of pure interest rates with maturity

Theoretically, therefore, as many average interest rates J_q can be imagined as there are periods (t_0, t_q). But only two rates are considered in practice: the short-term rate, being the average of the rates for short-term loans (whose period is a few months at most) on the money market, and the long-term rate, being the average of the rates for long-term loans on the financial market (whose period is of several years).

Moreover, as we shall see,[3] the rates quoted do not represent the corresponding pure interest rates, and, in so far as can be judged, the short-term rate must be assumed[4] to be lower than the corresponding pure rate of interest owing to the advantage of easier negotiability offered by short-term debt, while the long-term rate must be assumed[4] to be greater than the corresponding pure rate of interest owing to the existence of a risk premium for long-term debt due to the uncertainty of the future.

The difference between the short- and long-term rates of pure interest is thus in general less than might appear at first sight. If the economic environment were stationary, it follows from what has already been explained that the difference would be strictly nil, and since, at least in periods of monetary stability, the economy can be compared as a first approximation to a stationary model, it is safe to assume that the difference between them is in reality very slight.[4]

Finally it appears that the generally observed higher level of the long-term over the short-term interest rate should probably be attributed to the existence of a higher liquidity premium for short-term debt than for long-term debt and a greater risk premium for long-term debt.[5]

3. No. 84.
4. At least in general.
5. These observations will be clarified later (nos. 82 and 84).

15. The Fable of the Golden Shilling (18)

The foregoing formulae show that compounded capital grows exponen-
tially, and it is easy to prove that, even for relatively low levels of annual
interest rates, capital on which the interest is continuously compounded
swiftly attains enormous values.

Suffice it to recount the Fable of the Napoleon gold shilling [*sou*][1] invested in the year zero of our era at an interest rate of 5.7%.

One thousand nine hundred and forty-five years later, the capital sum
in gold accumulated by the continuous compounding of the interest derived from this modest shilling would constitute a mass equivalent to as
many Earth-sized globes of pure gold as the time elapsed in the interval
measured in billionths of a second.[2]

1. The [1803] Napoleon gold shilling remained the French *sou* until the 1928 monetary
reform. [It was worth five centimes or one twentieth of a gold Franc and contained 0.016125g
of 90% pure gold.—Trans.]

2. This is easily demonstrated by a simple calculation.

Let d be the density of the gold, R and M the length in meters of the earth's radius and
meridian, p the weight in grams of the gold shilling of Germinal, and P the weight in grams of
a globe of standard gold of the size of the earth; we have

$$P = 10^6 \frac{4}{3}\pi R^3 d = \frac{10^6 M^3}{6\pi^2} d \text{ grams.}$$

Let N be the number of billionths of seconds that have elapsed since the year 0; we have

$$N = 1{,}945 \times 365 \times 24 \times 60 \times 60 \times 10^9.$$

If I is the rate of interest such that the reinvested golden shilling yields in 1945 a gold
capital of weight NP, we shall have

$$p(1+I)^{1{,}945} = NP,$$

i.e.,

$$\log(1+I) = \frac{1}{1{,}945} \log \frac{NP}{p}.$$

Taking into account the expressions of N and P and the values

$M = 40 \ 10^6$ meters, $p = 0.0161$ grams, $d = 19.3,$

we find that

$$\log(1 + I) = \frac{51.88}{1,945} 0.0267,$$

hence

$$I \sim 6.34\%.$$

If the calculation were made in terms of seconds, rather than billionths of seconds, i.e.,

$$N = 1{,}945 \times 365 \times 24 \times 60 \times 60,$$

the value found for I would be slightly less: 5.14%.

16. Monetary interest rates, wage interest rates, real interest rates, gold interest rates, true interest rates (19)

To designate the level of the interest rate I have respectively used the terms[1] the *monetary* interest rate, the *wage* interest rate, the *real* interest rate, the *gold* interest rate, or the *true* interest rate, depending on whether the standard of value used in each case is the unit of circulating money, the hourly wage *s* of unskilled labor, the value whose nominal level is equal to the price index *P*, the unit of weight of gold, or the unit value of any good or service.

I shall designate these different standards or measures of the interest rates by attributing to the corresponding nominal measures the superscript prime ['], double prime ["], triple prime ['''], quadruple prime [''''], and v.

All these notions are in fact very simple. For instance, the distinction between the nominal interest rate and the real interest rate corresponds to the familiar distinction between nominal wages and real wages.

The real rate of interest is the rate of interest as evaluated by reference to the purchasing power of nominal capital. Thus it can be said that in a period when prices are rising by 1% per year a nominal interest rate of 5% is equivalent, when measured in goods, to a real interest rate of 4%.

In short, the real interest rate is the rate of interest yielded not by the nominal capital but by its purchasing power.

Since the different measures of interest rates obviously have comparable properties,[2] we need only examine, for example, the properties of real interest rates.

Average discontinuous real interest rate

By the definition of this rate we have

(1) $$C''' = C_0''' (1 + J''')^t,$$

where C''' represents the real measure $\dfrac{C}{P}$ of the capital whose nominal measure is C. Thus we have

---

1. No. 5.

2. In fact all that has been set out in nos. 15 and 16 relative to nominal interest rates and nominal capital applies unchanged to real interest rates and real capital.

(2)
$$(1+J''')^t = \frac{P_0}{P}(1+J)^t.$$

Real continuous instantaneous interest rate

By definition we have

(3)
$$dC''' = i'''C''' \, dt,$$

and since

(4)
$$C''' = \frac{C}{P},$$

we also have

(5)
$$\frac{dC'''}{C'''} = \frac{dC}{C} - \frac{dP}{P},$$

and hence

(6)
$$i''' = i - \frac{\frac{dP}{dt}}{P}.$$
                                                                                    3

Thus the real continuous instantaneous interest rate is equal to the nominal continuous instantaneous interest rate minus the relative rate of variation of the price index.

The same would be found for the continuous instantaneous wage rate of interest:

(7)
$$i'' = i - \frac{\frac{ds}{dt}}{s}.$$

3. This expression shows that, when the value unit changes, the new value for the different interest rates is obtained by *adding* a specific quantity to them. So the magnitude of the interest rate relative to the unit of value is quite distinct in form from the values usually met in the physical sciences, in which translation from one unit of measurement to another is made by multiplying by a certain factor, and its study calls for more widespread knowledge of the classical theory of measurement. (Readers interested by this subject may find further information in my general work *À la recherche d'une discipline économique*, 220–67.)

From this it can be seen that there are as many distinct expressions of the rate of interest as there are possible standards of value. In theory there is nothing to prevent our replacing the money of account in the usual interest formula by wheat or any other good, but in practice only money is negotiated between present and future.

If the purchasing power of the standard legally established in the shape of the unit of account was always stable in relation to different goods, the rate of interest calculated using this unit would be the same as if it were calculated in terms of purchasing power. But when the value of the unit of account appreciates or depreciates in relation to goods, the numbers that express the two interest rates—the one calculated in terms of the unit of account and the other on the basis of some specific good—are quite different.

Of course, as already indicated,[4] when the unit of account is the value of the unit of money, as it is in our own economy, the monetary interest rate, i.e., the measure of the interest rate calculated in terms of circulating money, is precisely equal to the nominal interest rate.

The case of a stationary model

When, as in a stationary model, the different prices remain constant,[5] the different expressions of the interest rate—whether wage interest, real interest, etc.—are, as has been shown above,[6] all equal to the nominal interest rate.

4. No. 6.
5. No. 13.
6. Equations (6) and (7) above.

17. The production process (20)

The set of operations necessary to production is termed the *production process*.

Production processes can be classified in two different categories: direct processes and indirect, or roundabout, processes.

Direct processes are those that serve to produce the finished product immediately out of its primary factors.[1] One example of such is fishing, which will be considered in chapter 3. Such processes are relatively rare in our days, and scarcely go beyond the supply of direct services (e.g., the services rendered by domestic servants).

Indirect processes are those that make use of capital.[2] They comprise several stages. The primary stages correspond to the creation of capital and the secondary stages to making use of the capital to produce consumer goods. I shall use the term *direct labor* for labor applied in the secondary stages and *indirect labor* for labor applied in the primary stages.

While direct processes correspond to a quasi-instantaneous production, indirect processes take time, and an interval is therefore necessary between the utilization of the primary factors and the emergence of the finished consumer products.

---

1. Land and labor.
2. By *capital* I mean reproducible capital, to the exclusion of land (see no. 42).

CHAPTER THREE

The Fable of the Fishermen

1. A fable (21)

A s the subject of interest raises some exceptionally difficult issues, it is useful to begin its study by considering a simplified economy presented in the guise of a fable in which a few key features can easily be highlighted.

Let us suppose that there are three fishermen on an island: Peter, who is 20 years old, Paul, who is 30, and James, who is 40.

Their conditions of life are quite difficult, as they must furnish 4,000 hours of labor per year to be sure of an annual catch, using their barely rudimentary means, of 200 kg of fish on which to live.

It is assumed that they have no means of preserving the fish and that they are also ignorant of the use of money and of the appropriation of natural resources.[1]

---

1. It will be seen later how these details should be modified, particularly with regard to the sign of the nominal interest rate, to take account of land ownership, the use of money, and the possibility of storing certain goods (chapter 9, "The Problem of Interest").

2. Possibility of a positive or negative real interest rate in the absence of any indirect process of production (22)

Although the economy we are studying has no indirect production process, it is easy to see that it may come to make use of an interest rate.

Let us suppose, for instance, that Paul falls ill and that, in order to subsist while waiting to recover, he needs 50 kg of fish. In such a case it is clearly in his interests to borrow these 50 kg, which he needs, from one of the other fishermen, even if he must undertake to reimburse a greater quantity, for example, 60 kg, i.e., even if he must undertake to pay real positive interest measured in fish.

Moreover, James, who is relatively old, may perfectly well prefer to reduce his immediate consumption of fish in order to diminish later on the amount of labor he performs. He may prefer, by increasing his present effort, to produce a further 50 kg, for instance, even with a view to receiving in exchange, in the future, a lesser quantity, for example, 40 kg, i.e., even if he has to lend at a negative real interest rate measured in fish.

It may well be imagined that, perchance after some debate between Paul, who wishes to borrow, albeit at a positive interest rate, and James, who is seeking to lend, albeit at a negative interest rate, a compromise is reached that seems to each party to be in his interests. Of course, the real interest rate chosen will in fact be positive or negative depending on whether James or Paul shows himself the more skillful bargainer.

Hence this example enables us to prove that, independently of any indirect operation of production, an interest rate may come into existence in the economy, and it is clear that a priori, *under the conditions assumed, there is no reason for this interest rate to be positive rather than negative.* Each possibility seems equally probable, and the observed outcome will essentially depend on the specific case involved.[1]

---

1. It will be seen later that, in the economies we are familiar with, imperious reasons (the private ownership of land and the possibility of storing certain goods such as money at no appreciable expense) ensure that the nominal interest rate (i.e., the interest rate measured in units of account) is necessarily positive (chapter 9, "The Problem of Interest"). (See the observations already made on this subject in nos. 3 and 14.)

3. Effects of technical progress (23)

Let us now assume that Peter is exceptionally ingenious and discovers that the use of a net makes fishing much more productive.

Let us also assume, for instance, that 4,000 hours of labor—the labor of one fisherman for one year—are needed to make a net and that, using a net, two fishermen can catch 2,400 kg of fish per year and finally that the net is entirely worn out by the end of the year.

It is plain that the new process, if it can be used, is much more profitable: it means that a total annual output of 600 kg of fish can be replaced by a total annual output of 2,400 kg, i.e., four times as much.

In the first case, the number of hours of labor corresponding to the production of one kilogram of fish, which might be termed the "labor intensiveness"[1] of the production of the kilogram of fish and could be measured in "man-hours," the *man-hour* being defined as the labor of one worker for one hour, is

$$\frac{12,000}{600} = 20 \text{ man-hours.}$$

But in the second case this labor intensiveness becomes

$$\frac{12,000}{2,400} = 5 \text{ man-hours.}$$

Recourse to an indirect process of production therefore has the advantage of decreasing labor input per unit of output, i.e., labor intensiveness.

However, in order for the new procedure to get underway, it is imperative that one of the fishermen should give up fishing altogether for a year and devote his time to manufacturing a net, which means that during this period the other two fishermen must supply him with the quantity of fish he needs to live on. Hence, if Peter has the idea of using a net, before embarking on his new method, he must necessarily borrow from the other two fishermen the quantity of fish necessary for his subsistence during the coming year. Since production will be considerably increased thereafter,

1. "Labor intensiveness," which I am using to translate the author's French neologism *laborité*, denotes the input of labor in man-hours per unit of output such that greater input means higher labor intensiveness (or lower labor efficiency).—Trans.

as he has foreseen, he can undertake to reimburse a greater quantity of fish than he will be borrowing, i.e., to pay a positive rate of real interest.

It is perfectly possible that, in light of Peter's proposals, the other two fishermen should think it in their interest to lend Peter the amount of fish he needs to subsist on while making the net. But as their life must temporarily become more austere, we must conclude that the real interest rate agreed on will prove to be at least as high as that which prevailed under the former conditions. For it is inconceivable for a greater restriction in consumption to be obtained on the basis of a lower real interest rate.

It emerges from this that the discovery of a technical process has the immediate effect[2] of inciting economic agents to decrease their present consumption with a view to increased future consumption and of provoking a rise in real interest.

Once the net has been made, Peter can put it to use with the help of the other two fishermen, and the output will be increased to 2,400 kg per year.

If, in order to make his net, Peter contracted a debt of 150 kg of fish, he will be able to reimburse it without difficulty, even if he committed himself to paying a relatively high rate of real interest, for instance, 100%; indeed, to persuade Paul and James to give up their former fishing method and come and work with him using his net, he could pay them a higher annual wage, for instance, 400 kg of fish. Moreover he could at the same time make the manufacture of a new net his own activity while Paul and James use the first one.

Finally, it can be seen that, taking account of the replacement of the net, and notwithstanding the very high rate of real interest and the increase in wages he must bear, at the end of the second year Peter will be left with a net annual income of

$$2,400 - 300 - 800 = 1,300 \text{ kg of fish,}$$

corresponding to the excess of the new output of 2,400 kg of fish over the payment of 300 kg by way of repayment of the debt contracted plus interest, and 800 kg of fish for wages.

It is thus verified that, thanks to a technical progress, an entrepreneur can at the same time incur debt at a relatively high rate of real interest, increase real wages, and, nonetheless, enjoy a substantial increase in income while simultaneously renewing his capital.

2. I.e., for primary effect in the sense of note 1 to no. 9.

4. Possibility of positive real interest under stationary conditions in the case of an indirect production process (24)

Having once paid off his debt, Peter may very well no longer wish to work after the end of the second year, in view of the considerable increase in his real income; and he might propose to lend his net[1] to one of the other two fishermen on condition that the latter undertakes (a) to renew it when it is worn out and (b) to pay, in addition, a certain real interest measured in fish.

We can thus imagine a steady state becoming established in which the capital of the economy in question, i.e., the net, is owned by Peter and loaned by him, against interest, to Paul, for instance, and in which Paul will be really able each year to honor the interest payment to which he has committed himself as well as periodically renewing Peter's net.[2]

We might, for instance, have each year the situation presented in table 3.1.

TABLE 3.1

Annual output: 2,400 × ⅔	1,600 kg of fish
Annual income of entrepreneur Paul	600 kg of fish
Annual wages of worker James	400 kg of fish
Positive interest paid annually by Paul for the use of Peter's net, the renewal of which is his responsibility at the end of each period of use (= Peter's annual income)	600 kg of fish
Value of capital held by Peter (= value of one net = annual wages of one worker)*	400 kg of fish
Rate of interest applied $+ \dfrac{600}{400}$	+150%

* Because in equilibrium price and cost of production are equal.

1. Made by Peter during the second year.
2. In this case, as two men working together are needed to use the net, it can be imagined that the production cycle will be 18 months. During the first 6 months Paul and James produce a net that they will use during the following 12 months. Then annual production will be reduced to 2/3 of what it was before, i.e.,

$$2,400 \times \frac{2}{3} = 1,600 \text{ kg of fish.}$$

5. Possibility of a real negative rate under stationary conditions in the case of an indirect production process (25)

However, it is possible that Peter, while lending his net to Paul, may continue to work as a fisherman[1] and that his solicitude for the future may be so great that he prefers—in order to have a constant reserve—to loan his net at a real negative interest rate, rather than to exchange it immediately for fish that could not be kept, or to put it in storage, which, under the supposed climatic conditions of the island, would risk leaving it unusable after a few years.

It might even happen that, in light of the increased production of fish, Paul and James insist on higher wages in fish for their personal labor.

It is conceivable that, in view of Peter's intense desire for possessions and Paul's and James's increased demands, a real negative interest rate in fish might at length become established.

We might, for instance, each year have table 3.2.

TABLE 3.2

Annual output	2,400 kg of fish
Annual income of entrepreneur Paul	1,230 kg of fish
Annual wages paid by Paul to workers Peter and James	1,230 kg of fish
Negative interest annually received by Paul for the yearly renewal of Peter's net	–60 kg of fish
Peter's annual income* 615 – 60	555 kg of fish
Value of capital held by Peter (= value of a net = annual wages of one worker)**	615 kg of fish
Rate of interest applied $-\dfrac{60}{615}$	–9.75%

* Equal to the excess of his annual wages of 615 kg over the negative interest he must pay Paul for keeping his capital (one net) in good condition.
** Because in equilibrium price and cost of production are equal.

1. In this case annual output again becomes 2,400 kg of fish and the production cycle 12 months.

6. Role of the rate of interest in production (26)

The role played in the economy by the rate of interest and by the use of roundabout processes of production thus becomes apparent.

A new process can be implemented if it enables output to be increased for the same input of the primary factors of production; but this implementation calls for temporary abstinence from consumption with a view to greater future consumption; it also calls for a change in the way these primary factors are used.

Once the necessary capital has been saved, the new process can continue to be applied only if the necessary capital is constantly renewed, i.e., if the owners of this capital refrain from consuming its value.

The real interest rate that becomes established is such that the capital that the public desires to own is precisely equal to the total capital used by the economy. A priori, for unexceptional structural conditions, this rate may equally well be negative or positive.[1]

Since in a stationary environment the different expressions of the level of the interest rate are equal, evidently the results obtained for the real interest rate remain valid for the nominal interest rate or the wage interest rate, which a priori may equally well be negative or positive.

---

1. Let us recall once more that the only reason why this result may seem surprising at first sight is our habit, based on immemorial experience, of thinking that the nominal rate of interest must necessarily be positive. One of the fundamental questions posed by interest is precisely *why* the nominal rate of interest always remains positive in our economy although a priori negative rates are perfectly conceivable (see the remarks already made in nos. 3, 14, and 22).

The argumentation presented shows that in fact "there is no absolutely necessary reason inherent in the nature of man or things why the rate of interest . . . should be positive rather than negative" (Fisher, *The Theory of Interest*, pt. 2, ch. 8, § 5). And our failure to find any example in the economic reality we live in of a zero or negative rate is due, as we shall see, to the fact that our economy is marked by different structural conditions from those that prevail in the fable — conditions that call for elucidation.

7. Characteristic diagram of production (27)

In the first method of production, the annual output of 600 kg of fish was obtained by a labor input, over the same year, of 12,000 hours.

When the new process is in place and each of the three fishermen continues to put in 4,000 hours of labor, each annual output of 2,400 kg of fish is obtained by (a) an input in the same year of 8,000 hours of labor and (b) an input of 4,000 hours of labor in the preceding year.

Each year continues to see 12,000 hours of labor input, but the year's output is obtained thanks to the input of 8,000 *present* hours and 4,000 *past* hours—since the 4,000 hours devoted the same year to producing a new net will in fact only bear fruit the following year.

Thus any production process can be represented by a diagram showing the distribution over time of the hours of labor necessary for the overall output (fig. 3.1).

In the first case, this diagram comprises a rectangle of which the base stands for a year and the area is equal to 12,000 hours of labor. In the second, it comprises two rectangles, the base of each of which is equal to a year and the areas of which respectively represent 8,000 hours and 4,000 hours, the first of them representing the labor input during the year in which the output becomes available and the second the labor input during the year immediately preceding. In both cases the total area of the

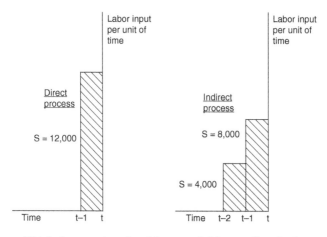

FIGURE 3.1 Distribution over time of work hours needed for overall production

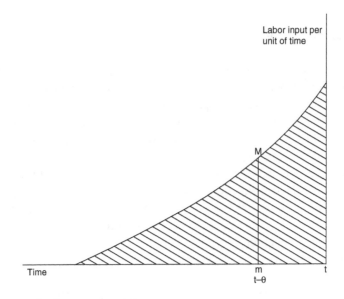

FIGURE 3.2 Continuous representation

diagram is still equal to the total amount of the annual labor input, i.e., 12,000 hours.

Hence it is clear that in a stationary model a production process can generally be represented, for a given annual labor input, by a curve I shall call *the characteristic curve of the process studied* (fig. 3.2), which encloses an area equal to the total annual labor input. This curve represents the distribution of labor over the different stages of production, leading, at the end of the period, to the finished product. Thus the line *mM* parallel to the y-axis represents the labor input, per unit of time, at time $t - \theta$ in order to produce the output that will be available only at time *t*.

CHAPTER FOUR

Interest, Capital, and Capitalization

1. Principles governing exchanges over time (28)

A s the components of the market are assumed to be given, every firm chooses, among the activities open to it, those that will leave it the largest revenue margin between the present, or discounted, value of expected receipts and necessary expenditure.[1]

It is clear that at the point of equilibrium this revenue margin must be zero. For if this condition were not fulfilled, every other firm would be able to engage in comparable activities and would in fact do so, as such activities would enable them to realize additional income. And thus the conditions of equilibrium would *not* be fulfilled.

---

1. In the dynamic disequilibrium of the real economy, the volume of activities carried out by each firm is naturally limited by the purchasing power available to it.

2. Price of durable goods (29)

Every durable good is capable of providing in the future a stream of income represented by its future use-values, and the recipient of this income stream can transfer it to someone else by selling the economic good to which it is attached. It follows from what we have already seen that *in equilibrium the value of a durable good at a given time is necessarily equal to the sum of the present values, at the time in question, of its future income stream.*

This is what I shall call *the law of present values.*

If we now consider at time t_0 a durable good $(\bar{A})$ of price $\bar{a}_0$ liable to last n years, and if we denote by $a_1, a_2, \ldots, a_n$ the prices of its future services $(A_1), (A_2), \ldots, (A_n)$ and if we take as the unit of service the services rendered per unit good per year, we shall necessarily have, in equilibrium,

(1)
$$\bar{a}_0 = \frac{a_1}{(1+J_1)} + \ldots + \frac{a_n}{(1+J_n)^n}.$$
[1,2]

Thus the rate of interest is seen to be the link between capital and income, the bridge that makes it possible to pass from one to the other.

For given interest rates the law of present values tends to be verified. For if the present value of future income were greater than $\bar{a}_0$, the good $(\bar{A})$ would be subject to increased demand at time t_0, which would tend to increase $\bar{a}_0$.[3]

This increase in $\bar{a}_0$ would itself bring about an increase in the production of $(\bar{A})$, assuming that it is a reproducible good. Thereupon the quantity of services rendered by this good would increase, and hence their prices would diminish.[3] Thus the market would develop in such a way that the law of present values would tend to be verified. Similar reasoning would apply in the opposite direction if the price of the durable good in question were greater than the present value of its future income stream.

---

1. It is crucial to note that in this equation a_p does not represent the price at time t_p of the service rendered by good $(\bar{A})$, but the price at that point in time of the service rendered by the good that good (A) has become after p years of service.

2. The income derived from a durable good is, in fact, received at the end of each period.

3. According to the well-known laws of supply and demand.

Likewise if we assume that the prices $\bar{a}_0$ and $\bar{a}_p$ are given and if the price $\bar{a}_0$ were less than the sum of the present values of good $(\bar{A})$, it would be worthwhile to invest present income in the purchase of goods $(\bar{A})$ in order to benefit from future income whose present value is greater. In order to take advantage of this profitable operation, firms would be induced to borrow the necessary sums, which would be repaid later at different times t_q. We shall see that such transactions would bring about an increase in the interest rates J_q. This increase would in turn lead to a decrease in the present value of the future income stream of the good in question. So it is clear that in the case we are considering, the movement of interest rates in the market would continue until the law of present values was verified.

Observed prices and estimated prices

Of course equation (1) will only be rigorously verified over time in terms of observed prices if there is perfect foresight.

If this condition is not fulfilled, these equations will *only apply to the prices estimated at the initial instant by the market as a whole*, i.e., the prices determined on the market at the initial instant for present or future goods. Naturally, they will not apply to the prices in fact observed in the future or to the prices estimated by any particular firm.

Moreover the estimated value of a good is generally not equal to its mathematical value, i.e., to its probable value, taking account of the different possible outcomes and of their respective probabilities.[4] The former may be higher or lower than the latter depending on whether the persons involved are more or less risk inclined. For it is by no means the same thing, from the point of view of the individual, to receive a promise to pay representing a mathematical expectation of 100 francs and to receive the 100 francs in cash: in the latter case, only one outcome is possible whereas in the former, the individual in question might in fact receive, for instance, 120 francs, 100 francs, 90 francs or nothing at all, each of those potential outcomes enjoying a certain probability. The market value of a good will in fact be greater or less than its probable value depending on whether the market as a whole is or is not risk inclined, i.e., on whether it is ready to gamble. Thus two factors play a role in the valuation of a good: the mathematical evaluation of the risks and the subjective cost of the risk itself.

---

4. This probable value is equal to the weighted mean of the expected values of the price, the weighting coefficients being equal to their probabilities as assessed by the market.

A gambler is usually someone for whom the estimated value is greater than the probable value. For him, the pleasure of gambling can be so strong that he does not hesitate to stake his fortune on odds that he knows are against him so that the subjective cost of the risk becomes negative. This is how the "bank" at Monte Carlo can make a profit although its victims know full well that they are paying, in order to play, more than the mathematical value of their chances. The outcome is of course that most of them are ruined.

Conversely, when insurance is taken out, the estimated value of the risk run is greater than its probable value; the subjective cost of the risk is positive. This is the circumstance that makes the phenomenon of insurance possible. If the insurance premium is greater than the probable value of the risk, it can be highly profitable to the insurer since for him, in view of the law of large numbers, there is little difference between the estimated value and the probable value of the risk.[5] But even if the discrepancy between the insurance premium and the probable value of the risk is high, the insurance contract can still be a worthwhile operation for the person insured if, *for him*, the estimated value of the risk is greater than the insurance premium.

As a matter of fact, the ordinary person will not consent to pay a sum equal to his mathematical expectation for a risky investment. He is risk averse and is in fact willing to make sacrifices in order to shield himself from risk.

Of course, the discrepancy between the market value and the mathematical value tends to decrease and to be reduced to a few administrative costs as the risk market develops with the establishment of specialized insurance companies or of large firms whose sheer size enables them to practice self-insurance.

Thus it becomes clear that in the case of stipulated prices (bonds, for instance), the value estimated by the market will generally be little different from the probable value, taking possible risks into account, and that it will consequently be lower than the stipulated price, so that the present value of the estimated price will be lower than the present value of the stipulated price, present values being calculated at pure interest rates. In fact, it is as though the current value of the probable price were calculated

---

5. Remember that in a game of chance the probable difference increases only as $\sqrt{n}$, where n is the number of throws. Consequently the insurer's unit risk decreases as $\frac{1}{\sqrt{n}}$, where n is the number of persons insured.

on the basis of the stipulated price using an interest rate higher than the pure interest rate: the difference between these rates represents the *risk premium*.[6]

In the marketplace, estimated prices are not in fact taken into account and the consideration of risk is introduced only by the use of interest rates higher than the pure interest rates. So equation (1) is verified in terms of stipulated prices only by applying interest rates that take account of risk premiums corresponding to the uncertainties of the investment.

Thus if a bond is issued at par at 7% by a firm, it means that the firm commits itself to paying at each due date interest of 7 francs per 100-franc bond (the stipulated price). Now if the pure interest rate is 5%, this means that the estimated value of each payment, or at least of *some* payments, is less than 7 francs, so that the present value of successive payments must be calculated on the basis of stipulated prices equal to 7 francs using a 7% interest rate equal to the pure interest rate plus a 2% risk premium.

Estimated-risk premium and cost-of-risk premium

From the foregoing analysis it follows that the risk premium that is added to the pure interest rate can be broken down into two components, of which the first corresponds to the difference between the stipulated price and the probable value and the second to the difference between the probable value and the commercial value.[7] These two components may, respectively, be called the *estimated-risk premium* and the *cost-of-risk premium*.

While the *estimated-risk* premium is always positive, the *cost-of-risk* premium might, at least a priori, just as well be negative as positive. In fact, we may take it as being generally positive, its value tending to restrict itself to the unit costs, which become ever lower as market organization improves.

6. See no. 11.

7. I.e., the value as estimated by the market.

3. Price of perpetual annuities (30)

In the specific case of land, which supplies income indefinitely,[1] the law of present values gives

(1)
$$\bar{a}_0 = \sum_{q=1}^{q=\infty} \frac{a_q}{(1+J_q)^q},$$

where a_q is the annual rental price of the land ($\bar{A}$).

If the land in question is able to yield the same income a indefinitely and if the different interest rates are equal to an identical rate I, as is the case in a stationary model, the present value of the land will be

(2)
$$\bar{a} = \sum_{q=1}^{q=\infty} \frac{a}{(1+I)^q},$$

[2]

i.e., if the interest rate is positive,

(3)
$$\bar{a} = \frac{a}{I}.$$

Thus, if a plot of land yields an annual income of 5,000 francs, and if the interest rate, for the various periods of the future, is 5%, the value of the land will be 100,000 francs. This value in fact becomes greater as the interest rate becomes lower and must increase indefinitely if the interest rate takes on lower and lower values tending toward zero.

It might seem astonishing at first sight that men, whose life span is naturally limited, should take account, in estimating the value of land, of infinitely remote incomes, and it might be thought that equation (2) could not be rigorously exact and that in particular the value of a plot of land could not become infinite if the interest rate tended toward zero.

But in fact it is easy to see how men take their infinitely distant income into account in estimating the value of land and to verify that, equation (3) is perfectly rigorous. Any plot of land of value $\bar{a}$ is able at any point in time

---

1. The income here considered is the income obtained by the land *as such, independently of any capital* (clearance, fertilizer, etc.) *that might be attached to it.*

2. In this case the common value of the average rates J is equal to the common value of the instantaneous rates I.

to yield, by sale, an income $\bar{a}$. It follows that according to the law of present values, the value $\bar{a}_0$ of a plot at time t_0 must be equal to the present value at t_0 of the sum of the income a_1 that it would make available at time t_1 and of the likely product $\bar{a}_1$ resulting from its sale at this time; in other words, we must have

(4)
$$\bar{a}_0 = \frac{a_1}{1+I} + \frac{\bar{a}_1}{1+I},$$

i.e., in the case of a stationary model such as we are considering,

(5)
$$\bar{a} = \frac{a}{1+I} + \frac{\bar{a}}{1+I},$$

an equation that translates into

(6)
$$\bar{a} = \frac{a}{I}.$$

It is thus verified that equation (3) may safely be taken as resulting *exclusively* from the estimates of individuals concerning a *limited* period, without direct involvement of infinitely remote incomes.[3]

Land rent and interest

It follows from equation (3) that in a stationary model the land rent a of a plot ($\bar{A}$) equates to the interest $I\bar{a}$ on its value $\bar{a}$. Some authors have inferred from this that land rent is nothing but a form of interest. This is downright confusion.

Indeed it is noteworthy that it is only so under stationary conditions. When land rent varies over time, equation (3) is no longer valid and land rent can no more be regarded as interest than can the price paid for the use of any other good.[4]

---

3. Naturally, these incomes are indirectly involved in equation (4) through the agency of the price $\bar{a}_1$, being the present value at time t_1 of all future incomes generated by the land subsequent to this time.

4. It will be seen later (no. 33) that a relation does indeed exist between the interest rate, the selling price, and the price paid for the use of a good, but that this relation cannot be

In fact it cannot be stressed enough that *the phenomenon of land rent is absolutely distinct from that of interest.* Hence, if by appropriate measures the interest rate were reduced to zero,[5] ground rent would continue to be determined by the same laws as before. Or rather, the only tangible change would be that the capitalized value of this rent would become infinite and private ownership of land would in this case be utterly inconceivable.[5] In the same way, if land rent as a source of private income were eliminated by suitable taxes or by public ownership of land, the phenomenon of interest would continue intact since it is essentially due, as we shall see,[5] to the preference (positive or negative) shown by Society as a whole, for present as opposed to future goods.[6]

Relation between instantaneous rates and average perpetual rates

The term *average perpetual interest rate* and the symbol J_∞ will be used to denote the level of the average interest rate J_q when the period (t_0, t_q) becomes infinitely great.

So let there be (fig. 4.1) two points of time, t_1 and t_0, separated by a year, let I^0 be the instantaneous annual rate of interest between times t_0 and t_1,[7] and let J_∞^0 and J_∞^1 be the perpetual rates of interest at these points. If foresight is perfect, it is easy to see that there is a necessary relation between the three rates I^0, J_∞^0 and J_∞^1. An identical annuity of 1 franc to be paid each year must have the same value whether it is calculated using rate J_∞^0 or rates I_0 and J_∞^1. According to equation (6) the annuities in question have values $\dfrac{1}{J_\infty^0}$ and $1 + \dfrac{1}{J_\infty^1}$ at times t_0 and t_1. Hence, we must have

(7)
$$\frac{1}{J_\infty^0} = \frac{1}{1+I_0}\left(1 + \frac{1}{J_\infty^1}\right).$$

It can be seen that the value attributed to the perpetual rates J_∞^0 and J_∞^1 determines the instantaneous rate I_0. Of course, this result immediately

---

reduced to identity between the price of its use and the interest on its value, and that it involves the variation of this value per unit of time.

5. See chapter 9, "The Problem of Interest."

6. Readers wishing to achieve a clear understanding of the distinct nature of interest and of land rent are advised to study what would happen to economic equilibrium if land ownership were public. (See the study of such an equilibrium in appendix II.)

7. Remember that according to the definitions given (no. 14) this rate represents the average rate between times t_0 and t_1.

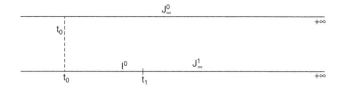

FIGURE 4.1

becomes general, and it is seen that prediction of the perpetual average rates for all future periods is equivalent to prediction of instantaneous rates for the same periods.

Now let us assume that the rate J_∞^0 has a given value while the predicted rate J_∞^1 varies, and let us inquire what the corresponding variations in rate I_0 will be.

By logarithmic differentiation of the second term we obtain

$$
(8) \qquad -\frac{\Delta I_0}{1+I_0} - \frac{\dfrac{\Delta J_\infty^1}{(J_\infty^1)^2}}{1+\dfrac{1}{J_\infty^1}} = 0,
$$

i.e., if the levels of the rates are low,

$$
(9) \qquad \Delta I_0 \sim \frac{\Delta J_\infty^1}{J_\infty^1}.
$$

This equation shows that, for a given value of the perpetual interest rate, the instantaneous rate of interest will undergo quite considerable variations when even minor variations are foreseen in the perpetual interest rate. If the rates I_0 and J_∞^0 both have the same value of 4%, assuming a predicted 1/2 point increase in the perpetual rate, the corresponding change in the instantaneous interest rate is a theoretical fall of 12.5%: 25 times greater. As far as can be judged, this fact contributes to explaining why the short-term rate is much less stable than the long-term rate.[8]

In fact when equilibrium is not attained and there are good grounds for long-term forecasts of a rise or a fall, profitable arbitrage opportunities are likely.

8. Another reason will be explained later (no. 89).

In the case already considered, as long as the fall in the short-term rate has not reached its theoretical value,[9] it would be in an investor's interest to postpone any long-term investment in favor of either short-term investments or simply hoarding his funds.[10] It can thus be seen that an expected rise in the long-term interest rate constitutes a powerful incentive to money hoarding.[11]

9. Which in present conditions will always be the case, since, as we shall see (nos. 81 and 137) the nominal interest cannot become negative.

10. On this hypothesis and in the case being considered, for an available capital of 100 francs one would lose $J_0^\infty = 4$ francs interest, but one would gain $\Delta J_\infty^1 / J_\infty^1 = 12.50$ francs in capital.

11. In particular it follows from the observations made both in the text and in note 10 above that a general expectation of a rise in the long-term rate, to which the short-term rate will not be able to adjust, necessarily leads to large-scale hoarding. Such circumstances are met with especially in cyclical periods of depression.

4. Capital and income (31)

The law of present values is the *essential* law by which the value of any good is determined at a given moment.

The value of a good is what it is worth *as a source of income*, and this is determined by discounting this income. "This principle . . . applies in any market to all property and wealth—stocks, land . . . buildings, machinery, or anything whatever. Risk aside, each has a market value dependent solely on the same two factors, the benefits, or returns, expected by the [enterprise][1] and the market rate of interest by which those benefits are discounted."[2]

When the values of the capital and income are considered, their cause-and-effect relationship is the reverse of that which applies to the tangible goods of which they are the monetary valuation. For while capital yields over time a stream of physical income, it is from the value of this physical income that capital (which is to say the value of capital goods) is derived.

The cause-and-effect sequence is represented by figure 4.2.

Thus, "it is true that the wheat crop depends on the land which yields it. But the value of the crop does not depend on the value of the land. On the contrary, the value of the land depends on the expected value of its

Capital goods
↓
Physical income
↓
Income value (or income)
↓
Capital value (or capital)

FIGURE 4.2

1. The notion of *an enterprise* is here a convenient abstraction that may very well stand for an individual whenever his activity has some other object than consumption properly so called. [Allais substitutes the French word *entreprise* for Fisher's original "investor."—Trans.]

2. Fisher, *The Theory of Interest*, pt. 1, ch. 1, § 11.

crops."[3] So the common expression "the income of capital" is to be taken as a whole, since it is not the income that comes from the capital but the capital that comes from the income.[4]

3. Fisher, *The Theory of Interest*, pt. 1, ch. 1, § 9.
4. The distinction between capital and income often occasions confusion, and many authors, faced with a given case, hesitate between the two terms. Yet the distinction is quite clear: capital is a value, whereas income is essentially a value given or received *per unit of time*. Hence no doubt can be possible in distinguishing between capital and income.

5. Determination of the value of goods (32)

Economists have discussed whether the market price of a good is determined by the cost of production, or whether it is the cost of production that is determined by the market price.

In reality, at a given moment, the value of a good is determined in the market by discounting its future services, at market rates, taking account of risk, and since the number of firms and the market price are both known, each firm develops its output until the marginal cost is equal to the market price.

So if *a short period of time* is considered, it is the value of a good as found by discounting its future services that determines the marginal cost of production. In this case there are as many average costs as there are firms. Hence it is established that neither the average cost nor the marginal cost determines the value of a good at a given moment; on the contrary, *they* are determined by *it*.

If the marginal cost thus determined is greater than the average cost, new firms will come into being and output will increase so that the greater number of future services of the good in question will lead to a fall in their price[1] and the market price will eventually revert to the value of the minimum cost.

If on the other hand the marginal cost is less than the average cost, a certain number of firms will disappear, output will thereupon decrease leading to a corresponding fall in the services later to be rendered by the good in question and thus, eventually, to a rise in the price of these services.[1] The ultimate outcome will be an increase in the present value of the future services of the good being considered, and hence an increase in the market price—and this will continue until this price is equal to the minimum cost.

In this way the actions and reactions form a recurring circuit. See the diagrammatical representation in figure 4.3. The direction of the arrows shows the direction of the cause-to-effect relationships.

This illustrates how the economic circuit functions. All economic action is propagated in a closed circuit and finishes by returning to its starting point.

We see then that the *variations* of the various economic parameters follow clearly determined *laws of cause and effect*, but that, conversely, *in*

---

1. On account of the well-known laws of supply and demand.

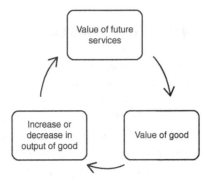

FIGURE 4.3　Diagram of the economic circuit

*equilibrium, there is no cause that assigns specific values to these param-
eters.* The determination of their values is the result of the mutual interdependence of the links in question.

In equilibrium it is therefore idle to discuss whether the natural price of a
good depends on the present value of its present and future services or on its
cost of production, for these magnitudes are in fact mutually interdependent.

This mechanism has given rise to somewhat vain discussions between
the mathematical school and the subjective school, the former denying the
causality and the second seeing therein the very foundation of economic
links. In reality, although the value represented by the price has no cause,
its variations always have well-determined causes; in other words, *although
dynamic equilibrium knows no cause-and-effect relations, dynamic disequilibrium is wholly based on such relations.*

Hence the value of a good at a given moment is essentially determined
by discounting its future services and not by its cost of production. Old
machines, even in good condition, cannot be valued on the basis of their
cost; their only value derives from the discounted value of the services it
is presumed they can still render.

The value of the future services of a given good depends in turn on the
quantity of this good that will be produced—hence on the comparison between its present or future cost and its present or future value. "Past costs
have no *direct* influence on value. Only indirectly do they enter to the
extent that they have determined the existing supply of goods and have
thus either raised or lowered the value of the services of these goods."[2]

2. Fisher, *The Theory of Interest*, pt. 1, ch. 1, § 10.

So the production cost is only indirectly involved but its influence is nonetheless considerable *in the long run*.

To follow the terminology I have adopted,[3] the law of present values is thus seen to be a primary law in the sense that it is always verified, whether in equilibrium or disequilibrium; by contrast, the law of average cost[4] is seen to be a secondary law that can only be rigorously verified in equilibrium.

In reality *the price of a good, which is always equal to the present value of its present and future income stream, is not determined by the cost of production, but the working of the economic mechanism leads the price to coincide with the production cost when equilibrium is attained.*

3. See note 1 to no. 9.
4. According to which price is determined by average cost.

6. Analysis of the price of use (33)

Equation (1) of no. 29 yields in particular

(0)
$$\bar{a}_q = \frac{a_{q+1}}{1+I_{q+1}} + \frac{\bar{a}_{q+1}}{1+I_{q+1}}$$

or

(1)
$$a_{q+1} = I_{q+1} + \bar{a}_q - \bar{a}_{q+1},$$

where a_{q+1} is the price paid for the use of the good in question during the year T_{q+1}, $\bar{a}_q$ is the price of this good at point t_q, and $\bar{a}_{q+1}$ its price at the point t_{q+1} when it has provided a year's service.

This equation can also be expressed in continuous notation:

(2)
$$a = i\bar{a} - \frac{d\bar{a}}{dt},$$

where $\frac{d\bar{a}}{dt}$ represents the variation in the sale value $\bar{a}$ per unit of time.

It can thus be seen that in equilibrium the price paid for the use of a good during a particular period T is the difference between the interest on its value and its increase in value during this period (if in fact it appreciates) and is the sum of the interest on its value and of its decrease in value (if in fact it depreciates).[1]

Using a more concise, though less rigorous, formulation, it may be said that *the price of use is equal to the difference between the interest and the value-gain, if the value rises, and to the sum of the interest and the value-loss if the value falls.*

---

1. This outcome is immediate if it is borne in mind that for the owner of a good the cost of its use per unit of time includes both the loss due to the interest $i\bar{a}$ he *could* have earned if he had invested the value $\bar{a}$ of this good at the market rate i, and the fall in price $-d\bar{a}/dt$ that the good undergoes during the same period.

Breakdown of value-yield

These findings can be expressed in a slightly different form that is more convenient in certain cases. For this purpose I shall use the term the *value-yield r* of a good $(\bar{A})$ for the ratio

$$(3) \qquad r = \frac{a}{\bar{a}},$$

relating its price of use to its value, which represents the instantaneous interest rate obtainable by this good, and I shall use *value-gain rate p* for its relative increase in value per unit of time:[2]

$$(4) \qquad p = \frac{\frac{d\bar{a}}{dt}}{\bar{a}}.$$

These notations give us in equilibrium

$$(5) \qquad r = i - p; \qquad\qquad [3]$$

in other words, in equilibrium, the value-yield of a good is equal to the excess of the market interest rate over its rate of increase in value.

Analysis of value-gain

The value-gain rate p may be considered as the sum of several components the consideration of which is, from the economic point of view, of the utmost interest and which is crucial to distinguish from one another. For, as we shall see, in the most commonly encountered case this increase in value p must normally take into account the general movement of prices, the fall in the value of goods due to wear and tear, the risks incurred, the greater or lesser propensity of the community to accept risks, and finally expected future variations in the interest rate.

---

2. Which may be positive *or negative.*

3. The existence of a value-gain p explains the difference to be found between the apparent interest rates (equal to value-yields) of shares and bonds in periods of rising, or falling, prices—the value-gain being relevant to shares only in first approximation.

Monetary value-gain

When monetary conditions vary, there exists for every price a component of increase or decrease in value that is due to the general rise or fall in prices and this is taken into account in the rate p of expected value-gain. I shall call the corresponding component of the rate p the *monetary value-gain premium* and I shall denote it by μ.

Value-loss due to use

As a rule, in consequence both of wear and tear and of technical progress, the value of durable industrial goods expressed in terms of wages[4] decreases over time. So there is generally a wage-value-loss for capital goods properly so-called[5] that is taken account of in the value-gain in the shape of a depreciation premium, which I shall denote by α.[6]

Risk estimate and subjective cost of risk

Generally speaking the various capital goods are exposed to certain risks, greater or lesser in each case. For instance, houses may be destroyed by fire, ships may be wrecked, firms against which claims are secured in the shape of shares or bonds may go bankrupt. The probable value $(\bar{a}_{q+1})_\pi$ of the corresponding good for the following period[7] naturally takes account of these risks. However, the estimated value $\bar{a}_{q+1}$ of a good of which the probable value is $(\bar{a}_{q+1})_\pi$ is not necessarily equal to this probable value, since individuals may be more or less inclined to take on the risks.

As we have seen, the estimated value takes two quite distinct components into account: the mathematical evaluation of the risks and the subjective cost of the risks.

These components also play a role in fixing the price $\bar{a}_q$ and the expected price $\bar{a}_{q+1}$, but as the role is different in each case, it follows that

4. I.e., in relation to the hourly wage of unskilled labor.

5. I.e., capital assets that are reproducible at will.

6. Not knowing how much depreciation will in fact be undergone by durable industrial goods, firms, in drawing up their accounts, set in advance a fixed-rate write-down called *depreciation* based on the findings of experience. Moreover each firm charges as expenditure the interest on its invested capital so that, in finally determining its production costs, the use-value of a durable good includes both interest and depreciation.

7. The index π means that the value in question is a probable one.

there are two components in the value-loss ($-p$): one that I shall call the *value-loss due to risk-estimation* or more simply the *estimated-risk value-loss* and that I shall denote by ε and the other that I shall call the *value-loss due to subjective risk cost*, or more simply the *cost-of-risk value-loss*, which I shall denote by ρ.

It is easy to prove that these two components are respectively equal to the estimated-risk premium and cost-of-risk premium as defined in no. 29.[8]

Capitalization value-gain

Since at every point in time the value of a good is equal to the present value of its future income stream, any fluctuation in the interest rate must lead to a fluctuation in the price and hence affect the rate of value-gain. I shall use the term *rate of capitalization value-gain* and the symbol γ to denote this component of the rate of value-gain p. Theory shows that this rate is positive or negative depending on whether or not a fall in the interest rate is expected.[9]

---

8. Returning to the example of a bond considered in no. 29, we have, according to equation (3) of the above text,

$$\bar{a} = \frac{a}{i + \varepsilon + \rho},$$

an equation that shows that rates ε and ρ are precisely the estimated-risk and cost-of-risk premiums discussed in no. 29.

9. Let us assume, for instance, that the predicted interest rate I has value I_0 from t_0 and t_1 during year T_0 and value I_1 thereafter. According to equation (3) of no. 30 we shall then have, in the case of a bond with an annual yield a,

(1)
$$\bar{a}_1 = \frac{a}{I_1}$$

and, in accordance with equation (1) of no. 33,

(2)
$$\bar{a}_0 = \frac{a + \dfrac{a}{I_1}}{1 + I_0},$$

whence

(3)
$$\gamma = \frac{\bar{a}_1 - \bar{a}_0}{\bar{a}_0} = \frac{I_0 - I_1}{1 + I_1},$$

Components of the value-gain

Finally it is seen to follow from the preceding definitions that

(6) $$p = \mu - \alpha - \varepsilon - \rho + \gamma,$$

meaning that the rate of value-gain is equal to the sum of the monetary and capitalization value-gain premiums, less premiums for depreciation, estimated risk, and cost of risk, so that finally, in equilibrium, we have

(7) $$r = i + \alpha + \varepsilon + \rho - \mu - \gamma,$$

---

i.e.,

(4) $$\gamma \sim I_0 - I_1 .$$

Hence if we have $I_0 = 3\%$, $I_1 = 4\%$, we shall have $\gamma = -1\%$. In other words, in view of the predicted change in the interest rate, the market will expect the bond to incur a value-loss of 1%.

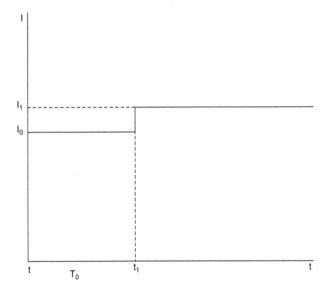

FIGURE 4.4 FOOTNOTE

an equation that gives the value-yield, i.e., the quotient of the income stream by the price, as a function of the pure interest rate and of the premiums of depreciation, risk, monetary value-gain, and capitalization value-gain.[10]

---

10. Of course, the classical analysis of the interest rate set out in nos. 10 and 11 remains applicable if we assimilate to risks the fall in value due to use and the general variations in prices and in the rate of interest, but in the interests of clarity it is better to distinguish carefully, as I have endeavored to do, the different components that correspond to circumstances of a different nature.

7. Basic components of prices (34)

The sale price of any firm can be reduced to the following seven items:

I.   Employee wages
II.   Value of the primary factors needed to make the finished product
III.   Rents or dues paid by the firm for the use of land or other natural resources
IV.   Depreciation of capital borrowed by the firm and corresponding to the depreciation of the durable capital goods that the firm has used these loans to procure
V.   Interest on this borrowed capital[1]
VI.   Taxes
VII.   The income of the firm

All these items can be reduced in turn to wages, rent, and interest. By their very definition this applies to items I, III, and V. Moreover, a firm's income has all the hallmarks of a rent, which we may term *disequilibrium rent*. Turning to items II and IV, they can be broken down into the wages, rental costs, interest, taxes, and the income corresponding to firms producing primary factors and machines. From this it emerges that all prices are composed of wages, rent, interest, and taxes. If we then note that taxes represent the firm's contribution to the expenses of the State[2] and that the latter correspond to the payment of wages, interest, rent, and supplies (themselves composed of wages, rents, interest, and taxes) it can finally be seen that taxes come down to wages, rent, and interest.

This step-by-step approach shows that the prices of goods that are reproducible at will break down into three components, which I shall call the *basic price components*, namely:

- A wage component
- A rent component
- An interest component

1. Interest and depreciation together correspond to the price paid for the use of capital (see no. 33).

2. Taxes can be regarded in a sense as the price paid by the firm for the services rendered to it by the State. The only distinctive character of this price is that it is arbitrarily fixed by the State. Thus considered, taxes are seen to be real overhead costs for the firm.

And the rent component can itself be broken down into two subcomponents: a land rent component and a disequilibrium rent component.

The wage components of prices so defined are those that would appear if there were a vast conglomerate of vertically integrated firms (public services included) and this single firm computed in a single account all wages paid out at the different stages of manufacture of the article in question.

8. Basic price components in equilibrium (35)

In equilibrium, in the absence of monopolies, business income is nil. Hence in equilibrium, analysis reveals that prices are exclusively composed of wages, land rent, and interest (the basic price components).

I shall denote these components by applying to the corresponding prices the sub-indices σ (wages), γ (income from capital), and φ (land rent). In general, we shall have

(1) $$a_q = a_{q\sigma} + a_{q\gamma} + a_{q\varphi}.$$

Taking the wage component $a_{q\sigma}$ of the price a_q of the service (A_q), this component can itself be broken down into partial components $a_{q\sigma}^r$ relative to the different moments t_r at which the wages were entered in the books. Partial components $a_{q\varphi}^r$ of the rent component $a_{q\varphi}$ could even be defined.

It can then be shown[1] that we have, in equilibrium,

(2) $$a_q = \sum_r (1 + J_r^q)^{q-r} (a_{q\sigma}^r + a_{q\varphi}^r). \qquad \text{2}$$

This equation displays *how prices are generated, in equilibrium, from wages, rents and interest*. It also brings out the importance of the interest component in prices,[3] which is often overlooked because at each stage of production the interest expense is relatively light.

1. See my general work *À la recherche d'une discipline économique*, 570–73.
2. From the identity in equilibrium of the price and the cost of production it follows that in equilibrium the price is equal to the capitalized value of wages and land rent expenditure incurred at different points in the production process.
3. Taking the example of a saucepan, there may be a considerable lapse of time between the moment when the first wages needed to produce the saucepan were paid and the final sale to the consumer.

For the saucepan includes an indirect wage component owing to its metal content, just as this metal itself involved an indirect wage component on account of the blast furnace used to smelt it, and so on. The further one goes back in time, the smaller these component parts are, but the greater is the binomial $(1 + J)^t$.

Hence for an interest rate of 10% over a period of eight years—figures widely observed in industry—we have

$$(1 + 0.1)^8 = 2.13.$$

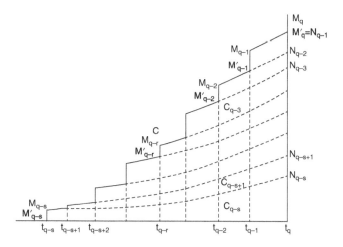

FIGURE 4.5 Geometrical representation of the formation of prices

In what follows I shall use the term *primary value* of a good to designate the sum of the wage and rent components of its price, representing
the primary factors of production (personal services from labor and natural resource services from the land) and the term *acquired value* for the
interest component of its price, equal to the sum of the interest yielded by
the secondary factors of production (capital equipment).

Geometrical representation

It is easy to reach a simple geometrical representation of the formation
of prices using capitalization curves.[4] In figure 4.5 I have assumed that
all the components $a'_{q\sigma}$ and $a'_{q\phi}$ are zero for $r < q - s$. In general the segment $M'_{q-r}M_{q-r}$ is equal to the sum $a'_{q\sigma} + a'_{q\phi}$. The curve C_{q-s} represents
the capitalization curve passing through the point M_{q-s}, and the differ-
ence in the ordinates at any time t between the curves C_{q-r-1} and C_{q-r}
represents the magnitude, capitalized at this point in time, of the initial

---

It can thus be seen that for periods of this order the interest component is greater than
the component from which it is derived.

As we shall see (note 39 to no. 47), the average percentage of interest included in the
price of final consumption goods is, so far as can be judged, of the order of 20%.

4. No. 15.

segment $M'_{q-r}M_{q-r}$ representing the primary component corresponding
to time t_{q-r}.

It can be seen that the composition of the value of the good in question
at any time during its production[5] is represented by the step-shaped curve
C drawn in continuous lines.

5. It is worth emphasizing that curve C does not represent the value of the good considered at different stages of its manufacture. For instance, in the case of refined salt, its pre-
refinement value is equal to the price of unrefined salt, but this value is lower than that represented by figure 4.5, which also includes, for example, the capitalized value at this point in time
of the wage and rent components incorporated in the refining machinery and that, by way of
depreciations, will comprise part of the final cost price.

9. Nature of capital (36)

It follows from what we have seen that at any point in time the value of any capital is simply the discounted value of its future income. Thus the price $\bar{a}_q$ of capital $(\bar{A}_q)$ must take the form

(1)
$$\bar{a}_q = \sum_r \frac{a_r}{(1+J_q^r)^{r-q}},$$

where a_r denotes the price of its service at time t_r and J_q^r denotes the average annual interest rate between times t_q and t_r.

But with regard to reproducible capital,[1] this is only one aspect of capital. For *in equilibrium* the value of all reproducible capital is equal to its cost of production,[2] which itself is equal to the capitalized value of past primary costs. For we have just seen that

(2)
$$\bar{a}_q = \sum_r (1+J_r^q)^{q-r}(a_{q\sigma}^r + a_{q\varphi}^r),$$

where $(a_{q\sigma}^r + a_{q\varphi}^r)$ represents the cost at time t_r of the primary factors needed for the production of the good $(\bar{A}_q)$ and utilized at time t_r.

Thus in equilibrium capital may equally well be expressed in relation to past costs (retrospective valuation) or to future costs (prospective valuation) and in each case its value depends essentially on the level of the rate of interest. For given future incomes its value is less, and for given past primary costs it is greater, as the level of the rate of interest is higher; equilibrium is struck when the two values are equal.

It follows that in the theory of interest the price of the services provided by capital is sharply distinguished from that of the price of the services provided by any ordinary good. For in the case of any given ordinary good, the quantity of its services has a physically well-determined value.

---

1. Which equates to capital goods excluding land and money. Land *per se*, independently of the capital goods that may be attached to it, has no cost of production. And as to money, its price cannot be deemed to be equal to its cost except under a gold standard, a case in which its value, being arbitrarily fixed, cannot be regarded as a function of the interest rate.

2. Of course, this equality applies only in equilibrium: in the real economy it is only an *underlying tendency*.

By contrast the quantity of services of a capital good[3] emerges essentially as a function of its price. This is one of the very points that make the study of interest theory so demanding.[4]

3. Which is equal to the quantity of the capital itself if we take as unit of services of the capital the services provided by the unit of quantity of the capital good per unit of time.

4. These remarks will be clarified later.

10. Aggregation of capital and income (37)

It is vital to the understanding of the theory of interest and of capital to have an exact view of the income flows that occur in the economy and of the link between capital and income. This can easily be obtained by aggregating (a) the capital that individuals have at their disposal and (b) the income stream that they receive and spend.

As a rule this study is quite intricate and, if it is to be rigorous, calls for detailed explanations. However, the essential links between capital and income may be understood using a simplified but sufficiently accurate outline of reality.[1]

General hypotheses

In the real economy, value may be stored by hoarding money, and a lag intervenes between the receipt of income and its expenditure such that the income received during one period is spent only during subsequent periods, the length of the lag varying from one economic agent to another.

However, to understand what is really happening *I shall assume as a first approximation that there is no circulating money and that the income of any one period is expended during the same period.*

These hypotheses typify what may be called an *account-based economy* — one in which there is an accounting currency (or money of account),[2] but no circulating money,[3] where value cannot be stored since *every receipt is immediately expended*, and where there is therefore *no lag* between receiving income and spending it.

---

1. Thus the explanations that follow make no pretense to scientific rigor: they disregard corrective factors in order to take account only of essential elements.

I expect shortly to publish a general and scientifically rigorous theory of the aggregation of capital and income in which the reader wishing to study this intricate topic in greater detail will be able to find all the complementary information he needs: the intended title is *Fondements comptables de la macrodynamique économique* (The accounting basics of economic macrodynamics). [Allais's *Les fondements comptables de la macro-économie* was published in 1954. — Trans.]

2. Having no physical counterpart, this accounting currency serves exclusively for reckoning values.

3. See the explanations already given concerning the distinction between money of account and circulating money (no. 6).

For the greater part of this presentation, I shall consider as a business activity any individual activity that does not reduce to using given income with a view to direct consumption. According to this definition, when an individual buys a durable good such as a house, this is considered to be a *business* activity; by contrast, the direct consumption of services provided by various goods, such as foodstuffs, will be considered as an individual consumption activity.

As a first approximation I shall assume that there is no State and that only firms and individuals exist together.

I shall consider only the flows of value between the set of firms (businesses) and the set of individuals. So flows of value occurring *within* each of these sets will be disregarded.

The value flows I shall be considering will be flows per unit of time.

Variation of national capital

I shall use the term *national capital,* and the notation C_N, to denote the value of all goods existing in the economy at a given point in time. The variation in value of the national capital at any point in time can be broken down into three components: the first of these is variation in value[4] due to changes in prices while the composition and quality of the goods involved remain constant; the second is due to the disappearance, or alteration in quality, of these goods while prices are constant, and the third is equal to the value of new real investments.[4] I shall call the first and the third *gross value-gain of the national capital* and *invested national income* respectively and I shall use P_V and R_I to denote them. As to the second, it is generally negative, and its absolute value is generally called *depreciation*; I shall use A to denote it. This gives us

(1)
$$\frac{dC_N}{dt} = P_V - A + R_I.$$

I shall use the term *net value-gain* for the excess $(P_V - A)$ of the gross value-gain over the depreciation.

4. Per unit of time.

Components of the national profit

I shall use the term *national profit* and the notation B to denote the sum of the profits of firms, minus interest on their net assets,[5] as these appear in the accounts. This profit is composed of two parts—one equal to the gross value-gain P_V in the national capital, immobilized in the form of capital goods, the other equal to the excess $B - P_V$ of the profit over its immobilized part, which represents the part of the national profit that can be distributed, which I shall denote by B_D. This will give us

$$(2) \qquad\qquad B = P_V + B_D.$$

Distributed national income

I shall use the term *distributed national income* and the notation R_D to denote the aggregate amount of income received per unit of time by individuals. Assuming as a first approximation that the depreciations and interest recorded in the firms' accounts are wholly distributed and that the same applies to the distributable profits, and using I to denote the aggregate interest recorded in the accounts[4,6] and S for the total amount of the wages,[4] we shall have

$$(3) \qquad\qquad R_D = S + A + I + B_D;$$

in other words, the distributed national profit emerges as the sum of the wages, depreciations, interest, and distributable profits.[7]

Use of the distributed income

I shall use the terms *consumed national income* and *financially invested national income* and the notations R_C and R_P to denote the aggregate expenditure devoted by individuals to consumption and financial investment, respectively.

---

5. Valued at the pure rate of interest.
6. Including interest on net assets.
7. I am here considering land rents as the interest on the capitalized values of the land.

In view of the assumptions made, the sum of the consumed income and the invested income is necessarily equal to the distributed income, giving us

$$(4) \qquad\qquad R_D = R_C + R_P.$$

Invested national income

I shall use the term *invested national income* and the notation R_I to denote the total amount of the real investment expenditure by firms. Bearing in mind the above assumptions, we necessarily have

$$(5) \qquad\qquad R_I = R_P.$$

Final output and overall output

I shall use the term *national produced income* or *final output*, and the notation P_F, to denote the value of the output[4] of finished products directly utilizable either for consumption or for investment.

Assuming, as a first approximation, that there is no storage, we necessarily have

$$(6) \qquad\qquad P_F = R_C + R_I. \qquad\qquad [8]$$

This final output must be carefully distinguished from the aggregate output P of the whole set of firms. For most firms produce only primary factors and half-finished products, which are not involved in the final output P_F.

---

8. Following from this equation and from equations (3), (4), and (5), we have

$$(1) \qquad\qquad P_F = S + A + I + B_D.$$

If we note that the value P_F of the final output is composed of wages, depreciations, interest, and profits, it is clear that the sum of the wages, depreciations, interest, and profits paid *prior to time t* toward the final output at time *t*, per unit of time, is precisely equal to the sum of the wages, depreciations, interest, and profits paid in the whole of the economy *at time* t. To this equation, which is valid only in an account-based economy, corresponds the famous "law of markets," according to which the whole purchasing power distributed at a given point in time corresponds precisely to the value of the final output at that moment.

Using F to denote the overall value of firm-to-firm supplies, we have, of course,

$$(7) \qquad\qquad P_F = P - F.$$

National income

I shall use the term *net national income* or, more simply, *national income*, and the notation R_N to denote the value of the output available to consumers either for consumption or for investment, when the value of the national capital is simply maintained.

As the net value-gain of the old capital is equal to the difference $(P_V - A)$, it can be seen that we have, by definition,

$$(8) \qquad\qquad R_N = P_F + P_V - A.$$

Thus the national income is equal to the sum of the final output and of the net value-gain of the old capital.

By introducing the value of P_F yielded by equation (6) into equation (8) we obtain, according to equation (1),

$$(9) \qquad\qquad R_N = R_C + \frac{dC_N}{dt},$$

meaning the national income emerges as the sum of the consumed national income and of the increase in the national capital.

Components of the national income

In light of equations (5) and (6), equation (8) gives

$$(10) \qquad\qquad R_N = R_D + P_V - A$$

or, from equations (2) and (3),

$$(11) \qquad\qquad R_N = S + I + B,$$

meaning the national income is equal to the sum of national wages, national interest, and national profit.

Gross national savings, total national savings, and net national savings

I shall use the term *gross national savings* and the notation E_B to denote the excess of the final output over consumed income R_C. Thus we have

(12) $$E_B = P_F - R_C$$

or, following equation (6),

(13) $$E_B = R_I.$$

Thus gross national savings are equal to the aggregate value of investments.

The *total value produced* by the economy includes, on the one hand, the final output P_F and, on the other hand, the value-gain P_V of the old capital.

So I shall use the term *total national savings* and the notation E_T to denote the excess of the total value produced over the consumed income R_C. This gives us

(14) $$E_T = P_F + P_V - R_C$$

or, following equation (6),

(15) $$E_T = R_I + P_V.$$

It thus appears that total savings are equal to the sum of the invested income and the value-gain of the old capital.

Finally I shall term *net national savings* and denote by E_N the excess of national income over consumed income R_C. Thus we obtain

(16) $$E_N = R_N - R_C$$

or, following equation (9),

(17) $$E_N = \frac{dC_N}{dt}.$$

Hence it appears that the net national savings is simply the increment of the national capital.

Now from equations (13), (15), (17), and (1) it can be seen that we have

(18) $$E_T = E_B + P_V$$

and

(19) $$E_N = E_T - A.$$

Total national savings are thus shown to be the sum of gross national savings and the gross value-gain of the old capital, while net national savings are shown to be the excess of total national savings over national depreciation.

The case of a stationary equilibrium

It is interesting to observe what happens to these different equations in the case of a stationary model. In this case, perfect foresight applies, there is no unforeseen income, and all present and future income has been capitalized once and for all at some original point in the past. Under these conditions, there are no profits, and we have

(20) $$B = 0.$$

Moreover, since prices are constant, the gross value-gain of the old capital is zero and we obtain

(21) $$P_V = 0.$$

Taking equation (2) into account, we may then write

(22) $$B_D = 0.$$

In other words, there is no distributable profit.
  Since the equilibrium is stationary, we also have

(23) $$\frac{dC_N}{dt} = 0,$$

a condition that, in light of equations (1) and (21), gives

(24) $$R_I = A.$$

It can be seen that in a stationary model new investments exactly offset depreciations at each moment.

Taking account of equations (3), (8), (9), (11), (13), (17), and (18) we then obtain

(25) $$R_D = S + A + I,$$

(26) $$R_N = P_F - A = R_C = S + I,$$

(27) $$E_T = E_B = R_I,$$

(28) $$E_N = 0.$$

Thus, in a stationary environment, the distributed income is equal to the overall total of wages, depreciations, and interest; the national income is equal to the excess of the value of the final output over the value of the depreciations, i.e., to the income consumed: it is also equal to the sum of wages and interest. Total savings are equal to gross savings and hence to invested income. Net savings are nil.

Finally, as interest includes both land rent[9] and the interest on capital, we have, from equation (26),

(29) $$R_N = S + R_\varphi + R_\gamma,$$

using R_φ and R_γ respectively to denote aggregate land rents and aggregate interest on capital.

Overconsumption

In general, net national savings are positive or negative depending on whether consumed income is greater or less than national income.[10] In the eventuality of negative national savings, the community is living in part on its capital; we say that there is overconsumption.

Of course there may be individual overconsumption on the part of certain persons without overconsumption on the part of the community. This situation can occur at the individual level when capital is consumed or when

9. In the shape of interest on the capitalized values of the land.
10. Equation (16).

debts are incurred to be repaid by future income.[11] In the first case, a part of the capital of the individual in question is exchanged against the net savings of other persons and, from the collective point of view, it is in fact the corresponding income that is spent. In the second case, the mechanism is the same but the diminution of the capital of the individual who overconsumes is replaced by an increase in his indebtedness.

It can thus be seen that the net savings of the community are equal to the algebraic sum of net individual savings, which may equally well be positive or negative.

Increase in real capital

Naturally, net positive savings lead to real enrichment only for real rather than nominal values.

It can then be seen[12] that, given the net value-loss $A - P_V$ of the previously existing capital, real investment can only be increased if, and to the exact extent that, the community temporarily forgoes the consumption of an equivalent fraction of final output, i.e., distributed national income.

Against this fact the most sophisticated techniques of credit expansion, the proliferation of banknotes and the anticipation of tax receipts, are powerless.[13] Investment can be achieved only by two processes: either, for a given consumption, by increasing the final output or, for a given national income, by decreasing consumption.[14]

The case of a monetary economy

In monetary economies, in which circulating money exists,[15] storage of value can occur, and the income spent over a given period is no longer necessarily equal to the income received during the same period. In this case, the preceding equations must of course be modified, and corrective terms are introduced that, in some situations, may be highly significant.

---

11. Such a situation naturally ceases to occur at the community level since all indebtedness of one individual is offset by an equal increase in the capital of another individual.

12. Equations (1) and (6).

13. Their only effect being to modify the distribution of income and the burden of investment (see later, no. 106).

14. Which of course is not to deny that the expansion of bank credit may enable a greater volume of investment to be achieved than would result from spontaneous savings (see no. 109).

15. Whether as cash or demand deposits.

FIGURE 4.6

Quite simply, the income that is distributed is not necessarily consumed or invested, as it may either be devoted to an increase in working capital or hoarded, so that we have

(30) $$R_D = R_C + R_I + R_E,$$

using R_E to denote the part of income devoted to increasing money balances, or again

(31) $$R_D = R_C + R_I + R_R + R_T,$$

using R_R and R_T to denote respectively those parts of the income that are devoted to increasing working capital or hoarded.[16]

Thus the use of income may be presented as shown in figure 4.6.

It is apparent that savings do not immediately and necessarily make capital available on the market. The capitalist who keeps millions in a safe has no influence on the capital market: he is hoarding. In normal times in modern societies hoarding is fairly slight and stays at a more or less constant level: hence its effects are minimal. But in troubled periods hoarding can become a significant phenomenon; in such cases it creates piles of uninvested capital withdrawn from monetary circulation and it can have a considerable effect on the economy.[17]

In the same way, income invested in financial assets is no longer, in this case, necessarily equal to income devoted to real investment, since a part of firms' resources may be devoted to increasing their money balances.

Moreover (a) firms may in fact distribute only a part of their distributable profits, and (b) banks may issue money in the form of unbacked demand deposits, which amounts to putting supplementary monetary income

---

16. I.e., stored beyond what is strictly necessary to constitute the working capital necessary to balance receipts and expenditure over time.

17. See below, chapter 8, "Interest and Money."

at the disposal of the business community; hence if we respectively denote by R_{ND}, $\dfrac{dM_S}{dt}$, and $\dfrac{dM_P}{dt}$ the distributable income not distributed by the firms, the quantity of demand deposits issued,[4] and the increase in money balances held by the whole of the production sector[4] we have

(32)
$$R_P + R_{ND} + \frac{dM_S}{dt} = R_I + \frac{dM_P}{dt},$$

a situation that may be diagrammatically represented as shown in figure 4.7.

Since the difference $R_{ND} - \dfrac{dM_P}{dt}$ represents that part of the undistributed income actually devoted to investments, it follows that real investment may be taken to comprise three components: *spontaneous investment* R_P from individuals, *self-financed investment* $R_{ND} - \dfrac{dM_P}{dt}$ from the production sector, and finally investment brought about with the help of new bank loans $\dfrac{dM_S}{dt}$, which I shall call, in accordance with current terminology, *forced investment*.

The composition of real investment can now be represented as shown in figure 4.8.

Finally, *taking State intervention into account*, we can formulate in this regard an equation parallel to equation (32). The issue of demand deposits is simply replaced by the issue of cash. However, the undistributed income is generally negative, as the State distributes more income than it

FIGURE 4.7

FIGURE 4.8

State borrowing
New issues
$\left\{\begin{array}{l}\text{State investment}\\[4pt]\text{Deficit cover}\\[4pt]\text{Increase in money balances}\end{array}\right.$

FIGURE 4.9

receives, the difference representing its operating deficit. Thus the aggregate of new investments in government securities and the increase in money supply due to inflation is allocated to (a) financing State investments, (b) covering the operating deficit, and (c) increasing the money balances held by the various State organisms,[18] so that the situation may be represented by the diagram in figure 4.9.

18. Which are here limited to working capital.

Determination of the Equilibrium Rate of Interest on Capital in an Account-Based Economy

Overview (38)

In an account-based economy,[1] the rate of interest, being the price paid for the use of capital, is determined, like every other price, by the supply and demand mechanism in the capital market where the use of capital is bought and sold.

---

1. The extension of this analysis to the case of a monetary economy, using circulating money as a medium of exchange, will be seen in chapter 8 ("Interest and Money"). It will be shown that in a monetary economy the interest rate constitutes essentially the price paid for the use of money and that this concept is noticeably different from the one expounded in this paragraph, which concerns an account-based economy. We shall also see how these two apparently contradictory points of view can and must be reconciled.

A. *The Supply of Capital*

1. Available capital and supply of capital (39)

Let us assume, to simplify this presentation, that time is divided into successive, equal periods of duration T (fig. 5.1) and that the various economic operations are concentrated at the end of each period.[1]

Let $C^{n,i}$ be the value of that part of the national capital in use during period T_n and held by individual (X_i), let $P_V^{n,i}$ and $A^{n,i}$ be the value-gain and the depreciation of the capital $C^{n,i}$ per unit of time during the period T_n, and let $R_D^{n,i}$ and $R_C^{n,i}$ be the income received and the income consumed per unit of time by the individual concerned during this same period. As it is assumed that the operations are concentrated at the end of the period, individual (X_i) has at his disposal at the end of period T_n a *total disposable capital* $C_D^{n,i}$ equal to the sum of the income $TR_D^{n,i}$ received during this period and of the value of the capital $C^{n,i}$ held during the same period, plus its net value-gain $T(P_V^{n,i} - A^{n,i})$. Thus we have

$$(1) \qquad C_D^{n,i} = C^{n,i} + TP_V^{n,i} - TA^{n,i} + TR_D^{n,i}.$$

A part of the available capital is used to cover expenses incurred during period T_n for the purchase of directly consumable services (food, lodging, and, generally, the services of direct fungible goods and the services of durable goods used for direct consumption). Their value represents income $TR_C^{n,i}$ consumed during period T_n by individual (X_i).

The other part goes to make up the capital $C^{n+1,i}$, which individual (X_i) intends to have at his disposal in the future. Hence, we have

$$(2) \qquad C_D^{n,i} = TR_C^{n,i} + C^{n+1,i}.$$

It can thus be seen that each individual is constantly choosing between immediate expenditure and deferred expenditure and that what affects this choice is the total capital available $C_D^{n,i}$, i.e., the overall value of income received and of capital possessed plus its net value-gain, and not only the income received $R_D^{n,i}$ as certain economists explicitly or implicitly main-

---

1. Such a simplistic assumption becomes scientifically rigorous if period T is very short, for example, equal to a single day.

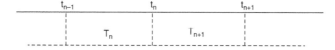

FIGURE 5.1

tain. For the capital $C^{n,i} + TP_V^{n,i} - TA^{n,i}$ may in fact be realized in whole or in part by its owner.

If we use the term *available national capital* and the notation C_D^n to denote the sum of the capitals $C_D^{n,i}$, we shall of course have[2]

(3) $$C_D^n = C^n + TP_V^n - TA^n + TR_D^n$$

and

(4) $$C_D^n = TR_C^n + C^{n+1}.$$ [3]

The capital C^{n+1} represents the value that, at time t_n, individuals mean to have at their disposal in the future. It therefore represents the total available capital at time t_n.

2. Using the notations of no. 37.

3. Combining equations (3) and (4) of course gives us

$$\frac{C^{n+1} - C^n}{T} = P_V^n - A^n + R_D^n - R_C^n,$$

an equation already found in no. 37 (equation [1]), since the difference $(R_D^n - R_C^n)$ represents invested income.

It is worth emphasizing here that while some differences $(R_D^{n,i} - R_C^{n,i})$ may be negative, i.e., while individuals considered in isolation can consume more than is possible for them by simply spending the wages, depreciations, interest, and profit they receive, nevertheless the difference $(R_D^n - R_C^n)$ can only be positive, since capital goods *collectively considered* cannot be sold.

2. Motives for saving (40)

Savings are determined both by man's desire to have capital in reserve that will be available to him in the future and by the income he can derive from this saved capital.

Man compares—more or less intuitively—the *present inconvenience* he experiences[1] in refraining from consuming economic goods available to him, with the *present pleasure* he experiences in thinking of the *future advantages* he hopes to derive from saving.

In fact, he chooses between immediate consumption and consumption that is delayed but accompanied by a certain quantitative increase[2] corresponding to interest as found in the market.

Thus the act of saving is in fact determined both by the desire to spread out consumption over time and by the wish to increase resources by financial investment.

When an individual has at his disposal capital C, he has the choice between consuming this capital at once or investing it in financial assets over a period of time t, which would enable him to consume at time t capital $C(1 + I)^t$ where I is the rate of interest.

There is no need to distinguish to what extent the individual's determination is affected by each of these two elements, the desire to *store* his capital and the desire to *make it bear fruit*, sharply differentiated though they are from the psychological point of view.

> Should an individual wish to set aside certain wealth for the future, he cannot fail to be interested in the quantity of this wealth which the act of setting aside will enable him to recover; as a rule, he will not fail to invest his resources in financial assets while waiting to consume them, so as to derive, subsidiarily, interest from them, and the consideration of this interest cannot leave him indifferent.[3]

Should another individual, by contrast, wish to make a part of his wealth fruitful and financially invest it with the principal intention of deriving income from it, he too must give up the possibility of immediate consump-

1. Or indeed the satisfaction that he forgoes.
2. Which, for that matter, would be negative if the rate of interest were negative.
3. F. Divisia, *L'épargne et la richesse collective* (Paris: Sirey, 1928), 119.

tion of his savings, allowing himself to consume them only at a later date; so the balance between the ability to consume at once and the ability to consume only in the future cannot leave him indifferent.

For explanatory purposes it is convenient to use the term "propensity to consume" to denote the set of motives that prompt the individual to immediate consumption and "propensity to save" for the set of motives prompting him to deferred consumption. If these definitions are adopted, savings will be proportionately greater as the propensity to consume is less and the propensity to save is greater.

Distribution of income over time and the maximization of present satisfaction

At a given time t_0 each individual (X_i) has available a total disposable capital C_D^i, which he divides between his present and future consumption. Let R_0^i be the amount of income he intends to consume during year n^4 and let $R_1^i, R_2^i, \ldots, R_p^i$ be the income he retains for the coming years $n_1, n_2, \ldots, n_p$.

For given prices, present and foreseen, his satisfaction S_0 at time t_0 is seen to be a well-determined function of his income $R_0^i, R_1^i, R_2^i, \ldots, R_p^i$, so that we can write

(1) $$S_0^i = S_0^i(R_0^1, R_1^i, \ldots, R_p^i).$$

Following the law of present values, we have, of course,

(2) $$C_D^i = R_0^i + \frac{R_1^i}{(1+J_1)} + \frac{R_2^i}{(1+J_2)^2} + \ldots + \frac{R_p^i}{(1+J_p)^p},$$

where $J_1, J_2, \ldots, J_p$ stand for the average interest rates between time t_0 and times $t_1, t_2, \ldots, t_p$. According to the theory of constrained maxima, maximum present satisfaction is obtained by distributing income over time so that

(3) $$\frac{\dfrac{\delta S_0^i}{\delta R_0^i}}{1} = \frac{\dfrac{\delta S_0^i}{\delta R_0^i}}{\dfrac{1}{1+J_1}} = \ldots = \frac{\dfrac{\delta S_0^i}{\delta R_p^i}}{\dfrac{1}{(1+J_p)^p}}.$$

---

4. The income R_0^i is the same as the consumed income R_C^i considered in no. 39.

These equations, in combination with equation (2), determine the unknowns $R_0^i, R_1^i, \ldots, R_p^i$ and hence the total capital C_0^i saved by this individual at time t_0, since we have

(4)
$$C_0^i = \frac{R_1^i}{1+J_1} + \ldots + \frac{R_p^i}{(1+J_p)^p}.$$

Variation of total capital saved with rate of interest[5]

For the sake of simplicity it is assumed that the different annual rates of interest $J_1, J_2, \ldots, J_p$ are all equal to the same value I. This being so, the foregoing explanations enable us to write, for given forecasts, using the notations of no. 39,

(5)
$$C = f(C_D, I).$$

In other words, saved capital C is shown to be a function of available capital C_D and of interest rate I.

It should also be stressed that as available capital C_D basically depends on the value of the capital previously invested[6] and as this value is simply the sum of the present values of its expected future income stream, available capital is itself a function of interest rate I.

In reality, when savers determine their savings as a function of the interest rate, they consider all the other prices as given, in particular those of the goods they possess. So to study the reactions of savers toward the situation of the capital market, the variation of the supply of capital C must be considered as a function of the interest rate, while available capital is assumed to be constant.[7,8]

5. This of course refers to the pure rate of interest and not to the various rates observed on the market, which include, in addition, risk premiums varying from one loan to another (nos. 10 and 11).

6. Equal to the expression $C^n + T(P_V^n - A^n)$ of no. 39.

7. In particular the indirect effect of the variation of the price of land with the interest rate is not to be considered here.

8. However, it should be borne in mind that the supply C of capital depends indirectly on the interest rate through the agency of available capital.

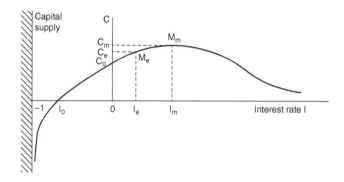

FIGURE 5.2 Variation of the supply of capital as a function of the annual rate of interest

When the rate of annual interest payable annually I is close to its minimum value (-1),[9] it is clear that the supply of capital C is negative (fig. 5.2) and that its absolute value is greater as interest rate I is closer to (-1). For a debt D contracted at this point would in these conditions bring about only a very slight liability $D(1 + I)$ the following year. So for a given propensity to consume, the indebtedness, if it were possible, would therefore be considerable.[10]

In the same way, if the interest rate I were extremely high, capital saved would certainly be very low. Indeed, whatever the value of I, present consumption R_0 cannot exceed the value of the available capital C_p, whereas the future income stream $R_1, R_2, \ldots, R_q$ increases indefinitely with I, for a given saved capital C, however slight it may be. This shows that, in order to achieve the best balance of present consumption and future consumption, the individual would be led to reduce indefinitely his saved capital C, if the rate of interest were also to increase indefinitely by very great values.

Thus when the annual rate of interest payable annually I increases from its minimum value (-1) to $+\infty$, saved capital C begins by being an infinitely great negative and ends by tending toward zero through positive values. It can therefore be assumed *as a first approximation* that capital C, initially an infinitely great negative, increases as rate I rises; becomes nil for a certain value I_0, passes through a maximum C_m for a value I_m, then decreases

9. No. 14.

10. In the extreme case, a debt D would bring about a zero liability $D(1 + I)$. In which case the capital the individual would be disposed to borrow at an interest rate equal to (-1) would certainly be infinitely great.

asymptotically toward zero through positive values while I increases indefinitely, so that the shape of the curve representing C as a function of I is ultimately as shown in figure 5.2.[11]

Naturally, the values of $I_0, I_m, \dfrac{C_m}{C_D}$ and of $\dfrac{C_0}{C_m}$ vary from individual to individual. Thus the interest rate I_0, which is far above zero for the very poor and the very improvident, is very close to –1 for the very rich and very cautious.[12] Similarly the ratio $\dfrac{C_m}{C_D}$ will remain relatively low for the former but will be close to unity for the latter.

It is also easy to see that rate I_m may be either lower or higher than the usual market interest rate values.

Thus it is understandable that under present conditions, among the recipients of income, the ordinary middle-class saver who is striving to build

11. This curve of supply of savings in no way prejudges the way in which the capital supplied would in fact be financially invested.

Hence, in the case of a monetary economy, it is possible that part of the capital supplied would be hoarded in the form of money. If so, the marginal value of the services rendered by the money would be equal to the rate of interest (see chapter 8, "Interest and Money").

12. In all these explanations it is of course assumed that in every economy there is a single interest rate I and that in consequence no available investment will yield a rate of interest different from this rate I.

So I am not examining at this point what would occur in the real economy in equilibrium if the interest rate fell so as to take on values close to (–1), but *only* what the supply of capital would be for an available capital assumed to be *given* if individuals were only able to invest their money at rate I.

In reality, the supply of capital depends both on how much capital is available and on the rate of interest I, and, under present structural conditions, if this rate were to fall toward zero, this would bring about in equilibrium an increase in the available capital C_D on account of the rise in land value (no. 30). The amount of capital supplied as a function of the rate of interest would then be quite different.

Moreover, for reasons that will be made clear further on, the rate of interest in equilibrium could not, under present structural conditions, have negative values (see chapter 9, "The Problem of Interest").

But it is one thing to examine the concomitant variations of the rate of interest and of capital *in equilibrium*, and quite another to inquire how the rate of interest would vary with the supply of capital alone for a total available capital *assumed to be given*—the only question discussed here.

up capital in order to live on its income[13] should be obliged, when the interest rate falls, to set aside greater capital in order to assure himself of a specific annual rent. In this case, the capital saved varies in inverse proportion to the interest rate and the value I_m will be low or even negative.

It is also understandable that, insofar as saving—which is an abstention from consumption—involves under present conditions the idea of a sacrifice accepted by the saver, the rate of interest on capital can be considered to be the necessary stimulant and reward for this sacrifice and, this being so, savings should be all the more abundant as interest rates rise. In this case the value I_m would be higher than the levels usually observed in the market.

The first case seems in general to be that of rich persons and the second that of poor persons.

Moreover, even if the interest rate were to fall for a long period to very low levels, the small saver would not for that reason give up saving. For his chief goal is to build up reserves for his old age and against the risks of life for himself and his family. His chief concern is the size of this reserve, not the interest, which in his eyes counts as no more than a minor accessory, indeed one that can be to some extent disregarded, in view of (a) the slight value of the capital saved and (b) the considerably greater income derived from his work. Let us take the case of a small saver who earns 20,000 francs per year and owns capital of 100,000 francs. If the interest rate should fall from 5% to 4%, he will lose just 1,000 francs in income, an amount that will not prevent him, if he so wishes, from keeping up the level of his net annual savings, i.e., continuing to increase his capital holding, as the fall in his total income is not too steep.

From this it may be concluded that a large part of current savings would still occur without interest or even at negative interest. Saving does not always and necessarily imply suffering or even deprivation, as was held by the old abstinence theories; indeed the chief care of human beings seems to be to make provision for their old age or for hard times.

From these remarks it can be inferred, with considerable likelihood, that for the market as a whole, the value I_m corresponding to the maximum supply of capital is probably of a magnitude close to that of the rates currently observed, that under present conditions the total supply of capital varies

13. In the case of life annuities, the income from the capital includes both depreciation and interest.

relatively little with the interest rate,[14] and finally that the level it would attain for a zero rate would not be so very different from its present level.

Psychological interest rates

In the most general case, when equilibrium is not necessarily attained, equations (3) above would define parameters that I shall denote by the notations $J_P^{i0}, J_P^{i1}, \ldots, J_P^{ip}$ and by the term *psychological interest rates*.

It is then easy to verify that if the psychological interest rate J_P^i relative to the period $(t_0 t)$ is below the market level, it would be in the interests of the individual (X_i) in question to exchange present income against future income, i.e., to save, and conversely, that equilibrium could only be attained if the various psychological interest rates were equal to the various market rates.[15]

Real psychological rates of interest

The psychological interest rates thus defined are nominal rates that depend on the general level of prices at times $t_0, t_1, \ldots, t_p$. To eliminate the

14. This is a finding that has already been pointed out by many economists. In my opinion the foregoing argumentation entitles us to deem it highly probable.

15. We have

(1)
$$\delta S_0^i = \frac{\partial S_0^i}{\partial R_0^i} \delta R_0^i + \frac{\partial S_0^i}{\partial R_q^i} \delta R_q^i,$$

i.e.,

(2)
$$\delta S_0^i = \frac{\partial S_0^i}{\partial R_0^i} \left[\delta R_0^i + \frac{\delta R_q^i}{(1 + J_P^{iq})^q} \right].$$

In the market an increase δR_q^i necessitates a decrease of R_0^i equal to $\delta R_q^i / (1 + J_q)^q$ where J_q represents the market's relative rate of interest at period $(t_0 t_q)$. Hence, we have

(3)
$$\delta S_0^i = \frac{\partial S_0^i}{\partial R_0^i} \left[1 - \frac{(1 + J_q)^q}{(1 + J_P^{iq})^q} \right] \delta R_0^i.$$

Thus it stands to reason that if $J_q > J_P^q$, *it will be in the interests of the individual* (X_i) *in question to diminish his present consumption* $(\delta R_0^i < 0)$, i.e., to save.

influence of variations in this level, we can consider, for example, the real psychological interest rates $(J_P^{ip})'''$ defined by the equations

(6) $$[1+(J_P^{ip})''']^P = \frac{P_0}{P}(1+J_P^{ip})^P.$$ [16]

It is easy to verify that these rates are no different from those that could be directly defined from equations of types (1), (2), and (3) above if the satisfaction functions were considered as functions of real income.

In fact, insofar as the *relative* prices of the various goods over each period may be assumed to be given,[17] the real psychological interest rates *may be considered to be physical entities, independent of general price trends.*

---

16. No. 19, equation (2).

17. Such an assumption can be validly made in interest theory since this theory is exclusively concerned with the study of the economic links between different periods and their effects.

3. The saver's rent (41)

When the market rate is at the equilibrium level I_e (fig. 5.3), the capital saved by a given individual has value C_e, but a part of this saving would still occur if the market interest rate were less than I_e. The result for the saver is a rent.

The sum dC by which the saver would have accepted to increase his capital for an annual income $I\,dC$ is in fact added to his capital for an annual income $I_e\,dC$.

The consequence for him is a free income equal to the integral

$$R = \int_0^{Ce} (I_e - I)\,dC$$
$$= \text{shaded area } I_0 I_e M_e,$$

which I shall call the saver's rent.

Some economists have claimed that the interest received IC is the reward for the effort of abstinence made by the saver in increasing his capital from value C_0, which it would have for a zero interest rate, to its equilibrium value C_e. However, it is clear that this reward is generally much greater than the real sacrifice involved, the value of which is equal to the area $C_0 C_e M_e$, which would correspond only to a reward for marginal saving. Hence Lassalle's indignant reaction to some of the more extreme contentions of the abstinence theorists: "The income on capital is *the reward*

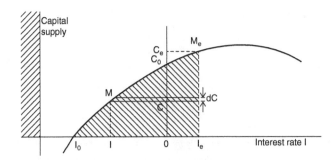

FIGURE 5.3

for doing without! A wonderful statement, a statement—worth its weight in gold! The millionaires of Europe, the ascetics, the Hindu penitents, the stylites perched on one leg atop their columns, their arms extended, their bodies bent, their faces pallid, all stretching out their begging bowl towards the people to collect the reward of their doing without! And in their midst, towering over all the other penitents, the most mortified ascetics of them all: the Rothschilds!"[1]

The saver's rent and the consumer's rent

In reality the saver's rent should be seen as a specific case of the rent enjoyed by every individual when he takes part in the market. For an individual (X) seeks to trade good (A) for good (B) only so long as, taking account of the market's rate of equivalence, the quantities of (B) received are for him of greater value than the quantities of (A) given in return; he ceases to trade when his psychological rate of equivalence becomes equal to the market rate. Hence every economic operation freely carried out provides the agent involved with free income, a rent, since only at the margin are the quantities received psychologically equivalent to the quantities supplied, and so long as this limit has not been reached the agent derives an advantage from the exchange.

So the saver's rent, insofar as it is a free income, is not a phenomenon specific to savings and is perfectly analogous to the rent of the consumer for whom the average psychological value of the goods he acquires is always greater than that of the sums he spends to acquire them—and the difference may be considerable—or indeed to the rent of the worker, for whom the psychological value of his wages is always greater than that of the work supplied.

And while, as has been shown, it would be false to maintain that the interest received is nothing but the strict reward for the saving effort, it would be no less unjustified to deny that part of the interest received constitutes a free income, seeing that the same applies to the consumer's purchases, to the worker's income and indeed to every economic act; hence however fair

1. W. Röpke, *Explication économique du monde moderne* (Paris: Librairie de Médicis, 1940), 79.

they may be as criticisms of certain abstinence theories, Lassalle's remarks cannot be accepted, *as expressed*, as arguments casting doubt on the social justification of the interest-bearing loan.[2,3]

2. However, while it is quite certain that there is no difference *in nature* between the rent of the consumer or the worker and the rent of the saver, there may in some cases be a difference of *scale*.

For instance, it is hardly possible to compare the rent of the worker for whom the value of the wages he receives for a given job of work at a rate of pay equal to his marginal psychological value may be five to ten times greater than its average psychological value, and the rent of the American millionaire who, on the basis of a pure rate of interest of the order of 4%, receives 40 million in interest for a level of savings that he would scarcely modify at all if the market's pure rate of interest fell to zero.

3. These observations will be completed in no. 157.

B. The Demand for Capital

1. Distribution of the factors of production over the different stages of production (42)

At any given moment, the available factors of production are distributed in a certain way among the different stages of production. Some are used in industries producing consumer goods,[1] others are used in industries of the immediately preceding stage, and others again are assigned to the production of semi-finished articles, raw materials, tools, and machinery.

The distribution of the factors of production between the production of consumer goods and earlier stages of production can be modified and is in fact continually being modified.

Economic progress, i.e., the increase in quantity and quality of output using constant techniques for given quantities of the primary factors of production,[2,3] *is largely attributable to the fact that an ever-greater proportion of available resources is devoted to the early stages of production.* New stages are introduced so that the production sequence is lengthened. In other words, production methods become more roundabout, more mediate, and more capital intensive in the sense that the production of consumer goods requires, per unit, more capital, i.e., more intermediate articles, machines, primary factors, or semi-finished products.[4]

In some cases, *time* alone is the main condition of the increase in the quantity or quality of the output. Examples are wines, cigars, violins, and all articles that, under present conditions, increase in value with the passage of time practically without human intervention. In the forests, trees grow just as well without human help, and this is the chief interest of forestry production. In the same way again, when, in times past, ice and snow were harvested in winter, it was enough to wait for summer for these products to increase in value. Indeed this was the main feature of the production process used.

1. I.e., goods intended for direct use by consumers.

2. Land and labor.

3. Economic progress so defined is distinct from technical progress, where output quantities increase for given quantities of the factors of production (whether primary or not).

4. The intermediate articles and the consumer goods are here measured in value.

As we have seen,[5] the national capital of the entire community is defined as the sum of the capital[6] held in the economy. It includes *monetary capital*, i.e., money balances, *land*, which has its own specific value,[7] and finally *reproducible capital*, which denotes the value of tangible capital goods other than money and land.

Reproducible capital includes all tangible goods other than land existing at a given moment. It includes, for example, the means of production, tools, stocks of merchandise, dwelling houses, etc.[8]

An overview of reproducible capital could be obtained if we had a photograph of the whole set of physical goods other than land. By this process there would appear, in addition to durable wealth, a great quantity of goods that are consumed rapidly. As Irving Fisher has so well pointed out, "this photograph would show trainloads of meat, eggs, and milk in transit, cargoes of fish, spices, and sugar, as well as the contents of private pantries, ice chests, and wine cellars. Even the supplies on the table of a man bolting his dinner would find a place. So the clothes in one's wardrobe or on one's back, the tobacco in a smoker's pouch or pipe, the oil in the can or lamp, would all be elements in this flashlight picture."[9]

The goods comprising reproducible capital may themselves be classified as either circulating capital or fixed capital.

Fixed capital is capital that exists in a durable form. Its use involves only gradual wear and tear. It includes buildings, tools, etc.

Circulating capital is that which is destroyed outright in a given production process. It includes all fungible goods.

Take, for example, the making of bread by the baker. "The water, the flour, the salt, the yeast, and the coal are circulating capital; they are entirely destroyed in the process of production. The kneading trough and the oven are fixed capital, which only wear out gradually, like the building in which the bakery is situated."[10]

---

5. No. 37.

6. Which may be negative in the case of debts, but which are then offset by the corresponding credits of equivalent amount.

7. Remember that we are here considering the land in itself, independently of capital (clearance, fertilizer, crops, etc.), which may be attached thereto (see note 1 to no. 30).

8. Following this definition, the economic meaning of the [French] term *mobilier* [here translated "reproducible"] is quite different from that which it commonly bears in French civil law [chattels].

9. Fisher, *The Nature of Capital and Income* (New York: Macmillan, 1919), ch. 5, § 1.

10. G.-H. Bousquet, *Institutes de science économique*, vol. 3 (Paris: Rivière, 1936), 42.

To produce a quantity of bread, from the moment when the flour is taken out of the sack to the moment when the bread emerges from the oven, a certain period of time is needed, during which the circulating capital is entirely destroyed while fixed capital is only partially destroyed.

Renewal of fixed capital in a stationary model

In a stationary model the different articles of fixed capital remain constant in total quantity. As they are continuously undergoing wear and tear they must be renewed whenever they are worn out.

Let us, for example, imagine a closed economy in which all dwelling houses are of the same type, all lasting for 100 years, and let us assume that the number of houses in existence is kept stable by regular new construction. "We can thus select in this stationary economic system, at any given moment, a group of 100 houses of which the oldest is 100 years old and therefore ready for demolition, the most recent was built during the preceding year, and in which each intermediate year is represented by one house. This group of houses is kept constant by the production of one house and the demolition of another during each year,"[11] and each of the houses in the group advances each year by one degree in the classification by age.

If we consider a large enough stationary economy, the stock of durable goods can be maintained in this way, practically unchanged in composition, by maintenance and new production, i.e., by a process of continual production. This process, by which the fixed capital of the stationary economy[12] is maintained intact can be called the *reproductive* or *circulation process of fixed capital.*

Capitalism and collectivism

Following the definition most commonly used, the term *capitalism* denotes an economic system in which ownership of the means of production (land and capital) is private, while *collectivism* denotes an economic system in which this ownership is collective.

---

11. G. Cassel, *Traité d'économie politique*, vol. 1 (Paris: Giard, 1929), 38. [English (adapted) from *The Theory of Social Economy*, translated by S. L. Barron, bk. 1, ch. 5.]

12. I.e., in an economy in which stationary conditions prevail.

By this definition, the terms *capitalism* and *capitalist* apply to the legal system of production and not to the use of indirect processes of production. Hence, to denote such use, I shall use the term *capitalistic*. So, for example, an economy making use of capital will be called *a capitalistic economy*.

2. Indirect processes of production and waiting (43)

A durable good can only be produced if the economy is in a position to wait for the services it will be able to render during its existence. Should neither the producer himself nor anyone else be willing to take on the burden of this waiting period, production would encounter an economic impossibility and be suspended.

In reality, for this production to be possible, a certain capital—in the abstract sense of the word—must be available: a capital corresponding to the cost of production. Thus anyone who builds a house must have available a sum equal to the cost of production, which he "immobilizes" in this construction. In the same way, anyone who buys a house after it is finished must have the purchase price available. He pays this price to the builder of the house who may thereupon do with it as he wills. But from his own point of view he has "immobilized" his capital in the house, and in this sense, he succeeds the builder of the house.

Waiting for the services of a durable good therefore requires a certain availability of capital.[1] *This is a necessary condition of every roundabout production process.* This wait essentially implies that someone refrains from consuming the value of his available capital in order to make the necessary purchasing power available for production.

1. No. 4.

3. Technical interest rate (44)

Let (T) be a roundabout production technology the setting up of which is expected to require total disbursements of $D_0, D_1, \ldots, D_p, \ldots, D_q$, and which is expected to generate receipts of $R_0, R_1, \ldots, R_p, \ldots, R_q$ per unit of time at times $t_0, t_1, \ldots, t_p, \ldots, t_q$ (on whatever account).[1]

The whole of these disbursements and receipts can be represented with continuous variables by figure 5.4. The disbursements are represented by curve $M_0 M_s$, receipts by curve $N_r N_q$, and net receipts R_P^N by the discontinuous curve $P_0 P_r P_s P_q$.

As every production process begins with investments and later brings in receipts greater than expenditure, we may conclude that the net receipts begin by being negative during an initial period (t_0, t_m) — the investment phase — and then become positive during a second period (t_m, t_q) — the operational phase.[2]

When the interest rate between instants $t_0, t_1, \ldots, t_q$ has a single value I, the operation yields an overall income of

$$\textbf{(1)} \qquad R_0^T = \sum_{P=0}^{P=q} \frac{R_p}{(1+I)^P} - \sum_{P=0}^{P=q} \frac{D_p}{(1+I)^P}$$

equal to the excess of the present value of expected receipts over the present value of intended expenditure.

The operation will or will not prove profitable depending on whether the overall income is or is not positive.[3]

Now if the net receipts curve has in reality the appearance shown in figure 5.4 — which is, as has just been stated, generally the case — it is easy to

---

1. Thus the expenditure D_p includes disbursements for investment made at time t_p, disbursements for maintenance of facilities made from t_0 and t_p and finally direct disbursements for labor and primary factors made at time t_p.

Similarly, receipts include all takings, whether due to the sale of main products or subproducts or indeed to sale of the facilities themselves.

2. Of course, these remarks by no means rule out the possibility that there may be some degree of operations during the investment phase; they simply specify that in the first period investments predominate while in the second period operations are more important.

3. These explanations are naturally applicable irrespective of whether or not operations have begun. In all cases only future disbursements and receipts are relevant (see no. 62 *in fine*).

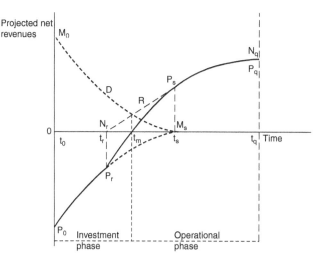

FIGURE 5.4 Economic diagram of a technical project

demonstrate that, as the annual interest rate payable annually I varies from -1 to $+\infty$, overall income R_0^T becomes zero for a certain value of I (fig. 5.5), below which it is positive and above which it is negative.[4]

4. The basic principles behind this demonstration are as follows:

First note that for values of interest rate I close to -1, R_0^T is an infinitely great positive, while for very high values of I, R_0^T is an infinitely small negative. From this we may conclude that it becomes zero at least once.

Moreover, if I_0 represents a value of I for which R_0^T is zero, we have

(1)
$$\int_{t_0}^{t_q} \frac{R^N(t)}{(1+I_0)^{t-t_0}} dt = 0,$$

where $R^N(t)$ denotes the net operating income per unit of time at time t. As we have

(2)
$$\frac{dR_0^T}{dI} = -\frac{1}{1+I}\int_{t_0}^{t_q}(t-t_0)\frac{R^N(t)}{(1+I)^{t-t_0}} dt,$$

since function $R^N(t)$ is negative in the initial stage and positive in a second stage and the different components of the second integral are only those of the first multiplied by the factor $(t-t_0)$, which has greater values in the second period than in the first, it can be seen that, in view of equation (1) the derivative $\dfrac{dR_0^T}{dI}$ is necessarily negative. So overall income R_0^T is therefore decreasing for every value of the interest rate that reduces it to zero. It follows from

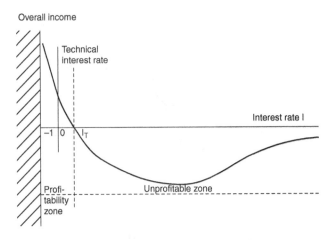

FIGURE 5.5 Variation of overall income as a function of the interest rate

Under these conditions, if we use the term *technical interest rate* to denote the rate of interest I such that overall income is nil,[5] it is seen that this income is positive or negative and hence that the intended process of production will prove profitable or not depending on whether the technical interest rate is greater or less than the market rate.[6]

The statement that the technical interest rate is equal to I amounts to saying that the corresponding investment can attract an interest I_T. This being so, it is fitting to term this rate I_T *the rate of value productivity* or more simply *the rate of productivity of capital.*[7]

Average technical interest rate and marginal technical interest rate

Let us suppose that disbursements D are increased by $\Delta D_0, \Delta D_1, \ldots, \Delta D_q$ and that the expected corresponding increases in income R are $\Delta R_0, \Delta R_1, \ldots, \Delta R_q$. We may use the term *marginal technical interest rate* or *marginal rate of productivity of capital* for the rate I_T^m such that we have

---

this fact that the curve representing R_0^T can cross the time axis only from high to low and hence can cross it *only once.*

5. The technical interest rate so defined is the same thing as Fisher's *rate of return over cost.*

6. It is worth emphasizing the similarity of this formula to the one already given for psychological interest rates (no. 40).

7. See no. 15.

$$(2) \qquad \sum_{p=0}^{p=q} \frac{\Delta R_p}{(1 + I_T^m)^p} - \sum_{p=0}^{p=q} \frac{\Delta D_p}{(1 + I_T^m)^p} = 0,$$

reserving the term *average technical interest rate* for the rate I_T, which reduces income R_0^T to zero.

It is easy to see that the average and marginal technical interest rates display properties similar to those of the average and marginal costs of a given firm.

First it can be shown that the average technical interest rate increases or decreases when investments are increased depending on whether the marginal technical interest rate is or is not greater.[8]

8. An increase in investment corresponds to an increase in disbursements during the investment period or to an increase in receipts during the operational period. Thus we have

$$(1) \qquad \delta R^N < 0 \text{ from } t_0 \text{ to } t_m, \qquad \delta R^N > 0 \text{ from } t_m \text{ to } t_q.$$

Now, by definition we have, in continuous notation,

$$(2) \qquad \int_{t_0}^{t_q} R^N(t) e^{-i_T(t-t_0)} dt = 0,$$

whence, when function $R^N(t)$ varies from $\delta R^N(t)$,

$$(3) \qquad -\delta i_T \int_{t_0}^{t_q} (t - t_0) R^N(t) e^{-i_T(t-t_0)} dt + \int_{t_0}^{t_q} \delta R^N(t) e^{-i_T(t-t_0)} dt = 0,$$

where i_T stands for the average continuous technical interest rate.

As the marginal technical interest rate is defined by the equation

$$(4) \qquad \int_{t_0}^{t_q} \delta R^N(t) e^{-\frac{i_T^m}{T}(t-t_0)} dt = 0,$$

it can be seen that if $i_T^m > i_T$ we have, in view of equations (1),

$$(5) \qquad \int_{t_0}^{t_q} \delta R^N(t) e^{-i_T(t-t_0)} dt > 0,$$

and since we also have (note 4 above)

$$(6) \qquad \int_{t_0}^{t_q} (t - t_0) R^N(t) e^{-i_T(t-t_0)} dt > 0,$$

it can finally be seen that we have $\delta i_T > 0$.

Moreover, it follows from what we have seen[9] that the marginal investment envisaged is or is not profitable depending on whether the marginal productivity of capital is or is not greater than the market interest rate.

Thus it will be seen that investments will be expanded up to the point at which the marginal productivity of the capital is precisely equal to the market interest rate.[10,11]

But then it is clear that in general the average productivity represented by rate I_T will not be equal to the market interest rate I, and as we know that in equilibrium there is only one interest rate on the market, this may seem to lead at least *prima facie* to a contradiction.

The reality is that this situation is very similar to that which is met in studying the equilibrium of firms. In any situation, a firm expands its output until its marginal cost is equal to the market price. It then enjoys income

---

9. Taking account of equations (1) of note 8. The demonstration is the same as in the case of mean technical interest (note 4 above).

It is sufficient to start from the equation

$$\delta R_0^T = \int_{t_0}^{t_q} \delta R^N(t) e^{-i_T(t-t_0)} dt.$$

10. It is easy to prove that the overall revenue R_0^T is then maximal. We have

$$\delta R_0^T = \int_{t_0}^{t_q} \delta R^N(t) e^{-i(t-t_0)} dt,$$

a quantity that is positive, zero, or negative according to equations (1) and (4) of note 8, depending on whether the marginal interest rate i_T^m is greater than, equal to or less than the market interest rate i.

11. The reader can easily prove that the marginal interest rate I_T^m is only independent of the variation $\delta R^N(t)$ if overall income R_0^T is maximal.

I simply point out that net income flows R_P^N are certainly not independent and that there necessarily exists a certain relation between them

(1) $\varphi(R_0^N, R_1^N, \ldots, R_q^N) + 0.$

So the variations δR_P^N must satisfy the equation

(2) $\dfrac{\partial \varphi}{\partial R_0^N} \delta R_0^N + \dfrac{\partial \varphi}{\partial R_1^N} \delta R_1^N + \ldots + \dfrac{\partial \varphi}{\partial R_q^N} \delta R_q^N = 0.$

It follows that in order for income

(3) $R_0^T = \sum_{p=0}^{p=q} \dfrac{R_p^N}{(1+I)^p}$

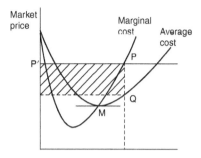

FIGURE 5.6 Variations in marginal cost and average cost as a function of output

equal to the product of the quantity produced by the excess of the marginal cost over the average cost (fig. 5.6).

New firms are then attracted, and the market price falls until it is equal to the absolute minimum of the average cost, corresponding to the intersection of the average and marginal cost curves.[12,13]

In the same way here, when the average productivity of a technique (T) is greater than the marginal productivity, new techniques (T) are implemented, which has the effect of increasing the demand for capital and hence, as we shall see,[14] of raising the market interest rate. This development continues until, for the various techniques involved, the average rate

---

to be maximal for a given market rate I, we must have

(4)
$$\frac{\frac{\partial \varphi}{\partial R_0^N}}{1} = \frac{\frac{\partial \varphi}{\partial R_1^N}}{\frac{1}{1+I}} = \ldots = \frac{\frac{\partial \varphi}{\partial R_q^N}}{\frac{1}{(1+I)^q}}.$$

It can be deduced that we then necessarily have

(5)
$$\delta R_0^N + \frac{\delta R_1^N}{1+I} + \ldots + \frac{\delta R_q^N}{(1+I)^q} = 0.$$

This equation shows that the marginal interest rate defined by equation (2) of the text is precisely equal to the market rate I and hence is independent of the variation $\delta R^N(t)$ in question.

12. Point M of figure 5.6.

13. See my $\grave{A}$ la recherche d'une discipline économique, no. 116.

14. No. 48.

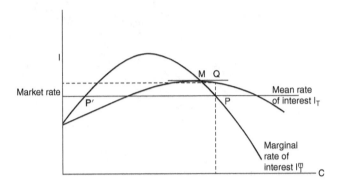

FIGURE 5.7 Variation of average and marginal productivity levels as a function of demand for capital

of productivity of capital is equal to the marginal productivity rate, which is itself equal to the market interest rate.[15]

Real technical interest rate

The technical interest rates that we have just been considering are nominal rates that depend essentially on *foreseen* variations in the general price level from one period to another. But it may be helpful for the line of reasoning being followed to eliminate this influence and replace these nominal rates with real rates. For this purpose it is sufficient to replace nominal values with real values in the foregoing explanations. All the results obtained will thereupon extend to the case of actual interest values.

In continuous notation we naturally have

$$i_T''' = i_T - \frac{\frac{dP}{dt}}{P},$$

15. Note that when the market interest rate *I* has a certain value, of the two points of intersection *P'* and *P* of the marginal productivity of capital curve and of the straight coordinate line equal to the market rate, only point *P* corresponds to a stable equilibrium. Any movement of the system around position *P'* in fact tends to distance it from stable equilibrium. Thus it is seen that an increase of *C* is advantageous since it corresponds to a productivity greater than the market rate.

where i_T''' denotes the real technical interest rate and $\dfrac{\frac{dP}{dt}}{P}$ denotes the expected relative rate of variation in prices.[16]

For the relative prices of different goods at the different periods *assumed to be given*,[17] the foregoing reasoning shows that the real technical interest rate *is a physical component independent of the general movements of prices.*

16. No. 19, equation (6).

17. Such a supposition can validly be made in interest theory, as has already been stated (note 17 to no. 40), since this theory is exclusively concerned with the study of the economic links between different periods and their effects.

4. Demand for capital (45)

It can thus be seen that some previously unprofitable production techniques become profitable when the market interest rate falls. For instance, some activities that proved unprofitable at an interest rate of 7–8% become profitable if the interest rate falls to 6%, and if it falls to 5%, additional activities will come into being.

The passage in which Turgot describes this effect of the variations in the interest rate has often been quoted: "The interest rate can be considered as a sort of level below which all work, all agriculture, all industry, and all commerce cease.[1] It is like a sea spread over a vast country: the mountain peaks rise above the waters and form fertile islands of cultivation.[2] If this sea should recede, as its level falls, the uplands, then the plains and the valleys gradually appear and are covered with productions of every sort. It is enough for the water to rise or fall by a foot to flood or restore to cultivation vast swathes of land."[3]

We may thus conclude that the demand for the availability of capital[4] is a decreasing function of the rate of interest. In which respect the availability of capital resembles every other service.

This demand becomes zero at a certain value of the interest rate beyond which there can be no profitable production process, and it becomes infinite for an annual rate very close to –100% since every process of indirect production whatsoever then becomes profitable (fig. 5.8).

These considerations show how strongly the level of the interest rate can influence the determination of investments. To take but one example, the overwhelming issue affecting the development of a country's hydroelectric resources is the enormous volume of capital that must be committed to set up the facilities.

Since hydroelectric power is the definitive rival to power derived from fossil fuels, the importance of the interest on the capital to be invested in penstocks for the development of hydroelectricity is evident.

1. These are the production techniques whose technical interest rate is lower than the market interest rate.

2. These are the production techniques whose technical interest rate is higher than the market interest rate.

3. M. Turgot, *Reflections on the Formation and Distribution of Wealth* (London: E. Spragg, 1795), § 89.

4. See no. 4.

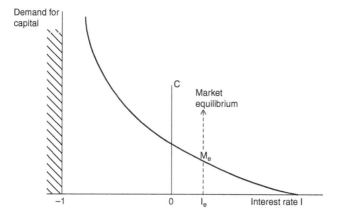

FIGURE 5.8 Variations in the demand for capital as a function of the interest rate

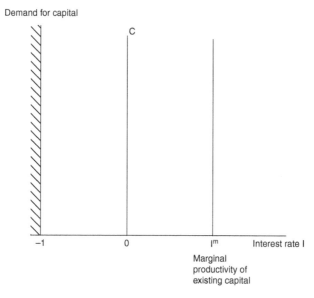

FIGURE 5.9 Variation in the demand for capital as a function of interest rate in a perfect market

Of course, apart from technical givens strictly so-called, the demand for capital depends on the level of information the market possesses and on the number of businesses able to implement the techniques envisaged. In fact, if the market were perfect, the slightest discrepancy between the market interest rate and the marginal productivity rate of existing equipment would lead to an infinite demand for capital. In this case, the demand for capital would be represented by a straight line, parallel to the y-axis, of abscissa equal to the marginal rate of productivity of the existing equipment (fig. 5.9).

In practice we may conclude that the shape of the capital demand curve is as in figure 5.8, but that the elasticity $\dfrac{\frac{dC}{C}}{\frac{dI}{I}}$ of the demand is very high so that as a first approximation the case of figure 5.9 may be adopted for the study of equilibrium.

5. Importance of forecasts in determining investments (46)

Every production is ultimately intended to satisfy a consumer. Now there is usually a time lag—sometimes a very substantial lag—between the moment when the firm advances the costs (on behalf of the consumer) and the moment when the finished product is purchased by the final consumer. Meanwhile the firm must predict as accurately as possible how much consumers will be willing to pay when, after this possibly substantial time lag, it is in a position, directly or indirectly, to satisfy them.

The firm has no alternative but to let itself be guided by these forecasts, at least when implementing production processes that take time.

The calculation of technical interest rates thus involves future prices predicted by the firm. So what counts for the firm are expected results. Present results are relevant only as part of the data on which the predictions are based.

Hence it is perfectly possible for a particular investment that would be profitable under present market conditions not to be made if an unfavorable price movement is expected. On the other hand, some other investment that current conditions would prove unprofitable may nonetheless be made if the expected price trend appears favorable. In fact, *only the future matters* and what must be compared with the market interest rate is the *expected* technical interest rate, not the currently observed technical interest rate.

Since reliable forecasts are possible only under relatively stable economic and social conditions, this highlights the importance of the stability of these conditions for the business spirit and for economic prosperity.

6. Rate of interest, production period, and distribution of the primary factors of production (47)[1]

Duration of a production process

Let A be a product available at time t_0 and the production of which requires, directly or indirectly, by way of expenditure on *primary factors of production* (land and labor) $\Delta_{-q}, \dots, \Delta_{-p}, \dots, \Delta_{-1}, \Delta_0$[2,3] per unit of time at times $t_{-q}, \dots, t_{-p}, \dots, t_0$.

We have seen[4] that with continuous parameters the production process being studied can be represented by a diagram (fig. 5.10), representing the distribution over time of the aggregate

(1) $\Delta = \Sigma \Delta_{-p}$

of the values of the primary factors of production used, which I have termed the *primary value* of product A.[5]

Under these conditions, if the discontinuous interest rate is I, value V at time t_0 of product A will be equal, in equilibrium, to the sum of expenditure (primary expenditure + interest),[5] i.e.,

(2) $V = \Sigma (1 + I)^P \Delta_{-p}.$

It is convenient to define this production process by the weighted mean interval Θ of supply of the primary factors of production. This gives us

---

1. For the present writer, the starting point of the reflections that follow was the penetrating analysis of selected indirect production processes by G.-H. Bousquet, in volume 3 of his *Institutes de sciences économiques* (Paris: Rivière, 1936), ch. 6, "Le temps et l'équilibre de la production," 111–73.

2. The estimation takes into account their respective prices.

3. Difficulties may arise in this determination owing to the existence of (a) durable goods used at different instants in the production of the same good and (b) related goods produced in the same production process (gas and coke, for instance). It is beyond the scope of this study to examine them. Suffice it to say for the present that they can easily be overcome. (On this intricate question, my *À la recherche d'une discipline économique* may be consulted with advantage.)

4. No. 27.

5. No. 35.

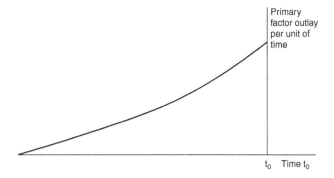

FIGURE 5.10 Characteristic diagram of a production available at time t_0

$$(3) \qquad \Theta = \frac{\Sigma(t_0 - t_{-p})\Delta_{-p}}{\Sigma\Delta_{-p}}.$$

The period Θ represents the average waiting interval between supply of the primary factors and availability of the finished product: i.e., it characterizes the average period of production, and I shall call it the *production period*.

Clearly under stationary conditions the primary value of the capital used in a given process is greater as period Θ is longer.[6] *We may therefore conclude that period Θ is characteristic of the amount of capital used.*

Production period and interest rates

As in general the more a factor of production costs the less it is used, and as the price of a factor of production (X_{-q}) supplied at time t_{-q} for price x_{-q} is equal to $x_{-q}(1 + I)^q$ at time t_0, it is clear that factor (X_{-q}) will be decreasingly used for product (A_0) as interest rate I rises.

It follows that, if the rate of interest is high, earlier factors of production will be relatively little used by comparison with recent ones, and vice versa. It can thus be seen that the production period, and consequently the degree of use of capital, will be proportionally less as the rate of interest is higher.[7]

6. This property will be clarified later.
7. This result confirms the findings of no. 45.

It can also be seen that when the interest rate rises, production processes are replaced by shorter ones and that the longer the processes in question, the more pronounced this shortening will be.

For example, in the case of the production of housing services, this means that the buildings will be proportionately more durable, i.e., built of more solid materials, as the interest rate is lower.[8] Hence in emerging countries, where interest rates tend to attain levels far higher than those found in developed countries, constructions tend to be of a shorter-lived kind; shanty-

---

8. It is easy to establish this in a completely different way.

Let there be two buildings rendering services that are comparable but of different duration: n_1 and n_2 years. Let a_1' and a_2' be their respective cost prices. If the economy is in a stationary state and if a is the price of the service rendered each year by these buildings, their present values are respectively

(1) $$a_1 = \frac{a}{1+I} + \ldots + \frac{a}{(1+I)^{n_1}},$$

(2) $$a_2 = \frac{a}{1+I} + \ldots + \frac{a}{(1+I)^{n_2}}.$$

It can be seen that

(3) $$a_2 - a_1 = \frac{a}{(1+I)^{n_1+1}} + \ldots + \frac{a}{(1+I)^{n_2}}.$$

If the rate of interest is high, it can be seen that the difference $(a_2 - a_1)$ will be slight and not enough to cover the supplementary expenses needed to increase the life of the buildings from n_1 to n_2 years.

For instance, taking $n_1 = 25$ and $n_2 = 50$ and an interest rate of 10%, we have

(4) $$\frac{a_2 - a_1}{a_1} = \frac{9.91 - 9.09}{9.09} = 0.09 \sim \frac{1}{10}.$$

Thus for a rate of 10%, the present value of the services increases by only about 1/10 when building life increases from 25 to 50 years whereas evidently the increase in the construction cost is much greater.

If we had $n_1 = 50$ and $n_2 = 100$, we should find, for $I = 10\%$,

(5) $$\frac{a_2 - a_1}{a_1} = \frac{9.99 - 9.91}{9.91} = 0.008 \sim \frac{1}{100}.$$

Thus the relative difference of present values would be only 1/100 and hence certainly out of all proportion to the relative increase in building costs.

towns and makeshift accommodation predominate. The same also applies to countries devastated by war.

Primary national income

I shall use the term *primary national income* and the notation $R_{N\omega}$ to denote the sum of the values of the primary factors of production used per unit of time in the whole economy at any given point.

In a stationary equilibrium, this income is constant and equal to the sum of wages and land rent.[9] Thus, using the previous notations,[10] we have

(4) $$R_{N\omega} = S + R_{\varphi}.$$

As a first approximation, the primary income calculated in terms of wage value under stationary conditions can be deemed to be independent of the capital stock, and hence of the prevailing interest rate.[11,12]

Distribution of primary national income over the different stages of production

For the economy as a whole, the distribution of the primary national income per unit of time, *at a given time*, over the different stages of production, can of course be represented by a diagram (fig. 5.11) similar to the one we used for a specific production.

I shall use $\varphi(\theta)$ to denote the quantity of primary income spent per unit of time, θ units of time before time t at which production is completed and the product is available for direct consumption.[13]

9. No. 35.

10. No. 37.

11. Quite simply, if $A(X, Y, \ldots, Z)$ represents a production function, we can conclude that the ratio of the prices y/x of factors (Y) and (X), equal to the ratio A'_y / A'_σ, varies little with the quantity Z used of factor (Z).

12. All the calculations that follow will thus be made in terms of *wage value*. However, to simplify the notations, I shall not be using a sub-index for these values (see no. 19).

13. With regard to the houses, note that the consumer product referred to is not the buildings themselves but the housing *services*, which alone can be consumed immediately and directly.

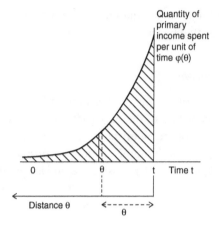

FIGURE 5.11 Diagram representing overall production at time t

By definition, the function $\varphi(\theta)$ thus characterizes the *distribution in the past of the primary value of the consumable product*[14] *available at time* t.[15]

If conditions are stationary, we shall then have

(5)
$$R_{N\omega} = \int_0^{+\infty} \varphi(\theta)\, d\theta.$$
[16,17]

14. Per unit of time.

15. Irrespective of whether or not the process is stationary.

16. As a rule I am assuming that the characteristic curve extends to infinity, but this may not always be so in practice. Indeed I think that above a certain value for θ the characteristic production function may be assumed to be zero.

17. This is easily established using a simple example.

Let us assume that there is only one production process, divided into three stages, each lasting a year. The quantities of raw materials used during each of these stages are respectively represented by rectangles S_1, S_2, S_3.

At the end of each year one part of the output is finished, another part is in a half-finished state, still needing a further year's transformation, and the remaining third part is still in the state of primary factors. The environment being stationary, the whole production system can be represented by three characteristic diagrams, identical but spaced one year apart. Naturally we have

(1)
$$R_{N\omega} = \theta_1 M_1 + \theta_2' M_2' + \theta_3'' M_3''$$

and, consequently,

(2)
$$R_{N\omega} = \theta_1 M_1 + \theta_2 M_2 + \theta_3 M_3.$$

This equation expresses the fact that the shaded area enclosed by the characteristic curve is equal to the primary national income and hence that function $\varphi(\theta)$ *also characterizes the distribution at a given moment of the primary national income over the various stages of production.*

I shall therefore call this function the *characteristic production function* and the curve that represents it the *characteristic curve.*

Shape of the characteristic production function

We may assume that on average the characteristic production function $\varphi(\theta)$ is under present conditions a decreasing function of θ. For on the one hand the existence of a positive interest rate under present conditions has

---

In this way we verify that the primary national income, being the sum of the values of the primary factors of production used during the year T preceding time t, is equal to the primary value of the output finished at time t.

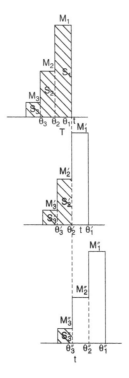

FIGURE 5.12 FOOTNOTE

the effect of making more distant primary factors of production more expensive and hence of making them relatively less used, and on the other, even if the interest rate were zero, it is safe to assume that the same would apply since we have fuller *technical* know-how concerning short-term production processes than long-term ones.[18]

National production period

I shall use the term *national production period* and the notation Θ_N to denote the average spacing of the different primary factor outlays concurring in the formation of the national income at time t.

18. This means that if

(1)
$$A = A(\Delta_0 \Delta_{-1}, \ldots, \Delta_{-p}, \ldots, \Delta_{-r}, \ldots, \Delta_{-q})$$

represents the output obtained from primary outlay $\Delta_0 \Delta_{-1}, \ldots, \Delta_{-p}, \ldots, \Delta_{-r}, \ldots, \Delta_{-q}$, we have on average

(2)
$$\frac{\partial A}{\partial \Delta_{-p}}(\Delta, \Delta, \ldots, \Delta) > \frac{\partial A}{\partial \Delta_{-r}}(\Delta, \Delta, \ldots, \Delta) \text{ for } p < r.$$

This means that, for an equal distribution of primary expenditure, the functions of production can be deemed on average to be such that an identical supplementary primary outlay generates an increase in output that becomes greater the earlier the outlay occurs.

Indeed, only if our technical know-how were perfect before could the characteristic function of the national output for a zero interest rate have a conventional shape, whereas in reality our technical know-how is much greater concerning short-term processes, and this for two reasons:

1. Long-term processes are more complex and on average more impervious to innovation.
2. Long-term processes can only be perfected by experimentation, and for that, considerable capital must already be available. Hence, knowledge of the efficiency of longer processes depends on the *prior* implementation of shorter ones.

However, the fact that the representative curve of the characteristic production function can safely be taken to have the shape shown in figure 5.11 of the text does not mean that it will be the same for all productions. For instance, in the case of the production of housing services examined in note 13 above, we may take it that the characteristic curve has the shape shown in figure 5.13. It can thus be seen that particular curves relative to certain services can differ sharply from the average curve relative to aggregate national output.

This gives us

(6)
$$\Theta_N = \frac{\int_0^{+\infty} \theta\varphi(\theta)\,d\theta}{\int_0^{+\infty} \varphi(\theta)\,d\theta}.$$
[19,20,21]

It follows from the foregoing that the national production period can be considered to be a reliable indicator of the economy's capital stock.

Variation of the distribution of primary income with the rate of interest under stationary conditions

As the primary national income can safely be taken as a first approximation to be independent of the rate of interest, the area enclosed by the characteristic curve remains constant as the rate of interest varies, and it follows from what we have seen that the characteristic curve draws closer to the time axis on the right and farther from it on the left as the rate of interest decreases,[22] as is shown in figure 5.14.

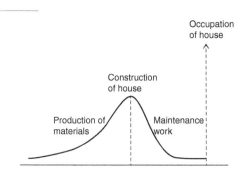

FIGURE 5.13 FOOTNOTE

19. As the reader can easily verify, the national production period so defined is simply the average of the durations of the various production processes, weighted according to the fractions of the primary national income respectively devoted to each.

20. It should be emphasized that, taking account of the definition of the function $\varphi(\theta)$, the definition given of the national production period is valid whether or not stationary conditions prevail.

21. From the definition of the function $\varphi(\theta)$ it naturally follows that the national production period depends on the relative prices of the different factors of production. It is therefore an *economic* concept and not a physical one.

22. Because earlier primary factors of production then become relatively less expensive.

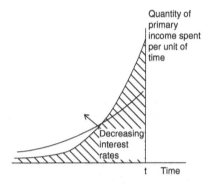

FIGURE 5.14 Variation of the distribution of primary income with the interest rate

Variation of the national production period with the rate
of interest under stationary conditions

It can thus be seen that the national production period increases as the
rate of interest falls (fig. 5.15). Very close to zero for very high interest rate
levels, it is naturally very great for values close to −1.[23]

The generation of national income under stationary conditions

We have seen[24] that in a stationary model the national income is expressed by

(7) $R_N = R_C,$

where R_C represents consumed income.

23. Some readers may be surprised to find me here considering the rate of interest as
a variable whereas experience shows that in fact it is determined by the conditions of the
equilibrium.

For this reason, it is worth emphasizing here that equilibrium is due to the combination
of conditions of a technical nature (in the production sector) and the other economic conditions (individual psychologies, system of ownership, State intervention, etc.). Hence different
equilibrium states are conceivable that correspond to a single technical state but involve different psychological conditions or a variable degree of State intervention (e.g., in the market).
Under these conditions production period Θ_N clearly emerges as a function of the rate of
interest. These statements will be clarified in greater detail in appendix II in which a specific
case will be studied.

24. No. 37.

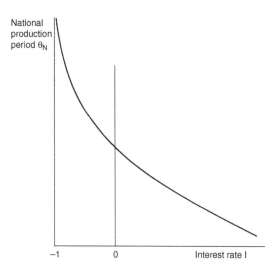

FIGURE 5.15 Variations of the national production period with the interest rate

As the primary expenses involved in income R_N are represented by the function $\varphi(\theta)$ and the value at time t of the primary national income $\varphi(\theta)\,d\theta$ spent at time $(t - \theta)$ is equal to $e^{i\theta}\varphi(\theta)\,d\theta$,[25,26] we have

(8) $$R_N = \int_0^{+\infty} e^{i\theta}\varphi(\theta)\,d\theta.$$ [27]

Value of national capital in a stationary economy

The national income at any point in time is composed of two elements: primary national income and interest on the national capital C_μ.[28] Thus we have

25. See nos. 15 and 35.

26. For the calculations I am here systematically using the continuous interest rate i, which is more convenient to manipulate. By contrast, in the diagrams I revert to the more commonly used annual interest rate payable annually.

27. Note that the national income R_N, though equal under stationary conditions to consumed income R_C, is not equal to the final output P_F of finished goods and is in fact less than in it by the aggregate of depreciations A (no. 37, equation [26]), which is itself equal to the sum total of investments (no. 37, equation [24]). Hence in the national income only *directly* consumable products are involved.

28. The national capital consists of the value of all capital goods except land (no. 42).

(9) $$R_N = R_{N\omega} + iC_\mu,$$

therefore

(10) $$C_\mu = \frac{R_N - R_{N\omega}}{i},$$

i.e.,

(11) $$C_\mu = \int_0^{+\infty} \frac{(e^{i\theta} - 1)}{i} \varphi(\theta)\, d\theta.$$

Hence this equation gives the value of the national capital as a function of the characteristic production function $\varphi(\theta)$.[29]

29. This expression for C_μ can also be discovered by two alternative methods of calculation that are much less simple but shed vital light on the link between capital, income, and the rate of interest.

a. *First method.*

At time t the capital is the sum of the values arising from expenditure on primary factors occurring before time t and that will lead to a final output only during period $(t + T, t + T + dT)$ subsequent to time t.

The primary value *spent prior to time t* of the final product of value $R_N dT$ of the period $(t + T, t + T + dT)$ has, at time t, (fig. 5.16) the value

(1) $$dT \int_T^{+\infty} \varphi(\theta) e^{i(\theta - T)}\, d\theta.$$

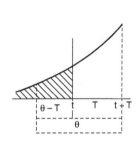

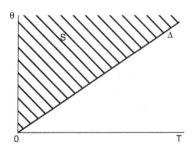

FIGURE 5.16 FOOTNOTE   FIGURE 5.17 FOOTNOTE

This gives us

(2)
$$C_\mu = \int_0^{+\infty} dT \int_T^{+\infty} \varphi(\theta) e^{i(\theta - T)} d\theta = \iint_S \varphi(\theta) e^{i(\theta - T)} dT d\theta.$$

where S represents the area enclosed by the 0θ axis and the bisector $0A$ of angle $T0\theta$ (fig. 5.17). Inverting the order of the integrations, we obtain

(3)
$$C_\mu = \int_0^{+\infty} e^{i\theta} \varphi(\theta) d\theta \int_0^\theta e^{-iT} dT = \int_0^{+\infty} \frac{e^{i\theta} - 1}{i} \varphi(\theta) d\theta,$$

which brings us back to expression (11) in the text.

b. *Second method.*

The capital in existence at time t can equally well be considered as the sum of the values at time t of the various primary incomes spent in periods $(t - T, t - T - dT)$ and that will be used for a finished production only after time t (figs. 5.18 and 5.19).

The part of the primary income $R_{N\omega} dT$ supplied during period $(t - T, t - T - dT)$ that will be used for a finished production after time t is expressed by

(4)
$$dT \int_T^{+\infty} \varphi(\theta) d\theta,$$

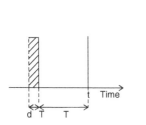
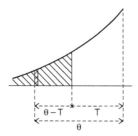

FIGURE 5.18 FOOTNOTE   FIGURE 5.19 FOOTNOTE

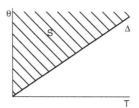

FIGURE 5.20 FOOTNOTE

Primary national capital

I shall use the term *primary national capital* and the notation $C_{\mu\omega}$ to denote the primary value[30] of the national capital C_μ. By definition, this value is quite simply what the value of the national capital would become if, all other things being equal,[31] the interest rate became zero. According to equation (11) we then have

(12)
$$C_{\mu\omega} = \int_0^{+\infty} \theta\varphi(\theta)\,d\theta,$$ [32,33]

i.e., taking account of equations (5) and (6),

---

and its value at time t is

(5)
$$e^{iT}\,dT\int_T^{+\infty} \varphi(\theta)\,d\theta,$$

so that the value of the national capital at time t emerges as

(6)
$$C_\mu = \int_0^{+\infty} e^{iT}\,dT\int_T^{+\infty} \varphi(\theta)\,d\theta = \iint_s e^{iT}\varphi(\theta)\,d\theta\,dT$$

(see fig. 5.20)

$$= \int_0^{+\infty} \varphi(\theta)\,d\theta\int_0^\theta e^{iT}\,dT,$$

i.e., finally,

(7)
$$C_\mu = \int_0^{+\infty} \frac{e^{i\theta} - 1}{i}\varphi(\theta)\,d\theta.$$

Thus once again we come back to expression (11) in the text.

30. No. 35.

31. In particular the function $\varphi(\theta)$.

32. Bear in mind that we have

$$\lim_{i=0}\left(\frac{e^{i\theta} - 1}{i}\right) = \theta.$$

33. This equation can easily be found again directly in the specific case studied in note 17 above.

For it can be seen at once that the primary capital $C_{\mu\omega}$ at the end of year t is equal to the sum of the shaded areas of figure 5.12 of that note.

So we have

$$C_{\mu\omega} = S_1 + 2S_2 + 3S_3,$$

(13) $$C_{\mu\omega} = \Theta_N R_{N\omega}.$$

From this it follows that the primary national capital is equal to the product of the primary national income by the average production period.[34]

As the primary national income can be considered to be constant and the national production period is a decreasing function of the rate of interest I, it emerges that the primary capital is itself a decreasing function of the rate of interest I. In fact, the representative curve of the relation of capital to interest rate I can be regarded indifferently either as that of the total demand for primary capital in equilibrium as a function of the rate of interest (fig. 5.21),[35] or as that of the marginal productivity of the capital[36] as a function of primary capital (fig. 5.22).

Approximate measurement of the national production period under stationary conditions

It is easy to give approximate formulae for calculating the national production period:

---

which is the same as equation (12) expressed in discontinuous terms.

Reasoning identical to that used in note 29 above generally leads back to equation (12) without problem.

34. If the amount of money is denoted by M, the flow of expenditure per unit of time in a money-based economy by Φ, and the average period of idleness of money by T, the quantitative relation can be expressed as

$$M = T\Phi.$$

This brings out the similarity of the relation between the primary capital and the primary income and the quantitative relation. However, whereas when we choose the year as the unit of time, the period T has values on the order of from 1/10 to 1/100, the period Φ_N has values on the order of from 5 to 10. Consequently, whereas the sum of money balances is far less than the flow of annual expenditure, the primary capital is far greater than the primary income.

35. This demand, which corresponds to the variations in equilibrium of the primary capital as a function of the rate of interest must be clearly distinguished from the instantaneous demand for capital out of equilibrium considered in no. 45.

36. At the moment of investment in the primary factors of production, the value capital and the primary capital are identical and their productivity is the same.

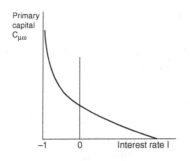

FIGURE 5.21 Total demand curve for primary capital as a function of interest rate

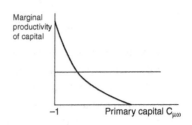

FIGURE 5.22 Variations in the marginal productivity of capital as a function of primary capital

(1) ON THE BASIS OF THE NATIONAL INCOME AND ITS COMPONENTS. According to equation (8) we have

$$(14) \qquad R_N = \int_0^{+\infty} \left(1 + i\theta + \frac{i^2\theta^2}{2} + \dots\right) \varphi(\theta)\, d\theta,$$

i.e., from equations (5) and (6),

$$(15) \qquad R_N \sim R_{N\omega} + i\Theta_N R_{N\omega}.$$

From this we infer that as a first approximation we have

$$(16) \qquad \Theta_N = \frac{1}{i}\left(\frac{R_N}{R_{N\omega}} - 1\right).$$

This equation provides a method of calculating the period Θ_N on the basis of the national income and its component $R_{N\omega}$.[37]

37. This formula was found by von Stackelberg using a specific case in his article "Kapital und Zins in der stationären Verkehrswirtschaft" [Capital and interest in the stationary exchange economy], in *Zeitschrift für Nationalökonomie*, vol. 10 (1941) (Centre Perroux collection).

In this article, von Stackelberg applies equation (16) to the case of Germany in 1913 on the basis of the following values in marks

$R_N = 46$ billion, $R_N - R_{N\omega} = 10$ billion, $i = 4$ to 5%,

whence

(II) ON THE BASIS OF NATIONAL CAPITAL AND NATIONAL INCOME.   According to equation (10) we have

(17)
$$C_\mu = \frac{R_N}{i}\left(1 - \frac{R_{N\omega}}{R_N}\right).$$

From this we may infer, on the basis of equation (15), that we have

(18)
$$C_\mu \sim \frac{R_N}{i}\left(1 - \frac{1}{1 + i\Theta_N}\right),$$

38

whence, as a first approximation,

$$\Theta_N = 5.5 \text{ to } 6.9 \text{ years.}$$

(The rate of interest considered here is the average rate of interest on investments and hence includes risk premiums.)

38. More exactly, equation (17) gives

(1)
$$\frac{C_\mu}{R_N} = \frac{1}{i}\frac{R_N - R_{N\omega}}{R_N}.$$

If we write

(2)
$$\Delta = \frac{\int_0^{+\infty}\theta^2\varphi(\theta)\,d\theta}{R_{N\omega}},$$

we then have

(3)
$$\frac{C_\mu}{R_N} \sim \frac{\Theta_N + \frac{\Delta}{2}i}{1 + i\Theta_N} \sim \Theta_N\left(1 + \frac{\Delta}{2\Theta_N}i\right)(1 - i\Theta_N),$$

i.e.,

(4)
$$\frac{C_\mu}{R_N} \sim \Theta_N + \left(\frac{\Delta}{2} - \Theta_N^2\right)i,$$

where Δ is a certain function of i. Thus we have

(5)
$$\frac{d}{di}\frac{C_\mu}{R_N} \sim \frac{d\Theta_N}{di} + \frac{\Delta}{2} - \Theta_N^2,$$

an equation that we shall make use of later (notes 39 and 47).

(19)
$$\Theta_N \sim \frac{C_\mu}{R_N},$$

an equation that enables us to calculate the period Θ_N on the basis of the national capital and the national income.[39]

39. According to the values of C_N and R_N for 1913 given for various countries in billions of marks by the "Economic Forces of the World" (a statistical publication of the Dresdner Bank, Berlin, 1930, pp. 177 and 179) and the average values of the short-term interest rate I_c (the discount rate of sound commercial paper) from 1896 to 1913, for different countries, *all comparable with one another*, that can be obtained from tables II, III, IV, and VII given by Fisher in his *The Theory of Interest* as an appendix to chapter 19, if we take the pure rate of interest I to be greater by 1% than the short-term rate (note 14 to no. 84 and note 19 to no. 94) and if we take the ratio $\frac{C_\varphi}{C_N}$ of land (*as defined in note 1 to no. 30*) to national capital to have the same value (33%) in the other countries that it has in France (according to figures given by Moulton, *Income and Economic Progress* [Washington, DC: Brookings, 1935], this ratio can be evaluated at 28% for the United States in 1939), table 5.1 can be drawn up in billions of marks for 1913.

TABLE 5.1 FOOTNOTE

	C_N	C_φ	C_μ	R_N	i
France	240	80	160	29.7	3.5
Great Britain	290	97	193	46	4.1
Germany	310	103	207	48	4.5
United States	831	277	554	150	5.7

The value of Θ_N can then be calculated on the basis of these two approximate ratios:

(1)
$$\Theta_N = \frac{C_\mu}{R_N},$$

(2)
$$\Theta_N = \frac{1}{i}\frac{R_N - R_{N\omega}}{R_{N\omega}},$$

i.e., according to equation (9) in the text,

(3)
$$\Theta_N = \frac{C_\mu}{R_N - iC_\mu}.$$

So far as can be judged by studying simple cases (note 47 below) it seems plausible that equation (1) gives Θ_N by defect. Moreover, it follows from equation (14) in the text that equation (3) gives Θ_N by excess. The best indication will therefore be to take the average of the two values so found. This gives us table 5.2.

It is thus verified that the average production period Θ_N does indeed vary in inverse proportion to the interest rate, and by plotting the different values obtained on a graph (fig. 5.23) it is clear that that they may be regarded as sufficiently consistent.

The reader may be surprised, at least at first sight, to see France thus figure at the head of the list in terms of capital intensity. But it should be remembered that the year is 1913, not 1945. Two successive wars and a nonsensical economic policy from 1919 to 1939 have ruined our industry, so that today we find it hard to imagine the status of France in the industrial world of 1913. Yet it is well known that French savings were so abundant as to be able to overflow massively into foreign countries. "There was no great business in the world in which

TABLE 5.2 FOOTNOTE

	Value of Θ_N			
	By Defect	By Excess	Average	Rate of Interest i
France	5.4	6.6	6	3.5
Great Britain	4.2	5.2	4.7	4.1
Germany	4.3	5.3	4.8	4.5
United States	3.7	4.7	4.2	5.7

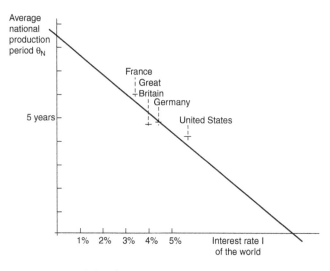

FIGURE 5.23 FOOTNOTE Variations in the average national production period as a function of the interest rate

French engineers were not to be found, often in dominant positions. The construction of ports and railways in new countries was most often undertaken by French engineers and French industrial groups then manufactured the equipment needed to run them" (A. Caquot, "La renaissance française, ses conditions techniques," *Bulletin de la société des ingénieurs civils de France*, 1945).

At home, our facilities were such that in 1917 "we were able to supply the young American army with all its warplanes and its field guns without prejudicing the massive manufacture of ammunition and equipment for the French army, while at the same time making a sterling contribution to re-arming the Italian army after its defeats. In 1918 France possessed the strongest aviation industry of all the belligerent powers" (Caquot, "La renaissance française"). Incredible though they may appear today, these are cold and certain facts.

Another surprise awaits the unprepared reader when we compare the above ranking by capital intensity with the following ranking of countries in terms of capital and income per person, which, in thousands of marks, looks as shown in table 5.3.

But it should be noted that there is no direct relationship between capital intensity and wealth, i.e., between the distribution of primary income (land and labor) over time and income per person. The rankings are quite different. Indeed, it seems legitimate to consider, at least as a first approximation, that the national production period depends chiefly on the rate of interest while the other factors entail only relatively slight variations.

Moreover, the quantities that are directly comparable here are not the capital per person values calculated using the same unit (in this case the mark), but the same capital values measured in national wage units. By making these calculations with the help of the statistical data published by the Statistique Générale de la France (Special Study on the purchasing power of workers in different countries from 1914 to 1938, *Bulletin de la S.G.F.* for June–September 1944, pp. 214 and 220, and the general indices of economic activity in France from 1901 to 1931, published by the S.G.F., p. 146), table 5.4 can be drawn up for weekly wages per person.

TABLE 5.3 FOOTNOTE

	Capital per Person	Income per Person
France	6	0.75
Great Britain	6.3	1
Germany	4.6	0.7
United States	8.6	1.5

TABLE 5.4 FOOTNOTE

	1929	1929 Index (Base 1914)	1914 col. 1 / col. 2	Exchange Rate (Marks)	1914 in Marks col. 3 / col. 4
France	—	—	32.5 francs	0.8	26.0 marks
Great Britain	60 shillings	194	31.0 shillings	1.02	32.0 marks
Germany	45 marks	163	27.5 marks	1	27.5 marks
United States	33 dollars	228	13.6 dollars	4.1	51.0 marks

This gives us, for the per person capital and income for each country expressed in terms of the value of a week's work, table 5.5.

Here we find that values for per person capital are ranked in the same order as the period Θ_N. That it decreases with the rate of interest is basically due to the fact that, as we shall see (note 48 below) national capital expressed in wage terms must be taken to be a decreasing function of the interest rate.

Turning to the per person income, it exhibits similar values. The differences observed are due to the fact that (a) the relative amount of land rents and the wage dispersion were not the same in 1913 for the national primary income in the four countries in question and (b) the national income expressed in terms of wages varies with the interest rate (equation [15]), although this variation is slight, as the product $i\Theta_N$ has values that differ little (from 0.19 to 0.24) for the four countries being studied.

Note too that the above ranking of pure interest rates derived by increasing the short-term rates by one point does not coincide with the ranking of the capitalization rates of government bonds—the exception being England. For in 1913 this country's capitalization rate was the lowest (2.81% as against 3.12% in France from 1901 to 1913, according to M. Dieterlen, *Les normes économiques* [Paris: Institut scientifique de recherches économiques et sociales, 1943], 132). In my view this is explained by the fact that British consols were an outstandingly safe investment, not only on a national level but also internationally, which led to a higher liquidity premium than was enjoyed by the government bonds of other countries (no. 84).

By comparing the respective values of Θ_N and of i, a first-approximation idea can be obtained of the order of magnitude of the variation of Θ_N with i, which will be used later. Assuming that the representative curve of Θ_N as a function of i reduces in the region studied to the tangent, by interpolating the values found by a straight line, we obtain

$$\frac{d\Theta_N}{di} \sim -80;$$

in other words, the production period increases by 0.8 years when the interest rate falls in absolute value by 1%.

Naturally the foregoing calculations are very approximate since the equations used are themselves approximate, as well as on account of the assimilation of the curve representative of Θ_N to its tangent, of the differences in natural wealth per person and in population sizes in the countries studied, of our lack of exact knowledge of the size of the national income and

TABLE 5.5 FOOTNOTE

	Capital per Person	Income per Person
France	6,000/26 = 230	750/26 = 29
Great Britain	6,300/32 = 190	1,000/32 = 31
Germany	4,600/27.5 = 168	700/27.5 = 25
United States	8,600/51 = 149	1,500/51 = 29

Variation of national capital with the interest rate

According to equation (11), for small values of the rate of interest i we have

(20)
$$C_\mu \sim \int_0^{+\infty} \left(0 + \frac{i\theta^2}{2}\right) \varphi(\theta)\, d\theta,$$
40

i.e., according to equation (12),

(21)
$$C_\mu \sim C_{\mu\omega} + \frac{i}{2} \int_0^{+\infty} \theta^2 \varphi(\theta)\, d\theta$$

or, according to equation (13),

(22)
$$C_\mu \sim \Theta_N R_{N\omega} + \frac{i}{2} \int_0^{+\infty} \theta^2 \varphi(\theta)\, d\theta.$$

As the primary national income $R_{N\omega}$ can as a first approximation be taken as constant, we then have[41]

---

capital as well as of the pure interest rate and, finally, the fact that only as a first approximation can the economies considered be regarded as stationary in 1913; hence these calculations
should be seen as *very crude estimates, subject to strong reservations, providing mere orders of
magnitude and to be taken as the starting points of a more thorough and absolutely essential
investigation.*

It goes without saying that *caution is called for in extrapolating to the present the values
found* for Θ_N and for $\dfrac{d\Theta_N}{di}$, since production techniques have evolved considerably since
1913; but the instability of economic conditions after the First World War *excludes any calculation based on more recent data.*

Finally it should be noted that the figures given above highlight the importance of
the interest component in prices (no. 35). The average percentage of interest in the prices
of final consumption goods is in fact equal to the ratio $\dfrac{iC_\mu}{R_N}$. This amounts respectively to 19%,
17%, 19%, and 21% for France, Great Britain, Germany, and the United States in 1914. So
we may safely conclude that this percentage is on the order of 20%.

40. In fact, we have

$$\frac{e^{i\theta} - 1}{i} = \frac{1}{i}\left[i\theta + \frac{(i\theta)^2}{2!} + \frac{(i\theta)^3}{3!} + \ldots \right].$$

41. Omitting the terms containing i as a factor.

(23)
$$\frac{dC_\mu}{di} \sim R_{N\omega}\frac{d\Theta_N}{di} + \frac{1}{2}\int_0^{+\infty} \theta^2\varphi(\theta)\,d\theta.$$

As the first term of the second member is negative (because the period Θ_N is a decreasing function of the rate of interest) while the second is positive, as a rule no conclusion can be drawn as to the sign of the derivative $\dfrac{dC_\mu}{di}$, which may equally well be positive or negative.[42,43]

So notwithstanding the common opinion, national capital,[44] cannot generally be accepted as a reliable indicator of the aggregate national equipment stock.[45] Indeed it emerges from what has just been seen that when the derivative $\dfrac{dC_\mu}{di}$ is positive national capital increases as the equipment stock decreases.[46]

It follows that in fact *only* the primary capital, which represents at a given point in time the aggregate value of the primary factors of production that were necessary for the production of the economy's capital equipment, can be deemed to be a reliable indicator.[47]

42. See note 47 below for an examination of two specific cases.

43. This result was predictable. For while raising the rate of interest has the effect of diminishing the stock of equipment, another of its effects is to increase the value of the capital-output ratios $e^{i\theta}$. Thus with regard to the value of the capital C_μ two opposing tendencies are produced, either of which may equally well prevail.

44. Note that this is a *value*, not a physical quantity.

45. This is essentially a physical quantity.

46. Naturally what is at issue in this case is the variation of the capital C_μ with the rate of interest i when the relevant stationary equilibrium is modified as a result of structural variations independent of conditions of a technical or psychological nature, for instance. So this result by no means contradicts the fact that the demand for capital is always a decreasing function of the rate of interest (no. 45). (See the very similar remarks about the supply of capital made in note 12 to no. 40.)

All that can be said is that, all other things being equal, the equilibrium interest rate will be proportionally greater as the primary capital is less.

It can thus easily be understood why the rate of interest in equilibrium should be much higher in new countries than it is in old ones that are already equipped. (In 1913, for instance, the rate of interest in the United States was higher than in Europe. See note 39 above.)

47. As we do not know the real shape of the characteristic curve, it is worth examining what happens in two particularly simple cases.

a. *Whatever the value of the rate of interest* i *may be, the function* φ(θ) *reduces to a constant* between θ and a limit value λ. This case was studied by Jevons in chapter 7 of his *Theory of Political Economy* (London: Macmillan, 1871), 316–26, of the French translation (Giard, 1900) and also, but with much greater precision, by Bousquet, *Institutes de science économique*, vol. 3 [Institutions of economic science] (Paris: Rivière, 1936), ch. 6, § 8, 157–69.

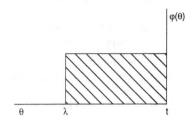

FIGURE 5.24 FOOTNOTE

We then have

$$(1) \qquad \varphi(\theta) = \frac{R_{N\omega}}{\lambda},$$

$$(2) \qquad \Theta_N = \frac{1}{R_{N\omega}} \int_0^\lambda \frac{R_{N\omega}}{\lambda} \theta \, d\theta = \frac{\lambda}{2},$$

$$(3) \qquad R_N = \int_0^\lambda \frac{R_{N\omega}}{\lambda} e^{i\theta} d\theta = \frac{R_{N\omega}}{\lambda} \frac{e^{i\lambda} - 1}{i} \sim R_{N\omega} \left(1 + \Theta_N i + \frac{2\Theta_N^2 i^2}{3} \right),$$

$$(4) \qquad C_\mu = \int_0^\lambda \frac{R_{N\omega}}{\lambda} \frac{e^{i\theta} - 1}{i} \, d\theta = \frac{R_{N\omega}}{i\lambda} \left(\frac{e^{i\lambda} - 1}{i} - \lambda \right)$$

$$\sim \Theta_N R_{N\omega} \left(1 + \frac{2\Theta_N}{3} i + \frac{\Theta_N^2}{3} i^2 \right),$$

$$(5) \qquad C_\mu = \frac{R_N}{i} \left(1 - \frac{R_{N\omega}}{R_N} \right) \sim R_N \Theta_N \left(1 + \frac{2\Theta_N^2}{3} i \right),$$

$$(6) \qquad \frac{dC_\mu}{di} \sim R_{N\omega} \left(\frac{d\Theta_N}{di} + \frac{2\Theta_N^2}{3} \right).$$

Equations (3) and (5) give us an idea of the errors committed in using equations (16) and (19). Moreover, equation (6) shows that as a first approximation, and for $\Theta_N = 6$, for example, the derivative $\frac{dC_\mu}{di}$ is negative or positive according to whether or not the increase in the period Θ_N for an absolute variation of 1% of the annual interest rate does or does not approximately exceed 3 months (the value corresponding to $\dfrac{d\Theta_N}{di}$ is then –24).

b. *Whatever the value of the rate of interest* i *may be, the function* $\varphi(\theta)$ *reduces to a decreasing linear function.*

We then have

(7)
$$\varphi(\theta) = \alpha - \beta\theta.$$

If we let λ denote the maximum value of θ, we shall obviously obtain

(8)
$$\alpha = \frac{2R_{N\omega}}{\lambda}, \quad \beta = \frac{R2_{N\omega}}{\lambda^2}, \quad \varphi(\theta) = \frac{2R_{N\omega}}{\lambda}\left(1 - \frac{\theta}{\lambda}\right).$$

This gives us

(9)
$$\Theta_N = \frac{1}{R_{N\omega}}\int_0^\lambda \theta\varphi(\theta)\,d\theta = \frac{2}{\lambda}\int_0^\lambda\left(1 - \frac{\theta}{\lambda}\right)\theta\,d\theta = \frac{\lambda}{3},$$

(10)
$$R_N = \int_0^\lambda \frac{2R_{N\omega}}{\lambda}\left(1 - \frac{\theta}{\lambda}\right)e^{i\theta}\,d\theta \sim R_{N\omega}\left(1 + \Theta_N i + \frac{3}{4}\Theta_N^2 i^2\right),$$

(11)
$$C_\mu = \int_0^\lambda \frac{2R_{N\omega}}{\lambda}\left(1 - \frac{\theta}{\lambda}\right)\left(\frac{e^{i\theta} - 1}{i}\right)d\theta$$

$$\sim \Theta_N R_{N\omega}\left(1 + \frac{3}{4}\Theta_N i + \frac{9}{20}\Theta_N^2 i^2\right),$$

(12)
$$C_\mu = \frac{R_N}{i}\left(1 - \frac{R_{N\omega}}{R_N}\right)$$

$$\sim R_N \Theta_N\left(1 + \frac{3\Theta_N i}{4}\right)$$

(13)
$$\frac{dC_\mu}{di} \sim R_{N\omega}\left(\frac{d\Theta_N}{di} + \frac{3}{4}\Theta_N^2\right).$$

Conclusions parallel to those in the preceding paragraph can be drawn from these various equations. (For $\Theta_N = 6$ the critical value of $\dfrac{d\Theta_N}{di}$ is then –27.)

Note too that the coefficients of the different powers of i involved in these equations, which depends on the shape of the function $\varphi(\theta)$, in reality differ relatively little even for shapes as distinct as the rectangular and the triangular.

Finally, note that in both cases we have respectively (equation [5] of note 38) for $\Theta_N = 6$

It seems nonetheless to follow from our statistical information that in the specific case of our own economies, the national capital C_μ is indeed a decreasing function of the interest rate i.[48] But this is a matter of fact that

(14) $$\frac{d}{di}\frac{C_\mu}{R_N} - \frac{d\Theta_N}{di} \sim \frac{\Delta}{2} - \Theta_N^2 = \begin{cases} -\dfrac{1}{3}\Theta_N^2 = -12 \text{ (rectangle)} \\ -\dfrac{1}{4}\Theta_N^2 = -9 \text{ (triangle).} \end{cases}$$

In both cases the assimilation made in note 39 between $\dfrac{d}{di}\dfrac{C_\mu}{R_N}$ and $\dfrac{d\Theta_N}{di}$ for a value of -120 for the first magnitude would be justified, the value of $\dfrac{d\Theta_N}{di}$ thus obtained being approximate by defect of about 10%.

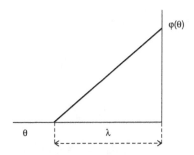

FIGURE 5.25 FOOTNOTE

48. It follows from equation (23) that, using the notations of note 38, we have

(1) $$\frac{dC_\mu}{di} \sim R_{N\omega}\left(\frac{d\Theta_N}{di} + \frac{\Delta}{2}\right),$$

i.e., from equation (5) of note 38,

(2) $$\frac{dC_\mu}{di} \sim R_{N\omega}\left(\frac{d}{di}\frac{C_\mu}{R_N} + \Theta_N^2\right),$$

from which, for the average point at which $i = 4.5\%$ and $\Theta_N = 5$ years, noting that the approximate value of the derivative $\dfrac{C_\mu}{R_N}$ is -80 according to note 39, (since the y-coordinates of the graph are precisely equal to $\dfrac{C_\mu}{R_N}$), we have

can in no way be deduced from general economic theory, at least in the present state of our knowledge.[49]

$$\frac{dC_\mu}{di} \sim (-80 + 25)\, R_{N\omega} \sim -55 R_{N\omega}.$$

These calculations, highly approximate though they are, therefore seem clearly to demonstrate that in our economies aggregate national capital, like primary national capital, is in equilibrium a decreasing function of the rate of interest.

49. It may be that this decrease is a necessary consequence of the stability of the general equilibrium.

C. The Capital Market

1. Determination of the rate of interest in disequilibrium dynamics (48)

In an account-based economy,[1] the rate of interest can be considered to set itself in the market at the value corresponding to the intersection of the curves of the supply of and demand for capital.[2]

It is essential to note that both the supply and demand curves (fig. 5.26) depend on market prices—especially on the prices of durable goods. It follows that the rate of interest is determined by the intersection of the two curves, which depend *directly* on this rate. This marks a crucial difference between the market for capital and the markets for all other goods.[3]

The process of determining the rate of interest is therefore schematically as follows. For an initial interest rate value I_0, there are two curves, C_1 and C_2^0, which determine a new rate I_1. To this rate there correspond two new curves, C_1^1 and C_2^1, which determine a rate I_2, and so on. Stable equilibrium can exist only when the rate of interest determined by the intersection of the supply and demand curves is precisely that from which they have been drawn.

Supply of and demand for new capital

From the point of view of the community it is noteworthy that the value $C + T(P_V - A)$ of old capital at the end of the period T we are here considering[4] cannot be consumed because it corresponds to fixed assets.[5] So instead of considering the aggregate supply

$$
\begin{aligned}
C^{n+1} &= C_D^n - TR_C^n \\
        &= C^n + T(P_V^n - A^n + R_D^n - R_C^n),
\end{aligned}
$$

(1)

1. See note 1 to no. 38.

2. Nos. 40 and 45. As a first approximation, I am at this stage disregarding the supply of capital originating in firms (internal savings) and forced savings, which in the context of a monetary economy correspond to bank inflation.

3. See what has already been said in no. 36 and in note 12 to no. 40 and note 46 to no. 47.

4. The notations are those of nos. 37 and 39.

5. See note 3 to no. 39.

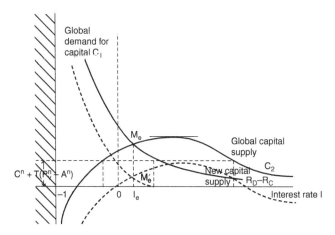

FIGURE 5.26 Capital supply and demand curves as a function of the interest rate

it is possible to consider only the supply

$$T(R_D^n - R_C^n)$$

of new capital.

Similarly, instead of considering the aggregate demand for capital, it is possible to take account only of the demand for capital minus the value of the old capital, i.e., the value of new investments R_I. The point of intersection of the two curves thus obtained naturally corresponds to the same level of the interest rate.[6]

6. Both presentations have their worth. But the former has the major advantage of recalling that every capitalist as an individual is continually confronted by the choice of whether or not to consume his capital. For there is nothing to stop him from selling the goods he owns and applying the proceeds to his day-to-day consumption.

2. Determination of the rate of interest in equilibrium dynamics (49)

The theory shows that for a given psychological and technical structure, economic equilibrium is well determined. In particular, it can be shown that for given structural conditions and aside from any State intervention there is *only one stationary state in stable equilibrium* in which the conditions of economic equilibrium are verified.

However, when the State intervenes, for instance, by acting on the capital market either as borrower or as lender, an additional degree of freedom is introduced, and there are an infinity of stationary states corresponding to a given psychological and technical structure, each of these states corresponding to a different equipment stock and interest rate for a given State intervention.[1]

---

1. These remarks will be confirmed by studying the simplified outlines examined in appendix II (nos. 177 and 196 in particular).

3. Accumulation of capital and the role of the banks (50)

It follows from the foregoing that two stages ought to be carefully distinguished in the process of capital accumulation, even though they may
sometimes be carried out by the same economic agent:

1. the accumulation of savings, corresponding to the supply of capital curve, and
2. the transformation of savings into capital goods by businesses, corresponding
   to the capital demand curve.

To mediate between savers and firms, there exist specialized enterprises
known as banks. Individuals save by refraining from spending the funds
they have available. The banks hire out the use of these savings and transform them into capital available for industry. Finally, firms hire the capital
and use its services for production. The sale of the goods produced enables
them both to renew their capital, worn out by production, and to cover the
interest charges corresponding to the use-value of the capital they have
borrowed.

Thus the accumulation of savings and their investment in capital are fundamentally different operations that must not be confused.

4. Role of savings (51)

Savings are essentially postponed consumption.

At a given moment, capital comprises the aggregate value available to individuals that they refrain from consuming and to which correspond the capital goods that will be used to contribute to their future needs.

Thus the act of saving means "voluntarily interposing an interval between the moment when one renders services to society and the moment when one withdraws equivalent services . . . it is the insertion of a lag between service rendered and service received."[1]

The role of savings consists in continually withdrawing part of the factors of production available to the economy as a whole from the production of immediately consumable services and devoting them to activities—the construction of dwellings, the production of machinery or tools—which, although not immediately consumable, will nonetheless, sooner or later, bring the community additional output,[2] and, hence, well-being. Thus, saving implies the continuous displacement of factors of production away from the use they would have been intended for if they had not been so displaced.

Creation of new savings

When there are net savings, i.e., when supplementary capital is created, an additional demand for nonconsumable products is substituted for the demand for consumable products. By this very fact, savings modify the distribution of the factors of production in the economy. They free from their previous use a certain quantity of these factors and divert them toward a new use. The previous use consisted in producing consumable capital or services; the new use consists in producing nonconsumable capital—new sources of consumer products. Thus, they prepare a future increase in disposable income for society.

The value of the new investments corresponds to the value of the consumable services that are not produced because the saver refrains from consuming them. This value is invested by the saver in industrial securi-

---

1. F. Bastiat. *Harmonies économiques* (Paris: Guillaumin, 1851), ch. 15, 417–19.

2. On account of the physical productivity of capital. (See below, chapter 7, "Interest and Social Productivity.")

ties. It thus passes into the hands of firms and enables them to exercise in the marketplace, in the savers' stead, the purchasing power that the latter have abstained from making immediate use of. The firms use it to pay for their investments and the factors of production they employ.

This mechanism has the noteworthy effect of modifying the distribution of available labor over the different production stages by diverting a greater number of workers away from the production of immediately consumable goods and toward the expansion of the stock of capital equipment available to the economy as a whole.

By increasing this equipment stock, savings, as will be seen, make the economy more efficient,[2] so it is easy to see how beneficial their effect can be on the system of production.

Role of the waiting period

It is obvious that in a barter economy, savers freely accept the unavoidable period of waiting for the fruits of the early stages of production. This waiting period can thus be identified as an independent economic function.

> It is, of course, conceivable that a group of workers, having built a house together, should wait to receive their wages in the form of the rent that gradually comes in the future. But as a rule they either cannot, because they need the means to satisfy unavoidable wants, or will not, because they prefer to enjoy the fruit of their labor now rather than in the distant and uncertain future.[3]

In this case, the role of the buyer of the house is to discount the stream of future rents. This enables the workers to receive at once, as soon as the house is built, the reward for their economic contribution to this construction, while the buyer shoulders the burden of waiting.

Renewal of capital

The value of capital constantly oscillates between immobilization in the shape of investment and mobilization in the shape of depreciation. The capital built up through savings and then invested should never be considered as wealth acquired once and for all by the economy as a whole. All capital invested is eventually freed up again by virtue of depreciation,

3. Cassel, *Traité d'économie politique*, vol. 1, 284 (bk. 2, ch. 22).

as the corresponding capital goods are gradually used up or worn out. Its holder can then decide whether he is going to "run through" the capital thus freed and at his disposal or reinvest it, thus renewing the savings operation for a second time. It is clear that the renewal of the capital equipment serving the economy can only be ensured if the freed-up capital is reinvested or else replaced by capital created elsewhere thanks to new savings.[4]

An economy in which sufficient renewal was not ensured would be "running down" its capital; it would be, as we say, "living off its substance." Its production plant and equipment would gradually decay, and its productivity would relentlessly decline, thereby progressively decreasing its real disposable income.[5]

It thus emerges that in an economy in which a certain amount of capital exists, some degree of abstinence from consumption is needed at every point. This rule remains valid, and if some overconsume, the economy can maintain its capital only if others save more.

Equalization of psychological and technical rates of interest in equilibrium

It follows from the foregoing that in equilibrium the market mechanism leads to the equalization of the various technical and psychological rates of interest.[6] Thus, as long as the technical rate of interest corresponding to a given technology is greater than the psychological interest rate of any particular individual, it will be in that individual's interests to save, and, in the same way, it will be in the interests of a firm to invest the savings thus generated in that technology.

In equilibrium, there is a single rate of interest, and the various technical and psychological rates of interest are equal to it.[7]

---

4. See no. 37, § "Overconsumption."

5. These concepts will be clarified later (chapter 7, "Interest and Social Productivity"). See the remarks already made in no. 23.

6. Nos. 40 and 44.

7. In reality there are as many rates of interest as there are periods (t_0, t_q) being studied. I shall here consider only a single rate of interest in order to simplify the presentation. Readers will have no difficulty in extending the reasoning applied in the text to the more usual scenario.

5. Technical progress and interest (52)

By continually making available more profitable production processes, technical progress raises the technical rate of interest on the available capital. For every level of the interest rate, this increases demand. Thus the primary effect of technical progress is to raise the interest rate.

However, this effect lasts only as long as the technical interest rate of the new investments remains high. In fact, there comes a point at which the greater abundance of the products brought about by the technical progress causes their prices to fall and thereby lowers the technical rate of interest. The market rate of interest then falls, and this fall may very well exceed its initial rise. It thus appears that the secondary effect of technical progress may equally well be either a rise or a fall in the rate of interest.[1]

It must also be stressed that, notwithstanding a claim often made, although technical progress has the immediate consequence of increasing capital, it does not necessarily bring about in equilibrium an increase in the economy's capital equipment stock. Technical progress may in fact make shorter production processes more profitable and thus reduce the average length of the production period.[1]

1. This will be confirmed by the study of the simplified economies presented in appendix II.

6. Accumulation of capital and transitions (53)

Some authors have observed that there is an internal principle of contradiction in the act of saving in the sense that saving bears within itself the causes of its own limitation. The saver restricts his consumption in order to transform part of his income into capital. But he can only find opportunities to invest his new capital, in so far as it will serve to make production goods, to the extent that takers can be found for the consumption goods. The *raison d'être* of production goods is to produce consumption goods and if the outlet for these falls off owing to excessive parsimony on the part of the consumer, savings in turn lose their outlets. So the act of saving contains the germ of a kind of economic contradiction.[1,2]

These remarks are judicious, and they raise a problem that calls for careful analysis. If, for example, there were but a single production—the production of shoes—supplementary savings this year would mean that at last year's price the products finished at the beginning of this year could not all find buyers. Hence the producers would bear losses, and, a priori, it is hard to imagine how, under such conditions, they could undertake new investments.

In fact, however, each manufacturer has his own particular projects, and, faced on the one hand by market problems and on the other by a fall in the interest rate, he will normally be induced to find a solution to his sales problems by lowering his production costs via an improvement in his equipment made feasible by the fall in the interest rate. This explains how the demand for new capital goods not only remains steady but can even increase.

Moreover, there is not just a single production; there are a great many, and they will not all be equally affected by the fall in purchasing power devoted to consumption. For some of them, the decline in activity will be imperceptible, and the only significant difference for them will be the fall in the rate of interest, which will prove decisive in inducing them to upgrade their production equipment in favor of more roundabout and productive processes.

1. H. Truchy, *Cours d'économie politique*, vol. 2 (Paris: Sirey, 1934), 209.
2. No few authors have been inclined to see therein a possible explanation of economic cycles.

So this difficulty does not reveal a contradiction in the way our economy works,[3] but it does highlight two important facts.

First, since the aim of all production is consumption, any restriction of present consumption *must sooner or later be followed by a corresponding increase in future consumption.* This is because the surpluses that can be obtained by an increase in productivity due to an increase in primary capital cannot be indefinitely converted to capital in order to increase this productivity yet further since, as we shall be seeing,[4] there is an optimal value of primary capital for which the increase in output due to the use of roundabout production technologies[5] is maximal. This increase in future consumption will normally occur in the wake of falling prices due to improvement in social productivity.

Second, the accumulation of capital—and the resulting use of more roundabout production processes—necessitates major transfers of factors of production from some industries to others. It also requires substantial changes in the techniques used.[6] Such modifications to the economy cannot be made without provoking serious imbalances that, though temporary, beyond a certain limit may become *unendurable*, no matter how profitable the capital accumulation may prove; and even granting that the restriction of consumption it calls for is easily borne, the accumulation of capital should nevertheless not proceed at too rapid a pace: to be innocuous it must be gradual.

---

3. Hence no satisfactory explanation of economic cycles can be drawn from it.

4. Chapter 7, "Interest and Social Productivity."

5. See no. 23.

6. For example, a significant fall in the rate of interest, by lowering the price of hydroelectric power, would lead to a considerable replacement of coal by water (see no. 71).

Interest and Social Efficiency

1. Definition of social efficiency (54)

It can be shown that for every individual there is a function $S(A, B, \ldots, C)$ of his various consumption sets $A, B, \ldots, C$ such that of two consumption sets $(A_1, B_1, \ldots, C_1)$ $(A_2, B_2, \ldots, C_2)$ it is the one having the highest value of index S that is preferred. This function is an increasing function of the parameters $A, B, \ldots, C$. I have called it the *satisfaction function*. So saying that an individual's satisfaction increases is equivalent to saying that the corresponding new consumption *is preferred* to the former, in other words, that the individual in question is in a preferable economic situation.[1]

Following Pareto, I consider that the optimal state of management of the economy for a given demographic structure and given capital equipment is any state such that any virtual change within it (compatible with its basic characteristics) that increases the satisfaction of some individuals, necessarily decreases the satisfaction of others.

---

1. The scope of the present study precludes further elaboration concerning this topic. Readers wishing to be rigorously convinced of the legitimacy of using satisfaction functions in economics may usefully consult my general work, *À la recherche d'une discipline économique*, nos. 52–70.

Such a state corresponds to what I have called the maximization of social efficiency.[2,3,4] The basic characteristics I have just referred to are the factors that define the structure of the economy (individual psychologies, existing production techniques, and capital equipment). Hence, they are *absolutely independent of any assumption concerning the economic and legal system of the community in question.* Clearly, then, a state cannot be considered optimal if changes could be made to it such that all satisfactions would increase.

And whenever social efficiency is not at its maximum, it is possible to modify the economic organization so that every individual can enjoy greater well-being, or at least so that the lot of *some* individuals can be improved without detriment to any others.

2. Social efficiency thus defined cannot be expressed in precise figures; it should be seen as *a purely qualitative concept that is highly convenient to use.*

Quite simply, if, under identical structural conditions, there are two states of the economy such that every individual receives greater satisfaction in the first than in the second, it can be said that the first state has higher social efficiency than the second.

But if in the second state some satisfactions are less while others are greater, it is no longer possible to draw any conclusion concerning the respective efficiency of the two states. For such comparisons would require a specific relationship of equivalence between the different satisfactions $S_1, S_2, \ldots, S_n$. However, no scientific criterion enabling us to establish such a relationship exists, so the idea of efficiency can only be qualitative.

When the economic state satisfies the above condition, it is not possible to find a state displaying higher efficiency, so it may be considered to be of maximum efficiency. And since this concept involves the economy taken as a whole, the efficiency in question is a collective one, an efficiency that is social in the sense of pertaining to the society as a whole—hence the term chosen.

3. The maximization of social efficiency does not suffice to determine completely the economic state under consideration. To a given psychological and technical structure there corresponds no single state of maximum social efficiency, any more than there exists a single way of achieving the optimal running of a paper mill, since the mill may produce any of several different qualities of writing paper without causing its efficiency to fall below the maximum.

Indeed, to a given psychological and technical structure there correspond an infinity of states of maximum social efficiency; each of these corresponds to a specific distribution among the various individuals of the consumer services produced.

4. Readers wishing to investigate this topic more fully may find all the information they need either in my simplified presentation *Économie pure et rendement social,* published in 1945 by the Librairie Sirey, or alternatively in my self-published general work *À la recherche d'une discipline économique* (604–82).

The aim of the present chapter is to complete and clarify the theory of social efficiency in its relations with the role of the rate of interest.

Thus, from the economic point of view, the existence of non-maximum social efficiency is like a steam leak due to a loose gasket in a machine. It is a dead loss due to the state of the system itself—one that can be remedied with no loss to anyone.

The above definition of maximum social efficiency may at first sight surprise unprepared readers. But in fact it corresponds very well to our intuitive idea of maximum efficiency when the functioning of the economy as a whole is under consideration.

Let us take the example of an economy comprising only a single product, A, and two individuals, X and Y, each working eight hours per day; and let us suppose that, depending on the suitability of the techniques used, total daily output varies between 0 and 100 units. Under these conditions, if the technology used is not the best, and only produces, say, 80 units per day, and if this output is divided in the ratio of one-quarter to three-quarters between X and Y, i.e., 20 units for X and 60 for Y, it will always be possible for *an improvement in technology* to increase simultaneously the quantity of product A allotted to both X and Y.

On the other hand, when the best technology is used, i.e., when total output equals 100, there is no way of increasing, for instance, the share of individual X, i.e., 25, without at the same time decreasing that of Y, i.e., 75.

This shows that the above definition of social efficiency closely coincides with our own intuitive idea of it.

Of course, if the economy really consisted of but a single product, it would be quite unnecessary to adopt such a sophisticated definition of social efficiency: it would suffice to say that the best technology ought to be employed. But in reality, things are not so simple: there are many products instead of just one, and every day the question arises whether to use coal power or hydropower, to manufacture shoes or wireless sets, consumer goods or machines that will only be able to satisfy men's needs in a more or less remote future. In such everyday cases, the problem of maximizing social efficiency cannot therefore be reduced to a simple problem of maximizing a specific quantity, and the only possible definition of social efficiency is the one I have given.

2. Theorem of social efficiency (55)

Given these definitions, the theory basically demonstrates that in any kind of economy[1] the necessary and sufficient condition for maximum social efficiency—*at a given moment*—for given psychologies and production methods, and for given land use, equipment, and demographic structure—is that there should be at that moment, explicitly or implicitly, a price system equivalent to that which would be found in an account-based economy characterized by free choice for individuals and perfect competition for businesses.[2]

These findings mean that, for any given structure of the economy, the best organization of production involves the explicit or implicit use of the price system found in a competitive economy and that, in this way, the inherent optimum coincides with competitive equilibrium.[3]

1. Competitive or not, collectivist or not. (Reminder: a collectivist economy is an economy founded on collective ownership of the means of production.)

2. Rigorous formulation of the theorem of social efficiency is much more complex, but the simplified definition above is enough to understand the rest of the analysis, even though it does not distinguish between the differentiated sector (in which the best production technology is obtained by the juxtaposition of separate but similar production units) and the undifferentiated sector (in which the best production technology is achieved from a single production unit) and thus assumes that there is no undifferentiated sector.

3. For this very reason such an economy constitutes *an indispensable reference system*. See the explanations provided above (note 3 to no. 2).

3. Social efficiency and the distribution of consumer goods and services (56)

The theory demonstrates that, for any economy having the same supply of land and equipment (durable industrial goods), there are an infinity of possible economic states of maximum possible efficiency that differ only in terms of the distribution of disposable incomes among the different individuals. Of course, to each of these different possible income distributions there corresponds an array of different economic situations that— since different individuals vary in how they dispose of a given income— may differ considerably even though all have maximum social efficiency.

The differences that may be found between any two given states of maximum social efficiency can only be attributed to the modes of distribution of consumer goods and services. For any given distribution, the maximization of social efficiency enables the best use to be made of technological possibilities, whereas lower efficiency causes a loss of possible satisfactions in exchange for no compensatory benefit of any sort.

Thus the pursuit of maximum social efficiency is fundamentally *a matter of economic technique*; its solution is, in principle, entirely *independent* of whatever political and sociological ideas may be held about the distribution of consumer goods and services.

In fact, the statement that a state (E), in which individuals $(X), (Y), \ldots,$ (Z) have satisfactions $S_x, S_y, \ldots, S_z$, has maximum social efficiency does not imply that this state is preferable to another state (E') in which individuals $(X), (Y), \ldots, (Z)$ would have satisfactions $S'_x, S'_y, \ldots, S'_z$, some greater and others less than the S satisfactions of state (E); it implies only that it is impossible in state (E) to increase, for example, S_x, without diminishing at least one of satisfactions $S_y, \ldots, S_z$, or indeed to increase simultaneously the whole set of satisfactions $S_x, S_y, \ldots, S_z$. *It means that the management of the economy in state* (E) *is optimal; it does not mean that its distribution is preferable to all others. It is management that is optimal, not distribution.*

If, for example, there were only two individuals (X) and (Y), the states of maximum social efficiency would be distributed along a line L such that each point on this line corresponded univocally to a given distribution of disposable income determined, e.g., by a certain distribution of ownership of durable goods.[1]

---

1. By the very definition of maximum social efficiency, line L forms the limit of the region R', which is the locus of the points representing *possible* economic states. In a given state

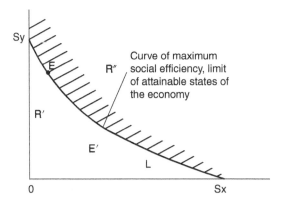

FIGURE 6.1 Curve of maximum social efficiency, limit of attainable states of the economy

Under these conditions, the statement that state (E) is one of maximum social efficiency would mean that point E representing this state is situated on line L, but not that this state is preferable to a state (E'), even if the latter is not one of maximum social efficiency; for while, in the latter case, we can affirm that the management corresponding to state (E) is better than that corresponding to state (E'), nothing entitles us to conclude that state (E) should be preferred to state (E').

On the contrary, it is perfectly possible for state (E') to be deemed—for example, on account of its more equitable distribution of incomes—preferable to state (E), even though the latter corresponds to optimal management. But this preference would not alter the fact that in state (E') the management of the economy could be improved, as satisfactions S'_x and S'_y could simultaneously be increased. Thus the management of the economy in state (E') could not be considered satisfactory, since the situation of each economic agent in it could be improved without prejudice to the principles of income distribution characteristic of state (E').

In fact, if it is deemed desirable to favor some individuals at the expense of others or to offset the disadvantages that may affect certain groups as a result of the management system or of the evolution of the economy, the most beneficial method consists in directly modifying the

_____

of technology and for a given capital equipment stock in the economy, line L thus represents the extreme limit of the consumption possibilities, *which cannot be exceeded in any case whatsoever.*

way in which consumer goods and services are distributed without changing the conditions of competition at all.

A simple example may illustrate this assertion. "It is sometimes argued that the state should arrange that those commodities which are bought mainly by the poorer members of the community should be sold at prices below their cost of production, so that at these abnormally low prices the real income of the poor would be increased. This could be brought about by the subsidization of the production of such commodities or by the socialization of their production, in order to sell them at prices lower than their cost."[2,3]

It is easy to see that such a policy could only compromise the maximization of social efficiency. For since most goods are bought by rich and poor alike, some subsidized goods will be bought by rich consumers and some unsubsidized goods by poor ones. "Each consumer, rich or poor, will consume the different goods in such quantities that the increase in satisfaction that the consumer obtains by spending an additional monetary unit will be identical, irrespective of the product purchased. However, the marginal cost of a subsidized good will be greater for the community than for the consumer. So if a consumer, rich or poor, were to spend one monetary unit less on a subsidized good, he would thereby make available factors of unsubsidized production worth more than a single monetary unit. The standard of living of each consumer could then be improved with no correlative diminution in the well-being of another consumer, if more unsubsidized goods were produced and fewer subsidized ones."[2,4]

Thus the distribution of the factors of production over their different uses would be defective, and it can be seen that the well-being of the wealthy could be improved without any corresponding decline in the standard of living of the poor and that the standard of living of the poor could be raised without any corresponding decline in the well-being of the wealthy.

The foregoing remarks *enable us to discern the kind of distribution policy that could be adopted without jeopardizing the maximization of social*

2. J. E. Meade, *An Introduction to Economic Analysis and Policy* (Oxford: Oxford Clarendon Press, 1936), 229, published in French as *Économie politique et politique économique* (Paris: Payot, 1939), 328–29.

3. In the case of wheat production, for example, this is actually practiced at the time of writing.

4. This purely intuitive argument becomes rigorous only in the context of the demonstrations I have given of the theorem of social efficiency. (See note 4 to no. 54.)

efficiency. In practical terms, the theory shows that a modification of the competitive distribution of income corresponding to a given ownership system that does not compromise social efficiency can be obtained only by a system of taxes or grants bearing either on land or on persons *irrespective* of their role in the economy and without changing this role.[5]

Finally it can be seen that *in the context of maximum social efficiency, the distribution of incomes is arbitrary, but the means used to bring about a given distribution are not. The management of the economy and the distribution of incomes can indeed be independent, but only on condition that appropriate means are used to bring about the desired income distribution. And if the maximization of social efficiency is not to be compromised, the desired distribution must be brought about using methods that have no bearing on the marginal functioning of the various economic mechanisms.*

---

5. Thus a tax of any kind (fixed, proportional, or of any nature whatsoever) levied exclusively on the trade of plumbers would diminish social efficiency. By contrast, a tax levied only on Protestants or Royalists would not diminish it.

Similarly, a tax on the land of the Beauce region would not compromise maximum social efficiency, but a tax on wheatland would diminish it.

Fuller information cannot be provided within the limited scope of the present survey.

4. Maximization of social efficiency, distribution of incomes over time, and organization of the system of production (57)

It follows from the theory of social efficiency that, in a competitive environment,[1] the distribution that individuals make of their consumption expenditure is *at every point in time* the most favorable to social efficiency.

The same applies to how available capital is distributed among its different possible uses in a competitive environment, in light of the rate of interest and the profitability principle.

The key role played by the rate of interest in maximizing social efficiency is at once apparent.

1. No. 55.

5. Conditions determining the proof of the theorem of social efficiency (58)

It is of the utmost importance to state correctly the conditions under which the theorem of social efficiency can be proved, in order to ensure the correct interpretation of these results and the future development of economic theory.

These conditions are essentially as follows.

Let us consider an economic state extending from initial time t_0 to final time t_p. Perfect foresight is assumed. Assumed *to be given are*: the demographic characteristics of this state at every point in time $t_0, t_1, \ldots, t_q, \ldots, t_p$, its land characteristics identical at every point,[1] the capital goods (machines, tools, etc.) existing at times t_0 and t_p, and finally all the physical characteristics (consumptions, productions, etc.) of this economic state that fall outside the period (t_0, t_p).

Let us consider the satisfaction characterizing the economic psychology of each individual either at time t_0, whenever his participation in economic life predates or starts at time t_0, or at time t_q, in the event that his participation starts only then.

Maximum social efficiency being defined as above, it is immediately verified that the necessary and sufficient condition for an economic state to have maximum social efficiency is that the satisfaction of a particular individual may be considered maximal while all other satisfactions are maintained constant. From this it follows that the maximization of social efficiency amounts to a classic problem of constrained maxima and that, when the corresponding conditions are formulated, we obtain conditions precisely identical to those characterizing a competitive equilibrium. The proof of the theorem is thereby complete.

---

1. Note that land is considered in itself, independently of capital attached to it (see note 1 to no. 36). As land is indestructible, the land characteristics of the economy are indeed constant over time.

6. Infinite-horizon model (59)

In light of these findings it can be seen how the proof of the theorem of social efficiency obtained using finite-horizon models can be extended to infinite-horizon models.

In fact, in the commonest infinite-horizon case, the boundary conditions considered above[1] disappear and the theorem of social efficiency can only be generalized with caution. In this case I shall say that an infinite-horizon model has maximum social efficiency if it can be regarded as such, in the meaning of the foregoing definitions, between any two points in time and for the boundary conditions that characterize them. With this definition, the stated theorem of social efficiency[2] becomes immediately applicable to infinite-horizon models.

By contrast, in the case of a *stationary* infinite-horizon model, the boundary conditions do not disappear since, as the process is assumed to be stationary, the structural conditions remain the same over time. The theorem of social efficiency can then be extended without difficulty, the boundary conditions being replaced by the structural conditions that characterize the stationary process.[3,4]

---

1. Comprising the capital goods existing at times t_0 and t_p and the physical characteristics outside period (t_0, t_p).

2. The proof of which has been given for the finite-horizon model.

3. I.e., those of any point in time characterizing this model.

4. I shall provide a specific illustration of the importance of these facts in an appendix (no. 197, § i).

7. Broadening the concept of social efficiency (60)[1]

The maximization of social efficiency as defined involves the satisfaction of individuals only during the first period T_1 of their economic life included within the interval (t_0, t_p) we are considering.[2,3]

This concept is in perfect harmony with the point of view of the classical economists as admirably clarified and completed by Pareto, but it is not yet completely satisfactory.

This is easily shown using a simple example. Let there be, in an economy of perfect foresight, an individual whose economic life is reduced to two periods T_0 and T_1 and who consumes only two services: (A) and (B). Let A_0, B_0, A_1, B_1 be his consumptions during these periods. At time t_0 his scale of preferences can be represented by a certain satisfaction

(1) $$S_0 = S_0(A_0, B_0, A_1, B_1).$$

The same applies at time t_1, but at that point the only variables are the parameters A_1 and B_1, so that the function representing the range of choice of the individual in question is reduced to a function

(2) $$S_1 = S_1(A_1, B_1)$$

of the consumptions A_1 and B_1 during period T_1.[4]

Now in the whole of the classical theory and indeed in the theory of social efficiency as it has just been set out, S_0 is the only satisfaction taken into account. No account whatever is taken of satisfaction S_1.

Yet in a world of perfect foresight,[5] *no logical reason can be found a priori for seeking to maximize satisfaction* S_0 *rather than satisfaction* S_1.

---

1. The following arguments are relatively complex, and the reader will probably arrive at a full understanding only after a second reading and after making himself familiar with appendix II (notably no. 197) and appendix III.

2. Which may be infinite.

3. Period (t_0, t_p) is assumed to be divided into equal small intervals $T_1, T_2, \ldots, T_p$.

4. It is easy to see that in the commonest case S_0 and S_1, although distinct, are not independent (no. 219).

5. As such an economy constitutes a first approximation of the real economy, the reasoning here set out can easily be extended to the case of our own economy in which foresight is imperfect.

It would be inadmissible to claim that under perfect foresight satisfaction S_0 takes account of satisfaction S_1—perfectly known to the individual in question during his youth T_0. For in fact what the young individual takes account of is the satisfaction he experiences at time t_0 at the idea of the satisfaction that he will experience at time t_1, and not this latter satisfaction itself.

In fact there is as much difference between satisfactions S_0 and S_1 of the same individual considered at two different times as between the satisfactions of two distinct individuals considered at the same time. They are magnitudes of a different nature, and they cannot be compared except by adopting an absolutely arbitrary convention.

However, it is easy to generalize the concept of maximization of social efficiency while taking these circumstances into account. I shall stipulate that the *generalized social efficiency* of a given economic state under perfect foresight[6] is maximal when any virtual modification of this state, compatible with its basic characteristics, that increases the satisfaction of certain specific individuals at specific times, necessarily diminishes the satisfaction of other individuals or that of the same individuals at other times.

Using this definition it can be seen that just as there are an infinity of economic states of maximum social efficiency, each defined by a certain distribution of disposable income among the various individuals,[7] so too there are an infinity of economic states of maximum generalized social efficiency, each defined not only by a certain distribution of disposable income among the various individuals but also by a certain distribution over time of the disposable income of the same individual.

I shall call this definition the "generalized definition of social efficiency" as opposed to the earlier, more restrictive definition, which I shall call the "restricted definition of social efficiency," and henceforth I shall speak of "restricted social efficiency" and "generalized social efficiency," *reserving for the latter the simpler term "social efficiency." In fact, I shall add the qualifier "generalized" only when it is necessary to distinguish it from restricted social efficiency.*

It follows from the foregoing analysis that while the restricted theory of social efficiency only takes into account the present satisfactions of the various individuals, the generalized theory takes into account at the same time their present and future satisfactions.

---

6. Which notably applies to stationary models.

7. These different states are represented in figure 6.1 of no. 56 by the different points on the curve (L).

8. Generalized theorem of social efficiency (61)

It is now possible to arrive at the following theorem:[1]

In an economy with perfect foresight, of whatever kind,[2] the necessary and sufficient condition for maximum generalized social efficiency—*for a determined period*, for given psychologies and production techniques, and for given land characteristics, *capital equipment* and demographic structure[3]—is that there should prevail throughout this period, explicitly or implicitly, a system of prices and of interest rates equivalent to that which would be found in an account-based economy defined by

1. perfect competition between firms in the production sector,
2. free choice for individuals in distributing among the various possible consumptions *within each sub-period* such of their income as is allocated to expenditure *during this period*,[4,5] and
3. the same distribution of consumer goods and services.

This theorem shows that, for any structure of the economy, the best organization corresponds to the use, at every moment in time, of a unique price system and *a unique technical rate of interest*[6] in the production sector and of the same price system in the consumption sector, whereas the

---

1. The demonstration presents no difficulties but calls for lengthy explanation, and for this reason I have taken the view that it is beyond the scope of the present study; however, its successive steps are exactly the same as those set out in my *À la recherche d'une discipline économique*, 604 and 682, and summarized in my study *Économie pure et rendement social*. The reader may verify the results in appendix II (see in particular nos. 186, 194, and 197, § i) and will find a simplified demonstration in appendix III, nos. 218–21.

2. Competitive or not, collectivist or not.

3. The psychologies, technologies, land, and demographic characteristics are given for each instant of the period in question; the capital equipment stock is given only at the limits of this period.

4. Thus, in the case of the individual considered in no. 60 above, a state of maximum social efficiency is characterized by the free choice of the individual in distributing his income $R_0 = aA_0 + bB_0$ between consumptions A_0 and B_0 and his income $R_1 = aA_1 + bB_1$ between consumptions A_1 and B_1, but the distribution of his disposable income between incomes R_0 and R_1 remains arbitrary.

5. For the sake of simplicity, this statement, like that made at no. 55, does not take the undifferentiated sector into account (see note 2 to no. 55).

6. No. 44.

psychological rates of interest[7] corresponding to the latter sector remain *arbitrary* and may have any value whatever.

From this it can be seen that, while the maximization of generalized social efficiency requires the use of a *unique* rate of interest in the production sector, it leaves *indeterminate* the psychological interest rates, at the different points in time, of the various individuals.[8]

Of course, provided that foresight is satisfactory, the theorem of generalized social efficiency may be taken to apply to the real economy.[9]

It is essential to emphasize that there is *no contradiction* between the restricted and the generalized theories of social efficiency. The latter simply *completes* the former.

Indeed any economic state that satisfies the conditions of maximization of restricted social efficiency also satisfies the conditions of maximization of generalized social efficiency.

The generalization effected simply shows that *the restricted theory is too restrictive*, since *it excludes states of the economy that should in fact be deemed to display maximum social efficiency in the fullest meaning of the term.*

7. No. 40.

8. This unavoidably brief account will be made more explicit in appendix II, nos. 194 and 197, § i.

9. Some readers may wonder why this complementary information was included neither in my article *Économie pure et rendement social* nor even in the chapter dealing with the study of social efficiency in my *À la recherche d'une discipline économique*, although I already had its main components at my disposal at that time.

The reason for this is basically that in its progress toward truth, the mind proceeds by stages, so that full understanding is only achieved gradually by proceeding from the particular to the complex; first a rough path must be hacked out through the undergrowth and only after successive clearance operations can this path become a thoroughfare by way of which solid and incontrovertible results can be reached. Hence, to provide at the outset a full statement of the theorem of social efficiency, introducing the successive satisfactions of each individual, would have run the risk of making it harder to assimilate the theory and of mixing up some very different aspects of economic reality. For, on the one hand, the concept of generalized social efficiency is accessible only to a mind that has already mastered the simplified theory of social efficiency (this was my own experience) and, on the other, the applications of the generalized theory of social efficiency relate much more to the particular study of the rate of interest than to the general theory of prices and of economic equilibrium.

By keeping my argument in step with the progress of my own thought and reserving this sensitive issue for combination with the general study of the rate of interest in which it plays a central role, I believe I have—if my own experience can be relied on—considerably facilitated the reader's task.

9. Interest, social efficiency, and production (62)

As we have just seen, the maximization of generalized social efficiency requires the use of a single interest rate in the production sector at every point in time. It is easy to see why this is so. *The role of the interest rate is in fact to make it possible to choose, among the array of possible investments, those whose profitability best suits available savings. Thus the interest rate draws a line between production methods that can be adopted and those that must be rejected.*

Technical optimum and economic optimum

If we use the term *labor intensiveness*[1] to denote the amount of labor needed, directly or indirectly, for the production of a given good, it follows that of two technologies making use of the same amount of land per unit produced, the more socially advantageous technology will be the one having the lower *labor intensiveness*. The minimum *labor intensiveness* can therefore be taken as the technical optimum from the social point of view. Experience shows that this minimum generally corresponds to production techniques that make use of more intermediate goods.

Now, in fact, as will be seen,[2] this technical optimum could be simultaneously achieved in all industries only if there were sufficient capital. But in general, *at any given moment*, this condition is not fulfilled, as the equipment stock is insufficient to ensure that the technical optimum is achieved in all industries.

The theorem of social efficiency shows that, *for a given equipment stock*, the socially optimal economic state corresponds to the existence in the production sector of a competitive system of prices and interest rates and that this system must be taken into account in selecting production techniques. This economic optimum is not to be confused with the technical optimum as it has just been defined. For in fact the technical optimum corresponds to a social optimum among several economic optima for a variable equipment stock. And it will be seen that among all stationary models that satisfy the conditions of maximum social efficiency (optimal

---

1. This term is fully explained by the author in chapter 3, no. 23, and in the accompanying translator's note. — Trans.

2. See chapter 7, "Interest and Social Productivity" (no. 68).

management) but that have a variable stock of capital equipment, there is one for which production is maximum for a given labor input and that thus fulfills the conditions of the technical optimum (optimal capital structure).[3]

Some authors continually accuse the present economy of being unable to exploit the productive capabilities of modern technologies to the full. But in reality, this reproach is based on a serious confusion between the collective viewpoint and the individual viewpoint. By simple multiplication, these authors transpose into the collective economy a technical optimum devised from the viewpoint of the specific firm. They are entirely forgetting that the capital available to the economy at any given point in time is limited and can only be increased by means of a *previous restriction of currently consumable services*. Indeed nothing could justify an individual firm in failing to equip itself in accordance with the technical optimum except the consideration of the limitation of existing capital relative to its needs, as determined in accordance with the rules of the technical optimum of the whole economy. But the fact is that, precisely by depriving itself of its technical optimum, a given firm can release the means of production more urgently needed in other branches of production: in a state of equilibrium the means of production it uses would only be able to yield an output of less value elsewhere.

Indeed, the complexity surrounding the choice of the most appropriate means of production would be crucially underestimated if that choice were treated as a purely technological problem, as though maximum social efficiency could be ensured simply by identifying the best production method in technical terms.

To choose the best production processes, a firm also needs to be guided by a price system. That organization of a firm that is the best from the technical point of view is not always the best from the economic point of view. No matter how great the perfection of the technology used in producing a given category of articles, it will always entail losses of possible satisfaction if the production is undertaken in disregard of the economic principles underlying the maximization of social efficiency. A technically inferior production process may be economically superior; this is the case, for instance, when the use of any less sophisticated equipment leads to a saving in value that offsets, and more than offsets, the loss due to subsequent inferior output in terms of quantity or quality.

3. See chapter 7, "Interest and Social Productivity" (no. 73).

"It is also possible for a specific investment, although it appears productive and useful from the technical point of view, to be rejected, exclusively because the expected return does not justify investing the capital at the going rate of interest. It must not be inferred from this that our present system of price-setting is flawed";[4] it simply shows that there are other improvements in the production system that enable a higher return to be expected and that these ought therefore to be given priority.

Interest rates and the discarding of obsolete facilities

It is often asked whether, following technical progress, existing facilities should be discarded; when the facilities are recent, public opinion often sees such discarding as a waste, to be written off as a liability in the competitive organization of the economy.

However, the theory of social efficiency shows that of two economic decisions the one that is more advantageous from the collective point of view is the more profitable one, i.e., the one for which the technical rate of interest on *future* returns relative to *future* outlay is higher. *Past costs are entirely irrelevant.*

As the technical interest rate only involves the operating expenses for the old facilities, whereas for the new facilities it takes account not only of operating expenses but also of interest charges and depreciation, it can be seen that, for identical output and quality, the old facilities should be discarded only if their partial cost price is greater than the total average cost corresponding to the new facilities; if that is the case, discarding the old ones will be worthwhile and ought to be carried out,[5] even if they are all recent and cost considerable sums. In this case, although scrapping the existing facilities may look like a waste to uninformed eyes, in reality it will correspond to a correct assessment of the interests of the entire community.

---

4. G. Von Haberler, *Prospérité et dépression* (Geneva: Société des nations, 1939), 44.

5. Alternatively it may be stated that, for identical output and quality, all obsolete technology should be immediately discarded as soon as the cost of installing new technology is less than the sum of the present values of the differences between the future costs of the old and the new.

10. Interest, social efficiency, and consumption (63)

It follows from the above that

1. *overall uniqueness of the rate of interest throughout the economy is by no means necessary for maximization of social efficiency and is only so in the production sector;*
2. *this uniqueness,* which is in principle a characteristic of the current competitive regime, *has the effect of generating, for each individual, one of the many possible distributions* over time of his disposable income,[1] but that this distribution can in no case be regarded as preferable to every other.

For the same capital equipment stock, different distributions of income over time could be envisaged, each of them being defined for each individual by a system of different psychological rates of interest, and in principle any distribution is possible. Given the capital equipment, only the rate of interest used in the production sector is not arbitrary and has a value clearly determined by the conditions that specify the maximization of social efficiency.

There is in fact a *perfect parallelism* between the single arbitrariness of the distribution of the aggregate income among different individuals, for a maximum restricted social efficiency, and the double arbitrariness of the distribution of the aggregate income among the different individuals and of each individual income over the different periods, for a maximum generalized social efficiency.

Technical interest rate and psychological interest rates

While the technical rate of interest, used in the production sector, stands out as a characteristic parameter of increasing capital intensity in the economy,[2] and must indispensably be unique for the maximization of social efficiency, the psychological rates of interest emerge as characteristic parameters determining, for each individual, the distribution of his in-

---

1. From which there results at every point in time a certain intergenerational distribution of the national income.

2. See nos. 45 and 47.

come over time, and their diversity is perfectly compatible with the conditions for the maximization of social efficiency.

Thus, *whereas setting the rate of interest in the production sector is a technical problem of economic management, setting the rates of interest in the consumption sector is a matter of distribution.*

Consequently, although the former can and should be determined exclusively on the basis of economic data, the determination of the latter necessarily involves *arbitrary* data, external to economics, belonging to the ethical and political spheres.[3]

Current competitive mechanism and the division of incomes

The competitive regime, in its current formulation, is such that at every point in time the day-to-day decisions of individuals determine the structural conditions of the immediate future.

Now, aside from any State intervention in the savings market, individuals assess their future needs only through their present psychology. So their economic activity tends to maximize only their present satisfaction[4] and indeed that is all they *can* take into account.[5]

It follows that, for each individual, the development of the economy leads to a certain distribution of his income over time, but—and it cannot be too strongly emphasized—this distribution cannot be regarded, from the viewpoint of maximizing social efficiency, as preferable to any other: it is just one of the many possible distributions.

In fact, within its current framework, *the competitive development of the economy* consistent with the maximization of restricted social efficiency *cannot jeopardize the maximization of generalized social efficiency; it simply brings about,* among all the possible distributions, *a certain distribution of disposable income over time that, as such, must be regarded as arbitrary.*

---

3. See my article "Économie pure et rendement social" [Pure economics and social efficiency], *Annales des mines,* no. 15 (January–February 1945).

4. Which of course also takes account of future consumptions. Thus, for the example given in no. 60, the present satisfaction $S_0(A_0, B_0, A_1, B_1)$ takes account of future consumptions A_1 and B_1.

5. Thus, for the example given in no. 60, the individual is unable to choose at time t_0 between maximizing satisfaction $S_0(A_0, B_0, A_1, B_1)$ and maximizing satisfaction $S_1(A_1, B_1)$ since in general he is only aware of satisfaction S_0. Even supposing he was aware of satisfaction S_1, as in the assumption of perfect foresight, he could take it into account only through his present psychology, represented by function S_0.

Need to take into consideration the different satisfactions of the same individual at different ages

The foregoing analysis shows that in order to maximize social efficiency in its most general sense, there is no need to attribute a special role to present satisfactions, *but there is every need to take future satisfactions into account.*

It also demonstrates that any claim of equivalence between these different satisfactions is *necessarily arbitrary* and can only be made on the basis of *information derived from the ethical and political spheres,* foreign to economics. For the science of economics can in any event only state the conditions for maximum efficiency that the economy must satisfy so that no satisfactions can be increased without at the same time decreasing other satisfactions in one or the other of the *twin sets* of satisfactions of the different individuals considered at different moments of their lives.

Need to correct the classical doctrine

At this point appears a first objection to the thesis propounded by liberalism, which champions laissez-faire as the best solution in the sphere of savings. In fact, the distribution of income over time obtained on the basis of maximizing present satisfactions, taking future satisfactions into account only through the present, can by no means be considered, from the purely economic viewpoint, as the best possible distribution.[6] In reality, it is just one of the possible distributions, and there is no reason a priori

6. It is easy to show that this is so, even limiting ourselves to the narrow viewpoint of classical theory. For example, consider a stationary competitive economy having only one consumable product (A), and in which there exists only one category of individuals, n in number, living through two periods T_0 and T_1 of satisfaction

$$S^i = S^i(A_0^i, A_1^i),$$

where the interest rate is equal to I and the production for each period T is equal to A. The output of A being given, it is clear that, in general, the competitive regime in question does not ensure the maximum satisfaction compatible with production of A. In fact, for a given output A, the maximization of S^i would require us to have

$$\frac{\partial S^i}{\partial A_0^i} = \frac{\partial S^i}{\partial A_1^i}.$$

to prefer it to all the others. In any event, any possible motives for preferring it do not belong to the science of economics and can only be ethical or political in nature.

Savings policy

Individuals see the future only through the present so that their decisions aim only at maximizing their present satisfactions.[7]

Indeed they cannot seek the maximization of their future satisfactions[8] for they do not know what they will be, and even if they could approximately foresee them, any equivalence they may establish between their present and future satisfactions is based on their present psychology.

As has already been pointed out, what must be emphasized is that *this equivalence is but one of many possible equivalences, and from an exclusively economic viewpoint it need not be mandatory.* Consequently, *bearing in mind the lessons of experience, the State may perfectly well deem preferable, for motives of an ethical or political nature,*[9] some other equivalence that leads to a different distribution of incomes over time. For the State has individuals of all ages within its purview and can infer from its observations, and by extrapolating from its experience of the psychology of the elderly, what the psychology of the young will become. The State alone can, in some measure, abstract from the arbitrariness that inevitably affects the economic decisions of the young, who see the future only through the present; it alone can have a clear perception of the relative urgency of future needs as compared with present needs, since experience enables it to identify the economic psychologies of both young and old, whereas the young, at any rate, can only glimpse their future

----

This condition, following equation (3) of no. 40 above, would require a zero rate of interest.

It follows that insofar as satisfactions S^i are to be maximized without otherwise altering the structure of the production sector, *there can be no alternative to a double interest rate.* (These inevitably brief observations will be clarified in appendix II, no. 197, § i.)

7. Functions $S_0(A_0, B_0, A_1, B_1)$ from the example in no. 60.

8. Functions $S_1(A_1, B_1)$ from the example in no. 60.

9. It is worth underlining here once again that, for an economist, these motives are essentially *arbitrary*, and that discussion of them *is beyond the scope of economics.*

psychology through their present psychology and thus cannot abstract from the present.[10]

It is plain that the solution given by the spontaneous competitive mechanism to the problem of distributing the income of a given individual over time is *conventional and arbitrary*, and it can easily be understood that the State, *for motives of an ethical or political nature*, and in a way that *from the purely economic viewpoint* is admittedly *no less conventional and arbitrary*, can legitimately intervene in the interest of the individuals themselves, with a view to acting on this distribution and to correcting whatever may be excessive therein.

Of course, from the ethical and political viewpoint only experience can show whether at a given point in time the distribution between young and old resulting from the spontaneous competitive mechanism is satisfactory. If, as a matter of fact, the young are so improvident that, though fully aware of the facts, they fail to save enough to provide for their old age—though, once old, they will complain bitterly of the community's indifference to their plight—it is understandable and legitimate that the State should intervene in order to ensure compulsory saving.[11] Such intervention, from the viewpoint of economic theory, must be deemed to be *quite as justified as the option of refraining from intervention*. The two policies are, from the purely economic viewpoint, absolutely equivalent. Only noneconomic motives, ethical or political in nature, can decide between them.

These points bring out the *profound analogy* between the policy of redistributing the national income among different individuals and the pensions policy, which aims at distributing the resources of the different individuals in a particular manner over time.

As to the former, economics can offer no criterion whereby to compare the satisfactions of two different individuals upon which a policy of distribution could be based, but it informs us (the theory of restricted social efficiency) that any intervention affecting the distribution of disposable income among individuals must be made by *direct* action on their incomes, leaving *unchanged* the competitive structure of the economy.[12]

---

10. Perfectly analogous is the case of parents, who are better placed to evaluate the future satisfactions of their children than these children themselves, since the latter cannot take into account their future psychologies as adults except as filtered through their present mentality as children.

11. In the form of compulsory pension contributions, for instance.

12. See the observations made in no. 56 *in fine*.

And as to the latter, economics offers no criterion enabling the satisfactions of the same individual to be compared at two different times so as
to provide a basis for a pensions policy, but it does inform us (the theory
of generalized social efficiency) that, *for a given stock of capital equipment*, any intervention intended to influence how individuals distribute
their income over time must be made through *direct* action, modifying
only psychological interest rates and *letting the technical interest rates* used
in the production sector *settle at the general level that is characteristic of the
competitive equilibrium* of this sector and that corresponds to its stock of
capital equipment.[13,14,15]

13. Remarks similar to those made in no. 56 *in fine* could be made here.

14. Under stationary conditions, such a policy would lead to a redistribution over time of
the income of *each* individual while leaving unchanged the distribution of the real national
income *at a given moment among the individuals*.

We shall see later what influence an investment policy could have on the real value of
national income (as opposed to a policy of private savings, whether free or compulsory, since
private savings may differ from investment owing to State intervention in the capital market).
(See chapter 7, "Interest and Social Productivity," particularly no. 74.)

15. We shall see later what economics has to teach us about the stock of capital equipment (no. 77).

11. Interest, social efficiency, propensity to own, and propensity to bequeath (64)

The range of choices taken into account so far has only involved consumption. In reality, however, individuals take account in their decisions not only of their consumptions but also of the goods they own and of the goods they intend to bequeath to others. These psychological dispositions can be designated in everyday language by the terms *propensity to own* and *propensity to bequeath*.

In both cases, extending the theory of social efficiency calls for careful handling and goes beyond the scope of the present study. Suffice it to say that this theory does in fact entirely cover the propensity to own but that in the case of the propensity to bequeath, although the conditions previously indicated for the maximization of social efficiency remain necessary, they are no longer sufficient.[1,2]

1. This can easily be understood using a simplified example. Assume a timeless economy, having only one consumable product (A) and reduced to two categories of individuals (X) and (Y), both equally numerous, whose satisfaction functions are respectively

(1) $$S_X = f(A_X),$$

(2) $$S_Y = f(A_Y, A_D),$$

where A_X and A_Y represent respectively the consumptions of individuals (X) and (Y) and A_D represents the quantity of service (A) given by an individual of category (Y) to an individual of category (X). In this case, to the satisfaction derived from their own consumption, is added for (Y) individuals a supplementary satisfaction derived from the gift to (X) individuals of a part of their consumable resources. The propensity to give exists.

If we use A to denote the aggregate production and n to denote the number of individuals in each group and if we write that the satisfactions S_X and S_Y are Pareto-maximal, i.e., that social efficiency is maximum, it immediately follows that the conditions for competitive equilibrium must in fact be fulfilled in the production sector but that we must have

(3) $$A_D = A_X.$$

Now, as the reader may easily verify using any example, this condition is not usually fulfilled in the most general case of competitive equilibrium, whatever the corresponding distribution of aggregate income may be.

This example clearly demonstrates that the conditions for competitive equilibrium in the production sector still remain necessary for the maximization of social efficiency but that they are no longer sufficient.

What also emerges is that the distinctive features that are introduced in the case of a propensity to bequeath are due to circumstances *independent of time* and that consequently do not involve the theory of interest.

2. Some complementary information, concerning a specific case, will be given later (appendix II, § B).

12. Interest, social efficiency, and State intervention (65)

The theory demonstrates that when the State intervenes in the savings
market so as to maintain a particular interest rate, either by borrowing
or by lending, using methods that do not jeopardize social efficiency,[1] the
only effect of this intervention from the viewpoint of consumption[2] is to
change the way individuals distribute their income over time,[3] thus making it possible to bring about states of the economy that, in the absence
of any intervention, would be impossible because total credits and debits
on the balance sheet must be constantly equal. *The role of the State in
such a case is absolutely equivalent to that of a simple catalyst in chemistry*, since it enables certain states to be realized that would otherwise be
impossible and yet does so without direct intervention in consumption or
production.[3]

1. The theory shows that in the event that the State's interest rate policy leads it to lend,
the necessary resources must be levied, in order to avoid compromising the maximization of
social efficiency, either by means of a general land tax or by means of a tax on capital accumulation independent of economic activity (see what has already been said on this subject in
no. 56 and in note 5 to no. 56).

2. We shall see later the effects such an intervention produces from the production
viewpoint.

3. Interested readers may find all necessary clarifications in the case of the specific examples studied in appendix II (see in particular no. 199, § i).

13. Interest, social efficiency, and classical theory (66)

The foregoing argumentation highlights the additional specifications needed
to make the classical theory rigorous. In fact, as we have seen, *there is no
reason to suppose that spontaneous competitive equilibrium*[1] *corresponds to
an inherent optimum,*[2] as this competitive equilibrium in fact only brings
about one of the many possible distributions over time of the disposable
income of the various individuals.

1. Corresponding to the absence of State intervention.
2. I.e., a physically preferable situation from the point of view both of the efficiency of
production and of the distribution of consumable services.

Interest and Social Productivity

1. Problem of social productivity (67)[1]

The theory of social efficiency specifies the conditions for optimal economic management under given structural boundary conditions (population, land, and capital equipment) and given conditions of distribution. These conditions fully determine the various economic parameters for times $t_1, t_2, \ldots, t_{p-1}$ intermediate between the boundary times t_0 and t_p. In particular they determine the savings made by individuals and the investments made by firms at these various times.

Given these conditions of maximum social efficiency, we may inquire whether a variation in the initial capital equipment at time t_0 might not bring about an increase in Pareto satisfaction.[2] A similar question may be asked regarding the capital equipment existing at time t_p. In both cases the inquiry bears on the link between the economy's stock of capital equipment and the satisfactions of individuals. This inquiry is the subject of what I shall call the theory of social productivity.

If, for instance, we vary only the capital equipment existing at time t_0, it can immediately be seen that the maximum sought corresponds to zero marginal production[3] of the various capital goods at time t_0. Hence the

---

1. As I have already mentioned (no. 3), what first pointed me in the direction of the reflections that follow, apart from my own private studies, was a chapter of J. E. Meade's *Economic Analysis and Policy* titled "The Optimum Supply of Capital," 394–403, in the French edition published in 1939 as *Économie politique et politique économique*.

2. The increase of at least one satisfaction while other satisfactions remain constant.

3. A condition corresponding to identities of type $\frac{\partial A}{\partial X} = 0$ where A represents one of the quantities produced and X one of the factors of production.

corresponding stock of capital may be deemed to be practically infinite. Indeed this result is so evident as to be of little practical interest.

But the same does not apply in the hypothesis of a *stationary* state. In this case, any change in the stock of capital equipment at time t_0 entails a parallel change in the stock of capital equipment at time t_p and it is not immediately apparent whether or not there is a maximum, and if so, what conditions characterize it.

In this case, this problem is of the greatest practical import since *in first approximation* our economic system is comparable to a stationary model, and *it is essential to inquire whether this stationary model can or cannot be deemed optimal from the viewpoint of its capital equipment stock.*

As this stock depends essentially on the quantities of primary factors of production[4] devoted to producing it, it can be seen that the problem before us comes down to whether or not there exists an optimum distribution of the primary factors of production, available at every moment, between the production of capital goods and the production of consumer goods and services. Thus each year a country such as France has about 40 billion hours of labor available,[5] and the problem arises whether there is a distribution of this total number of hours between direct and indirect labor (in the meaning of no. 20) that would enable satisfactions to attain their maximum potential.[6]

I shall consider that the social productivity of a stationary economy having maximum social efficiency is itself maximal when its satisfactions[7] are maxima in the meaning of Pareto for a variable stock of real capital,[8] i.e.,

4. Land and labor.

5. On the basis of a 40-hour working week and an active population of 20 million inhabitants, and supposing as a first approximation that there is only a single quality of labor. (This approximation is made here only to facilitate comprehension in posing the problem and is not involved in what follows.)

6. In the meaning of Pareto.

7. The reference is to the twin sets of satisfactions of different individuals considered at different points in time (no. 60).

8. I remarked earlier (no. 49) that in the absence of State intervention there exists only one stationary competitive state corresponding to given psychologies and technologies. The reader may therefore be surprised at first view that I should consider the volume of real capital to be a variable.

So let me state at once that *what is here considered are all possible economic states and not only those that correspond to the spontaneous competitive equilibrium of an economy based on private ownership.* So nothing prevents me from considering as independent, *from the physical viewpoint* I have adopted, parameters that must be considered *from the economic*

when there exists no virtual modification of this stock such that at least one satisfaction could be increased while the others remain constant.[9]

Thus the theory of social productivity can be seen to relate to the pursuit of a *structural optimum*, by contrast with the theory of social efficiency, which concerns the pursuit of a *management optimum*.[10]

---

viewpoint, under certain conditions, to be restricted—"under certain conditions," since it will be seen that some economic states that are unrealizable in a competitive economy without State intervention would become realizable in the context of such intervention.

This distinction is exactly parallel to the distinction currently used in physics between real displacements, which in fact occur, and virtual displacements, which could occur only if the constraints alone were involved and no action was exercised by the forces characterizing the system in question. To the real and virtual displacements of physics there correspond respectively the displacements that arise, or could in fact arise, in the economy and the displacements that could occur if only constraints *of a physical nature* applied (production technologies, individual scales of choice, etc.) in the absence of any economic action (use of prices, pursuit of maximum income, etc.).

These unavoidably brief remarks will be made clearer by what follows (see in particular appendixes I and II and especially no. 197). (See too the observations made above in note 23 to no. 47.)

9. Social productivity so defined is no more capable of being quantified than is social efficiency; once again it must be understood as *a purely qualitative concept*, the use of which is highly convenient. Readers will be able to transpose here without difficulty the remarks made about social efficiency in note 2 to no. 54.

10. The observations that follow, which I have made as general as possible, may at first strike the reader as somewhat abstract. For this reason, and to avoid all ambiguity, I have deemed it necessary to illustrate the theory expounded by the study of specific cases (see appendixes I and II).

2. Physical productivity of indirect processes of production (68)

We saw in the Fable of the Fishermen[1] that the use of a net, i.e., of a roundabout process of production, makes it possible to obtain a greater output for the same input of labor, or alternatively the same output for less labor. In current terminology the use of roundabout processes of production is said to be *physically productive*. More simply still, we can speak of the physical productivity of capital.

This physical productivity can be defined as the increase in output obtained using the roundabout process in question for the same unit input of primary factors of production.[2]

Thus if we denote by A_d and A_i the outputs of a good (A) obtained from an identical input C_ω of primary factors of production, the physical productivity can be characterized by the ratio

(1)
$$\pi = \frac{A_i - A_d}{A_d}.$$

Experience shows that under stationary conditions physical productivity begins to increase with the coefficient Θ_N characterizing the use of capital,[3] passes through a maximum, and then decreases generally as the period Θ_N increases. Thus, output of shoes indeed increases for a given labor input when machines are used, but it is clear that if the use of direct labor is gradually decreased, for instance, by recourse to highly sophisticated automation, the quantity of output obtained per quantity of labor input would decrease eventually to zero, since the progressive replacement of direct by indirect labor would call for the use of increasingly sophisticated machines, the production of which would itself demand an increasing amount of labor. At this point the productivity of capital would become negative.[4]

It is clear that *in a stationary model the necessary and sufficient condition for maximization of social productivity* as defined above *is that the physical productivity of the various production processes employed should be maximal.*

This condition is necessary, for if it were not realized, it would be possible to conceive of a virtual displacement consisting in a change in the stock

---

1. No. 21 *et seq.*
2. See no. 23.
3. First paragraph of no. 47.
4. These general remarks can easily be verified for the case of my Fable of the Fishermen.

of capital equipment that would enable at least one production to be increased at every point in time—and thus at least one satisfaction to be increased too[5]—while the others remain constant.

And it is sufficient, for if it is fulfilled, no such virtual displacement is conceivable.

In that case, we have

$$\pi = \frac{A_i - A_d}{A_d}$$
$$= \frac{2,400 - 600}{600} = 300\%.$$

In this example, if, instead of manufacturing one net per year, only a half a net were made, it would be possible to fish using a net for only half the time, since a net lasts only one year, so that the annual catch would only be

$$1,200 + 300 = 1,500 \text{ kgs,}$$

and we should then have

$$\pi = \frac{1,500 - 600}{600} = 150\%.$$

On the other hand, if, instead of manufacturing one net per year, two were made, one net would necessarily remain unused since the labor of two men is required for a single net. The annual catch would only be

$$2,400 \times \frac{1}{2} = 1,200 \text{ kgs,}$$

and we should then have

$$\pi = \frac{1,200 - 600}{600} = 100\%.$$

Finally, if the fishermen did nothing but manufacture nets, the output of fish would fall to zero and we should have

$$\pi = -\frac{600}{600} = -100\%.$$

5. Assuming that the satisfactions depend only on the quantity of the various consumer goods and services actually consumed. It will be seen further on how the theory can be generalized when the satisfactions involve elements other than quantities of services consumed, such as quantities of goods possessed or bequeathed (no. 75).

3. Conditions for maximization of physical productivity of indirect processes of production (69)

The observations just made show that in a stationary model there exists an optimal degree of use of capital or indeed an optimal distribution of the available factors of production between direct and indirect use[1] that makes social productivity maximal.

It is easy to identify the conditions that characterize this optimal distribution and to show *that the necessary and sufficient condition for maximum social productivity[2] in a stationary economy having maximum social efficiency, i.e., for the physical productivity[3] of the various production processes to be maximal, is that the rate of interest characterizing the competitive equilibrium in the production sector be zero.* To this end I now proceed to a twofold presentation: the one direct, starting from the definition of the maximization of social productivity, and the other, indirect, starting from consideration of the physical productivity of roundabout processes of production. The direct presentation can itself be subdivided into two forms.

Direct presentation — first form

The theory of social efficiency shows that any virtual modification of an economic state that makes a surplus value available is liable to increase satisfactions in the meaning of Pareto.[4,5] Let $(\overline{H})$ be one of the durable goods used by the stationary economy studied, assumed to be of maximum social efficiency, and let $(H_1), (H_2), \ldots, (H_n)$ be the future services that it will successively render. Social efficiency being assumed to be maximal, the conditions of competitive equilibrium are verified, and we know[6] that

(1) $$\overline{h} = \frac{h_1}{1+I} + \frac{h_2}{(1+I)^2} + \ldots + \frac{h_n}{(1+I)^n},$$

---

1. In the sense of no. 20. It should be borne in mind that the direct use of the primary factors of production relates not to the implementation of direct processes but to their use in the final production stage of an indirect process.

2. In the meaning of no. 67.

3. In the meaning of no. 68.

4. See my study *Économie pure et rendement social*, nos. 22 and 39.

5. See note 5 to no. 68.

6. No. 29, equation (1).

where $\bar{h}, h_1, \ldots, h_n$ and I denote the prices of the good $(\bar{H})$ and of its services (H) and the rate of interest prevailing in this stationary state.[7]

Let us suppose that at every instant we cause the quantity of good $(\bar{H})$ produced to vary by $\delta\bar{H}$. As the conditions are stationary, the quantities $H_1, H_2, \ldots, H_n$ of the services (H) used at each point in time will vary by quantities $\delta H_1, \delta H_2, \ldots, \delta H_n$, equal to δH.[8] Since at every point in time the production of $\delta\bar{H}$ requires expenditure $\bar{h}\delta\bar{H}$, while the supplementary quantities available of services (H) generate the surplus value $h_1\delta H_1$, $h_2\delta H_2, \ldots, h_n\delta H_n$, *at every instant there results a net surplus value equal to*

(2) $$\delta\Omega = (h_1\delta H_1 + h_2\delta H_2 + \ldots + h_n\delta H_n) - \bar{h}\delta\bar{H}.$$

Now according to equation (1) and the identity of the various δ values this surplus value can be expressed as

(3) $$\delta\Omega = \left[h_1\left(1 - \frac{1}{1+I}\right) + h_2\left(1 - \frac{1}{(1+I)^2}\right) + \ldots + h_n\left(1 - \frac{1}{(1+I)^n}\right) \right]\delta H.$$

As prices $h_1, h_2, \ldots, h_n$ are positive, it can be seen that, depending on whether interest rate I is positive or negative, an increase or a decrease in the capital $\bar{H}$ makes it possible to generate surplus value and hence to bring about an increase in Pareto-satisfactions.[9] Consequently the maximization of social productivity can be achieved only if the interest rate *corresponding to the production sector in competitive equilibrium* is zero.

7. No. 19.

8. Bear in mind that the unit of service rendered by a durable good has been defined as the service rendered per unit of this good per unit of time (no. 29).

9. In view of what has been said in note 8 to no. 67, the reader may be initially surprised that in studying a question relating to *physical* quantities I should use prices—specifically *economic* quantities.

The reason is that *when social efficiency is maximal, the ratios between any two prices represent physical quantities*; the coefficients of marginal equivalence, and the sign of quantities of type $\delta\Omega$ depends only on these ratios.

It should be recalled that if production A is a function

(1) $$A = A(X, Y, \ldots, Z)$$

of the quantities consumed $X, Y, \ldots, Z$ of the factors of production $(X), (Y), \ldots, (Z)$, the variation dA is said to be equivalent to the variation dX if

It is easy to see that this is also sufficient, i.e., that if the rate of interest is zero, the social productivity that is stationary is indeed maximal. Equation (3) shows that if interest rate I is positive, an increase in capital yields a positive surplus value. However, we have seen that such an increase corresponds to a decrease in the equilibrium interest rate.[10] It follows that social productivity increases as the interest rate tends toward zero through positive values. It would be found that the same applies when the interest rate tends toward zero through negative values. Hence the maximum is truly achieved.

Direct presentation—second form

This presentation may also be presented in a way that is different, though identical in principle, linking it directly to the explanations that have been given concerning stationary models.[11]

Let B and b be the quantities produced and the prices of final consumption goods in an economic state assumed to have maximum social efficiency. It has been seen[12] that we have

(4) $$R_N = \sum bB,$$

where R_N is the national income.

If we now suppose that to a slight virtual modification of the distribution of the primary factors of production over the various stages of the production cycle[11] there correspond the increments dB, it can be seen that, overall, the economy will have at every instant a surplus value available, which I shall denote by (dR_N) *and which is expressed by*

---

(2) $$dA = \frac{\partial A}{\partial X} dX,$$

and that the quantity A'_X may be called the coefficient of marginal equivalence of (A) to (X). (It is the quantity of A that is equivalent at the margin to a unit of X.) As in competitive equilibrium the price x of factor of production (X) is equal to the value of the marginal production A'_X, it is verified that the ratio of price x to price a is precisely equal to the coefficient of marginal equivalence A'_X of (A) to (X).

10. Nos. 45 and 47.

11. No. 47.

12. No. 37, equation (26).

(5) $(dR_N) = \sum b \, dB,$

and it follows from what has already been set out that social productivity cannot be maximal unless the surplus (dR_N) is zero for all virtual displacements compatible with the constraints.[13,14]

As the surplus (dR_N) is the same as the differential of the national income *for constant prices*, and as we have[11]

(6) $R_N = \int_0^{+\infty} e^{i\theta} \, \varphi(\theta) \, d\theta,$

it can be seen that we have

(7) $(dR_N) = di \int_0^{+\infty} e^{i\theta} \frac{d\varphi(\theta)}{di} \, d\theta,$

since this expression represents precisely the variation of the national income when prices are assumed to be given. In equation (6) prices are characterized by the values of the interest rate and of each component $\delta\varphi$ of the primary income, with no specification as to the stage at which this component is employed and the structure of the production, i.e., its higher or lower degree of capital-use, is characterized by the shape of the function φ.[15]

Now we have seen that for low values of the rate of interest we have[16]

(8) $R_N \sim R_{N\omega}(1 + \Theta_N i).$

So equation (7) can be written in first approximation

(9) $(dR_N) \sim R_{N\omega} \frac{d\Theta_N}{di} i \, di,$ [17]

13. Readers wishing to study this question in greater depth may find complementary information on the differential (dR_N) in my *À la recherche d'une discipline économique*, nos. 263 and 270 *bis*.

14. See note 5 to no. 68.

15. Any reader still prey to doubts on this subject will be able to dissipate them by examining the specific case studied in appendix II, which enables this calculation to be illustrated on a concrete example (note 9 to no. 197).

16. No. 47, equation (15).

17. It is worth emphasizing here that, since the differential (dR_N) is calculated at constant prices, the constancy of the primary income $R_{N\omega}$, which in no. 47 was only an approximate

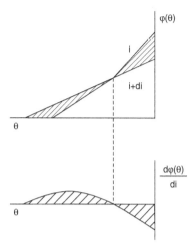

FIGURE 7.1

an equation that results from the differentiation at constant prices of equation (8).

As we know that the production period is a decreasing function of the rate of interest,[18] this equation shows that social productivity increases or decreases depending on whether the rate of interest is negative or positive.

It can thus be seen that the necessary and sufficient condition for social productivity to be maximal is that the interest rate *characterizing the competitive equilibrium in the production sector be zero*.[19]

Indirect presentation

Let A be the production of good (A) in the stationary model assumed to have maximum social efficiency that we are considering, and let $X_{-p}^A, \ldots,$

---

property (note 11 to no. 47), is here a rigorously established fact, which subsists even if in equilibrium the primary national income varies considerably with the rate of interest.

18. No. 47, fig. 5.15.

19. The basis on which (dR_N) is calculated from prices assumed to be constant amounts to assuming that all the data concerning the *physical* functions of production remain constant (note 9 above) while envisaging a virtual displacement, also physical, of the factors of production. This displacement is here characterized by the variations $d\varphi$ or again in the approximate equation (9) by the variation $d\Theta_N$ in the period of production.

$X_{-q}^A, \ldots, X_0^A$ be the quantities of primary factor of production $(X)^{20}$ used for production A during periods $T_{-p}, T_{-q}, \ldots, T_0$, which precede time t, at which production A becomes available. We then have

(10) $$A = A(X_{-p}^A, \ldots, X_{-q}^A, \ldots, X_0^A).$$

Naturally, quantity A also depends on the quantities of type Y_{-q}^A representing the quantities of the other primary factors of production (Y) necessary for production A and supplied at different times, but these quantities are here assumed to be given.

As conditions are assumed to be stationary, the sum

(11) $$X^A = X_{-p}^A + \ldots + X_{-q}^A + \ldots + X_0^A$$

represents *the total quantity of factor of production* (X) *used at each point in time directly or indirectly for production* A.

We may next inquire under what conditions production A may be deemed to be maximal for a total quantity X^A of factor X assumed to be given. This means finding out which distribution of quantity X^A *at each point in time* over the different stages of production maximizes production A, and hence maximizes the physical productivity of the indirect process of production leading to production A.

The theory of constrained maxima shows that for this we must have

(12) $$\frac{\partial A}{\partial X_{-p}^A} = \ldots = \frac{\partial A}{\partial X_{-q}^A} = \ldots = \frac{\partial A}{\partial X_0^A}.$$ 21

As social efficiency is assumed to be maximal, the price x_{-q} at time t of factor (X_{-q}) is equal to the value $\dfrac{a\partial A}{\partial X_{-q}^A}$ of its marginal product at the same point in time. So we have

20. Labor or land.
21. We must in fact have

$$\frac{\partial A}{\partial X_{-p}^A} dX_{-p}^A + \ldots + \frac{\partial A}{\partial X_{-q}^A} dX_{-q}^A + \ldots + \frac{\partial A}{\partial X_0^A} dX_0^A = 0$$

for every system of values $dX_{-p}^A, \ldots, dX_{-q}^A, \ldots, dX_0^A$ that satisfies the condition

$$dX_{-p}^A + \ldots + dX_{-q}^A + \ldots + dX_0^A = 0.$$

(13) $$x_{-q} = a\frac{\partial A}{\partial X_{-q}^A}.$$

As we also have

(14) $$x_{-q} = x(1 + I)^q,$$

since the cost at time t of a disbursement made at time t_{-q} is equal to the product of this disbursement by the binomial $(1 + I)^q$, it finally emerges that

(15) $$a\frac{\partial A}{\partial X_{-q}^A} = x(1+I)^q$$

and hence

(16) $$\frac{\dfrac{\partial A}{\partial X_{-p}^A}}{(1+I)^p} = \ldots = \frac{\dfrac{\partial A}{\partial X_{-q}^A}}{(1+I)^q} = \ldots = \frac{\dfrac{\partial A}{\partial X_0^A}}{1}.$$

These conditions, in combination with those of (12), show that the necessary condition for production A to be deemed maximal for a total quantity X^A of primary factor (X) assumed to be given is for interest rate I to be zero.[22]

Taking into account the general properties of functions of satisfaction and of production and the fact that social efficiency is assumed to be maximal, it can be shown that this necessary condition is also sufficient.[23,24]

22. The same condition could also be found by seeking the minimum quantity X^A of factor of production (X) allocated to production (A) for a given output.

23. Readers can find the demonstration in a specific case in appendix I, no. 173.

24. An intuitive idea of this demonstration can be obtained in the following way, suggested to me by one of my students, M. Jacquelin, a Corps des Mines senior civil servant and engineer.

If, for a given total labor input, all possible distributions (R) of this labor between the manufacture of machines and the manufacture of directly consumable products are envisaged, it is clear (no. 68) that one of these distributions gives maximum output. Let this distribution be R_m.

As the firm makes its decisions on the basis of value and seeks to minimize its unit cost, it is clear that for a positive rate of interest, the distribution that is most in the firm's interests cannot be distribution R_m, for if it were, it would be possible for the firm, by devoting a slightly lower amount of labor to capital investments and increasing direct labor (in the meaning of no. 20), to decrease its interest charges, while losing very little production, which

It is essential to note that the condition thus found is independent of production (A) and of the primary factor (X) of production in question. Hence, when the rate of interest is zero, the physical productivity of the production processes is *simultaneously* maximal for the different productions and for the different primary factors of production used.

Ultimately it emerges that the necessary and sufficient condition for the physical productivity of capital, and hence the social productivity of a stationary model having maximum social efficiency, to be maximum, is for the rate of interest *in the production sector* to be zero.[25]

The case of quasi-stationary models

We have seen that under stationary conditions, prices being constant, the level of the rate of interest remains the same irrespective of the unit of value chosen. So there would be no distinction between the nominal interest rate, the wage-denominated interest rate, and the various real interest rates.[26]

However, if the various productions and consumptions remain constant, i.e., if the *physical* characteristics of the economy in question remain invariable, while monetary conditions vary—a model that may be called quasi-stationary—only the various real interest rates, and notably the wage interest rate, have a common value, the nominal rate of interest being equal to this common value plus the rate of variation of prices.[27] In such a situation the foregoing reasoning shows that the necessary and sufficient condition for social productivity to be maximal is for the common value of the real rates of interest—equal to the wage interest rate— to be zero.

---

by assumption would be in the vicinity of its maximum. The firm is therefore led to choose a labor distribution R intermediate between distribution R_m and the distribution corresponding to the absence of machines.

There is only one case in which the firm would choose distribution R_m, viz. when the rate of interest is zero. In this case it cannot be in the interests of the firm to modify the distribution R_m.

This shows that the necessary and sufficient condition for the physical productivity of capital to be maximal is for the interest rate to be zero.

25. Readers wishing to study the demonstration of the theorem of social productivity in greater depth will find the complementary information they need in the detailed study of specific cases provided in appendixes I and II.

26. No. 19.

27. No. 19, equation (6).

Social productivity and labor intensiveness

When social productivity is maximal, all output obtained from a given labor input may be regarded as maximal. Hence the labor intensiveness of the production in question,[28] i.e., the quotient of the labor input by the output quantity, is minimal. Thus the maximization of social productivity brings about the minimization of labor intensiveness.

It is nevertheless essential to note that the minimum in question is a *relative* one, which itself varies with the total labor input allocated to the production in question.[29]

Social productivity and independent parameters

It has already been stated[30] that for given psychologies and technologies and in the absence of any State intervention, there exists only one stationary state, and its equipment stock is thus perfectly determined as a function of the conditions of psychological and technical structure.

Under these conditions the reader may at first sight wonder how it is possible to seek the conditions of maximization of a system of which all the parameters are well determined: but this objection is easily parried.

On the one hand, this determination is applicable only to a spontaneous competitive economic equilibrium, whereas there is no a priori reason obliging us to consider only spontaneous competitive economic states. On the contrary, it is both possible and *necessary* to inquire whether, among *all* possible physical systems (i.e., those whose conditions of psychological and technical structure have been specified) there may not be some that are preferable in the absolute, and noncompetitive regimes cannot be excluded from this inquiry. Indeed, there is no a priori reason why the inherent optimum should be identical to the spontaneous competitive economy. It is quite conceivable that it may be so under some circumstances, but the result is by no means evident a priori, and its acceptance is absolutely dependent on demonstration.[31]

---

28. Nos. 23 and 62.

29. This point will be clarified in appendix II (no. 197, § iii).

30. No. 49 and note 8 to no. 67.

31. It has already been pointed out (nos. 3 and 66) and will be seen farther on (nos. 76 and 77), that while the concepts of competitive equilibrium and inherent optimum are connected, they are nonetheless distinct, and neither can be reduced to the other.

As the theory shows that among all the physically possible economic states those with maximum social efficiency are preferable, there are grounds for limiting to these states our quest for the particular states whose capital equipment stock is optimal. Now it is easy to verify that the conditions of being stationary and having maximum social efficiency *do not sufficiently specify* an economic state of given psychological and technical structure; for there remain independent variables, including the stock of capital equipment used[32] in the relevant production processes. Thus it is possible and appropriate to study the variation of social productivity in relation to this stock.

On the other hand, even supposing that our inquiry is limited to competitive systems, the complete determination of the competitive stationary economic state corresponding to given conditions of psychological and technical structure is in any event only valid in the absence of any State intervention. If the State intervenes, for instance, on the savings market, a supplementary parameter is introduced (equal, as the case may be, either to the amount of the public debt or to the aggregate of its claims on private persons), and it is both possible and advisable to study, as a function of this parameter, the variations of social productivity corresponding to a variable stock of capital equipment.

Indeed, experience entirely bears out this view, for it shows that the capital equipment available to a community is by no means the result of circumstances beyond that community's control or influence. Thus, in the case of Soviet Russia, the government has been able, in 20 years, entirely to change the industrial plant and equipment available to the Russian economy. So it is perfectly legitimate in economic theory to consider the stock of capital equipment as a variable.

National wage-denominated income and national real income

We have seen that the national income calculated in wage terms[33] is in fact proportionally greater as the rate of interest is higher,[34] i.e., for positive

32. Which can be characterized by the primary national capital $C_{\mu\omega}$ (no. 47), or again by the average duration Θ_N of the production processes (no. 47), or indeed by the rate of interest used in the production sector (which, from equation [16] above, is seen to be a physical quantity).

33. Note 12 to no. 47.

34. It follows from equation (15) of no. 47 and from the properties of the average production period Θ_N, which remains finite for $i = 0$, that the national income calculated in wage terms R_N is an increasing function of the rate of interest.

values of the interest rate, social productivity decreases and hence output is lower. The national wage-denominated income therefore constitutes a poor indicator of the community's real standard of living.[35,36]

It follows from the foregoing analysis that as a function of the rate of interest, the variation in real national income could be well expressed as

(17) $$(dR_N) = \Sigma\, b\, dB,$$

being the differential, at constant prices, of the national income. Or, as a first approximation, as we have seen, it could be expressed as

(18) $$(dR_N) = R_{N\omega}\frac{d\Theta_N}{di}\, i\, di.$$

---

35. When i decreases, the quantities B increase, but wage prices b decrease, so that overall, as we have just seen, output falls in wage terms. The value of the differential

(1) $$dR_N = \sum_B b\, dB + B\, db$$

is thus negative.

36. This is but a manifestation of a general phenomenon that can be called "the paradox of value": the value of a good is greater in proportion to its rarity, i.e., as society is poorer (see my general work *À la recherche d'une discipline économique*, no. 251).

4. Variation of the physical productivity of production processes with their capital intensity and the rate of interest (70)

The foregoing[1] shows that as capital intensity (degree of use of capital) Θ_N increases, the physical productivity of the production processes first increases,[2] then passes through a maximum, then decreases and finally becomes negative.

As capital intensity Θ_N increases from zero when the rate of interest falls beneath a certain value I^3 and physical productivity is maximal for level $I = 0$,[4] it can be seen that when the rate of interest decreases, physical productivity, initially zero, rises, passes through a maximum for $I = 0$, then falls gradually until it reaches its limit value of -100%.[5]

The different results obtained can thus be represented by the diagram in figure 7.2.[6]

Value productivity and physical productivity

When the market interest rate is 5%, a present capital of 100 francs can be exchanged against a capital of 105 francs available in one year's time. It is said that the capital is productive of value and that the interest received of 5 francs represents the capital's value productivity.[7]

The foregoing shows that, as Böhm-Bawerk had pointed out, the value productivity of capital must not be confused with its physical productivity—indeed physical productivity can exist where there is no value productivity. All that can be said is that if there is value productivity, there is certainly physical productivity, and if there is physical unproductivity, there is certainly value unproductivity.

1. Nos. 68 and 69.
2. So let us agree to say that "social productivity" increases.
3. No. 45.
4. No. 69.
5. No. 68.
6. These results will be confirmed in the study of a specific case in appendix II (no. 197, § ii).
7. No. 15.

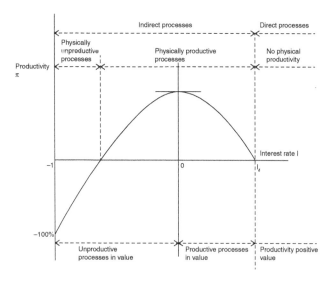

FIGURE 7.2

"Physical productivity" is the value productivity of financial investments, not of direct investments, since the production processes are in this case direct.

Optimal capital stock

Contrary to the more or less intuitive belief of many economists, the capital stock corresponding to a zero interest rate does not correspond to an infinite value.

In fact, since the representative points of typical economies—in which the pure interest rate can be deemed to have a value of a few percent—are extremely close to the point that corresponds to a zero level on the curve representative of the average duration Θ_N of processes of production,[8] we may safely conclude that

(1) $$\Delta\Theta_N \sim I\left|\frac{d\Theta_N}{dI}\right|,$$

where I represents the pure rate of interest, $\left|\dfrac{d\Theta_N}{dI}\right|$ the variation of Θ_N with I in the vicinity of point M, and $\Delta\Theta_N$ the average lengthening of production processes as the interest rate falls to zero.

8. No. 47, fig. 5.15.

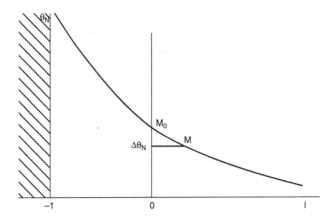

FIGURE 7.3

As we have[9]

(2) $C_{\mu\omega} = \Theta_N R_{N\omega},$

and as the primary national income $R_{N\omega}$ can be taken to be approximately constant, we deduce

(3) $\Delta C_{\mu\omega} = I \left| \dfrac{d\Theta_N}{dI} \right| R_{N\omega}.$

This equation enables us to evaluate, in relation to the primary national income, the approximate increase in the initial capital stock that would be brought about if the pure rate of interest fell to zero.[10]

---

9. No. 47, equation (13).

10. If we take 80, as found previously (notes 48 and 39 to no. 47), as the value of $\left| \dfrac{d\Theta_N}{di} \right|$, we find for France, on the basis of a pure interest rate on the order of 4–5% (the prewar situation), that

$$\Delta C_{\mu\omega} = R_{N\omega}\Delta\Theta_N \sim 3 \text{ to } 4 \ R_{N\omega}.$$

The increase in equipment that would have been necessary to bring the interest rate down to zero would thus have been on the order of 3.5 times the annual national income. On that basis, if average annual investments, representing about 1/5 to 1/7 of national income, had been doubled, which would have been more or less equivalent to keeping constant the investments corresponding to high-growth periods, it can be seen that a maximum lag of 15 to 30 years would have been necessary, and this without any decrease in the national standard of living or even a partial reassignment in favor of equipment of the increases in production due to technical progress, in order to reach an optimum level of capital equipment in a full-employment economy.

It is worth recalling that in 1938, a difficult period for the French economy and one in which savings were low on account of the rapid rise in prices, total national savings represented about 60 billion as against a national income of 300 billion (Report no. 16, May 1944, of the French Institut de Conjoncture).

The figures for other countries would be found to be comparable. For instance, in the United States, according to Mitchell, investments represent on average 1/7 of the national income (Gaétan Pirou, *Les nouveaux courants de la théorie économique aux États-Unis,* fasc. 3 [Paris: Domat-Montchrestien, 1938], 99).

Of course, these calculations represent *only very rough approximations* since for the prewar period they use the value $\dfrac{d\Theta_N}{di}$ corresponding to the period preceding the First World War. I cite them only to give the reader an idea of the orders of magnitude involved.

5. Significance of the results obtained (71)

Every day the overall economy has a certain number of hours of labor available, and the question arises how best to distribute this labor over the different stages of production (final goods and intermediate goods) so that satisfactions are Pareto-maximal, i.e., in simple terms albeit approximate and imprecise, so that the output of consumer services obtained is maximal.[1] The reasoning I have set out shows that this maximum is attained when the rate of interest is zero.

What this means can be simply grasped using a specific example: energy.

A kWh generated by hydroelectric power needs many fewer hours of labor for its production than a kWh derived from coal. The failure to develop hydroelectric power to the detriment of coal despite this advantage is due to the price per kWh of hydroelectric energy, which, under present conditions, is equal to the price per kWh of coal. This is so even though the labor costs for hydroelectric power are lower because hydroelectricity is burdened with interest charges that hamper its development.

The results obtained imply that for a given output of kWh the number of hours of labor directly or indirectly necessary to produce a single kWh is minimum when the rate of interest is zero.

Now it is precisely possible to verify at once using this example that, if the rate of interest were zero, there would indeed be a gain, in labor terms, for a given output of kWh since on this hypothesis hydroelectric energy would succeed in supplanting coal in every field because it would be cheaper.[2]

Advantages corresponding to maximization of social productivity

The advantages attaching to the maximization of social productivity obviously depend on the shape of the curves representing the average physical productivity of the various production processes in the range of variation of the rate of interest from zero to current levels of from 4% to 8%. In the event of a *flat maximum* (fig. 7.4 left), the advantages that could be derived from maximization of social productivity would obviously be negligible,

---

1. What this means is explained in the foregoing.

2. The use of coal would no longer be necessary except for certain operations such as metallurgical processes, for which it is indispensable on account not of its calorific power but of its chemical properties.

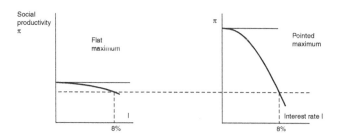

FIGURE 7.4

whereas in the case of a *pointed maximum* (fig. 7.4 right), they would be considerable.

As a matter of fact, there is every reason to think that we are rather in the scenario of a pointed maximum. Suffice it to consider the transformations that would result in both energy and in town planning in the event of reduction of the interest rate to zero.[3]

In the case of the energy sector, in France, for instance, a radical transformation of present conditions would occur. It is plausible that the production of hydroelectric energy would be increased in the ratio of 10 to 1,[4] coal production would be reduced to 1/5 and coal imports would cease altogether; indeed it is likely that energy costs would fall by about 4/5. The economic consequences of such a development would be immense and can only be indicated approximately.

In the town-planning sector the transformation of present economic conditions would be no less far reaching; it is plausible that, on the basis of a 50-year depreciation period for buildings, rental costs would fall by a proportion in the vicinity of 30%.[5,6,7]

3. Or to a level in the region of zero such as 0.25% or even 0.5%.

4. This very rough estimate will at first sight appear somewhat overstated to those who are competent in the field of hydroelectric energy production, but *the profitability calculations involved are of course based on a zero interest rate.* Hence the figure quoted is of course greater than current estimates of our hydroelectric possibilities, which are calculated on the basis of profitability depending on an interest rate of 5% to 6% or more; it also takes into account the use of tidal energy, which would be profitable at a zero interest rate.

5. This figure does not take land rent into account.

6. Of course, this remark does not apply to current French rentals, which the law keeps artificially low, but to the costs that the community *really* bears in one way or another for its housing services.

7. It can easily be seen that the effect of lowering the rate of interest would in fact be all the more pronounced given that, in the sectors affected, the investment period is longer.

Evaluation of advantages corresponding to maximization
of social productivity

Evaluation of the gain in real income that could be obtained by reducing
the rate of interest is in fact possible thanks to the equation specified above,
which gives the surplus value produced.[8]

It can be shown in this way that a fall in the rate of interest from 5% to
zero is likely to yield a minimum increase in real income on the order of
20%, and the gain thus obtained would be almost entirely achieved by lowering the pure interest rate from 5% to 1.5%. If the initial pure interest rate
is only 4%, a decrease to 1.5% still brings about a gain on the order of 10%.

In any event, it is apparent that losses become very high when the pure
rate of interest exceeds 5%.[9,10,11,12,13]

As the annual price of use a of an investment ($\bar{A}$) of cost $\bar{a}$ is equal to the sum of the interest and of its depreciation in value, we have, in first approximation, on average

$$a = I\frac{\bar{a}}{2} + \frac{\bar{a}}{n},$$

where n denotes the duration of the investment and assuming that all depreciations are equal.
We infer that for the ratio α of the relative variations of a and I, we have

$$a = \frac{\dfrac{da}{a}}{\dfrac{dI}{I}} = \frac{1}{1 + \dfrac{2}{nI}},$$

where it is assumed that cost $\bar{a}$ remains largely unaffected by variation in I.

For an interest rate of 5% and depreciation periods of 2, 5, 10, 50, and 100 years, the
values of a are respectively 0.05, 0.11, 0.20, 0.55, and 0.71. So the same fall in the interest rate
to 1%, representing a fall of 80% in relative value, would bring about price falls respectively
equal to 4%, 8%, 16%, 44%, and 57%. Thus these falls in price would be greater—and hence
the effects of the contemplated decrease in the interest rate more substantial—as the periods
of the investments being considered were longer. These effects would be especially marked in
the building and hydroelectric energy sectors.

8. No. 69, equation (9).

9. Thus if we seek the gain likely to be obtained by reducing the interest rate to zero a
rough and ready calculation on the basis of equation (9) of no. 69 gives

(1) $$(dR_N) \sim R_N \frac{i^2}{2}\left|\frac{d\Theta_N}{di}\right|$$

---

or, for $i = 5\%$ and the value 80 found for $\left|\dfrac{d\Theta_N}{dI}\right|$ (note 39 to no. 47),

(2) $$\frac{(dR_N)}{R_N} \sim 10\%,$$

a relatively low value. But in reality, it seems that the gain would be considerably greater. For in light of the observations made in note 47 to no. 47 *in fine*, it seems reasonable to estimate $\left|\dfrac{d\Theta_N}{di}\right|$ at 90. Moreover, considering that Θ_N increases indefinitely as i tends toward -1 and that consequently $\left|\dfrac{d\Theta_N}{di}\right|$ increases as i decreases, we may take it that the value 90 is approximate by defect.

Finally, expression (8) of no. 69 disregards some higher-order terms, all of them positive according to equation (14) of no. 47. If second-degree terms are taken into account in i, we have (from equation [14] and the notations of note 38 to no. 47)

(3) $$R_N = R_{N\omega}\left(1 + \Theta_N i + \Delta\frac{i^2}{2}\right).$$

Now it follows from the calculations of note 47 to no. 47 that Δ is equal to $4\dfrac{\Theta_N^2}{3}$ and to $3\dfrac{\Theta_N^2}{2}$ depending on whether the characteristic curve is triangular or rectangular in shape. We thus see that the value of $\dfrac{\Delta}{\Theta_N^2}$ is greater as the shape of the characteristic curve is flatter. And it is a fact that flattened shapes of type A (fig. 7.5) seem a priori more likely.

If this is so, a measurement that is approximate by defect can be obtained by writing

$$R_N = R_{N\omega}\left(1 + \Theta_N i + \frac{3}{4}\Theta_N^2 i^2\right)$$

and, taking account of the values found for the product $i\Theta_N$ close to 20% (note 39 to no. 47),

$$\frac{(dR_N)}{R_N} = \frac{1}{1.2}\left(i + \frac{3}{2}\Theta_N i^2\right)\frac{d\Theta_N}{di}\,di.$$

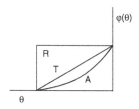

FIGURE 7.5 FOOTNOTE

By lowering the interest rate to zero, we thus obtain, for the gain in income g, using for Θ_N its average value of 7 in the (0–5%) range, the value

$$g \sim 37i^2 + 264i^3.$$

Hence table 7.1.

TABLE 7.1 FOOTNOTE

i	$37i^2$	$264i^3$	g
%	%	%	%
0.5	0.1	0.003	0.1
1.0	0.4	0.030	0.4
1.5	0.8	0.100	0.9
2.0	1.5	0.200	1.7
3.0	3.3	0.700	4.0
4.0	5.9	1.700	7.6
5.0	9.2	3.300	12.5
6.0	13.0	5.700	18.7
7.0	18.0	9.200	27.2
8.0	24.0	13.400	37.4

These figures still disregard the following terms, which take on a significant value as soon as the level of i becomes appreciable. They can therefore be regarded as minima.

Finally, account must be taken of the fact that in reality the economic calculations of firms are not made on the basis of the pure rate of interest but on the basis of that rate plus the risk and management premiums (nos. 11, 29, and 33). When the pure rate of interest is increased by a risk premium, this serves to eliminate technologies that, according to the known probabilities, would not be profitable. This must therefore be borne in mind by deducting the risk premiums from the rates used.

By contrast, the effect of the management premiums is to eliminate technologies that would normally be profitable. So if the estimate of g was made on the basis of the pure interest rate, the loss obtained would be lower than it is in reality.

In the same way it will be seen that as a result of the market mechanism certain risks and management charges are counted *twice* (note 6 to no. 84). Once again, the effect of this is that technologies that would be profitable at the pure market interest rate are in fact eliminated.

For these reasons, calculation of the loss g must be made not on the basis of the pure interest rate but on the basis of an intermediate value between this rate and the average rate really used by firms in their profitability calculations. *On average*, in my judgment, the basis used for this calculation should be the pure interest rate plus at least one point.

It can be seen that a fall in the pure interest rate from 5% to 1% probably corresponds to an increase in real national income of some 15 to 20% and that a fall from 5 to 2% still corresponds to a gain of about 15%.

These figures show that maximum social productivity is practically attained as soon as the pure interest rate attains levels on the order of 1.5% (losses lower than 2%), but that losses in productivity become highly significant as soon as the pure interest rate exceeds 4%.

Of course we have so far been assuming equilibrium, so in order to transpose these results into the real context of disequilibrium it is not the nominal rate of interest that must be considered but the marginal productivity of capital in real terms (no. 44).

Finally, it is worth reiterating the reminder of note 39 to no. 47 that *these different estimates are very rough and ready*. They are included here exclusively to provide the reader with bases of appreciation and to point him in the direction of how the issue can be treated statistically. It goes without saying that further study would be absolutely necessary to endow these estimates with truly scientific value. But I have taken the view that twilight is better than total darkness and that it would be worthwhile to show the reader straight away how the loss of social productivity can be calculated and to give him some idea of its order of magnitude.

The very fact that such a computation can be envisaged is a source of encouragement given that, at least in the present state of our knowledge, there exists no means of estimating the losses of social efficiency corresponding to a given state of the economy.

Indeed, it opens great possibilities for the analysis of certain problems that remain hitherto unsolved: for instance, the comparison of the efficiency of the American and Russian economic models. For if we admit, *as a first approximation*, that these countries are comparable from the point of view of their demographic characteristics and natural resources (population size and natural wealth per person), the differences in living standards between them must be primarily attributed to differences of social efficiency and social productivity. This granted, if the impact of social productivity can be quantified, the *differential* comparison of social efficiency becomes possible, even if the losses in social efficiency in absolute terms remain beyond our reach. Clearly this provides econometricians with an exceptionally promising line of research.

10. This reasoning coupled with the fact that the percentage of interest included in prices is on average on the order of 20% (note 39 to no. 47) leads to the conclusion that *the fall in prices, in wage terms, to be expected from maximization of social productivity starting from a point at which the pure interest rate was 5% would be on the order of 40%*.

11. These figures may appear relatively modest to some readers if they are measured against the promises of those who cheerfully paint in glowing colors the tenfold increase in income that, they assure the crowds, could easily be obtained. But keeping our feet firmly on the ground, no sensible person will fail to appreciate what a great improvement in well-being could be achieved by a *permanent* 20% increase in national income in real terms. For what lends our life its charm is in fact the surplus income that is left over after our vital needs have been provided for. And a simple increase of 20% in total real income would undoubtedly in many cases enable this surplus to be multiplied by 10 if not more.

It is also worth pointing out that an improvement on this scale would have been equivalent, for France in 1938, to a technical innovation that would have enabled the country—other things being equal—to increase its annual output of coal from 46 million to 300 million tons.

12. As the maximum is probably reached in practice for an interest rate level of 1.5%, it can be seen that, in light of the information provided in note 10 to no. 70, the increase in primary capital needed to reach this practical maximum from an initial level of about 4% to 5% (the prewar situation) would be

Implications of the theory

It is worth noting that the results obtained were by no means evident a priori, at least at first sight. It might have been thought, on the contrary, that the more capital there is, the greater the output and that the lower the rate of interest (even to the extent of negativity) the more roundabout processes of production would be socially advantageous in view of the low user cost of capital under such conditions.

But in reality, this inference is valid only from the individual viewpoint of the isolated firm; it is not applicable to the economy as a whole, in which the upkeep and renewal of a greater capital stock requires the use of a larger share of the available primary factors of production.

The use of ever-greater quantities of capital would only be advantageous if capital were a free commodity the production of which called for no input, or at most only a very slight input, of the primary factors of production. But this is not the case, and there is a point at which indirect labor becomes less advantageous than direct labor.[14] This point corresponds to a limit beyond which expansion of the stock of capital equipment is no longer desirable.

$$\Delta C_{\mu\omega} = 2 \text{ to } 3\ R_{N\omega},$$

the corresponding time lag being from 10 to 20 years if annual average investments were doubled (see note 10 to no. 70).

Thus these figures are significantly lower than those found in note 10 to no. 70. However, it follows from what is said in note 9 above that they must be considered to be approximate by defect.

13. Since the last world war brought about for France a decrease in its capital on the order of two years' worth of national income, the rise in the equilibrium interest rate in terms of the value of the national capital in 1913 is on the order of

$$\Delta_i = \frac{2}{80} = 2.5\%.$$

Since the pure equilibrium interest rate in 1939 was at least 5%, the estimates made in note 9 above show that failure to rebuild our national capital to its 1938 level would correspond, in equilibrium, to a permanent loss of at least 20% of national income (see also note 14 of no. 164).

14. See note 1 to no. 69.

6. Social productivity and distribution (72)

It is important to emphasize that the conditions for maximizing social productivity leave untouched the question of the distribution of consumer services, whether in the shape of the distribution of the aggregate income among the different individuals or the distribution of individual incomes between the different periods.

Just as increasing social efficiency does not necessarily improve the condition of a given individual,[1] so too improving social productivity, though it increases output per person, will not necessarily have the effect in reality of enhancing the satisfaction of any given individual at any given time. In both cases the improvements obtained are distributed, in a competitive economy, according to the laws of the functional distribution of income and of how ownership is distributed.

In fact, in the context of the present system of ownership, the maximization of social productivity would mean the disappearance of the income of capitalists—since the rate of interest would then be zero—and hence a decrease in their satisfactions.

Moreover, as we shall see,[2] in a competitive system this maximization would not be possible without prior collectivization of land ownership and consequent State appropriation of income derived from land.

The situation of the workers in a competitive equilibrium of maximum social productivity would thus be simultaneously improved in three different respects on account of the increase in social productivity, the elimination of pure interest on capital, and the appropriation of land rent by the community. So far as can be judged, this improvement, assessed on the basis of a competitive equilibrium with a pure rate of interest of 5% can be reckoned at about 50% of the income corresponding to the present situation.[3]

Similarly, in the case of a stationary model, a zero interest rate in a competitive system would not necessarily have the effect of simultaneously

1. See my article entitled "Économie pure et rendement social," *Annales des mines*, no. 15 (January–February 1945).

2. No. 139.

3. In view of the statistical indications given in note 39 to no. 47 and in note 10 to no. 71, this percentage breaks down as follows: the elimination of pure interest on capital, 20%; appropriation of land-rent by the community (equal to the product of land by the pure interest rate), 10%; maximization of social productivity, 20%.

increasing the different satisfactions of the same individual at different periods, and it is perfectly possible that some would diminish while the others increased,[4] but — and this is the crucial point — *it would still be technically possible*, by suitably modifying the distribution over time of the income of the individual in question,[5] to make an increase in social productivity achieved by modifying the economy's stock of capital equipment correspond to an improvement in the different satisfactions of the same individual.

The differences that may exist between this or that state of maximum social productivity in reality consist only in how consumer goods and services are distributed.[6] For a given distribution, maximization of social productivity enables the best use to be made of what is technically possible; by contrast, lower social productivity leads to a loss of possible satisfactions without any form of compensation.[7]

4. See appendix II, no. 198.

5. Obtained, for instance, by using in the consumption sector interest rates different from the zero interest rate used in the production sector (see appendix II, nos. 194 and 198).

6. Once again it should be recalled that this distribution has two sides since it includes both the distribution of aggregate disposable income among the various individuals and the distribution over time of their disposable income by those various individuals.

7. In order to highlight the analogy between the theories of social efficiency and of social productivity in respect of distribution, the same formulation has deliberately been used here as in the second paragraph of no. 56.

7. Social productivity and social efficiency (73)

The foregoing explanations clearly bring out the link between the theory of social efficiency and the theory of social productivity.

The theory of social efficiency seeks optimal conditions for managing the economy for given initial and final capital structures.[1]

The theory of social productivity seeks the optimal structural conditions when social efficiency is already optimal and the variable is the stock of capital equipment.[2]

Clearly there is a close analogy between these two concepts of social efficiency and social productivity. The former relates to operating conditions and the latter to structural conditions, but both relate to the pursuit of a certain optimum of the technical conditions of production, abstracting from any question of the distribution of the aggregate income among the various individuals, or of the distribution of individual incomes over different time periods.

Maximization of social efficiency refers to an operational optimum, while maximization of social productivity concerns a structural optimum; both constitute purely economic issues the study of which is a duty for any community whatsoever.

It is easy to form an exact idea of the link between the notions of social efficiency and social productivity on the basis of the previously defined areas of maximum social efficiency.[3]

For a given stock of capital equipment, i.e., for a given primary national capital stock $C_{\mu\omega}$, all possible economic states are enclosed by a line Σ_ρ of maximum social efficiency at each point of which economic management must be deemed to be optimal (fig. 7.6).

Whenever—social efficiency being maximal—primary capital $C_{\mu\omega}$ increases, the foregoing explanations show that it is possible to increase satisfactions in the sense of Pareto.[4] This means that the line Σ_ρ moves away from the origin. When social productivity is maximal, line Σ_ρ attains a

---

1. Note that in the case of a stationary equilibrium the given boundary conditions are in effect the assumptions concerning the stock of capital equipment at a given moment.
2. Bear in mind that only under stationary conditions does this optimum correspond to a zero interest rate.
3. No. 56.
4. Note 1 to no. 67.

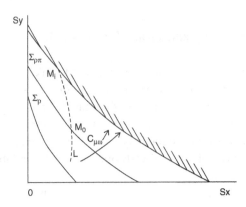

FIGURE 7.6

boundary position $\Sigma_{\rho\pi}$ that represents the limit of all possible economic states having *variable* economic management and *variable* capital equipment.

It can thus be seen that there is not just one point of maximum social productivity but an infinity and that the area of maximum social productivity corresponds to a *maximum maximorum* situation.

Moreover, when, *for a given ownership distribution*, the primary capital $C_{\mu\omega}$ increases as a result of State intervention, for instance, in the context of a single interest rate, the representative point of the economy assumed to have maximum social efficiency follows a line L, and it is obviously possible that along this trajectory certain satisfactions Sy may increase rapidly while others Sx may increase less or even diminish.[5]

If, instead of considering the distribution of the national income among different individuals, we turn to the distribution of the income of a single individual over the different time periods, analogous results are obtained.

For instance, let us assume a stationary economy including two identical groups of individuals, the one young and the other old, and let S_0 and S_1 respectively, be the satisfactions of the young and the old; and for the sake of simplicity let us also suppose that there is only a single consumer good A.

For a given stock of capital equipment, i.e., for a given technical interest rate, all economic states of maximum social efficiency are on a line Σ_ρ of equal productivity, at each point of which economic management must be deemed optimal.

5. No. 72.

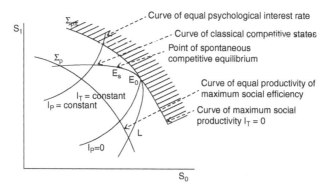

Curve of equal psychological interest rate

Curve of classical competitive states

Point of spontaneous competitive equilibrium

Curve of equal productivity of maximum social efficiency

Curve of maximum social productivity $I_T = 0$

FIGURE 7.7

Whenever—social efficiency being maximal—primary capital $C_{\mu\omega}$ increases, line Σ_ρ moves away from the origin and attains a boundary position $\Sigma_{\rho\pi}$, at which social productivity is maximal.

For a given distribution of property, assumed, for example, to be equal among all the individuals in the same group, there is only one point E_S of spontaneous competitive equilibrium characterized by a single rate of interest and the absence of State intervention.[6] When the State intervenes in the capital market while maintaining the uniqueness of the rates of interest, the point representing equilibrium follows a line L, which may be called the line of classical competitive states.

The equilibrium point will always be on the line L unless the psychological and technological rates of interest separate. Assuming the uniqueness of the psychological rates of interest,[7] there is thus a twofold network of lines: the lines of equal technical interest rate (or equal productivity) and the lines of equal psychological interest rate. To each line of equal productivity there corresponds a twofold technical interest rate.[8] Line L is naturally tangential to line $\Sigma_{\rho\pi}$ at point E_0 where the psychological and technical rates of interest are both zero.

It is clear that in the context of the single interest rate, which characterizes classical competitive equilibria, an increase in social productivity can lead S_0 and S_1 to vary in opposite directions, but it is also clear that

6. No. 49.

7. Which, it is worth emphasizing, *is not a necessary condition of maximum social efficiency* (no. 61).

8. As follows from figure 7.2 of no. 70.

from any initial state whatever, it is always possible to ensure that to an increase in social productivity there corresponds a simultaneous increase in both satisfactions S_0 and S_1. For this, it is only necessary to separate the psychological and technical rates of interest.[9]

Twofold problem posed by investments

Real investments pose two problems: the first concerns the distribution, orientation, and specialization of the means of production in the various branches for a given total volume of investment—it falls within the province of the theory of social efficiency; the second concerns the overall volume of investment itself—it falls within the province of the theory of social productivity.[10]

9. All these points will be confirmed and clarified in appendix II by the detailed study of a specific case (nos. 186, 194, and 197, § vi and vii).

10. These two aspects can be simply represented by figure 7.8.

Let there be n communicating containers $A, B, \ldots, C$ containing a liquid of total mass M, and let us assume that we are seeking to distribute the liquid so that the mean distance

$$z_m = \frac{1}{M} \int_v z \, dm$$

of the particles of liquid counted vertically downward from a horizontal plane P is maximal.

It is obvious that (a) the distribution obtained by the action of gravity will bring about this distribution for a given mass of liquid, while (b) the absolute maximum will be obtained when the total mass of the liquid is such that the upper surface of the liquid in the different containers coincides with plane P (since above P the zs become negative).

In this comparison the mean distance z_m stands for social productivity, and the different masses $M_1, M_2, \ldots, M_C$ found in the different containers $A, B, \ldots, C$ represent the capital invested in the various industries $A, B, \ldots, C$.

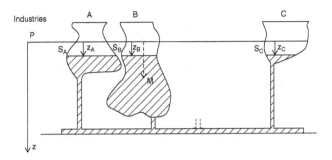

FIGURE 7.8 FOOTNOTE

For a given total equipment stock (represented by a given total mass of liquid), satisfactions (represented by mean distance z_m) are Pareto-maximal when the different technical interest rates (represented by distances $z_A, z_B, \ldots, z_C$ of surfaces $S_A, S_B, \ldots, S_C$) are the same in the different industries. This equality corresponds to a certain distribution of the capital among these industries (represented by the distribution of the liquid among the containers) and the relative maximum obtained corresponds to the maximization of social efficiency.

When the total mass of investments (represented by mass M of the liquid) increases, social productivity (represented by z_m) first increases, passes through a maximum, and then decreases. The absolute maximum attained for a zero interest rate (represented by the common distance $z_A = z_B = \ldots = z_C$) corresponds to the maximization of social productivity.

8. Transition from one stationary state to another (74)

It follows from the foregoing that to a given stationary state whose stock of capital equipment is less than the optimum, we should prefer, from the viewpoint of the structure of its production equipment—and abstracting from any question of distribution—any stationary state[1] whose social productivity is closer to its maximum.

However, it goes without saying that transition from the former stationary state to the latter calls for a prior accumulation of the capital needed for the contemplated increase in social productivity to be possible, and hence for net savings[2] to be made for a certain time, or an increase in gross savings, and this necessarily entails a fall in the output of consumer goods and services over the same period.[3]

A schematic representation of the transition from a stationary economic process in which the output of consumer goods and services is Q_0 to one in which it is Q_1 is shown in figure 7.9.

It can be seen that to a *temporary* restriction of the output of consumer goods and services during the transition period, there corresponds later a compensatory increase *of unlimited duration* in this output for equal labor input.[4] This highlights the social importance of savings in achieving a higher economic life.

---

1. Corresponding, of course, to the same conditions of psychological and technical structure.

2. Note that under stationary conditions net savings are nil (no. 37, equation [28]).

3. It is also clear that, while the transition from a positive interest rate to a zero interest rate entails a certain abstention from consumption, the transition from a negative interest rate to a zero interest rate is always possible, since the second state requires only a lower volume of capital. From this it emerges that *to set up a stationary equilibrium with a negative interest rate would be socially disadvantageous* in the sense that, with present capital, the same consumable output could be obtained for less labor input. (See appendix II, no. 197, § vi.)

4. Remember that, as the technical structure is assumed to be constant, there is no technical progress, and once the effort needed to increase the stock of capital has been made, it need not be made again. Thereafter only ongoing renewal of the existing capital is involved, and the calculation of level Q_1 takes account of this.

Further technical progress does not change this conclusion, for the equipment effort once made will suffice for the implementation of new technologies. For instance, it is quite certain that as technical progress makes it desirable for an economy to turn to atomic energy, it will only be able to do so if it already possesses sufficient capital equipment.

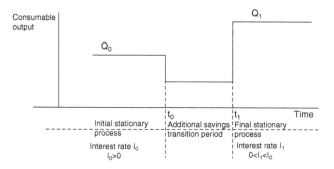

FIGURE 7.9

Moreover, while the passage from one stationary state to another, more advantageous, one necessarily involves a transition period of restricted consumption, it is evident that there is no need to sacrifice a generation; in other words, the consumption of a given generation is not necessarily decreased to the exclusive advantage of succeeding generations.

For ways can always be found of ensuring that in the interim period of increased savings the consumption of the old is left unchanged while only the consumption of the young is diminished, and that the surplus output obtained subsequently is assigned to the old, who had been the young of the immediately preceding period, so that during the interim period the total disposable income allocated to *each generation*[5] remains constantly greater than it was in the initial stationary state.

Thus it is clear that *transition to the optimal stationary economic process can always be effected by a simple redistribution over time of the income of each generation*—the conventional and arbitrary nature of this distribution has already been stressed.[6]

Of course when technical progress occurs, to the advantages that would result from maximization of social productivity under constant technological conditions there accrue the advantages due to the technical progress itself (see also note 21 to no. 77).

5. Which results from the addition of the disposable income corresponding to the different ages (see no. 197, § v).

6. No. 63.

It will be seen later on that the implementation of the policy of increasing capital equipment required by this transition would in fact only be possible under competitive conditions if land ownership had *previously* been collectivized (no. 139).

9. Interest, social productivity, and propensity to own and to bequeath (75)

It can be shown that when the scales of choice involve an *intrinsically definable* propensity to own[1] or to bequeath—i.e., one that can be defined irrespective of any system of prices—and when storage of goods is possible, the theorem of social productivity remains fully valid.[2]

When the scales of choice involve the *values* of capital owned or bequeathed measured against a certain price system, the physical pursuit of the maximization of social productivity[3] becomes *meaningless*, since the values owned can only be defined in terms of a specific price system and hence cannot be held to have any intrinsic significance.

When the propensity to own or to bequeath involves *physical* quantities, the *physical* pursuit of maximum social productivity remains meaningful, but it can be shown that the theorem of social productivity is not valid if storage is not possible.[4,5]

In reality, of course, the greater the propensities to own and to bequeath, the higher—in equilibrium and other things being equal—savings will be, the lower will be the interest rate and hence the greater will be the physical productivity of the processes of production when the rate of interest is not negative.[6]

1. I.e., when ownership, in itself and independently of any use made of the possession, tends to provide satisfaction.

2. Readers wishing to study this question more fully will find the information they need in the study of the specific case presented in appendix II, § C.

3. In the meaning of no. 67.

4. In the real world, of course, storage *is* possible.

5. Whenever the *physical* problem of social productivity no longer makes sense, or, though making sense, the theorem of social productivity no longer holds good, the satisfactions are no longer Pareto-maximal for a variable stock of capital equipment and a zero technical interest rate. It can only be said that the physical productivity of the various production processes is maximal when the technical interest rate is zero. But this too is a *crucial* result.

6. This condition is realized, as we shall see, when storage is possible without significant charges (no. 136).

10. Social productivity and classical theory (76)

Classical theory holds that of all possible stationary economic states, the state[1] that arises spontaneously in the context of competition and in the absence of any State intervention is to be preferred, as it ensures the Pareto-maximization of satisfactions.

In fact, however, there is no a priori[2] reason why this stationary state should comprise precisely the conditions of maximum social productivity that a comprehensive analysis—in light of the generalized theory of social efficiency—indicates as preferable to all others. Indeed theoretical analysis shows that nothing of the sort applies.[3] Plainly, then, the classical theory, according to which competitive equilibrium corresponds to a Pareto optimum, must be subject to new reserves.[4]

---

1. It has already been pointed out that there is only one stationary state, which corresponds to given conditions of structure and to a given distribution of the ownership of capital assets (no. 49).

2. Hence, as we shall see later, it is absolutely impossible for the rate of interest to take on zero values in a competitive economy with private ownership of land (see no. 135 as well as the points already made in nos. 3 and 13 and note 1 to no. 22).

3. No. 139.

4. See the remarks already made in no. 66.

11. Social efficiency, social productivity, and interest rate policy (77)

The explanations just given of the role of interest considered from the twofold viewpoint of social efficiency and social productivity make it possible to sketch the outline of a possible interest rate policy.

Interest rate policy: the facts

The basic facts underlying every interest rate policy seem to be as follows:

1. *At every point in time* the distribution of the available income of consumers among the various consumptions then available so as to attain Pareto-maximal satisfactions corresponds to their free choice in the context of the competitive mechanism.
2. The interest rates used in the consumption sector, which determine the *distribution over time* of the various individual incomes, are *arbitrary*, in the sense that from the purely economic viewpoint there is no inherent reason for preferring one system of values to another. Only ethical or political considerations can cause any one system to be deemed preferable.
3. The structure of the production system most favorable to the Pareto-maximization of satisfactions corresponds to the free play of the competitive economy, whether the economy is considered at a given point or over time. Hence, this maximization requires that there should be *a single pure rate of interest in the production sector*.[1]
4. Of all possible stationary economic states of maximum social efficiency, the one that must be judged preferable[2] from the viewpoint of Pareto-maximization of

---

1. I.e., throughout the various production sectors.
2. Subject to what is said in no. 75.

There can in fact be cases, as has been pointed out, in which the propensity to own may be a factor militating, for Pareto-maximization of satisfactions, in favor of a non-zero technical interest rate.

But, in the opinion of the present writer, between satisfaction of the propensity to own value (as opposed to physical goods, concerning which the theorem of social productivity remains true) and satisfaction of the propensity to consume, nobody will be found ready, in a world in which there is so much misery, to yield precedence to the former rather than to satisfy *first* the propensity for consumption, even if the maximal satisfaction of this propensity leads to a decrease in the *value* available to be owned and hence to a lesser satisfaction of the

satisfactions is the one that corresponds to maximal social productivity, i.e., to the use of a zero interest rate in the production sector.

This condition does not imply, incidentally, that it suffices for the State to reduce the pure rate of interest to zero in order for this maximum to be achieved; it implies only that for the maximum to be achieved the pure interest rate must necessarily be zero.

5. *Some of the foregoing conditions*[3] *are not spontaneously fulfilled in a spontaneous competitive stationary environment.*

In any event, even supposing that structural conditions did not conflict with a zero interest rate,[4] the use throughout a stationary economy (i.e., in both the consumption and the production sectors) of a single pure interest rate and the bookkeeping necessity for individual assets and liabilities to be constantly balanced between the generations make some economic states impossible to realize.[5]

Given equal capital equipment, these economic processes differ from one corresponding to spontaneous equilibrium only as to (a) how the aggregate income is distributed among the various individuals[6] and (b) how the income of a single individual is distributed over the various periods of his life.

In reality *there is no purely economic reason why the spontaneously occurring distribution should be deemed preferable to other distributions that are excluded by the stated conditions.* Only motives of an ethical or political nature can influence the choice to be made, and there is no a priori reason why taking these motives into consideration should specifically lead us to prefer the economic state corresponding to spontaneous equilibrium, even if structural conditions therein are such[7] that social productivity is indeed maximal.[8]

---

propensity to ownership. For it is undeniable that the propensity to own is relatively artificial in character by comparison with the physical, and hence natural, character of the propensity to consume.

3. § 2 and 4 above.

4. I.e., as will be seen, that land is publicly owned and money depreciates over time in terms of the unit of account (no. 139).

5. In the case of figure 7.7 to no. 73, these economic states are those whose representative point is located outside line L. Hence, they include all states of maximal social efficiency and social productivity except those that correspond to point E_0.

6. Whether or not they belong to the same generation.

7. Note once again that this can only be so under collective land ownership (see chapter 9, "The Problem of Interest").

8. Thus in the case of figure 7.7 to no. 73, there are no a priori grounds for preferring point E_0 to any of the other points on line $\Sigma_{\rho\pi}$.

6. *The real economy can, as a first approximation, be regarded as stationary when the conditions for maximum social efficiency are fulfilled.*[9]

Such are the objective data that must be taken into consideration by any interest rate that aspires to be rational.

State intervention: ethical and political angle

Aside from the maximization of social efficiency and of social productivity the State can legitimately[10] undertake, for motives of an ethical or political nature, to bring about, by appropriate means, a certain distribution of individual incomes over time.[11]

Possible modes of State intervention

In order to bring about the distribution it deems preferable, the State can intervene, for a given psychological structure[12] and stock of capital equipment, in two different ways.

9. Suffice it to point out that in periods of monetary stability—which alone are compatible with the maximization of social efficiency (see chapter 8)—the various consumptions and productions remain, in most sectors and for periods extending over several years, more or less constant and of the same nature. Statistically speaking, the tastes of individuals in fact undergo relatively little change from one year to the next. And as for technical progress, it is generally *much lower* than a superficial examination might lead one to expect. (Research undertaken by the French Institut de Conjoncture has shown that technical progress was on average only 1.5% per year both in the period 1900–1940 and in the period 1860–1900. *Le progrès technique en France depuis 100 ans* [Paris: Imprimerie Nationale, 1944].)

10. At a given moment some individuals may feel aggrieved by such a policy, considering it to be an intolerable intrusion into their private life. Such is the case of national insurance contributors who protest against the old-age pension contributions that they are obliged to pay.

The incomplete theory of our orthodox economists of yesteryear upheld this protest, claiming that such State interference was unjustified on the grounds that it would diminish social efficiency. But in reality, the reasoning that has been set out shows that this is quite untrue and that social efficiency in the broad sense of the term—the only sense that should be retained—is in no way diminished by such a policy and that *there is no reason for the State to show preference toward the man whom a given individual represents at a specific point in time rather than to the man he will be 10 or 20 years later.* For the State, both are citizens equally worthy of regard.

11. These observations will be clarified in the appendix II, in a study of a specific case (see in particular, no. 199, § ii).

12. Of course, the State can always decide to act directly by propaganda, or by any other means, on individual psychologies (represented at a given point in time by certain satisfac-

The first would consist in keeping the spontaneous savings sector rates of interest[13] different from the single rate of interest in force in the production sector.

However, the maintenance of different rates of interest in the consumption and production sectors does not appear to be possible in an absolutely rigorous manner, at least[14] in a competitive economy of private ownership; such a policy is only conceivable in a collectivist economy in which ownership of the means of production is collective. In this case, indeed, the only financial investments available to individuals are State bonds, and the consequent separation of individual savings from the financing of real investment makes the maintenance of a double interest rate conceivable.[15,16]

The second conceivable kind of policy would entail compulsory saving of a minimum amount levied by taxation.

---

tion functions), but such modes of intervention lie outside the scope of the present considerations, which are limited to cases in which individual psychologies considered as such are *given*. Hence they apply to any psychologies whatsoever, irrespective of whether or not they have previously been affected by propaganda.

13. Which, in the context of maximum social efficiency, may be distinct from one category of individuals to another and may differ with the loan period (no. 61).

14. See no. 145 below (note 8 in particular).

15. In fact the interest rate policy in force in the USSR is implicitly based on this principle.

16. However, it is obvious that in this case the maximization of social efficiency would require a certain organization of the risk market, for collectivization of the means of production alone would not suffice to eliminate the risks inherent in the uncertainty of the future. In the event of a new technological breakthrough, for instance, no calculation, no matter how sophisticated, can provide certainty of its economic consequences. Only trial and error will enable a definitive judgment to be made, but such experimentation inevitably involves risks.

Now by extending the theory of social efficiency to the case of risks it can be shown that its maximization requires that responsibility for risks should be borne precisely by those who, with a view to possible profit, are inclined to bear them and that the cost of risk should be precisely that which corresponds to a competitive organization of the risk market.

It follows that a collectivist economy, whose citizens, in the absence of other arrangements, would have no access to the capital market, would from this point of view incur considerable losses in social efficiency.

This could be avoided only if the collectivist State financed all of its investments involving risk by a national lottery system that would enable the cost of the various risks to be borne by the same individuals who were willing to take them on.

(On this subject, readers may profitably refer to my "Le problème de la planification dans une économie collectiviste" [The problem of planning in a collectivist economy], *Kyklos: International Review for Social Sciences*, July 1947.)

Such a solution is compatible with maintenance of a single rate of interest throughout the economy and is practiced in the form of national insurance in Western economies in which the means of production may be privately owned.

Indeed, it is clear that in this case the policy adopted amounts to using for a certain number of individuals[17] a psychological interest rate different from the single technical interest rate used in the production system. This rate is the same as that which, under a free savings regime, would induce the individuals in question to make spontaneous savings equal to the compulsory savings. Naturally, it differs from one individual to another.

In fact, it can be seen that in both cases the legitimate concern of the State to bring about a certain distribution of individual income between the present and the future can equally well be satisfied, so, *in this respect, the choice between the system of private ownership of production goods and that of their collective ownership remains unaffected.*

Maximization of social productivity and temporary restriction of consumable output

As has been pointed out, the maximization of social productivity starting from a normal situation,[18] in which the equilibrium rate of interest was on the order of 4%–5%, would demand prior restriction of consumption, but it should not be concluded from this that such a policy would necessarily involve unbearable sacrifices.

It should be recalled that insofar as can be judged the transition to an interest rate close to zero would hardly require more than to maintain over 20 or 30 years the volume of investment observed during periods of prosperity.[19] This effort can therefore be borne without any hardship if the conditions of full employment are sustainable.

Moreover, it is safe to assert that if the public had a clearer perception of the considerable advantages that the expansion of capital would bring them in the future, they would save much more. Evidently, an individual saves because he has balanced what he could currently procure with his

17. Those for whom spontaneous savings at a rate equal to the rate of interest used in the production sector are inferior to compulsory savings.

18. No account is taken here of the supplementary restrictions at present exceptionally imposed on countries devastated by the war in order to rebuild their 1938 equipment stock.

19. Note 10 to no. 70.

savings against what he expects to obtain in the future with his savings plus the interest accrued. But he generally bases this comparison on the implicit assumption that the relative prices of the different goods will remain the same. Now this entails a fundamental fallacy since the accumulation of capital causes prices to fall in wage terms.[20] If his information were complete, the individual ought therefore to add to the advantage of interest accrued the increment due to the fall in prices, which genuinely constitutes additional interest. Hence we may conclude that, under present conditions, the savings of individuals are generally inferior to what they would be if they had more exact information about the future and a clearer perception of the advantages these savings would subsequently represent for them.

Moreover, it will be seen that if present structural conditions were modified[21] so as to allow a zero pure rate of interest—which is currently impossible, at least under stationary conditions—the equilibrium rate of interest would spontaneously fall to a lower value than that corresponding to current structural conditions.[22] This value might even be negative.[23,24]

Note too that if current structural conditions, suitably modified, failed spontaneously to bring about a zero or negative rate of interest, it would remain technically possible to implement a policy of increasing savings so that no generation would feel that it had been unduly sacrificed.[25]

Only if none of the abovementioned factors applied would a significant effort[26] be required to bring about the supplementary savings and would it be necessary to weigh the sacrifice imposed on the present generation against the permanent advantages that future generations would derive

20. I.e., the quotients of nominal prices by the basic unit wage.

21. It will be seen later that this modification consists in the collectivization of land and in the depreciation of money in relation to the unit of account (no. 139).

22. See no. 139.

23. Note 4 to no. 139 and no. 198, § iii. In this case, of course, spontaneous savings would be too great, and disincentive would be called for.

24. It cannot be too strongly emphasized that the insufficiency of savings observed in France over recent decades is chiefly due to the fact that the real rates corresponding to the nominal rates have been strongly negative owing to the rise in prices. It would therefore be a mistake to conclude that a zero rate would lead to absolutely *insufficient* savings.

My own opinion is that if the State were today to borrow at a zero, or even negative, rate of interest, *while guaranteeing the purchasing power of sums saved*, it would immediately receive considerable savings. Contrary to what might be thought, *the chief incentive to saving is much more the maintenance of purchasing power than the interest premium.*

25. No. 74.

26. Which in any event should not be exaggerated.

from it.[27] Such a comparative judgment could of course only be made on the basis of data that are not specifically economic, but ethical or political in nature.[28,29,30]

27. The judgment involved would in fact be analogous to that which must be made by an underpopulated society wishing to attain its optimum demographic size. For the average standard of living of such a society can only increase if its population increases, but this increase in population would entail for the present generation a restriction in its average consumption owing to the heavier burdens that would weigh upon it on account of its more numerous youth. So the State would have to balance the increased satisfactions to be obtained by future generations against the decrease in satisfactions present generations will enjoy. This judgment could be made only on the basis of arbitrary motives unconnected with economic methodology per se and belonging rather to the ethical or political orders.

28. Note that if the State has equal regard to the present generation and future generations, i.e., if it deems that all generations are equivalent from the point of view of assessing their gains and losses in satisfaction, it will inevitably be led to seek the maximization of social productivity irrespective of whatever sacrifices this may demand of the present generation. It has been seen that the necessary supplementary savings once in place enable the real aggregate income to be increased *indefinitely* for all future *generations* and that, thus, for every policy of lowering the rate of interest that has equal regard for present and future generations, the possible suffering of the present generation in order to build up the necessary supplementary savings will be superabundantly offset by the gain in satisfactions to be enjoyed by future generations.

29. At this point the reader may be inclined to object that since the theory of social productivity is applicable only under constant technical structure, technical progress might well, from one day to the next, nullify the efforts made by one generation in order to attain the maximization of social productivity in a given state of technical development.

This objection is not without weight, but it is equally applicable to every economic state. For whatever its stock of capital equipment and its pure interest rate may be, the question always arises whether a new investment ought to be made in view of the *ever-present* possibility that unexpected technical progress might lead to the abrupt abandonment of plant and equipment built up at the cost of considerable effort (see no. 62). The advantages that the new investments are expected to bring must therefore be weighed against the risks run in making them. But this is precisely the role of the risk premium that is added to the pure interest rate: to enable the risks entailed by the various possible investments to be compared and to discourage those involving significantly higher risks.

Now it must be stressed that the maximization of social productivity, which requires a zero pure interest rate, in no way implies a zero risk premium. Whether or not the pure interest rate is zero this premium must continue to play its role in the evaluation of risks.

So the technical progress factor leaves intact the thesis that it is advantageous to maximize social productivity.

30. Of course, all these statements are valid for individual psychologies assumed to be given, and it is certain that the modification of these psychologies in the direction of increasing the propensity to save by means of appropriate propaganda always remains possible.

General position of interest policy in terms of view of savings and of Investments contrasted with classical theory

The argumentation presented in this chapter and in the previous one shows the complexity of interest policy in relation to savings and investments and that, in any event, the laissez-faire solution cannot be considered the best.

It emerges that in the usual case of a nonstationary environment the State confronts a twofold problem, *ethical and political in nature and hence arbitrary in solution*:

1. Setting the level, at every point in time, of the technical interest rate, which determines the volume of investment.
2. Distributing consumable output in the best way between the generations—a policy that amounts to adopting directly or indirectly one or several psychological rates of interest different from the single technical interest rate adopted in the production sector.

For the fact is that *no a priori economic motive* can be found that would enable a position to be taken on these two problems exclusively from the classical point of view of the Pareto-maximization of satisfactions. In both cases, what is at issue is essentially a distribution problem.

It is clear how far from the classical theses our reflections have led us.

A priori, one might well wonder whether, from the viewpoint of savings and investments, spontaneous competitive equilibrium really corresponds to an intrinsic optimum and whether a competitive economy is not in fact in conflict with the realization of the highest possible level of Pareto satisfaction.[31]

These remarks show that the problem is only simple when time is disregarded. Without time, from the viewpoint of investments, intrinsic optimum and competitive equilibrium coincide.

But when time is taken into account conclusions must be more nuanced.

31. A priori, in my opinion, the coincidence of spontaneous competitive equilibrium with the intrinsic optimum alleged by classical economics ought at the very least to have been found astonishing.

Given the state of classical economic knowledge, this could only be a bold extrapolation to the field of economics of the fact that in the physical sciences spontaneous equilibria correspond to maximum situations of certain functions.

In reality, it is shown in the text that this coincidence exists only in limited form, but even so reduced it remains highly remarkable.

It remains true that the intrinsic optimum corresponds to the implementation of a spontaneous competitive economy with regard to the distribution of investments among the different industries, but it is not true that extension of the spontaneous competitive economy to the entire economy (savings and investments) automatically leads to the intrinsic optimum.

In fact, as has been seen, substantial reservations can and must be made that show how insufficiently the liberal school of economics has explored the problem of interest.

Interest and Money

Overview (78)

So far, we have examined how the interest rate is determined in a money-less account-based economy. We must now examine to what extent the existence of circulating money modifies the conclusions we have reached.

Circulating money comes in two forms: cash, represented by the notes and coins in circulation, and deposit money, represented by the banks' unbacked demand deposits.[1] As those economic agents who have bank accounts draw practically no distinction between whether their available funds take the form of cash or of demand deposits, I shall consider these two forms of money to be equivalent in first approximation, and I shall consider the aggregate quantity of both together, which will be denoted by M.[2]

As will be seen, money comprises an intermediate good *exactly like every other intermediate good*, and its utility consists in providing economic agents with purchasing power that is *always immediately available at no cost*. This utility may be called "the liquidity of money."

However, some important particularities occur in the economies we are familiar with owing to the fact that money also serves as unit of account and that the price paid for its use is therefore equal to the nominal rate of interest.[3]

---

1. The aggregate of *unbacked* demand deposits is equal to the excess of demand deposits over cash in vault plus reserves at the Central Bank; it will be seen (no. 91) that the existence of unbacked demand deposits amounts to actual creation of money by the banks.

2. See the remarks already made in note 2 to no. 6.

3. See nos. 6, 7, 8, 9, and 81 below.

The first part of this chapter will specify the value of the service rendered by money and the factors influencing how the various economic agents determine their money balances.

In the second part an overall description of the economic mechanism will be given that will endeavor to highlight the main sub-mechanisms in which the rate of interest plays a role.

The third part will examine what determines the rate of interest, and for the sake of clarity, this examination will comprise two successive stages corresponding respectively to processes in dynamic equilibrium and in dynamic disequilibrium.

Once this overall view has been put in place, a fourth part will analyze some exceptionally interesting aspects of the link between the theory of interest, the special theory of money, and the general theory of prices. One key issue will be how far the rate of interest can really play the role of regulator needed to achieve stable equilibrium in our monetary economies.

For simplicity, the context of inconvertible money will generally be adopted.

What is about to be set out concerns one of the hardest subjects in economics, namely the link between the classical theory of the equilibrium of an account-based economy—where the rate of interest serves as the regulating parameter of savings and investment—and the theory of money and price levels—where the rate of interest can also be considered as the price paid for the use of money.

Between these two theories there is a *very close interdependence* that economists have not yet succeeded in *fully elucidating* and that has been the subject of impassioned debate in recent years. This alone shows how difficult the question is. For this reason, the reader is requested to redouble his attention and is advised that a second reading may be necessary if he is to arrive at full understanding.[4]

---

4. In order to keep this presentation within reasonable limits I have systematically striven, here more than elsewhere, to confine myself to the essential. So *the concision of the following brief presentation is intentional* and has cost much effort and sacrifice, as I have had to resist the constant temptation to be led into highly interesting details about the theories properly so-called of money and of economic cycles, since in economics all problems are closely interdependent, and I was therefore constantly brought up against the questions that have been most discussed by the world's economists in recent years.

But I have taken the view that each point must come in its own time and that a succinct presentation of a general theory of interest absolutely excluded analysis, even stripped to the basics, of monetary disturbances or of economic cycles.

A. *Liquidity Premium of Money*

1. Working capital (79)

I shall use the term *the working capital of an economic agent* to denote the sum of money that he uses to balance over time his income and expenditure occurring at different points.

For instance, a worker who each week earns and spends 700 francs must distribute his weekly pay over the seven days, and if his daily expenditure amounts to 100 francs, his working capital will present the successive values of 700, 600, 500, 400, 300, 200, 100 francs, and will then begin anew the cycle of the same values on the different days of the following week and so on, so that its mean value will be equal to $2,800 \div 7 = 400$ francs.

The working capital of an economic agent generally includes two components respectively intended to enable him

1. to balance his normal receipts and expenditure over time; and
2. to take advantage of opportunities he may unexpectedly encounter or to cope with unforeseen needs. What are involved here are merely possibilities, but they are *normal* possibilities, in the sense that their likelihood must be assumed to remain relatively constant over time.

Let M_R^Y be the average working capital of an economic agent (Y): this quantity can be seen to be a certain function[1] of the market prices $a, b, \ldots, c$, and it is clear that this function is necessarily homogeneous in the sense that, *all other things being equal*,[2] the sum M_R^Y must be n times greater if all prices are n times higher.

So if we use P to denote the price index, we may write

(1)
$$M_R^Y = Pf\left(\frac{a}{P}, \frac{b}{P}, \ldots, \frac{c}{P}\right),$$

where f is a certain function of real prices. Let us write

---

1. Which of course depends on other factors such as the forecasts of individual (Y).

2. *Particularly with regard to the market's dynamic development* (the development of prices being considered here in relative terms).

(2) $$M_R^Y = PK_R^Y,$$

so that K_R^Y represents a magnitude independent of the absolute price level.[3]

If we use M_R to denote the total sum

(3) $$M_R = \sum_Y M_R^Y$$

of working capital we may then write that

(4) $$M_R = PK_R,$$

where K_R stands for the total sum, *independent* of price levels, of working capital reckoned in real terms.

---

3. It is therefore a constant with regard to this level, *but it is not an intrinsic constant depending only on the economy's structural characteristics, since it also depends on the dynamic development of the economy.*

2. Speculative reserve (80)

In addition to his working capital, every economic agent holds a certain amount of money that may be called a speculative reserve or hoard and that is intended to enable him

1. to cope with exceptional circumstances,[1] and
2. to take advantage of the price and interest rate disparities that constantly occur over time on account of the unpredictability and inertia of various economic parameters.[2]

These motives are both in constant play, but while the former requires a sum whose real value is usually subject to little variation, the latter may lead to considerable variations in the real value of the speculative reserve.

For instance, if the economic agent in question foresees a fall in prices, it will be in his interests to postpone certain purchases; this will induce him to store money, i.e., to hoard, raising his real speculative money balance above its normal value.

As before, if we use M_T^Y to denote the hoarded funds of economic agent (Y), we can write

(1)
$$M_T^Y = PK_T^Y,$$

where K_T^Y is a magnitude independent of the absolute price level.[3]

If we write

(2)
$$K_T = \Sigma_Y K_T^Y,$$

---

1. This applies, for instance, to the worker who foresees possible redundancy and therefore seeks to increase the liquid resources he has available.

2. By postponing his purchases.

This motive may come into play in two quite distinct cases. Taking the example of an expected price variation, in the first case a fall in prices is foreseen by the market as a whole, while in the second a fall is foreseen only by the economic agent we are considering. So too, a variation in the long-term rate of interest may be foreseen either by the market as a whole or by the economic agent alone (see no. 30).

3. *But which, unfortunately, depends on the observed and foreseen variations in that level.*

we also have

(3) $M_T = PK_T,$

where K_T is a quantity *independent* of price level P representing the real value of all speculative reserves in the aggregate.

It should be noted that according to these definitions what distinguishes hoarding is not the fact of holding money, but the fact that the money held is earmarked for speculative reserve purposes.

Finally, if we use M^Y to denote the total money balance of economic agent (Y) and M to denote the total amount of money, including both cash and demand deposits, we have

(4) $M^Y = M_R^Y + M_T^Y$

with

(5) $M^Y = P(K_R^Y + K_T^Y)$

and

(6) $M = M_R + M_T$

with

(7) $M = P(K_R + K_T).$

3. Interest as price paid for use of money (81)

It has been seen[1] that for any good (A) we have, in equilibrium,

$$(1) \qquad\qquad a = \bar{i}\bar{a} - \frac{d\bar{a}}{dt},$$

in other words, the price paid for the use of a good is equal to the sum of (a) the interest on its value and (b) its value-loss.

In the case of the money ($\bar{M}$) of the monetary economies we are familiar with, whose price $\bar{m}$ is by definition equal to unity, this equation becomes

$$(2) \qquad\qquad m = i;$$

in other words, the nominal price m paid in the market for the use of money is equal to the market's nominal rate of interest.[2]

As money can be stored without appreciable expense, it is clear that the price paid for its use cannot be negative since, rather than lending money at a negative price, it would always be in one's interests simply to retain it. It is for this reason that in our monetary economies, in which the unit of account is identical to the unit of money, the nominal interest rate i cannot become negative either.[3]

---

1. No. 33.

2. The rationale of this use-value will be analyzed in no. 82.

3. I shall return to this question later. For the present, suffice it to remark that this property constitutes in any event a *crucial* point in any discussion of the rationale of interest, a discussion that seeks to discover why the observed nominal interest rate has always had positive values in the various known economies (see what has already been said in nos. 3, 14, and 26).

4. Liquidity preference and money balances (82)

The term *liquidity preference* will be used to denote the whole array of motives that incline economic agents to hold money.[1]

As we have just seen, these motives include both the need to balance receipts and expenditure and the desire to take advantage of the opportunities, foreseen and unforeseen, arising from price movements.

Yet whatever the weight of these motives, *the decision to hold money rather than to lend it remains in appearance a disadvantageous one* as long as the pure interest rate is positive. For it is not inconceivable, at least a priori, for economic agents to lend out their money balances at the market rate while calling in their loans as and when needed.

So there remains a circumstance to be explained that, as Professor Hicks has underlined in a noteworthy article,[2] constitutes the key point of the pure theory of money. The issue is to explain why economic agents prefer to store assets in the form of sterile money[3] rather than to acquire financial assets that could provide them with pure interest,[4] and exactly how the value of this monetary asset stock is determined; in other words, what must be shown is why the specific good comprised by the sum of money ($\overline{M}$) has use-value m and how the quantity held by each economic agent is determined.

It is not really difficult to perceive the reasons why it is preferable to keep liquid assets in the form of money. For if an economic agent (X) kept all his assets invested in capital, it would be constantly necessary for him, in order to have available the exact purchasing power necessary for his expenditure, either to liquidate a part of his assets or to make new investments, according to whether his net income at each point in time was negative or positive. It is easy to see how disadvantageous such a practice would be to him. On the one hand it would involve continual trouble and waste of time representing a very high management cost,[5] and on the other it would call for either a selection of financial investments able to be made or unmade by tiny fractions, or else recourse to a loan. Now such in-

1. Whether in the form of demand deposits or of cash (see no. 78).

2. J. R. Hicks, "A Suggestion for Simplifying the Theory of Money," *Economica*, February 1935.

3. Or at least apparently sterile.

4. Equal to the value-yield minus premiums for depreciation, estimated-risk, and cost-of-risk, and plus the monetary and capital premiums (no. 33, equation [7]).

5. Nos. 10 and 11.

vestments either do not exist or, where they do, yield only a very low pure rate of interest and, in any event, entail costs[6] that are relatively very high, so that in the long run such investments would be equivalent to a negative pure rate of interest and hence would be less profitable than simply holding money. Similarly, recourse to a loan could only be had at a rate of interest higher than the market's pure rate of interest by an amount equal to the lender's risk and management costs. This rate would be much higher than the net interest rates that agent (X) obtains by investing at a rate of interest equal to the market's pure rate of interest less (X)'s management costs.

It can thus be seen that *the reason why economic agents retain money balances is on account of the costs*, which may be extremely high, *of acquiring or liquidating financial assets or obtaining loans as and when needed. Thus it can be seen that money is an intermediate good needed to balance receipts and expenditure in a world in which credit availability is limited by its associated costs.*

This shows that the retention of monetary capital offers certain permanent advantages[7] the value of which per unit of time and relative to the quantity of monetary capital held may be called the *use-value of money*, or, indeed, in the expression consecrated since the work of Keynes, "*the liquidity premium of money.*"[8]

Thus, if we say that the liquidity premium of money for an individual (X) holding an average monetary capital of 10,000 francs is 50% per year, this simply means that the advantages obtained by the liquidity of this capital are worth 5,000 francs per year, or alternatively that the cost of negotiating financial assets possessed, or of borrowing from third parties in order to obtain the necessary day-to-day purchasing power,[9] would represent a value of 5,000 francs per year.

Of course, as with every asset, a distinction should be made here between the *mean* liquidity premium, which applies to the whole of the average money balance we have been considering, and the *marginal* liquidity premium, which corresponds to the annual value of the advantages obtained by the last franc of the average money balance, and it can easily be verified that, since the costs entailed by lending, liquidating, or borrowing

6. Bank charges.

7. These consist in avoiding (a) very high liquidation or borrowing costs and (b) subjective inconvenience.

8. It will be seen later that money is not the only asset to enjoy a liquidity premium (no. 84).

9. For regular or exceptional purchases.

are deemed *as a first approximation* to be independent of the amounts involved,[10] the marginal liquidity premium l_M of the average money balance M is a decreasing function

(1) $$l_M = l_M(M)$$

of this balance.

It is clear that the value of the advantages obtained by a supplementary money balance of 100 francs when the average balance is already of 10,000 francs is much lower than when the average holding value is zero. If, for instance, the consumer thoughtlessly invests all he has in financial assets, "he is practically certain to be inconvenienced as soon as his first needs make themselves felt, and some of these may be essential and may not even allow the time to obtain credit. The retention of a simple sum of 100 francs will thus already spare him countless minor inconveniences enabling him to have lunch, to return home by bus, buy a newspaper, give a tip, etc."[11] and this balance may have for him a far superior annual value, e.g., 500 francs, which would represent a 500% liquidity premium. On the other hand, if his average balance is already high in value, e.g., 100,000 francs, a supplementary balance of 100 francs will obviously be of only slight value to him, on the order of a few percent or per mille.[12]

It then becomes easy to see what determines the amount of the average balance M_E in equilibrium of an economic agent. For as long as the marginal liquidity premium l_M of the average balance is greater than the

10. Thus, in the case of a stock market investment, these costs include (a) the fixed costs (time lost in choosing the right investment, in giving instructions, in correspondence and in inconveniences of every kind) and (b) the proportional costs (the actual stock market purchase costs); but it is clear, given the figures involved, that the latter may be ignored by comparison with the former, at least as a first approximation.

11. R. Florin, *Théorie des encaisses et théorie de l'intérêt* [The theory of money balances and the theory of interest], typed MS, 1945, p. 5.

12. It is easy to add precision to these intuitive but obviously somewhat vague indications by taking a specific example.

Let us, for instance, consider an economic agent who receives a continuous stream of net income, each receipt being equal to R (fig. 8.1) per unit of time, and let us suppose that he invests the money so received only at intervals of time equal to T, when his money balance attains a certain value. Under these conditions, the curve representing his money balance as a function of time will comprise a series of linear segments and will oscillate between values 0 and RT, so that its mean value will be

(1) $$M = \frac{RT}{2}.$$

pure rate of interest, it is in the interests of the agent to keep his capital
in the form of money. This money balance is "barren" only in appearance,
for in reality it yields advantages per unit of time whose value is equal to
the liquidity premium. But when the liquidity premium falls below the
pure rate of interest, it becomes more profitable to invest available capital
instead of keeping it in the form of money. *The optimal situation corresponding to equilibrium is achieved when the amount of money held is such
that its marginal liquidity premium is equal to the pure rate of interest.*[13]

It can thus be seen that the use of money is profitable but that no price
is directly paid for it. Its cost is an *indirect* result of the loss of the interest

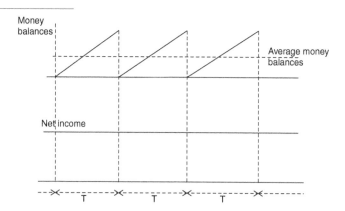

FIGURE 8.1 FOOTNOTE

If we then denote by $F(V)$ the costs corresponding to an investment of value V, the cost
of the investment per unit of time will be equal to $\dfrac{F(RT)}{T}$ or in other terms $\dfrac{RF(2M)}{2M}$. If the
mean balance increases by ΔM, the saving per unit of time, being equal to the marginal liquidity premium of the average balance, will be equal to the derivative of this quantity, giving us

(2)
$$l_M = -R\frac{d}{dM}\frac{F(2M)}{2M}.$$

If F is constant, we shall have

(3)
$$l_M = \frac{RF}{2M^2},$$

which is indeed a decreasing function of balance M.

This extremely simple example has the advantage of making the matter very easy to
understand and of showing how a rigorous general theory of liquidity may be constructed.

13. In the case of the example examined in note 12 above, balance M_E, held in equilibrium, will naturally be determined by the equation

242

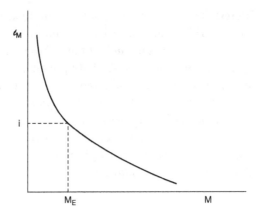

FIGURE 8.2

(1)
$$-R\frac{d}{dM}\frac{F(2M)}{2M}=i.$$

This equation can easily be rediscovered. Let C be the capital held by the agent in question. At the end of each period T, we have

(2)
$$\Delta C = iTC_0 + RT - F(RT),$$

where C_0 denotes the capital held at the start of period T. This equation gives

(3)
$$\frac{\Delta C}{T} = iC_0 + R - R\frac{F(2M)}{2M}.$$

It might be tempting to compare as a first approximation the ratio $\frac{\Delta C}{T}$ to the derivative $\frac{dC}{dt}$, but such an approximation would amount to supposing that income R is invested in a continuous manner, whereas in reality the investment is discontinuous, and to taking for dC too great a value of the amount of interest on the balance during each period T, approximately equal to the product iM of its average value M by the market's pure rate of interest. In fact, we clearly ought to write

(4)
$$\frac{dC}{dt} = iC + R - R\frac{F(2M)}{2M} - iM.$$

Thus the most advantageous situation will be obtained when the growth of capital C is most rapid, i.e., when the sum

(5)
$$R\frac{F(2M)}{2M} + iM$$

that would have been earned if the money held had been invested. Equilibrium occurs when the marginal value of liquidity, the service rendered by the money, is precisely equal to the interest lost and the balance is increased or decreased depending on whether its marginal liquidity premium is or is not greater than the market interest rate.

Determination of money balances and imperfect competition

In the real world, of course, the foregoing estimates can only be approximate, but it emerges from this reasoning that in every case the determination of their money balances by the various economic agents is due to a more or less unconscious economic calculation in which the marginal liquidity premium of the funds is weighed against the market's pure rate of interest. As a rule, the components of this calculation are the inequality of receipts and expenditure, the uncertainty of the future, expected income

---

is at its lowest, a point that will be reached when we have

(6)
$$\frac{d}{dM}\left(R\,\frac{F(2M)}{2M} - iM\right) = 0,$$

an equation equivalent to equation (1) for a market interest rate i assumed to be given.

So, should F be a constant, the size of the balance will be determined by the equation

$$\frac{RF}{2M^2} = i.$$

Hence, if we have

$R = 100{,}000$ francs, $F = 200$ francs, $i = 5\%$,

we shall have

$$M = 14{,}000 \text{ francs.}$$

This shows that the average money balance enjoys significant value as a result of the costs of financial investment, even if these costs are fairly low.

As we have

$$\frac{M}{R} = \sqrt{\frac{F}{2iR}},$$

it can be seen that in the case in question the ratio of the average money balance to annual income decreases as the income itself becomes greater. This result holds good even if F, increasing with income R, grows less rapidly than R. This fact seems to be of general application.

and expenditure and their expected probability, the costs of investment in financial assets, liquidation costs, loan costs, and the conditions of imperfect competition.[14]

Rationale of the liquidity premium and foresight

It is clear that the liquidity premium of money is exclusively due to the costs of investing, selling, or borrowing[15] and that, notwithstanding the opinion of some writers,[16] it would continue to exist even if foresight were perfect. In this case, speculative reserves would obviously be zero, but working capital would remain.[17,18]

Working capital and interest rates

Cases may occur in which the real working capital held by an economic agent, if not actually independent of the rate of interest, is only very tenuously dependent on it. Thus in the case of the worker considered in no. 79, it is quite certain that, *within the usual range of interest rate levels*, the working capital remains entirely unaffected by any variation in this rate.

Only when the working capital reaches high levels or when there are substantial intervals between receipt of income and its expenditure does the interest rate play an important role in its determination.

So our overall conclusion is that the sum total of the real working capital of the various economic agents is closely connected to the interest rate, although its influence in some cases is slight or even negligible.

14. Needless to say, the present explanations are but summary indications, quite insufficient to establish a general theory of liquidity. Indeed, the text has been limited to only those explanations that are indispensable for the general understanding of the present study.

15. Whether these costs correspond to real outgoings or to the opportunity costs due to diverse inconveniences (loss of time, anxiety, etc.).

16. P. N. Rosenstein-Rodan, "The Coordination of the General Theories of Money and Price," *Economica*, August 1936.

17. Only if costs were zero and foresight were perfect would the liquidity premium of money be nil. In that case, money would be an unwanted good whose use-value and hence price would be zero. Neither could it in that case act as unit of account for expressing the various prices; it would be necessary to use some other commodity as a reference—one whose value was not zero.

18. Of course, it follows from these observations that the liquidity premium corresponding to a given money balance is greater, as foresight is less perfect.

Moreover, as the future can never be fully foreseen, it is clear that if it cost nothing to hold money, it would be worthwhile to have very substantial, if not infinite, working capital, which alone would enable the agent to make the most of every opportunity, even those most unlikely to arise in practice. It must be inferred that the demand for money to serve as working capital increases sharply as the rate of interest falls.

Speculative reserves and interest rates

Naturally, for given forecasts concerning the probable development of prices, interest rates, and the economic situation in general, the speculative reserves that are built up to cope with the possibility of unusual events or to take advantage of interest rate or price disparities will be greater as the rate of interest is lower.

Representative curve of aggregate demand for money balances

We have seen that the money balance of a given economic agent is a well-determined function of the pure rate of interest. By aggregating the functions relating to the different economic agents, the total demand for money balances as a function of the rate of interest is obtained. It follows from the foregoing observations that this demand can be represented as in figure 8.3 and that it becomes very great, if not infinite, for a zero rate.[19]

Of course, as the demand for money balances is itself proportionate to the price level,[20] it may be concluded that figure 8.3 *also represents desired money balances in real terms*.

Representative curve of demand for new money

Instead of representing the total desired money balances of economic agents, it is possible to consider only the demand for new balances arising

---

19. The rate of interest considered here is of course the pure rate of interest that the economic agent in question must accept in order to borrow in the market. It is thus equal to the stipulated interest rate minus—in particular—the risk premium corresponding to the risks as assessed by the most favorable lender (nos. 29 and 33). Only in the event that the borrower is very well established can this risk premium be considered negligible.

20. No. 80.

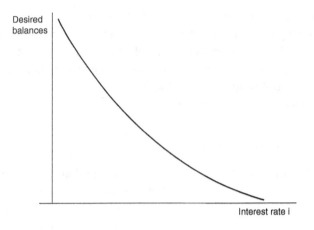

FIGURE 8.3

during a given period T, of which the total is equal to TR_E.[21] This of course gives us

(2) $$M^{n+1} = M^n + TR_E^n,$$ [22]

using M^n to denote the balance at the beginning of period T_n.

It can be seen that the representative curve of the new balances TR_E^n can be deduced from the representative curve of total balances M^{n+1} by a translation parallel to the y-axis of amplitude equal to M^n.

Here again the real demand for new balances seems to be equally well represented by figure 8.4.

Theoretical representation

It is easy to see how the consideration of money can be introduced into the general theory of equilibrium. For instance, let

(3) $$S = S(A,B,\ldots,C)$$

be the satisfaction function of an individual (X), and let R be his income. By assuming that his expenditure equals his receipts per unit of time, we shall have

21. The notations are from no. 37.
22. An equation parallel to equation (1) of no. 48.

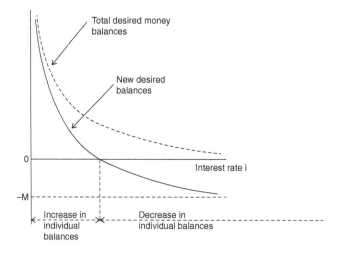

FIGURE 8.4

(4) $$aA + bB + \ldots + cC + iM = R,$$

since to hold balances M costs a sum iM per unit of time.[23]
   Following from this we shall have

(5) $$l(M,A,B, \ldots ,C,a,b, \ldots , c) = i,$$

using l to denote the marginal liquidity premium of money. The economic behavior of individual (X) results almost instinctively in the maximization of the S function under constraints (4) and (5), where prices a, b, c, and i are assumed to be given. We then find the following conditions:[24]

---

23. Assuming that income R here considered includes interest on the total capital owned.
   Thus, for instance, in the event that an individual receives wages X and owns capital T (including money), we have

$$aA + bB + \ldots + cC = X + i(T - M),$$

i.e.,

$$aA + bB + \ldots + cC + iM = X + iT = R.$$

24. According to the general theory of constrained maxima, the maximization conditions for S under conditions (4) and (5) can in fact be obtained by maximizing the function

$$S(A,B, \ldots ,C) - \lambda(aA + bB + \ldots + cC + iM - R) - \mu[l\,(M,A,B, \ldots , C,a,b, \ldots ,c) - i],$$

$$
\textbf{(6)} \qquad \dfrac{\dfrac{\partial S}{\partial A}}{a - i\dfrac{\dfrac{\partial A}{\partial l}}{\dfrac{\partial M}{}}} = \dfrac{\dfrac{\partial S}{\partial B}}{b - i\dfrac{\dfrac{\partial B}{\partial l}}{\dfrac{\partial M}{}}} = \ldots = \dfrac{\dfrac{\partial S}{\partial C}}{c - i\dfrac{\dfrac{\partial C}{\partial l}}{\dfrac{\partial M}{}}}.
$$

As the money balance M is generally low in value in comparison with annual income, and as annual interest rate levels are generally low, it follows that, *as a first approximation*, conditions (5) and (6) are reduced to the classical conditions

$$
\textbf{(7)} \qquad aA + bB + \ldots + cC = R,
$$

$$
\textbf{(8)} \qquad \dfrac{\dfrac{\partial S}{\partial A}}{a} = \dfrac{\dfrac{\partial S}{\partial B}}{b} = \ldots = \dfrac{\dfrac{\partial S}{\partial C}}{c},
$$

which are independent of money.[25]

The generalized case of a monetary economy

In its most general form, the monetary economy has a unit of account that is distinct from the unit of circulating money.[26] So the unit of money $(\overline{M})$ has a price $\overline{m}$, and its use-value m is expressed, in equilibrium, like that of any good, by the equation

$$
\textbf{(9)} \qquad m = i\overline{m} - \dfrac{d\overline{m}}{dt}.
$$

---

where λ and μ are deemed to be constants.

We then find the equations

$$
\textbf{(2)} \qquad \dfrac{\partial S}{\partial A} - \lambda a - \mu\dfrac{\partial l}{\partial A} = 0 \qquad \dfrac{\partial S}{\partial C} - \lambda c - \mu\dfrac{\partial l}{\partial C} = 0,
$$

$$
\textbf{(3)} \qquad -\lambda i - \mu\dfrac{\partial l}{\partial M} = 0,
$$

whence, eliminating of λ and μ, come the conditions of (6).

25. We shall see later on what happens when rate i assumes very low levels and money balances M become very great (no. 97).

26. No. 6.

The marginal liquidity premium of money represents, in accordance with the definition given above, the value of the advantages pcr unit of time of holding a sum of money whose overall value is one unit of account. Thus, the value of the advantages of holding one monetary unit is equal to the product $\overline{m}l_M$ so that we have in equilibrium

$$(10) \qquad\qquad l_M = \frac{m}{\overline{m}},$$

since m represents the market price paid for the use of one monetary unit. Thus, in equilibrium we have

$$(11) \qquad\qquad l_M = i - \frac{\dfrac{d\overline{m}}{dt}}{\overline{m}}.$$

It can be seen that *in the most general case, in equilibrium, the liquidity premium of money is not equal to the pure rate of interest, but to the excess of the latter over the relative rate of increase in the nominal price of money. Only when the unit of account is precisely equal to the unit of money is the liquidity premium of money in equilibrium equal to the pure interest rate.*

This finding is intuitive, for in the commonest case it is naturally necessary to add to the advantages of liquidity those due to the appreciation $\dfrac{\dfrac{d\overline{m}}{dt}}{\overline{m}}$ of money so that investment in money is truly comparable to an investment in the market at pure interest rate i.[27]

The representative curve of the aggregate demand for money balances as a function of the market rate of interest i thereupon assumes, both in

27. It should be noted that *unlike the rate of interest (no. 19), the liquidity premium is an intrinsic magnitude independent of the unit of value chosen.* Thus, for instance, we have for its expression in wage terms

$$(1) \qquad l_M'' = i'' - \frac{\dfrac{d\overline{m}''}{dt}}{\overline{m}''} = \left(i - \frac{\dfrac{ds}{dt}}{s}\right) - \left(\frac{\dfrac{d\overline{m}}{dt}}{\overline{m}} - \frac{\dfrac{ds}{dt}}{s}\right) = i - \frac{\dfrac{d\overline{m}}{dt}}{\overline{m}},$$

i.e., ultimately

$$(2) \qquad\qquad l_M'' = l_M.$$

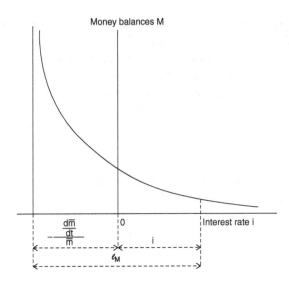

FIGURE 8.5

real and nominal terms, the shape indicated in figure 8.5, and it can be seen that for a given nominal rate of interest, desired balances fall sharply in real terms when money depreciates in nominal terms.

Moreover, it can be immediately verified that the conditions of the individual equilibrium become

$$(12) \qquad aA + bB + \ldots + cC + \left(i - \frac{\dfrac{d\overline{m}}{dt}}{\overline{m}} \right) M = R,$$

$$(13) \qquad l(M, A, B, \ldots, C, a, b, \ldots, c) = i - \frac{\dfrac{d\overline{m}}{dt}}{\overline{m}},$$

$$(14) \qquad \frac{\dfrac{\partial S}{\partial A}}{a - \left(i - \dfrac{\frac{d\overline{m}}{dt}}{\overline{m}} \right) \dfrac{\frac{\partial l}{\partial A}}{\frac{\partial l}{\partial M}}} = \frac{\dfrac{\partial S}{\partial B}}{b - \left(i - \dfrac{\frac{d\overline{m}}{dt}}{\overline{m}} \right) \dfrac{\frac{\partial l}{\partial B}}{\frac{\partial l}{\partial M}}} = \ldots = \frac{\dfrac{\partial S}{\partial C}}{c - \left(i - \dfrac{\frac{d\overline{m}}{dt}}{\overline{m}} \right) \dfrac{\frac{\partial l}{\partial C}}{\frac{\partial l}{\partial M}}}.$$

These equations are, of course, *intrinsic* equations, which do not depend on the unit of account used.[28]

28. It is worth emphasizing that *only* these equations are intrinsic in character, independent of the particular unit of account chosen as unit of value. Equations (4), (5), and (6) are in fact only applicable when the value of the unit of account is not haphazard but is identical to that of the circulating money. Thus, if the hourly wage of unskilled labor is taken as unit of account, equation (12) becomes

(1)
$$a''A + b''B + \ldots + c''C + \left(i'' - \frac{\frac{d\overline{m}''}{dt}}{\overline{m}''}\right)M'' = R'',$$

where $a'', b'', \ldots, c'', i'', \overline{m}'', M'', R''$ respectively denote prices, the pure rate of interest, the price of money, the value of money balances, and the value of income all expressed in wage terms.

In the specific case of our conventional monetary economies, we have

(2)
$$\overline{m} = 1, \quad \overline{m}'' = \frac{1}{s},$$

hence

(3)
$$a''A + b''B + \ldots + c''C + \left(i'' - \frac{\frac{ds}{dt}}{s}\right)M'' = R'',$$

and not the incorrect equation

(4)
$$a''A + b''B + \ldots + c''C + i''M'' = R'',$$

which one might be tempted to derive from equation (4), which is not intrinsic, i.e., it depends on the units used.

B. General Structure of the Economy

General outline of the economic mechanism (83)

As we have seen, the aggregate income R_D distributed to consumers in the form of money is divided by them into three parts: the first part R_C is devoted to the purchase of final goods (consumed income), the second part R_E to the increase of money balances (increased working capital and hoarding), and the third to the purchase of financial assets[1] (invested income[2]).

The first part acts to determine the market demand[3] for final goods and, by balancing what the firms supply, to determine the prices and quantities produced of these goods. The notations P_D and Q_D will be used to denote, respectively, the price index and the business activity index in the final goods sector.

The second part corresponds to variations in individual money balances. It is, of course, a function of price levels, of interest rates, and of the expected development of both.[4]

The third part is intended for the purchase of debt instruments on the securities market, also called the financial market. If only aggregate demand is considered, as will be the case here, and if it is supposed, for the sake of simplicity, that firms do not themselves hold financial assets, the supply and demand of existing financial assets, whatever the price may

1. Comprising corporate debt instruments. This part is usually, but *improperly*, termed "supply of capital." *In reality it is* money *that is supplied and* capital *or* financial assets *that are demanded.*

In order to study dynamic disequilibrium, therefore, it would be preferable from the viewpoint both of logic and of conformity with the facts to invert the classical terminology as hitherto used in the present work (chapter 5, "Determination of the Equilibrium Rate of Interest on Capital in an Account-Based Economy"). However, to avoid the risk of confusion I shall retain the classical definitions of supply and demand of capital, simply adding the notion of supply and demand of financial assets. Following this terminology, the demand for and supply of financial assets will correspond respectively to the supply of and the demand for capital in the classic sense.

2. Following the notations of no. 37 and disregarding in first approximation the existence of the State.

3. This demand is naturally represented by the various demand curves corresponding to the relevant aggregate amount of the consumption expenditure R.

4. As follows from the foregoing explanations. Further clarifications will be made at several points later in the text (nos. 85 and 98 in particular).

be, are exactly balanced in equilibrium and the aggregate demand relates exclusively to new issues.

The net demand for new financial assets balances the supply of new share or bond issues on the part of firms. For in tandem with their productive activity, firms are constantly anxious to replace their outworn or out-of-date equipment. For this reason, as we have seen,[5] they consider the technical interest rates corresponding to the various possible investments, so that for each interest rate they are disposed to borrow a certain capital for real investment purposes. This is what determines the supply of new securities. Thereupon, the interaction of the supply and demand of financial assets determines in the long term the volume of shares and bonds issued and the interest rates.

Firms devote the funds thus levied to new real investments and thus determine the market demand for intermediate goods.

The combination of this demand and the supply of equipment by firms determines the prices and quantities produced of the various production goods. The indices of price and activity levels in the intermediate goods sector will be denoted respectively by P_I and Q_I.[6]

---

5. Nos. 44, 45, and 46.

6. The distinction between savings, investment in financial assets [French *placement*], and real investment in capital goods [French *investissement*] is often neglected. Yet the distinction is essential and absolutely necessary in order to understand how the economy works.

For it is possible to have savings without financial investment and hence without investment in equipment, and there can be financial investment, and therefore investment in equipment, without savings (see the explanations given in no. 37). Savings depend essentially on the psychological dispositions of consumers, whereas real investment in capital depends on the psychological dispositions of firms. These dispositions cannot by any means be considered as reducible to one another. Real investment is not made for the pleasure of investing, but in order to take advantage of a production situation deemed favorable. Whether savings are abundant or not, and hence whether the instantaneous interest rate is low or high, is a circumstance that cannot be decisive on its own, since investment will only occur if the marginal productivity expected from capital is high enough to exceed this rate. Hence, in a period of depression, money is cheap (the rate of interest is low), but the marginal productivity expected from capital is still lower, if not negative, with the result that there is no real investment even though, as a matter of fact, there may be very abundant savings (see the explanations given on this subject in no. 53).

In reality, the propensity to save, the propensity to invest in financial assets, and the propensity to invest in real capital are three distinct notions. In equilibrium, of course, financial investment is equal to real investment, but the motives for financial investment are quite different from those for real investment.

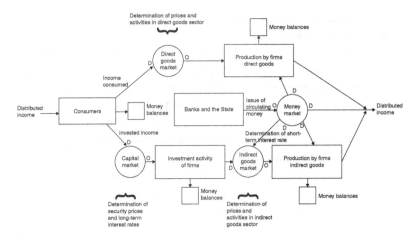

FIGURE 8.6 Outline of circulation of money flows in the economy
Arrows indicate direction of money flows.
"O" indicates the origin of supplies, and "D" indicates the origin of demands.
On the "capital market" claims in capital are supplied and demanded.
"Issue of circulating money" may be positive or negative.

In the same way, there may be issues[7] of money either by the State in the form of cash or by the banks in the form of demand deposits. These issues have a direct or indirect influence on the money market where money is lent. Discounting bills of exchange by the banks on this market amounts to placing the corresponding sums at the disposal of the firms prior to the maturity of the bills discounted. Thus, the discount operation is tantamount to lending money for the period between the discount date and the maturity date.

Naturally, at every level, monetary outflows are equal to monetary inflows minus the increase in money balances. Figure 8.6 represents this circulation in diagrammatic form.

For the sake of simplicity, it will be assumed in part (a) of what follows that banks have no unbacked demand deposits.[8] It will be granted that demand deposits exist and that the banks engage in credit operations, notably discount operations, but it will be assumed that the aggregate of each

7. Negative or positive.

8. For the sake of simplicity, all issues of money have been represented as passing by the money market.

bank's demand deposits is backed by an equal amount of cash in vault or in reserve, available on demand, at the central bank.

In part (b) the more complex case will be examined in which the banks are able to issue unbacked demand deposits. In this case, it will be seen that the exercise of this power introduces into the theoretical discussion, especially from the point of view of the discount rate, difficulties that require specific examination.

(a) 100% backing of demand deposits

1. Value-yields and pure interest rate (84)

Liquidity premiums of the various assets

While money is of course the only asset having perfect liquidity, i.e., that is immediately available at no cost, other assets are characterized by variable liquidity depending on the various costs involved in their *immediate* liquidation.[1] For instance, since the cost of selling housing at short notice can be very high, the liquidity of a house is very low by comparison with the liquidity of Treasury bonds, which can be swiftly realized at little cost by means of discount.

Here again, the term *marginal liquidity premium* of any asset can be used for the value per unit of time of the liquidity advantages provided by holding one further value unit of this asset.

Naturally, this liquidity premium will always be lower than that of money because the liquidity advantages provided by any asset are necessarily lower than those offered by money itself.[2]

---

1. Let a be the market value of an asset A and let us suppose that the probable value, net of all costs, that can be derived by the immediate realization of A is $a' < a$ (because of the imperfection of the market and the costs entailed by immediate liquidation). The liquidity of asset A can be characterized by a liquidity coefficient K such that

$$K = \frac{a'}{a}.$$

Perfect liquidity is characterized by a value equal to the unit of the liquidity coefficient; zero liquidity ($a' = 0$) is characterised by a zero value for this coefficient.

2. The liquidity advantages of a given asset in fact become closer to those of money as the cost F of *immediate* realization of this asset becomes lower. If the corresponding annual liquidity premiums are denoted by l and l_M we can conclude that

$$l = l_M - pF,$$

where p denotes the probability, calculated over a year, of using the asset in question as ready money.

Naturally, this equation is valid only when the product pF is less than the premium l_M. If it were greater, we could safely conclude that the liquidity premium l was zero.

All these explanations bring out the complexity of the notion of liquidity and the sort of difficulties presented by its analysis. Unfortunately, the limited scope of the present study makes it impossible to enter into greater detail here.

Storage and management costs of the various assets

It is a fact that holding a given asset entails certain storage costs[3] and that, as we have seen, certain management costs must be added to these.[4]

Components of value-yield

The breakdown of the value-yield already carried out[5] can now be completed by consideration of the liquidity and of the costs of storage and of management. If l, c, and g denote the premiums of liquidity, storage, and management, the rate of interest really yielded by a financial investment is seen to be equal to

$$r + l + \mu + \gamma - \alpha - \varepsilon - \rho - c - g,$$

so that in equilibrium we must have

(1) $$r + l + \mu + \gamma - \alpha - \varepsilon - \rho - c - g = i.$$

In other words, for any asset, the sum of the value-yield r and of the premiums of liquidity l and of the monetary μ and capital γ value-gains, minus the premiums of depreciation α and of estimated risk and cost of risk, ε and ρ, and costs of storage c and of management g is equal, in equilibrium, to the pure market interest rate i. This equation adds completeness and gives general applicability to equation (7) of no. 33, which did not take into account the premiums of liquidity, storage, and management.[6,7]

3. Comprising, for instance, storage fees.

4. Nos. 10 and 11. The taxes directly levied on the income deriving from these assets may be deemed to belong to the same category.

5. No. 33.

6. Of course, the classical analysis made in nos. 10 and 11 remains valid if we add to the category of risks (both favorable and unfavorable eventualities) the loss of value due to wear and tear, general variations in price and interest rates, and the advantages of liquidity, and if we consider administrative costs to include the costs both of storage and of management. But, for the sake of clarity, it is preferable carefully to distinguish the various components involved in determining the value-yields (see the explanations already given in note 10 to no. 33).

7. It follows from these explanations that when an economic agent (X) extends a monetary loan to agent (Y) to enable the latter to make a specific real investment, we must have, on the one hand, for the lender

$$r + l + \mu + \gamma - \alpha - \varepsilon - \rho - c - g \geq i,$$

The immense variety of value-yields observed in the market is explained by the considerable variations in the various premiums from one financial investment to another.

Moreover, in the absence of equilibrium, the price disparities corresponding to the disequilibrium are of course added to these diverse elements of differentiation.

The case of money

In the case of money, of course, we have

(2) $r = \mu = \gamma = \alpha = \varepsilon = \rho = g = 0.$ [8]

---

using i to denote the pure market interest rate and $r, l, \mu, \gamma, \alpha, \varepsilon, \rho, c,$ and g to denote the value-yield and the premiums of liquidity, monetary and capital value gain, depreciation, estimated-risk and cost-of-risk, of storage and of management for agent (X)'s claim on agent (Y) (it is worth noting that, as the loan is made in money against a recognition of liability, we have $\mu = \alpha = \gamma = 0$), while, on the other hand, for the borrower,

$$r' + l' + \mu' + \gamma' - \alpha' - \varepsilon' - \rho' - c' - g' \geq r,$$

where $r', l', \mu', \gamma', \alpha', \varepsilon', \rho', c',$ and g' denote the value-yield and the premiums corresponding to the intended investments.

In equilibrium and at the margin, these inequalities of course become equations so that we have

$$r' + \mu' + \gamma' - \alpha' = i - (l + l') + (\varepsilon + \varepsilon') + (\rho + \rho') + (c + c') + (g + g').$$

As the sum $(r' + \mu' + \gamma' - \alpha')$ is the same as the marginal technical interest rate corresponding to the real investments made (no. 44), it can be seen that the only investments actually made are those whose marginal technical interest rate exceeds the pure market interest rate by the excess of the premiums of risk, storage, and management over the liquidity premiums of lender and borrower, and it can be seen that there are risks that are counted twice. This is a circumstance that prevents many investments from being made even though available information indicates that they would prove profitable overall.

In any event, it is clear that *exact risk assessment* can be of the greatest importance for the implementation of a technology. A well-known example is that of the small firm of little standing for which it is technically possible to make highly profitable investments, but which is prevented from doing so by the excessive risk premium required by potential lenders (X).

8. The value of the premium ε is zero, as it corresponds to the risk of non-repayment of the funds invested.

So if we assume that storage costs are negligible, we obtain

(3) $$l = i,$$

an equation that, as we have seen,[9] characterizes every equilibrium scenario in the absence of storage costs.

Whereas in the case of money the sum $(\alpha + \varepsilon + \rho + c + g)$, which is
equal to the storage premium, is generally negligible compared to the sum
$(r + l + \mu + \gamma)$, which is equal to the liquidity premium, other goods are
generally characterized by a value $(\alpha + \varepsilon + \rho + c + g)$, which is far greater
than their liquidity premium. It follows that it is not profitable to own
them unless their use generates sufficient value or unless the excess of the
premiums of depreciation, risk, storage, and management over the liquidity premium is more than compensated for by the premiums of monetary
and capital value-gain $(\mu + \gamma)$, respectively, due to the expected rises or
falls of prices and interest rates.

The case of stock exchange securities

In the case of stock exchange securities, the premiums of depreciation,
storage, and management may be deemed negligible *as a first approximation*. So for these securities we can state that

(4) $$r + l + \mu + \gamma - \varepsilon - \rho = i.$$

The liquidity premium l of a security is of course so much the greater,
as its transaction costs and its risk of depreciation at sale are lower, i.e.,
as its market is deeper. Thus a deep market security whose liquidity premium may be substantial will by this very fact be of greater value than a
security in other respects comparable but with a shallow market.

In the case of shares, the monetary appreciation premium μ may reach
very high levels, whereas it is, of course, zero for bonds.

The capital value-gain premium γ may also reach very significant levels
when the market is expecting major variations in the rate of interest.[10]

The estimated-risk premium may be taken as a function of the risk of
nonpayment of the stipulated interest and of non-repayment in the case

9. No. 82.
10. Note 9 to no. 33.

of bonds, and of payment of higher or lower dividends for shares (abstracting from price variations due to variations in the value of money, which are already included in premium μ).

In the case of shares, the estimated-risk premium is naturally negative if a rise in dividends is expected.

If we use a and $\bar{a}$ to denote the income and the price of a security at time t, equation (4) may be written

(5)
$$\bar{a} = \frac{a}{i - l - \mu - \gamma + \varepsilon + \rho}.$$

This expression makes it possible to see how the price of a security is determined from its instantaneous income, the instantaneous pure market interest rate, and the premiums of monetary and capital value-gain, and of estimated risk and cost of risk as evaluated by the market.

Equation (5) enables us to explain, for example, the high prices that may be fetched by a share offering only a mediocre income if an increase in dividends is expected.

Instantaneous pure interest rates

It follows from this analysis that for each investment bearing at time t a value-yield r, there will correspond a pure instantaneous interest rate i, when equilibrium is not attained. The pure instantaneous interest rates thus corresponding to the various investments are naturally equal only in equilibrium.

At every point in time, countless arbitrages tend to bring about this equality, either in the financial market for the various long-term securities, in the money market for the various short-term securities, or indeed between both markets for both short- and long-term securities. All this arbitraging, of course, takes place *at the same time*, but to reach a clear understanding of what occurs it is *convenient* that the markets should be sharply distinguished and studied separately.

The pure instantaneous interest rates corresponding on average[11] to the monetary and financial markets will be denoted by i_M and i_F.

---

11. The different pure interest rates are, of course, only equal in a given market when arbitraging has actually brought about equilibrium.

Short- and long-term interest rates

Rates i_M and i_F are, of course, distinct from the interest rates commonly called short- and long-term interest rates, which will be denoted here by i_c and i_l, and which are in fact *averages of the value-yields* for a certain number of debt instruments.[12]

From the foregoing, we thus have

(6)
$$i_c = i_M - l_c - \mu_c - \gamma_c + \alpha_c + \varepsilon_c + \rho_c + c_c + g_c \qquad [13]$$

and

(7)
$$i_l = i_F - l_l - \mu_l - \gamma_l + \alpha_l + \varepsilon_l + \rho_l + c_l + g_l,$$

where l_c, l_l, μ_c, μ_l, γ_c, γ_l, α_c, α_l, ε_c, ε_l, c_c, c_l, g_c, and g_l, respectively, denote, in the monetary and financial markets, the average premiums of liquidity, of monetary and capital value-gains, of depreciation, of estimated risk and cost of risk, of storage, and of management. As a first approximation it may be assumed that in the financial market

(8)
$$\alpha_l = c_l = g_l = 0$$

and

(9)
$$i_l = i_F - l_l - \mu_l - \gamma_l + \varepsilon_l + \rho_l.$$

12. The short-term rates being considered here are the rates corresponding to short-term debt instruments in an economy having no recourse to the issue of unbacked demand deposits (no. 83 *in fine*). They do not therefore include the discount rate, which, under usual conditions, is precisely and closely connected to the conditions of this issue.

The short-term debt here considered includes only those instruments that do not involve the banks: short-term loans between individuals or firms, Treasury bonds, and repos.

But it will be seen later that in equilibrium the discount rate cannot differ significantly from the rate corresponding to these debt instruments (no. 94). Thus it will be possible to extend the following explanations to the more usual case, and they will become valid for the short-term rate, which is the average of the short-term rates corresponding to the various types of debt instrument, including bills discounted following the issue of unbacked demand deposits.

13. Note that the value-yield i_c of short-term securities is calculated not on the basis of their market value a_q (notations of no. 3) but of their stipulated value. Under these conditions the risk premiums ε_c and ρ_c take into account the whole of the risks involved and not only, as is usually the case, their changes over time.

In the money market, the securities are short term and of a given nominal amount so that as a first approximation we may assume that

(10) $$\mu_c = \gamma_c = \alpha_c = \varepsilon_c = \rho_c = c_c = g_c = 0$$

and consequently

(11) $$i_c = i_M - l_c.$$ [14]

We therefore have

(12) $$i_l - i_c = (l_c - l_l) + \varepsilon_l - \rho_l - \mu_l - \gamma_l + (i_F - i_M)$$

and, when equilibrium is achieved between the monetary and financial markets,

(13) $$i_l - i_c = (l_c - l_l) + \varepsilon_l + \rho_l - \mu_l - \gamma_l.$$

These equations enable us to explain why the long-term rate is *generally* higher than the short-term rate. In normal circumstances, rates i_M and i_F are in fact equal, and on account of the stability of prices and of interest rates the premiums of monetary and capital value-gains μ_l and γ_l are low on the long-term market. It can then be seen that, *as a rule*, the difference between the long- and short-term rates of interest is chiefly due to the

---

14. For everyday values of i_c on the order of 2% to 5% it is reasonable to suppose that, in view of the considerable liquidity advantages offered by short-term securities, the liquidity premium l_c must be on the order of 25% to 50% of the liquidity premium of money, which is theoretically equal to the pure interest rate i_M. This premium can therefore be estimated, for everyday values of i_c, to be on the order of 1%.

Of course, equation (11) can only be deemed valid in so far as the risk and management premiums—which, so far as can be judged, are on the order of 0.5%—remain negligible, at least as a first approximation. Indeed if the equilibrium pure interest *rate* $i = i_M$ were to fall to a very low level, the liquidity premium l_c, which is naturally less than the liquidity premium i of money, would itself become very slight. Under these conditions only the premiums μ_c, γ_c, α_c, and c_c could be deemed negligible and according to general equation (1) we should have

(1) $$i_c \sim \varepsilon_c + \rho_c + g_c.$$

The short-term rate would then be reduced substantially to the risk and management premiums and would be greater than the pure interest rate.

higher liquidity premium of short-term securities and to the risk premium $(\varepsilon_l + \rho_l)$ of long-term securities. As might have been expected a priori the constant tradability of long-term debt instruments means that the difference in the expected rates of interest depending on maturity,[15,16] notwithstanding the commonly accepted opinion,[17] *normally* plays no role.[18]

It can also be seen that, notwithstanding the common opinion, the short-term interest rate i_c is generally not representative of the market's pure interest rate in equilibrium $i = i_M = i_F$ and that it is generally less than the average liquidity premium of short-term securities, which can have significant values.[19] In fact it is safe to assume that under normal conditions the most likely level of the pure instantaneous interest rate is the average of the short- and long-term rates.[20]

Under exceptional circumstances, the long-term rate i_l may become equal to the short-term rate i_c or even fall below it. In the first place, this may occur if, in the absence of equilibrium between the monetary and financial markets, the difference $(i_F - i_M)$ becomes strongly negative on account of a sharp credit squeeze. The same thing may also happen if equilibrium prevails between the two markets and the future instantaneous interest rates are expected to be much lower than the interest rates currently observed.[21] Indeed, in this case, the capital value-gain premium γ_l

15. Which, according to the foregoing, can intervene only indirectly through the medium of the capital value gain premium (see note 9 to no. 33 and note 21 below).

16. Nos. 10 and 14.

17. Thus, Irving Fisher, notwithstanding his usual lucidity, maintains that the main reason for the difference between short- and long-term rates is the variability of average pure interest rates depending on maturity (*The Theory of Interest*—French edition: *La théorie de l'intérêt* [Paris: Giard, 1933], 298, 310, 311). The present writer also subscribed to this error until 1943 (*À la recherche d'une discipline économique*, no. 212).

18. See the explanations given above in no. 17.

19. On the order of 1% for common levels of the short-term rates as has been observed above (note 14 above).

20. However, if the equilibrium pure interest rate $i = i_M = i_F$ fell to a very low level, we should have, as we have seen (note 14 above),

$$i_c \sim g_c.$$

The short-term rate would then be greater than the pure interest rate and the latter could no longer be regarded as occupying an intermediate level between the short and long-term rates.

21. Instead of considering the aggregate of the instantaneous rates $i(t)$ foreseen at time t_0 for the various times t, it would of course be possible to consider the different average rates

may be strongly positive.[22] Finally the same may occur if a sharp monetary value-gain due to a price rise is foreseen for long-term securities.[23]

Definition of pure interest rate

The definition of the pure interest rate given in chapter 2^{24} could not, of course, take account of liquidity theory.

It can be seen from the foregoing that the pure nominal interest rate must be defined as the nominal value yielded by a debt instrument for which the various premiums l, μ, γ, α, ε, ρ, c, and g are 0. Such a debt must specifically involve no management or storage costs, *offer no liquidity advantage*,[25] and its repayment in nominal value must be certain. This is the case, as a first approximation, of the rate of interest yielded by a substantial loan secured by a very sound mortgage, always provided that the mortgage market is sufficiently well organized for the unit management premium to be negligible.

$j(t)$ foreseen at time t_0 for the different periods (t_0, t) (no. 17) or indeed the different average perpetual rates $j_\infty(t)$ foreseen at time t_0 for the various times t (no. 30).

22. Note 9 to no. 33.

23. At this stage of the analysis I must state once and for all that the exact breakdown of the value-yield into its different components, their symbolic representation, and the use of formulae are not intended to introduce evaluations in terms of precise figures, which would certainly be impossible in the present state of our knowledge, but to facilitate explanation and analysis by providing them with a concrete support and symbolic representation.

24. No. 11.

25. This is in particular the case of "frozen" debts.

2. Consumers' decisions (85)

On the basis of the prices and interest rates that they observe in the present and foresee for the future, individuals determine[1] their consumption expenditure R_C, the increase in their money balances R_E, and the total fraction of their income to be invested in financial assets R_P.

The representative curve of income invested in financial assets R_P as a function of the interest rate I[2] is then determined by the difference between the representative curves of unconsumed income $R_D - R_C$[3] and of the demand for new money balances R_E.[4] Various circumstances may then arise depending on the level of market interest rate I in relation to the significant levels $0, I_0, I_1, I_2,$ and I_3 of interest rate I shown in figure 8.7.

If $-1 < I < 0$, the demand for money would be infinite (positive) and the net demand for financial assets would be infinite (negative).

For it would be in the interests of individuals to borrow as much as possible by obtaining money (with a near zero interest rate) against promises to pay (whose rate of interest, for them, would be negative).

In such a situation any economic agent would be willing to receive money, but none would want to supply it. Upon which the interest rate would inevitably rise to a positive level.[5]

If $0 < I < I_0$, invested income R_P is negative. This means that, in the aggregate, individuals are selling financial assets. The price of these assets will then necessarily fall, and, in consequence, the interest rate will rise[6] to a level higher than rate I_0.[7]

---

1. Nos. 40 and 82.

2. Which is assumed for the sake of simplicity to be unique.

3. Fig. 5.26 of no. 48.

4. Fig. 8.4 of no. 82.

5. These explanations will be expanded on later (nos. 87 and 88). But it is already possible to see why the nominal interest rate could not become negative in our economies in which the monetary unit serves as unit of account (see the explanations already given in nos. 3 and 13 and note 12 to no. 40, as well as in chapter 9, "The Problem of Interest").

6. For given expected future incomes, a fall in one asset necessarily entails an increase in the rate of interest (no. 29, equation [1]).

7. This is one reason why, in the economies we are familiar with, the rate of interest not only cannot fall to zero but cannot normally even fall to a very low level. At first sight, it may be considered that the interest rate I_0 must be on the order of 0.25% to 0.5%. At such a value for I, investment in money would certainly be deemed preferable to any other investment.

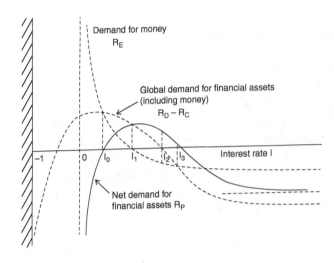

FIGURE 8.7

If $I_0 < I < I_1$, unconsumed income $(R_D - R_C)$ is devoted partly to increasing money balances and partly to new financial investment.

If $I_1 < I < I_2$, money balances decrease, and the decrease is added to unconsumed income $(R_D - R_C)$ to supplement the invested income R_P.

If $I_2 < I < I_3$, the difference $(R_D - R_C)$ is negative; individuals spend more on their consumption than they receive and continue to invest $(R_P > 0)$. All their expenditure is financed by the decrease in their money balances.

Finally, if $I_3 < I$, invested income R_P will be negative. It has already been pointed out above that such a situation, in which individuals in the aggregate are sellers of financial assets, could not occur in the real world.

3. Decisions of firms (86)

We have already seen[1] what determines the level of new financial assets: the supply rises or falls depending on whether firms are expecting a favorable or unfavorable price trend.[2]

As a first approximation, this supply curve can be represented by a straight line, parallel to the y-axis, whose abscissa is equal to the nominal marginal productivity of the old assets.[3] This marginal productivity, which is very high in a boom period, may fall to negative levels during a period of depression.[4]

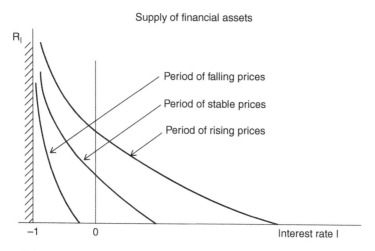

FIGURE 8.8

1. Nos. 45, 47 and 48.
2. No. 45.
3. Equal to the rate of value productivity of a small supplementary investment.
4. This nominal marginal productivity is equal to the marginal productivity in real terms, as determined by the volume of existing investments, augmented by the rate of price increase $\dfrac{\frac{dP}{dt}}{P}$. (This will be expanded on below, no. 106.)

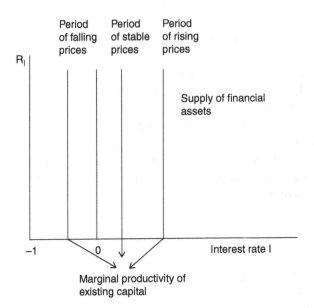

FIGURE 8.9

4. Financial market (87)

Two kinds of transaction take place in the financial market: (a) new issues of financial instruments and (b) sales of earlier issues at prices different from their issue price.

For new issues, a pure equilibrium rate of interest tends to become established corresponding to the intersection of the financial asset supply and demand curves (fig. 8.10). *As a first approximation*, this rate may be taken to be equal to the marginal productivity rate of the old assets.[1]

In the case of existing financial assets, a price is established for each of them that takes account both of its expected future returns and of expected future interest rates. To these various assets there naturally correspond as many specific instantaneous pure interest rates, tending to settle

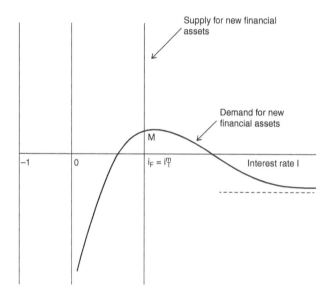

FIGURE 8.10

1. For the sake of simplicity, the supply of new financial instruments on the part of the State (bonds) is overlooked here. Readers will easily be able to see how the explanations that follow can be extended to take account of this case and to confirm that they hold good. Suffice it to point out at present that the market rate tends to settle at whichever is higher of the government borrowing rate and the marginal rate of productivity of capital.

at the same level as a result of arbitraging.[2] It will be assumed that this leveling out occurs continuously.

In the same way, arbitraging occurs between the new issues and the old instruments so that there is a tendency toward equalization of the corresponding pure interest rates.

It will be assumed in what follows, as a first approximation, that a single, unique instantaneous pure rate of interest i_F continuously prevails in the financial market, whether for new issues or for old securities.

In most cases, whether new or old instruments are involved, what is traded is not the use of the capital but the promises to pay on maturity an amount that may or may not be stipulated depending on whether bonds or shares are involved. In the case of old bond issues or shares, only their market prices as quoted on the stock exchange are involved, and the corresponding interest rate is merely an *implicit result* of that. Only in the case of new bond issues does the accent, by contrast, fall on the stipulated interest rate and hence on the price of use of capital.[3]

2. No. 84.

3. And even then, many bonds are issued below par, so that their price of issue plays just as significant a role as the stipulated rate.

5. Money market (88)

Transactions on the money market, be they discounts, loans against security, current account credit facilities, repurchase transactions, etc., all amount to short-term monetary loans. By nature they are secured loans.

In this light the money market emerges as, in essence, a market in which what is traded is the use of money, either in the form of cash or of demand deposits.

Of course, for each specific transaction there is a specific instantaneous pure rate of interest, but, as a result of arbitraging, the different pure interest rates constantly tend toward a common value. I will assume *for the sake of simplicity* that this common value prevails in reality so that the money market uses a single pure interest rate i_M, which is the price paid for the use of money.

On this assumption it is easy to see how the pure interest rate i_M is determined. It settles at a level such that total money demand (on the part of both consumers and firms) is precisely equal to the total quantity M of money actually in circulation, which is itself equal to the sum of cash M_M plus demand deposits M_S.[1] In light of the desired money balance curve[2] shown in figure 8.11 it is necessarily positive.

Using the terminology adopted,[2] it can be seen that, for a given total quantity of money, the monetary interest rate is higher as liquidity preference is stronger.

1. In reality the direct intervention of consumers on the money market is negligible, and it is taken into account here only for ease of explanation and as a first approximation.

Consumers, in fact, act on the money market only indirectly by their decision to increase or decrease their money balances (for the justification of the assumptions adopted, see no. 98, § "Simplifications used," as well as note 1 to no. 90).

2. No. 82.

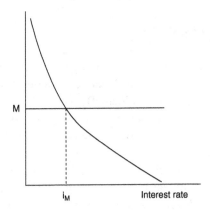

FIGURE 8.11

6. Arbitraging between financial investments (89)

At every point in time arbitraging is taking place between different financial investments, as economic agents strive to take advantage of the most profitable ones. This arbitraging can be divided according to whether it occurs within the same market or between markets.

The first sort has already been considered, and it has been assumed *for the sake of simplicity* that following this arbitraging the same pure interest rate was in force on both the monetary and the financial markets. This hypothesis rests on the assumption that the liquidity premiums of all money balances are equal to a single rate i_M and that all pure technical interest rates are equal to a single rate i_F. It now behooves me to examine arbitraging between the money market and the financial market.

This arbitraging naturally stems from evaluation of the pure interest rates i_M and i_F. For instance, if the pure interest rate i_M in the money market is greater than the pure interest rate i_F in the financial market, it will be profitable to invest one's capital in money rather than in financial assets, since the liquidity advantages of increased money balances are worth more than investment in a financial asset. The effects of such arbitraging will be examined later on.[1] Meanwhile, it is worth emphasizing that studying them is *of the highest importance* for understanding the link between interest theory, the classical theory of prices, and the theory of money.

It should be recalled that the level of the instantaneous rate i_F depends chiefly on forecasts concerning the future levels of this rate, which are themselves deduced from forecasts of the average perpetual interest rates.[2] When a lasting fall in these rates is foreseen, the capital value-gain premium γ has a high positive value, while the pure interest rate in the financial market i_F is low and may fall below the pure interest rate in the money market i_M. It is then more profitable to hoard money, though only briefly, for once the fall in the average permanent rate takes effect, the capital value-gain premium will again become zero and the rate i_F will rise once more to a level above rate i_M. Investment in financial assets will thereupon become once again more profitable than hoarding.[3]

1. No. 98.
2. Note 21 to no. 84.
3. See the remarks already made in no. 84 *in fine*.

This helps explain why short-term interest rates are subject to much greater fluctuations than long-term rates. It is chiefly because even slight variations in long-term rate forecasts lead to major variations in short-term rates.[4]

Moreover these variations in short-term interest rates are all the wider for the fact that transactions in the money market are cushioned by a total monetary mass that falls far short of the total capital serving to cushion the financial market.

Hence, while a credit squeeze corresponding to a few percentage points of total money can bring about a rise of several points in short-term interest rates, we have seen that a variation of total capital equal in value to the annual national income—which in France is roughly equal to the total monetary circulation[5]—corresponds to a variation on the order of only one point in long-term rates.[6]

It is important to realize that the various arbitrages, whether on one market or between markets, *are taking place at the same time* and that it is only by an *arbitrary* simplification that all the rates on the financial market and the money market have been reduced to two unique pure interest rates i_F and i_M. But this simplification seems both *convenient and justified.*

In the first place it is convenient, because, as we shall see, it makes it easy to bring out the general economic repercussions of arbitraging between the financial and the money markets, and between hoarding and investment, which is particularly important for the understanding of the economic mechanism.

And it is justified because it is an accepted scientific procedure to isolate a specific mechanism in a system while assuming that equilibrium prevails in its other parts. In economics, for instance, a given market is studied by assuming that the prices corresponding to other markets are well determined, i.e., that equilibrium prevails in them. In the same way, when we were considering the distribution of a consumer's income over time, it was implicitly assumed that at every point in time the income was distributed as well as possible between the different consumptions available.[7]

4. No. 30.
5. Cash plus demand deposits.
6. Note 10 to no. 70.
7. No. 40.

7. Money market and financial market (90)

Debt instruments, whether long- or short-term, always constitute promises to pay upon maturity, and both are financial assets, so the reader may initially be surprised to see me attribute essentially distinct roles to the short- and long-term markets, considering the former as the market for the use of money and the latter for the use of capital.

The reason for this is essentially as follows. It is quite certain that when firm (A) pays firm (B) with a draft that firm (B) draws on it, it borrows from (B) capital of the same amount, and, aside from the time period involved, this operation is absolutely parallel to the long-term loan that firm (A) may take out in order to purchase its equipment. Indeed, from this angle alone, there would be no reason to distinguish between the instantaneous pure interest rate yielded by a short-term loan and the instantaneous pure interest rate yielded by a long-term loan. *Both cases concern financial assets.*

But the parallel breaks down when confronted with the possibility of discount in the money market, which is in practice reserved for short-term debt instruments. This is what makes the money market seem much less like a market for short-term loans than like *a market for the use of money.* The best proof of this is the fact that advances against collateral can be obtained in the money market secured by long-term financial assets deemed to be reliable.

However, it must be admitted that this observation is of limited significance since the use of money is really only the use of a specific capital asset. Indeed *the capital market and the money market are in reality almost inextricably mingled because (a) all capital loan operations, whether short- or long-term, are effected by the medium of monetary payment and (b) the value of money, which is simply a specific intermediate good, itself constitutes a part of total capital considered collectively.*

Nevertheless, as it is convenient, from a theoretical point of view, to distinguish between the use of capital and use of money, the money market may be taken, *as a first approximation,* to represent the use of money, while the financial market represents the use of capital.[1]

1. For the benefit of any readers who may be reluctant to admit this simplification, the following theory could be presented in an alternative form by distinguishing three forms of arbitrage: (a) those that tend to equalize the instantaneous pure interest rates corresponding

to short- and long-term debt (between which no distinction would be made), (b) those that tend to equalize the various liquidity premiums, and (c) those that tend to equalize the pure rates of interest on debt and the liquidity premiums.

As only this last form of arbitrage makes a significant contribution to the explanation of economic development, we would assume, for greater clarity, that the various pure interest rates on debt were all equal to the same value i_F and that the different liquidity premiums were all equal to the same value i_M (a hypothesis that, of course, is not verified in reality but that would make it possible to isolate—so as to simplify the reasoning—the arbitrages between rates i_F and i_M), and the economic effects of a difference between rates i_F and i_M would be examined.

This approach would naturally be more abstract, but it would have the advantage of elimi-nating any dissymmetry between trade in short-term debt and in long-term debt. In any event, from the viewpoint of money balances and long-term debt, it would be absolutely equivalent, being based on the same simplifying assumption of the equality of liquidity premiums and of pure interest rates for long-term debt. The only difference would be that the first approach would assume that the pure interest rates corresponding to short-term debt and the liquidity premiums had attained equality at value i_M, while the second would assume that the pure interest rates of both short- and long-term debt had attained equality at value i_F.

Hence, the situation could be summarized in table 8.1.

Thus the first approach places side by side short-term loan capital and monetary capital while the second places side by side long-term loan capital and short-term loan capital. Each is *equally distant from reality*, for all the arbitrages are taking place simultaneously, but *each is equally justified*, for it is always permissible, in order to study a given mechanism, to isolate it, while assuming that the effects of *certain* other mechanisms have already been achieved. (Needless to say, the overall interdependence of economic phenomena forbids us to assume that the effects of *all* the other mechanisms have been achieved. Indeed, as we shall see, vari-able parameters do remain: the price levels of consumer and producer goods.)

In both cases the objective is to identify, by isolating them and supposing other disparities to be nonexistent, the effects of disparity between the price paid for the of use of capital (long-term or short-term depending on the case—it is worth noting here that the overall short-term value of capital is generally slight in comparison with that of long-term capital) and the price paid for the use of money: effects that are *crucial* to understanding what determines the gen-eral price level.

TABLE 8.1 FOOTNOTE

			First Approach	Second Approach
Capital	Loan capital	Pure interest rates on long-term debt	i_F	i_F
		Pure interest rates on short-term debt	i_M	i_F
	Monetary capital	Money balance liquidity premiums	i_M	i_M

Notwithstanding its dissymmetry as to loan capital, preference has been given to the first approach in the text, since I take the view that in reality *there is less difference between the liquidity premiums of firms* (which account for a great part of money balances) *and the short-term pure interest rates than there is between the latter and the long-term pure interest rates,* on account of (a) the physical separation of the money and financial markets and (b) the identification of money held by firms and of the short-term loan market with the money market alone, so that, as a first approximation, the money market may be taken to be characteristic of the liquidity premiums of money balances, while the financial market may be taken to characterize the marginal productivity of capital.

(b) Partial backing of demand deposits

1. The credit mechanism (91)

When a firm presents a bill of exchange to be discounted by a bank (B^i), the bank does not usually pay the discounted value of the bill of exchange in cash; it simply credits its customer's account with the appropriate amount.

For the firm, this sum is available on demand; it can be drawn on at any moment without cost and is in practice absolutely equivalent to liquidity directly held as ready cash.[1]

But for the bank, as a rule, there is no available liquidity corresponding to this sum, in the sense that the total of its demand liabilities is far higher than its total cash balance.

The bank knows by experience that, owing to the interplay of bank clearances, in order to have no difficulty in meeting all repayment demands, a reserve in ready cash[2] far less than its total demand liabilities[3,4] is enough. The ratio of this ready cash to demand liabilities is called the reserve ratio.

So, for the firm, the discount operation has the effect of substituting, among its assets, an immediately available sum of money, for the present value of a financial claim only available in the future. Its net assets have not changed in value, but they have changed in nature.

---

1. In reality this interchangeability is not perfect, for some payments can only be made using ready cash while, on the other hand, there are many payments that can be made more cheaply using deposit money than cash. However, these differences are only minor, and while they must be taken into account in order to construct a rigorous theory (no. 94), they may be disregarded as a first approximation.

2. Or on demand with the Central Bank, which amounts to the same thing.

3. Thus, when part of the cash balances of a large number of firms are grouped together in a bank, this enables the overall balances to be substantially diminished. There is a reduction in the total amount of ready cash needed for any given price level.

This phenomenon is very similar to the system prevailing in the distribution of electricity, where the instantaneous power demands of subscribers can at any given moment be satisfied with a total power availability equal to a quarter, at most, of the sum of the power levels specified in each subscriber's contract.

4. These explanations, of course, apply only to the national currency: banks usually hold foreign currency cash reserves equal to their demand liabilities in each of these currencies.

As to the bank, its assets have been increased by the present value of the discounted bill of exchange. But this asset increase is offset to the same value by the creation of a demand deposit in favor of the firm. The bank's net assets do not change in value and neither do its reserves; there is simply a parallel addition of the same value to its total assets and its total liabilities.

But for the community as a whole it is clear that this operation has the effect of increasing the total volume of actual money by an amount equal to the present value of the discounted bill. For although the bank's money balance has not changed, that of the firm that presented the bill for discount has increased by the amount involved. It can thus be seen that the discount operation, when it is achieved by creating a demand deposit, is equivalent to the issue of money to the same amount.[5]

The mechanism is the same if, as often happens, the discount operation is effected by the bank (B^i) in favor of a person (X) who is not one of its own customers. In this case, the reserve of the bank (B^i) is indeed decreased by the amount of the bill, but as a rule this sum is immediately paid out again and credited to the customer's account (X) in another bank (B^j). *So for all the banks together, considered as if they comprised a single bank, the mechanism remains identical, since the total reserves of the banks have not changed, notwithstanding the fact that the total amount of money available to firm* (X) *in the form of a demand deposit has simultaneously increased by the amount of the discounted bill.*[6]

It is clear that a bank (B^i) *can only carry out unbacked discount operations to the extent that customer deposits on its balance sheets enable it to do*

5. *It is crucial not to imagine,* as some outstanding thinkers seem to, *that credit necessarily leads to unbacked demand deposits.* In a world in which all bank credit available on demand had to be backed by an equal amount of money held by the bank in question, credit would still be possible, but it would be *limited* to a ceiling represented by the banks' aggregate money balance. It would thus be subject to *prior* borrowing, by each bank, of the sums it needed in order to extend the credit. This is precisely the scenario examined in the first part of this presentation (nos. 84 to 90) (see too nos. 113 and 162).

6. For a given bank, the sequence of credit operations can be schematically represented as follows.

In the initial scenario, customers have deposited a sum of cash totaling M^1_{MB}, and the balance sheet looks like table 8.2.

TABLE 8.2 FOOTNOTE

Balance Sheet 1	
Assets	
Cash in vault	M_{MB}^1
Liabilities	
Demand deposits	M_S^1

Using its reserves, the bank discounts bills totaling E_B^2. Its balance sheet now reads as in table 8.3.

TABLE 8.3 FOOTNOTE

Balance Sheet 2	
Assets	
Cash in vault	$M_{MB}^2 = M_{MB}^1 - E_B^2$
Portfolio	E_B^2
Liabilities	
Demand deposits	$M_S^2 = M_S^1$

By the interplay of the bank clearing new deposits, Δ_{MB}^3 come into being, and the bank's balance sheet now reads as in table 8.4.

TABLE 8.4 FOOTNOTE

Balance Sheet 3	
Assets	
Cash in vault	$M_{MB}^3 = M_{MB}^2 + \Delta_{MB}^3$
Portfolio	$E_B^3 = E_B^2$
Liabilities	
Demand deposits	$M_S^3 = M_S^2 + \Delta_M^3$

This is how the balance sheet changes over time until the ratio of the volume of demand deposits to the vault cash reserve reaches the level deemed desirable by the bank.

It can be seen that whenever the bank discounts a bill, from the bank's own viewpoint, *the transaction looks like the redistribution of money it actually holds and not like the creation of money*. This goes to explain *the illusion frequently entertained by bankers* that their loan operations are not inflationary.

so.[7] Quite obviously, if all discounted sums were withdrawn by the firms in the form of cash and kept in their own safes, it would be impossible to extend unbacked credit. Of course, the banks could continue discount operations, but they would have to do so using their own capital or capital borrowed for this purpose, which would thus be constantly reinvested in the short term.

As a rule, lending banks do not use their own capital to fund their reserve. Indeed it may be substantially lower in value and is generally represented either by real estate or by marketable securities. The reserve of a lending institution is generally comprised of the deposits of its own depositors. In theory, such a bank could function with no capital of its own. The sole role played by the capital of a lending institution is (a) to finance its plant and equipment and (b) to provide a guarantee to its customers.

This being so, if we use M_S^i to denote the total demand deposits of bank (B^i), and if κ is the percentage reserve requirement in force, the banks will only hold the amount κM_S^i of these deposits in liquid form. The rest, i.e., $(1-\kappa)M_S^i$, will be devoted to discount operations. From this it can be seen that *the volume of deposits determines the volume of bills discounted.*

But it is of course equally clear that the opposite also applies: the volume of deposits is itself determined by the volume of bills discounted. Firms divide the money at their disposal in a certain proportion between cash and deposits. Since the overall quantity of money depends, for the reasons we have just seen, on the volume of bills discounted, it can be seen that the same applies to the overall volume of deposits. As these deposits are divided among the various banks according to the convenience of the economic agents, it ultimately emerges that *the deposits with each bank depend on the overall volume of bills discounted in the economy.*[8]

Hence the successive cause-and-effect links can be represented as shown in figure 8.12.

7. Remember that loans made by the bank via discount may be extended to economic agents other than its own customers and that in this case an equal decrease in its vault cash corresponds to each such loan. Even if these loans are made to customers, they are generally used by the customers to make payments.

So discounting is only possible if the outlays it involves are constantly offset by new deposits.

8. And this is the justification for Mr. H. Withers's expression "loans make deposits." Bearing in mind that the loans themselves are brought about by the deposits, it could even be said that deposits make deposits.

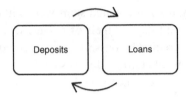

FIGURE 8.12

Finally, it can be seen that there is a twofold cause-and-effect link between deposits and the volume of bills discounted. For each bank considered individually, *the volume of bills discounted depends on the volume of
its deposits, but for the economy as a whole, the volume of deposits depends
on the volume of bills discounted.* As will be seen later, this double link
between deposits and discounted bills means that each reciprocally determines the other.[9]

---

9. This is but one further example of the *interdependent phenomena* that are typical of the
economy. It is comparable to the relationship between consumer income and expenditure.

For each economic agent, expenditure depends on income, just as discounted bills depend
on deposits, but following the economic circuit, income depends on expenditure, just as deposits depend on bills discounted.

2. Lending banks: their income and policy (92)

It is easy to see why lending operations can be highly profitable for a bank, for if the bank had constantly to keep a reserve equal to the total amount of its demand liabilities, discount operations would only be possible with its own capital or capital borrowed for this purpose. Under these conditions, discount operations would amount, for the bank, to lending operations closely parallel to long-term investments in financial assets and, as such, would be neither more nor less profitable than any other investment.

But as things stand, banks are *not* in fact required to possess monetary capital equal to the demand deposits on their books. A bank can extend credit without immobilizing an equal amount of immediately available monetary capital. For its demand deposit holders collectively, it is as if the bank were lending money that it has not got. Loan operations thus enable the bank to realize a net gain equal to the interest on the unbacked credit it has extended.

If, for instance, M_B^i is the total reserve held by a bank (B^i) and if the total of its demand deposits is M_S^i, the total of its unbacked demand liabilities is $(M_S^i - M_B^i)$. If i_B is the discount rate,[1] the bank thus receives in theory an income of $i_B(M_S^i - M_B^i)$ for lending its customers the sum $(M_S^i - M_B^i)$, which it does not possess.

However, as pointed out above, discount operations are only possible insofar as the bank has sufficient deposits available. *In order to be able carry out an operation as profitable as discounting, each bank is thus induced to seek and attract deposits.* To this end, it pays interest[2,3] to its depositors and provides them with certain facilities the remuneration for which is generally lower than their cost[4] and the value of which is comparable to supplementary interest. The notation i_D will be used to denote the *overall* interest rate thus paid to depositors. If, for a reserve ratio κ each

---

1. In practice, of course there is more than one discount rate, for the rate varies according to the quality of the bills of exchange. However, to simplify the explanation it will be assumed, in the bulk of what follows, that there is only one discount rate in force.

2. Usually on the order of 0.5% to 1% for fairly substantial deposits.

3. This explains the *seeming paradox* that depositing in the bank funds *that remain available on demand* not only costs nothing but can even yield modest interest.

4. Keeping accounts, safeguarding funds, managing security portfolios, paying dividends, cash in-payments, transfers, safe facilities, etc.

franc deposited enables the amount $(1 - \kappa)$ to be discounted, there results a unit cost of $\dfrac{i_D}{1-\kappa}$ for every franc of bills of exchange discounted.

Moreover, discount operations entail certain administrative costs, certain risks,[5] and certain liquidity advantages[6] for the bank, such that if the corresponding premiums are denoted by g_B, ε_B, ρ_B, and l_B, the overall unit cost of the operation for the bank is

$$\frac{i_D}{1-\kappa} + g_B + \varepsilon_B + \rho_B - l_B$$

and its income r_B equal to the excess of the discount rate i_B over the cost is

$$r_B = i_B - \left(\frac{i_D}{1-\kappa} + g_B + \varepsilon_B + \rho_B - l_B\right).^{7}$$

Of course, for given values of these different rates, the lower the reserve ratio—i.e., *the more loans are made relative to the available liquid reserve*—*the higher the profit, but also the greater the risks.*[8]

In practice, a bank succeeds in maintaining its indispensable reserve *by varying as circumstances require the rate of interest* that it charges on its loans. "If it has few loans and a reserve large enough to support loans

---

5. These risks include (a) the risks of non-repayment of discounted bills and (b) the risks attendant upon the possibility—which can never be entirely excluded—of inability to meet demand liabilities in the event of massive withdrawals that cannot be satisfied owing to the existence of unbacked demand deposits.

6. Due to the possibility of rediscounting bills that have been discounted either by other banks or, especially, by the Central Bank (see no. 93 below).

7. It should be specified that rate i_B is typically between 2% and 5%, while i_D is from 0.25% to 1% and g_B from 0.5% to 1%.

The estimated-risk premium ε_B will usually be very low if not zero. It is only in periods of depression, when, for purely monetary reasons, numerous bankruptcies occur, that it can attain high levels.

Premium ρ_B corresponds to the greater or lesser tendency of bankers to take on at its mathematical value the twofold risk of nonpayment of drafts and the possibility of being unable to meet their demand liabilities.

From this premium, of course, we must deduct the liquidity premium l_B, which specifically corresponds to the possibility of successfully countering the second risk by rediscount.

8. The risks in question here are those of the bank's inability to meet all possible withdrawal demands using exclusively its reserve.

of much greater volume, it will endeavor to extend its loans by lowering the rate of interest. If its loans are large and it fears too great demands on the reserve, it will restrict the loans by a high interest charge. *Thus, by alternately raising and lowering interest, a bank keeps its loans within the sum that the reserve can support, but endeavors to keep them (for the sake of profit) as high as the reserve will support.*"[9]

It is only experience that guides banks as to the average figures that should be adopted for reserve ratios, in view of the habits of their customers, and the nature and scale of their activities. The figure the banks deem optimal for these rates naturally varies with circumstances: under normal economic conditions it is about 10%.

For given rates i_B, κ, g_B, ε_B, ρ_B, *and* l_B,[10] *competition between banks normally leads them to fix the average rate yielded in favor of their depositors at a level close to that at which the price of discount and its cost would be equal.*[11]

Finally, it should be pointed out that when normal equilibrium conditions prevail, the value of the new bills discounted each day is precisely equal at every point of time to the value of previously discounted bills now reaching maturity.

9. Fisher, *The Purchasing Power of Money*, ch. 3. Emphasis mine.

10. It will be seen later how the discount rate i_B is set.

11. Of course, this tendency, which resembles the tendency of the selling price of each commodity to become equal to its cost of production, *exists only if there is competition*. In reality, as for all activities, *monopolistic conditions are not excluded*, as the banks can collude in order to avoid paying their depositors rates of interest that they deem too high. This, of course, is in each specific case a question of fact, examination of which falls outside the scope of this study.

3. Central Bank discount rate (93)

A similar policy is practiced by the Central Bank, which accepts for discount exceptionally reliable bills of exchange or for rediscount bills that have already been discounted by private lending banks. However, it is established practice that the Central Bank does not in principle compete with lending banks in the discount market; hence it does not pay interest to its depositors.

Just as for lending bank depositors a demand deposit is equivalent to cash, so for a lending bank itself its reserves on deposit with the Central Bank are equivalent to immediately available liquidity.

The Central Bank generally fixes the discount rate at which it accepts for discount — without limitation[1] — all bills fulfilling certain conditions. It will be denoted by i_E.[2]

In practice, in countries where lending banks customarily apply to the Central Bank to rediscount part of their commercial portfolios or to make them a loan, the official discount rate i_E acts as a benchmark against which other banks can set their discount rate i_B. As they may be led to have the bills they receive rediscounted, they only accept them — to avoid running the risk of losses — at a rate slightly higher than the official rate.

On the other hand, when commercial banks have abundant monetary reserves and do not intend to rediscount, the discount rate i_B may fall below the official rate i_E. In this case the volume of bills discounted by the Central Bank is naturally low.[3]

The fact that the Central Bank does not pay interest to its depositors enables it to realize substantial revenues, but as the State imposes various responsibilities on the Central Bank,[4] and they are roughly equivalent in value, these revenues may in practice be considered to be interest whose beneficiary is the State itself and hence all individuals collectively.

---

1. If the number of bills presented for discount becomes too great, the Central Bank of course has the option of reducing it by raising its discount rate, but what interests us here is what occurs for a given discount rate.

2. The subscript index E [French *émission* = issue] is a reminder that the rate in question is the Central Bank's discount rate.

3. All of these remarks will be clarified in no. 94, where the determination of the discount rate will be studied.

4. Notably the duty of carrying out, free of charge, all the State's fund transfers from one point of the territory to another.

4. Pure interest rate, discount rate, liquidity premiums, and volume of money balances (94)

The foregoing summary clarifies the link between the instantaneous pure interest rate and the discount rate when banks are able to issue unbacked demand deposits.

In order to understand what happens, several hypotheses will be considered in turn, starting with simpler but less real models and moving on to scenarios that are more complex but closer to reality.

Case one

Let us first assume that for economic agents cash and demand deposits are perfectly interchangeable, that debt instruments cannot, even partially, replace money, i.e., they have zero liquidity,[1] that lending institutions have zero administrative costs, that the sale of securities entails no costs, that all transactions are risk free, that there are no Central Banks, and that there is perfect competition.

Under these conditions, banks' income per franc discounted is equal to

$$(1) \qquad r_B = i_B - \frac{i_D}{1 - \kappa},$$

so obviously lending banks will keep their reserve ratio as low as possible.

Moreover, as we have seen, for a given discount rate i_B, a bank's income rises as the volume of its discounts increases. As this volume depends directly on deposit levels, each bank will seek to attract deposits by raising the rate of interest they bear. Ultimately, competition between banks will have the effect, under the conditions assumed, of raising the rate of interest i_D earned by depositors to a level at which the discount price is equal to its cost, thereby canceling out the income of the individual banks,[2] and we shall have

$$(2) \qquad i_D = (1 - \kappa)i_B.$$

1. In the sense of no. 84.

2. As has already been remarked (note 11 to no. 92) what is stated here about the discount price also applies to the price of any other good. In both cases, competition has the effect of equalizing price and cost.

Moreover, on the assumptions stated, discount rate i_B cannot exceed the instantaneous pure interest rate i, for if it did, it would be more profitable for firms to pay for their purchases in ready money by borrowing the sums needed on the market at rate i.

Nor indeed could discount rate i_B fall below rate i, for if it did, it would be in the banks' interests to use their available deposits not for buying bills of exchange, which would bring them remuneration of only i_B, but for buying financial assets,[3] issuing secured loans, or for repo investments,[4] which would bring them a remuneration of rate i.[5]

Thus, *in equilibrium under the conditions assumed*, the discount rate must obviously be equal to the instantaneous pure interest rate so that we have

$$\textbf{(3)} \qquad\qquad\qquad i_B = i.$$

Finally, as cash and demand deposits are assumed to be perfectly interchangeable, every economic agent will prefer to hold his balances in the form of demand deposits in order to take advantage of the return i_D paid to depositors. Moreover, as we have seen, since he has the choice of whether to keep his money or to invest it at rate i, he will fix the level of his money balance so that its marginal use-value plus rate i_D is equal to rate i. Hence, from equations (2) and (3), the liquidity premium of the money balance emerges, in equilibrium, as

$$\textbf{(4)} \qquad\qquad\qquad i - i_D = \kappa i,$$

and total demand deposits M_S will be a well-determined function

$$\textbf{(5)} \qquad\qquad\qquad M_S = M_S(\kappa i)$$

of rate i.

---

3. This is only possible on account of our initial assumptions, which exclude risk. In the real world, using bank deposits to invest in stocks and shares is absolutely ruled out because of (a) their insufficient liquidity and (b) their price variations.

4. Note that repo transactions are economically equivalent to secured loans.

5. Thus, for instance, *under the conditions assumed* of absence of costs, the repo rate could not, *in equilibrium*, fall below the instantaneous rate i of long-term debt, for if it did, it would be profitable to purchase securities under repo thus pocketing the difference between the interest yielded and the repo costs.

Neither could the repo rate exceed rate i, for if it did so, it would be preferable to invest funds in repos rather than in securities.

Case two

Let us now assume that demand deposits are not completely interchangeable with cash but that a degree of interchangeability exists.

The reader will easily be able to satisfy himself that, in this case, the results obtained in case one regarding the discount rate and the rate paid to depositors remain entirely valid.

However, as cash and demand deposits are not entirely interchangeable, the quantity held of each will depend on the price paid for their respective use and, in each case, on the volume of the other.

As the use-value of each economic agent's cash balance depends both on its quantity M_M^i and on the quantity M_S^i of demand deposits that he holds, and as he sets his cash balance at a level such that its use-value is equal to the pure interest rate i in the market,[6] we must have in equilibrium

(6) $$M_M^i = f(M_S^i, i).$$

As the user cost of demand deposits[7] is equal only to the product κi, it also follows that

(7) $$M_S^i = g(M_M^i, \kappa i).$$

In equilibrium this gives us

(8) $$M_M^i = M_M^i(i)$$

and

(9) $$M_S^i = M_S^i(i);$$

6. If this use-value were greater than i, it would be in the agent's interests to decrease his real investments and increase his money balance, and vice versa.

The use-value of the balance, whether it is held as cash or as demand deposits, cannot in equilibrium be different from i.

Of course, the use-value of the demand deposits can be broken down into two components: (a) their liquidity premium κi and (b) their income $i_D = i - \kappa i$.

7. Equal to the opportunity cost corresponding to holding a demand deposit of 1 franc, i.e.,

$$i - i_D = i - (1 - \kappa)i = \kappa i.$$

in other words, cash and demand deposit balances are well-determined functions of the rate i.[8]

Case three

Let us now maintain the assumptions of case two but add the costs and risks involved in economic reality.

As before, competition between banks encourages them to raise the rate of interest paid to their depositors until the price of discount is equal to its cost. In equilibrium this gives us

$$(10) \qquad\qquad i_B = \frac{i_D}{1-\kappa} + g_B + \varepsilon_B + \rho_B - l_B. \qquad\qquad \text{9,10}$$

This equation determines the rate i_D paid to depositors as a function of the discount rate i_B.

This leaves the link between the discount rate i_B and the market's instantaneous pure interest rate to be determined. This link seems to be due to the alternatives available (a) to firms and (b) to banks in their decisions.

To begin with, a firm (X) resorts to discount only if this operation is more in its interests than direct borrowing in the market. So let g^x, ε^x, and ρ^x be the management, estimated-risk, and cost-of-risk premiums that firm (X) would have to pay if it borrowed in the capital market, and let g_e^x be the management premium it incurs for the discount operation.[11]

It is clear that the discount operation will only be in the interests of firm (X) if we have

$$(11) \qquad\qquad i_B + g_e^x < i + g^x + \varepsilon^x + \rho^x.$$

8. These explanations will be illustrated in the case of a specific example in appendix II, § B (nos. 211 and 212).

9. Using the notations of no. 92.

10. Although we are assuming that there is no Central Bank, a liquidity premium l_B must still be taken into account, since rediscount by other banks remains possible.

11. This premium includes the subjective cost corresponding to the greater or lesser reluctance of every firm to resort to discount on account of the doubts this course may raise as to its solvency.

This premium is certainly not insignificant, and the sharp fall in discount operations over the last 20 years is unquestionably due to its increase.

This condition determines, for a given discount rate i_B, the volume $C_{\mu e}$ of bills actually presented for discount, which is thus seen to be a well-determined function

$$(12) \qquad C_{\mu e} = C_{\mu e}(i_B) \qquad \qquad \text{[12]}$$

of the discount rate i_B, but of course it cannot tell us the relative values of rates i and i_B.[13]

If instead we turn to the options banks enjoy of using their deposits to buy Treasury Bonds, to finance repo (sale and repurchase) transactions, or to issue secured loans, it is easy to see how the relative levels of rates i and i_B are determined.

First, some Treasury Bonds are directly bought by individuals and firms. This being so, if we use i_T and l_T to denote their interest rate and their liquidity premium for these agents, we necessarily have in equilibrium[14]

$$(13) \qquad i_T = i - l_T.$$

But if, at the same time as discounting bills of exchange the banks use their deposits to buy Treasury Bonds, we have

$$(14) \qquad i_T + l_{TB} - g_{TB} - \varepsilon_{TB} - \rho_{TB} = i_B + l_B - g_B - \varepsilon_B - \rho_B,$$

where l_{TB} and l_B, g_{TB} and g_B, ε_{TB} and ε_B, ρ_{TB} and ρ_B, respectively, denote the bank's liquidity, management, and risk premiums for Treasury Bonds and bills of exchange.

This gives us

$$(15) \qquad i_B = i - l_T + (l_{TB} - l_B) + (g_B - g_{TB}) + (\varepsilon_B - \varepsilon_{TB}) + (\rho_T - \rho_{TB}).$$

---

12. The subscript indices μ [French *valeurs mobilières* = securities] and *e* [French *escompter* = discount] remind us that we are discussing the discounting of financial assets.

13. This would be so only under the assumptions of case two where $i_B = i$.

14. No. 84.

As the liquidity, management, estimated-risk, and cost-of-risk premiums for Treasury Bonds and bills of exchange must normally[15] be little different[16] *in equilibrium*,[17] it can be seen that in practice we must have

(16) $$i_B \sim i_T \sim i - l_T;$$

in other words, *the discount rate of bills of exchange must normally be equal, in equilibrium, to the rate of interest on Treasury Bonds and, hence, less than the market's instantaneous pure interest rate for the liquidity premium of the latter.*

Exactly analogous reasoning also applies to repos (sale and repurchase agreements). As some individuals and some firms use their funds for such transactions, if we use i_r to denote the repo rate and l_r to denote the liquidity premium offered by such investments,[18] we must normally[15] have, *in equilibrium*,[17]

(17) $$i_r \sim i - l_r.$$

As in the case of Treasury Bonds, it can be shown that, since banks use their funds *at the same time* in both rediscount and repo transactions, the rate for the latter must *in equilibrium*[17] be little different from the discount rate, and hence we must have *in equilibrium*[17]

(18) $$i_B \sim i_r \sim i - l_r.$$

A similar conclusion could also be obtained for the rate i_A on secured loans. For the banks, this rate can obviously differ little from the discount rate. Neither can it be significantly different from the pure instantaneous

---

15. I.e., in periods of relatively stable prices.

16. Note that while we must take the estimated-risk premium ε_{TB} for Treasury Bonds to be strictly zero, since the risk of non-repayment is practically nonexistent, premium ε_B, for bills of exchange, is, in any event *usually* about zero too, as has already been pointed out (note 7 to no. 92).

Regarding premiums ρ_{TB} and ρ_B, it is obvious that the risk of inability to meet all demand liabilities owing to the issue of unbacked demand deposits is substantially the same whether it is bills of exchange or Treasury Bonds that are being discounted.

17. *This expression implies that what is at issue is a general tendency that can be verified only over a long period.*

18. This premium must be estimated to be of the same order as that for Treasury Bonds.

interest rate i, for if it were too far above it, borrowers would prefer to sell their securities and forgo their interest at pure rate i, and if it were too far below it, they would prefer to invest their money balances in securities, rebuilding them by secured loans. In reality, the former scenario does not usually arise, whereas a certain number of economic agents do in fact invest part of their money balances in securities even if this entails rebuilding their balances through the mechanism of secured loans. For these agents, at the margin, we thus have

$$i_B \sim i_A \sim i - g_A,$$

where g_A denotes a management premium corresponding to the costs incurred by this practice and policy.

In the long run, it emerges that the *equilibrium discount rate, notwithstanding the peculiarities due to the issue of unbacked demand deposits, usually differs little from the other short-term rates* already studied in no. 84.[19]

This crucial finding entitles us to extend to the case of discount rates all the reasoning presented in no. 84[20] *relating to other short-term interest rates.*

19. The practical outcome of this discussion is that the different short-term rates (discount rate, Treasury Bond rate, repo rate, etc.) necessarily have, in equilibrium, very similar values, while their average value would have to be lower than the pure rate of interest on the liquidity premium represented by short-term debt for the finances of economic agents other than banks. As we saw earlier (note 14 to no. 84), for habitual values of short-term rates, a safe estimate of the average value of this liquidity premium would be 1%. (This estimate seems to be empirically confirmed by the fact that the discount rate is usually 0.5% to 1.5% below the rates yielded by illiquid long-term and relatively risk-free investments.)

This is the hypothesis upon which I based my estimate of the pure interest rate in note 39 to no. 47. *But I stress that this estimate is only approximate.* Once again, all these questions entail *considerable difficulties* and to treat them adequately would call for a minute examination of facts that this writer has not yet been able to undertake; hence all the numerical applications given in this work are presented with *all due restrictions*; their real interest is to show how practical calculations can be made on the basis of empirical data. No doubt the future will bring major changes to these estimates (see the remarks already made in note 39 to no. 47 and in note 9 to no. 71).

20. As also in nos. 17, § "Variation of pure interest rates with maturity," and 30, § "Relation between instantaneous rates and average perpetual rates."

Case four

Let us now assume that the general assumptions of case three remain unchanged but that there is a Central Bank at which lending institutions can
rediscount their portfolio at the official rate i_E.

For rediscounting to be profitable *in a normal economic environment*,
the revenue from the new discounts made possible by funds obtained by
rediscounting must be greater than the cost of rediscounting. Now when
a bank rediscounts 1 franc's worth of bills of exchange, it forgoes the corresponding interest—i_E—as well as the ready availability of these bills, the
use-value of which is equal to their liquidity premium l_E plus the management costs g_E of the rediscount, and it gains the possibility of discounting
up to 1 franc's worth of new bills,[21] which, in light of the foregoing, earns
it the sum $(i_B - g_B - \varepsilon_B - \rho_B + l_B)$. So rediscounting is only profitable if

$$(19) \qquad i_B - g_B - \varepsilon_B - \rho_B + l_B > i_E + l_E + g_E,$$

i.e., if we disregard in first approximation the terms $(g_B - g_E)$, ε_B, and ρ_B
as being certainly very slight,

$$(20) \qquad i_B + l_B > i_E + l_E,$$

and equilibrium and rediscount can only coincide if

$$(21) \qquad i_B + l_B = i_E + l_E. \qquad\qquad [22]$$

Of course if

$$(22) \qquad i_B + l_B < i_E + l_E,$$

rediscounting cannot occur in equilibrium.

Two scenarios can therefore be envisaged depending on whether the
rediscount rate i_E is equal to or lower than the sum $i_B + (l_B - l_E)$. In the

---

21. If initially its reserve ratio was at its lowest level, this sequence of operations causes
the sum of 1 franc in cash to be removed from its vaults and replaced by an equivalent credit
with the Central Bank, leaving its portfolio of bills of exchange and its demand deposits unchanged. Thus the reserve ratio remains equal to its maximum κ_0.

22. On the assumptions of case two above, this equation of course becomes $i_B = i_E$.

first case, a certain volume of bills is rediscounted,[23] but in the second the volume of bills rediscounted is zero.

In the first case, the foregoing explanations show the close link between the official rediscount rate, current short-term rates and the pure instantaneous interest rate. There, too, they enable the substance of the findings of no. 84 to be extended to the short-term rates on loans not involving unbacked bank deposits.

Of course, for every franc of bills discounted, the Central Bank earns income equal per unit of time to the excess

$$i_E - g_E - \varepsilon_E$$

of its discount rate over the management costs g_E and the actual cost ε_E of the risks run.[24] As we have seen,[25] this income usually goes to cover the costs of services freely provided for the benefit of the State, i.e., for the community.

The Paris discount rate for "open-market" bills, eligible bills,
and ineligible bills

In Paris, *open-market* bills comprise drafts bearing the signature of major banks or of front-ranking firms. Their discount rate represents the open-market rate.

Eligible bills are those that fulfill the conditions required in order to be rediscounted by the Central Bank, even if they are not guaranteed by names as well-known as *open-market* bills.

Ineligible bills are those that do not fulfill the conditions required for admission to the portfolio of the Central Bank.

When there is a certain volume of rediscounted bills,[26] we have, from the foregoing

$$i_B + l_B = i_E + l_E,$$

23. What determines this volume will be seen later.
24. The unit cost ε_E is equal to the quotient of the losses incurred per unit of time divided by the average volume of bills discounted during this period.
  Note that the cost-of-risk premium ρ_E, as it represents a psychological cost that corresponds to no real cost, is not involved in estimating the real costs borne by the Central Bank.
25. No. 93.
26. The first possibility considered in case four above.

where i_E denotes the official rediscount rate, l_E the liquidity premium of the rediscounted bills, i.e., of the eligible bills, and where i_B and l_B denote the discount rate and the liquidity premium of a given bill for the lending bank.

If this bill is an *open-market* bill, in which case its liquidity will be greater than that of an eligible bill, its discount rate will obviously be slightly lower than the official rate.

If the bill is an ineligible bill, in which case its liquidity will be less than that of an eligible bill, its discount rate will of course be higher than the official rate.

If the bill is an eligible bill, premiums l_B and l_E will be equal and premiums g_B, ε_B, ρ_B, and g_E will no longer be negligible in comparison with the difference $(l_B - l_E)$, giving us

$$i_B = i_E + g_E + g_B + \varepsilon_B + \rho_B,$$

so that the discount rate will be slightly higher than the official rate.

In light of the foregoing explanations, this confirms that *the market rate on open-market bills is either slightly lower than the discount rate (when the volume of rediscounted bills ≠ zero), or independent of, but slightly lower than, this rate (when the volume of rediscounted bills = zero).*

Bank profits, justified and unjustified

While in theoretical competitive equilibrium bank income is strictly nil, as the price of discount is equal to its cost, in reality, banks are like any manufacturing firm.

On the one hand, equilibrium is never in fact reached, since structural conditions are constantly changing, thus giving rise to continual adjustments, and on the other hand, monopolistic situations may arise making it possible for prices to remain durably higher than costs.

In particular, it is quite certain that depositors will prefer to entrust their funds to well-known banking establishments even if the rate of interest they are paid is less, so, obviously, if the limited number of major lending houses collude, they can keep the interest rate they pay their depositors below the level that would correspond to competitive equilibrium.

It follows that (a) the equality between the price and the cost of discount exists only as a tendency and (b) it is perfectly possible for monopolistic action on the part of the major lending institutions to enable them to realize substantial excess profits,[27] but this is a straightforward question of fact that can only be settled by observation.

In any event, it would be a major error to think that the excess

$$[(1 - \kappa)i_B - i_D]M_S$$

of the interest $(1 - \kappa)i_B M_S$ earned by lending a fraction $(1 - \kappa)M_S$ of deposits M_S, over the interest $i_D M_S$ paid to depositors, constitutes net earnings that would represent "free income" for the banks—an "enrichment without cause" in the meaning of Roman law. The reality is that this difference normally covers the administrative costs of the lending banks and the risks they run. This would be entirely the case under competitive conditions and partially so in the case of a monopolistic market.

So if in some cases banks can make unjustified profits owing to monopolistic conditions, this should not be seen as an inescapable consequence of the banking structure but rather as a sign of a competitive dysfunction.[28,29]

27. The term *excess profit* here denotes that part of a firm's earnings that cannot be considered as the reward for a service rendered by the firm to the economy as a whole. (Concerning this concept see my *À la recherche d'une discipline économique*, no. 158.)

28. Under prevailing conditions, it would be sufficient for the Central Bank to offer greater direct discount facilities to firms (which it can always do since, in its case, discount operations do not require prior deposits) in order to put an end to any such monopolistic scenario.

This is why in France, for instance, lending banks have often put pressure on the Central Bank not to practice a low discount rate policy.

29. By the end of this discussion, notwithstanding *the excessive brevity imposed by the scope of the present study*, the reader will surely be left in no doubt that the subject of discount rates and short-term credit is *much more complex* than is thought by some superficial thinkers who are never assailed by the slightest doubt bearing on the specious clarity of the view they have so complacently embraced. The reality is that the subject is *especially difficult*, and calls for thorough analysis, both from the theoretical and the practical viewpoints.

5. Credit and financing (95)

If manufacturer (X) supplies retailer (Y) with merchandise to be paid for in three months' time, these terms mean that manufacturer (X) is in effect financing a part of retailer (Y)'s working capital. If manufacturer (X) then has the corresponding bill of exchange (E) discounted by bank (B), bank (B) replaces manufacturer (X) in financing retailer (Y)'s stock. The merchandise in reality belongs to bank (B) and its ownership is attested by the inclusion of the bill of exchange (E) among bank (B)'s assets.

But it should not be inferred that it is bank (B) that bears the real cost of this financing. Such a view would be quite mistaken, as can easily be seen from what follows.

Let C_φ and C_μ denote the economy's capital in the form of land and physical assets, respectively; let M_{MA} and M_{MB} denote the amounts of cash held, respectively, by all economic agents other than banks (i.e., by individuals and firms) and by the banks; let M_S denote the aggregate demand deposits for all banks collectively and M_{ME} the supplementary cash issued by the Central Bank, in addition to cash already in circulation, when the banks rediscount a part M_{ME} of their portfolio; and let M_M denote the total quantity $M_{MA} + M_{MB}$ of cash in circulation. It follows from the foregoing explanations that the respective balance sheets of all economic agents other than banks, of the banks and of the Central Bank stand as shown in table 8.5.[1]

Combining these equations shows that the total capital C owned by individuals[2] is given by the condition

(1) $$C = C_\varphi + C_\mu + M_M - E.$$ [3]

---

1. It is assumed *for the sake of simplicity* that the banks are the only customers of the Central Bank, that the private capital of the banks and of the Central Bank are negligible (no. 91), and that the banks have no current account with the Central Bank.

It should be recalled that we are also assuming inconvertible money.

2. This is the capital C of no. 39.

3. Of course, in the event that the Central Bank was a private organism and its income was not used to render free services to the community, it would be reinvested, and under the Central Bank's liabilities there would appear a further item, under the heading *Capital*, corresponding to the amount of this reinvestment. But at the same time, under the Central Bank's liabilities a new item of equal value would appear corresponding to the capitalized value of its future income. Thus it can be seen that equation (1) would in the long run remain unchanged.

TABLE 8.5

All Economic Agents Other Than Banks (Individuals and Firms)	
Assets	Liabilities
Land and physical assets $C_\varphi + C_\mu$ Cash balances M_{MA}	Capital C Promissory notes $V = M_S - M_{MB} + E^*$ (accepted bills)
Demand deposit balances M_S	

All Banks	
Assets Cash balances M_{MB} Portfolio of discounted bills $M_S - M_{MB}$	Liabilities Demand deposits M_S

Central Bank	
Assets Advances to the State $M_M - E$ Portfolio of discounted bills E	Liabilities Cash in circulation M_M

All Banks and Central Bank Together	
Assets Advances to the State** $A = M_M - E$ Cash balances M_{MB} Portfolio of discounted bills $V = Ms - M_{MB} + E$	Liabilities Cash M_M Demand deposits M_S

* This value is derived from the balance sheets of all banks together and of the Central Bank.
** This account usually corresponds, in the context of inconvertible money, to the amount of cash issued by the Central Bank other than for rediscount. If the Central Bank's bookkeeping is independent, this account is equal to the amount of cash successively put into circulation by the State, which has been advanced to it by the Central Bank.

Now the total capital C_T the economy requires to function is equal to the sum of land and reproducible capital plus the overall total M of money needed, i.e.,

$$(2) \qquad M = M_{MA} + M_S = M_M + (M_S - M_{MB}),$$

an equation that means that the aggregate quantity of circulating money is equal to the sum of the cash and of the unbacked demand deposits issued by the lending banks. This gives us

$$(3) \qquad C_T = C_\varphi + C_\mu + M.$$

It can then be seen that the use of credit *spares individuals the burden of financing* a fraction

(4) $$C_T - C = (M_S - M_{MB}) + E$$

of the capital required, equal to the sum of the unbacked demand deposits issued by all the banks collectively plus the amount of cash issued by the Central Bank in rediscount operations.[4] *This financing is not in fact paid for by anybody and is simply covered by the promissory notes for the same amount issued by the firms.*

If we use $C_{\mu e}$ to denote the fraction of financial capital that has been discounted,[5] we shall have

(5) $$C_{\mu e} = M_S - M_{MB} + E = C_T - C,$$

so that the credit mechanism may *equally* well be said to have the effect of sparing individuals the burden of financing *either* the discounted capital $C_{\mu e}$ *or* the part of their money balances $(M_S - M_{MB} + E)$, which corresponds to the issue of unbacked demand deposits by the banks and of cash by the Central Bank via rediscount.

If, in light of these explanations, we now return to the example given at the beginning of the present no. 95, the balance sheet provided shows that the ownership by the banks and the Central Bank of the discounted capital $C_{\mu e}$ represented by the sum $(M_S - M_{MB} + E)$ of the total portfolio of discounted bills is offset in their liabilities to an equal amount by demand deposits or by money. This sum, which also figures among the assets on the collective balance sheet of all economic agents is offset, under their liabilities, by the sum $(M_S - M_{MB} + E)$ of the promissory notes issued by firms. Finally, it is seen that *the financing of the discounted capital $C_{\mu e}$ is borne not by the banks but by the firms themselves via the issue of promises to pay in the future.* Hence, this financing is not included in the capital C, and the overall savings C of individuals are spared this burden. *In this way, the credit mechanism ultimately relieves the economy of the burden of financing a part of its capital.*

But, as indicated above, it can equally well be considered that the mechanism ultimately relieves the economy of the financing of a part of its money balances. From this viewpoint, the opinion of the classical

4. Note once more that demand deposits with the Central Bank are perfectly equivalent to cash and that for the sake of simplicity only the issue of cash has been considered here (note 1 above).

5. See previous no. 94.

economists that credit leads to a *saving of money* turns out to be entirely
justified.[6,7]

Finally, it can be seen that *every discount operation has two quite dis-*
tinct aspects: a monetary aspect and a financing aspect; the former of which
consists in the issue of a sum of money equal in value to the sum of bills

6. The fact that paper money, which we are considering here, entails practically no production cost makes no difference to this result. For the value of money does not in fact stem from
its cost of production; as for any good, it is exclusively due to the present value of its future
use — a value that is itself derived from its liquidity advantages.

Hence, we must conclude that the value of the money used by the economy is or is not
borne by the community depending on whether or not it is financed by savings.

7. This analysis only takes account of capital assets, but it is obvious that identical conclusions would be reached by adopting the viewpoint of the cost in terms of income (i.e., of the
interest charges corresponding to financing), instead of the viewpoint of capital.

For, considering all individuals and firms collectively, the financing of land, other capital
assets, and aggregate money balances costs at every point in time — assuming for the sake of
simplicity, equilibrium and cost-free, risk-free discount — the amount expressed by

$$iC_T = i(C_\varphi + C_\mu + M).$$

But from this cost must be deducted (a) the interest

$$i_D M_S = (1 - \kappa)i M_S$$

paid by the lending banks to their depositors and (b) the cost i of the services freely rendered
by the Central Bank. Hence, the final cost of financing the ongoing action of the economy that
must be borne by individuals is

(2) $$iC_T - (1 - \kappa)i M_S - iE = iC,$$

since we have

(3) $$(1 - \kappa)M_S = M_S - M_{MB}.$$

Thus it can be seen that in the long run individuals are spared the cost

(4) $$i(C_T - C) = (M_S - M_{MB} + E) = iC_{\mu e}$$

corresponding to financing either the discounted capital or the part of money balances that
correspond to unbacked demand deposits and to issues of cash via rediscount by the Central Bank.

Thus it becomes clear that *money issued on the occasion of a loan is money that, in the*
last analysis, costs nothing. It does not entail a burden to be borne by savings either as capital
or as a source of cost.

discounted and the latter in relieving individuals of the burden of financing—to an equivalent amount—part of the real investments made by firms.[8]

---

8. Of course all the foregoing explanations concerning discount operations could be transposed without difficulty to the case of loans extended by banks to their customers. The only fundamental difference from the theoretical point of view here adopted is that a loan cannot be rediscounted.

Loans play a major role, one that—as in England, for instance—can be greater than that played by discount.

C. Determination of the Rate of Interest

Equilibrium and disequilibrium (96)

The role played by the interest rate in the process of dynamic disequilib-rium[1] *that characterizes the real economic world cannot be understood without first having a clear idea of the conditions of economic equilibrium, for they typify the basic tendencies of economic development.* They are also much easier to study than the complex, multifaceted interplay of actions and reactions observed each day in the dynamic disequilibrium process we live in, and *without the solid foundations provided by their prior study, the inquirer is exposed to the danger of misunderstandings that in the long run may prove highly pernicious.*

This, of course, is a preparation for, and not an alternative to, the study of real-world conditions, full understanding of which will require analysis of the cause-and-effect sequences involved in actual economic develop-ment. Indeed elucidation of the role of the rate of interest under dynamic disequilibrium—a task that *bridges* the divide between the classical the-ory of the savings-investment equilibrium and modern theories of money and price levels—undeniably comprises the *central issue* around which the whole of contemporary economic thought gravitates.

The final resolution of this difficulty seems set to be one of the most important milestones in economic theory. For, once it has been completed, bright light will be shed on fundamental phenomena that at present still lie in the half-dark.

As the limited scope of the present study rules out the detailed ex-planations that a complete analysis—entailing a general theory of money and cycles—would require, once again a brief outline must suffice whose only goal will be to clarify the main links between interest theory and the theories of money and of the general price level.

I shall begin by assuming that banks have no unbacked demand de-posits and that cash is inconvertible;[2] then I shall examine how the re-sults obtained must be completed when unbacked demand deposits are issued both by private banks and by the Central Bank and when money

---

1. Note 2 to no. 9.
2. I.e., its value is not pegged to that of any other good, such as gold.

in circulation is convertible.[3] In both cases I shall first assume a process of dynamic equilibrium and then of dynamic disequilibrium.

3. This division parallels the division adopted in nos. 84 *et seq.*

(a) 100% backing of demand deposits

1. Determination of the rate of interest in the dynamic equilibrium process of an economy having no unbacked demand deposits and in which cash is inconvertible (97)

Generally speaking, as for account-based economies, theory shows that for a given psychological and technical structure,[1] the dynamic economic equilibrium of a monetary economy having no unbacked demand deposits and using a given volume of inconvertible cash is well determined. In particular, it can be shown that for given structural conditions in the absence of State intervention there exists *only one* stationary state in which the conditions of economic equilibrium are verified.

In the same way, when the State intervenes, for instance, by acting on the capital market either as borrower or as lender, a further degree of freedom is introduced and there are an infinity of stable stationary equilibria corresponding to any given psychological and technical structure, each of these equilibria corresponding to a different stock of capital equipment and a different interest rate.[2]

An examination of the characteristics of the dynamic equilibrium of a monetary economy having no unbacked demand deposits and whose cash volume at each instant is given, may be carried out in three successive stages, the first assuming stationary conditions,[3] the second quasi-stationary conditions,[4] and the third conventional structural conditions.

Stationary model

In a stationary equilibrium, the different expressions of the same interest rate are all equal and independent of the yardstick adopted[3] while the different interest rates themselves—psychological interest rates,[5] technical

---

1. Including the percentage costs of the borrowing, investment in, and liquidation of physical assets (no. 82) involved in determining money balances.

2. This is confirmed by perusal of the simplified models set out in appendix II, § B (no. 208 in particular).

3. No. 19.

4. No. 69.

5. No. 40.

interest rates,[6] liquidity premiums of money[7]—are all equal to the same value, here termed the real equilibrium interest rate and denoted by i_r.

As a first approximation, as seen above,[7] *the equilibrium equations may be replaced by those that would characterize an account-based economy*. It follows that the first approximation values of the various physical parameters,[8] the relative prices of the various goods, and the real equilibrium interest rate are *independent of the monetary conditions* represented by the liquidity functions l and of the total amount of money in circulation.

As to the general price level, it settles at a level such that the sum of individual money balances—which is itself a function of the rate of interest[7] and proportional to the general price level[9]—is precisely equal to the total quantity of money in circulation. *The real money balances, which in this case reduce to the real working capital,[10] are determined by the real equilibrium interest rate while the price level is determined by the ratio of the quantity of money to real money balances.[11]*

6. No. 44.

7. No. 82.

8. Production and consumption per unit of time, inventory, etc.

9. No. 80.

10. Since structural conditions stay the same and a physically stationary process prevails, foresight may be assumed to be perfect.

11. As rate i is given by the equilibrium conditions, which as a first approximation are independent of monetary conditions, the real level

$$M''(i) = M_R''(i) + M_T''(i)$$

of total money balances, which here reduces to $M_R''(i)$, is well determined, and price level P follows from the equation

$$M = PM''(i).$$

When money consists exclusively of ready cash and its physical quantity (e.g., the number of coins or of bank notes) is well determined, its aggregate level M follows from the price set for the monetary unit. This confirms that *in the case of a monetary economy the determination of the price level basically depends on the price set for the specific intermediate good used as money*.

And this is absolutely parallel to what occurs in an account-based economy in which there is no money and the determination of the price level can only depend on setting the price of a particular good or set of goods.

In any event, it is clear that the nominal price level is determined by the definition of the unit of account, i.e., by specifying the price of a single good selected as benchmark.

In second approximation the equilibrium equations can no longer be replaced by those which would characterize an account-based economy. For as we have seen,[7] in this case corrective terms are introduced in which the interest rate i is a factor,[12] so that the real equilibrium interest rate depends on the liquidity functions l, but here too the values of the different physical parameters, the relative prices, the interest rate, and real money balances $\dfrac{M^y}{P}$ are independent of the quantity of money M.

Finally, it can be seen that *in a stationary equilibrium, the order of magnitude of the rate of interest is absolutely independent of conditions of a monetary nature, for it depends only on the equilibrium between consumers' propensity to save and firms' propensity to invest, while the greater or lesser liquidity preference does not determine the interest rate*—as many authors seem to think—*but the price level. This level is in fact greater as the total amount of money* M *is greater and as liquidity preference[13] is weaker.*

Of course, strictly speaking, the level of the interest rate depends on liquidity preference, but as a rule this dependence involves only a differential variation. In any event, the rate of interest is independent of the total amount of money.

Moreover, it is easy to see the impact of the differential action of money on the interest rate, for the desire to hold money in real terms diminishes proportionally the propensity to save, which seeks its satisfaction in the form of investments, i.e., the propensity to invest in financial assets. So, in equilibrium, *the existence of circulating money may be taken to have the effect of raising the interest rate to a level higher than that which*

In the specific case of an economy using money but having as unit of account some good other than the unit of circulating money, the price level P would be determined by the definition of the unit of account, and the price $\overline{m}$ of the unit of circulating money existing in quantity N would be determined by the equation

$$N\overline{m} = M = PM''(i),$$

where the function $M''(i)$ is independent of the quantity N of monetary units in circulation.

12. Such as the terms $iM, i\,\dfrac{\frac{\partial l}{\partial B}}{\frac{\partial l}{\partial M}}$ of equations (4) and (6) of no. 82.

13. Which can be measured, for a given interest rate, by the level of actual money balances.

it would have had in its absence.[14,15] The effect of this on the spontaneous
equilibrium corresponding to the absence of any State intervention is a
fall in social productivity.

These results may be confirmed in the following way. In equilibrium
the real capital C^r held by individuals is equal, as we have seen,[16] to the
sum of the real value $C_\varphi^r(i)$ of the land plus the real value $C_\mu^r(i)$ of the
reproducible capital plus the real value M_M^r of the cash, here equal to
the real value M^r of money in circulation, i.e., to the overall desired money
balances $M(i)$ where i is the real equilibrium interest rate of the stationary
process under consideration. So let $C_0^r(i)$ be the supply of capital in real
terms by the consumers. This supply is equal to the amount of real capital
they wish to hold in order to balance over time their flows of expected
income and intended expenditure.[17] *In equilibrium* this gives us[18]

(1) $$C_\varphi^r(i) + C_\mu^r(i) + M^r(i) = C_0^r(i).$$

If there were no money (as in an account-based economy), this equation would become

(2) $$C_\varphi^r(i) + C_\mu^r(i) = C_0^r(i).$$

These equations may be represented by the graph shown in figure 8.13.

14. Since the interest rate is proportionately higher as the value of invested capital is
lower (no. 47).

15. The reader will have realized that this intuitive reasoning implicitly assumes a stable
equilibrium.

It can also be said that if the equilibrium is stable, a fall in the propensity to financial
investment must bring about a variation in the interest rate I that, of itself, would tend to
counter the equilibrium change, i.e., that, of itself, would liberate savings. This variation would
necessarily be upward. (This is just a particular application of a general law of stable equilibria, the law of systematic displacement, concerning which readers may find all useful information in my general work *À la recherche d'une discipline économique*, no. 183.)

16. No. 95, equation (1), where $E = 0$ (i.e., there are no unbacked demand deposits).

17. It is worth emphasizing that this function is *absolutely independent of conditions of a
monetary nature*. It depends only on the expected structure of receipts and on the greater or
lesser psychological propensity of economic agents to use them in this or that way by postponing or advancing the date of consumption of their incomes.

18. The supply of capital here considered, for conditions of dynamic equilibrium, should
not be confused with the supply of capital corresponding to dynamic disequilibrium. (See
what has already been said about this distinction in note 12 to no. 40 and notes 46 and 48 to
no. 47.)

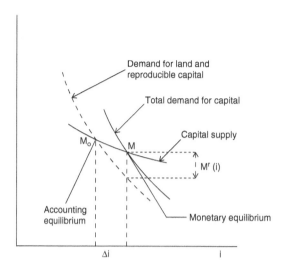

FIGURE 8.13

If we assume that the equilibrium is stable, i.e., that for a rate lower than the equilibrium rate demand falls short of supply and vice versa, it is clear that *the use of money has the effect of raising the rate of interest to a higher level than it would otherwise have had.*

But it also transpires that if the real demand for money balances is low in comparison with overall demand for land and capital—as is usually the case in reality—*the rate i corresponding to monetary equilibrium is little different from what it would be under moneyless conditions.*[19]

When interest rate *i* is determined in this way, the price level follows from the equation

(3)
$$P = \frac{M_M}{M^r(i)},$$

---

19. In fact, as experience shows that for different countries and different periods since 1910 aggregate money balances are of the order of magnitude of three quarters of national income, it can be inferred that the level of the equilibrium interest rate corresponding to the use of ready cash, *to the exclusion of all demand deposits*, would be on the order of 1.5% (in light of the analysis presented in no. 70). Since the order of magnitude of the pure interest rate is normally on the order of 3% to 5%, it is clear how much influence the use of cash may have on the equilibrium position. We shall see later (no. 99) how these observations should be completed when demand deposits are used as money.

where M_M denotes the amount of cash in circulation and $M^r(i)$ the aggregate demand for real money balances. This confirms that the equilibrium interest rate normally depends relatively little on liquidity preference,[20] which in fact is what chiefly determines the price level.[21]

Quasi-stationary model

In a quasi-stationary model,[4] all conditions of a physical nature remain unchanged. Only the amount of money in circulation M varies with time, and its variations are assumed to be known so that foresight may still be assumed to be perfect.

It is worth noting that under these conditions real money balances

$$(4) \qquad M_Y^r = \frac{M_Y}{P}$$

are decreasing functions of the marginal liquidity premiums[22] and are *independent* of price levels. For this scenario the fact that the various physical elements are stationary entails perfect foresight so that in real terms the marginal advantage presented by a real money balance depends only on the flow of real values.[23] If we also assume this flow of values to be constant as a first approximation,[24] real money balances may also be taken to be independent of variations in price levels.

Finally as a first approximation we may assume that in equilibrium

$$(5) \qquad M_Y^r = M_Y^r(l_M),$$

20. Represented by the function $M^r(i)$.

21. All these assertions will be confirmed by the study of a specific case (appendix II, § B, no. 208).

22. Which, as we have seen, are equal to their real value (equation [2] of note 27 to no. 82).

23. In the case of the example in note 12 to no. 82, a closely analogous calculation could be made in the event of variation of any kind in the price level.

This would give us

$$P = P_0 \frac{\varphi(t)}{\varphi(0)}, \quad R = R_0 \frac{\varphi(t)}{\varphi(0)}, \quad F = F_0 \frac{\varphi(t)}{\varphi(0)}.$$

But the calculations would all remain *unchanged* if carried out in real terms.

24. I.e., as independent of relative price variations. (See note 35 below.)

where l_M is the common value of marginal liquidity premiums, M_Y^r is the real value of the money balance of economic agent (Y), and $M_Y^r(l_M)$ is a decreasing function independent of the price level and its variations.

Now, we know[25] that *in dynamic equilibrium* the nominal equilibrium interest rate i_e is equal to the real equilibrium interest rate i_r plus the relative rate of price increase so that we have

(6)
$$i_e = i_r + \frac{\frac{dP}{dt}}{P},$$
[26]

and hence, in the most general case, when the unit of account is different in value from the unit of money,[27]

(7)
$$l_M = i_r + \frac{\frac{dP}{dt}}{P} - \frac{\frac{d\overline{m}}{dt}}{m},$$

25. No. 19, equation (6).

26. It follows from equation (7) of no. 33 that the value-yield of an asset (A) is given by the equation

(1)
$$r_A = i_e + \alpha_A + \varepsilon_A + \rho_A - \mu_A - \gamma_A.$$

Now, in a quasi-stationary model, the capital value gain premium γ_A is zero, risk premiums must also be assumed to be zero, and rate μ_A is equal to the rate of rise in price level P. So under such conditions we have

(2)
$$r_A = i_r + \alpha_A,$$

which means that under quasi-stationary conditions the real interest rate is equal to the usual value of the surplus of value-yields over depreciation premiums.

If we then use i_A to denote the market interest rate expressed in terms of good (A), we obtain, in light of the findings of no. 19,

$$i_A = i - \frac{\frac{d\overline{a}}{dt}}{\overline{a}} = i_r + \frac{\frac{dP}{dt}}{P} - \frac{\frac{d\overline{a}}{dt}}{\overline{a}} = i_r,$$

since, under quasi-stationary conditions, all prices vary in the same way. This confirms that in such a model all expressions of the interest rate in real terms have an identical common value.

27. No. 82, equation (11).

where $\overline{m}$ denotes the nominal value at each instant of the unit of money and P the level of nominal prices.[28]

If, as is the case in present-day economies, the unit of circulating money is at the same time the unit of account $(\overline{m} = 1)$, we naturally have

$$(8) \qquad\qquad l_M = i_r + \frac{\frac{dP}{dt}}{P},$$

and hence

$$(9) \qquad\qquad M_Y^r = M_Y^r \left(i_r + \frac{\frac{dP}{dt}}{P} \right).$$

This shows that the real values of the money balances are decreasing functions of the relative rate of price variation. It follows that all the physical conditions characterizing the equilibrium, which may be deemed to be determined by the general equilibrium equations expressed in real terms,[29] turn out to be functions of the relative rate of price variation.[30] So *the equilibrium can be quasi-stationary only if this rate of variation is itself constant.*

It thus becomes clear that there are infinite quasi-stationary equilibria, each of them characterized by a given value of the relative rate

$$(10) \qquad\qquad \pi = \frac{\frac{dP}{dt}}{P}$$

of price variation.

28. I.e., expressed in units of account.

29. As well as by the general equations of the equilibrium expressed in nominal terms.

30. Thus intrinsic equation (12) of no. 82 expressed in real terms is

$$a_r A + b_r B + \ldots + c_r C + \left(i_r - \frac{\frac{d\overline{m}_r}{dt}}{\overline{m}_r} \right) M_r = R_r,$$

i.e.,

$$a_r A + b_r B + \ldots + c_r C + \left(i_r - \frac{\frac{dP}{dt}}{P} \right) M_r = R_r.$$

In each of these economic states the level of real money balances rises as rate π falls. Now it follows from the equation

(11) $$C_\varphi^r(i_r) + C_\mu^r(i_r) + M^r(i_r + \pi) = C_0^r(i_r)$$

that the greater the real value of money balances, the higher the real interest rate i_r—a circumstance explained by the fact that holding real money partially satisfies the propensity to save and thereby diminishes investment in capital.[31] It follows that the real interest rate i_r in equilibrium is greater, as rate π is lower.

But as long as the overall real value of money remains low in comparison with the overall real value of the nation's aggregate physical assets, the variations in rate i_r may naturally be taken to be slight in comparison with rate π.[32] This is particularly so in the economies we are familiar with.[33,34]

---

31. Note that under stationary conditions the real interest rate may be deemed to be proportionately higher, as real reproducible capital is less (note 48 to no. 47).

These cursory observations will be illustrated by the study of a specific case in appendix II, § B (see in particular nos. 208 and 210).

32. Thus, if the level of aggregate money balances is one-tenth of the level of national real capital, doubling money balances will lead to a variation on the order of 10% in capital and hence to a relatively slight change in rate i_r.

33. As a first approximation, average aggregate real money balances may be taken to be equal to a year's real national income—which is, as we have seen 1/6 or 1/8 of real national capital (note 39 to no. 47).

34. What happens can easily be grasped using a simplified example. For instance, let us assume that national wealth consists only of physical assets and money (no land) and that, using wage terms to express the various values involved (no. 19), we have

(1) $$M'' = \frac{\alpha}{i'' + \pi},$$

(2) $$C_\mu'' + M'' = K,$$

(3) $$\frac{dC_\mu''}{di''} = -\beta.$$

These equations express, respectively, (1) that the aggregate money balance in wage terms M'' is infinite for a zero nominal interest rate $i = i'' + \pi$, (2) that the capital of individuals in wage terms $(C_\mu'' + M'')$ remains constant when the wage-denominated interest rate varies (no. 40), and (3) that physical capital in wage terms C_μ'' is a decreasing linear function of the wage-denominated rate of interest i'' (note 48 to no. 47).

If we choose plausible values for coefficients α, β, and K so that for values $i'' = 5\%$ and $\pi = 0$ we have

(4) $M'' = \dfrac{3}{4}R_N''$, $\Theta_N = \dfrac{C_\mu''}{R_N''} = 6$, $\beta = -55R_{N\omega}''$,

equations that are broadly confirmed by experience (note 28 above and notes 39 and 48 to no. 47) and taking into account equation (15) to no. 47, which here becomes

(5) $R_N'' = 1.3R_{N\omega}''$,

we obtain

(6) $M'' = 0.049\dfrac{R_{N\omega}''}{i'' + \pi}$,

(7) $C_\mu'' + M'' = 8.8R_{N\omega}''$,

(8) $C_\mu'' = R_{N\omega}''(10 - 55i'')$.

These assumptions mean that figure 8.13 in the text now looks like figure 8.14.

For a given rate π, the equilibrium rate i'' is located at the intersection of the straight line representing the difference $K - C_\mu''$, with the curve C_π, which is deduced from the curve C_0, representing the function

(9) $M'' = 0.049\dfrac{R_{N\omega}''}{i''}$

by a translation toward the right equal to $-\eta$.

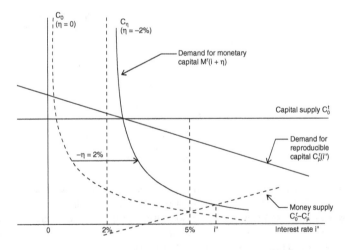

FIGURE 8.14 FOOTNOTE

From conditions (6), (7), and (8) we can immediately deduce the equation

(10)
$$\eta = \frac{0.049}{55i'' - 1.6} - i''.$$

And as the nominal interest rate

(11)
$$i = i'' + \pi$$

must be positive, it can be seen that the wage-denominated interest rate i'' must remain higher than the value $\dfrac{1.85}{55} \sim 3.5\%$ and that the shape of the representative curves of rates i'' and i as a function of rate π is as shown in figure 8.15 below.

The level of 3.5% for i'' is simply the level of rate i'' that would correspond to equilibrium in an account-based economy of the same structure as the economy we are considering. And in the absence of circulating money, we should in fact have

(12)
$$C_\mu'' = K = 8.8 R_{N\omega}'',$$

an equation that, in combination with equation (8), would give

$$i'' \sim 3.5\%.$$

Thus, when the rate π of price increase rises indefinitely, the real equilibrium interest rate tends through higher values toward the level it would have under moneyless conditions. This tendency is of general validity: equation (1) in the text tends toward equation (2) as, when rate π increases, the level of aggregate demand for money balances $M^r(i)$ tends towards zero (but of course the interest rate limit is not necessarily positive and may be negative, depending

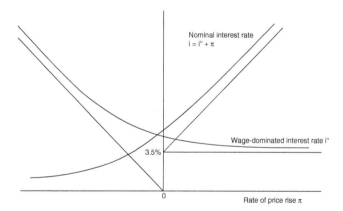

FIGURE 8.15 FOOTNOTE

These facts are illustrated in figure 8.16.

Curve C is the representative curve of money balances as a function of nominal interest rate i. The economic state corresponding to $\pi = 0$ is represented by point M_0, while states corresponding to a continuous rise $\pi = +\alpha$ or to a continuous fall $\pi = -\alpha$ are respectively represented by M_1 and M_2. In the first case, the real interest rate $i_r(\alpha)$ is inferior to interest rate $i_r(0)$, corresponding to price stability, and in the second the real interest rate $i_r(-\alpha)$ is superior to it, but in both cases the difference is slight.

Clearly *in both cases the real level of money balances undergoes considerable variations.*[35]

---

essentially on the structures involved). (See chapter 9, "The Problem of Interest," no. 137; see also appendix II, § B, no. 209.)

It is confirmed that for $\pi = 0$ we have

$$di'' \sim -\frac{d\pi}{4},$$

an equation that shows that the variations of i'' are lower than the values of π (which are equal to $d\pi$, since π varies in the vicinity of zero).

Note, too, that when rate π increases through negative values, the wage interest rate rises enough for the nominal rate to remain positive and that, in the vicinity of the conditions corresponding to price stability, a given increase in π has a much weaker influence on the equilibrium wage-denominated rate i'' than a decrease of the same size.

When rate π reaches -17.4%, the interest rate expressed in wage terms reaches 18% and real capital in wage terms C_μ'' falls to zero. This means that, *on the assumptions made*, values of π lower than -17.4% bring about the absence of all real capital, implying exclusive recourse to direct production processes. Money balances will then be the only form of capital in private hands.

It should be borne in mind that under quasi-stationary conditions the different real expressions of the interest rate are equal (no. 69). The above calculation was made in wage terms because this yardstick enables the primary national income $R_{N\omega}''$ to be assumed constant while the wage-denominated interest rate i'' varies.

Note that the shape of the curves obtained *would remain the same* in the usual case in which the expressions of functions M'' and C_μ'' are *unexceptional*, assuming simply that demand for balances becomes infinite in real terms for a zero nominal interest rate and that real capital in terms of wages is a decreasing function of rate i''.

35. These results are of course subject to the fact that aggregate money balances $M(l_M)$ can be deemed *as a first approximation* to be a function independent of wage-level fluctuations, i.e., of wage-denominated interest rate i''. Now, however, when rate i'' falls, the structure becomes more capital-intensive, so that production comprises more successive stages, and hence, for a given value of l_M, more money is required; by contrast, the amount of income in circulation falls in wage terms (we have seen in no. 47 *in fine* that national income R_N decreases

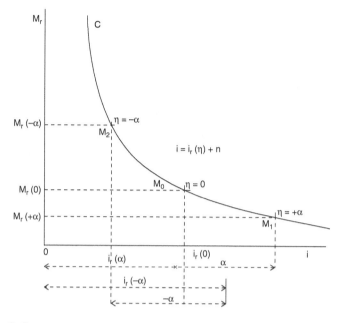

FIGURE 8.16

The general price level naturally stabilizes in both cases at a value P such that we have

(12) $$P = \frac{M}{M_r},$$

where M denotes the volume of the circulation.

If π remains constant, M_r does too, and we have

(13) $$\pi = \frac{\dfrac{dM}{dt}}{M}.$$ 36

---

when the rate of interest falls). So as a first approximation these two effects may be deemed to cancel one another out.

36. The foregoing remarks show that in dynamic equilibrium the proportionality coefficient relating prices to the amount of money is so much the greater as the relative rate of price increase is higher. Thus it is clear that *even in equilibrium* it would be a mistake to believe that there is a simple proportionality between prices and the quantity of money. In fact this would only be so in a stationary equilibrium.

Finally, it is clear that, as long as price variations remain on the same order as the real equilibrium interest rate, it is safe *as a first approximation* to take *the order of magnitude* of the real interest rate, as in the stationary model, as determined by the equilibrium between individuals' propensity to save and firms' propensity to invest, while the nominal interest rate depends only on the relative variations in the volume of money and remains independent of its absolute amount.[37] Thus, *in equilibrium the determination of the rate of interest results as a first approximation from the addition of two components, the one concerning the physical conditions of the economy and the other its monetary conditions.*

Of course, *strictly speaking*, here once again, the level of the real equilibrium interest rate depends on liquidity preference, but this dependence normally affects it only differentially.

It also depends on the rate of price variation, but so long as this rate does not reach significant levels it entails only slight variations in the real interest rate.

Finally the nominal interest rate, like the real rate, depends only on the rate of variation in the quantity of money and not on its absolute amount.

It should be emphasized that under quasi-stationary conditions the real interest rate is proportionately lower—and hence social productivity is proportionately greater[38]—as the rate of increase in the quantity of money is higher.

It may be inferred that, *provided equilibrium prevails (the inflation remains moderate), inflation, by lowering the real equilibrium interest rate, favors an increase in social productivity.*

Conversely it is also clear that *a policy of deflation, even if it is possible to maintain the dynamic economic equilibrium, would in the long run be disadvantageous,* since by increasing the real value of capital held in the form of money, it would decrease the real value of capital invested in production and hence bring about a *fall in social productivity.*

A noteworthy consequence of this is that, on average, lengthy periods of rising prices are, other things being equal, more prosperous than lengthy periods of falling prices.[39]

---

37. Equation (6) above.

38. No. 71.

39. This motive of prosperity is of course not the only one: it comes on top of others, which may indeed have greater influence—such as the fact that, on average, firms realize a profit when prices are rising and a loss when they are falling (see note 3 to no. 107).

Conventional model

The foregoing findings can readily be extended to a model displaying everyday structural conditions, neither stationary nor quasi-stationary, and having imperfect foresight. The only difference will be that in this case *real money balances cannot be reduced to working capital: they must also include speculative reserves.*

As before, *in equilibrium* it is safe to take *the order of magnitude* of the *real instantaneous interest rate* as due not to monetary conditions, but to the equilibrium between consumers' propensity to save and firms' propensity to invest.[40]

The instantaneous nominal interest rate is of course equal to the instantaneous real rate plus the relative rate of increase in the quantity of money. It is independent of the absolute quantity of money.

It is this interest rate that, in combination with liquidity preference, determines the level of money balances in real terms, and this level, in combination with the total quantity of money, is what determines the price level.

Hence, the price level is greater as the quantity of money M is higher and as liquidity preference is lower.

Naturally, as before, the exact level of the real interest rate in equilibrium depends both on liquidity preference and on the rate of variation in the quantity of money, but this dependence normally causes it to vary only differentially.

What chiefly emerges from this is the *complexity of identifying exactly what determines the equilibrium interest rate,*[41] depending as it does on the simultaneous interaction of psychological, technical, and monetary conditions. There is no possible comparison between the attention needed to grasp the theory of the price of a specific good—the market for which may

40. Of course, this result is valid only so long as liquidity preference remains inconsiderable, as is generally the case. If liquidity preference becomes strong enough to make the real value of money balances much greater than the real value of capital assets, the order of magnitude of the equilibrium interest rate might not only depend on liquidity preference but even depend on it almost exclusively.

41. Remember (no. 96) that this study is crucial for anyone wishing to disentangle, in the dynamic process of the economy out of equilibrium, the basic trends that constantly tend to appear and whose underlying action, though sometimes unseen, may nonetheless produce highly significant effects.

in first approximation legitimately be considered in isolation from the rest of the economy—and the mental effort required to understand the complex and simultaneous interrelations that lead to the determination of the interest rate. Faced with such complexity, the outrageously simplistic theories we are all familiar with have gravely distorted reality, deliberately or otherwise, by concealing crucial difficulties. *And we are dealing only with the theory of dynamic equilibrium!*

Pure interest rate and rising prices

We have just seen that *in equilibrium* the pure nominal interest rate is equal to the pure real rate plus the relative rate of increase in the quantity of money.

This confirms that the pure interest rate, as I have defined it, implicitly contains, as pointed out above,[42] a premium reflecting general variations in prices, whether upwards or downwards.

42. No. 11.

2. Determination of the rate of interest in the dynamic disequilibrium of an economy having no unbacked demand deposits, no hoarding, and using inconvertible cash (98)

We have outlined the conditions that characterize equilibrium. We must now inquire how this equilibrium can be achieved. And this, as has already been pointed out, is a much harder question.

It follows from what has been said that (a) *in equilibrium* the order of magnitude of the real interest rate is determined, independently of monetary conditions, by the equilibrium between consumers' propensity to save[1] and firms' propensity to invest; (b) the nominal interest rate is equal to the sum of the real interest rate and the rate of variation in the quantity of money; and (c) the money balances of the different economic agents are well determined as a function of the nominal interest rate. Now, the sum of these money balances must be precisely equal to the total quantity of money M, which raises the question of *how this adjustment takes place in equilibrium*. The foregoing analysis has shown that the requisite adjustment occurs through variation in the price level, which stabilizes at a level such that the nominal value of the balances, whose real value is determined by the real equilibrium interest rate,[2] is in fact equal to the total quantity of money M.

Thus, *in equilibrium*, the sequence of these determinations would *in first approximation* be as follows. The equilibrium between consumers' propensity to save and firms' propensity to invest determines the real interest rate. The real interest rate and the rate of increase in the quantity of money determine the nominal interest rate. The nominal interest rate determines the real value of money balances. The real value of money balances in combination with the total quantity of money determines the price level.

But the question that calls for an answer is how such a delicate and complex adjustment actually happens, as a continuous process, under the dynamic disequilibrium prevailing in the real world. And finding the answer is undoubtedly the *most serious challenge* facing the ongoing progress of economic science. In the present state of our knowledge, although there

---

1. A propensity that, *in equilibrium*, would *in first approximation* be the same as the propensity for financial investment, with real money balances remaining more or less constant.

2. Nos. 82 and 97.

is no consensus among economists as to the solution, it may at least be agreed that the problem has been clearly defined and it is to the great credit of the contemporary Anglo-Saxon school, and of John Maynard Keynes in particular, to have stressed the need for this problem to be resolved and to have tried to formulate it comprehensively.[3]

3. On this subject the reader is recommended to read Keynes's *General Theory of Employment, Interest, and Money.*

The merit of J. M. Keynes, in my opinion, is not to have solved the difficult problem of the link between the classical interest rate theory and the theories of money and price levels—a task in which he has not in fact succeeded; it is to have shown that this link is a subject deserving thorough debate and to have endeavored (though to my mind without full success) clearly to state its conditions. But even thus reduced to proportions much more modest than those claimed for him by some of his admirers (not to say worshippers), Keynes's contribution to the progress of economic thought is undeniably a major one.

For although as an economic construct the *General Theory* displays inconsistencies and cannot bear thorough examination by any exact and systematic thinker, the value of Keynes's work—even aside from his justified attacks on the failure of the classical school to give sufficient recognition to the link between the theories of interest and of money and on the barren prejudices of the orthodox liberals—remains of the highest order. Wonderfully set out, with rare humor and an unequalled polemical talent, almost always brilliant, sometimes even dazzling, the work teems with judicious observations and original insights. There is *no better instrument for stimulating thought*, and its perusal is certainly the foremost duty of any serious economist. Almost every page offers new stimulus for reflection.

Though inadequate as a rigorous overall theorist, J. M. Keynes displays an unrivalled intuitive mind, offering fruitful topics for reflection to exact thinkers who are unsatisfied by woolliness.

Such are the true scope and the real merits of Keynes's work, but I fear that they are not widely recognized, as most of his readers have based their admiration on the *General Theory*'s new synthesis—i.e., on what is undeniably its worst aspect.

What is the explanation of this error? Apart from the difficulty generally found in isolating the positive contributions of a work that is unusually broad in scope, and apart from the natural mental sloth that attracts readers more to eye-catching creations painted with broad strokes of the brush that the first-comer can comment on without effort than to the analyses of specific questions, which, no matter how penetrating, are quite beyond either the understanding or the discussion of the simplistic, the error is due to causes quite similar to those admirably stated by Pareto with regard to Karl Marx in his *Systèmes socialistes*, vol. 2 (Paris: Giard, 1926), 394—indeed his strictures can be applied almost word-for-word to Keynes.

The truth is that Keynes's attacks on savings and income inequality—his inflationary theses—seduce minds susceptible to demagogic agitation or embittered by life's trials—the minds of those who find any inequality unbearable if they are not its beneficiaries. It is so convenient to believe that the action of the rich alone is responsible for our ills!

Against a background where sentiment and intuition are paramount, "vigorous reasoning and subtle sophistries stand out. The daydreams of utopians, metaphysicians, and ethicists may make us smile, but [Keynes's] powerful dialectic imposes the respect due to every

The chief difficulty is as follows. Whereas in equilibrium the sequence of determinations can be taken in first approximation as going from the real equilibrium interest rate to the nominal interest rate, via the real value of money balances, in dynamic disequilibrium, where the rate of interest constitutes, depending on the case, the price paid for the use either of money or of capital, the cause-and-effect sequence starts from a diversity of nominal interest rates, which, for the purposes of theoretical presentation, may be reduced to two: (a) the nominal interest rate on the money market, which is determined by the condition of equality between aggregate money balances and the total quantity of money M, and (b) the pure interest rate on the financial market, which is determined by the instantaneous equilibrium between the propensity to investment in financial assets and the propensity to real investment, in order to arrive, finally, at the real interest rate, which balances consumers' propensity to save and firms' propensity to invest.

If the initial nominal interest rates in the monetary and financial markets are not equal, there is disequilibrium, and we must examine whether this disequilibrium can be eliminated and what series of actions and reactions it leads to.

For a tendency toward stable equilibrium to exist, it follows from the foregoing that any disequilibrium in the nominal interest rates in the

---

adversary whose strength is of no common order; and this respect helps to increase the faith of the adepts in their master. The obscurity, in certain points of [Keynes's] works contributes to producing the same effect; mystery appeals to man, and when we begin to admire a work, the very obscurities we find in it increase this admiration. Moreover, we end up by convincing ourselves that we have penetrated them, that we have lifted the veil covering the author's thought. On the one hand, this interpretation, being the fruit of our imagination, is necessarily in agreement with our sentiments—we find in the work of the author we are interpreting what we put there and, needless to say, these ideas strike us as excellent. On the other hand, the thought that, while the true meaning has escaped most men, we alone have succeeded in discovering it, affords delightful thrills to our vanity—thrills that attach us more and more to the work we are interpreting and to its author." Finally, as for Marx, Keynes's want of precision makes him unduly difficult to refute and this lends him considerable strength. For though the overall frailty and inadequacy of his edifice can readily be realized, it is much harder to catch him in any specific flagrant error, since his defenders can always claim that he meant something else.

This digression about Keynes may at first sight seem somewhat long, but at a time when efforts are being made to lay the foundations of a French economic policy and when some economists seem to be deeply influenced by the construct of the *General Theory*, I have thought it worthwhile to express here a judgment that is undeniably different from the commonly accepted opinion.

monetary and financial markets must lead to changes in the general price level such that the interest rate in the money market—the price paid for the use of money—and the interest rate in the financial market—the price paid for the use of capital—tend toward the same value, which represents the common price paid for the use of money and of capital when equilibrium prevails between consumers' propensities to save and firms' propensity to invest.

The fundamental difficulty of this explanation arises from the fact that, whereas in the different classical economic mechanisms of supply and demand there is only one variable parameter—price—the evolution of which is explained by consideration of the supply and demand curves, in this case there are *two parameters—interest rate and price level—the determination of which must be explained at the same time.* We still have two series of supply and demand curves, the former relating to money and the latter to capital, but on the one hand these two series of curves relate to a single parameter, the rate of interest, and their intersections can correspond to the same value for this rate only for an appropriate value of the price level, and on the other hand it is possible, as we have seen,[4] for the supply and demand curves of capital to intervene in the practical order only implicitly, with lending and borrowing occurring in the shape of sales and purchases of financial assets at given prices.

To clarify the state of the problem and how best its solution should be sought, I shall first give an overview of the principles of economic development when monetary structure is constant, then I shall specify the nature of the general problem of the stability of the overall system, and finally I shall indicate how these results are affected when the quantity of money varies.[5]

Principles of general economic development

As previously indicated, it will be assumed that all differences are zero between (a) the different pure rates of interest on long-term debt and (b) the different liquidity premiums and pure rates of interest on short-term debt. In the same way price differences will be assumed to be zero be-

---

4. No. 87.

5. Only variations in cash are involved since no. 98 deals only with cases in which there is no issue of unbacked demand deposits. This analysis will be completed below in nos. 99 and 100.

tween (a) the various final goods and (b) the various intermediate goods and, in accordance with the notations system adopted,[6] their respective levels will be denoted by two indices P_D and P_I and their common level by index P. *Finally, it will be assumed that the total quantity of money and the conditions of psychological and technological structure remain constant, that money is not hoardable[7] and that money balances are invariably restricted to the necessary amount of working capital.*[8]

Under these conditions it is easy to see how the economy develops starting from an initial difference $(i_F - i_M)$ between pure interest rates in the financial and money markets.

Let us first suppose that rate i_F is higher than rate i_M and that a stationary equilibrium is in place, by assuming, for instance, that there is a watertight separation between the financial and the money markets. Under these conditions, the level of money balances remains constant and the income and expenditure cycles of the various economic agents remain unchanged over time.

Hence, for instance, the way in which these agents distribute their income R_D^0 between consumption expenditure R_C^0 and financial investments R_P^0 remains constant so that

(1) $$R_D^0 = R_C^0 + R_P^0$$

with

(2) $$R_E^0 = 0,$$

where R_E^0 denotes the share of income devoted to increasing money balances.[9] With regard to the physical structure of the economy, it too remains unchanged under these conditions. The various outputs remain constant as do the various consumptions and investments. The notations Q_D^0 and Q_I^0 will denote the indices of activity of the final and intermediate goods sectors under these conditions.

---

6. No. 83.

7. The conditions under which money could not be hoarded will be clarified below (see in particular note 9 to no. 100 and note 5 to no. 113).

8. Economic development occurring when these assumptions are no longer applicable will be examined below (no. 100).

9. Notations of no. 37.

Now let us suppose that the watertight separation between the financial market and the money market is eliminated. Since rate i_F is superior to rate i_M, financial investment is more worthwhile than holding money; so it is in the interests of economic agents to alter the distribution of their capital between their financial capital and their monetary capital by decreasing the latter.

The crucial question is how this decrease can take place given that, by assumption, the sum total of money balances remains constant, so that any decrease in the money balance of one economic agent must be offset by an increase in the balance of another agent. And as we shall see, the answer is, in summary, that the efforts made by the various economic agents to decrease their money balances, which will take the shape of greater expenditure per unit of time, will lead to an increase in general price levels so that in the long run there will be a decrease in the overall real value of money balances, although their nominal value will remain constant.

Faced with the fact that rate i_F is greater than rate i_M, consumers will in reality continue to save the difference $R_D^0 - R_C^0$, but they will decrease their money balances so that their liquidity premium i_M will increase, and they will increase their expenditure on financial investment, which will thus become

$$R_P^1 = (R_D^0 - R_C^0) + (-R_E^1).$$

This increased expenditure on financial investment for a business capital demand curve that has remained unchanged (since prices have not yet altered) will have two effects: (a) a fall in interest rate i_F and (b) an increase in firms' direct investment expenditure. The increase in expenditure will also entail an increase in the price level P_I of intermediate goods and an increase in activity Q_I in this sector, leading in turn to an increase in distributed income, which will thus pass from level R_D^0 to a higher level R_D^1. This increase in income will mean greater expenditure on consumption and on investment in financial assets, but also a greater need for money balances, so that a share of the increased income will be devoted to increasing them. Finally, this increased expenditure will entail an increase in the price of final goods.

It is worth noting, incidentally, that when a new stationary state is established, it is safe to assume that the different money balances whose overall nominal value has remained constant will be distributed in a roughly analogous manner so that there will be little change in each individual balance. Similarly, the distribution of each balance between working capital and hoarded funds will remain largely unchanged so that the different payment flows keep much the same value.[10] Thus income R_D, after rising, will tend to settle at a level little different from its starting point.[11]

In summary, the development that takes place basically leads to a rise in prices, which increases the liquidity premiums l_M of money balances,[12] and to an increase in real investment, which diminishes the pure interest rate i_F in the financial market.[13] Finally it emerges that the difference $(i_F - i_M)$ tends to decrease — an adjustment that in monetary terms occurs by means of a general increase in prices.

A similar development would take place in the event that the pure interest rate i_M in the money market was initially greater than rate i_F. In this case, it would be more worthwhile to hold money than to invest in financial assets; there would be a fall in prices, a drop in aggregate capital, an increase in the real value of cash balances, a fall in rate i_M and a rise in rate i_F.

All this entitles us to conclude, with a high degree of probability, that under constant structural conditions the economy as a whole would evolve

---

10. Once hoarded funds are excluded, the velocity of circulation V_R of working capital M_R alone would remain approximately constant (since it basically depends on time lags intervening between receipts and expenditure; see no. 79) so that the flow of payments defined by Irving Fisher's equation

$$(1) \qquad\qquad \Phi = M_R V_R$$

would also be approximately constant. (Since M remains constant and its division between M_R and M_T is assumed to be largely invariable, total working capital M_R would be constant.)

11. The same conclusion can be reached by a different process if we argue that the need for money consequent on the rise in prices has the effect of decreasing the income flow that had initially increased.

12. Our assumption that money is not hoarded becomes relevant at this point. For this is only so because the propensity for liquidity represented by the function $M^r(i_M)$ — real desired money balances at rate i_M — remains *by and large unchanged*, and hence a reduction in real balances M^r corresponds to a rise in rate i_M.

If hoarding *was* possible, since experience shows that an initial positive difference $(i_F - i_M)$ is generally accompanied by hoarding due to the previous stage (beginning of a period of cyclical prosperity), the price rise provoked would lead to dishoarding, i.e., a decrease in function $M^r(i)$. And from this it would follow that a fall in real money balances M^r would not necessarily lead to a rise in rate i_M.

13. Since total invested capital increases.

toward what the theory defines as the general equilibrium position, at which price differences are no longer found.[14]

Simplifications used

Of course, the foregoing analysis is based on the assumptions that the various pure long-term interest rates constantly retain the same value i_F and that the liquidity premiums of money balances all have the same value i_M—assumptions that are not verified in reality since all the arbitraging really takes place *at the same time*, but the remarks made, by isolating the effects of a single difference $(i_F - i_M)$, make it possible to determine the specific effects of arbitraging between holding money and investing it. As the effects of other arbitrages analyzed by the classical theory of prices are well known and change nothing in the overall pattern, we can now grasp the tendencies that are at work in real economic evolution when there is on average a difference between the pure interest rates in the financial market and the pure interest rates in the money market and when, among all the arbitraging taking place at a given point of time, some of it is endeavoring to take advantage of this difference. There is therefore no reason why the economic explanation should not now be put back into the context of complex initial assumptions more in conformity with reality whereby we may reach an overall understanding of economic development.[15]

Closing of monetary circuits and interdependence

The highly condensed analysis just presented nevertheless brings out the complexity of the actions and reactions that develop in the economy in the wake of disparities involving money and the rate of interest. With regard to consumers, for instance, it is not only the distribution of their income flows among the different possible uses that is modified, but also the volume of these income flows. For although this volume in the long run returns to a level little different from its starting point, the changes that it undergoes in the interim play a key role.

14. No. 97.

15. Thus it is ultimately confirmed that the simplifying assumptions introduced at the start of this presentation concerning the uniqueness of pure interest rates i_F and i_M (no. 89) have no influence on the results obtained, which remain exactly the same when the perspective of complex reality is adopted instead. This should reassure any readers who may have found my initial approach somewhat disconcerting.

However, this complexity is much greater still, for my analysis has systematically disregarded certain effects that, though of secondary importance, have temporary repercussions that make the explanation considerably more complicated.

For example, the decrease in the pure interest rate i_F for long-term debt brought about by the evolution of the economy considered entails an increase in the value of long-term debt[16] and hence an increase in available capital, leading to a different distribution of income—one more favorable to consumption expenditure.

In the same way, the increase in the price of consumption goods, by increasing the profits of the firms that produce them, tends to strengthen the trend toward direct investment and thereby to increase rate i_F.

And again, observed price trends may be extrapolated into the future by the various economic agents in many different ways, and to each of these there naturally corresponds a specific development.

These few remarks suffice to show how delicate and difficult it can be to explain general economic evolution fully and to emphasize that the above presentation is no more than a *cursory outline*.

It should nonetheless be pointed out that the order of magnitude of these different effects is on average less than that of the main effects analyzed.

For instance, it is well known that the increase in available capital due to appreciation in the value of capital owned translates mainly into an increase in capital saved and leads only to a slight increase in consumption expenditure. So the first effect indicated plays a role that is relatively secondary.

In the same way, a certain lapse of time is needed for the increase in profits to generate an increase in demand for investment. It may be assumed that this period is normally longer than that called for by the previous stage. It may also be inferred that it can only be a corrective effect, leaving the evolution unchanged in its principles.

Finally it is quite certain that rising expectations, for instance, can lead to a generalized increase in investments and a persistent increase in the rate i_F, but such expectations can only emerge if a *persistent* upward trend is *already* underway. Now, in the context of our assumption that the quantity of money is constant, no such persistent rise could occur, for the price level is automatically limited beyond a certain level by the impossibility

---

16. Since this value varies in the opposite direction to the rate of interest i_F.

of satisfying an increasing demand for money balances, while the overall volume of money remains unchanged.

These few remarks show that in every case only second-order effects are involved and that the general explanation set out above *remains entirely valid in its principles.*

General problem of equilibrium stability

Our analysis so far has only enabled us to determine

1. the cause-and-effect links within the economy;
2. the conditions that any equilibrium must necessarily satisfy.

Thus the complete and rigorous demonstration, in the most general case, of exactly how the overall economy develops, starting from any initial state, toward a state of stable equilibrium corresponding to the stated conditions of equilibrium, *remains to be made and constitutes a major challenge for the immediate future of economics.*[17,18,19]

However, a simple and intuitive idea of the principles of such a demonstration can be reached as follows. Consider any initial state and examine how the economy will develop from this state.

Two kinds of mechanism will be involved.

On the one hand, each market, with external conditions assumed to be given, will develop in accordance with the well-known classical principles of supply and demand.

On the other, the development of each market will modify the external conditions considered as given by the other markets. Thus in a given mar-

17. In this regard, the remarks made above should be taken merely as an intuitive starting point for further research.

18. Of course, such a demonstration is only feasible under constant structural conditions (notably of a monetary nature). If these conditions change and if the speed at which they change is greater than the speed at which the economy is developing toward equilibrium, it is clear that no stable equilibrium can come about. This is particularly so when the total quantity of money varies (see my general work *À la recherche d'une discipline économique*, no. 227).

19. I have undertaken this demonstration for the case of an account-based economy having no productive operations but assuming no other unusual conditions (see my general work *À la recherche d'une discipline économique*, no. 193). This demonstration has the fundamental advantage of showing what the general problem of equilibrium stability consists in and how it can be resolved.

ket the supply and demand curves that emerge depend in essence both on prices observed in the other markets and on the income at the disposal of the suppliers and demanders, the level of which depends on how these other markets develop.

This brings to light a much more complex cause-and-effect relationship whose careful study, notwithstanding its key importance, has only recently begun. And this study is rendered more difficult by the fact that it bears on the general interdependence of the different markets and hence involves them *all at the same time.*

As the physical functioning of the markets takes a certain amount of time, this dependence implies that the value of any parameter over period T_n would be a function of the values of the parameters characterizing the overall economy during the preceding period T_{n-1}.[20] Hence the position of the economy over period T_n can be regarded as a consequence of its position during the preceding period T_{n-1}. It can then be seen that we are faced with a *linked succession* of different states $(E_0), (E_1), \ldots, (E_{n-1}), (E_n)$ connected one to another by a set of equations that may be *symbolically* represented by the equation

(3) $$E_n = f(E_{n-1}).$$ [21]

The fundamental problem is then to find out whether this succession leads to a well-determined equilibrium and whether this equilibrium is stable. It will only be so, of course, if the equation

(4) $$E = f(E)$$

has one, and only one, solution and if the sequence of states $(E_1), \ldots, (E_n)$ obtained starting from any initial state (E_0) would in fact tend toward state (E).[22]

---

20. The duration of period T is of course unique to each case, and this gives rise to an essential difficulty. How this difficulty can be avoided will be explained below (note 22).

21. In reality such an equation would comprise, if made explicit, as many equations as there are economic parameters.

22. In reality, allowing for the diversity of period T depending on specific mechanisms envisaged, it would be necessary, in the most general case, to consider state (E_n) as a function not of a single state (E_{n-1}), but of a certain number of previous states $(E_{n-p}), \ldots, (E_{n-1})$ so that we should have

The general, complete, and precise study of this question—which *inescapably* implies the systematic use of mathematics—still appears *inaccessible* in the present state of our economic knowledge, but it is at least possible to use simplifying approximations *to form an idea* of the probable appearance of the phenomena. Thus, since consumers adjust to new conditions of income and prices only after a certain lag, it may be assumed that the consumed income R_c^n of period T_n is a function of the prices and incomes of period T_{n-1}, consequent upon the maximization of satisfactions during this period according to classical theory. Thus income R_c^n is shown to be a function mathematically determinable from the satisfaction functions and the representative parameters of state (E_{n-1}). This illustrates how the problem could be posed, and thereafter it will only be a matter of pure mathematics to establish whether the development in question does or does not bring about a stable equilibrium.[23,24]

Hence, the only real difficulty is to formulate the problem correctly. Once this has been achieved mathematical reasoning alone will suffice to settle it without difficulty.

Causality and interdependence

The above presentation makes it possible to reconcile two points of view that have hitherto led only to vain quarrels ceaselessly embittered, alas, by muddled thinking: the viewpoint of the partisans of causality and that of the partisans of general interdependence. For the former, only cause-and-effect links exist, and it would be *a grave mistake* to think that the economic parameters of a period T_n are determined by relations of interde-

---

(1) $$E_n = f(E_{n-p}, \ldots, E_{n-1}),$$

every position of equilibrium being characterized by the equation

(2) $$E = f(E_0, \ldots, E).$$

23. This being so, it may be safely predicted that, like physics, as soon as it is treated as a science, economics will confront the mathematical sciences with *new* problems the study of which will be of value both to economists and to mathematicians. But, as with physics, only those educated *both* in economics and in mathematics will be able to undertake these studies. Thus progress in economics is *utterly dependent* on the formation of such scholars.

24. It is worth drawing attention here to the highly interesting studies presented by Swedish economist Erik Lundberg in his *Studies in the Theory of Economic Expansion* (London: P. S. King, 1937).

pendence connecting them one to another; for the latter, the causal links are but a cloak concealing a deeper reality: the general interdependence of the economic parameters and their mutual determination by functional relationships linking them one to another.

The truth is that neither party is entirely right nor entirely wrong.

It is first and foremost undeniable that *economic development is at every moment dominated by cause-and-effect relations* and that the value of every parameter at time t_n is determined not by the value of the other parameters at *that* point but by their value at preceding points of time.[25]

But it is no less certain that, if a stable stationary equilibrium is in place, we may safely conclude that equation (2) above determines it outright,[26] so that the values of the different parameters that characterize it are determined by relations of mutual interdependence. *In such an equilibrium, the causal links subsist but in such a way as to mask an underlying interdependence that constitutes the real innermost characteristic of the economy.*[27]

As a first approximation, the conditions of the real economy may be regarded as stationary.[28] Consequently, still in first approximation, interdependence may be assumed. This means that *the order of magnitude* of the parameters is determined by the underlying relationships of interdependence so that they come into play only through their values at the time in question, but this is only a matter of orders of magnitude — the *differential corrections* that should be applied to them to obtain their exact values

25. It is impossible, for instance, to accept that the price of paper at Marseilles at a given time *t* is a function of the market price of lead in Paris at the *same* moment, for, manifestly, the latter cannot in any way, directly or indirectly, influence the supply and demand of paper at the time in question owing to the inevitable information lag.

26. In light of what has been said in note 21 above, the equation once made explicit in fact contains as many relations as unknowns.

27. Similar situations are found in physics. For instance, the potentials of Newton and Maxwell that introduce functional relations of interdependence between physical parameters *belonging to the same point of time* by no means suggest that the corresponding physical phenomena do not obey causal links. These causal links exist, and their action implies the existence of time lags, but the lags are usually so slight in relative terms that they may be disregarded.

When the lags are no longer negligible, physical theory must include delayed potentials to take account of the propagation period of physical actions. *So the causality is manifest but, once again, by no means excludes the possibility of stationary equilibria* (for example, the equilibrium of two electrically charged balls, suspended from threads, that attract one another) *where the causal relations are equivalent to relations of interdependence.*

28. Note 9 to no. 77.

depend fundamentally *on causal links that are not reducible to relation-ships of interdependence.*[29]

Exterior aspects of the monetary mechanism

What characterizes, from the practical viewpoint, the intricate mecha-nism of adjustment of the different rates of interest and the price level "is that nothing reveals its existence to the layman, or even to the specialist who treats of it. For what activates it are the differences between rates or prices. These differences are tempting to brokers in quest of profit."[30] But in their pursuit of profit margins they have no inkling of the indispensable public service they are at the same time rendering by providing for the community's monetary needs. Neither does such an idea cross the mind of the bankers who supply or demand money.

The mechanism operates in silence, but with unfailing accuracy. It con-tinuously raises the real value of the various kinds of money in existence, both demand deposits and cash, to the level of real money demand. It is what ensures that monetary circulation always has the real value that its users want it to have.

Stability, inflation, and deflation

Of course, the foregoing remarks about the stability of the equilibrium no longer apply when the quantity of cash is undergoing constant increase or decrease.

For as we have seen, the adjustment mechanisms that lead the econ-omy toward equilibrium involve complex and delicate circuits. Not only does the adjustment of supply to demand in every market take time,[31] but market-to-market reactions, which also play a key role in the process, all take time too—sometimes substantial periods. *For it is only when the monetary circuit is completely closed that the existing disparities can be gradually absorbed and that the economy can evolve toward a stable equi-*

29. I believe that systematic adoption of this point of view could eliminate many of the difficulties hampering the debate over contemporary economic theories. Readers wishing to pursue the issue will find further information in my general work *À la recherche d'une disci-pline économique*, nos. 557–64.

30. J. Rueff, *L'ordre social* (Paris: Sirey, 1945), 301.

31. This period may be exceptionally protracted in cases such as the adjustment of real investment or money balances to the interest rate.

librium. Whenever the circuit is closed the economy draws closer to the final equilibrium position corresponding to the relevant structural conditions, but this equilibrium can be achieved only after whatever lapse of time is needed for a certain number of successive closures of the circuit.

Hence, if the quantity of cash varies more rapidly than the pace of the economy's continuous but unhurried advance toward the equilibrium position corresponding to that instant's structural conditions,[32] there can no longer be any question of reaching stability.

Indeed, theoretically, stability could only occur if the relative rate of increase in the quantity of money were constant,[33] a situation rarely found.

For both these reasons, the continuous increase or decrease in the quantity of cash, when they take place at a significant rate,[34] prevent any stable equilibrium from being realized. The economy is abandoned to disorder and to permanent instability.[35]

32. Readers wishing to study in greater depth the concepts of the speed of adjustment (development toward equilibrium) and of the distortions (variations in structural conditions) of a system may usefully consult my *À la recherche d'une discipline économique*, no. 227.

33. No. 97.

34. The case of credit inflation will be examined later on.

35. Variations in the quantity of cash are due to the issue or cancellation of money by the State in a paper money system, and to the monetization or demonetization of gold under a gold-standard system.

It should be noted that under a gold standard, all other things being equal, the gradual exhaustion of the gold mines should raise production costs and slow down production for a given legal price. When this happens, gold production is no longer sufficient to meet both monetary and industrial needs for gold, so demonetization of gold in circulation takes place. But this demonetization, by lowering prices, and in particular the cost of gold production, tends to create the conditions for a new equilibrium.

The opposite is observed, of course, in the event of a fall in the cost of gold production owing to technical progress or the discovery of new seams.

(b) Partial backing of demand deposits

1. Determination of the rate of interest in a dynamic equilibrium process (99)

At the outset I assume, for the sake of simplicity, a stationary model in which cash is inconvertible, discount operations are risk free and cost free,[1] the liquidity of the various debt instruments is zero, and there is no Central Bank; demand deposits and cash, are not, however, perfectly substitutable.[2]

Under these conditions we have seen that the different instantaneous interest rates are all equal, in equilibrium, having the same value i.

As the capital saved by individuals is equal to the sum

(1) $$C = C_\varphi + C_\mu + M_M,$$ [3]

equation (1) of no. 97 here becomes

(2) $$C_\varphi^r(i) + C_\mu^r(i) + M_M^r = C_0^r(i),$$

where M_M^r denotes the real value of the cash.

As has been seen, the cash M_{MA}, and demand deposits M_S, held by economic agents other than banks[4] are well-determined functions of the interest rate i, proportional to price level P.[5] Consequently, their real values M_{MA}^r and M_S^r are also well-determined functions

(3) $$M_{MA}^r = M_{MA}^r(i),$$

(4) $$M_S^r = M_S^r(i)$$

of the interest rate i.

---

1. But of course it is assumed that investment in financial assets and the sale of assets entail costs, since it is precisely these costs that underpin the use value of money, whether cash or deposits (no. 82).

2. These are the same assumptions as in the second case considered in no. 94.

3. No. 95, equation (1), where E is zero (there is no Central Bank).

4. Notations of no. 95.

5. Nos. 82 and 94.

Finally we have

(5) $$M^r_{MA} + M^r_{MB} = M^r_M$$

and

(6) $$M^r_{MB} = \kappa M^r_S,$$

equations that respectively express in real values that the total amount of cash is equal to the sum of the cash held by the banks and by other economic agents and that the banks' cash balances are equal to the product of the aggregate of demand deposits by the reserve ratio.

From equations (3), (4), (5), and (6) we can infer that

(7) $$M^r_M = M^r_{MA}(i) + \kappa M^r_S(i),$$

and thence

(8) $$C^r_\varphi(i) + C^r_\mu(i) + M^r_{MA}(i) + \kappa M^r_S(i) = C^r_0(i).$$

This equation determines the interest rate i in equilibrium. The real values of the cash and demand deposits held then depend on equations (3) and (4) and the real value of overall cash on equation (5). Price level P is then determined by the equation

(9) $$P = \frac{M_M}{M^r_M}.$$

Since in first approximation equation (2) reduces to the equation

(10) $$C^r_\varphi(i) + C^r_\mu(i) = C^r_0(i),$$

it appears that *here too the interest rate may be taken as a first approximation to depend only on the propensities to save and to invest, the price level being determined by the respective volumes of liquidity desired at this rate in the form of cash and of demand deposits.*

It could also be demonstrated here[6] that the equilibrium interest rate in is in fact greater than it would be in the absence of money (cash and

6. As in no. 97.

demand deposits), as the propensity to own is in part satisfied by owning money, which also diminishes to some extent the propensity to invest.

Finally, as we have[7]

(11) $C_{\mu e}^r = M_S^r - M_{MB}^r,$

an equation that states that the overall value of discounted bills is equal to the excess of the total amount of demand deposits over the total money balances of the banks and that the values of M_S^r and M_{MB}^r are well determined as a function of rate i, it becomes clear what determines the volume, in equilibrium, of bills discounted.

This volume in fact *settles at a level such that total actual demand deposits exactly match total desired demand deposits.*[8]

Of course, as the discount rate is, under the conditions assumed, equal to rate i, the rate i_D paid to depositors is here determined by the equation

(12) $i_D = (1 - \kappa)i.$ [9]

Effects of credit

Experience shows that the distribution of money balances between cash and demand deposits remains fairly constant, allowing us to write

---

7. Under the approximate conditions of no. 95 where, for the sake of simplicity, bank capital is assumed to be zero (no. 95, equation [5]) as we are assuming here that there is no Central Bank.

8. Remember that in the *theoretical equilibrium* here considered, in which discount rate i_B is equal to the pure market interest rate i, it is irrelevant for a firm whether it finances its investments via discount or not. It might thus seem that discounted capital is indeterminate under these conditions.

But the explanations in the text show that this is not so and that this capital is strictly determined by the conditions of the general economic equilibrium.

In *economic reality*, in which costs and risks are involved, this logical difficulty does not apply, as the volume $C_{\mu e}$ of discounted capital is determined by the sum of the bills that fulfill the condition

$$i_B + g_e^x < i + g^x + \varepsilon^x + \rho^x$$

indicated in no. 94 (condition [11]).

9. No. 94, equation (4).

(13) $$M_S = \alpha M_{MA}.$$

Moreover, it can be accepted *as a first approximation* that total real money balances

(14) $$M^r = M^r_{MA} + M^r_S$$

are a function $M^r(i)$ of interest rate i, independent of the intensity α of use of demand deposits.[10]

If this is so, it follows that we have, in light of equations (5), (6), (13), and (14),

(15) $$M^r_M = \frac{1 + \kappa\alpha}{1 + \alpha} M^r,$$

so that equation (8) becomes

(16) $$C^r_\varphi(i) + C^r_\mu(i) + \frac{1 + \kappa\alpha}{1 + \alpha} M^r(i) = C^r_0(i),$$

whereas in the absence of demand deposits it would be

(17) $$C^r_\varphi(i) + C^r_\mu(i) + M^r(i) = C^r_0(i).$$

---

10. Aggregate real money balances break down, as we have seen (no. 82), into two components: (a) real working capital and (b) real speculative balances.

Since component (a) varies little with the user cost of the balance, it is not very responsive to a fall in this cost in value i to value κ^i for total demand deposits.

Moreover, although component (b) is indeed sensitive to the user cost of the money balance, it must be noted that the interest rate yielded by the part of it held in the form of demand deposits is little else but the interest directly paid by the banks, i.e., a very low rate of interest, for the indirect advantages enjoyed by a depositor depend almost exclusively on the level of his activity, i.e., on the size of his working capital. Hence the user cost of speculative monetary reserves held in the form of demand deposits differs little from their cost when held as cash.

So, ultimately, it is clear that although for any value of i real aggregate money balances increase in consequence of the potential use of demand deposits (a fact confirmed in the study of a specific case in appendix II, § B, no. 212), this increase remains relatively slight and may be disregarded as a first approximation.

This reveals, in light of the foregoing, *that recourse to credit has the effect of reducing the equilibrium interest rate to a value lower than it would have if there were no demand deposits. Thus the use of demand deposits has the effect of moving the interest rate closer to the rate it would have under moneyless conditions.*[11]

This result is mainly due to the action of the credit mechanism in relieving the economy of the task of financing money balances held in the form of demand deposits, a responsibility now borne by no one (no. 95), so that the propensity to own, being no longer satisfied in monetary form except by cash, is correspondingly redirected toward capital investment.

This leads to a gain in social productivity, which, when credit is expanded, can become significant,[12] and it can be seen that in this way, re-*course to credit offsets to some extent the disadvantages associated with the use of money.*

Turning now to the price level, it depends on the equation

(18)
$$P = \frac{M}{M^r(i)} = \frac{1+\alpha}{1+\alpha\kappa} \frac{M_M}{M^r(i)},$$

---

11. Whereas for a country such as France, where α is on the order of 1/4 and κ on the order of 1/10, this effect, expressed by the ratio

$$\frac{1+\alpha\kappa}{1+\alpha} = \frac{1+\dfrac{1}{40}}{1+\dfrac{1}{4}} \sim \frac{4}{5}$$

is not very significant, for countries like Great Britain or the United States, by contrast, it is substantial, since the ratio

$$\frac{1+\alpha\kappa}{1+\alpha} = \frac{M_M}{M} = \frac{M_M}{M_{MA}+M_S}$$

of cash to demand deposits can reach values on the order of 1/8.

If we note that the real value M^r of total money balances is of the order of magnitude of 3/4 of the national income, it can be seen that in the case of Great Britain or of the United States the corresponding fall in the rate of interest would be on the order of 1.5% in light of the explanations given in no. 70 and in note 19 to no. 97.

12. Note 9 to no. 71.

This is certainly a factor that makes an appreciable contribution to the high labor productivity in the United States, where credit is exceptionally highly developed.

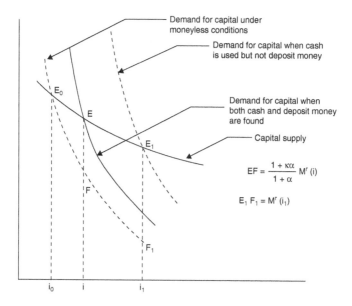

FIGURE 8.17

whereas in the absence of demand deposits it would depend on the equation

(19) $$P_1 = \frac{M_M}{M^r(i_1)},$$

where i and i_1 represent respectively the equilibrium interest rate with, or without, recourse to demand deposits. This gives us

$$\frac{P}{P_1} = \frac{1+\alpha}{1+\alpha\kappa} \frac{M^r(i_1)}{M^r(i)},$$

i.e., in light of figure 8.17,

$$\frac{P}{P_1} = \frac{E_1 F_1}{EF},$$

and since $EF < E_1 F_1$ it is clear that $P > P_1$, since ratio $\dfrac{P}{P_1}$ becomes greater as point E draws closer to point E_0, i.e., as the ratio $(1 + \kappa\alpha)$ to $(1 + \alpha)$ becomes smaller.

Thus we confirm that *credit has the effect of raising the price level to a point higher than it would have in the absence of demand deposits, for an identical amount of cash in circulation.*

Role of the Central Bank

This explanation is easily adapted when there is a Central Bank able to rediscount bills of exchange that have already been discounted by the commercial banks.

In this case, equations (3), (4), and (5) remain unchanged, but equation (2) becomes[13]

$$(20) \qquad C_\varphi^r(i) + C_\mu^r(i) + M_M^r - E^r = C_0^r(i),$$

where E^r denotes the real value of bills discounted by the Central Bank so that equation (8) becomes

$$(21) \qquad C_\varphi^r(i) + C_\mu^r(i) + M_{MA}^r(i) + \kappa M_S^r(i) - E^r = C_0^r(i).$$

It can be seen that, as a result of rediscounting, the equilibrium interest rate is lower and that it is a function of the real value E^r of bills rediscounted by the Central Bank, or—which amounts to the same thing—that the real value of bills rediscounted by the Central Bank is a function of the interest rate that emerges as an *arbitrary parameter.*

Nonetheless, it is clear that *the Central Bank's control over the interest rate in equilibrium*—by setting its rate of discount i_E, which, *under the conditions assumed*, is equal to or greater than the instantaneous pure interest rate i depending on whether bills are or are not presented for rediscount[14]—*is arbitrary only within fairly narrow limits.*

For, on the one hand, it is observable that, since the real value E^r of bills rediscounted is necessarily positive and the real value of unbacked demand deposits cannot be negative, the interest rate in equilibrium cannot be set at a level higher than would obtain in the absence of any rediscount—a point examined above.

And on the other hand, it is obvious that the credit mechanism itself limits the volume of bills that can be rediscounted and hence introduces a lower possible limit for the interest rate. In fact, since the entry "Advances

---

13. In combination with equation (1) of no. 95.
14. No. 94, equations (20) and (21), where $l_B = l_E = 0$.

to the State" on the Central Bank's balance sheet, which represents the amount of cash that would be in circulation if there were no rediscounting, cannot be negative, we necessarily have[15]

$$(22) \qquad\qquad E^r < M_M^r,$$

from which, in combination with the above condition,[16] which remains unchanged, we obtain

$$(23) \qquad\qquad E^r < \frac{1+\kappa\alpha}{1+\alpha} M^r.$$

As equation (21) can be expressed as[16]

$$(24) \qquad C_\varphi^r(i) + C_\mu^r(i) + \frac{1+\kappa\alpha}{1+\alpha} M^r(i) - E^r = C_0^r(i), \qquad\qquad [17]$$

it is clear that in any event the fall in the interest rate cannot be greater than the rise in the equilibrium interest rate consequent on the use of money,[18] this maximum being achieved when the entire circulation is due to rediscounting: $M_M = E$.[19,20]

---

15. No. 95.

16. In light of our previous findings (equation [16]).

17. According to the equation $M_M = A + E$ of no. 95 this equation could also be expressed

$$C_\varphi^r(i) + C_\mu^r(i) + \frac{A}{A+E} \frac{1+\kappa\alpha}{1+\alpha} M^r(i) = C_0^r(i).$$

It can thus be seen that the fall in the equilibrium interest rate is maximal when the ratio $\frac{A}{E}$ is zero, i.e., when the volume of monetary circulation M_M depends wholly on the volume of bills discounted by the Central Bank.

18. It is obvious that when the volume of monetary circulation rests entirely on rediscounting ($M_M^r = E^r$) the economy is, as indicated above (no. 95), entirely relieved of the financing of money balances. The equilibrium position is then that which corresponds to the complete absence of money.

19. As total money balances M^r are on the order of 3/4 of the national income, it is clear that, in light of what has been said in note 11 above, the maximum possible fall in the interest rate through the action of the Central Bank is *in equilibrium* only on the order of 1.5%.

20. When the discount rate is lowered from level i_M, corresponding to zero rediscount to its minimum level i_m corresponding to a moneyless equilibrium, the value E^r of rediscounted bills increases from zero to

But this is a *theoretical* limit that could not be attained in practice, as the value of bills discounted by the Central Bank never in fact comprises more than a small fraction of total circulation. Finally, it follows that *the potential for lowering the rate of interest via the policy of the Central Bank is in fact very limited.*

$$\frac{1+\kappa\alpha}{1+\alpha} M^r(i_m).$$

(It should be recalled that total money balances $M^r(i)$ are an increasing function of rate i.) So the real value of advances to the State

$$A^r = M_M^r - E^r = \frac{1+\kappa\alpha}{1+\alpha} M^r - E^r$$

tends toward zero. As their volume A is assumed to remain constant, price level P rises indefinitely. Of course, the ratio of the nominal value of rediscounted bills to minimum volume A of monetary circulation

$$\frac{E}{A} = \frac{E^r}{A^r}$$

increases indefinitely.

It is clear that *in equilibrium* for the rediscount rate to fall to rate i_m is conceivable only as an asymptotic limit that cannot be exceeded.

In each situation the real value V^r of the total volume of bills discounted is equal to

$$V^r = M_S^r - M_{MB}^r + E^r = (1-\kappa)M_S^r + E^r = \frac{(1-\kappa)\alpha}{1+\alpha} M^r + E^r.$$

The limit value of this total volume thus turns out to be equal to

$$\frac{(1-\kappa)\alpha}{1+\alpha} M^r + \frac{1+\kappa\alpha}{1+\alpha} M^r = M^r,$$

i.e., to aggregate real money balances.

It can thus be seen that an asymptotic fall of rate i toward rate i_m is only conceivable if the real value of *discountable* bills is greater than aggregate money balances $M^r(i_m)$. Otherwise, the possible fall in the interest rate would no longer be limited by rate i_m but by the higher rate at which the value of discounted bills would attain its maximum possible.

Moreover, as in practice the ratio $\frac{E}{A}$ is normally kept below unity by the Central Bank, it is clear that the fall in the interest rate will be considerably less than its possible maximum— which would correspond to a ratio $\frac{E}{A}$ equal to infinity.

It is thus clear that *two different scenarios may arise depending on whether the rediscount rate* i_E *is greater or less than the equilibrium level corresponding to a zero rediscount volume. In the former case, the level* i_E *of the official rediscount rate is too high and allows no rediscount so that the equilibrium interest rate remains unchanged; in the latter case, the equilibrium interest rate falls to a level corresponding to rediscount rate* i_E.

So the fall in the interest rate obtained via the discount rate policy is in fact *limited*, and it is easy to verify that no stationary equilibrium is conceivable for a discount rate lower than or equal to its minimum level.[21]

Here too, when the Central Bank rediscounts a part of the discountable portfolio by a supplementary issue of money—strictly equivalent to the issue of unbacked demand deposits by the banks—with the effect of relieving savings, to an equivalent amount, of the financing of money balances, the outcome is a *pro rata* redirection of the propensity to save toward the financing of capital. This enables the interest rate to be lowered, pursuant to the rediscount policy of the Central Bank.

Rise and fall of the discount rate and price levels

It is obvious[21] that *in equilibrium the effect of a fall in the discount rate is to raise the price level and that the relative rise in the price level is much greater than the relative fall in the discount rate.*[22]

And needless to say, the opposite is observed in the event of a rise in the discount rate.

These findings are summarized in table 8.6.

TABLE 8.6 FOOTNOTE

i	E^r	A^r	P	E/A	E	M_M	V^r	V
i_M	0	$\dfrac{1+\kappa\alpha}{1+\alpha} M^r(i_M)$	$\dfrac{1+\alpha}{1+\kappa\alpha}\dfrac{M_M}{M^r(i_M)}$	0	0	A	$\dfrac{(1-\kappa)\alpha}{1+\alpha} M^r(i_M)$	$\dfrac{(1-\kappa)\alpha}{1+\kappa\alpha} M_M$
↓	↓	↓	↓	↓	↓	↓	↓	↓
i_m	$\dfrac{1+\kappa\alpha}{1+\alpha} M^r(i_m)$	0	$+\infty$	$+\infty$	$+\infty$	$+\infty$	$M^r(i_m)$	$+\infty$

21. See note 20 above.

22. It follows from note 20 above that to a finite variation $i_M - i_m$ in the interest rate there corresponds an infinite variation in the price level.

*Keeping the discount rate constant in the event of a change
in liquidity preference*

Equation (24) can be written

(25) $$C_\varphi^r(i) + C_\mu^r(i) + A^r(i) = C_0^r(i),$$

where $A^r(i)$ denotes the real value of that part of the monetary circulation
that does not correspond to rediscount operations and the nominal value
of which therefore remains constant.

This implies that if liquidity preference, represented by function
$M^r(i)$—which represents the real demand for money balances at a given
interest rate—changes,[23] keeping the discount rate i_E and hence the interest rate i at a constant value has the effect of maintaining at the same level
the real value A^r, in other words, the price level (since nominal value A
remains constant).

From this it follows that *if, in equilibrium, the Central Bank keeps the
discount rate at a given level, this exercises a twofold stabilizing influence
since this policy enables both the interest rate and the price level to be kept
at constant values at the same time.*

This avoids either a fall in the interest rate and a rise in the price level[24]
if liquidity preference falls, or a rise in the interest rate and a fall in the
price level if liquidity preference increases.

23. Upward or downward.

This increase and decrease, respectively, correspond to a general rise or fall in the curve
representing real desired money balances $M^r(i)$.

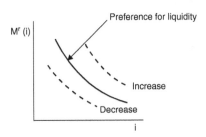

FIGURE 8.18 FOOTNOTE

24. It follows from equation (25) and from our findings so far that a fall in the rate of
interest decreases the value of A^r and thus increases the price level $P = \dfrac{A}{A^r}$.

In the first case, the decrease in desired money balances is offset by the decrease in bills rediscounted, while in the second case, the increase in desired balances is made possible by increased rediscounting.

Naturally, this stabilizing influence is only possible to the extent that, for the interest rate in question, changes in liquidity preference do not have the effect—for a constant interest rate—either of canceling out the volume of bills discounted or of setting the ratio $\frac{E}{A}$ of this volume to the minimum volume of monetary circulation at a level deemed undesirable by the Central Bank.

In the first case, reducing the value of discounted bills to zero may not suffice to offset the fall in the demand for balances. As the official discount rate kept at its previous level is greater than the equilibrium interest rate corresponding to a zero volume of rediscount, the interest rate disconnects from the official discount rate and falls to the level of the equilibrium interest rate. Of course, in the final equilibrium, the price level settles at a higher level than it had originally.[25]

In the second case, the maximum rise in the volume of rediscounting authorized by the Central Bank is insufficient to satisfy the increased demand for money balances. Since the rediscounting demand is deemed too high, the Central Bank raises its discount rate until the rate of interest reaches the equilibrium level corresponding to the target volume of rediscounting. Of course, in the final equilibrium, the price level will settle at a level lower than it had originally.

Thus *the stabilizing influence of the discount rate can only be limited*, but understandably it may be especially effective in the event of only slight variations in liquidity preference. This is particularly the case for seasonal liquidity variations.[26]

Of course, when liquidity preference decreases, the real value of demand deposits falls. If the ratio of deposits to cash remains fairly constant, as occurs in reality, the *nominal* volume of demand deposits remains constant and the drop in real value results from a rise in prices.

In the absence of a Central Bank policy of stabilizing the interest rate, the adjustment of the economic equilibrium to a fall in liquidity preference takes place via both a fall in the interest rate—which, of itself, increases liquidity preference—and a rise in the price level, which decreases the real value of money, both cash and demand deposits.

25. Because part of the decrease in the real value of desired balances is obtained via the rise in prices (see note 24 above).

26. Seasonal variations in liquidity preference, represented by the real value $M^r(i)$ of desired balances, are due to the fact that the unequal distribution of settlement dates over time is not offset by the number of economic agents and that it presents on average common characteristics for the different kinds of money balance. For instance, the end of the month is

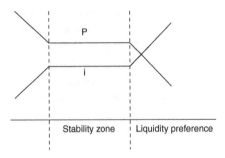

FIGURE 8.19

Clearly for a given range of variations in liquidity preference the stabilization policy based on the discount rate will be all the likelier to succeed the further the normal equilibrium volume of rediscounting is from its extreme limits, i.e., the more closely this volume approaches to a level on the order of one-half of the maximum volume accepted for rediscount by the Central Bank.[27]

The case of convertible money

When money is convertible, for instance, into gold, *the quantity of cash, which does not correspond to the rediscount of bills of exchange,[28] is no longer given but is determined by the further condition of being equal to the unit of the gold value of the unit of account.*

---

a time when most economic agents have payments to make: for a given price level, demand for balances is minimal at the mid-month, rises as the end of the month approaches, then falls from its peak toward the new minimum level. In the same way it is well known that the average monthly demand for money balances varies depending on the month in question.

27. Note that all these explanations would remain unchanged in the event that the lending banks' reserve coefficient κ could not differ from unity, i.e., if lending banks were unable to issue demand deposits. (See note 5 to no. 91 and nos. 113 and 162.)

Thus *the stabilizing influence of the rediscount rate normally depends only on possible variations in rediscount volume* and would be quite unaffected in the event that lending banks were unable to issue unbacked demand deposits.

28. Corresponding to "Advances to the State" on the Central Bank's balance sheet in no. 95. In the present case, if we assimilate reserves at the Central Bank to cash, the Central Bank's balance sheet will resemble table 8.7.

Subject to this qualification, the foregoing explanations remain entirely valid, and the reader will be readily able to generalize them.[29]

Note, however, that for a given real value $M^r(i)$ of total money in circulation, *the amount of gold needed for the system to operate*, corresponding to a fraction of the real value of the cash circulation M_M^r, *is less as credit is more extensive* both at the level of lending banks and at the level of the Central Bank.[30]

Moreover, under this system, the price level may be taken, as a first approximation, to be independent of the level of the discount rate. For it can be assumed as a first approximation that for a given general price level the marginal cost of gold is a well-determined function of its output.[31] Now, in a stationary equilibrium the output of gold is constant and equal to its industrial consumption. And as the legal price of gold is kept at a constant level, it follows from these conditions that *a first approximation of the general price level in equilibrium depends only on the general conditions that characterize the production and consumption of gold and is independent both of the general level of interest rates and of liquidity preference.*

Here too, the Central Bank's rediscount volume, i.e., the ratio of banknotes issued to reserves held, remains an independent variable that can be arbitrarily set by the Central Bank. As the quantity of money must in first

TABLE 8.7 FOOTNOTE

Assets	Liabilities
Gold reserves	Money in circulation
Advances to the State	
Portfolios of discounted bills	

29. Once again, I recall that, as a complete analysis would involve a general theory of money, this presentation remains succinct, being basically limited to explaining the role of the rate of interest.

30. In this case, too, credit leads to a saving, but in the present case, the saving is more visible than in the case of paper money (note 8 to no. 95) since, as a result of the convertibility mechanism, the value of money—equal to the present value of its future liquidity services—is also equal, in equilibrium, to its marginal cost of production.

31. In reality this may not be the case, owing to rapid exhaustion of known seams, the discovery of new seams, technological progress, etc., but under normal circumstances the stability of structural conditions may be accepted as a valid approximation *at least over a short period of time.*

approximation be taken to depend, in equilibrium, on the price level,[32,33] the variability of the reserve ratio is here equivalent to variability in the level of the precious metal reserves, which could in theory vary from zero to a level equal to the entire quantity of money.

It follows from what we have seen that the more money is issued against bills of exchange, i.e., the lower the gold and silver reserves, the lower the rate of interest can be and vice versa. This shows *that in a closed gold-backed monetary economy setting the rediscount rate and hence the general level of the interest rates enables the monetary authorities to control the level of their gold reserves or rather of the proportion these reserves represent with respect to the total volume of money.*[34]

Finally, note that here too, *when liquidity preference increases*, keeping the discount rate constant can—by increasing the rediscount volume and decreasing the gold backing of paper money—maintain price levels unchanged, but if the increase in liquidity preference is too great, the gold reserve ratio cannot fall below a certain minimum, the discount rate is raised, and the price level falls. As this fall entails a parallel fall in the cost of production of gold, it leads to an increase in the output of gold, the effect of which is naturally to curb the fall in prices.[35]

When a new equilibrium is achieved, the output of gold is once again devoted exclusively to industrial uses, so it is normally at the same level. This is because the marginal cost of gold has reverted to the same value, at least under constant structural conditions,[36] so that the nominal price

32. Itself determined by the legal price of gold.

33. For slight variations in the rate of interest there is in fact relatively little change in plant and equipment structure and hence in the aggregate real demand $M^r(i)$ for money balances.

34. It is easy to see which sequence of primary effects draws such secondary effects in its wake.

In a closed economy a rise in the discount rate leads to a rise in the pure interest rate i_M and hence to a fall in prices (no. 98). This fall in prices stimulates gold production, and to cope with this increased gold output, the Central Bank must, if it is to maintain the legal price of gold, absorb this surplus—hence an increase in the amount of money in circulation, which raises the price level and restores equilibrium.

In an international economy of fixed gold exchanges, a fall in prices stimulates export growth and hence gold imports, the effect of which is of course identical to that of an increase in national gold production.

35. Remember that throughout this presentation *my remarks relate exclusively to equilibrium, independently of the time it takes to become established.*

36. See note 31 above.

level[37] has returned to its former level. As gold circulation has increased, the real value of cash circulation has risen, and it can therefore be shown that at a constant reserve ratio for cash, the interest rate has necessarily risen durably,[38] but it follows from the foregoing that this rise is relatively slight so that the interest rate may in practice be deemed unchanged.

On the other hand, *if liquidity preference falls* below a certain level, it can easily be seen that for an interim period price stability can no longer be ensured, prices rise, and industrial consumption of gold is made possible in part by demonetizing gold. Thus, when equilibrium is restored, gold output returns to its previous level as does the price level, while the interest rate is somewhat lowered.

In this way under the gold standard the economic mechanism in equilibrium and under constant structural conditions achieves practical stability of prices and of the rate of interest; slight variations in liquidity preference are offset by the rediscount rate policy, and major variations are offset by variations in the monetary gold reserve achieved by temporary variations in gold output.[39]

37. I.e., gold prices, in the present case.

38. When the liquidity rate is constant, the real value of rediscounted bills must increase in proportion to the real value M_M of ready cash. So the same applies to the difference $(M_M^r - E^r)$ and it follows from the equation

$$C_\varphi^r(i) + C_\mu^r(i) + M_M^r - E^r = C_0^r(i),$$

where M_M denotes the total amount of cash (notes plus coins) — an equation which is still applicable — that the equilibrium interest rate i is higher in light of the assumed initial stability of the equilibrium (see no. 97).

39. Readers familiar with M. Rueff's *L'ordre social* (Paris: Sirey, 1945) cannot fail to notice the agreement of my conclusions with M. Rueff's as to the stabilizing role both of the discount rate policy — whether or not in a convertible money system — and of the convertibility policy under a gold standard. This agreement is all the more striking as these conclusions are not commonplace, and I reached them, for my part, as is apparent from the text, by *entirely different paths* from those of M. Rueff.

With regard to the discount rate policy, note that M. Rueff's text deals only with primary effects, whereas the remarks made above show that the stabilizing quality of the discount rate policy also applies to *secondary effects*.

Quasi-stationary model and conventional model

In light of what is set out above,[40] the reader can easily verify that these different results can be immediately extended to a stationary model or to a model whose structural conditions are quite different, as the twin effects of unbacked credit and of variations in nominal prices are simply added one to the other.

Extension to cases involving costs and risks

All the foregoing findings can also be readily applied to cases presenting costs and risks and in which management and risk premiums occur.

The different discount rates, the official rediscount rate and the pure interest rate are dissociated but remain closely connected, and their general level is strictly determined by the whole set of conditions of economic equilibrium for a given discount policy adopted by the Central Bank.

This policy is in some degree arbitrary and can in fact aim to stabilize the pure interest rate and the price level, thus sparing the economy the disturbances due to accidental or seasonal variations in liquidity preference, but this action is strictly limited and can only manifest itself within a narrow range of variation in the rate of interest near and above the level corresponding to equilibrium in an account-based economy having no circulating money.

The case of international equilibrium

Hitherto I have tacitly confined myself to a closed economy, but if we are to understand the interest mechanism, it is vital to grasp how the above findings can be extended to the case of the international equilibrium.

The first point to remember is that *competition between banks on the different national markets continuously tends to equalize the pure interest rates*. It follows that in a world without costs or risk the different instantaneous pure interest rates would be equal in the different marketplaces.

When costs and risks are involved, however, permanent differences of level may subsist owing to the costs and risks involved in all overseas in-

40. No. 97.

vestment: these differences in the level of the rates of interest are equal to the corresponding premiums.[41]

Of course, this leveling out of instantaneous pure interest rates acts only as a trend, but the country-to-country short-term loan mechanism is so sophisticated that the leveling out of the pure interest rates corresponding to discount between two such marketplaces as London and Paris is usually much more reliable than the leveling out of short- and long-term pure interest rates within each of these marketplaces.

Hence, it is clear that in equilibrium the different national pure rates of interest are so *closely connected* that it would not be conceivable for one of them to rise or fall for any significant length of time without the others behaving in the same way.[42]

Admittedly each Central Bank exercises a certain influence on the international level of the rates of interest, since each bank's volume of rediscounting figures as an *arbitrary datum* among the general conditions of international equilibrium, but it is easy to show[43] that the spread in the international interest rate level due to the rediscount policy of any particular Central Bank is in fact *very slight*.

So, although a given country may sometimes follow an apparently independent discount rate policy, this can only be on account of the adjustment lags of the economic mechanism—which are particularly pronounced in the long-term market—and of purely speculative capital movements due

41. This means that the production period and social productivity vary depending on the country considered (note 39 to no. 47).

42. Hence, under free trade the social productivity of a given country cannot be maximized at home by a policy of lowering the rate of interest unless a similar policy is simultaneously applied in the other countries.

So if a given country were seeking to maximize its social productivity, it would have to apply a suitable policy (such as a tax on overseas financial investments, for instance) to offset the lower levels of the interest rates in force (which of course would be lower than national pure interest rates on account of the risk premiums to which overseas investments are subject).

Note that if overseas financial investments were risk-free or involved only limited risks, a policy of overseas investments at a positive interest rate would enable real national income, for an equal volume of savings, to reach a higher level than would correspond to the maximization of social productivity, i.e., to zero-interest domestic investments, but (a) overseas investment risks are generally underestimated, and (b) a zero interest rate at home is so socially advantageous (see chapter 10) that in my view the maximization of social productivity ought to take priority in every national financial investment policy.

43. Using fairly lengthy but uncomplicated reasoning of the kind provided above in the sub-section entitled "Role of the Central Bank," but which are beyond the scope of the present study.

to forecast inconsistencies in a highly unbalanced economy. Either such a policy simply reflects the leveling-out tendency in the face of persistent disparities or else it will inevitably create new imbalances for the future that will prove worse than those it was intended to remedy.[44]

a. *As a first approximation, it is safe to assume that in equilibrium the international level of the rates of interest depends only on the equilibrium between international savings and investment.* And once this interest rate is determined, the level of *real* demand for money balances $M^r(i)$ in each country necessarily follows. Hence, two scenarios can be envisaged, one for a gold standard model and the other for a floating exchange rate model.

Under a floating exchange rate, if we take as given the amount of paper money in circulation and the volumes $E_1, E_2, \ldots, E_n$ of bills rediscounted by the Central Banks, each country's total *nominal* circulation is well determined. In combination with its own real value as determined by the rate of interest, this total amount of money, in turn, is what determines the corresponding price level. *Thus, exchange rates are well determined as a function of rediscount volumes* $E_1, E_2, \ldots, E_n$. *Conversely, it is clear that for a given country the exchange rate may be set at an arbitrary level provided that the volume of bills rediscounted may freely settle at the corresponding level.* For a given international price level and exchange rate, the nominal domestic price level is well determined and the basic role of the rediscount volume then becomes—*taking into account, of course, multiplier effects due to the credit mechanism*—that of leveling out the difference between (a) the nominal value of the product of the real demand for balances by the price level and (b) the nominal value of banknotes in circulation.

Under a gold standard the legal price of gold is what determines the nominal price level and the exchange rates in each country. The rediscount volume in this case plays the same role as under floating exchange rates and serves to level out—*taking into account, of course, multiplier effects due to credit*—the difference between the nominal value of (a) the product of the real value of desired balances by the nominal price level and (b) total paper money in circulation.[45] Thus, for a given quantity of paper money, the reserve ratio of each Central Bank, i.e., the level of its

44. I shall return to this question below (no. 109).
45. Assuming, for the sake of simplicity, that gold does not circulate. This hypothesis corresponds to the gold bullion standard. It can be extended without difficulty to a model in which gold does in fact circulate.

nominal liabilities (money in circulation and rediscounting) relative to its gold reserve, is what determines the value of that reserve.

Needless to say, these are relationships of interdependence in dynamic equilibrium between the different characteristic economic magnitudes; they are not cause-and-effect links acting in dynamic disequilibrium, *which can be very different.*

b. *As a second approximation, in equilibrium, every Central Bank exercises, via its rediscount policy, a certain influence on the international level of interest rates, but this influence is limited.* Moreover its effects also differ, depending on whether the exchange rate is floating (paper money) or fixed (gold standard).

In the first case, if a fall in the rate of interest occurs simultaneously in every country, it will lead, *in equilibrium*, to a credit expansion, a decrease in the real value of cash balances and an increase in the price level, *in all the countries.* As these effects will naturally differ in scale from country to country, price variations in equilibrium will bring about corresponding variations in the exchange rate.

In the second case, a fall in the rate of interest—leaving unchanged the marginal costs of gold, exchange rates and hence nominal price levels— will have the exclusive effect of decreasing the worldwide circulation of gold and expanding overall credit.[46]

But here once again it is only the aggregate fall in worldwide gold circulation that is determined, and this fall may be distributed arbitrarily among the different countries depending on the individual credit policies adopted by their Central Banks.

And of course, the opposite secondary effects would be observed in the event of a rise in the international level of interest rates.

Broadly speaking, the international level i_i *of interest rates is a strict function of the volumes* $E_1, E_2, \ldots, E_n,$ *of bills rediscounted by the various Central Banks, which are thus shown to be independent parameters that can be arbitrarily set*, giving us

$$i_i = f(E_1, E_2, \ldots, E_n).$$

---

46. These facts are easily explained in light of the foregoing explanations.

As has been pointed out several times, the expansion of credit encourages a "saving" of cash and thereby enables the rate of interest to fall.

For given values of volumes $E_2, \ldots, E_n$, rate i_i depends only on volume E_1, and vice versa. Since the different rates of interest tend to level out, it becomes apparent how the rediscount rate set by a given Central Bank can, in equilibrium, determine the volume of bills it rediscounts.

Under inconvertible money, this setting of the rediscount rate leads, for given values of $E_2, \ldots, E_n$, to a change in the national price level and in the national exchange rate. So there is a relation of interdependence between the rediscount volume and the exchange rate.

When money is convertible, however, it leads, for given values of $E_2, \ldots, E_n$, to a change in the volume of national gold reserves, assuming that the national price level and exchange rate remain unchanged.

We must therefore conclude that *in equilibrium* the following will hold true:

1. *The different national rates of interest are closely linked and the possible variations in international interest rate levels via modification of the monetary policy of any given country are very limited.* Hence, the scope for variation of the different national official rediscount rates is itself very limited.
2. *Under a floating exchange rate* each country is master, for a given cash circulation, *either* of its exchange rate — via a suitable adjustment of its rediscount volume — *or* of the said rediscount volume — via an appropriate adjustment of its exchange rate.
3. *Under the gold standard*, with prices and exchange rates remaining fixed, each country is master of its gold reserves — or rather of the percentage of gold backing its money. The level of demand for gold is set through the gold production mechanism.

Relation of short to long term

The above analysis has shown how close the links are between the financial and money markets and, in the money market, between the discount rates and the other short-term rates.

As we have seen, when banks are able to issue unbacked demand deposits, peculiarities are introduced affecting how the discount rate is set, making it necessary, in studying both market structure and the determination of the rate of interest, to distinguish between (a) the relatively simple case in which unbacked demand deposits cannot be issued and (b) the more complicated case in which they can.

In the first, relatively simple, case, the link between short- and long-term depends on arbitraging by the different economic agents between long-term capital investments and short-term financial investments (such as Treasury Bonds and loans between individuals and firms other than banks) as well as on arbitraging between holding money—which constitutes a short-term internal investment—and external financial investment, whether short- or long-term.

The second case involves a further stage, linking the setting of the discount rates and the setting of the various other pure rates of interest, both short- and long-term. We have seen that this stage involves the Treasury Bond market, the repo market, and the secured loan market. Thus, for instance, the discount rate and the repo rate could not be very far apart, since if they were, it would be in the banks' interests to increase or decrease their repo investments. Similarly the repo rate could not differ greatly from the instantaneous pure long-term interest rate, for if the former were greater than the latter it would be profitable for speculators to invest their funds in repos, whereupon the repo rate would fall, or, if it were less, it would be profitable for them to buy securities under repo.

In a free market all this arbitraging occurs spontaneously and automatically, as thousands of speculators are always ready to take advantage of the slightest differences between current rates.

This explains the very close connection between the different pure instantaneous long- and short-term interest rates: the differences between actually observed yields are proportionally less, as there is less difference between the premiums corresponding to liquidity, monetary and capital value-gain, depreciation, estimated risk and cost of risk, storage, and management costs.

2. Determination of the rate of interest in a dynamic disequilibrium process (100)

Readers will have no difficulty in verifying that all the findings of no. 98 based on consideration of the difference $(i_F - i_M)$ between the pure rates of interest in the monetary and financial markets can be readily transposed to the general case in which money is hoardable and banks can issue unbacked demand deposits—*at least with regard to the general principles of economic development.*

In this case too, a pure interest rate i_F in the financial market that is greater than the pure interest rate i_M in the monetary market means that · it is more worthwhile to use money to acquire financial assets than to store it, so money balances fall, investments are made, prices rise, the real values of money balances fall, rate i_M rises, and rate i_F falls. And the opposite process takes place if it is rate i_M that is greater than rate i_F.

"Hoardability" of money and the issue of unbacked demand deposits

At this point certain peculiarities arise owing to the facts that (a) in the real world, money can usually be hoarded and (b) bank reserve ratios κ only descend to their minimum levels in equilibrium, displaying variable levels under dynamic disequilibrium, while the Central Bank's rediscount volume has no fixed value but depends on the Central Bank's own policy, which is itself subject to variation.

For the study of a dynamic disequilibrium process, this means (a) that *aggregate demand for money balances* $M^r(i)$ *in terms of real value can no longer be assumed to be broadly constant* and (b) that *the total quantity of money* M *available to the economy can no longer be assumed to be given, for it is itself variable.*

It is easy to foresee how the economic system will evolve under such circumstances starting from an initial difference $(i_F - i_M)$ between pure interest rates in the financial and monetary markets.

Generation of continuous and accelerating prosperity

For instance, let us assume an initial situation in which rate i_F is greater than rate i_M, the banks' reserve ratios are above their minimum permissible level, the Central Bank's rediscount volume is lower than its maximum possible, there is a degree of unemployment, and the various industries are running below their production capacity—*all circumstances normally found in economic cycles at the beginning of a period of prosperity.*

Under these conditions, *financial investment is more advantageous than holding money, so expenditure increases and prices rise.*

This rise in prices is naturally dampened by the general recovery, but owing to economic inertia, prices have a tendency to forestall the recovery. In any event, the increase in prices and the recovery lead to major profits for firms.

But in these circumstances *this development will lead to no immediate fall in rate i_F or rise in rate i_M.*

After all, expenditure is increasing, prices are rising, and profits are being made: business is booming. With optimism in the air, the banks are inclined—in order to take advantage of the margin between their discount rate and their expenses—to increase the volume of their discounts and—in order to attract bills—to keep their discount rate low. Under these conditions, rate i_M will not rise.

The increase in the volume of bills discounted leads to an increase in deposits. *So demand deposit money increases, and this increase itself helps to stimulate activity and raise prices.*

This rise in prices and activity, along with the resulting prosperity, now induces the various economic agents to decrease their money balances by the amounts hitherto hoarded either as a hedge against an uncertain future or with a view to taking advantage of expected lower prices. *This dishoarding further stimulates activity and contributes to raising prices.*

The continuing surge in prices and activity leads economic agents to think it will last—a prediction encouraged as prices do in fact continue to rise. The consequence is a continuing increase in the expected profitability and in the technical interest rates on real investments[1] and hence in the corresponding pure interest rate i_F.

This tends to bring about a continuous rise in activity and prices[2] and thus an acceleration of prosperity.

---

1. Throughout this analysis the rates referred to are of course forecast rates and not observed profitability rates (see no. 46). This underlines the crucial importance of forecasts in economic evolution.

2. Whereas this increase was only *momentary* in the model examined in no. 98, in which the quantity of cash was constant and hoarding was absent.

Widespread confidence and optimism usher in maximum dishoarding, short-term credit growth, and the maintenance of a low level for rate i_M, while increased profitability keeps rate i_F high.

Thus, so far, the initial difference ($i_F - i_M$), *far from decreasing, goes on widening.*

As firms have no difficulty in obtaining the credit they want—for bank reserves are above the minimum required—applications to the Central Bank for rediscount remain moderate and the official rediscount rate remains unchanged.

End of the boom and onset of the depression

But a development of this kind must reach the end of its course when dishoarders have nothing left they can part with, when the unrestrained issue of demand deposits has reduced banks' reserve ratios to their lowest authorized levels and when the possibilities of rediscounting by the Central Bank are also exhausted.

In pure theory we might imagine that, once money balances have been reduced to working capital, and total money available to the economy has reached its ceiling, a stable equilibrium might set in at this new level, but it is evident that this could not happen in practice. For the run of prosperity has given rise to latent imbalances the effects of which have so far been masked by the ongoing inflation. Thus, for instance, owing to the well-known acceleration principle, the capital goods industry has expanded to an extent that is unsustainable in a stationary equilibrium. The economy is over-supplied with capital goods.[3]

When credit expansion and dishoarding come to a halt—*and they cannot but stop sooner or later* when bank reserves have plummeted to minimum levels and the money held by economic agents is reduced to necessary working capital—*the inevitable adjustments, which have hitherto been postponed, begin to take effect.* Some firms, especially in the production goods sector, can no longer find a market for their products; they find themselves in difficulties and are unable to meet their commitments. Faced with these nascent difficulties, *to avoid incurring losses banks tend to raise their liquidity levels and restrict credit.* To this end, they raise their discount rate and rediscount part of their portfolio at the Central Bank.

---

3. See in particular nos. 109 and 111 below.

Whereupon the Central Bank, in order not to exceed its assigned rediscount limits, must itself raise the official rate.

The depression spreads and gains speed

This abrupt rise in the money rate is seen as a harbinger of hard times and moves the various economic agents to increase their cash in hand in order to forestall cash-flow difficulties. *Hoarding begins.*

The fall in the volume of circulation, brought about by the credit squeeze in combination with cash hoarding, *provokes a fall in income spent, and it becomes impossible to sell products at break-even prices.*

Widespread overproduction may then ensue in the sense that each industry finds it impossible to clear all its output even at cost price.

The breakdown of the monetary circuit induces a breakdown in the goods circuit.

Obviously once such a trend is underway it *spreads progressively.*[4] Faced with surplus production, firms reduce their activity, decrease their purchases of raw materials, and lay off part of their personnel. Income flows are thereby suppressed, which decreases the purchasing power of those affected and the initial disturbance spreads.

As aggregate income flows are equal to

$$PQ = M_R V_R,$$

where P and Q, respectively, denote the price level and the volume of activity and where M_R and V_R, respectively, denote the aggregate value and the velocity of circulation of working capital, it is clear that when the velocity of circulation of the fraction M_R of money that in fact continues to circulate[5] is constant, a decrease ΔM_R[6] leads, if the various prices remain unchanged, to the elimination of a quantity of income flows totaling $V_R \Delta M_R$. Thus, for instance, if annual velocity of circulation is 50, to a hoarding of one billion there will necessarily correspond the interruption of a total payment flow of 50 billion.

4. Spreads, not accelerates, notwithstanding the apparent opinion of many authors. For if the fall in the volume of deposit money (or hoarding) should cease, the tendency is swiftly checked as soon as the price level adjusts to the new monetary conditions.

5. As a first approximation, we may treat as a constant the velocity of circulation V_R of non-hoarded money M_R used as working capital.

6. Corresponding either to a fall in the supply of deposit money or to hoarding.

Once this tendency is underway, *it can only accelerate*.[7] Indeed the widespread insecurity created by the interruption of money flows to the amount of $V_R \Delta M_R$ leads to new hoarding on the part of individuals and firms and induces banks not to renew their credit. *Thus the fall in* M_R *quickens its pace*, which leads—notwithstanding a certain fall in prices—to the breakdown of numerous circuits of money and of goods. Prices and economic activity fall together.

This development leads to a rise in rate i_M and a fall in rate i_F.

First of all, to try to maintain their liquidity levels threatened by a decrease, sometimes very substantial, in receipts, firms seek to borrow, and this at the very moment when the banks are decreasing the volume of their discounts and their loans. A rise in rate i_M results.

Moreover, the losses incurred by most firms and the worsening predicament usher in a pessimistic outlook for the future. The consequence is a fall in the rate of interest i_F corresponding to marginal financial investments: it may even become negative.

Thus rate i_M *will ultimately rise, but only after long delays, and when this adjustment does take place, it tends to be abrupt. Similarly, rate* i_F *finally falls, but it too does so sharply, so that the initial difference* ($i_F - i_M$), *far from gradually diminishing and tending gently toward zero, crosses the zero threshold very swiftly and takes on a substantial negative value thereby immediately giving rise to the opposite phenomena.*

In the early days of the crisis, widespread liquidity troubles and the tightening credit squeeze lead to a major increase in rate i_M, and the risk entailed by any investment is such that rate i_F may fall to negative values.

When the crisis is over, the volume of credit has been greatly curtailed and firms' cash balances have been substantially restored, the reduction in the volume of business means that cash is once again abundant. Rate i_M falls, but rate i_F remains very low if not actually negative, so that the difference ($i_M - i_F$) is still positive.

The depression stops and the recovery gets underway

However, with unbacked demand deposits much diminished and the liquidities of economic agents increased, it is theoretically conceivable that in the absence of any change in these monetary conditions, the interplay of

---

7. This acceleration must be carefully distinguished from the propagation movement we have just studied (see note 4 above).

economic adjustments might lead the economy to a durable equilibrium. Yet clearly this could not be so in practice.

For the decreasing costs observed during the depression, the continuance of a certain volume of incompressible activities corresponding to basic needs, the relatively slight fall in the prices of those goods (food, clothing, etc.) and in those corresponding to long-term contracts (housing, for instance) ultimately create conditions of profitability in some sectors, thus raising rate i_F.

When rate i_F becomes greater than rate i_M, the conditions for a recovery of the above kind are once more in place: dishoarding occurs, accompanied by a general expansion of credit, and a new cycle begins.

Causes of economic cycles

This explains the disturbing phenomenon whereby an economy passes successively through phases of prosperity, in which output and consumption enjoy continuous growth and entrepreneurs reap rising profits in a general surge of prosperity, and periods of depression, in which output and consumption relentlessly decline while firms bear ever-greater losses amid an ever-worsening general depression. Upward trends, as they accelerate, end in crises, while the depression phases, as they grow, gradually generate the conditions for new phases of prosperity. A regular sequence of these cycles ensues, each cycle differing from the previous one only by the scale and length of its phases.

Finally, it emerges that the highly complex regulatory mechanism of monetary and financial interest rates, instead of leading, as before,[8] to a stable equilibrium, here leads to a situation that is constantly unstable and that this instability must therefore be attributed to the two basic facts that we had not been taking into account so far: the fact that banks can issue unbacked demand deposits and the fact that economic agents can hoard money.[9] These two factors must therefore be recognized as the determining causes of the permanent inherent instability of the economic system and of the cycles it begets.

---

8. No. 98.

9. Note that this only occurs in practice because in our modern economies the value of circulating money is invariably tied to the value of the unit of account so that whenever prices fall it becomes profitable to hoard.

Indeed, it can easily be shown that either of them alone is capable of bringing cycles into being.[10]

Lagged adjustment of the economic mechanism

In the real world, adjustment still takes place, but this adjustment is delayed, so that the economic system, instead of constantly tending toward a state of stable equilibrium, swings regularly back and forth between two extremes like a pendulum oscillating under the influence of gravity.

The existence of a credit margin[11] implies that the total volume of money in circulation is not fixed but varies between two limits. And the possibility

---

10. Let us first consider an economy such that no hoarding can occur *but in which credit can legally be granted in the form of demand deposits not backed by an equal amount of liquid assets*. It is clear that this possibility is liable to give rise to cycles.

In the case of a preexisting established equilibrium in which the banks' reserve ratio was 100%, banks would have, as we saw in no. 92, a powerful incentive to extend credit in the shape of unbacked demand deposits; this would lead to a rise in prices, and as reserve ratios could not without danger fall below the minimum values dictated by experience, the observed price rise would necessarily stop at a given point. At this point, any disequilibrium jeopardizing public confidence would encourage economic agents to withdraw all or a part of their demand deposits and the banking system would collapse. Credit would be reduced, and, after a shorter or longer period, the situation would return more or less to its starting point from which a new credit expansion could develop.

Now let us consider an economy in which it is not possible to issue unbacked demand deposits *but in which money can be hoarded*. It is plain that here too cycles will arise.

For if we begin with a situation of full employment but in which certain structural disequilibria (unsuitable circuits, earlier errors of economic management, etc.) are present, sooner or later economic difficulties of one sort or another arise, when some firms are unable to find outlets for their product at a price equal to its cost. The resulting insecurity induces some economic agents to increase their money balances, i.e., to hoard. This hoarding causes prices to fall, the fall in prices increases the insecurity and the insecurity launches a new wave of hoarding.

But of course with the rise in the real value of money balances, there comes a point when they are considered sufficient to cope with any risk whatever. And at that point, the fall in prices necessarily stops, which inevitably stimulates renewed confidence and renewed economic activity, leading in turn to dishoarding. This dishoarding sends prices up and it takes place at an accelerated rate. The consequence is the formation of structural disequilibria.

When money balances are reduced to the minimum levels of working capital compatible with structural conditions, the rise in prices will necessarily stop. The halt in the rise coupled with the appearance of difficulties due to structural imbalances brings the situation more or less back to its starting point whereupon a new expansion can get underway.

11. The credit margin owes its existence to the banks' ability to create unbacked demand deposit money (having no counterpart in legal money).

of hoarding money implies a variable level of aggregate demand for balances, for any given rate of interest—a level that also varies between two limits.[12]

Under these conditions, the economy's self-adjusting mechanisms act only when the limits are reached, whereas the accelerative mechanisms of disequilibrium are constantly at work, which is what explains the wide swing movements we observe.

In fact what happens is *exactly parallel* to what would be observed in the running of a steam engine if it were equipped with two centrifugal governors, the one powerful but operating only when certain limits were attained (the regulatory mechanism) and the other weak but operating in the opposite direction and in all positions (the accelerative mechanism). Under such conditions, it is easy to demonstrate that the engine, instead of running smoothly, would run cyclically.[13]

12. Thus, whereas in no. 98 the total volume of monetary circulation M and the function $M^r(i_M)$ denoting real desired money balances as a function of the interest rate i_M in the money market were considered to be constant, in the present case they are variables whose value depends on the state and evolution of the economic system at the point in question.

13. *Naturally, in view of the limited scope of the present study, the account of the cycle mechanism has been reduced to its simplest form.*

Indeed this highly simplified account by no means claims to be a complete theory of cycles, which would call for a volume in itself; its only aim is to bring out the link between the cycle phenomenon and interest theory by emphasizing the serious disturbances suffered by the highly complex and delicate regulatory mechanism of the monetary and financial interest rates owing to the possibility of hoarding money and of issuing unbacked demand deposits, and by thus explaining how cycles arise.

The present writer hopes to set out in a forthcoming study a detailed analysis of economic cycles, far more exact and complete than the above rough presentation of the basic underlying principles. This study will be based on a successive examination of the different factors of disequilibrium liable to be involved in cycles, in order to identify which of these factors should be classified as *induced* and which as *drivers*. This study will show that only the two factors isolated in the above analysis can be considered to be true drivers. [The analysis of economic cycles was the subject of Professor Allais's Innsbruck (1953) and Uppsala (1954) papers. See also *Les fondements de la dynamique monétaire* (The foundations of monetary dynamics) (Paris: Éditions Clément Juglar, 2001).—Trans.]

3. Classical point of view and modern theory (101)

The foregoing analysis[1] brings out the close interdependence between the determination of the interest rate and the determination of the price level and the intricacy of the link between the money market and the capital market.[2]

The classical theorists were undoubtedly right when, *in studying equilibrium*, they considered money to be a "veil" that had to be drawn aside because it masked the deeper and more fundamental relations linking (a) human needs and the effort required to satisfy them and (b) the propensities to consume and to invest.

But their position became *absolutely untenable* when they insisted on applying the same method to explaining *economic development outside equilibrium*. For money is then so fundamental a factor that it cannot be disregarded without running the risk of distorting reality so gravely as to render it almost incomprehensible.

In fact the separation of general price theory from the theory of money introduced by the classical authors is undoubtedly a key step in the analysis of economic reality, but it is only a step, for (a) the study of equilibrium must be completed by introducing the specific intermediate good known as money and (b) the study of disequilibrium must be fundamentally based on consideration of the interplay of the various economic factors, with a deliberate focus on the relative modifications not of the flows of *real* values that alone are considered by the classical theory, but of the flows of *nominal* values, i.e., the flows of circulating money. *Otherwise economic theory is condemned to struggle with insurmountable difficulties.*

1. Nos. 97 to 100.

2. Readers wishing to study this subject further are recommended to consult no. 197 *bis* of my *À la recherche d'une discipline économique.*

D. The Theory of Money, the General Theory of Prices, and the Theory of Interest

1. Theory of money, general theory of prices, theory of interest, and viewpoints (102)

The results so far obtained have given us an outline of the main links between interest and money. The argumentation has been set out in a planned sequence, as demanded by the rules of logical presentation; hence, economic reality has been considered only in the form of successive approximations, while the overriding need to present an overview may have prevented some aspects of theoretical and practical importance from being sufficiently analyzed or emphasized.

The time has now come to rectify such omissions or at least the more important of them.

The following presentation will complete the overview the reader already possesses, giving him a fuller grasp of the general mechanism by linking it closely with actual observation.

Full understanding of the issue, with all its aspects seen in perspective, depends on this diversity of approaches, so the reader should not be deterred by occasional, unavoidable repetition.

2. Interest, money, and quantity theory (103)

It is well known that in its classical form Fisher's equation

(1) $MV = PQ,$

where M, V, P, and Q, respectively, denote the quantity of money, the velocity of circulation, the price level, and the volume of activity, *is in fact simply a defining equation for the velocity of circulation*, which could not be determined in any other way.

The law of circulation expressed by equation (1) is illusory; it can have no deductive value except by taking the velocity of circulation if not as given at least as an element of only slight variability.[1]

Indeed what has been said above makes it easy to state the exact scope and meaning of the quantity theory. For by writing that total working capital plus speculative reserves equal total money M, we obtain the equation

(2) $M = P(K_R + K_T),$ [2]

i.e.,

(3) $$P = \frac{M}{K_R + K_T},$$

an equation expressing the interdependence of price level, volume of circulation, and the real individual money balances of economic agents (working capital plus hoarded reserves).

---

1. In fact Fisher's equation could only have explanatory value if it were presented in the form

(1) $(M - M_T)V_R = PQ,$

where M_T denotes the portion of balances allocated as speculative reserves, i.e., the quantity of hoarded money, and V_R denotes the velocity of circulation of working capital. Velocity V_R may in fact be deemed constant as a first approximation (see the remarks made in no. 79 and in note 10 to no. 98).

2. In view of the remarks made in nos. 79 and 80. We have seen (no. 82) how coefficients K_R and K_T depend on the rate of interest.

Unlike Fisher's equation, this equation has very high explanatory value, for the real levels of working capital and hoarded reserves are directly observable and, as has been shown, the motives that govern these levels can easily be determined as a function of the general theory of prices.

3. Money, credit, and social efficiency (104)

We have seen[1] that the necessary and sufficient condition for the social efficiency of a given economy to be maximal is that the competitive equilibrium conditions of the account-based economy having the same psychological, technical, and capital structure be verified.

However, in economies that use money, the competitive equilibrium conditions are in fact different from those of an account-based economy,[2] except when the equilibrium interest rate is equal to zero.[3] For this reason it is generally inevitable that the use of money compromises the maximization of social efficiency.[4] However, if the other conditions of this maximization are realized, it is safe to assume that the corresponding loss in social efficiency is of second order. For it has been shown that while the competitive equilibrium of a monetary economy undoubtedly differs from that of the corresponding account-based economy, the difference is relatively slight, and it is known that in the vicinity of the maximum, a first-order difference in the variable leads only to a second-order differ-

1. No. 55.

2. No. 82, § "Theoretical representation."

3. For in this case, parameters of a monetary nature (money balances and liquidity functions) for which the rate of interest is a factor disappear from the system of the general conditions of the equilibrium (no. 82, § "Theoretical representation"), which is thereupon reduced to the system corresponding to an account-based economy.

Indeed, as will be seen in chapter 9, "The Problem of Interest," the rate of interest *cannot* be zero in an economy in which the currency unit also serves as unit of account.

4. No. 55.

ence for the function. Of course, when the interest rate is zero the loss of social efficiency is also zero.[5,6]

Brief as they are, these observations show that from the monetary viewpoint, contrary to the claims—past and present—of the liberal school, *optimal management and competitive equilibrium are not equivalent concepts*.[7]

---

5. It might be thought that credit, by economizing cash, improves social efficiency, but in fact this is not so at all, at least not in any lasting way, as what matters from the point of view of social efficiency is the gap between a given state and the nearest state of maximum social efficiency. Now, although the use of deposit money spares *the overall economy* a certain financial cost and thereby improves social productivity, it leaves unchanged the corrective terms that are introduced into each equation considered *individually*, since the user cost of deposit money is identical in equilibrium to the user cost of cash. Consequently, for a given rate of interest, the order of magnitude of the loss of social efficiency remains the same.

And in this respect it is irrelevant whether the cash in question is paper money or gold. If money were not subject to wear and tear, a constant quantity of gold would be sufficient, under constant structural conditions, to provide for monetary needs. Once this quantity had been produced, there would be no greater loss of social efficiency than in the case of inconvertible paper money.

However, the fact remains that replacing a convertible currency system by an inconvertible currency system would mean that the quantity of metal previously reserved for monetary purposes could now be put at the disposal of industry. This shows that when gold is used as money there is a clear threefold loss in social efficiency: (a) the *permanent* loss due to the use of the money (convertible or not) as such, (b) the *permanent* loss due to wear and tear of the gold coins in circulation, and (c) the *temporary* loss corresponding to the opportunity cost due to the use for monetary purposes of the supply of gold on which the currency is based. Loss (c) is of course less, as credit is more extensive. Thus the saving of money achieved does indeed correspond to a gain in social efficiency, but it is a one-off gain and a temporary one.

6. But of course this result applies only when the selected unit of account is equal to the currency unit, as in our present monetary economies.

If the currency unit were distinct from the unit of account, i.e., if the twin functions of money were separated (see note 1 to no. 6 and nos. 113 and 161 below), the loss in social efficiency would only be zero if the liquidity premium of money l_M (which, it should be remembered, is an intrinsic magnitude: see note 27 to no. 82), and not the nominal interest rate i, was zero. As we have

$$l_M = i - \frac{\frac{d\overline{m}}{dt}}{m},$$

it can be seen that in a model in which the nominal rate of interest was kept at zero and money depreciated over time (the policy I advocate in chapter 10, nos. 160 to 164), while a loss in social efficiency would occur, this loss would be (a) of second order, as shown in the text, and (b) *impossible to eliminate* since, as will be shown, although a zero nominal interest rate is possible, a zero liquidity premium for money is unattainable (no. 136).

7. See no. 56.

Under a monetary regime, competitive equilibrium as a rule does not correspond to optimal management; there is a loss of social efficiency. Though slight, this loss is real, and this fact is enough to show *the inconsistency of the purely verbal reasoning on which is based the alleged demonstration that competitive equilibrium always corresponds to optimal management.* This highlights the absolute necessity of recourse to the methods traditionally used in the physical sciences, and to mathematics as the indispensable extension of ordinary logic. In the case in point, only a rigorous theory can show to what extent and under what conditions optimal management coincides with competitive equilibrium. *Any other approach can comprise only gratuitous assertions liable to bring economics into disrepute.*

4. Specific characteristics of money as an economic good (105)

In light of their fundamental importance, I think it worthwhile at this point to summarize and make a few remarks about the basic characteristics of money as an economic good.

Interest rate and money stock in equilibrium

Savings in quest of investment opportunities appear in the market in the shape of a flow of money—a fact that has naturally led to the belief that the equilibrium interest rate depends on the total quantity of money,[1] falling as the amount of money rises and rising when then the amount of money falls.

Observation of how the credit market develops outside equilibrium strengthens this belief, for the rate of interest in the financial market is indeed low when money is abundant and high when it is hard to come by.

Nonetheless, the notion that the equilibrium interest rate depends on the quantity of money is inexact and must be eradicated.

Anyone believing that there is a cause-and-effect relationship in equilibrium between the quantity of money and the interest rate is the victim of an illusion. Money is only a means of exchange and a symbol of wealth. Its greater or lesser abundance in equilibrium can modify neither the level of real savings nor the level of opportunities available to new capital nor the total amount of real balances but only the monetary expressions of these magnitudes, all of which are proportional to the quantity of money so that the equilibrium interest rate would remain unmodified.

The fundamental fact is that variations in the quantity of money act simultaneously and equally on the magnitudes whose equilibrium determines the rate of interest and do not therefore have any effect on the rate itself.

This common misunderstanding is due to confusion between the primary and the secondary effects of an increase in the quantity of money. For the primary effects of inflation do indeed include a fall in interest—one that is followed, as we shall be seeing, at the upper end of the inflationary curve, by a rise; but once equilibrium is restored (secondary effects), the rate of interest settles at a level independent of the quantity of money.

1. Both cash and deposit money.

There is simply no way that multiplying the instruments of exchange can, in equilibrium, multiply the means of production. Double a nation's money stock if you will; you will produce no generalized increase in natural resources, tools, or products being processed: fuels, metals, cloth, etc.

It is therefore natural to wonder what the effect of increasing the volume of monetary circulation really is. The answer is either (a) if the money is issued as cash intended to finance the State's expenses, it will act directly on market exchanges leading to a rise in prices, or (b) if it is issued by the banks, it temporarily increases the resources of the borrowers. In the latter case the rate of interest begins by falling. Entrepreneurs then increase their indebtedness and compete more and more aggressively in their efforts to acquire means of production. So the price of capital goods will rise. After a certain time, equilibrium is restored between the resources made available to borrowers and the goods they are seeking. The rise in the price of these goods diminishes the purchasing power of money, and *everything occurs just as if the quantity of money had returned to its original level.*

Moreover, common sense ought to tell us that *in the long run* it is not the increase in the quantity of money that will exercise the overriding influence on the rate of interest, but the increase in savings.

Interest rate and money stock in disequilibrium

We have seen[2] that the real *equilibrium* interest rate i_r depends *as a first approximation* only on the psychological and technical conditions of structure and that although, strictly speaking, it depends on the functions of liquidity and the rate of increase in the quantity of money, as a rule the influence of these factors is quite slight; in any event, rate i_r is strictly independent of money M.

We have also seen that in equilibrium the nominal interest rate i_e is equal to the sum of the real equilibrium interest rate and of the relative rate of increase in the price level—an equation expressed as follows:

(1)
$$i_e = i_r + \frac{\dfrac{dP}{dt}}{P}.$$
[3]

2. No. 97, § "Quasi-stationary model."

3. No. 97, equation (6).

As this equation is only strictly valid in equilibrium, the law it expresses is naturally applicable to the real economy only *as a trend*; i.e., the conclusion is that when prices rise, the interest rate must sooner or later tend to rise and vice versa.

As the price level is itself connected to the quantity of money,[4] clearly the interest rate must tend (secondary effect) to rise as amount of money increases.

This effect acts in the opposite direction to the corresponding primary effect. As the rate of interest acts, in the money market, as the price paid for the use of money, a fall must evidently be observed when the amount of money increases (primary effect).

These remarks are fully borne out by experience. At the start of an *inflationary episode*, the interest rate begins by falling. Only when the effects of the inflation begin to make themselves felt (tendency toward equilibrium) does the interest rate increase.

Similarly at the start of a *period of deflation* the rate of interest begins by rising and only when the effects of the deflation become manifest (tendency toward equilibrium) does the rate of interest decrease.

Characteristics of circulating money

When the price level is stable, the nominal interest rate is equal to the real equilibrium interest rate and hence *is independent of the quantity of money*. Thus, money is a good that enjoys the remarkable property that under stable price conditions *the price paid for its use is independent of its quantity. The same applies of course to its selling price*, which by definition is equal to one monetary unit.

If the price level is variable, the interest rate depends only on the relative variations in the quantity of money and remains independent of the quantity itself.[5]

These facts highlight the *peculiarities* of money as an intermediate good since its price of sale and the price paid for its use are always independent of its absolute quantity,[6] whereas for all other goods prices decrease as quantity increases.[7]

4. No. 97.

5. This property is equally applicable under dynamic equilibrium or disequilibrium.

6. Reminder: it follows from these remarks that the price paid for the use of money depends, of course, on the speed of variation in its quantity.

7. This decrease, which is very pronounced in the case of the primary factors of production (labor and land), is relatively slight in the case of goods reproducible at will (see nos. 249

These characteristics, specific to money as an intermediate good, should be compared with those of capital considered as an abstract good.[8] For both money and capital display peculiarities that give rise to specific difficulties in studying their respective markets and oblige the student of interest to adopt radically different approaches and analytical methods from those used when studying the price paid for the use of ordinary goods.

---

and 259 of my *À la recherche d'une discipline économique*), but in any event, there is always a variation in prices of use and selling prices depending on quantity.

8. No. 36.

5. Inflation, deflation, and the rate of interest (106)

It follows from what has just been said that *if forecasts were perfect, the nominal interest rate would be adjusted so as to neutralize or counterbalance the effect of variations in the price level, thereby stabilizing the real interest rate at the level of the real equilibrium interest rate.*[1] Thereupon,

> continuously rising prices would be associated not with a continuously rising [nominal] rate of interest but with a continuing high [nominal] rate of interest, and falling prices would be associated not with a continuously falling rate of [nominal] interest but with a continuing low [nominal] rate of interest, and a constant price level would be associated with a constant [nominal] rate of interest—assuming, in each case, that influences other than price change remained the same. . . .
>
> One obvious result of such an ideally prompt and perfect adjustment would undoubtedly be that [nominal] money interest would be far more variable than it really is and that when it was translated into real interest this real interest would be comparatively steady.[2]

In reality, however, *we observe* that it is rare for the nominal interest rate to adjust promptly and exactly enough to prevent the real interest rate from becoming abnormal and, contrary to what would occur if foresight were perfect, what emerges in the absence of foresight and adjustment is *relative stability in the nominal interest rate and great instability in the real interest rate*, while the insufficient variations in the nominal interest rate cause the real interest rate to vary in the opposite direction to the price level.

In fact, Irving Fisher has shown[3] that the real interest rate is from 7 to 13 times more variable than the nominal interest rate. This shows that we do not adapt nominal interest rates swiftly and accurately to price level variations, the requisite adjustments being in fact obstructed by our inability to forecast future variations in the purchasing power of money as

---

1. A rate that strictly speaking depends on the relative rate of variation in the money stock but that, as a first approximation, may be taken to be independent of it (no. 97).

2. Fisher, *The Theory of Interest*, pt. 4, ch. 19, § 5. [Bracketed terms added by Maurice Allais—Trans.]

3. Fisher, pt. 4, ch. 19, § 5.

well as by custom, law, the impossibility of a negative nominal interest rate,[4] and by the slowness with which the structure of the production system[5] adapts, or indeed by any other obstacle.

What does exist is the constant tendency — variable in strength — toward this adjustment. Thus, during an inflationary episode, the nominal interest rate ends by rising, so that at the end of the period, when price levels are high, the nominal interest rate is high too.

> It would doubtless in time revert to normal if the new high [price] level were maintained, but this seldom happens. Usually prices reach a peak and then fall. During this fall the interest rate is subject to a cumulative downward pressure so that it becomes subnormal at or near the end of the fall of prices.
>
> Thus, at the peak of prices, [nominal] interest is high, not because the price level is high, but because it has been rising and, at the valley of prices, [nominal] interest is low, not because the price level is low, but because it has been falling.[6]

Thus, the apparent irregularity of the nominal interest rate at these various periods *is an inevitable consequence of the efforts to stabilize the real interest rate.*

What brings about the movements in the nominal interest rate is not, in fact, so much the rise or the fall itself as the expectation of a rise or of a fall, taking into account all possible price movements and their probability. For instance, if prices have risen, but no new rise is expected, the nominal interest rate will tend to fall; only if further depreciation is expected will the rise in the nominal interest rate tend to continue.

Nominal interest rate and real interest rate under inflationary conditions

What matters to the businessman is not so much the nominal interest rate as the real interest rate, calculated in terms of goods for sale. This rate is expressed by the equation

---

4. No. 81.

5. Note: when prices display a continuous upward or downward trend, equilibrium would require a lower or higher real interest rate and hence an increase, or a decrease, in the average production period (no. 92).

6. Fisher, *The Theory of Interest*, pt. 4, ch. 19, § 10.

$$i''' = i - \frac{\frac{dP}{dt}}{P}.$$

(1) [7]

If the nominal interest rate is 7% but prices are rising at a rate of 10%, the real interest rate is negative: −3%. Obviously, it will be well worthwhile to borrow in order to invest the sums borrowed in real goods.

If, in these circumstances, I borrow 100,000 francs and use the sum to buy scrap iron, I shall have 7,000 francs interest to pay at the end of the year, but my scrap iron will then be worth 110,000 francs, so my investment will have yielded 10,000 francs, leaving me a net gain of 3,000 francs financed by my lender.

But if the money borrowed is invested in an industrial venture yielding a technical[8] interest rate of 5% when prices are stable, the rate of return becomes

$$5\% + 10\% = 15\%,$$

and the investment remains profitable as long as the yield remains higher than the nominal interest rate.

Alternatively, we may say that the investment is profitable as long as the real rate of interest on the loan, i.e., −3%, is lower than the real technical interest rate, i.e., 5%.

It can thus be seen that when prices rise and there is a lag before the adjustment of nominal interest rates, the businessman who borrows can repay his loan with a sum that in real terms not only involves no interest whatever but is in fact lower than the capital loaned in the first place. The real rate of interest falls to a negative value and the borrower thereby derives a potentially substantial profit.

This is why, when prices are rising, great fortunes can be made on the back of public misery, and the biggest gains are made by those who are the first to realize that they must borrow, borrow, and borrow again in order to take fullest advantage of the profit to be made from the difference

7. Rate i''' here considered is the real rate equivalent to the nominal rate *observed* in a dynamic disequilibrium process. It is of course distinct from the real rate of interest i_r, which *would prevail in equilibrium* and which I have called the *real equilibrium interest rate* (no. 105, equation [1]).

8. No. 44.

between the nominal interest rate and its theoretical value, which would correspond, in equilibrium, to the rate of price variation.

Admittedly, if a price rise is on the horizon, the increase in loan volume leads to an upward movement in the nominal interest rate. This is one reason among many why to a period of rising prices there corresponds, as we have seen, a high interest rate, while a low rate corresponds to periods when prices are moving downward; but this adjustment is never complete and never instantaneous; it only partly compensates for the fall in the purchasing power of money, it always sets in belatedly and it is always very slow.

When prices begin to move upward, the nominal interest rate is hardly affected. For it to rise significantly, the rise in prices must either have lasted some time or be substantial.

It is easy to grasp the mechanism that activates the law of the secondary effect whereby the nominal rate becomes equal to the sum of the real equilibrium interest rate and the rate of monetary depreciation. For every economic agent endeavors to adjust the various real interest rates of his investments to one another. As soon as he becomes aware of the inflation mechanism and its effects he tries, more or less consciously, to reduce[9] his real money balances to a value such that their liquidity premium is equal to the sum

$$i_e = i_r + \frac{\dfrac{dP}{dt}}{P}$$

of the real technical interest rate, the effects of which continue to act, though latently, and of the rate of monetary depreciation. Since, mean-

---

9. It should be remembered from no. 97 that in equilibrium real demand for balances falls as the price level rises. As we have

$$P = \frac{M}{M_r(i)},$$

it can be seen that in times of inflation prices must normally rise *more than in proportion to the quantity of money*. This finding helps explain the observation that the velocity of circulation increases in times of inflation. This is because, for a *given* propensity to hold money (represented by a given function $M_r(i)$), inflation corresponds to a fall in real money actually held. This effect *is added* to the action exercised *in the same direction* by the propensity for liquidity in times of inflation (decrease in function $M_r(i)$ for each value of i).

Similar observations of course apply in the case of deflation.

while, the real technical interest rate varies comparatively little,[10] the nominal interest rate now rises and tends toward its equilibrium level.[11]

However, during prolonged inflationary episodes, some members of the public, in their anxiety to avoid losses, may be led to overreact by reducing the amount of real resources they hold in the form of money beneath the level they *normally* need.[12] In this case, they have to provide for their day-to-day payment needs by borrowing, and rates may then *accidentally* rise to prodigious levels, far in excess of the equilibrium rate

$$i_r + \frac{\dfrac{dP}{dt}}{P},$$

corresponding to the *expected* rate of monetary depreciation.

Observation shows that the rapid depreciation of money gives rise, however paradoxical it may appear at first sight, to periods of monetary shortage accompanied by abnormally high short-term interest rates "because the public, in their anxiety not to hold too much money, will fail to provide themselves even with the minimum that they will require in practice."[13] This was the case in Germany at certain moments in the inflation that followed the 1914–18 war.

---

10. Reminder: if equilibrium were attained, the existence of a constant relative rate of price variation π would lead to a variation in the real interest rate i_r, but we have seen that, at least for moderate values of π, this variation would remain comparatively slight (no. 97).

11. By bearing in mind that *lending money means keeping it for the future*, it is easy to understand why it is precisely when everyone is seeking to unburden themselves of their money that no one agrees to lend except at very high interest.

12. I.e., lower than the real money balances that would correspond to a liquidity premium equal to the sum

$$l_M = i_r - \frac{\dfrac{dP}{dt}}{P}$$

of the real technical interest rate and of the foreseen relative rate of price variation. This behavior of course has the effect of accelerating the rise in prices.

13. J. M. Keynes, *A Tract on Monetary Reform* (New York: Macmillan, 1923), ch. 2, § 1.

If equilibrium prevailed at all times, it is quite certain that the rate of interest could not exceed the sum of the real interest rate and of the *expected* rate of monetary depreciation. But equilibrium does *not* so prevail. So it may happen that *some* economic agents who have reduced their money balances below their normal level fail to find *immediately* in the market,

During this inflation, Germany furnished an example of how the nominal interest rate can rise when prices have increased so greatly and so persistently that, rightly or wrongly, everyone thinks they will continue to do so. Yet even in Germany the nominal interest rate never rose high enough to keep pace with *the actual rise in prices*.

> In the autumn of 1922, the full effects were just becoming visible of the long preceding period during which the real rate of interest in Germany had reached a high negative figure, that is to say during which anyone who could borrow marks and turn them into assets would have found at the end of any given period that the appreciation in the mark-value of the assets was far greater than the interest he had to pay for borrowing them. . . .
> But after this had been good business for many months, everyone began to take a hand, with belated results on the money rate of interest. At that time, with a nominal Reichsbank rate of 8 per cent, the effective gilt-edged rate for short loans had risen to 22 per cent per annum. During the first half of 1923, the rate of the Reichsbank itself rose to 24 per cent, and subsequently to 30 per cent, and finally 108 per cent, whilst the market rate fluctuated violently at preposterous figures, reaching at times 3 per cent *per week* for certain types of loan. With the final currency collapse of July–September 1923, the open market rate was altogether demoralized, and reached figures of 100 per cent per month.[14]

But although the rates quoted sometimes exceeded the rate of monetary depreciation that could normally be *foreseen*,[15] they were still low in comparison with the *actual* progress of that depreciation, and borrowers continued to make profits.

---

at the rate that ought to bring about equilibrium, the liquidities they need. Under these conditions it is understandable that the rate of interest may rise to abnormally high levels, even though the very existence of such abnormal levels shows that there still exist in certain sectors of the economy sums of money potentially available, but which are momentarily unable to influence the market because of its imperfection.

14. Keynes, *A Tract on Monetary Reform*, ch. 1, § 1. Emphasis mine.
15. In accordance with the mechanism explained above.

Nominal interest rate and real interest rate under deflationary conditions

When prices fall, comparable phenomena are observed but in the oppo-site direction.[16]

For a relative rate of decrease in the quantity of money assumed to be given, equilibrium would require, as we have seen, (a) a fall in the nominal interest rate to a level

$$i_T^m - \left| \frac{\frac{dP}{dt}}{P} \right|$$

equal to the excess of the real marginal productivity rate of capital[17] over the absolute value of the relative rate of fall in prices and (b) a rise in the real marginal productivity rate of capital.[18]

However, such adjustment may in fact be absolutely impossible be-cause (a) it is impossible for the nominal interest rate to become nega-tive[19] and (b) it is impossible for the production sector to adapt its struc-ture rapidly so as to increase its average production period Θ_N.[20]

And as long as this adjustment has not taken place, the money market's real interest rate

$$i + \left| \frac{\frac{dP}{dt}}{P} \right|,$$

which is equal to the sum of the nominal market interest rate and the absolute value of the rate of fall in prices, remains higher than the real

16. However, notwithstanding the perfect symmetry between the explanations of the mechanisms of deflation and inflation, I here use, to help the reader to understand the issue, a somewhat different form of explanation from that used in the previous paragraph.

17. This rate must be considered to be at every instant a *physical* datum resulting from the industrial structure of the production sector. It has been seen that in equilibrium it takes the shape of a well-determined function of primary national capital (no. 47).

18. On account of the fall in capital brought about by the increase in the real value of money balances (no. 97).

19. No. 81.

20. No. 47.

marginal productivity rate of capital. *In this situation, no investment is profitable and only money hoarding makes sense.*

When firms begin to realize the situation, an adjustment tends to occur (a) by a fall in the nominal interest rate due to the abundance of hoarded capital and (b) by a rise in the real marginal productivity rate of capital due to the cessation of investments and the decrease in primary national capital.[21,22]

As long as this adjustment has not taken place, the borrowers must lose and the lenders must win. However, when borrowers are crushed beneath a very high real interest rate they are generally unable to meet their commitments and their loans are simply written off. Which is why, faced with this risk, potential lenders prefer to keep their capital in the form of money by hoarding. Hence deflation is accelerated.[23]

When prices are falling at 15%–20% per year, as was the case in France in 1930–31, a bank interest rate of 1% is still a crushing burden for business because it is equivalent to a real interest rate of 16–21%. It would have been in the interests of anyone able to anticipate the movement to liquidate his assets and withdraw from business for a time.

Real market interest rate and equilibrium of investment and savings

The foregoing findings have shown that *the real interest rate, whose role should be to determine the equilibrium between savings and investment and whose importance for the economy is therefore fundamental, is in fact influenced more by monetary instability than by key factors such as the economy's psychological and technical structure, a fact that leads to extremely severe troubles in the operation of the economic system—troubles the importance of which cannot be too strongly emphasized.*

---

21. It should be recalled that in equilibrium the real marginal productivity of capital is greater as primary national capital is less.

22. Thus, a series of phenomena arises that tend to bring the economy to the state of equilibrium described in no. 97. As explained in no. 81, whereas the pure rate of interest can tend toward zero while remaining above it, the fall in the short-term interest rate is limited in its downward movement by the risk and management premiums (note 14 to no. 84).

23. In addition to the fall in prices that *in equilibrium* would result from (a) the decrease in the quantity of money and (b) the increase in real money balances (no. 97), there now supervenes a further fall due to an increase in real balances on account of the increased risks—a fall *greater than would occur exclusively as a result of the conditions of the dynamic equilibrium.*

6. Inflation, deflation, and competition (107)

Although competition stands out in periods of price stability as the basic factor in the normal interplay of the interest rate and the maximization of social efficiency, when price instability prevails, it cannot be too strongly emphasized that, although competition still plays a role, *it can become ineffective or downright harmful.* This is so when the conditions that determine the value of the unit of account vary rapidly and prices undergo substantial variations—upward or downward—in a short space of time. As we have seen,[1] such situations occur when the overall economy, for monetary reasons, experiences a period of rapid inflation or deflation.

Competition and inflation

When inflation prevails, all prices rise rapidly and business is easy. *When money is stable,[2] the sum of the gains and losses realized by entrepreneurs in a competitive environment is strictly zero, entrepreneurs as a whole do not diminish the national income, and profits accrue to ventures that are beneficial to the community* (lower cost prices, sound forecasts of market conditions, risk coverage), *but under inflationary conditions all firms, even the worst, may make gains and on average the sole cause of profits is the increase in the means of payment.[3] Considerable excess profits[4] are realized in this way.*

1. No. 100.
2. See no. 113 below.
3. An *intuitive* idea of what takes place may be formed as follows:

Note first that the profits and losses in question naturally take into account the *prior* deduction of interest on capital invested at the market rate and the remuneration of the entrepreneurs' activity (taken as equal to what they could have earned by working in a salaried post).

Bearing this in mind, let us first consider a *stationary equilibrium,* remaining identical over time. Under such economic conditions—which are purely *ideal,* as in reality structural conditions evolve constantly—there could be neither profits nor losses, since any field of activity that showed a profit would attract new firms, while any loss-making activity would in due course lead to the disappearance of the firms engaged in it, and thus no stationary equilibrium could subsist as initially supposed.

As the conditions are taken to be stationary, the quantity of money remains constant. The same applies to the money held by the various economic agents, whose expenditure remains constantly equal to receipts and bears a constant ratio to their money balances. Each year, the output of merchandise produced at a given cost encounters an equal expenditure flow enabling the market to be cleared. Prices remain stable and monetary neutrality prevails—a concept that will be explained below, no. 113.

a. Under these conditions *competition immediately becomes partly if not completely ineffective.*

First, during the period of rapidly rising prices, any attempt to compare prices, any estimate of potential investments, becomes either illusory or impossible. As anyone who buys becomes richer, there is a tendency to buy anything at any price. And as the situation is also very unstable, peo-

---

Let us now suppose that, under these conditions, *structural changes* occur, for instance, that consumer preferences alter so that more wireless sets are wanted and fewer clothes. Consumer expenditure will alter accordingly and during 1946, for instance, 100 million francs more will be spent on wireless sets and 100 million francs less on clothing, while the output of commodities, whose production took months during the years prior to 1946, has remained the same. This will lead to a rise in the price of wireless sets and a fall in the price of clothing, and, as sale prices have hitherto been strictly equal to costs, the wireless trade will show an overall profit of 100 million and the clothing trade will record a loss of 100 million. Under these conditions, *one's gain is strictly offset by another's loss.*

The profits realized by the wireless manufacturers are their reward for wisely concentrating their activity in a sector corresponding to consumer needs, while the losses incurred by the clothing manufacturers penalize their unwise decision to allocate factors of production to an activity less desired by consumers. *The overall deduction made from the national income by entrepreneurs as a whole is zero.*

Now let us suppose that, in addition to these structural modifications, monetary inflation takes place. In this case the aggregate flow of consumer spending in 1946 increases by comparison with 1945. This increase normally tends to be spread uniformly over all the expenditures. If clothing expenditure was formerly double what was spent on wirelesses, for instance, there will be, for example, supplementary expenditure of 200 million francs on clothing and supplementary expenditure of 100 million francs on wireless sets. Thus the total expenditure variation between 1945 and 1946 will be +100 million in the clothing industry and +200 million in the wireless industry. *In this case, all firms are simultaneously profitable*, their aggregate profit being equal to the increase of 300 million francs in consumer spending. The poor foresight displayed by clothing manufacturers is rewarded just as the good foresight of the wireless-manufacturers is.

This analysis is simplified; it cannot be extended rigorously to the case of a complex economy in constant evolution *without raising great difficulties* that exceed the scope of the present analysis. Suffice it to say for the present that these difficulties are exclusively due to the complexity of the monetary circuits and the very different forms that economic development may take: they make no change to the principles of the foregoing simplified analysis.

I intend to provide a rigorous demonstration of these various findings in a forthcoming study to be published under the title *The Accounting Foundations of Economic Macrodynamics.* [This work appeared (in French) in 1954—Trans.]

4. Reminder: what is here termed *excess profit* is that part of a firm's profits (as they appear in its profit and loss account) that cannot be considered to be the reward for a *service rendered* by the firm to the Economy as a whole (note 27 to no. 94). (Readers wishing to study in greater detail these two concepts of profit and excess profit, so defined, are recommended to consult nos. 157–62 of my *À la recherche d'une discipline économique.*)

ple live from hand to mouth and long-term projects tend to be abandoned as too risky. Under such conditions, *the regulatory effect of prices and the interest rate*, which is so essential for the maximization of social efficiency, *tends to fail*.

Secondly, as even the most second-rate firms find outlets, they not only survive but even make substantial excess profits; *the elimination of the unfit no longer takes place*, and the selection of the best is entirely illusory.

Thirdly, which is worse, the highest profits fall *not to those who devote patient efforts to cutting their costs* but to those who devote all their energy to speculation, now unfailingly lucrative.

b. Furthermore, *profits tend to lose their social significance*. Whereas in a time of price stability the highest profits are the mark of the greatest services to the community,[5] when prices are rising, they are generally at best due only to the fact that the overall trend is upward.

Under such conditions, the entrepreneur is no longer the bulwark of society and the architect of its future but, in the eyes of all, a mere profiteer. "In his heart he loses his former self-confidence in his relation to society, in his utility and necessity in the economic scheme."[6] By depriving the greater part of his profits of their merit and social justification, inflation deprives them of any social significance and brings the very principles of the competitive system into utter disrepute.

Competition and deflation

In a period of deflation *all* prices fall rapidly, business is difficult, and *all* firms, even the best, *may incur a loss*. Overall, the various industries suffer major losses and many firms, even among the best, go bankrupt.[7]

---

5. On this topic readers may usefully consult no. 159 of my *À la recherche d'une discipline économique*.

6. Keynes, *A Tract on Monetary Reform*, ch. 1, § 1.

7. This can of course be illustrated by an intuitive argument parallel to the one used in note 3 above.

Thus: if we assume that monetary deflation is added to the structural changes, the total consumer expenditure flows for 1946 will be less than in 1945. This decrease tends to be spread uniformly over the whole range of expenditure. Thus, for instance, we shall have falls of respectively 300 million and 150 million francs in spending on clothing and wireless sets. So the total variation between 1945 and 1946 will be minus 400 million francs in the clothing industry and minus 50 million in the wireless manufacturing industry. *Here all the firms will be making losses simultaneously*, their total loss being equal to the 450 million-franc decrease in overall consumer spending. The sound forecasting of the wireless producers will be penalized just as much as the poor forecasting of the clothing producers.

a. *Under such conditions it is easy to see that competition may become harmful.*

First, although all prices fall, they do so unequally, as resistance to the fall is very variable from one point of the economy to another.[8] Under these conditions *all economic calculations are distorted*, and precisely insofar as the interplay of prices and the rate of interest takes effect, it is liable to give rise to misinterpretations. The price-and-interest-rate mechanism no longer plays its regulatory role, indispensable for the maximization of social efficiency.

Secondly, *any firm*, no matter how good, may fail to break even. So competition is no longer the effective stimulant that, under stable price conditions, ensures progress. Instead, it becomes *a brutal and excessive incitement* to a veritable struggle for survival in which the financially weakest elements—which, on the strictly technical and economic level, are not necessarily the worst and may even number among the best[9]—invariably succumb. The accelerated fall in prices that results from this ruthless struggle for survival merely accentuates the deflation and can only bring whole industries to ruin. In such a conjuncture, the formation of powerful cartels or trusts tending to regulate manufacturers' prices *unquestionably* offers advantages that outweigh the drawbacks due to the monopolistic situations thus fostered—very often, it must be admitted, by force of circumstances and in opposition to the initial intentions of the firms involved. This explains why the public authorities, far from opposing the establishment of such agreements, often facilitate them or even promote them. The cut and thrust of competition thus leads to its ultimate elimination, and the fundamental principle of the economic system turns out to be self-contradictory.

Thirdly, under deflation, the competitive mechanism, instead of encouraging the spirit of enterprise and initiative, *offers a reward to all who slacken or liquidate their business activities*. The goal is no longer to work as well as possible but to safeguard one's capital by converting it into cash.

b. *Moreover, losses incurred by firms tend to lose their social significance.*

When prices are stable, losses can only be the sanction visited on error or incompetence. But when deflation prevails, such losses become the rule, striking even the most able and careful.

8. Thus the flexibility of wholesale prices often confronts a quasi-rigidity of interest rates and especially of wages.

9. This applied to the Citroën corporation in the depression that followed the 1929 crisis.

Whereas under inflation the unwarranted inflationary profits allocate to some a share of the national income that others will consider unfair, and thus exercise a demoralizing influence that saps the very foundations of the economic mechanism, under deflation, deflationary losses oblige entrepreneurs to bear the weight of circumstances they could not have anticipated and thereby seriously distort the economic functioning of the markets. In the first case, entrepreneurs are unjustly enriched at the expense of the community while in the second the community is unjustly enriched at the expense of the entrepreneurs.

Although very often they have been quite without fault, badly informed public opinion tends to blame the spectacular business failures on management incompetence. Faced with the scale of the ensuing difficulties, the State is indeed led to help the most precarious of the large firms, but to compensate for this risk sharing, public opinion calls for a share in their earnings and in their management.

And entrepreneurs themselves, overwhelmed by the scale of risks past all bearing, turn to the State as a permanent crutch. They go so far as to repudiate competition, sometimes without even realizing that it is the *only* justification for their existence. Thus they abdicate their entrepreneurial role and appear to a part of public opinion as parasites.

Problem of competition

Thus it is clear that in times of price instability, whether inflation or deflation, competition becomes meaningless and hence impossible or harmful. *It cannot suffice alone to ensure the maximization of social efficiency.* But this, I stress, carries no weight against competition itself, which is indispensable in one form or another[10] in order to ensure the normal free play of interest rates and optimal economic management; it argues only against circumstances that inhibit the normal operation of competition.

There can be no doubt that, as a response to the excesses of periods of inflation or deflation, *central planning*, either at State level or at industry level by way of cartel agreements, can be entirely justified. But it is no less evident that suppressing the normal free play of competition is likely to lead to deplorable conduct and to involve substantial losses for the entire community. Hence, though sometimes both necessary and inevitable, it

10. See the explanations given in chapter 6 (particularly no. 55) above.

remains an *evil* and must be exposed as such. So it is not competition that should be put in the dock—for in a stable price environment its effects can only be beneficial—but the underlying causes of generalized price movements that need to be identified and combated.

The competitive economy is and remains the only economic technique capable of leading to optimal management, but price stability emerges as the necessary precondition for any effective competition to be introduced.

7. Discount rate policy (108)

Principles of discount rate policy

The pure interest rate i_M in the money market *at a given moment in a dynamic disequilibrium process* differs little in practice from the Central Bank discount rate, which can be set by the Central Bank at a higher or lower level.

If this rate is cut, the use of money can be had for a lower price: money is said to be cheaper and increasing use is made of it. The demand for credit grows more substantial, and the amount of deposit money increases. Hence the total volume of money increases as the rate of interest falls.

Conversely total money decreases when the interest rate increases.[1]

Since at any given moment the market interest rate is proportionately lower as money is more plentiful,[2,3] it is clear that *in dynamic disequilibrium the cause-and-effect link between the quantity of money and the interest rate is identical irrespective of whether it is the volume of money that is modified first or the interest rate*: these facts are the basis on which Central Banks determine their credit policy.

Since banks always have the option of rediscounting part of their portfolio with the Central Bank, it is the discount rate applied by the Central Bank that controls, as we have seen, the entire issue of money in the economy whether by way of cash issued by the Central Bank itself or as deposit money created by the lending institutions.

Effects of altering the discount rate under inconvertible money

By combining these findings with the preceding analysis, we can identify what happens in an inconvertible money model when the Central Bank changes the discount rate. If the discount rate is cut, the use of deposit money grows, total money increases, and the result is an increase in prices.

---

1. In a dynamic equilibrium process the same applies if we consider no longer the nominal value of money but its real value $M^r(i)$ since the real value is a decreasing function of the rate of interest.

2. We have seen, in particular, that an increase in the amount of deposit money, starting from equilibrium, begins by causing a fall in the rate of interest.

3. It should be remembered that in *dynamic equilibrium*, for any given distribution of money between cash and deposits, the rate of interest is independent of the quantity of money and that it falls when the use of deposit money expands.

This is due to an increase in investments both in capital goods and in financial assets, which in turn is due to the differences $(i_F - i_M)$ between the pure interest rates in the financial and money markets.[4]

Quite simply, *cutting the discount rate* brings about a daily rise in the general price level, which is proportionately greater as the difference $(i_F - i_M)$ is greater. But of course this daily rise remains slight in so far as a new equilibrium quickly becomes established. At the end of this adjustment period the general price level settles, as we have seen, at a new plateau, higher than the preceding one, which, for given structural conditions, remains unchanged as long as the discount rate is not changed again,[5] since the relative rise in the price level thus produced is generally much greater than the fall in the discount rate that provoked it.

When the discount rate is raised, on the other hand, opposite effects are observed except that whereas in the foregoing case daily credit growth is unlimited, in the present case the daily curtailing of credit is in fact limited to the volume of earlier discounts arriving at maturity and not renewed by the banks. So the phenomena of adjustment are proportionately slowed down as the average term of discounted bills is longer. *The shorter this term, the more flexible the system.*

Of course, raising or diminishing the discount rate is limited for the former by the maximum rediscount volume fixed by the Central Bank and for the latter by the minimum—zero—level of this rediscount. *When the maximum has been reached it is impossible for the discount rate to be cut, and when the rediscount portfolio is zero any rise in the discount rate would be ineffectual.*

Stabilizing role of the discount rate under inconvertible money

When the official discount rate is higher than the value at which it is in the banks' interests to have part of their portfolio rediscounted, any *increase in the real demand for money balances*[6] sends prices down and the interest rate up.[7] Of course, if the rise in the market interest rate is not enough for

---

4. As explained in nos. 99 and 100.

5. No. 99.

6. Represented by an increase in the function $M^r(i)$ for each value of i (note 23 to no. 99).

7. This rise can initially be quite pronounced in the money market, but following arbitraging between the financial and money markets, the relative rise in the rate of interest *once equilibrium is reattained* is, as we have seen, much less than the relative fall in prices (no. 99).

it to be profitable for banks to rediscount part of their portfolio, the possibility of rediscount has no effect.

But as soon as the rise in the interest rate is such that rediscount becomes worthwhile, the pure interest rate settles at a level corresponding to the rediscount rate and, as we have seen,[8] the price level tends to stabilize. From then on, any further demand for balances is supplied by the monetization of bills of exchange via discounting. In nominal value, this monetization is equal to the product of the price level by the corresponding increase in real desired balances.

These remarks are equally applicable to the case of primary or secondary effects of increase in money demand.[9]

As the discount rate is almost always close to the level at which rediscount becomes worthwhile, the fall in the general price level corresponding to a moderate increase in desired balances will always be slight, if not zero, depending on the initial level of the discount rate.

In the case of a major increase in *desired money balances*, however, stabilization can no longer take place when the rediscount volume reaches the maximum level fixed for, or by, the Central Bank. From then on, the rediscount rate is increased so that the price fall and the interest rate rise hitherto blocked by the stabilizing action of rediscount can recommence.

Of course, all these explanations concerning the issue of deposit money via rediscount suppose a situation in which the reserve ratio of the lending banks is at its minimum.[10] If, for whatever reason, this minimum has not been reached,[11] the increased demand for balances can be satisfied, with no fall in prices or rise in the interest rate, simply by expanding credit and without any action on the part of the Central Bank.

When real demand for money (balances) falls, instead of rising, the market rate tends to drop to a level lower than that at which it is in the interests of the banks to turn to rediscount.

Hence the rediscounted portfolio decreases in size, and if the daily drop in desired balances is less than the daily amount of previous discounts maturing, the monetary adjustment takes place without any change in the

8. No. 99.

9. In the case of the *primary effects*, this is due to the fact that the main seasonal variations in demand for money balances come from firms and can therefore be *directly and immediately* satisfied via discount, and in the case of the *secondary effects* the cause is analyzed in no. 99.

10. Corresponding to the prevailing situation (no. 92 *in fine*).

11. Such a situation cannot be considered normal, as the desire to increase their income provides a constant incentive for banks to keep their reserve ratio as low as possible (no. 92).

general price level or of the short-term interest rate, by straightforward demonetization of discounted bills.

If, on the other hand, the daily drop is greater than the daily volume of previous discounts maturing, the short-term interest rate falls and prices rise. But should the fall in money demand cease, the interest rate fall and price rise may in due course be reabsorbed insofar as the rediscount volume may continue to be diminished.[12] When this limit is reached the fall in the short-term interest rate and the rise in prices become inevitable. But it should be noted that the links between the money and financial markets then have the effect of considerably reducing the fall in the interest rate so that *in equilibrium*, as we have seen, the fall in the interest rate due to decreased money demand is relatively slight. Here too it is confirmed that the market's adjustment capacity is proportionately greater as the average term of discounted bills is shorter.

Herein lies the explanation of

the characteristic monthly cycle of the markets: the market rate falls below the official rate as the end of month maturity date recedes into the past, while the quantity of money decreases. Then the market rate ceases to fall and begins to rise as, with the approach of the next due date, demand for money (balances) begins to grow. As soon as the market rate has drawn level with the official rate again[13] it ceases to change as all further money requirements are satisfied by discounting.[14]

So when the Central Bank's official discount rate is on par with the short-term market rate the general price index and the interest rate remain unchanged whenever the demand for money balances is growing, irrespective of how much extra money is in fact wanted,[15] just as they do in periods of decreasing money demand when the daily amount of unwanted money

12. There is nothing surprising in the dissymmetry between the effects produced by a rise and a fall in real desired money balances. "It is due to the dissymmetric character of the Central Bank's intervention [for slight variations in market conditions]. For the Central Bank 'takes' without limit, but only 'gives' to the extent that prior discounts fall due" (Rueff, *L'ordre social*, 250).

13. Note that the equilibrium value of the market rate is generally little different from that of the official rediscount rate (no. 94).

14. Rueff, *L'ordre social*, 249.

15. Within the limits, of course, as stated above, imposed by what the Central Bank's policy makes possible.

is lower than the daily volume of earlier discounts falling due. Only when the former is greater than the latter does the market discount rate fall while the overall price level rises.

Effects of variation in the discount rate under convertible money

As adjustments in gold production[16] are relatively slow, *the primary effects of variation in the discount rate under convertible money conditions are much the same as when money is inconvertible.*

But the secondary effects are different. For it follows from the explanations given above for dynamic equilibrium that when equilibrium is reestablished *the price level returns, more or less, to its previous level.*

Thus an increase in the discount rate under the gold standard, though it has the primary effect of bringing down prices, would not lead to any long-term price change.

From the secondary point of view, moreover, *the possible changes in the discount rate that can actually be made by the Central Bank during a long-term equilibrium are extremely slight.*[17] Consequently, the discount rate of one country's Central Bank cannot be sustainably held at a level significantly different from that implied by the general conditions of the economic equilibrium for determined average rediscount volume levels of other Central Banks.[17]

Stabilizing role of the discount rate in the case of convertible money

When money is convertible all the foregoing explanations concerning the stabilizing role of the discount rate under inconvertible money remain valid as to the primary effects, but with regard to the secondary effects there is, as we have seen,[17] an additional stabilizing effect, due to the steadiness of the gold price and to possible variations in gold production, which is added to the stabilizing effect of the Central Bank's rediscount operations whenever the scale of money demand variations exceeds the adjustment possibilities provided by rediscount alone.

As we have seen,[17] convertibility has the effect of substituting an increase in gold and silver balances for the general fall in prices that would occur in the case of inconvertible money, and vice versa.

---

16. Or country-to-country gold movements in the case of an international economy.
17. No. 99.

However, as input transfers are not instantaneous in the real economy, this *stabilizing effect of gold convertibility* can only come into play after a significant interval; this is why *it leaves unchanged the primary effects mentioned above and acts only as a secondary tendency.*

> Thus the convertibility mechanism is not instantaneous. It does not act as soon as increased money balances are called for but only later, after falling prices have produced their economic effect of increasing gold production to the extent needed to restore the price level to the point assigned it by the legal definition of money.[18]

Goal of the monetary policy of the Central Banks

The permanent goal of any monetary policy *is to reduce to a minimum the disturbances due to accidental or seasonal variations in desired money balances, i.e., the variations in prices, interest rates, or precious metal reserves, which they are liable to induce,* by counteracting them insofar as possible via an increase or a decrease in the volume of bills of exchange rediscounted.[19]

It follows from the above analysis that this goal can be achieved if the rediscount rate is held at a suitable level *as determined experimentally,* no change being introduced unless there are grounds for believing that a permanent change in the economic equilibrium has occurred.

Advantages of rediscount policy

Our findings also highlight the advantages of the Central Bank's rediscount policy for the normalization of short-term interest rates. In the absence of such a policy, these interest rates would undergo much greater variations owing to the regular changes in average liquidity preference — both in the course of the month and in the course of the year.

The effect of this stabilization is to avoid disturbances in the long-term market and in the various markets for commodities, notably raw materials, which sharp changes in the short-term interest rate would certainly lead to.

18. Rueff, *L'ordre social,* 260.

19. A policy of open market sales and purchases by the Central Bank in the free market is in theory absolutely equivalent to a policy of rediscounting bills of exchange (see below, § "Limits of rediscount policy").

No one can fail to recognize how precious this stabilization of interest rates and prices proves in enabling the free play of economic mechanisms to proceed as it ought.

Experimental principles of the Central Bank's policy

The normalization would of course be maximal if the average level of desired money balances corresponded to about half the possible maximum rediscount volume, i.e., if the discount rate were set at a level such that the corresponding pure interest rate was precisely that which would occur in a spontaneous equilibrium in which the rediscount volume was equal to half its maximum level and in which desired balances were equal to their average level.

This rate can only be identified by trial and error. The Central Bank cannot directly observe at what level to maintain its discount rate for maximum stabilization; it can only deduce it from movements observed in the market.

When there is a continuous upward trend in the general price level while the market discount rate is on a par with the official rate, this means that the difference $(i_F - i_M)$ between the respective rates of the financial and money markets is positive and the official rate is lower than its lowest possible level and should be raised.

When, on the other hand, the general price level is falling at a time when the market discount rate is moving downward away from the official discount rate, this means that the official rate is higher than its maximum possible level and must be lowered.

Thus discount policy cannot be subject to a priori decisions; it can only be determined in practice.[20]

In fact *any policy of stable prices and interest rates involves keeping the official discount rate of the Central Bank within fairly narrow limits, well determined by the general conditions of the equilibrium.* Fixing it at a level higher than the upper limit of this range deprives its action of any useful purpose, while keeping it below the lower limit cannot be achieved at all except by continuous increase in the quantity of money and indefinite price inflation.

20. Rueff, *L'ordre social*, 256.

Limits of rediscount policy

It must be emphasized that *rediscount policy cannot have a genuine stabilizing effect unless the reserve ratios of the lending banks are kept constant.*

Let us assume, for instance, that we are at the start of a period of prosperity and that credit margins are only partly used. Bank credit expands and prices rise. According to the explanations just given, the Central Bank should raise its discount rate. *But such a rise will in fact have no effect*, because, when the banks' credit margins are only partly used, there is normally no recourse to rediscount by the Central Bank. So the situation is one in which *the stabilizing influence of the rediscount policy cannot come into play.*

This stabilizing influence could be obtained only if the lending banks raised their discount rate, but doing so would amount—aside from seasonal variations—to leaving part of their credit margins unused and, at least in the present state of legislation, this is inconceivable because it is in the interests of every bank to issue unbacked demand deposits.

So it is clear that, under present structural conditions, the Central Bank is quite unable to control a business boom from a starting position in which unbacked deposit money issued by banks is not at its maximum. In such a case any hope that the discount rate might exercise a stabilizing influence would be illusory.

Similarly, at the onset of a crisis, when difficulties begin to be felt, banks cut back their credit and launch a deflationary trend that thereafter can only gather speed. Short-term money becomes expensive, and its rate rises. *According to the principles of rediscount policy the Central Bank should then freeze its rediscount rate,* so as to prevent a rise in the short-term interest rate and, by rediscounting bills *to an unlimited extent,* to allow banks to honor their demand liabilities without feeling the need to restrict the volume of their loans.

But this policy is not generally followed by the Central Bank, *which in fact feels called upon to raise its rediscount rate exactly when it ought to leave it unchanged.*

In this case, *the Central Bank has a genuine power to stabilize the economy, but* for fear of losing the value of a part of the rediscounted bills owing to potential drawer insolvency or of encouraging a boom it believes to be artificial, *it fails to use its power, and to avoid a lesser evil it helps to precipitate a depression a hundred times worse.*

Finally, it is clear that *the possibility of creating unbacked deposit money*, whose key role in cycles has already been shown, *neutralizes the stabilizing*

*action of the rediscount policy in time of prosperity. This inefficacy would
be but a temporary evil if the Central Bank had the courage relentlessly to
implement the stabilizing policy of the rediscount rate as soon as the first
difficulties became apparent.*

Clearly such a policy would by no means prevent the economic losses
that necessarily arise on account of investment errors committed when
times were too easy; but it would erect an effective barrier against the
general collapse of the credit system the first result of which is to render
artificially unviable firms that, under normal monetary conditions, would
be perfectly profitable.

In my opinion, however, such unlimited support of the banks by the
Central Bank is the best solution only *in so far as banks are entitled to
issue unbacked deposit money.* For if they are certain of receiving the support of the Central Bank, they will inevitably grant loans indiscriminately.

In recent years efforts have been made—in England particularly between 1925 and 1931—to palliate the insufficiencies of rediscount policy
whose stabilizing influence, in the case of large-scale movements, is only
effective against falls, *assuming it is in fact pursued,* by the "open market
policy." The theoretical goal of this policy is to keep short-term rates unchanged by decreasing or increasing the volume of cash in circulation by
selling or buying bonds in the open market.[21]

But this policy can only be effective *within fairly narrow limits;*[22] for
instance, the sales of bonds that would be necessary during a period of
prosperity to prevent a rise in prices due to the issue of demand money

21. Aside from its direct effect of monetary deflation or inflation, this policy also has a
downward or upward effect on bond values and hence an upward or downward effect on
instantaneous interest rates. The efficacy of these indirect effects is added to that of the direct
deflationary or inflationary effects.

22. Although its effects are amplified by the graduation of credit in countries where credit
is developed. For since we have (no. 99, equation [15])

$$M = \frac{1+\alpha}{1+\kappa\alpha} M_M,$$

and hence

$$\Delta M = \frac{1+\alpha}{1+\kappa\alpha} \Delta M_M,$$

when the ratio $\frac{1+\alpha}{1+\kappa\alpha}$ takes on substantial values, on the order of 8, as is the case in the United
Kingdom and the United States, evidently the secondary effects of an open-market policy

by the lending banks may be quite beyond the real power of the Central Bank.

The real solution, in my view, would be the absolute prohibition of the issue of unbacked demand deposits by the banks: the 100% money recommended by Irving Fisher. If this policy were put into practice, it would not prevent banks from discounting bills of exchange or from granting credit, but these operations would be conducted using capital entrusted to the banks either by their shareholders or by investors for this purpose. This capital would therefore not be withdrawable on demand and would have to be loaned to the banks for the long term and reloaned out by the banks at short term.[23] Under these structural conditions the stabilizing

---

may be eight times greater than its primary effects. In France, by contrast, where the ratio $\frac{1+\alpha}{1+\kappa\alpha}$ has a value of 5/4, i.e., little more than unity, this gearing effect is hardly noticeable.

23. Let us consider, for example, a credit institution whose balance sheet stands currently as given in table 8.8.

After the reform, assuming that its credit and its demand deposits remain the same, its balance sheet would be table 8.9.

It would not be possible to pass from state I to state II without economic disturbance unless, when the reform was about to be undertaken, the State made the banks a long-term capital loan equal to the amount of their unbacked demand deposits (i.e., 900 million in the case of the foregoing example).

To borrow such sums, whether from the State or in the financial market would naturally entail costs for the banks that would be added to their operating costs and would in due course oblige them (a) to cancel interest payments to their depositors and (b) to require depositors to pay for the services they rendered them. While this would lead to profound modifications in current habits, these modifications would be neither impossible nor abnormal.

TABLE 8.8 FOOTNOTE

Assets		Liabilities	
Cash balance	100 million	Demand deposits	1 billion
Discounted bills and loans	900 million		

TABLE 8.9 FOOTNOTE

Assets		Liabilities	
Cash balance	1 billion	Equity and borrowed capital	900 million
Discounted bills and loans	900 million	Demand deposits	1 billion

effect of the Central Bank's rediscount policy would once more become fully effective.[24,25]

24. See no. 162 below.

25. These proposals seem already to have had their first application in the Argentine Republic where decree no. 11594 of 24 April 1946 stipulates a 100% reserve ratio to back the banks' demand deposits. To the extent that the banks are unable to provide this backing using their own available assets, they must procure the required liquidities by rediscounting their reinvestments (Treasury Bonds and Drafts, discounted bills, loans, etc.) at the Central Bank.

8. Bank inflation and forced savings (109)

By lowering their discount rate, banks can increase the volume of their loans. This creates new purchasing power that enables firms to finance their short-term investments (raw materials and inventory) and hence *indirectly* to increase to the same extent their long-term (fixed capital) investments.

Moreover, this low short-term rate policy also tends—via arbitraging—to keep long-term interest rates down and *directly* to increase real investments accordingly. But it can easily be shown that in the long run this financing tends to diminish accordingly the sums put at the disposal of firms on a short-term basis so that *ultimately the new purchasing power made available to firms* for further investment in the short or long term *is equal to the volume of unbacked deposit money issued by the banks.*

If the initial economic state considered is taken to be in full-employment equilibrium, the demand for goods in the market is thus increased without the possibility of any concurrent increase in supply. This leads to a price rise that forces consumers to cut back their consumption and enables production to devote itself to developing capital goods. This is called *forced saving.*

"Forced saving" has the same primary effects as voluntary saving, i.e., it restrains consumption and liberates factors of production in favor of the creation of supplementary means of production. In fact, *the real capital needed for the new investments is levied on the consumer by means of the price rise.*

Thus the creation of money by the banks in the form of demand deposits and the issue of cash by the State have identical effects on prices, which rise in both cases, but their effect on social productivity differs greatly since the former leads to an increase in capital goods while the latter diminishes capital in favor of unproductive State spending.

However, although a certain increase in social productivity can be obtained in this way, our conclusions to date show that inflation of bank loans leads to *structural imbalances* in the vertical production system that will, *sooner or later*, give rise to difficulties in some sectors and, as a secondary effect, to a credit squeeze, which will thereupon gather speed in the way outlined above.

It is therefore clear that, far from improving the general economic situation, the only effect of bank inflation is to bring about a factitious and unhealthy prosperity. *No doubt social productivity can be provisionally increased, but sooner or later it will become necessary to return to the former state.* Thus inflation of deposit money succeeds only in producing serious disturbances in the economy, generating disorder. *It is therefore just as harmful as cash inflation on the part of the State.*[1]

1. Suitable means of bringing about a stable and *lasting* increase in social productivity will be examined later (no. 164).

9. Exchange rates and discount rates (110)

When, under a gold standard, gold outflow becomes a constant trend or, under floating exchange rates, ongoing depreciation of the national currency tends to set in, the Central Bank endeavors to remedy the situation by raising its discount rate. This rise has the effect, as we have just seen, of diminishing the volume of loans granted both by the Central Bank and by the main lending institutions, which leads to a fall in the overall quantity of money and hence to a fall in prices, which tends to restore the situation.

Though this policy has become standard, it is none the less highly questionable.

First, it is not certain that it will in fact produce the hoped-for price movements. Admittedly, a rise in the rediscount rate normally brings about a rise in short-term rates[1] and hence a demand for outside capital attracted by the higher return. This inflow of capital, which translates into increased demand for money or for national currencies has the twofold effect of halting the outflow of gold or the fall in the exchange rate on the external front and *slowing down the tendency of falling prices at home.* But such a policy cannot be sustained indefinitely for it implies an ongoing increase in national indebtedness to compensate for the balance of payments deficit—the cumulative total of which is so much the more dangerous as it is short-term debt, which can be called in at very short notice. This shows not only that a rise in the rediscount rate does not succeed in lowering prices as required, but also that it gives rise to a *highly unstable situation.* In fact, when exchange rates are constant, only a fall in prices at home can put an end to the current account deficit, but this fall in prices cannot be achieved rapidly except by acting *directly* on domestic means of payment (the open-market policy, for instance) to bring about the desired deflation at once.

In any event, a rise in the discount rate cannot on its own, as a rule, bring a stable equilibrium into being. For, as we have seen,[2] the evidence is that, by modifying its volume of rediscount E_1, a given country may act on its price level and restore its current account equilibrium. To this

1. Provided, however, at the risk of repetition, that in the preexisting equilibrium the volume of the rediscount portfolio should not be zero. If this condition were not verified, the rise in the rediscount rate would have no effect.

2. No. 99.

modification ΔE_1 of its rediscount volume there corresponds, in equilibrium, a modification Δi_i in the international interest rate level and hence a modification Δi_E in the rediscount rate. Thus, it is *theoretically* conceivable that by acting on rate i_E prices may be brought to the desired level, but we have seen that to a very substantial modification ΔE_1 of the rediscount volume there corresponds only a very slight variation Δi_i in international interest rates and hence only an equally *slight* variation Δi_E in the rediscount rate.[2] Under these conditions, it is quite certain that, even supposing it brought about the desired price movement, any appreciable rise in the discount rate would sooner or later be followed, once price levels had adjusted, by an approximately equal fall.[3] *The desired price level may indeed have been achieved, but only at the cost of serious disturbances to the capital market in the shape of two interest rate changes in opposite directions.*

In reality, discount rate policy must be considered inadequate, if not harmful, for it can restore equilibrium in one sector of the economy only by producing new imbalances, comparable in scale, elsewhere. Current account equilibrium can in fact only be brought about by direct modification of the exchange rate or, under fixed exchange rates, by direct adjustment of the quantity of money (for instance, by means of an open-market policy). *Manipulation of the interest rate for this purpose is quite useless. It can only generate new disorders.*[4]

3. This fall will not lead to a new credit expansion and thus to a new rise in prices because meanwhile the fall in price levels will have led to a fall in the nominal value of the money demand.

4. See no. 111.

10. Interest rate disparities (111)[1]

In theory the rate of interest is what regulates savings and investment. If the propensity to save is greater than the propensity to invest, the interest rate falls and this fall tends to balance savings and investment; conversely, if the propensity to invest is stronger, the interest rate rises and the difference between planned investment and the supply of savings decreases. The equilibrium interest rate determines the level of real money balances, and the latter in combination with the total volume of money determines the price level. This, as we have seen,[2] is a *first approximation* outline of what determines a stable equilibrium in a closed economy.

We have seen[3] that this outline in fact remains unchanged in the case of an international economy, as the international interest rate level can itself be regarded, *in first approximation*, as due to the global equilibrium between savings and investment.

In reality, however, the interest rate plays no such regulatory role, indispensable though it is to general economic equilibrium.

(i) Imperfection of the long-term capital market

As a rule, the depreciation of assets written down by firms is not paid to shareholders but directly reinvested in capital by the firms, and this applies not only to the renewal of existing assets but also in great measure to net investment.[4]

This *self-financing* on the part of firms is chiefly due to their directors' desire to ensure, whatever may befall in an economic world subject to permanent instability, the stability of their own position, which depends on the continuance of the ventures they manage as well as on the strengthening of their economic power and *often takes no account of the contrast between expected profits and the market interest rate.* This accumulation on

---

1. The reader is once more reminded that here and elsewhere I am systematically limiting myself to a simplified presentation, not presenting a thoroughgoing analysis of every aspect of all the issues addressed. My sole purpose at present is to provide a broad outline of interest theory. Specialists are therefore requested to forgive a degree of concision that may seem excessive in their eyes.

2. Nos. 97 and 99.

3. No. 99.

4. No. 37.

the part of firms thus takes place intuitively, automatically, impulsively: it does not obey the guiding principles of a genuine competitive economy.

This leads not only to considerable losses in social efficiency, but also to grave imbalances. Self-financing on the part of firms withdraws capital from the law of the market and the action of competition; it fosters capital investments that later turn out to be unprofitable, as they bear no relation to the potential market outlets that in fact exist. It prevents consumption from orientating production, as investments cease to be undertaken with a view to final consumption. Hence, situations can continue and even intensify *that lead, sooner or later, to economic dead ends.*

(ii) Inertia of the nominal interest rate

Moreover, economic equilibrium would require, when the price level is variable, that the nominal interest rate i should remain constantly equal, *as a first approximation*, to the sum of the real equilibrium interest rate i_r—corresponding to an equilibrium of stable monetary conditions—plus the relative rate of price variation, in accordance with the equation

(1) $$i = i_r + \frac{\dfrac{dP}{dt}}{P}.$$ [5]

This equation is in fact only valid as a tendency, and considerable discrepancies are found between the rises or falls of prices and those of the interest rate.[6]

It follows that, as a rule, *when the trend is upward, the nominal interest rate is much too low, high though it is, and that when the trend is downward, it is much too high, even though it is low.*[7] In the former case, investment is artificially encouraged and in the latter it is artificially kept at a level below that which would prevail in a stable equilibrium.

---

5. No. 97.
6. No. 106.
7. This explains the twin paradox of the coexistence at the end of a period of prosperity of a high rate of interest with a limited number of lenders and in a period of depression of a low rate of interest with a limited number of borrowers.

(iii) Monetary impossibility of negative nominal interest rates

To this inertia of the nominal interest rate must be added the fact that in our monetary economies in which the unit of account is defined as the value of the monetary unit, the nominal interest rate cannot in any circumstances have a negative value.[8] This makes it entirely impossible for equation (1) to apply when prices are falling rapidly.

When this is the case, the nominal interest rate is necessarily held at much too high a level; *the savings level remains excessive—far above the investment level—and as the excess savings become immobilized in the form of hoarded money,*[9] *this hoarding in turn gradually brings the economy to a standstill.*[10]

8. No. 81. See also no. 136 below.
9. The hoarding observed in times of low prices is due to the fact that, since there can be no economic disadvantage in holding money, we necessarily have

$$l_M \geq 0,$$

whereas the pure rate of interest corresponding to real investments in times when prices are falling sharply, equal to

$$i = i_r - \left| \frac{\frac{dP}{dt}}{P} \right|,$$

becomes negative.

Indeed it would only be possible to combat this hoarding by depreciating the nominal value of money, i.e., by lowering its nominal price $\overline{m}$, a condition that of course implies that the unit of money be other than the unit of account. The pure rate of interest corresponding to holding money would then become (no. 82, equations [10] and [11]) equal to the value

$$i_M = \frac{m}{m} + \frac{\frac{d\overline{m}}{dt}}{m},$$

i.e.,

$$i_M = l_M - \left| \frac{\frac{d\overline{m}}{dt}}{m} \right|.$$

The nominal rate of interest yielded by money could thus be aligned on the nominal rate of interest yielded by investments or if appropriate be made inferior to it thus preventing hoarding.

10. No. 100.

(iv) Non-adjustment of stipulated interest rates

Moreover, the interest rates stipulated in short-term contracts remain legally enforceable even when prices are rising or falling. Hence, *the futures mechanism is grossly distorted* when prices are moving upward, because the real interest rate in force

$$i''' = i_0 - \frac{\dfrac{dP}{dt}}{P}$$

becomes very much lower than the initially stipulated interest rate i_0, and when prices are going down because the real interest rate is far above it and leads to burdens that may be unbearable.[11,12,13]

(v) Credit policy of banks and of the Central Bank

Lastly, the nominal interest rate *is very often deflected from its fundamental mission of balancing savings and investment*, either by the banks, when they use it to act on the volume of their unbacked loans, or by the Central Bank when it uses it to prevent outflow of gold under the gold standard or to prevent the national currency from depreciating under a floating exchange rate.

---

11. It is curious to note that the *problem of a rational adjustment of contractual interest rates to prevailing monetary conditions has not yet been clearly addressed.*

12. Consequently, *when prices are rising*, prevailing interest rates may be considered to be at the same time too high and too low: *too high* for the future because sooner or later the upward trend will inevitably be reversed and *too low* for the present because of the artificial encouragement of the propensity to invest.

For analogous reasons, the rates of interest *when prices are moving downward* may be considered to be at one and the same time both *too low* and *too high*.

13. For equilibrium to be attained *from this viewpoint* the nominal rates of interest yielded at each point in time by the various *capital assets* would have to be equal. It follows that if a loan C is granted at time t at a contractual nominal interest rate i_c^t, whereas the pure nominal rate of interest is i^t, and if at time t' the market's pure nominal rate of interest has become $i^{t'}$, it would be necessary, assuming that the other components of the value-yield (no. 84) represented at time t by the difference $(i_c^t - i^t)$ remained the same, for the interest rate i_c^t to be adjusted, at time t', by a correction $(i^{t'} - i^t)$, i.e., for the nominal rate of interest yielded by capital C at that time to be

(1) $$i_c^{t'} = i_c^t + i^{t'} - i^t.$$

In the first case, this policy, at the end of a period of prosperity, leads to a rise in the interest rate at the point when the upward price movement has halted or gone into reverse, and at the beginning of the prosperity period it sends the interest rate down just when prices are moving upward. This policy must therefore be deemed *counterproductive*.

Similarly, *in the second case*, the Central Bank's policy causes the interest rate to rise when prices need to be lowered and to fall when the balance of trade takes a favorable turn, i.e., when prices at home begin to rise. The outcome is that although this policy indeed tends to bring the amount of deposit money into harmony with overseas price conditions at given exchange rates, it eventually gives rise to major imbalances in the basic activity of capital accumulation at home[14] and *once again proves counterproductive*.

Interest rate disparities and economic adjustment

The outcome of these various factors is that, in reality, determination of the rate of interest operates in accordance with principles very different from those that would be needed to realize equilibrium and thus gives rise to major imbalances that are not corrected by any swift and effective adjustment.

Thus the savings and investment market is certainly the most imperfect of all the markets, although it is the most essential of all, as its sound operation concerns the whole economy in its very foundations.

However, although these different disparities seriously compromise the realization of a stable equilibrium, it must be emphasized that *the origin of them all lies in the general price movements and economic cycles* of which the basic causes have been analyzed above. *The interest rate mechanism in itself can by no means be regarded as an autonomous disequilibrium factor and it would surely be effective in its basic role of regulating savings and investment* if the nominal price level remained stable,[15] i.e., *if the economy remained money-neutral*. Thus the neutrality of money emerges as the necessary condition of an effective interest rate mechanism.

---

14. No. 109. Note that for foreign trade the control parameter par excellence is the rate of exchange and that the fundamental role of the rate of interest is to regulate the accumulation of capital whether in the form of savings or of investment.

If changing the exchange rate were deemed undesirable, the only solution would be to bring about the required price movement by directly increasing or decreasing the total volume of ready cash in circulation, for example, by an open market policy (nos. 107 and 109).

15. Or only very mildly variable.

11. Basic factors of economic instability (112)

It follows from the foregoing that *the general price movements that are behind all large-scale economic disorders are directly related either to the amount of cash in circulation*[1] *or to (a) the volume of deposit money issued by the banks or (b) the volume of money hoarded by the various economic agents.*[2]

First of all, by resorting to inflation under conditions of inconvertible money, the State irremediably compromises the establishment of a stable equilibrium. The same applies under the gold standard if the circulation of gold coins rises sharply following the discovery of new deposits.

Secondly, the arbitrary and anarchical way in which the banks issue unbacked credit in quantities depending on whether the public at large happens to be expecting an upward or downward trend—an expectation sparked by chance events—creates a state of permanent instability. Any widespread fall in prices or any widespread pessimism causes loans to be curtailed, leading to a decrease in the total quantity of money, thereby accelerating the fall in prices. In the same way, rises induce further rises, by stimulating the expansion of unbacked credit. Bank reserve ratios are thus constantly oscillating between their maximum value, close to unity, and a minimum value determined by trial, which is very different.

Finally, widespread belief in an upward or downward trend may induce economic agents to modify in real terms the quantity of their hoarded funds in such a way as to accelerate those very price movements. For example, when a downward trend is expected, hoarding is increased in real terms, thus hastening a fall in prices.

Indeed it cannot be too strongly emphasized that widespread *rapid* price movements, whether upward or downward, parallel to activity trends *in the same direction*,[3] *would be absolutely inconceivable* barring either (a) an increase or a decrease in the total quantity of money (cash plus demand deposits) or (b) widespread hoarding or dishoarding.[4]

---

1. No. 98, § "Stability, inflation, and deflation."
2. No. 100.
3. This parallelism must be considered to be an empirical fact.
4. Without embarking on a detailed analysis at present, I note simply that the equation

$$M - M_T = \frac{PQ}{V_R}$$

Thus we have three factors capable of accounting for the generation of widespread price movements: (a) the possibility of variations in the quantity of money owing either to State-inflation under inconvertible money or, under the gold standard, to an increase or decrease in global gold production, (b) the banks' ability to issue unbacked deposit money, and (c) the hoardability of money; and no generalized price movement is conceivable in the absence of at least one of these factors.

Hence it is quite certain that only these three factors can be considered to be autonomous generators of economic fluctuations, whether in the short term (economic cycles) or long term (long-term price movements). *All the other disequilibrium factors,* and they are extremely numerous, that have been put forward in turn to explain these fluctuations (production period, underconsumption by certain social categories, speculation, etc.) *must in fact be classed not as autonomous factors—for of themselves they could not give rise to any general price movement—but simply as accelerating factors of the original imbalances allowed or triggered by the three autonomous disequilibrium factors revealed by this brief analysis.*[5]

---

given in note 1 to no. 103, in which the velocity of circulation V_R of working capital may, *as a first approximation,* be taken as a constant, shows, for instance, that a simultaneous increase in factors P and Q *necessarily* implies either a parallel increase in total money M (the sum of the values of cash and of unbacked deposit money) or else a decrease in hoarded money.

This is a *crucial* fact that in my opinion many economists, *even among the best,* have not sufficiently addressed. This neglect has led them to retain, for instance, as capable of explaining economic cycles, such factors as the length of the production process, or underconsumption on the part of certain social classes: factors whose action, considerable though it is, would be quite unable, in the absence of appropriate monetary conditions, to generate such cycles, and that in reality are merely accelerating factors of the large-scale imbalances induced by the interaction of unbacked credit and the hoardability of money.

5. Deeper analysis reveals that the short-term fluctuations we call economic cycles are in fact due only to the latter two factors (the possibility of issuing unbacked deposit money and the hoardability of money).

But in the context of the present study, the analysis provided here is limited to examining the basic factors of economic disequilibrium *in their relations with the rate of interest,* thereby showing

1. that economic fluctuations cannot be attributed to the phenomenon of interest;
2. how interest does in fact affect these fluctuations;
3. exactly what role the phenomenon of interest ought to play in any economic stabilization policy (see no. 113).

12. Principles of an economic regulatory policy in relation to the phenomenon of interest (113)

The above explanations give us the outline of the principles an economic regulatory policy must follow *with regard to the interest mechanism* if it is to be effective. These principles concern (a) elimination of the main factors of disequilibrium and (b) improvement of the actual performance of the various markets directly connected with the occurrence of interest.[1]

(i) Elimination of the main disequilibrium factors

NEED FOR 100% COVERAGE OF DEMAND DEPOSITS. To eliminate the banks' power of issuing unbacked demand deposits as an autonomous factor of disequilibrium, it is essential that loans in the form of demand deposits be fully backed by an amount of circulating money equal in value.[2]

NEED FOR MONETARY DEPRECIATION AND A SEPARATION OF THE FUNCTIONS OF MONEY. Moreover, there is no way of counteracting the possibility of hoarding money except by separating the functions of money as unit of account from those of money as medium of exchange (both at present filled by the same instrument), accompanied by continuous depreciation of circulating money in relation to the unit of account in order to keep money demand constant at the level required for working capital.[3,4,5]

The scale of this depreciation could evidently only be fixed by trial and error in light of circumstances, but I think that in a normal economic environment depreciation on the order of 10% per annum would be

1. I return to these explanations and expand on them in chapter 10, nos. 160–62.
2. Naturally, if demand deposits were fully secured, the liquidity premiums of cash and of deposit money, which are currently different because of the direct or indirect rate of interest paid by the banks to their depositors, would become equal (no. 94).
3. See note 9 to no. 111.
4. Note that it is by no means necessary for the accounting currency and the circulating currency to coincide and that they have not always done so (see note 1 to no. 6).
5. As in equilibrium we have (no. 82, equation [11])

$$l_M = i - \frac{\frac{d\overline{m}}{dt}}{m},$$

sufficient. As demand deposits comprise a part of circulating money, they must naturally be devalued at the same rate.

NEED FOR NEUTRAL MONEY.   To eliminate the troubles due to inflation or deflation of the amount of cash in circulation[6] the nominal value of this quantity in units of account must be kept, if not constant, at least only slightly variable, its variations having the exclusive function of keeping at the legally established level[7] the value of the benchmark commodity used to define the unit of account.

(ii) Improving the performance of the various markets in relation to the exchange rate

A policy of economic regulation adopted under dynamic disequilibrium should have no other purpose than to seek equilibrium, and to this end it must select among the means available those that will prove quickest and surest in achieving that end.

Since in equilibrium general interdependence prevails, it is conceivable, in order to bring about equilibrium in the market for good (*A*), to act not on its price *a*, but on the prices *b* of such and such other factors (*B*). But such a roundabout approach has the disadvantage of being time consuming and difficult to implement. Thus, when a commodity becomes scarce, its supply and demand can be balanced either by increasing its price or by decreasing pro rata all other prices. Needless to say, the latter approach, though theoretically possible, offers such difficulties that no one would seriously consider adopting it.

Yet it is just this kind of policy that is chosen when, under the gold standard or a fixed exchange rate, the attempt is made to balance the supply

---

it follows that for a positive rate of interest a depreciation of money on the order of $n\%$ would have the effect of raising the liquidity premium of money above $n\%$. Since working capital varies relatively little with the liquidity premium whereas speculative reserves undoubtedly vary in close correlation with it (no. 82), it is clear that for a high enough value of n, money balances would be *practically reduced to working capital.*

6. Whether under convertible or inconvertible currency.

7. Note that where circulating money is devalued by $n\%$ per year in relation to the unit of account, in order to keep the *nominal value* of circulating money constant (i.e., its value in terms of units of account) an equal annual relative increase of $n\%$ in the *quantity of cash* would be needed.

and demand of a given country's money, not by varying its price, i.e., the exchange rate, but by overall variation of all the country's prices.

Moreover it may happen that in a dynamic disequilibrium process equilibrium can indeed be brought about in the market of good (A) by acting on the price b of good (B) instead of on its own price a, but that the variation thus induced in price b destroys the equilibrium in the market for good (B). And if this occurs, the policy is certainly a bad one, since it succeeds in correcting certain imbalances, though only temporarily, at the cost of introducing new disturbances.

Yet this is the policy that is practiced when the attempt is made to counter disequilibrium in the exchange rate market due to a current account deficit by raising the discount rate. It follows from the foregoing that in the most favorable case,[8] when it succeeds in harmonizing price levels and exchange rates, this rise — unless it equalizes the national interest rate with international interest rates, which is not generally the case — far from steering the economy toward a general equilibrium is merely driving it farther away.

This shows that *if an economic stabilization policy is to be effective, it must act directly on the market it aims to balance.*

The main applications of this principle, with regard to the interest rate, are as follows.

STABILIZATION OF THE UNIT OF ACCOUNT.   In the economies we are familiar with, with their close links between present and future, the market on which available capital is traded between different dates cannot possibly function soundly unless there is a stable unit of value *remaining economically the same over time.*

And since the basic factor of production is unquestionably labor, it seems clear that the best[9] standard of value to be found is the hour of unskilled labor in a particular place, for instance, Paris in the case of France.

8. Which in fact seldom occurs (no. 110).
9. Or, rather, the least bad.

Such a reference means that the monetary policy followed is such that the nominal value of the man-hour selected as standard will remain fixed.[10,11]

Insofar as this objective can be attained, disturbances that are monetary in origin will be kept to a minimum so that money itself may be considered *"neutral."*[12]

STABILIZATION OF THE CAPITAL MARKET. *As monetary needs are relatively variable in relation to the propensities to save and to invest, the goal of monetary policy must be to shield the interest rate from the influence of accidental and seasonal variations in liquidity preference.*

If desired money balances are maintained at the level of necessary working capital by ongoing depreciation of the unit of money in relation to the unit of account, this policy can be implemented, in light of what has been said above, by keeping the Central Bank's discount rate at a certain level determined by trial and error.

The level in question should be periodically reviewed in order to maintain a sustainable equilibrium between the money and financial markets, but these revisions would naturally remain relatively minor since their only object would be to follow variations in the long-term interest rate determined by the relatively slow variations in the propensities to save and to invest.

STABILIZATION OF THE FOREIGN EXCHANGE MARKET. Every fundamental disequilibrium in the foreign exchange market that is due to a permanent current account disequilibrium ought to be corrected by *direct* modification of the exchange rate.

Seasonal current account imbalances should be offset by movements of gold or foreign currency.

10. Thus every monetary economy must confront two equally imperative necessities: (a) the availability of a unit of value that remains the same over time, and hence of a fixed wage-unit, and (b) the use of circulating money whose value decreases over time (see above).

These two requirements cannot be fulfilled at the same time unless the accounting currency is dissociated from the circulating currency.

11. The main point of this policy is to keep the nominal value (*i.e., in units of account*) of cash at a level corresponding to the legal definition of the unit of account. *Naturally, this level can only be determined by experience.*

12. In a neutral money economy, *prices are not fixed*, because only the nominal price of the benchmark commodity is kept constant, and there is no reason why the ratios one to another of the different prices should remain constant.

If the hourly price of unskilled labor is kept constant, it is safe to conclude that the price of other goods will *gradually fall* owing to technical progress.

Thus the exchange rate should be stabilized at such a level as to ensure on average a balance of payments equilibrium, any accidental or seasonal variations in this balance being compensated by gold or currency movements. This policy ought to be *strictly parallel* to the policy that stabilizes the pure interest rate at its average level to achieve equilibrium between the savings and investment propensities, offsetting variations in money demand by rediscounting.

The reader will have no difficulty in verifying, in light of the foregoing explanations, that if the principles just set out were put into practice, they would practically eliminate the various factors of disequilibrium that have been successively identified, and that, in such a context, *the action of the interest mechanism would be fully effective and economic stability would be ensured.*[13]

13. I realize that the reader may be astonished to see issues as complex as those involved in identifying an effective policy of economic regulation dispatched in a few lines, but *while I fully appreciate the difficulties entailed by such analysis, once again, the scope of this study is strictly limited to understanding the role of interest.* Hence explanations have been limited to those needed to show which measures can and should be adopted to ensure proper functioning of the rate of interest.

CHAPTER NINE

The Problem of Interest

A. *State of the Problem*

1. Existence of a problem (114)

Long experience shows that the sum of the income flows that any real asset can earn over the various periods of its existence subsequent to a given time[1] t is always greater than the market value of this asset at the same time t; the difference between the two represents the interest yielded.

To take the example of a parcel of land, we know that its value is finite, whereas it is capable of generating an infinite stream of income. Similarly, in the case of reproducible capital assets,[2] as a rule, the income stream exceeds depreciation so that the total value of the future income is greater than the value of the asset itself.

Note that in both cases, an asset of finite value could theoretically provide an infinite stream of income; this is a fact that calls for explanation.

In fact, this problem occurs in two different forms, depending on whether land or capital is involved. In the case of land, there is no difficulty in seeing that the income stream is infinite, but it is unclear why this infinite income stream has a finite value. In the case of capital, on the other hand, it is clear why the value is finite, because it is produced from a finite quantity of factors of production, but it is harder to understand why it can always generate income greater than the value of its own depreciation.

In reality, if this income is constantly reinvested, these two aspects are but two sides of the same question, and in both cases what needs explain-

---

1. The income flows themselves; not their current value at time t.
2. Plant and equipment, etc.

ing is why the observed value of any capital is less than that of its future income stream, or—which amounts to the same thing—why capital that is finite in magnitude can yield an unlimited stream of interest without being exhausted, i.e., why the use-value of capital is always positive.

It is important to emphasize that the problem of interest involves not so much why interest exists as why it settles at such and such a level and, more especially, why that level is *always* positive.

For there is no obvious reason why a value available in one year's time should be exchangeable for the same value available at once, i.e., why the prices of the two should be equal, since two different goods are involved and there is no a priori reason why the prices of two different goods at a given moment should be equal. So there are no grounds for surprise at the fact that interest exists, and indeed it would be surprising if it did not.

But while the existence of a rate of interest is self-explanatory, it is difficult to understand why at every place and time this rate has always been positive. Indeed, a priori, it would be reasonable to expect that the price $\frac{1}{1+I}$ of the unit of value available in a year's time might just as well be greater than 100% as lower, i.e., that the interest rate might just as well be negative as positive. As shown earlier in the Fable of the Fishermen, it is not hard to imagine theoretical examples of economies in which the interest rate might be negative.

So the fact that in every known economy an interest rate has always been found that is invariably positive raises a question that cannot be eluded and that must be explained by the theory. This is the problem of interest.[3]

---

3. Some explanations bearing on this problem have already been given above (nos. 3, 14, 26, and 81). The present chapter is specifically intended to expand on those explanations.

2. Analysis of the problem (115)

The problem posed by the existence of an invariably positive interest rate can be reduced to the following three questions:

1. Why, at a given moment, do lenders demand interest?
2. Why, at a given moment, do borrowers agree to pay interest?
3. How, as time elapses, are borrowers in fact able to make their interest payments?

The two first questions concern the instantaneous equilibria occurring at a given moment; but the third concerns the sustained equilibrium that tends to become established over time. The two first belong to the theory of primary effects and the third to that of secondary effects.[1]

It may at first sight seem quite easy to answer these questions:

In the case of borrowing and lending between individuals with a view to balancing their needs over time (consumption loans) it is indeed understandable, if X agrees to lend Y 100 francs repayable in a year, that he should require an interest payment in exchange as the price of the service rendered. And it is also understandable that Y should agree to repay later more than he borrowed in view of the urgency of his present needs. And finally it is easy to see how Y can reimburse his loan plus the interest on it since in order to do so he need only restrict his consumption.[2]

In the same way, in the case of a production loan, it is natural for a firm intending to implement a manufacturing technique that will enable it to reduce its costs to agree, in light of the supplementary income it will thus be able to earn, to pay interest. It is also natural that, in view of the risks run and of the opportunities for profit they might meet elsewhere, investors who lend funds should require interest. It is also easy to see how real progress in technology can make it easier for firms to pay the interest they owe, thanks to lower production costs.[2]

On closer examination, however, these questions turn out to be much less easy to analyze.

In the first place, the interest involved is pure interest, i.e., the interest yielded by a loan whose value-for-value reimbursement is certain, so risk cannot provide an explanation of the interest.

1. Note 1 to no. 9.
2. See the explanations given in the Fable of the Fishermen (nos. 21–27).

Furthermore, it is *not* the case that all individuals at every moment have urgent needs to satisfy. On the contrary some may wish to use their present income to lay up reserves for future use. If the number in the latter category is greater than the number in the former—a possibility that cannot be excluded a priori—it is not so clear why interest should still exist. Indeed it is quite conceivable that the interest rate might become negative. In that case interest would resemble a storage charge paid by the saver to have his capital kept as "principal."

Finally, though it is easy to see how firms can promise interest payments, in light of the savings they hope to realize, and how they can in fact pay them as long as the new technology they use has not been widely adopted, it is much harder to see how this possibility can persist as time goes on.

In fact, experience shows that competition between firms tends to lower the sale price of their products until a point is reached at which it barely covers, in addition to the cost of raw materials, the wages of labor, land costs, and depreciation and interest on reproducible capital. But why, we ask, does competition not lower prices to the point at which they no longer suffice to pay positive interest on the firm's capital?

Production remains technically possible so long as output suffices to make good the capital consumed in production operations. So why, aside from depreciation, do we find this surplus that we call interest?

It is easy to see that the cost of planks must include the value needed to maintain or replace the sawmill's machinery (i.e., the depreciation premium), but it is not so clear what "natural law" requires it to include a further value comprising the interest on the value of this machinery.

As long as the machinery brings in more than it costs, the firm generates income that enables it to pay interest. But the existence of this income, we might suppose, would lead to an increase in the number of comparable machines until competition had entirely wiped out the income. Instead of which, the competition stops sooner: why? Why, when equilibrium prevails, is the price regularly sufficient to cover the interest on the capital investment as well as depreciation?

Indeed, it is not even clear why, once the depreciation of worn-out capital goods has been taken into account, there should not remain a negative balance that capital lenders would agree to bear if their preference for future income over present income were strong enough.

Thus, whether we look at the behavior of individuals or that of firms, fundamental difficulties remain to be resolved. It is clear from what we have just seen that *these difficulties boil down to explaining interest in a stationary equilibrium model having no technical progress*, i.e., under constant conditions of technical structure and where there is no risk, foresight being perfect.

If it is possible to explain interest under these conditions, the three questions posed above will be answered.

First, obviously, the existence of invariably positive interest in equilibrium and under perfect foresight makes it possible to explain how interest can subsist in an economic world comprising a succession of instantaneous equilibria and having imperfect foresight. This is because the observed fact that it is possible to make regular payments of the agreed interest proves that a certain foresight and a certain equilibrium do in fact exist in the real world, and hence the problem of the existence of interest in the real economy is reduced to the corresponding problem in the context of an economy in equilibrium and having perfect foresight. This provides the answer to the third question.

And the answer to the first two can be immediately deduced from it. For if at a given moment lenders demand interest this is because borrowers accept this condition, and their doing so is due to their past experience, which has shown them that, under certain conditions, the commitment can be honored.

Thereupon, the general confidence, founded on experience, of being able to pay interest inclines people to find the requirement normal, which sheds light on the psychological reasons why a positive interest rate can arise at a given moment.

Hence the explanation of why there is a constantly positive interest rate must *in particular* be valid for a stationary model of constant psychological and technical structure and having perfect foresight.

For this reason, if a theory of interest is to give satisfaction, it must be just as applicable to the dynamic equilibrium of a stationary model having constant structure as to the dynamic evolution in disequilibrium of an economy of variable structure.

Nominal rate of interest and true rate of interest

We have seen that the nominal rate of interest may be considered as the sum of the true rate of interest in terms of the selected economic standard[3]

---

3. There is no need to specify what this standard may be: that is irrelevant to the analysis that follows.

and of the rate of depreciation of the unit of account in terms of the same standard.[4]

It is plain that in reality the interest problem only concerns the true interest rate; that part of the interest rate that is equal to the depreciation of the unit of account[5] serves only to offset the depreciation of the unit of value so that in real terms the corresponding unlimited stream of interest has only a finite value, precisely equal to the initial real value of the relevant capital. There is therefore no difficulty in understanding why the nominal sum of the indefinite sequence of depreciation interest is only finite in value.

Any explanation of interest must concern true interest. Since, in a stationary model, the different rates of interest are all equal to the nominal rate, it is confirmed from this angle that any interest rate must *specifically* provide an explanation of interest in a stationary equilibrium model having constant technical structure and no risk, i.e., perfect foresight.

4. Nos. 19 and 97.

5. Equal to the second term of the second member of the equation

$$i_e = i_r + \frac{\frac{dP}{dt}}{P}$$

(no. 97, equation [6]).

3. The problem of interest from the ethical and economic viewpoints (116)

From the ethical viewpoint, it may be asked whether it is just for the owner of capital to be able to receive indefinitely a share of society's annual output independently of any personal labor input. The question is an entirely reasonable one.

But if we are to avoid grave confusion, it is essential to distinguish carefully between this ethical problem and the theoretical problem of the existence of interest: before examining whether interest is just, beneficial, and useful, and hence whether it ought to be modified or abolished, we ought first to examine why it exists and what determines its level. *This is a purely scientific issue the solution to which is entirely independent of any value judgment.*

The fact is that interest theory must be established on its own terms and not, as too many authors have unfortunately done, with a view to finding an acceptable theoretical basis for their preexisting opinions as to whether interest is good or bad on the basis of religious, moral, or political considerations.

B. Erroneous or Incomplete Interest Theories

Overview (117)

To shed further light on the problem of interest, I will now examine several prominent theories.[1] By illustrating the difficulties of the problem and the pitfalls to be avoided in seeking its solution, this study will enable us to clarify the statement of the problem and to reach a completely clear understanding of it.

---

1. This examination is intended only to facilitate the reader's understanding, so its explanations will be simplified and only the most important theories will be considered, emphasizing the errors to be avoided. This is not the right place to embark on a complete critical study of interest theories: their name is legion and many of them are differentiated only by nuances. Any such study would take up many volumes and, however concise, would far exceed the scope of the present work.

(a) Crude theories of interest

1. Risk-based theories (118)

Many authors maintain *that interest is simply compensation for the risks of every sort run by the lender.*

Others, admittedly, recognize that, after deducting a risk premium, there remains a residual interest or "net interest," but as a rule they are unable to give an acceptable definition of it and having made their distinction between risk premium and net interest they hasten to add that there is scarcely any investment that does not involve some risk for the lender and that under these conditions pure interest is practically impossible to define. Whereupon they abandon this notion and content themselves with observing the average rate of interest yielded by a certain number of sound fixed income financial assets.

In reality, all of this is mere muddled thinking. And to avoid confusion there can be no alternative to giving a precise definition of pure interest — one that can be applied in practice — and stating the theory of it. The present writer has defined the pure interest rate as the rate of interest yielded by a non-liquid loan of which the money-for-money repayment is certain.[1] This rate has an exact meaning, both in the real economy and in the pure, perfect-foresight economy, which excludes any notion of risk as to the money-for-money repayment of the loans involved.

Its explanation must therefore also be independent of the notion of risk, so risk theory as a theory of interest must be deemed to rest on a crude notion of interest.

1. No. 84 *in fine.*

2. Progress-based theories (119)

According to these fairly recent theories, which incidentally have received widely differing expressions, *the existence of interest is connected with economic and technical progress.*

Interest can only occur at a given moment owing to new processes then available to firms that enable them to expect substantial income in the future thanks to the lower costs thus achieved.[1]

Some authors even state that when population is constant, the interest rate expressed in terms of gold tends, in a conventional model, to level out at the gold optimization rate.[2,3]

1. A theory elaborated by Austrian economist Schumpeter in his *Theory of Economic Development.*

2. I.e., the rate of technical progress in the gold industry.

3. A theory elaborated by the Guillaume brothers in G. Guillaume and E. Guillaume, *Économique rationnelle* [Rational economics] (Paris: Hermann, 1937) (see in particular pp. 290 and 343).

It is easy to grasp the intuitive idea behind this theory. Using the notations of no. 19, let i'' be the wage interest rate, i''' the gold interest rate, and o'' the wage price of gold. From no. 19 we have

$$(1) \qquad i''' = i'' - \frac{\frac{do''}{dt}}{o''}.$$

Now if ρ_o is the optimization rate of gold, we have, assuming constant population (i.e., constant labor scarcity),

$$(2) \qquad \frac{\frac{do''}{dt}}{o''} = -\rho_o,$$

and hence

$$(3) \qquad i''' = i'' + \rho_o.$$

From which it follows that the theory of equality between the gold interest rate and the gold industry's optimization rate is equivalent to the theory of the zero wage-denominated interest rate.

Others assert that the rate of interest expressed in real terms should in a conventional model be equal to the average optimization rate of the whole set of industries.[4,5]

For others again the rate of interest in wage terms must always be zero.[6]

As may easily be verified, all these theories are fundamentally equivalent and all of them link the existence of the interest rate to technical progress.[7]

One and all affirm that an interest rate level higher than the optimization rate can only lead the economy into dangerous dead ends, for in such circumstances the value created by financial investment has no real basis; some of them even refer to internal contradictions in the economy.[8]

4. J. Ullmo, "Recherches sur l'équilibre économique" [Inquiries into economic equilibrium], *Annales de l'Institut Poincaré*, vol. 8 (1938), 60.

5. Using i'' and i''' to denote the wage-denominated and real rates of interest and P'' for the price level in wage terms, no. 19 gives us

$$\textbf{(1)} \qquad\qquad i''' = i'' - \frac{\frac{dP''}{dt}}{P''}.$$

Now using ρ to denote the average optimization rate across the whole range of industries, we have

$$\textbf{(2)} \qquad\qquad \rho = -\frac{\frac{dP''}{dt}}{P''},$$

and this gives us

$$\textbf{(3)} \qquad\qquad i''' = i'' + \rho.$$

So once again the thesis that equates the real interest rate and the optimization rate turns out to be equivalent to the zero wage-interest rate thesis.

6. A theory elaborated by Pierre Doyen in his *Essai d'une théorie sur l'intérêt du capital* [Outline of a theory of interest on capital] (Paris: Domat-Montchrestien, 1938), especially 41, 48, 164.

7. See notes 2 and 3 above.

8. Thus, according to Maurice Aeschimann, *Le rôle économique et social de la monnaie stable* [The economic and social role of stable money] (Lausanne: Librairie de droit; Paris: Sirey, 1939), 71, "Accumulated capital is invested in a geometric progression. This progression, since in theory it encounters no obstacle, tends to infinity. But this infinity can be conceived only when the purchasing power of money has fallen to zero, otherwise *invested savings would be so great, in-credit bank depositors would be so rich and borrowers would be so indebted, that business relations would long since have become inconceivable.* It would then be necessary to establish a new scale of physical values."

Explicitly or implicitly, the partisans of these theories *deny that interest is possible in a stationary equilibrium having perfect foresight and stationary technology.*[9]

It is therefore not possible to accept that such theories explain interest, since what specifically calls for explanation is the existence of a positive interest rate under such stationary conditions.[10]

Thus development-based theories entirely misunderstand the innermost nature of interest and remain in reality, notwithstanding the scientific mode of presentation used by some of their champions, absolutely untenable.

This new scale is precisely obtained by the monetary readjustment that occurs during devaluations, with, without or despite the agreement of economists and governments.

"*In this way, devaluation exercises a corrective action on the cost of borrowing savings.*"

9. As we shall see, this thesis is refuted outright by theoretical study of simplified models. For it is possible to conceive in the abstract stationary economies that correspond in all other respects to the logical conditions admitted in the economic reasoning in general use, but that have a positive rate of interest (see appendix II, nos. 185 and 196, § i).

10. All we can say is that technical progress facilitates profitability in certain sectors of the economy, but on the one hand, profit and pure interest comprise two quite distinct notions that cannot be considered equivalent, and on the other, in a money-neutral economy (i.e., one in which prices display no tendency to rise or fall), the profits made by some firms are necessarily offset by the losses incurred by others (note 3 to no. 107).

3. Exploitation theories (120)[1]

According to this theory, all goods that have value are the product of human labor and, from the economic point of view, are the *exclusive* product of this labor. Labor is thus held to be the source of all value. Yet the workers do not receive the whole of the product that they alone have created. Capitalists take advantage of the fact that the institution of private property guarantees them a right over the auxiliary means that are indispensable to production to arrogate to themselves a part of what the workers have produced. In reality, interest on capital consists of a share of the product of someone else's labor acquired *by exploiting the precarious position of the workers*. It is due to the pressure exerted by the propertied classes on the unpropertied in the field of the price-war, thanks to the advantages of their position.

For instance,

> suppose that a tree twenty-five years old is worth $15 and was planted at a cost of $5 worth of labor. The laborer was paid $5 when the tree was planted. The capitalist who pays him receives the $15 twenty-five years later and thereby enjoys $10 increase of value, which is interest on his $5 investment, the cost of planting the tree.[2] Why does not the laborer who planted the tree get this increase of $10 instead of the capitalist?[3]

It is not enough to answer the partisans of the exploitation theory by asserting that capital assists labor and that the capitalist who owns a plough earns the interest paid in exchange for the use of this plough just as the worker who uses it to plough the field earns his wages by working. For the proponents of the exploitation theory apply the same reasoning to an earlier phase, claiming that the payment made for the use of the plough ought in turn to belong not to the capitalist who owns it but to the workers who originally made it, including those who made the tools with which it was put together.

---

1. A theory elaborated by many socialists, including Rodbertus, Lassalle, Marx, et al.
2. In this example, the rate of interest is about 4.5%. At this rate, a capital sum triples in value in 25 years if interest is constantly reinvested.
3. Fisher, *The Theory of Interest*, pt. 1, ch. 3, § 2.

Take the case of the tree that was planted with labor worth $5, and that, 25 years later, was worth $15. The [proponents of the exploitation theory] virtually ask, "should not the laborer receive $15 instead of $5 for his work?" *The answer is: "He may receive it, provided he will wait for it 25 years."*[3]

For in fact,

the perfectly just proposition that the laborer should receive the entire value of his product may be understood to mean either that the laborer should *now* receive the entire *present* value of his product, or should receive the entire *future* value of his product in the *future*. But [the partisans of the exploitation theory] expound it as if it means that the laborer should *now* receive the entire *future* value of his product.[4]

This makes it clear that the proponents of the exploitation theory entirely overlook *the waiting period* that the capitalist must bear between paying for the labor and receiving the income when he sells the product of the labor.[5,6]

The exploitation theory must therefore be considered to repose on a false conception of interest and may hence be dismissed.[7]

4. E. von Böhm-Bawerk, *Capital and Interest*, in Fisher, *The Theory of Interest*, pt. 1, ch. 3, § 2.

5. No. 51.

6. In reality, the labor theory of value, which makes labor the sole source of value and which has been championed by the exploitation theorists, can only be considered valid for certain primitive societies in which very little capital exists while land is so abundant as to have practically no value. In such societies, it is quite true that the exchange value of goods would be almost exclusively determined by the amount of labor devoted to producing them.

7. However, from the fact that the exploitation theory is entirely valueless as an explanation of the rate of interest it should not be concluded that it contains no underlying truth. For it is quite certain that at the beginning of the 19th century workers were often unequally placed for discussing employment terms with their employers. But the exploitation that this led to concerns the theories of monopoly and of wages, not the theory of interest.

4. Spontaneous productivity of nature theory[1] (121a)

This theory attributes the fact that there is always a positive rate of interest to nature's spontaneous productivity. For instance, wine in a cellar improves without any need for labor input. Similarly, a swarm of bees yields
honey and new swarms. And in the same way, a flock of sheep increases
of itself.

It is therefore unsurprising that 100 francs available today should be
worth more than 100 francs available next year. It is directly due to the
fact that a flock of sheep available today will, by next year, have become
a larger flock, not to mention the fleeces meanwhile obtained at shearing
time, and the fact that, since different wealth forms are interchangeable
in the market, if one of them yields interest this will necessarily mean that
the others yield interest too.

The inadequacy of such a theory is easily spotted. It can be shown by
verifying that the facts put forward are by no means incompatible with
the existence of a zero interest rate. Since in equilibrium the value of every good is equal to its production cost, if the rate of interest were zero,
the value of the annual increase in a flock of sheep[2] would be equal to
the cost of shepherding and shelter for a year—a value that is *never* zero.
There is nothing remotely impossible about such a hypothesis.

*Only if these costs were nonexistent would the flock's natural productiv-
ity necessarily bring about a positive interest rate,*[3] but such a hypothesis is
purely imaginary and never in fact occurs in the real economy.

---

1. A notable supporter of this theory was Henry George, in his work *Progress and Poverty*
(French edition, Paris: Guillaumin, 1887), 172.

2. Disregarding, for the sake of simplicity, the wool produced by shearing.

3. This is easily shown as follows. Assume a stationary economy and let n be the number
of heads in a flock that spontaneously increases each year by Δn animals, used for consumption, and assume that

$$\frac{\Delta n}{n} = \lambda.$$

Let a be the value of a single animal and F the annual upkeep cost for a flock of n sheep.
In equilibrium, if we denote the annual rate of interest by I, the law of cost of production
gives us

$$a\Delta n = Ian + F,$$

It can thus be seen that the theory of the spontaneous productivity of nature is inconsistent and falls apart on first examination. It must therefore be classified among the crude theories.

---

i.e.,

$$I = \lambda - \frac{F}{an}.$$

If F is zero, therefore

$$I = \lambda.$$

But when F is not zero, the value of I is not fixed by the value of λ and it is quite conceivable that I should be zero, in which case we obtain

$$a = \frac{F}{\Delta n},$$

a possibility that nothing rules out.

434

CHAPTER NINE

5. Capital demand theory (121b)

This theory, *implicitly* formulated by very many authors even among the most up-to-date, maintains that if the interest rate ever fell to zero, the demand for capital would become infinite and that hence it never can fall to zero (or become negative) since an infinite quantity of capital is entirely inconceivable.[1]

In reality, this theory takes for its starting point a hypothesis that, though very widespread, is grossly erroneous. As has been shown,[2] demand for capital would by no means be infinite under a zero interest rate, and there is therefore no necessary reason based on capital demand why the interest rate could not in fact fall to zero or even become negative.

1. Indeed it can be seen from figure 5.26 of no. 48 that if curve C_1 were asymptotic to the y-axis, the interest rate could not become zero irrespective of any State intervention whatsoever.

2. Nos. 45 and 69.

6. Capital supply theory (121c)

According to this theory the interest rate can never become zero or negative because if it did, there would be no savings.

Once again, though widespread, this opinion is wholly gratuitous. For in fact, as we have seen, there are no grounds for claiming that the supply of capital would become extremely slight, if not nonexistent or negative, under a zero interest rate. On the contrary everything leads us to suppose that with a zero interest rate the supply of capital would still be considerable.[1]

So, as this line of argument provides us with no explanation of the existence of an invariably positive interest rate, the corresponding theory must be rejected as being based on an utterly crude analysis.

1. No. 40.

(b) Theories based on misconceptions

1. Capital stock theory (122)[1]

This theory regards the rate of interest as the price paid for the use of capital, but capital is considered to be a stock of means of subsistence making it possible to "expend labor in advance."[2] This stock consists of food, clothing, furniture, etc., and its main role is to "enable the laborer to await the result of any long-term labor"[2] called for by more profitable roundabout production processes. In other words, capital is what keeps the workers alive during the production period.

In reality, however, this theory is based on an entirely erroneous notion of capital. Nowhere in the economy is there any stock of means of subsistence that would enable workers to be kept alive during roundabout production processes; in reality what enables the exchange economy to allow a given lapse of time to pass between labor input and its eventual output is not any *prior* accumulation of the means of subsistence but *the fact that the economy is so organized that the part of the population working to produce intermediate goods is supported by the part working to produce final ones.*

It is perfectly true that wages paid to laborers constitute an advance made by the firm on the value of the product of their labor, which may not be available until much later, but this advance owes nothing to any previous accumulation of means of subsistence; *it is simply the right to use at the time in question a part of the continuous stream of society's output.*[3]

We may therefore deem the capital stock theory to be based on an erroneous conception of capital and hence to have no explanatory value.

---

1. A theory elaborated notably by John Stuart Mill and by W. S. Jevons.
2. W. S. Jevons, *The Theory of Political Economy*, ch. 7.
3. Capital could only be validly equated with a store of means of subsistence in an economy having but a single producer. In this case it would be quite true that the production of capital goods would be conditional upon the *previous* accumulation of a reserve to live from. But in the complex economies of our days this condition entirely disappears.

2. Time theory (123)

For some authors, the rate of interest is simply the "price of time."[1] What is bought and sold on the capital market is time itself.

But this is a vague and inconsistent idea that cannot be too vigorously combated. The only good that interest theory has to deal with is the use of capital. This use of capital is naturally related to a certain waiting on the part of the owner of the capital since savings constitute deferred consumption,[2] but *wait* and *time* are not interchangeable terms. *Time as such is not an economic good.* So to call interest the price of time is to indulge in empty metaphor that hinders instead of advancing the explanation.

If it is to be fertile, a theory must rely not on images and figures but on concepts that are exactly defined and adapted to the facts. Otherwise there can be only verbiage and multiplied dangers of error. Interest theory, being particularly subtle, needs this rule to be respected more than elsewhere.

1. Louis Baudin, for instance, in his *Manuel d'économie politique*, vol. 2 (Paris: Librairie générale de Droit et de Jurisprudence, 1944), 175, a little book that is in other respects very clear and precise, has no qualms about adopting this concept.

2. No. 51.

(c) Primary theories of interest[1]

1. Supply-and-demand theory (124)

This theory considers interest as the price paid for the use of capital, and without further analysis declares that interest, like any other price, is determined by the supply-and-demand mechanism.

So far as it goes, this is undeniable, but it is a primary theory and fails to meet the conditions of validity for any effective theory.[2] For what needs to be explained is why supply and demand are always such as to give rise to an interest rate that is invariably positive. *For this to be so, the regular interaction of supply and demand must be due to deep-lying causes that need to be elucidated.*

In reality, the capital market comprises but a single juncture of the economic system. So supply-and-demand considerations can only provide an interest theory for given values of the other parameters (price, quantities) and can only have explanatory value to the extent that these parameters may be taken, owing to their inertia, as constants. It is easy to grasp that at a given moment goods produced may be sufficiently scarce relative to consumer requirements for their prices to exceed gross production costs[3] by a margin that encourages firms to commit themselves to making interest payments; but what specifically calls for explanation is why, under conditions of sustained equilibrium, there remains a discrepancy between prices and gross costs. It therefore remains to be shown why, when all constituent markets have attained equilibrium, the capital market gives rise to interest that is invariably positive.[4]

---

1. Reminder: in the present study the term *primary theory* designates a theory that relates only to primary effects (note 1 to no. 9).

2. No. 115.

3. *Gross costs* here means the firms' outlay minus the interest payments they make.

4. It is noteworthy that for supply-and-demand theorists, the rate of interest depends only on the supply and demand of *new capital*: existing capital plays no role whatever. While this point of view may be justifiable when studying the capital market at a specific point of time in a dynamic disequilibrium process, it is by no means acceptable when studying dynamic equilibrium. For the supply of new capital depends essentially on capital *already* possessed; similarly, the demand for capital takes account of marginal technical interest rates that themselves depend on *preexisting* capital investments, so that *in equilibrium* account must be taken of the supply and demand of *total capital* and not only of the supply and demand of new capital.

2. Relative wage and interest level theory (125)[1]

This theory states as its departure point that "it is almost always possible to obtain the same results using plentiful labor and basic equipment or using sophisticated equipment and a low labor input. . . . Hence, though capital and labor are both indispensable to a firm, the proportion in which they are used is not necessarily determined by the nature of the venture. While always using both, the firm can nonetheless, up to a certain point, substitute one for the other."[2]

For

> what guides each firm in choosing the proportions of capital and labor to be used in each of its projects is the cost-price factor: firms always choose the proportion that ensures the lowest cost price. This being so, let us suppose that to diminish by one the workforce assigned to a certain project, a capital investment of 100,000 francs is needed. If the annual rate of interest is I, the investment will cost 100,000 I francs per year;[3] and it will save the annual wages S of one worker, so it will or will not be in the entrepreneur's interests to make the investment depending on whether

(1)   100,000 $I < S$ or 100,000 $I > S$.

> If the $\frac{S}{I}$ ratio is exactly 100,000, it will make no difference which manufacturing process is adopted; if the ratio is greater than 100,000, it will be profitable to acquire the equipment, and if it is less, it will be more profitable to keep the worker.[4]

1. A theory elaborated by Clément Colson in volume 1 of his *Cours d'économie politique*, and taken over by François Divisia in his *Économique rationnelle*.

2. Clément Colson, *Cours d'économie politique*, vol. 1 (Paris: Gauthier-Villars, 1917), 362–63.

3. The author states at this point that he "is disregarding maintenance and depreciation costs for the sake of brevity but that they could easily be included." In fact, however, if these elements were taken into account, parameters S and I would no longer be involved exclusively by their ratio $\frac{S}{I}$; they would now be connected by a linear relation. This would require *considerable modification* to the author's analysis.

4. F. Divisia, *Économique rationnelle* (Paris: Doin, 1928), 188–92.

In other words, of two processes respectively needing, per unit of output, labor inputs of T and T' hours, and reproducible capital of C and C', such that $C < C'$ and $T > T'$, the former will be adopted if we have

(2) $ST + IC < ST' + IC',$

i.e., if

(3) $$\frac{C' - C}{T - T'} > \frac{S}{I}.$$

It can be seen that the market value of the ratio $\dfrac{S}{I}$ is the decisive factor in the firm's decision.[5]

> The influence of this ratio on the conditions of use of labor and of capital is ultimately what determines the ratio itself, if it is assumed that the available workforce and capital must be used in their entirety.[4]

Indeed, let us suppose that once a certain equilibrium is in place the wage level is artificially increased, while the rate of interest stays the same. The ratio $\dfrac{S}{I}$ will increase and it will become profitable to replace labor with equipment for a certain number of productions.

> To this change in production processes, which cannot fail to occur if the rise in wages is sustained for long enough, there will correspond an increased demand for capital and increased availability of labor; this labor might find employment for a time in manufacturing the new equipment, but once this has been done it will be redundant and will weigh on the labor market; this will lead to unemployment and a consequent fall in wages. Hence the combination of the upward movement of interest and the downward movement of wages will tend to lower the ratio $\dfrac{S}{I}$.
>
> But if the interest rate were kept artificially high in relation to wage levels, use of capital would cease to be profitable for some productions and the equipment involved would no longer be replaced. This would lead on the one hand

---

5. In view of the point made in note 3 above it would be more accurate to say, "... comparison of the market values of S and I is ..."

to a fall in the demand for capital and in the interest rate and on the other hand to increased demand for labor and a rise in wages, i.e., an overall tendency for the ratio $\dfrac{S}{I}$ to increase.[4]

This shows that the economic mechanism constantly tends to bring the value of the ratio $\dfrac{S}{I}$ back to its equilibrium level, corresponding to "use of capital and labor in proportion to the size of the population and its habits with regard to labor and savings."[1]

This theory undoubtedly sheds light on how firms behave at a given moment and for given prices,[6] but clearly it cannot constitute an explanation of what determines the relative values of interest and wages in a sustained equilibrium.

For its underlying supposition is that the prices of production goods are independent of the wage level,[7] whereas *in equilibrium* the facts rule out this hypothesis, as all prices are proportional to the wage level. It is evident that if quantities C and C' used above are themselves proportional to S, the theory collapses: wages S become indeterminate[8] and only the rate of interest can be regarded as being determined by the mechanism described.

And even then it must be emphasized that *this determination itself only concerns an intermediate equilibrium and does not explain the long-term subsistence of interest in a long-term equilibrium.*

To take but a single example, while it is true that a rise limited to agricultural wages leads to increased use of agricultural machinery, it is no less certain that a simultaneous rise in all other wages will in the long run bring about a proportional rise in the cost of agricultural machinery and in the price paid for its use. So *in the long run and of itself* a generalized rise in wages will not cause a decrease in the size of the agricultural workforce for any given interest rate level.

In fact, the theory here set out could be of real value in explaining the determination of the relative levels of interest and wages only if capital and labor comprised two *entirely distinct* production factors, but in reality

6. Particularly of capital goods.

7. I.e., that parameters C and C' in equation (3) are independent of S.

8. The wage level is directly linked to the price level and can only be determined *in equilibrium* by the action of conditions of a monetary nature (nos. 97 and 99).

capital in the shape of equipment is still labor, and even if an entrepreneur replaced workers with machines, the machines would themselves require labor so that their prices could not *in the long run* be independent of wage levels.

In fact, it follows from the foregoing[9] that *the relative share of invested capital and direct labor in equilibrium is absolutely independent of wage levels and is determined exclusively by the rate of interest*, high interest rates favoring labor-intensive production methods and low interest rates favoring increased mechanization.[10]

What emerges is that the theory of relative wage and interest levels is a fundamentally primary theory[11] that undertakes to complete the supply-and-demand theory by explaining why, for a given wage level and interest rate level, one technique is chosen rather than another and why, by way of reaction, this choice tends to make the rate of interest rise and the wage level fall or vice versa.[12] *It shows why differential variations in wages and interest rates tend to occur but it leaves their absolute levels undetermined.*[13] In particular it does not explain why an invariably positive interest rate is necessary, whether in a stationary equilibrium or even at any moment in the dynamic evolution of a system that is out of equilibrium. Such a theory is in reality strictly analogous to a theory in physics setting out to explain the formation of waves on the sea without reference to an average sea level.

9. Nos. 45 and 47.

10. While everyday economic experience admittedly shows that rising wages encourage mechanization, this is exclusively due to the hysteresis exhibited by market prices, based on accounting costs, in comparison with reproduction costs and because, during an upward trend, the rise in the nominal rate of interest is generally not sufficient (no. 106) to offset the rate of increase in wages, so that the wage-denominated interest rate—which is the only relevant rate—falls. But these are primary, not secondary, effects.

11. In the meaning of note 1 to no. 124.

12. This theory emphasizes that it is in a firm's basic interests to expand its equipment stock in the wake of rising wages before the price of machinery has fully reacted. In this case the cost of the advantage is borne by the capitalists who finance the machinery production, in accordance with the well-known mechanism typical of periods of rising wages (no. 106).

13. See the explanations given in no. 32.

3. Quantitative theory of interest (126)

The quantitative theory applies only to traditional monetary economies in which circulating money also serves as the unit of account. According to this theory the rate of interest is simply the price paid for the use of money and its level depends mainly on the money stock.

In reality, as we have seen,[1] while in a monetary economy the nominal level of the interest rate does indeed depend on *variation* in the quantity of money, it remains nonetheless always independent of the absolute level of this quantity.

This means that in a stationary equilibrium in which the quantity of money remains constant, the level of the interest rate is *absolutely independent* of the quantity of money.[2]

In reality, the quantitative theory of interest concerns how the nominal interest rate evolves in a monetary economy subject to price variation. *It provides no explanation of interest in a stationary equilibrium*, yet, as has been shown, this explanation is one of the fundamental conditions that must be fulfilled by any meaningful interest theory.

1. No. 105.
2. Nos. 97 and 99.

(d) Incomplete secondary theories

1. Theories based on the physical productivity of capital (127)[1]

These theories link the rate of interest chiefly to the increase in physical production that results, for a given quantity of primary factors of production, from the use of capital, and they see this increase as the basic rationale of interest.

However, as we have seen, the *physical* productivity of capital must be carefully distinguished from its *value* productivity represented by interest. *Since physical productivity can in fact exist without value productivity,[2] physical productivity can by no means be accepted as an explanation of interest.*[3]

Admittedly there can be no value productivity unless there is physical productivity[2] at the same time, but explaining the necessary existence of value productivity means discovering its sufficient cause, not merely describing one of the circumstances that accompany it while leaving the others unexplained. Proving that value productivity is accompanied by physical productivity is not *explaining* it in terms of this productivity "any more than it would explain land-rent if we showed that, without the fruitfulness of the soil, there could be no land-rent; or than it would explain rain if we showed that water could not fall to the ground without the action of gravity."[4]

In any event, without any need for in-depth analysis of the role of interest in production, it would be enough, in order to eliminate any theory of productivity as a fundamental theory of interest, to observe that no such theory can explain the undeniable fact that a positive rate of interest can exist in an economy that has no roundabout production processes and therefore practices only consumption loans, when there is a systematic preference for present goods.[5]

1. Theories elaborated in particular by J.-B. Say, Roscher, and Carey.
2. No. 70.
3. The physical productivity theories could only explain why there is always a positive rate of interest if nature endowed certain goods with a spontaneous productivity *needing no expenditure* (note 3 to no. 121a). But no such productivity is found in the real world.
4. Eugen von Böhm-Bawerk, *Capital and Interest: A Critical History of Economical Theory* (London: Macmillan, 1890), bk. 1, ch. 7.
5. See the explanations given concerning the agio theory (no. 130 below).

By insisting on the physical productivity of capital, productivity theories have justly drawn attention to *an absolutely essential and inescapable aspect of interest*, but even in their most finished form, they are and must remain no more than partial theories that in themselves are quite unable to constitute an explanation of the phenomenon of interest.

2. Abstinence theories (128)[1]

According to these theories, the rate of interest is positive because all savings require sacrifice, and this sacrifice will only be made if it is rewarded
by the payment of a surplus.

We have already seen what this thesis is worth.[2] For on the one hand
savings do not necessarily entail sacrifice and some savings would be
made even with a zero interest rate and on the other hand the value of the
interest paid is far greater than the sacrifice made, when sacrifice there is.

Some authors have softened what is excessive and manifestly inexact
in such theories by speaking of *waiting* instead of *abstinence*.

In order to make use of roundabout production processes some consumption expenditure must be deferred until later, a waiting period is inevitable, and the rate of interest is simply the necessary compensation for
this wait.

While this change of vocabulary lends the theory a more acceptable
external appearance, it changes nothing essential. Some people would still
be disposed to postpone a possible consumption and wait even if the rate
of interest were zero. So we cannot recognize the need to reward this waiting period as the basic reason why a positive rate of interest exists; hence,
as an interest rate theory, any theory based on waiting must be deemed
inexact.

However, by insisting on the psychological aspect of the phenomenon
of interest, these theories have directed attention toward *a facet of the
problem that is absolutely fundamental and inescapable*. For this reason,
such theories should be considered rather as incomplete than merely
inexact.

1. Elaborated in particular by Senior, Bastiat, and Marshall.
2. No. 41.

3. Perfected capital-based theory of interest (129)

This theory,[1] which represents the most sophisticated of the classical capital-based interest theories, holds that the reason why any capital good is worth more than the primary factors of production needed to produce it and why there exists interest corresponding to the difference between the two, comes down to *scarcity*. And if in fact the capital equipment stock is not more extensive, notwithstanding its great advantage of making it possible to earn interest, this is because its expansion would require supplementary savings that, to occur under the relevant conditions, would require higher interest than is offered in the market. Thus it is the relative scarcity of capital—itself due to the insufficient propensity to save—that is the ultimate reason why there is a positive interest rate.

Thus borrowers want capital because it produces value, and they agree to pay interest because the technical interest rate of their investments[2] enables them to do so.

But the supply of capital is limited because saving is burdensome and lenders demand interest because, for this very reason, capital is scarce in relation to the needs of production.

Interest induces individuals to save until the point is reached at which the supply and demand of capital, for this rate of interest, are evenly balanced.

Under these conditions, we may set out the following step-by-step explanation of the interest phenomenon:

1. The existence of interest in production implies that capital is sufficiently productive of value for firms to agree to pay interest for its use.
2. The existence of interest implies that the accumulation of capital requires sacrifice, for otherwise its value productivity would tend toward zero.
3. "Not all saving involves a sacrifice, but . . . a sacrifice appears only when the saving has been carried so far as to cut so deeply into present enjoyments and to add so little to prospective future enjoyments that, in present estimation, the prospective future enjoyments are less than the surrendered present enjoyments.

---

1. Elaborated in particular by Carver.
2. No. 44.

4. "Saving would normally stop at this point unless a premium in the form of more goods in the future than are now surrendered—i.e., interest—were offered as an inducement to further saving.

5. "If all the needs of production were met by such an amount of capital as could be saved without sacrifice, there would be no occasion for the payment of interest.

6. "But since the needs of production are not met by this amount of capital, interest must be, and is, paid as an inducement to such further saving as will more fully supply these needs.

7. "*Both productivity and abstinence are necessary to an explanation of interest*, the productivity of capital being the basis of the demand for it, while the increasing sacrifice of saving larger and larger amounts puts an effective check upon its supply."[3]

Sophisticated as it is, this theory can only be found satisfactory if we accept a priori that the propensity to save is relatively insufficient. Is it really enough to declare that this assumption is indirectly confirmed by observation? *Indeed, is not the problem precisely that of showing why this propensity to save is and always has been, in every time and place, such that the observed rate of interest has invariably been positive although a priori, as has been shown,[4] one might have expected that it could become negative?*

As with every other good, the rate of interest, being the price of the availability of capital, is evidently the result of its quantitative insufficiency relative to the absolute demand for it that would prevail if the price were zero. But why then is the capital that individuals seek to accumulate never superabundant? Why does it never exceed the absolute demand for it?

Is it really due to chance that over the centuries in every known society the rate of interest has always been positive? Such an occurrence must surely appear quite incredible unless some other explanation for it can be found. For it is hard to admit that at no time and in no place does the thought of the future ever weigh enough for the absolute supply of capital to exceed the absolute demand for it, i.e., for the rate of interest to become negative. Is the creation and expansion of capital always so laborious? The Fable of the Golden Shilling[5] suffices to cast doubt on this by

3. T. N. Carver, "The Relation of Abstinence to Interest," *Quarterly Journal of Economics* 18, no. 1 (1903): 142–45.

4. Nos. 114 and 115.

5. No. 18.

showing how easily even a very small capital grows even if a very modest rate of interest is maintained.

Indeed is it not clear that by claiming that the propensity to save has always been exactly such as to ensure a positive rate of interest, the theory explains nothing whatsoever? What should we say of a theory of gravitation that explained that bodies fall because they are subject to gravity?

However eminent they may be, the partisans of the perfected capital-based theory of interest are deceiving themselves. Their account of the mechanism by which interest is formed is irreproachable and their explanations ought therefore to be considered fully satisfying if as a matter of fact we observed rates of interest of all values, both negative and positive. But that is exactly what we do *not* observe. So there must be some factor or factors missing in this theoretical edifice, no matter how brilliant and penetrating it may otherwise be. *It is not enough to explain how the rate of interest becomes fixed—we also need an explanation of why it settles at such and such a level.* The theory suffers from deficiencies that must evidently, and imperatively, be made good. Notwithstanding its sophistication, this perfected theory of interest, which is now classic, cannot be regarded as providing a profound and satisfying explanation of the rate of interest, and it must be classified among the incomplete theories.

The fact is that astute thinkers have been more or less explicitly aware of this inadequacy for a long time now and have been striving to remedy it. I shall now examine four particularly thought-provoking such attempts, each of which has endeavored in its own way to make good the insufficiencies of classical interest theory.[6]

---

6. In the more or less definitive form that it had reached when they were elaborated.

4. Agio theory (130)

The agio theory was brilliantly constructed by one of the 19th century's most penetrating economic thinkers: Eugen von Böhm-Bawerk.

According to him, the rate of interest is explained by the agio in favor of present goods when they are exchanged against future goods. Thus, interest exists because people prefer present goods to future goods of the same quality and in the same amount: this is in his view the sole reason for interest.

And indeed if this preference for present goods could be regarded as a structural datum, the existence of positive interest would be its immediate and necessary consequence. For instance, let us suppose a simplified economy peopled by individuals who consume only one good (A) and whose economic life can be reduced to two periods T_0 and T_1, and let the functions of satisfaction $S(A_0, A_1)$ at time t_0 be of the form

(1) $$S(A_0, A_1) = S(A_0 + \lambda A_1),$$

where λ is a coefficient less than unity.

This would mean that the identical supplementary quantity ΔA consumed at time t_1 would *always* procure a lesser satisfaction than the same quantity consumed at time t_0, irrespective of the values of A_0 and A_1.[1] And this in turn would mean that the psychological structure of the economy in question was such that present goods were always preferred to future goods.

---

1. Conversely, it can in fact be shown that if this condition is met, i.e., if we have

(1) $$S(A_0 + \Delta A, A_1) - S(A_0, A_1) > S(A_0, A_1 + \Delta A) - S(A_0, A_1),$$

i.e.,

(2) $$S(A_0 + \Delta A, A_1) > S(A_0, A_1 + \Delta A),$$

for any *positive* value of ΔA, the satisfaction is necessarily of type (1) as per the text. This demonstration takes as its starting point a thorough analysis of the properties of the indifference surfaces, especially in the region of satiety (see my *À la recherche d'une discipline économique*, no. 64), but it exceeds the limited scope of the present study.

If we assume a stationary model and we use a to denote the constant price of service (A) and I to denote the rate of interest in force between the two points of time, we shall have in equilibrium[2]

(2)
$$\frac{S'_{A_0}}{a} = \frac{\frac{S'_{A_1}}{a}}{1+I}.$$

And as

(3)
$$S'_{A_1} = \lambda S'_{A_0},$$

we obtain

$$1 + I = \frac{1}{\lambda}.$$

This proves that for a value of λ less than unity the rate of interest would *necessarily* be positive[3] and thus that Böhm-Bawerk's theory is irrefutable provided that its starting premises are correct.

Yet nothing, in fact, is less certain than that there is a constant preference for present goods. It may fairly be observed that present goods do not always have greater psychological value than future goods of the same quality and in the same quantity. The desirability of a good varies with circumstances. A man who has just dined or a sick man who must diet cares little for an immediate meal that he is offered; he would prefer an invitation to dinner on a day when he will be able to take advantage of it.[4]

---

2. This condition corresponds to maximization of satisfaction S for given resources and prices (see no. 82).

3. And conversely, a value of λ greater than unity, i.e., a constant preference of individuals for future goods over present goods, would lead to a negative rate of interest.

4. All it seems possible to say, in light of our psychological introspection, is that if $A_0 \leq A_1$, the same increment ΔA will procure in general a greater increment of satisfaction if it affects present consumption than if it affects future consumption, i.e., we have (from note 1 above)

(1) $S(A_0 + \Delta A, A_1) > S(A_0, A_1 + \Delta A)$ where $\Delta A > 0$ and $A_0 \leq A_1$.

Thus if (A) denotes food and if $A_0 = A_1 = 0$, this condition implies that for a hungry man a present meal is always preferred to a future one.

But if A_0 is such that the man is at present sated and if $A_1 = 0$, i.e., if he has no intention of eating before the next time period, an extra meal in the future may be preferred to an extra meal in the present. In this case condition (1) is clearly no longer verified.

This condition shows that if we use M' and M'' (fig. 9.1) to denote the points derived from a single point M not located lower than the bisector Δ of the coordinate axes, by any identical increase in the x- and y-coordinates, we always obtain

(2) $$S(M'') > S(M').$$

From which it follows that to every point M_1'' symmetric to a point M_1' located above bisector Δ there corresponds a greater satisfaction.

By considering an infinitely small increment ΔA, we can further deduce from condition (1) that for every point M not located below bisector Δ, we have

(3) $$S'_{A_0} > S'_{A_1},$$

i.e., from condition (2) in the text,

(4) $$I > 0.$$

This shows that if the point M corresponding to general economic equilibrium is not below bisector Δ, the rate of interest is necessarily positive, but in fact there is no reason why the equilibrium point M should not be below bisector Δ at one of the points where the slope of the tangent is less than unity, points that *necessarily* exist since the tangents to the indifference curves become horizontal as satiety for commodity (A_0) is approached.

In short, *everything depends on the technical structure of production*. For instance, assume that the community in question includes only one category of individuals, consuming only

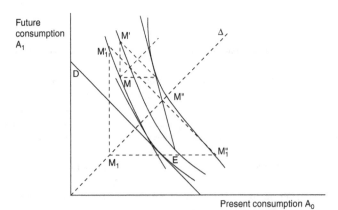

Future consumption A_1

Present consumption A_0

FIGURE 9.1 FOOTNOTE

commodity (A), *which is assumed to be storable*, that their economic life lasts only two periods of length T, and that individuals are capable of working only during the first of the two periods of their life. Using A to denote the quantity produced over this period, we have

(5) $$A_0 + A_1 = A.$$

Competitive equilibrium would then be reached at the point of contact E between the curves of indifference and straight line D representing equation (5). At this point the tangent to the line of indifference would be perpendicular to the bisector Δ, giving

(6) $$I = 0.$$

The rate of interest would be zero.

But if we assume that commodity A is only storable subject to a loss of 10%, we obtain

(7) $$A_0 + \frac{10}{9} A_1 = A,$$

and at the point of contact of the straight line representing this equation with the cluster of indifference curves the slope of the tangent would be $-\frac{9}{10}$ so that the rate of interest would be expressed by the equation

(8) $$\frac{S'_{A_0}}{S'_{A_1}} = \frac{9}{10},$$

which, in light of equation (2) in the text, gives us

(9) $$I = -10\%.$$

It is clear that, on the assumptions stated, *irrespective of the degree of preference for present goods* (which may, for example, be characterized by the average of the absolute value of the slope of the tangents along bisector Δ or indeed by the relative size of the area where the slope of the tangent is greater than unity), the rate of interest would be entirely independent of it and would instead depend exclusively on the technical structure of production. Hence the preference for present goods cannot be accepted as the reason why there is a positive rate of interest. (Fuller and more precise explanations of this point will be found in appendix II.)

Assuming now a case in which the shape of the satisfaction functions is

(10) $$S = S(A_0 + \lambda A_1)$$

(perfect substitutability) and structural conditions correspond to

(11) $$A_0 + A_1 = A,$$

the maximum for satisfaction S would be attained at point E (fig. 9.2) where straight line D representing equation (11) intersects the A_0-axis.

And that being the case, the whole of Böhm-Bawerk's theory falls to the ground and a new question mark floats over the entire subject. There is no denying that under present conditions, which include a positive rate of interest, present goods are preferred to future goods. But this must be regarded as a *consequence*, not an explanation, of the existence of a positive rate of interest. It could only be otherwise if the preference for future goods were a structural datum *independent* of market conditions, which is not the case. *By thus reducing its explanation of why there is a positive interest rate to the constant preference for present goods, which is precisely due to the existence of this positive interest rate, Böhm-Bawerk's theory turns out to be a mere vicious circle.*

However, while Böhm-Bawerk's psychological theory cannot be accepted as an explanation of the problem of interest, it rightly emphasizes *the*

At this point we should indeed have

(12) $$1 + I = \frac{1}{\lambda};$$

in other words, $I > 0$ for $\lambda < 1$ although along line D we have $I = 0$. In this case the maximum of S corresponds to the immediate consumption of all available output. Thus a condition of type (11) would lead to a zero interest rate only if a tangential point with a line of indifference existed on the corresponding line D. In short, when psychological conditions (condition [12]) and technical conditions (condition [6]) are in conflict, the psychological conditions prevail. (On this subject, readers may consult my *À la recherche d'une discipline économique*, no. 248.)

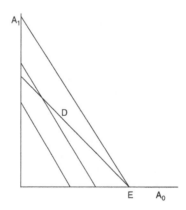

FIGURE 9.2 FOOTNOTE

importance of the psychological dispositions of individuals, consideration of which must be an indispensable element of any satisfactory theory of interest.

Moreover, while it is manifestly inexact to affirm a constant, systematic, and universal preference for present goods, analysis nonetheless reveals that if our present consumption of a good is lower than our future consumption of it, an increase at the present time in the quantity of this good consumed will in general obtain for us a greater satisfaction than will the same increase bearing on our future consumption.[5] From this it may be deduced that with regard to most of the set of possible consumptions, present goods are preferred,[6] and hence that *the probability in equilibrium of a positive rate of interest is greater than that of a negative rate.*[7]

Finally, beyond any question, Böhm-Bawerk was intensely aware of the need to explain why there is an invariably positive interest rate and *he thus made a powerful contribution to posing the problem of interest clearly.*

For these reasons Böhm-Bawerk's theory should much rather be regarded as incomplete than false. *And it represents in any event a seminal contribution to economic theory.*

5. Note 4 above.

6. In the case of figure 9.1 of note 4 above, the slope of the tangent to a line of indifference is greater than unity throughout the part of the $A_0 0 A_1$ quadrant located above the bisector $0A$, as well as in a part of the quadrant located beneath $0A$.

7. Irrespective of the average preference for present goods, points in the plane are always found (those at which present consumption is close to the point of satiety) at which there is a preference for future goods (i.e., in the case of figure 9.1 of note 4 above, where the slope of the tangent is less than unity), but the greater the average preference for present goods, i.e., the greater the area of consumptions in which this preference is found, *the greater the probability of a positive rate of interest for any technical structure of the economy.*

Indeed it will be established by studying a specific example in appendix II (no. 198, § i) that, for a given technical structure, the equilibrium interest rate is higher as the average preference (as defined above) for present goods is stronger.

By contrast it will also be established (no. 198, § ii) in the study of the same example, that for a psychological structure assumed to be given (i.e., for given satisfaction functions), the equilibrium interest rate is not necessarily higher in proportion to the capacity for physical productivity of roundabout production processes (defined as the maximum physical productivity capable of being achieved). Comparison of these two properties shows that Böhm-Bawerk's agio theory is much more penetrating than the productivity theories.

5. Fructification theory (131)[1]

According to this theory, all forms of interest owe their existence to the fact that the owner of capital has the option of making it fructify by exchanging it for a plot of land yielding a rent.

Obviously, *in the form in which it is expressed*, this explanation depends on a vicious circle. For it remains to be explained why a plot of land that, abstracting from unforeseen circumstances, yields a rent over an infinite horizon, is only of finite value. And this raises anew the question why, in the specific case of land, the present value of a future good is less than the future value of that good, i.e., the selfsame problem of interest.

The attempt to explain interest on capital in business and industry by the possibility of acquiring land using limited capital simply swaps the phenomenon of interest on capital in one guise for the same phenomenon in another guise that is just as much in need of explanation as the former. Obtaining interest via capital and discounting future income flows at a given rate are in reality two different aspects of the same phenomenon; neither can be explained simply in terms of the other.

Indeed this is confirmed by straightforward observation. In dynamic disequilibrium, interest is seen to be not so much the effect of the exchange ratio between the indefinite income stream provided by land and the capital that land represents as the cause of this exchange ratio. The reason why a plot of land that yields an annual rent of 5,000 francs is worth 100,000 francs is precisely because the rate of interest on capital is 5%. The plot would be worth 50,000 francs if the rate were 10% and 200,000 francs if capital yielded only 2.5%. Hence instead of trying to explain the rate of interest by the land-to-capital exchange ratio, it is the exchange ratio that should be explained by the fact that there is a rate of interest on capital.

In its classical expression, the fructification theory is therefore a *vicious circle* and does not explain interest on capital at all.

However, as will be shown, *by taking as its starting point the fact that the value of land is finite, this theory has made a potentially valuable contribution to understanding the phenomenon of interest*. For this reason I consider the fructification theory, not (as Böhm-Bawerk did) as an utterly crude theory, but simply as an *incomplete theory* that has hitherto been insufficiently analyzed and *the deeper study of which might easily have made a great contribution to solving a problem that has given rise to so much discussion*.

---

1. Elaborated in particular by Turgot.

6. Theory of the availability of money (132)

Like the quantity theory of money, this theory applies only to traditional monetary economies in which the money that circulates is also the standard of value. For this theory, it is an economic advantage to receive monetary income earlier rather than later. If this is so, "it is not due to an alleged tendency of human nature to prefer present goods to future ones; it is due to the fundamental fact that, since money can be stored without loss, if I receive on 1 July 1945 a sum that was only due on 1 October, I obtain a twofold advantage instead of a single one. For not only am I able to secure the *same advantages* as if I had received it on 1 October, but I can secure *in addition* whatever advantages may accrue from the use to which I put this sum between 1 July and 1 October. By receiving the same sum on 1 July instead of on 1 October, I am enabled to choose among *a wider range of uses for it*, and that is reason enough for me to prefer the earlier date of receipt."[1] It follows that the rate of interest is necessarily positive.

It is not difficult to see that, *as presented*, this theory, as a theory of interest in a perfect-foresight model, is a *vicious circle*. For when the reimbursement of loans is certain, it cannot be more advantageous to receive the same sum sooner rather than later unless the price paid in the market for the use of capital, i.e., the rate of interest, is in fact positive.

If, for instance, the market rate was zero, the immediate availability of a sum of money could not have greater value for me than the future availability of the *same* sum, as meanwhile I can always borrow if I need to, free of charge, at the zero market rate.

Thus the theory of the availability of money amounts to explaining interest by interest and thus constitutes a vicious circle.

All that can be deduced from this theory is that in an economy of stable prices the nominal rate of interest could not become negative, a finding that is, however, of fundamental importance. But it by no means explains why the rate of interest could not be zero but instead remains positive.[2] Thus the availability of money theory cannot be accepted as a satisfactory theory of interest.

---

1. C. Rist, *Essais sur quelques problèmes économiques et monétaires* (Paris: Sirey, 1933), 220.

2. Fuller explanation will be found farther on in this chapter (note 15 to no. 136).

However, this theory has the outstanding merit of pinning down the need to explain why there is necessarily a positive rate of interest and of insisting on a phenomenon of the highest importance for understanding the problem of interest, namely *the liquidity advantages provided by money and its ability to be stored at no significant cost*; for which reasons this theory must be numbered among the incomplete theories that *have contributed to finding a satisfactory solution to the problem of interest.*

.

7. Annuity theory (133)

This theory, devised by Swedish economist Gustav Cassel, maintains that it is not accidental that the rate of interest is not only always positive but moreover stays within a range of values normally on the order of 4% to 10%.

It inquires why interest does not fall to 1% or even 1‰. For there does not seem to be any a priori reason why the rate of interest could not have such values. But, says Cassel,

if we take the number of years' purchase of a fixed annuity instead of the rate of interest, we can show the present character of the rate by saying that a perpetual annuity costs twenty-five or thirty-three times the annual value.[1] When the matter is expressed in this way, it is easy to see that there is a definite relation between the rate of interest and the length of human life. Men, at the age at which they have control over their own capital, cannot generally count on more than another twenty-five to thirty-three years of life, and will not, consequently, sacrifice much more than twenty-five to thirty-three years of returns to secure a perpetual annuity.

Those who believe an interest of 1% to be possible are really supposing that, for instance, an estate with a net yield of £10,000 could be bought at the price of £1,000,000! But the millionaire, by consuming his million, can be much better off during his remaining years than by buying an income of £10,000 a year.

In reality, it is quite impossible to suppose that, with the present length of human life, absolutely durable goods would be paid for at the rate of a hundred or even fifty times their annual returns. A rate of interest of 1‰ would be possible if people were inclined to save £100,000 and then give it away in order to obtain an annuity of £100. That kind of economizing would only be done by a Methuselah.[2]

In the context of what has been set out in the foregoing chapters, Cassel's thesis could be summarized as follows: Men save for two motives: (a) they distribute their income over time so as to harmonize their consumptions at different periods,[3] and (b) they endeavor to maintain their

1. This method of calculation was used in the past when a loan of 4% or 3% was said [in French] to be repayable "au denier 25" or "au denier 33" i.e., at a rate of 25 or 33.
2. Cassel, *Traité d'économie politique*, vol. 1, 364 (bk. 2, ch. 26).
3. This distribution was studied in detail in no. 40.

capital at a certain level so as to satisfy their propensities to own and to bequeath.[4]

Now a saver can in principle proceed in either of two ways: (a) he may strive to build up a given capital, the income from which will serve to provide for his old age and which he can bequeath to his heirs, or (b) he may invest in a life annuity of which he will be sole beneficiary. The latter approach, for a given starting capital and market rate of interest will ensure higher income but will give less satisfaction to the propensity to own and none at all to the propensity to bequeath.

How, in practice, does the saver make his choice? In Cassel's view he does so chiefly in light of the prevailing rate of interest and of the probable length of his remaining life at the time of deciding. Assume a saver who at age n has the disposal of capital C. If he puts his capital into perpetual annuities[5] at rate of interest I, his annual income will be

$$R_0 = IC.$$

But if he buys a life annuity, he can receive each year an income R_1 the amount of which is well determined in the market in light of probable life expectancy at age n,[6] which will of course be greater than R_0 and will vary with n and with I. The values of the ratio $\dfrac{R_1}{R_0}$ are summarized in table 9.1.

TABLE 9.1

n \ I	$\frac{1}{8}\%$	$\frac{1}{4}\%$	$\frac{1}{2}\%$	1 %	2 %	4 %	10 %
10	19	10	5.2	2.8	1.7	1.22	1.01
20	22	11	6.1	3.3	1.9	1.30	1.03
30	28	14	7.4	4.0	2.3	1.50	1.06
40	35	18	9.2	4.9	2.7	1.70	1.12
50	47	24	12.0	6.4	3.5	2.00	1.24
60	73	37	18.0	9.6	5.1	2.90	1.50
70	134	67	34.0	17.0	8.9	4.80	2.20
80	205	133	67.0	34.0	17.0	9.00	4.00
90	400	201	100.0	51.0	25.0	13.00	5.70

4. For the sake of simplicity this point was disregarded in no. 40. Only in nos. 64 and 75 have I inquired how the theory ought to be completed to take account of it.

5. The hypothesis allows the investment to take any form provided the capital is left intact and only the interest is consumed.

6. See the *Nouvelles tables pour les calculs d'intérêts composés* [New tables for calculating compound interest] by P.-A. Violeine (Paris: Gauthier-Villars, 1930), 160 and 100 ff.

This table shows that for a rate of 4% a life investment made at age 40 increases annual income by only 70%. This being so, if his propensity to bequeath is strong enough, the saver will prefer to sacrifice this potential increase of 70% in his annual income in order to be able to bequeath his capital C to his heirs in its entirety.

If the rate was only 1%, the purchase of a lifetime investment at the same price would enable him to increase his annual income by 390%. It is likely that this level will incline him, for an equal propensity to bequeath, to invest part of his capital in a life annuity.

And if the rate was just 0.125%, by buying a lifetime investment at the same price he could increase his annual income in the proportion of 35 to 1, which makes it very likely that in this event he would invest almost the whole of his capital in life annuities.

Thus,

> ... let us suppose a capitalist who lives entirely upon the interest on his capital. If he possesses £100,000 and has received 4% up to the present—that is, £4,000 per annum—and, further, has adjusted his standard of living to this income, a reduction of the rate of interest to 3½% will probably make him stop some of his customary expenditure and confine his budget to the still handsome figure of £3,500. A further economy might still seem possible to him if the rate fell to 3%.
>
> If we assume, however, that the rate fell to ½%, our magnate would then certainly find the reduction unbearable, and would prefer, instead of living on a paltry £500 per year, to consume his capital gradually. If he calculated that he will live for another twenty-five years, he can in this manner enjoy his original income of £4,000.[7] If he wishes to provide for his children too, he will, perhaps, find a period of fifty years sufficient, and so consume his capital in that time— that is, at the rate of one-fiftieth per year. Without reckoning interest, that will still give him an income of £2,000 a year.
>
> From this simple example we see how to answer the question whether a man who lives on the interest on his capital, and uses the whole of it, shall, if the rate of interest falls, live on his capital. The decisive point is, clearly, the relative increase in income he can obtain by choosing the latter course. This relative increase evidently becomes much greater as soon as the rate of interest falls below its usual level. It also depends to a great extent on the length of time his capital must last. The shorter this period, the more the man gains by living on his capital.

7. Since £100,000 divided over 25 years gives £4,000 per annum.

This is the reason why, at the present rate of interest, much of the capital possessed by elderly and not very wealthy people is used for the purchase of annuities; by using their capital, these people obtain a considerable increase in their annual income.[8]

This behavior would inevitably spread to all capital owners if the rate of interest fell to very low levels.

Cassel declares that for a 4% rate of interest, a life annuity acquired at age 40 costs 1.7 times less in capital than a perpetual annuity and at 1% it costs 4.5 times less. Since for each class what the average saver chiefly seeks is to provide a given income for his old age, it is clear that the popularization of investment in life annuities that would be inevitable if the rate of interest fell to low values would lead to a substantial fall in the supply of capital. And this decrease would be so much the greater as almost all capital is held by the elderly,[9] to whom the transformation of perpetual annuities into lifetime annuities is particularly attractive. "With a rate of 1.5%," says Cassel, "income could be more than trebled for people of 40, quadrupled for people of 50, and increased sixfold for people of 60, and the owners of by far the greater part of the total wealth would have a very strong, and in some cases an irresistible, incentive to live on their capital."[10]

Since the corollary of this is that a fall in the rate of interest would lead to a sharp increase in demand for capital,[11] this double movement would bring powerful forces into action that would inevitably send the rate of interest back up to its usual levels. And as the order of magnitude of these effects would become, for low rates, far greater than the increase in the supply of capital that could be obtained by the extension of and possible

8. Cassel, *Traité d'économie politique*, vol. 1, 345 (bk. 2, ch. 25).

9. Cassel states that for Sweden, "in the towns, people over 60 years old own more than half the wealth, and that this is the case with people over 50 in the country. We can calculate approximately that, as a whole, over half the total wealth is owned by people more than 55 years old. People over 40 own not less than 89.5 percent in the towns, and 72.5 percent in the country, of the total wealth" (*Traité d'économie politique*, vol. 1, 349 [bk. 2, ch. 25]).

10. Cassel, *Traité d'économie politique*, vol. 1, 350 (bk. 2, ch. 25).

11. It follows from the analysis of notes 39 to no. 47 and 10 to no. 70 that in France in 1913 a fall of 3% in the rate of interest would have led to an increase in the demand for capital on the order of 2.5 times the national income, i.e., on the order of 50% of total reproducible capital.

increase in the inclination to save, it is clear that low interest rates are quite inconceivable.

> Every increase in the period for which the capital must last is, of course, a factor working against the consumption of capital. If the average length of human life were increased to a considerable extent, the rate of interest would, on that account, be able to fall much more than is possible with the present average length. If we imagine people living for several hundred years, there would be no extensive consumption of capital until the rate fell to a fraction of one per cent. From this point of view there would be nothing to prevent the rate of interest being calculated as so much per thousand instead of, as now, at so much per hundred. The dependence of the rate of interest upon the length of human life is thus made very clear.[12]

> . . . The increasing concern for the future which accompanies the advance of civilization has undoubtedly, in the course of centuries, made it possible to lower the rate of interest to a certain extent[13]—a process which may still be observed when semi-barbarous countries are lifted to the realm of civilization. This fall in the rate, it is true, is by no means as one-sided and pronounced a tendency as was sometimes represented; it is not an unlimited tendency which we may continue to expect. As shown in the preceding sections, it is already checked by powerful forces, and has only a rather narrow margin for free play.[14]

It is unsurprising that this fall in the interest rate

> led the general public to believe that the rate of interest had a general tendency to fall. But that this belief should be accepted by the foremost representatives of economic science as the result of research is not really very creditable to that science.

> Schmoller expresses himself rather cautiously when he says that "it is not inconceivable that the rate of interest, which fell in the eighteenth century to 3% and in the nineteenth to 2.75 and 2.5%, may, in the twentieth century, fall below 2%, and even as low as 1.5%."

---

12. Cassel, *Traité d'économie politique*, vol. 1, 347 (bk. 2, ch. 25).

13. "Working in the same direction," continues Cassel, "there has been the lengthening of human life, due especially to modern hygiene. The man who can count on living for another thirty years must definitely be more willing than a man who can only count on another ten or fifteen years to sacrifice some of his present wants so as to provide for the future" (Cassel, vol. 1, 359 [bk. 2, ch. 26]).

14. Cassel, vol. 1, 360 (bk. 2, ch. 26).

This conclusion that, because a certain movement is taking place, it is bound to continue in the same direction, is without any scientific basis. . . . Our analysis, on the contrary, has shown that in all probability the suppositions that the rate could reach 1.5% are entirely unjustified.

Cassel further remarks that

Before describing such a development as probable, it ought to be made clear how it would be possible to maintain a state of affairs in which the owners of by far the greater part of the total wealth could generally treble, and frequently more than treble, their incomes by living on their capital.[15]

This theory of Cassel's shows *considerable penetration*, but although his remarks concerning the behavior of savers under low interest rates seem unquestionable, *his conclusions as to the total supply of capital are in fact entirely wrong.* It is quite true that for a given rate of interest the cost of a life annuity is less than the cost of an equal perpetual annuity, but this does not allow us to conclude that a fall in the rate of interest would automatically lead to a decrease in the supply of capital, for the cost of any given life annuity[16] is so much the greater as the rate of interest itself is lower. *Hence while the supply of capital is decreased by the transformation of perpetual annuities into life annuities, it is increased owing to the fact that the cost of life annuities rises as the rate of interest falls. So far as can be judged, these effects ought to be of the same order of magnitude, so no conclusion is possible.*[17]

15. Cassel, vol. 1, 362 (bk. 2, ch. 26).

16. Or indeed of any given perpetual annuity.

17. This can easily be shown using a simple example. Let us assume a stationary economic model having only one category of individuals, all of whom live 70 years, and let us suppose that all children are born when their parents are 25 years old. If N is the total population, each year there will be $\frac{N}{70}$ deaths offset by $\frac{N}{70}$ births. Each couple who dies is assumed to leave their possessions to their two children, then aged 45. Finally, psychologies are assumed to be such that each individual works from 20 to 45 and wishes to provide himself with an income for his old age equal to R in real terms.

Now let us take two cases.

In the first case, the rate of interest is 6%. Each individual spends all his earnings between ages 20 and 45. At 45, he inherits capital, amounting to C in real terms, of which each year he consumes the annual income

$$R = IC.$$

At 70, he dies, bequeathing in turn capital C. In these circumstances, the average capital held by each individual during his life is

$$\frac{25}{70}\frac{R}{I} \approx 6R,$$

i.e., for the community's aggregate capital at a given point in time,

$$C_1 \approx 6NR.$$

In the second case, the rate of interest is zero.

Each individual saves each year, from age 20 to age 45, a sum R so as to make up a capital $25R$, which he then spends by equal annual installments equal to R. At 70, he dies, leaving no estate. In this case the community's capital is constantly equal to

$$C_2 = N\frac{12.5 \times 50}{70}R \approx 9NR.$$

This shows that, in the case considered, the transformation of perpetual annuities into life annuities not only does not diminish the community's stock of capital but in fact increases it.

It should be emphasized that for the same given psychological and technical structure, both cases examined are of equal antecedent probability. Firstly, the rate of interest may indeed settle at zero in the second case if the demand for capital only increases by 50% when the rate of interest falls from 4% to zero (which is not unlikely: see note 39 to no. 47 and

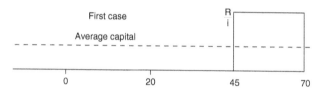

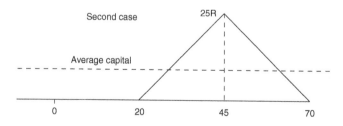

FIGURE 9.3 FOOTNOTE

Hence, in the form it has been given, the annuity theory cannot be deemed to offer a satisfactory explanation of the rate of interest, but it has the merit of highlighting the conditions that must be fulfilled by any theory of interest[18] and, *by insisting on the psychological data showing that the relation between average capital owned and average annual income consumed cannot exceed certain limits directly linked to the human life span, it provides,* as will be seen, *a sturdy foundation upon which to build a satisfying explanation of the rate of interest.* For this reason, it definitely ought to be classified rather as an incomplete interest rate theory than an inexact one.

------

note 10 to no. 70). And secondly, if it is admitted that the increase in social productivity is 10% when the rate falls from 4% to zero (note 9 to no. 71), and if we admit, for the sake of argument, that in the first case the average income consumed from 20 to 45 is equal to $R_1 = 3\dfrac{R}{2}$ (the consumption of children from 0 to 20 is assumed to be frozen at the same level as that of adults of 25 to 45), average income consumed from 20 to 45 in the second case is equal to R_2 such that

$$\frac{25R_2 + 25R}{50} = 1.1\left(\frac{25 \times 1.5R + 25R}{50}\right),$$

i.e.,

$$R_2 = 1.75R \approx 1.16R_1.$$

Thus, in the second case the non-satisfaction of the desire to bequeath is compensated for by (a) an increased satisfaction of the desire to possess (average capital of $9R$ instead of $6R$) and (b) an increase of approximately 16% in income consumed between ages 20 and 45.

It is clear that either case may in fact occur depending on whether the propensity to bequeath does or does not outweigh the propensities to consume and to own. In any event, it would be absolutely false to assert, as Cassel does, *on the exclusive basis of the facts presented,* that the second case is impossible.

18. I.e., the merit of stressing that the reason why the rate of interest settles at such or such a value needs to be explained.

C. Rationale of the Existence of an Invariably Positive Interest Rate

1. Exact statement of the problem (134)

It has been shown above[1] that for an interest theory to be acceptable it must offer a valid explanation of why there is an invariably positive rate of interest, both in a stationary economy in equilibrium and in an evolving economy in disequilibrium.

What calls for explanation is not just the existence of a rate of interest and how it is determined, but also why this rate settles at such and such a level. The explanation must therefore be quantitative as well as qualitative. As Cassel has well remarked, "A theory of interest that fits either of [two widely differing rates] is, strictly speaking, no theory at all."[2]

The foregoing critical analysis of certain highly typical interest theories, together with the explanations I have set out in the first seven chapters, make it possible to define the problem exactly and to locate the lacunae that economic theory must fill.

The explanations already given have, in fact, explained why there is a rate of interest and what determines its level.

There is a rate of interest because, just as two physically distinct goods will have different prices at the same moment, so two goods that are physically identical but available at different moments, will normally have different present values. The level of the rate of interest that becomes established in the market corresponds to the equilibrium reached between the propensity to save—which is due to the psychological conditions of individuals—and the propensity to real investment—which is due to the physical and psychological conditions of firms[3] and to liquidity preference.

Yet, as experience shows that the rate of interest is and always has been positive, whereas a priori negative levels might equally well be expected, *the underlying reasons why this is invariably so remain to be explained.*

Since the positive interest rate is found whether or not technical progress is rapid and whether foresight is good or poor, these reasons will only

1. No. 115.
2. Cassel, *Traité d'économie politique*, vol. 1, 364 (bk. 2, ch. 26).
3. Technical conditions, conditions of foresight, etc.

be valid if they explain why an invariably positive rate of interest is necessary both in the extreme case of an economy having stationary technology and perfect foresight and in the case of the dynamic evolution of the real economy in disequilibrium.

Such reasons cannot be traced, as we have seen, to the average psychological preference that people indubitably display for present goods over future goods. For even granting that in some cases a strong average preference for present goods may make a positive interest rate highly probable, it cannot suffice to establish a general rule: it remains perfectly conceivable either that the average preference for present goods should be relatively slight—thus decreasing the likelihood of a positive rate—or else that technical conditions should be such that equilibrium, corresponding to a tangential contact, should be precisely realized at a point at which there is a preference for future goods.[4]

In any event, what is involved is only ever a *probability*, not a necessity, whereas the constant existence of an invariably positive nominal interest rate is a *permanent* phenomenon whose explanation must be derived from *equally permanent* structural data and not from probabilities that are contingent in nature.

In fact, my intention is to show *that the reasons why our economies invariably incorporate a positive interest rate can be found in two quite different ways, one of them based on the private ownership of land and the other on the possibility of storing certain economic goods, money in particular, without appreciable cost.*

As these two explanations are theoretically independent, my presentation will be divided into three parts: the first will assume that there are no storable goods and therefore specifically no money, and that land ownership is entirely in private hands; the second will assume public land ownership and the possibility of storing certain goods, including money; and the third will comprise a synthesis of the first two approaches.

I will then complete my presentation by (a) analyzing how a capital accumulation fund works—an analysis of the greatest value for interest theory—and (b) examining the various kinds of intervention on the capital market available to the State.

4. Note 4 to no. 130, in particular.

2. Rate of interest and private ownership of land (135)

Let us first consider an account-based economy having no money and, we assume, no storable goods.

We have seen that Turgot's fructification theory takes as its starting point the fact that land has a finite value, although regrettably it fails to explore the reasons for this.

Now it is easy to see that in a stationary economic model in which land is privately owned, land value cannot exceed certain maxima, and hence the rate of interest not only cannot become zero or negative, but remains necessarily above an inferior limit.

For as the human life span is limited, it is not conceivable for the ratio of capital owned to annual income to exceed certain values. Hence, as Cassel has rightly underlined,[1] even the most provident find it practically inconceivable that this ratio should reach values on the order of $1000 : 1$. For instance, should an individual have an annual income of 100,000 francs, it is hardly probable, however great his propensity to own and to bequeath,[2] that he should keep intact a capital of 100 million. Even on the hypothesis that he hopes to live another 100 years, he could still multiply his annual income by five while reserving for his children a comfortable legacy of 50 million.

So even if all individuals were provident in the highest degree, we may take it that we should still have for each of them

(1)
$$\frac{C^i}{R^i} < \lambda,$$

using C^i and R^i to denote the capital and the income of the individual in question[3] and using the notation λ for a certain value directly related to the human life span.[4] This would give us

---

1. No. 133.

2. Unless, of course, he is extremely avaricious. But that can only be an exceptional case and cannot be taken to be an average phenomenon.

3. Income R^i includes wages, land rents, and interest payments on capital received by the individual in question.

4. Equation (1) could only be inexact for some individuals if there were a level of income for which they arrived at total satiety. For, if so, once that income had been attained, they would no longer have any further interest in consuming part of their capital, no matter how great that capital might be. However, experience seems to show that even for the wealthiest

$$(2) \qquad \frac{\sum_i C^i}{\sum_i R^i} < \lambda,$$

i.e.,

$$(3) \qquad \frac{C}{R} < \lambda,$$

using C and R to denote total capital and total income for all individuals collectively. Then if the State neither owned nor consumed anything, we should have

$$(4) \qquad C = C_N, \qquad\qquad R = R_N,$$

where C_N and R_N denote the national capital and the national income. From this we obtain

$$(5) \qquad \frac{C_N}{R_N} < \lambda.$$

Now we have

$$(6) \qquad C_N = C_\mu + C_\varphi,$$

if we use C_μ to denote national reproducible capital and C_φ to denote national land capital, and we have

$$(7) \qquad C_\varphi = \frac{R_\varphi}{I},$$

where R_φ denotes the part of the primary income[5] comprised of income derived from land and where we assume stationary conditions with a positive market interest rate I.[6]

---

billionaires, total satiety is practically never reached. For spending possibilities are infinite and while the desire to spend can be rapidly exhausted when personal expenditure is involved, it finds unlimited openings available to it in the distribution of income to others. Under these conditions it is psychologically difficult to imagine that it should in fact be impossible to find a number λ that does not satisfy condition (1).

    5. Equal to the value of the primary factors of production (no. 35).

    6. No. 30. This analytic expression is of course not applicable when rate I is negative, for in that case the capitalized value of land is infinite.

From this, if magnitudes C_μ, R_φ, and R_N vary with the rate of interest it can be taken that they vary relatively little for low interest rate levels.[7] *In first approximation*, they may be taken to be constant. As equation (1) may also be written

(8)
$$C_\mu + \frac{R_\varphi}{I} < \lambda R_N,$$

we necessarily have

(9)
$$I > \frac{R_\varphi}{\lambda R_N - C_\mu}.$$
8,9

This means that *for a given psychological and technical structure of the economy, private land ownership and the existence of a limit superior to the ratio of national capital to national income give rise to the existence of a rate of interest that is not only positive but even superior to a certain*

It will be seen later how the assumption of a positive rate of interest is justified.

7. Equations (15) and (19) and note 11 to no. 47.

8. Note that it follows implicitly from equation (8) where I is by hypothesis positive, that the quantity $(\lambda R_N - C_\mu)$ is also positive.

9. Of course, the inferior limit of I is so much the lower as the influence of private ownership of land (as represented by R_φ) is less, as the preference for future goods (represented by λ) is greater, as income received (represented by R_N) is greater and as the influence of reproducible capital (represented by C_μ) is less.

minimum—even if the different individuals are all particularly provident.[10,]
[11,12,13]

10. So if the rate cannot fall below a certain positive minimum, it is clear a fortiori that it cannot take on negative values. Hence the assumption of a positive interest rate considered at the start is found to be justified (see note 6 above).

11. I stress that even assuming absolute satiety for certain income levels and hence no incentive to decrease the value of the capital owned, no matter how great its value (note 3 above), such a circumstance could only arise, as experience shows, for extremely high income levels. And as the national income is *limited*, it is *impossible* for *all* individuals to enjoy such high income. Hence, if we suppose—as experience attests—that the ownership of tangible capital (including land as well as equipment) is not precisely concentrated in the hands of the few individuals whose satiety would be absolute, all the above observations could be repeated while considering only goods owned by individuals who had not reached satiety.

Finally, it is clear that *even if we admit* (though personally I do not consider it possible) *that there could be an income level that guaranteed absolute satiety*, the result obtained (i.e., the inferior limitation of the rate of interest) would remain entirely valid provided only that we assume—as experience confirms—*that a certain distribution of ownership prevails.*

From this standpoint it would not be so much *private* land ownership that hindered a zero pure rate of interest as the *distribution* of land ownership.

12. If conditions were not stationary, equation (7) would no longer be applicable, but assuming, as is the case in reality, that land yielded an indefinite income in wage terms, we should have, if we use $R_{\varphi m}$ to denote the minimum level of this income,

$$C_\varphi \geq \frac{R_{\varphi m}}{I},$$

and all the points made would remain valid.

Thus it is only the *permanent* quality of land income that matters and not its constancy. *This is precisely what distinguishes land-derived rents from other rents.*

13. It can be shown using these explanations that Cassel's reasoning (no. 133) is insufficient *alone* to demonstrate the impossibility of a zero interest rate. In reality Cassel's argument only yields the following condition

(1) $$\frac{C_N}{R_N} < \lambda,$$

but it does not prove that the ratio $\dfrac{C_N}{R_N}$ necessarily increases indefinitely as the rate of interest tends toward zero, and hence it cannot of itself provide a valid reason for a necessary inferior limitation of the rate of interest. That must involve the variation of land capital with the rate of interest under conditions of private land ownership.

If land ownership were in fact public, everything would depend on how the ratio $\dfrac{C_\mu}{R_N}$ (capital to national income) varied with the rate of interest, i.e., on the technical structure of the economy. But as this ratio remains finite for a zero rate of interest (nos. 45 and 69) the impossibility of lowering the rate of interest to zero would not constitute, under such conditions,

In the event of State intervention in the savings market to increase the supply of capital, it is easy to see that this minimum would be lowered but, as long as land ownership remained private, would never reach zero. For, using C_E to denote the capital owned by the State, condition (3) would become

(10)
$$\frac{C_N - C_E}{R_N} < \lambda,$$

i.e.,

(11)
$$C_\mu + \frac{R_\varphi}{I} - C_E < \lambda R_N,$$

and hence

(12)
$$I > \frac{R_\varphi}{\lambda R_N - C_\mu + C_E}.$$

It is clear that as C_E increases, the second term decreases, but as long as land ownership is private, C_E can never exceed C_μ, so that in any event we shall always have

(13)
$$I > \frac{R_\varphi}{\lambda R_N},$$

a condition that shows that under private land ownership State intervention in the capital market could never lower the rate of interest below a certain minimum.[14]

Indeed, it is easily shown, using a method that is less precise but more direct and intuitive, that when land ownership is in private hands a very low rate of interest cannot be sustained over a long period. For in this case landowners, having all become very rich, would wish to sell part of their land to use the proceeds for immediate expenditure.

---

an ineluctable necessity, at least in an account-based economy. It would then be no more than a possibility.

14. Of course, if the State consumes a part R_E of the national income, inequality (12) becomes

$$I > \frac{R_\varphi}{\lambda(R_N - R_E) - C_\mu + C_E},$$

and the inferior limit of the rate of interest is raised.

But all of these landowners would find themselves in the same dispositions at the same time, whereas non-owners of land would not have the
substantial capital they would need to buy land. And thus the sale price of
land could only fall, and financially motivated investment in land would
thereupon bear a technical interest rate higher than the official interest
rate, which the Government could henceforth only maintain by itself
loaning money over the counter at that rate. Hence the State would be
gradually led to finance the economy's entire stock of capital equipment
as individuals would prefer to put their capital into more lucrative land
investments.

To acquire the necessary funds, the Government would then have to
levy heavy taxes on wealth, the greater part of which would ultimately be
borne by the landowners, since most reproducible capital would then be
owned by the State; this would give the landowners a new, and imperious,
motive for selling their land,[15] which in turn would lead to a new fall in
land prices and an increase in its technical interest rate, thus aggravating
the disequilibrium.

Naturally, this fall in land prices could only be avoided if the State itself
became a buyer in the land market, but such a policy would lead it gradually to buy up all the land, an event excluded by the hypothesis, which
assumes that land ownership remains private.[16,17]

This shows that any systematic lowering of the rate of interest in an
economy retaining private land ownership would swiftly be checked by
physical impossibility. This is one of the underlying reasons why the rate
of interest could never be negative or zero, nor even descend below certain positive values. This reason applies, of course, to every economy having private land ownership, whether in terms of the trends underlying a

15. For the income derived from the land would not suffice to pay the relevant taxes.

16. Granted the initial enrichment of landowners corresponding to the fall in the rate of
interest would not be able to occur if the taxes levied on land-derived income transferred a
sufficient proportion of this income to the State. But such taxation would be tantamount to
indirect appropriation of the land by the State, which is excluded by the hypothesis.

17. Note that this argument alone is not a sufficient proof of the inferior limitation of
the rate of interest as a result of private land ownership. In any event, it can only provide an
intuitive starting point enabling the reader to grasp the underlying psychological reasons for
the inferior limitation of the rate of interest. Readers anxious for rigor are referred to the
simplified models given in appendix II (no. 198, § iii, in particular).

dynamic equilibrium process or the instantaneous movements that characterize dynamic disequilibrium.[18,19]

Possible levels of the rate of interest

We have seen that Cassel endeavored to show that there are intrinsic reasons, connected with the human life span, for the rate of interest to be

18. These observations receive corroboration from consideration of the representative curves of the different values of the rate of interest for the supply and demand of capital C_μ *in equilibrium.*

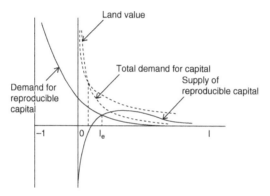

FIGURE 9.4 FOOTNOTE

We have seen (equation [5] to no. 40) that the supply C of capital is a function

$$C = f(C_D,I)$$

of available capital and of the rate of interest, and we have studied the variations of C with I for an available capital assumed to be given. In reality, when the rate of interest varies, the equilibrium value of C_D also varies, and it increases indefinitely when the rate of interest tends toward zero under conditions of private land ownership, owing to the increase in land values. For low levels of I, land value is very great, and the capital individuals want to save is less than the value of the land. This means that the net supply of reproducible capital for low values of the rate of interest is negative: which necessarily entails that the rate of interest is positive. Indeed it is clear that, whatever the demand curve may be, the rate of interest is necessarily higher than the level at which total capital demand is equal to total land value.

   (I stress that the supply and demand curves involved here, which relate to equilibrium values, are naturally different from those considered in no. 48 under disequilibrium dynamics. See the remarks made about this distinction in notes 12 to no. 40, 46 to no. 47, and 18 to no. 97.)

   19. All the points made appeal to intuition, but they may be readily verified by rigorous mathematical study of simple economic models. (See appendix II.)

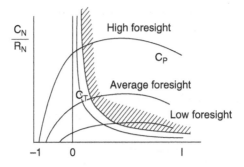

FIGURE 9.5

expressed in hundredths, rather than in thousandths or tenths. *This is a tempting idea but nonetheless wholly false.* The truth is that the equilibrium interest rate depends not only on conditions of a psychological nature but also on conditions of a technical nature.

If we take the values of the ratio $\dfrac{C_N}{R_N}$, the equilibrium interest rate is determined by the intersection of the curves representing this ratio from the technical point of view on the production side and from the psychological point of view on the consumption side.

For production we have

(14)
$$\frac{C_N}{R_N} = \frac{\dfrac{R_\varphi}{I} + C_\mu}{R_\sigma + R_\varphi + IC_\mu},$$

where R_σ denotes the sum of wages paid annually.[20] Hence we must clearly have

(15)
$$\frac{C_N}{R_N} > \frac{1}{I},$$

and we may take it that the curves representing the ratio $\dfrac{C_N}{R_N}$ for production are of hyperbolic shape and in every possible case are located below the equilateral hyperbola $xy = 1$ (fig. 9.5).

In the case of consumption, as the ratio of average capital owned to av-

---

20. No. 37, equation (29).

erage income owned is zero both for very low and very high interest rate levels,[21] it is safe to conclude that the curves representing $\dfrac{C_N}{R_N}$ in terms of consumption display a maximum and are asymptotic to the I-axis.

This means that in theory any value of I is possible; the only positive statement we can make is that if average psychology is such that the ratio $\dfrac{C_N}{R_N}$ is greater than a value λ, the rate of interest is necessarily lower than $\dfrac{1}{\lambda}$.

Thus in an economy in which individuals on average wish to own a reserve equal to five times their average annual income, the annual rate of interest is necessarily lower than 20%. Irrespective of the economy's technical characteristics, *this is the only intrinsic datum the theory allows us to infer.*

More specifically, it is plain that for the present psychology assumed to be given (represented by a certain curve C_P), the rate of interest could perfectly well be expressed in thousandths or even ten-thousandths. Everything depends on the curve C_T representing the technical ratio $\dfrac{C_N}{R_N}$ as a function of the rate of interest.

It is quite clear that, contrary to Cassel's claim, *a superior limitation of the ratio* $\dfrac{C_N}{R_N}$ *does not of itself imply any condition as to the level of the rate of interest.*[22,23]

Finally, it emerges from what has been set out that for every level of the rate of interest, private land ownership has the effect of raising the ratio $\dfrac{C_N}{R_N}$ above the level $\dfrac{C_\mu}{R_N}$ that it would otherwise have. Hence private land ownership has the effect of raising the equilibrium interest rate to a level I higher than level I' that it would have if land were publicly owned.

---

21. No. 40.

22. See the explanations given in note 17 to no. 133.

23. It does indeed seem that hitherto curve C_T has always been characterized by high values for the ratio $\dfrac{C_N}{R_N}$ for the very low values of I (on the order of 1/1,000) and by low values for this ratio for values of I on the order of 1/10. In my opinion, this is the only factor that explains the relatively slight range of variation observed for the rate of interest.

Note that for such a technical structure *supposed unchanged*, multiplying the human life span by ten would increase the value of ratio $\dfrac{C_N}{R_N}$ and thereby certainly lead to rates on the order of 1/1,000, just as dividing it by 10 would lower the value of this ratio and thereby lead to rates on the order of 1/10. *In this sense, and only in this sense, Cassel's point of view is defensible.*

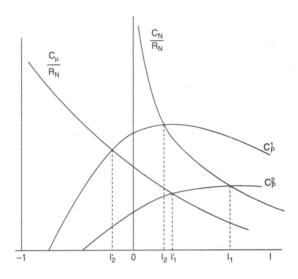

FIGURE 9.6

And this means that public land ownership has, other things being equal, the effect of increasing spontaneous investment C_μ in reproducible capital.[24] In other words, private ownership of land, while satisfying in part the propensities to own and bequeath, entails a proportionate decrease in the incentive to invest.

It also shows that the equilibrium interest rate corresponding to public land ownership is not necessarily negative, i.e., the preference for present goods may suffice on its own to keep the interest rate positive, though, contrary to what Böhm-Bawerk maintains, this need not be the case.[25,26]

24. Since in this case the corresponding rate of interest is lower.

25. All these general observations are confirmed with precision by the simplified economic models studied in appendix II (see in particular no. 198).

26. By this stage, I expect that the reader will realize the fecundity of Turgot's fructification theory and Cassel's annuity theory as starting points for study of the rationale of interest.

The fructification theory starts from the fact that land value is limited, to deduce that a positive rate of interest must necessarily exist, but it does not explain why the value of land necessarily remains finite.

The annuity theory explains why very high values for the ratio of average capital owned to average income are quite inconceivable, but it does not justify the infinite increase in this ratio, on the technical side, when the rate of interest falls owing to the consideration of private land ownership.

Possibility of negative nominal interest rates in equilibrium in the case of price deflation

The foregoing explanations have assumed that the use-value of land remained constant,[27] or at least greater than a certain minimum,[28] thus enabling no conclusion to be drawn except that real interest rates must be positive.

However, if we assume a quasi-stationary model[29] in continuous deflation characterized by a real interest rate i_r, we should only have the condition

(16) $$i_r > 0$$

and the corresponding nominal interest rate

(17) $$i = i_r - \left| \frac{\frac{dP}{dt}}{P} \right|$$

could become negative.[30]

Thus these theories have stressed the basic components of the problem, but they have not made full enough use of them and have not succeeded in establishing an effective link between these components and the theory of why interest exists.

True this link is not an immediate one and for my own part it was only after managing, in a personal way, to make the connection between private land ownership and the necessity of a positive rate of interest in an account-based economy that I realized how close to the real solution were the fructification and annuity theories, although they had not previously retained my special attention.

It is worth pointing out here that Irving Fisher also realized the impossibility of a zero or negative interest rate in an economy having private land ownership (*The Theory of Interest*, pt. 3, ch. 13, § 10), but failed to follow through his idea systematically or even to emphasize it adequately, so that in reading his work I failed to realize its potential.

27. Assuming stationary conditions.

This assumption enables us to write that the value of lands yielding income R_φ is equal to $\frac{R}{I}$.

28. See note 12 above.

29. No. 69.

30. Nos. 97 and 106.

3. Rates of interest, storage, and hoarding (136)

Let us now consider an economy in which land ownership is public, but in which there are goods that can be stored without significant expense. We shall see that this factor necessarily entails a positive level for the rate of interest.

Two cases will be considered, the one moneyless and the other having circulating money.

(i) The case of an account-based economy having public land ownership

Let us assume a good $(\overline{A})$ that is storable from time t to time $t + dt$ subject to a cost of $\sum_A dt$ paid at time t, corresponding to storage charges, and that good $(\overline{A})$ displays liquidity advantages[1] whose value over period $(t, t + dt)$ is equal to $L_A dt$. Let $\bar{a}$ be the price of $(\overline{A})$ at time t, let $\bar{a} + d\bar{a}$ be its expected price at time $t + dt$, and let i be the instantaneous interest rate between t and $t + dt$.[2]

If we have

(1) $$\bar{a} + \sum_A dt - L_A dt < \frac{\bar{a} + d\bar{a}}{1 + i\,dt},$$

i.e., if the present value calculated at the market interest rate of the expected price for time $t + dt$ is greater than the going price at time t plus the costs of storage over $(t, t + dt)$ and minus the liquidity advantages exhibited by good $(\overline{A})$ over the same period, it is worthwhile to store it over that period $(t, t + dt)$.

From this it is clear that as long as inequality (1) obtains, equilibrium cannot exist, as it is profitable for firms to buy or produce good $(\overline{A})$ at time t in order to store it and sell it again at time $t + dt$.

Conversely, if we have

(2) $$\bar{a} + \sum_A dt - L_A dt > \frac{\bar{a} + d\bar{a}}{1 + i\,dt},$$

it is in the interests of firms having a certain quantity of good $(\overline{A})$ in store, to sell it off straight away at time t for price $\bar{a}$. Of course, if there is no

1. No. 84.
2. Notations of no. 33.

stock, inequality (2) does not of itself lead to any particular economic modification.

Finally it can be seen that equilibrium is only possible if we have

(3)
$$\bar{a} + \sum_A dt - L_A dt \geq \frac{\bar{a} + d\bar{a}}{1 + i\,dt},$$

where the equation corresponds to the case in which there is a quantity of good $(\bar{A})$ in storage and the inequality to the case in which there is none.

The implication of condition (3) is plain. If we use p_A to denote the value-gain rate of good $(\bar{A})$ and l_A and σ_A to denote its premiums of liquidity $\dfrac{L_A}{\bar{a}}$ and storage $\dfrac{\Sigma_A}{\bar{a}}$, the condition[3] becomes

(4)
$$i \geq p_A + l_A - \sigma_A.$$

This condition means that equilibrium can obtain only if the value-gain rate plus the liquidity premium and minus the storage premium is less than or equal to the market rate of interest, as the equation necessarily obtains when there is storage.

For instance, if the rate of interest is 4%, it is impossible for a hundred-weight of wheat to be worth 100 francs today and 110 francs next year in a manner foreseeable by everyone today. For if such prices could exist, anyone taking a long position would realize a guaranteed gross profit of 10% (disregarding in first approximation liquidity advantages and the relatively low storage costs). This would lead to wheat hoarding and so many people would be seeking to acquire wheat that its present price would rise to a level equal to the present value of its future price, i.e., $\dfrac{110}{1.04} = 106$ francs, thereby reducing its value-gain to 4%.[4]

Noting that the excess of interest rate i over value-gain rate p_A is the same as i_A, the prevailing market interest rate, if we take good $(\bar{A})$ as unit of value,[5] we can also express condition (4) as

---

3. The storage premium σ_A is simply a particular instance of the conservation premium c considered in no. 81.

4. If a rise superior to the rate of interest was expected for all goods and if the rise in their present prices could not take place because of the insufficiency of the money supply, *it would necessarily be the market interest rate i that would adjust upward*. This fact helps explain why the nominal interest rate rises in time of inflation (no. 106).

5. No. 19.

(5) $$i_A \geq l_A - \sigma_A.$$

From this it emerges that equilibrium can obtain only if the level of the market interest rate expressed in terms of good $(\overline{A})$ is greater than the excess of the liquidity premium over the storage premium.

If stationary conditions are assumed, nominal price $\overline{a}$ is constant, and we have

(6) $$i_A = i;$$

in other words, the different expressions of the rate of interest are equal.[6] This shows that *a stationary equilibrium can prevail only if the market interest rate is greater than the greatest difference* $(l_A - \sigma_A)$.

As some storage premiums are exceedingly low, for instance, those of precious metals, and liquidity premiums are always positive, it follows that in practice the rate of interest can never be negative.

And this shows that *the possibility of storing certain goods without significant cost is a factor that would suffice alone to explain the necessity of a rate of interest that is practically always positive.*[7,8,9]

---

6. No. 19 *in fine*.

7. As the possibility of storing goods prevents the rate of interest from becoming negative, it is worth inquiring whether the use of roundabout production processes that are *physically more productive than storage* (in the meaning of no. 68) is not also, even on its own, able to maintain the rate of interest at a positive or zero level. This is the thesis of the physical productivity theorists already examined in no. 127.

Further, to the points made in no. 127, note that while storage transforms a good available at a given point of time into the *same* good available at a *different* point, roundabout production processes transform goods available at a given point into *different* goods available at a *different* point of time. But, unlike what happens in the case of storage, in this case there is no reason for the value of these goods to be greater than or equal to their primary value (in the meaning of no. 35). And there is therefore no intrinsic reason for the rate of interest to remain positive or zero either.

8. Notable among goods that can be stored at no significant cost is land. The theory of storage thus provides direct corroboration of part of the findings obtained in the previous no. 135 (viz. the impossibility of a negative rate of interest under private land ownership).

9. These findings were stated with precision by Fisher in his fundamental work *The Theory of Interest* (pt. 1, ch. 2, § 3, and pt. 3, ch. 11, § 9), but in my opinion he failed to make sufficiently systematic use of them in his explanation of the rationale of interest.

Note, however, that this necessity would apply only if price levels were not falling. For otherwise the various rates of value-gain are negative and nothing prevents the nominal interest rate from reaching negative levels.

(ii) The case of a monetary economy having public land ownership

If money (M) exists and the circulating currency also serves as accounting currency, we have

(7) $$p_M = 0,$$

so that, since the money is necessarily stored, condition (4) becomes

(8) $$i = l_m - \sigma_M,$$

a condition we have already obtained by a different approach.[10] And this means that if the cost of money storage is negligible, we shall necessarily have

(9) $$i \geq 0,$$

since the liquidity premium of money can only be positive or zero.

As in the case of money it may be taken that adjustment to the conditions of individual equilibrium always occurs, this confirms that the pure market interest rate can never become negative.[11]

Indeed it is plain that *when general economic equilibrium prevails the rate of interest not only cannot become negative but cannot fall below a certain positive minimum either.*

For we have seen that, for a zero interest rate, the demand for money balances is in real terms exceedingly high if not infinite and, hence, certainly greater than the real value of total capital demand.

Under these conditions the net supply of capital for low interest rate levels is certainly negative, and it is clear that *the equilibrium interest rate*

10. No. 84.

11. This finding was noted by Fisher in the first of the passages already cited (note 9 above). Fisher even remarks that in times of rioting or invasion, when the cost of storing money may become substantial, the nominal rate of interest may perfectly well become negative. However, as just indicated, Fisher did not sufficiently expand this subject.

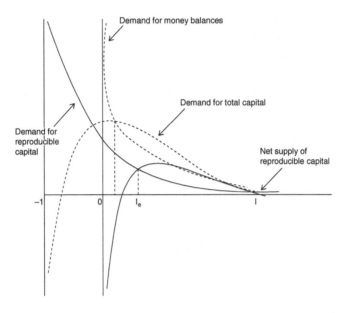

FIGURE 9.7

could never—however low the production sector's demand for reproducible capital might fall—*descend below a certain positive minimum equal to the rate below which individuals prefer to keep all their capital in the form of money.*[12,13,14,15,16,17]

Evidently a policy of lowering the nominal interest rate would swiftly encounter opposing forces, which, in the absence of State funding, would soon become significant.

Indeed a fall in the nominal rate would necessitate progressive State funding of the production sector. This would lead to increased hoarding and a deflation would follow that could be avoided only by massive issuing of new money by the State.

12. This finding has already been noted by Keynes in chapter 17 of his *General Theory*, on "The Essential Properties of Interest and Money," but his text contains numerous errors, chiefly due to a continual want of precision in the explanation.

13. These remarks are easily confirmed using a simple example. Let us assume a stationary model in which land values are zero and total capital demand is independent of interest rate I, being equal to a constant K. Let us further assume that desired money balances increase as rate I decreases, taking, for instance, the following shape:

(1) $$M = \frac{\alpha}{I}.$$

Let us also assume that the demand for reproducible capital C_μ is of the form

(2) $$C_\mu = \gamma - \beta I,$$

and let us use C_E to denote the total capital financed by the State. This gives us

(3) $$M + C_\mu - C_E = K,$$

i.e.,

(4) $$\frac{\alpha}{I} + \gamma - \beta I - C_E = K.$$

(These assumptions are exactly parallel to those made in note 34 to no. 97. However, in the present example conditions are stationary.) It is clear that even if the State financed all reproducible capital, the rate of interest could not fall below the limit value

$$I = \frac{K}{\alpha},$$

for which demand for money would be precisely equal to demand for capital. The rate of interest could only fall lower than this level if the State satisfied money needs by monetary loans, for instance, by issuing demand deposits.

14. It should be specified that the net supply of capital is obtained by deducting total desired money balances from total desired capital, i.e., liquidity needs are met *first*. This is because for a financial investment in the market, the average rate is equal to the market rate, while for money balances the average rate really yielded is higher than the marginal rate equal to the market rate (no. 82). This is why demand for money balances is always satisfied first and justifies the expression "liquidity preference."

15. Indeed to keep the rate of interest above zero it is sufficient that for a zero rate the demand for money balances be greater than the excess of total capital demand over demand for capital in the production sector.

This condition is certainly fulfilled when foresight is imperfect, since in this case the demand for money balances at a zero rate is certainly very great, but this might no longer be so under perfect foresight—a hypothesis that, of course, is of only theoretical interest. In this case, the rate of interest might fall to zero but could not, as has been explained, become negative.

This shows in which respects the theory of the availability of money examined in no. 132 is incomplete. By omitting to specify that the demand for money balances in the vicinity of a zero rate is, under stable prices and imperfect foresight, extremely great, this theory,

CHAPTER NINE

The case in which the unit of account differs from the unit of money

Naturally, these observations are valid only if the circulating currency is identical to the accounting currency. Otherwise they only enable us to write the condition

(10) $$l_M \geq 0,$$

i.e.,[18]

(11) $$i \geq \frac{\frac{d\overline{m}}{dt}}{\overline{m}}.$$

So if money is losing value, there is no reason, from this point of view, why the nominal interest rate could not become negative.[19,20,21]

Moreover, when we note that demand for money balances becomes very great if not infinite as its liquidity premium tends towards zero, it is plain[22] that in any event the liquidity premium of money must always remain higher than a certain positive minimum, *irrespective of monetary policy*. Hence, while it still appears possible for the interest rate to fall to zero, it is *absolutely impossible* for the liquidity premium to do so.

---

considered in itself, cannot in fact demonstrate the impossibility of a zero interest rate. It only proves the impossibility of negative interest rates.

16. These explanations are similar to those already given in no. 85 (see in particular note 5 to no. 85). However, the present subject is overall demands, not variations in these demands.

17. The reader will notice the parallel between this presentation and that of no. 135. Of course, figure 9.7 above supposes public land ownership just as figure 9.4 of no. 135 supposes moneyless conditions.

18. According to equation (11) of no. 82.

19. Figure 8.5 of no. 82 enables us to verify that in this case the demand for money balances at a zero rate of interest remains relatively low.

20. All that can be said is that the monetary interest rate, i.e., the market interest rate calculated in terms of money (no. 19)

$$i' = i - \frac{\frac{d\overline{m}}{dt}}{\overline{m}}$$

is necessarily positive.

21. These observations will be clarified in appendix II, § B (nos. 209 and 210) using a specific case.

22. Using reasoning parallel to that presented above in relation to figure 9.7.

4. Why there is an invariably positive interest rate (137)

What follows from the foregoing is that *the fact of an invariably positive rate of interest must be deemed to be simultaneously due to private land ownership and to the possibility of storing at negligible expense certain goods, particularly money when it is also the unit of account.*

Hence this positive interest rate should not be taken to be a mere contingency due to specific psychological or technical conditions, but rather the outcome of objective conditions, and absolutely inevitable in any economy in which either land is privately owned,[1] or certain goods can be stored at no significant cost, or indeed which uses circulating money as its unit of account.[2]

But it is no less certain that *the existence of an invariably positive interest rate is not an inevitable result* of conditions inherent in human psychology or in the technical structure of production processes, for in an economy with public land ownership, no cost-free storage of goods, and, above all, money undergoing continual depreciation in terms of the unit of account, negative rates of interest might perfectly well be normal.[2]

Of course, even in such a case a strong psychological preference for present goods[3] might *suffice* to bring about a positive rate of interest, but there would be nothing inevitable about it, and no matter how strong the preference for present goods, it would always remain possible, under public land ownership without goods able to be stored at insignificant cost, for the equilibrium interest rate to be negative.[4]

These two factors—private land ownership and the presence of certain goods able to be stored at negligible expense—to which money must be added when it does not lose value over time, are in action at the same time and in the same direction in every dynamic equilibrium with stable prices. But while land ownership and the existence of storable goods apart from money are present only as tendencies in disequilibrium dynamics, owing to economic inertia, the possibility of storing money whose nominal value

1. Provided that the economy is not in continuous deflation (see no. 135 *in fine*).

2. Reminder: the possibility of storing certain goods at no significant cost simply means that the rate of interest cannot in practice become negative; it generally leaves open the possibility that its level might be zero. The same applies to the identity of circulating currency and accounting currency, unless the demand for the latter becomes too strong for a zero rate.

3. In the meaning of note 4 to no. 130.

4. Note 4 to no. 130.

does not decrease over time is constantly at work to prevent the nominal interest rate from becoming negative.

Pure interest rates and value-yields

The remarks just made apply of course to the pure nominal interest rate. We must now examine to what extent their application can be extended to *the rates of interest observed in practice.* We have already seen[5] that these rates are obtained by the equation

(1) $$r = i - l - \mu - \gamma + \alpha + \varepsilon + \rho + c + g;$$

in other words, each of them is equal to the pure interest rate minus the premiums of liquidity, monetary value-gain, and capitalization value-gain, plus the premiums of depreciation, estimated risk and cost of risk, conservation, and management.

When prices and foresight are stable, this equation reduces to the condition

(2) $$r = i - l + \alpha + \varepsilon + \rho + c + g,$$

which, for money, gives

(3) $$0 = i - l_M + c_M.$$ [6]

From this we may deduce that

(4) $$r = (l_M - l) + \alpha + \varepsilon + \rho + (c - c_M) + g.$$

However, as stated above,[7] all liquidity premiums are lower than monetary premiums. And money is certainly the good whose storage cost is the lowest. Since premiums α and g are always positive and it is safe to take the sum $(\varepsilon + \rho)$ as generally positive, it is easy to see why observed value-yield rates r are positive.

5. No. 84, equation (1).

6. Reminder: since c_M is negligible and l_M is positive or zero, this condition led us to the inference that the rate of pure interest i is also necessarily positive or zero.

7. No. 84.

This circumstance, *necessarily* found under conditions of price and foresight stability, has given rise to the *habit* of specifying only positive value-yield rates, *even when price, interest rate, and foresight conditions are undergoing rapid change.*

This is why, in my view, observed rates *r* always remain positive even when prices are moving rapidly upward or a sharp fall in the rate of interest is expected. In this case, rates μ and γ may reach high positive levels, and there is a *theoretical* possibility that *r* rates may become negative as we have

(5) $r = (l_M - l) + \alpha + \varepsilon + \rho + (c - c_M) + g - \mu - \gamma.$ [8]

It should be noted that for certain goods the *r* rates are always necessarily positive or zero. This applies to land and storable goods. In this case, it is clear in particular that when the μ rates are strongly positive, powerful forces necessarily act to raise the corresponding pure interest rates to the levels imposed by the price rise.[9,10]

Rate of interest and real investment

Finally, it should be noted that the normal effect of private land ownership and of the existence of circulating money also serving as unit of account is to keep interest rate *i* not only positive but also above a certain minimum. *Since in equilibrium reproducible capital is a decreasing function of interest rate* i,[11] *the effect of private land ownership and of the use of circulating money as unit of account is to keep its growth constantly below a certain ceiling.* This ceiling is lower as the risk premium associated with investment in reproducible capital is higher, i.e., as foresight and social organization are more imperfect.[12] *It is here, and not in any alleged tendency*

---

8. Reminder: in the case of a general rise in prices we have seen that the consequent increase in nominal interest rate *i* and hence in the liquidity premium l_M only occurs after a certain delay, so that the l_M rise may not suffice to offset the subtractive term $-\mu$.

9. According to equation (1) a positive value for *r* generally leads to a positive value also for the difference $(i - \mu)$.

As to the difference $(i - \gamma)$, it is easy to demonstrate that it is always necessarily positive when rate μ is zero (see, for instance, the case of stable prices in note 9 to no. 33).

10. This mechanism was described in detail in no. 106.

11. No. 47 *in fine.*

12. Note that this risk premium was very high in antiquity.

of mankind to improvidence, that the underlying reasons must be sought
why, after several thousand years of uninterrupted saving, the world has
accumulated so little capital.[13]

13. My opinion, like that of Keynes (*General Theory*, bk. 4, ch. 17, § 5), differs in this respect from the older view of Böhm-Bawerk, as expressed with unusual dogmatism by Marshall in his *Principles of Economics* (581), "Everyone is aware that the accumulation of wealth is held in check, and the rate of interest so far sustained, by the preference which the great mass of humanity have for present over deferred gratifications, or, in other words, by their unwillingness to 'wait.' "

(I note, however, that in the passage referred to, Keynes attributes the exceptionally high risk premium formerly associated with investments in reproducible capital to the alleged existence of a high liquidity premium affecting land ownership at that time. This is but a single instance among a hundred of the kind of confusion constantly met with in Keynes.)

In fact, quite contrary to the opinion of Böhm-Bawerk and Marshall, *I think there are grounds for believing it highly likely that for identical psychological and technical conditions, the spontaneous interest rate that would arise in the event of public land ownership and the continuous depreciation of money over time would have no inferior limit except that due to the possibility of storing certain physical goods such as metals and that it would be practically zero* (see no. 139 below).

5. Effects of indefinite accumulation of capital (138)

Further useful light will be shed on what has been set out above by examining what happens when capital is indefinitely reinvested by an independent organism.

We have seen the astounding speed at which a capital sum increases when the interest thereon is continuously compounded.[1]

> The prodigious sums which result from the reckoning of compound interest always surprise those who have never made such computations. One dollar put at compound interest at 4 per cent would amount, in one century, to $50, in a second century to $2,500, in a third century to $125,000, in a fourth century to $6,500,000, in a fifth century to $325,000,000, and in a sixth century to $16,000,000,000. Beyond this the figures are almost unthinkable in magnitude.
>
> Yet we have few instances in which anyone has endeavored to set aside even one dollar for the benefit of posterity six centuries removed! There is too much reluctance to build for the remote future, even though the attainable results are enormous.[2]

However, more recent times furnish some exceptional examples of such investments. For instance,

> Benjamin Franklin, at his death in 1790, left $1,000 to the town of Boston and the same sum to Philadelphia, with the proviso that it should accumulate for a hundred years, at the end of which time he calculated that at 5 per cent it would amount to $131,000. In the case of the Boston gift, it actually amounted, at the end of the century, to $400,000, and has since accumulated to about $600,000. The sum received by the city of Philadelphia has not increased nearly as fast.
>
> Another interesting case of accumulation is that of the Lowell Institute in Boston, which was founded by a bequest of $200,000 in 1838, with the condition that 10 per cent of the income from it should be reinvested and added to the principal. The peculiarity of this provision is that it applies in perpetuity. There is, therefore, theoretically no limit to the future accumulation thus made possible. The fund, after sixty-seven years, amounts already to $1,100,000.[3]

1. The Fable of the Golden Shilling, no. 18.
2. Fisher, *The Nature of Capital and Income*, pt. 3, ch. 13, § 11.
3. Fisher, pt. 3, ch. 13, § 11.

However, the Fable of the Golden Shilling shows that the indefinite growth of a capital sum so invested is absolutely inconceivable. The question of what would happen if such accumulation were systematically pursued is easily answered.

The case in which land ownership is public and there is no money

Let us first assume, for the sake of simplicity, that land is publicly owned and that there is no circulating money. Let us further assume that the value of the basic wage remains constant and that the State does not intervene on the capital market.

Under these conditions, the total capital owned by individuals reduces to reproducible capital. If the initial capital of the independent Capital Accumulation Fund is C_0 and the rate of interest is $i(t)$, the capital owned by the Fund has a value at time t of

(1)
$$C = C_0 e^{\int_{t_0}^{t} i(t)\, dt}.$$
                                                                    4

Now it follows from what has been set out above that capital used for production remains of finite value in wage terms as long as the rate of interest is positive or zero.[5] It is therefore certain that

(2)
$$C_0 e^{\int_{t_0}^{t} i(t)\, dt} < K,$$

where K represents a certain constant. From this it is clear that inequality (2) can only remain valid if interest rate $i(t)$ decreases toward zero over time.

When the rate of interest reaches zero, capital C has reached its maximum value and can no longer grow.

The speed at which rate $i(t)$ falls naturally depends both on the initial values of C_0 and i_0 and on the propensity to save of other economic agents. If this propensity is strong, the fall in rate $i(t)$ is rapid, as the total supply of capital is, at every point in time, composed of (a) the Fund's capital C and (b) the aggregate of individual supplies.

4. No. 15, equation (2).
5. Nos. 45 and 70 and note 48 to no. 47.

When the rate of interest touches zero, the national capital is well determined by the technical conditions of the production sector[6] and the Fund's capital is equal to the excess of this aggregate capital over the capital supplied at a zero rate by the other economic agents.

The case in which land ownership is private and there is no money

These findings can easily be extended. Let us first assume private instead of public land ownership. In this case, total capital is equal to the sum of reproducible capital plus land, and the latter is equal to the quotient of total land rents by the rate of interest. It therefore rises indefinitely as the rate of interest falls. Condition (2) no longer obtains, but it is still clear that the rate of interest can only fall and tend toward zero. For if it remained higher than a value i_m, capital C would increase indefinitely while reproducible capital plus land remained lower than given values, which is self-contradictory.

It may be inferred that the Fund would be gradually led to buy up all land to use its funds.[7] When all land was owned by the Capital Accumulation Fund and the rate of interest was zero, the Fund would own, in addition to the land, reproducible capital equal to the excess of the demand for capital at a zero interest rate over the aggregate supply of capital at this rate by other economic agents.

The Fund's income from capital assets would now be zero, as the rate of interest would be zero, but it would continue to receive income from its land assets. If the Fund chose to continue to reinvest this income, the capital would increase and the rate of interest would become negative and would fall to the point at which the loss due to negative interest on capital owned by the Capital Accumulation Fund, equal to the excess of aggregate demand for capital at this rate over the supply of capital at the same rate by other economic agents, was precisely equal to the land rent received.

6. Aggregate capital demand for $i = 0$.

7. The capital held by the Fund would be constantly equal to aggregate national capital minus capital held by other economic agents, which remains finite; when rate i fell, this capital would therefore include, in value terms, an ever-greater proportion of land.

The case in which land ownership is private and money exists

Let us now assume a case in which land ownership remains private but there also exists circulating money, the unit of which also serves as unit of account. In this case too it can be shown that the rate of interest must tend toward zero.

It should be noted here that as the nominal interest rate falls, the demand for money balances in real terms increases. Hence if the total quantity of money is taken to be constant, a fall in prices would necessarily result. This deflation, by increasing the real value of the rate of interest, would accelerate the effects of the capital accumulation and bring forward the moment when the nominal interest rate would reach zero.

At that point, the Fund would own, in addition to the land, capital equal to the excess over individuals' supply of capital at a zero rate of (a) the aggregate value of the real capital in industry corresponding to a zero rate and (b) the monetary capital.

Let us take by way of example the case in which this capital is less than total real capital.[8] If the Fund wanted to continue to accumulate its land-derived income, its desire for accumulation could only be satisfied, given the unaltered propensity of individuals to save, by hoarding money, for as the nominal interest rate could not fall below zero because individuals could always store money, real capital could not be increased. On the contrary, as the nominal interest rate could not become negative, the real interest rate could not, in light of price deflation, remain at zero; it would rise, and real capital could only fall.[9] The price deflation would pursue its course and the fall in the nominal value of land rents received by the Fund would check to a certain extent the effects of the accumulation. Since the

---

8. In the other cases, the reader can easily determine, in light of the following explanations, how the economy would develop.

9. We have (from no. 97, equation [6])

$$i_e = i_r + \frac{\dfrac{dP}{dt}}{P},$$

and as i_e remains zero, it is clear that the real technical interest rate i_r would necessarily be positive and that reproducible capital, as a decreasing function of this rate, would fall. This shows that social productivity could not be maximal even though the nominal rate were kept constantly at zero.

value of the capital held by individuals would certainly remain at every moment greater than the aggregate value of land rents, the consequence would be that the continuous accumulation of these rents would never exhaust individuals' capital or, consequently, money, the amount of which would tend toward zero without ever reaching it. Indefinite price deflation would ensue.

Thus in every case the systematic accumulation of the income from capital would bring about a progressive concentration of ownership[10] *and a continuous fall in the market interest rate.* These findings are in fact intuitive. For it is easy to see that the administrators of such a Fund, after the passage of some centuries, would have ever-increasing difficulty in reinvesting its interest payments and that their efforts to do so would have the effect of gradually lowering the market interest rate until it reached zero. From this it would follow that the increase in capital accumulated would become less and less, tending toward zero.

Of course, *these effects would not occur if, parallel to the accumulation, the State became indebted to an equal amount.* In this case, for a constant price level, the effect of the accumulation on the rate of interest would be canceled out, as the increase in the supply of capital would be constantly offset by an equal State debt. The increase in the Accumulation Fund's capital would consist exclusively in Government bonds and there would be no change in the balance of ownership.

In the same way again, supposing that no dynamic equilibrium became established[11] owing to economic hysteresis, a continuous inflation would entirely cancel out the effects of continuous accumulation of the interest accruing on a capital sum. But the explanations given above show that, contrary to what many writers seem to think,[12] such an inflation can by no means be taken to be an inevitable consequence of continuous accumulation. This would only be so if the decision were made to offset the deflationary effect that the accumulation[13] would sooner or later necessarily lead to by adopting continuous inflation of the money stock.

10. Of which the continuous increase in Church property prior to the French Revolution certainly provides an example (even taking account of the legacies that the Church regularly received).

11. I.e., supposing that the nominal interest rate was not equal to the real technical interest rate plus the rate of price increase (no. 97, equation [6]).

12. Note 8 to no. 119.

13. See above.

Independent Capital Accumulation Fund and the repurchase of
land or of public debt

The above explanations have shown that the State could undeniably
buy up the land, if it so wished, by establishing an independent Accumulation Fund.[14]

Notwithstanding the apparent opinion of many writers, it could also
use the same means to redeem the public debt. However, it would obviously be an essential condition of this redemption that the State should
not continue meanwhile to increase its indebtedness and that it should
regularly raise by taxation the sums needed to service its debt. A point
would necessarily arrive at which all Government bonds were held by the
independent Capital Accumulation Fund.

14. Taking the 1913 figures as a convenient starting point, when we had (note 39 to no. 47)

$$I = 3.5\%, \qquad C_\mu = 160 \text{ billion}, \qquad C_\varphi = 80 \text{ billion}, \qquad R_N = 30 \text{ billion},$$

and assuming as a first approximation, also for convenience, a supply of capital independent
of the rate of interest (no. 40), it is clear that State appropriation of land in 1913 would have
had the effect of increasing reproducible capital from 160 to 240 billion.

From there, in light of note 39 to no. 47 and of note 10 to no. 70, it is plain that the rate of
interest corresponding at this period to an equipment stock of 240 billion, can be estimated at
a level of about 1%. At this rate, the land would have been worth about 280 billion.

As the land buy-up is gradual, its cost can be estimated at the average value of
$\frac{80 + 280}{2} = 180$ billion. Now at the average rate of 2.25% a capital sum constantly accumulated from annual payments of 1 billion reaches the value of 180 billion in 72 years. This enables us to estimate that an autonomous Fund annually endowed with a sum equal to 1/30 of
the national income would be able to buy up all land over a period of about 70 years.

Of course if the value-gain of the land brought about by the fall in the rate of interest —
which would truly be excess profit — were subjected to a corresponding tax, the land redemption period would in fact be much shorter, since at an annual rate of 2.25% an annual payment
of 1 billion would enable a capital of 80 billion to be built up in 45 years and this redemption
period corresponding to the sole resource of 1 billion paid each year would be further lowered thanks to rents derived from the tax on the land's value-gain (see volume 1 of my *À la
recherche d'une discipline économique*, no. 163).

When all is said and done, it can be shown that the combination of a capital accumulation
policy with a policy of taxing surplus land profits corresponding to the fall in the rate of interest would enable the land to be bought up in a period of some 20 years.

6. Rate of interest and State intervention (139)

We have seen that the condition on which the maximization of social productivity—i.e., of the output of roundabout production processes—depends is that the rate of interest should be zero. Now as has just been shown, under current structural conditions the rate of interest not only cannot be zero but must necessarily remain greater than a certain positive minimum. *So the question arises whether it is possible to bring the rate of interest down to zero by a judicious modification of structural conditions and by appropriate State intervention.*

Let us recall first of all that under present structural conditions the rate of interest depends in great measure on State intervention.

On the one hand, it has been seen that via rediscount with the Central Bank, the State can finance a proportion of real investments. However, the corresponding range of variation of the rate of interest remains relatively slight.

On the other hand, by acting directly on the capital market, i.e., by adding a supplementary supply to the existing private supply, the State can undoubtedly exert considerable influence on the rate of interest, but it follows from the explanations given above that under private land ownership, with money that does not lose value over time, the consequent fall in the rate of interest would inevitably be limited.[1]

---

1. From the findings of nos. 135 and 136 it follows that the rate of interest could not in fact fall below the level for which the total value of land and desired money holdings exceeds that of total desired wealth.

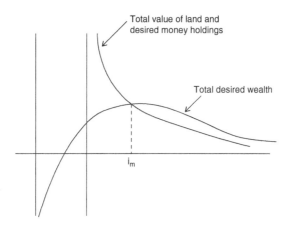

FIGURE 9.8 FOOTNOTE

In fact, it follows from the foregoing that *an effective zero interest rate policy necessarily implies as preconditions public land ownership and depreciation of money in terms of the unit of account.*[2]

If such structural modifications were made, not only would a zero rate of interest be possible, but it is safe to conclude that the spontaneously arising rate of interest would probably be zero or even slightly negative.[3]

In any event it would be considerably less high because the propensity to save previously satisfied by land ownership and by that part of money balances that would be eliminated as a result of monetary depreciation would now find an outlet in capital assets, so that State intervention in the

---

2. We have already seen that this depreciation must be recognized as a precondition of any effective policy of economic stabilization (no. 112).

3. Taking the example of France in 1913, we have seen that for $I = 3.5\%$ we have

(1) $C_\mu = 160$ billion, $C_\varphi = 80$ billion, $R_N = 30$ billion.

In light of the values found for the national production period Θ_N in note 39 to no. 47 and by combining the equations

(2) $C_\mu = \Theta_N R_N, \quad R_N = R_{N\omega}(1 + i\Theta_N),$

it can be deduced that if the rate of interest had fallen to zero this would have implied the following values for R_N and C_μ,

$$R_N = \frac{30}{1 + \dfrac{3.5 \times 6}{100}} \approx 25 \text{ billion}, \qquad C_\mu = 8.5 \times 25 \approx 220 \text{ billion},$$

assuming no change in the basic wage level.

Hence, disregarding money, the real value of which may be taken (under the assumed conditions of continuous depreciation in nominal value) to be unchanged, the total capital available to be owned would have passed from 240 to 220 billion. As we have seen that, insofar as can be judged, the total supply of capital varies little with the rate of interest, it is clear that for a zero rate the supply of capital in 1913 would probably have been superabundant relative to demand.

The fall in the rate of interest would then have been limited only by the possibility of storing at no significant cost certain goods other than money (which, under the conditions assumed, would have been paper, not gold) such as metals.

In any event, bearing in mind that calculations of this kind are *approximate*, it can be seen that the spontaneous rate of interest that would have emerged in France in 1913 in the context of public land ownership and depreciation of money in terms of its nominal value would certainly have been little different from zero.

capital market to keep the rate of interest down to zero, if needed at all, would only be slight in scale.[4,5,6]

4. These remarks will be confirmed in the study of particular cases (appendix II, no. 198, § iii, and no. 210).

5. As maximization of social productivity is practically attained as soon as the rate of interest reaches 1.5% (no. 71), some readers may be wondering whether collectivization of land is really necessary and whether a fall in the pure rate of interest to a level of 1.5% could not be achieved simply by State intervention on the capital market under conditions of private land ownership.

In reality, a fall in the rate of interest to 1.5% in 1913, would have led—assuming unchanged structural conditions (see note 4 above)—to the following values:

$$C_\mu = 200 \text{ billion}, \qquad C_\varphi = 180 \text{ billion}, \qquad R_N = 27 \text{ billion}.$$

In this case, total capital would have passed, in wage terms, from 240 to 380 billion, an increase of 140 billion or 60%. In the absence, for reasons already given, of any grounds for supposing a significant change in total capital demand with the interest rate, we may conclude that lowering the rate of interest to 1.5% would have called for State financing to the tune of 140 billion, i.e., 70% of capital goods then existing (and even then this takes no account of the increase in the real value of desired money balances, assuming unchanged gold-standard monetary conditions, which would further diminish spontaneous savings invested in reproducible capital).

Thus the actual maximization of social productivity under conditions of private land ownership would have meant, in addition to gratuitous enrichment of landowners to the tune of some 100 billion, State appropriation of at least 70% of total reproducible capital.

Detailed discussion, from the economic viewpoint, of the desirability of maximizing social productivity and of collectivizing ownership of land or capital, in whole or in part, is beyond the scope of the present study. I will simply observe that, should it be deemed desirable to maintain private land ownership, such massive collectivization of reproducible capital would in my opinion give rise to much more serious disadvantages than total land collectivization (via buy-up, of course). For experience shows that although it is fairly easy to separate the productive use of land by independent economic agents in conformity with the principles of maximum social efficiency (no. 55) from its ownership, it is much more difficult to realize comparable separation in the case of reproducible capital.

Moreover, *land collectivization and zero interest rates would offer invaluable social advantages*, for in a neutral-money economy having private ownership of capital but not land, all income received would be logically reducible to wages. (For it can be demonstrated, as shown in note 3 to no. 107, that in a neutral-money economy aggregate business profits are zero.)

Finally, land collectivization would also offer considerable advantages in terms of land consolidation and urban and rural planning. (These remarks will be expanded on in § F of chapter 10.)

6. If the pure interest rate i were held at zero and money depreciated at a rate of

(1)
$$\delta = -\frac{\dfrac{\overline{dm}}{dt}}{\overline{m}},$$

we should have, from equation (11) of no. 82

---

(2) $l_M = \delta.$

Thus the liquidity premium of money would be equal to the rate of its own depreciation so that real demand for money balances would be given by the condition

(3) $M^r = M^r(\delta),$

where $M^r(l_M)$ denotes the total real desired balances as a function of the liquidity premium l_M of money (no. 97).

From equation (1) of no. 81, which can be written

(4) $i = \dfrac{a}{a} + \dfrac{\dfrac{da}{dt}}{a},$

it is verified that nominal interest rate i_M corresponding to monetary investment, given by the equation

(5) $i_M = \dfrac{m}{m} + \dfrac{\dfrac{dm}{dt}}{m} = l_M - \delta,$

would indeed be zero, as for any other financial investment.

CHAPTER TEN

Significance of the
General Theory of Interest

A. *Key Aspects of the Phenomenon of Interest*

1. Interconnected roles of the theory of interest (140)

It follows from the foregoing that the rate of interest plays four sharply distinguished but interdependent roles, *viz. in equilibrium*:

1. *In the field of capitalization*, the value of a capital asset at a given point in time may be regarded either as the sum of the present values of its future services,[1] or, for reproducible capital, as the capitalized value of its past primary costs.[2]
2. *In the consumption sector*, the amount of capital saved depends on the level of the rate of interest.[3]
3. *In the production sector*, the level of the rate of interest varies with the amount of capital in existence.[4]
4. And *in conventional monetary economies* the price paid for the use of money is equal to the rate of interest.[5]

Thus the theory of interest is inevitably complex and multifaceted. No single explanation of the interest phenomenon can or ever will exist, any more than hydraulics can admit an explanation of the equilibrium pressure

---

1. No. 36, equation (1).
2. No. 36, equation (2).
3. No. 40.
4. No. 45.
5. No. 81.

in one of a series of communicating vessels that takes only that one vessel into account.

The phenomenon of interest can only be understood by successive analyses of its interactions with the key variables in each field in which it plays a role, followed by a systemic approach in order to obtain an overview of how the whole mechanism works. Nothing, I think, could be harder to achieve, but nothing is more necessary.

Some authors, such as Fisher, have compared the interest mechanism to the operation of a pair of scissors. This analogy argues that just as it is the relative movement of the blades that alone enables the scissors to work, not the movement of one blade alone, so the rate of interest is determined by the interaction of the propensity to save and the propensity to invest, and thus any theory that takes account only of the psychological dispositions of individuals or of the technical characteristics of production must be false.

But in reality this point of view is itself quite inadequate. The phenomenon of interest is much more complex yet. There are not just two interacting processes to take into account, there are four. And even then the phenomenon of interest cannot be reduced to these four without giving an oversimplified impression of reality.

In the first place, each of these main interactive processes cannot be reduced to a single element: each one comprises a great many. Thus the rate of interest earned by a firm depends on the volume of capital invested in it. Similarly, the rate of interest in a given country depends on the volume of capital invested in that country. And in the same way again, the total amount of real capital investment in the world corresponds to a well-determined level of the international rate of interest. Only in equilibrium do these different rates coincide.

Moreover the different pure interest rates, which are equal in equilibrium and are the only rates that can be compared to one another, do not act directly at all. Their action is only indirect and implicit for they are merely specific components of the observed rates of interest or of capitalization, which also include every kind of premium.[6]

---

6. It should also be stressed that the equality of the pure interest rates is only realized in equilibrium in the case of perfect foresight; when foresight is imperfect the effect of these premiums in equilibrium is to maintain the different pure interest rates at *unequal* levels.

Thus the pure interest rate yielded by a firm, i.e., the marginal productivity of the capital invested in it, minus the corresponding risk premium, is not equal to the pure interest rate

Both these reasons make the phenomenon of interest a highly complex one.

Of the four roles enumerated above, only the one concerning the relation between saved capital and the rate of interest has so far been the subject of serious study. But however great their intrinsic interest, they are clearly inadequate as the basis for a theory of interest. Analysis of provision for the future and the propensity to save is interesting, but it is not of itself essential for comprehension of the *mechanism* of interest, any more than it is necessary to analyze why people prefer beef to mutton in order to understand price theory.

Hitherto the role of the rate of interest in production has been insufficiently analyzed, though Böhm-Bawerk's penetrating analyses, especially regarding the distinction between value productivity and physical productivity and the notion of the production period, have considerably cleared the ground. Yet this is a role that it is quite essential to understand completely.

Again, one of the greatest difficulties in the theory of interest arises from the fact that *the magnitude called "capital" is not a physical magnitude, like a quantity of wheat or of wine, but an economic magnitude, the value of which depends directly on the level of the rate of interest.* This difficulty has not been widely grasped.

The classical authors used to say that the rate of interest is determined by the intersection of the supply and demand curves for capital, which is true, but its failure to point out that these supply and demand curves were themselves directly dependent on the rate of interest constitutes a major lacuna in their theory. For in reality capital supplies and demands are functions not only of the rate of interest I but also of the prices of durable goods that depend directly on this rate. To every level of interest rate I there correspond well-determined prices of the various durable goods and hence also well-determined capital supply and demand curves. Their intersection gives the instantaneous equilibrium rate I_e of the capital market, *but this rate* I_e *can only correspond to a durable equilibrium if the rate of interest characterizing the corresponding supply and demand curves is precisely*

---

yielded for the saver, since in equilibrium, simply owing to the risk factor, marginal productivity must be greater than the pure rate of interest by an amount equal to a *double* risk premium as the risks are counted twice (note 7 to no. 84).

   This difference between the interest rates implies the substitution of conditions of inequality for conditions of equality and recourse to complex arithmetic reasoning instead of much simpler differential reasoning.

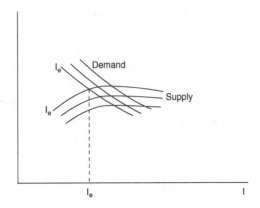

FIGURE 10.1

the rate I_e.[7] The economic mechanism has the effect of bringing about this adjustment, but the factors that bring about the adjustment are by no means so simple as those that the classical analyses seem to suggest.

Finally, the monetary role of interest theory, although it has been sufficiently analyzed *in itself*, has not been the subject of the much-needed analyses that alone could fully bring out its absolutely fundamental relation with the other three interconnected roles. As stated above,[8] a thorough understanding of this role and its interconnections comprises the central difficulty around which gravitates the whole of contemporary economic thought.[9]

An accurate overview of the simultaneous interplay of these four basic roles is made harder to obtain by the fact that *the differences between the properties of dynamic disequilibrium, representing immediately observable reality, and those of dynamic equilibrium, representing its underlying tendencies, are more pronounced here than in any other sector of the economy.*

As we have seen, whereas in dynamic equilibrium the rate of interest depends, as a first approximation, only on the balance of the first three interconnected roles, being largely *unaffected* by the fourth, i.e., the money stock, in dynamic disequilibrium, by contrast, the monetary effect *preponderates* and the observed rate of interest depends closely on variations in

7. See no. 48.

8. No. 96.

9. In view of its importance this issue will be the subject of a specific analysis in the following section (no. 141).

the quantity of money, so that although the rate of interest indeed appears in equilibrium as the regulatory parameter par excellence of savings and investment, this factor acts only as a tendency in the dynamic disequilibrium process of the real economy.

This brings out the complexity of the role played by the rate of interest in our economy and the fact that any theory involving only one of these aspects cannot in reality be more than a part of the complete explanation. In particular, as recalled above, the theory of the determination of the rate of interest by the intersection of the supply and demand curves for capital cannot be accepted as more than a partial theory, for these curves themselves depend on the level of the rate of interest; but though it is insufficient of itself to provide a complete and therefore satisfactory explanation of interest, this theory is nonetheless necessary insofar as it relates to the study of one of its most fundamental aspects.

In fact it is to the diversity of the aspects of interest, whether concerning its different fields of action (capitalization, consumption, production, money balances) or its modalities (use or exchange premium, capital, or money) that we must attribute the basic reason for the considerable difficulties constantly confronted by theoreticians of interest.

2. Capitalistic and monetary aspects of
the phenomenon of interest (141)

I have already pointed out more than once[1] that one of the most important difficulties facing economists is how to explain clearly the relationship between the general theory of prices in an account-based economy having no actual money and the general theory of money, between the capital-based theory of the rate of interest as the use-value of capital, determined by the balance between the propensities to save and to invest, and the monetary theory of the rate of interest as the use-value of money determined by the relation between the amount of money in circulation and desired money balances; and I think it may be stated without rashness that this is the *last fundamental obstacle* to be surmounted by economic theory for it to become a genuinely coherent whole.

It should be borne in mind that *for an initial period* lasting until about the middle of the 18th century, the monetary theory of interest was dominant. As loans tended to be made in money, it is all too comprehensible that money should at first have been taken to be the essential object of loans and that variations in the rate of interest should have been attributed to an excess or a lack of specie.

During the ensuing *second period*, which may be situated between the middle of the 18th century and the end of the First World War, the dominant conception was that, all things considered, money plays only an intermediate role in loans and that loans essentially consist in a temporary transfer of claims on capital. Throughout this period, interest theory was founded on the hypothesis that money was merely an accidental and very secondary form of the transfer of capital and that any clear explanation of the dependence of the rate of interest on the capital market must abstract from money altogether. There is no doubt that this was a fruitful theory, as it enabled interest theory to emerge from the earlier confusion between money and capital and, by emancipating it from the theory of money, made it possible to study the balance between savings and investment separately.

But it is no less certain that this theory cannot be accepted except as a first approximation. For any theory of interest that disregards the influence of monetary conditions (money stock and liquidity preference) on

---

1. Nos. 9, 78, 96, and 101.

the rate of interest is assuming, consciously or otherwise, a stationary equilibrium, which makes it quite unable to take cognizance of the link between the interest rate and monetary conditions and hence to grasp the intricate cause-and-effect mechanism that characterizes real economic life and tends to fix the rate of interest and the general price level at their equilibrium values.

The classical system only made sense, as a *direct* representation of concrete reality, under very special conditions, which are hard to bring about in the real world. For it is only in an environment of stationary equilibrium that the rate of interest coincides with the real interest rate and may be taken to result, in first approximation, from the balance between the propensities to save and to invest. By assuming such conditions, the theory is overwhelmingly simplified because expected prices are equal to present prices and the interest rates of one period need not be distinguished from those of another.[2]

Such a simplification could be justified only as a first approximation, and in order to come to closer grips with reality it is indispensable in second approximation—as has been rightly emphasized in a *third economic period* by the contemporary school and as I have myself tried to do—to take account of variable structural conditions and the uncertainty of the future. *Only* this second approximation, which brings into simultaneous play the psychological propensity to save (consumption sector), the psychological evaluation of the future yield of capital and the propensity to invest (production sector), and finally the psychological attitude to liquidity and the determination of money demand (monetary sector), can make it possible to weave into a coherent whole the general theory of the formation of the different prices, the theory of money, and the theory of the rate of interest.

I hope I have succeeded in showing how intricate and demanding such a synthesis must be.

If it is to be fully understood, the theory of interest calls for the successive and minute analysis of its various interconnected roles, under both dynamic equilibrium and dynamic disequilibrium. It is closely connected with monetary theory, from which it can only be separated in first approximation.

It also requires the rejection of the outrageously simplistic views of those who see in the interest rate nothing but the price paid for the use of capital as well as the views of those who insist on taking it only as the price paid for the use of money.

2. No. 17.

Such a synthesis shows that all the discussions that have taken place between the partisans of the capital-based theory of interest and those of the
monetary theory are perfectly parallel to those in which the theoreticians of
marginal value were opposed to those of the "production cost" value, that
they are quite as vain and are generally based on confusion between the
dynamic equilibrium of a stationary economy, where it is right to stress the
interest rate as use-value of capital, and the dynamic disequilibrium of an
economy of variable prices, where the stress rightfully belongs on the interest rate as use-value of money.

In studying the phenomenon of interest, no partial theory can be true
except insofar as it is a part of a whole; considered in isolation it can lead
only to errors. Thus in the dynamic development of an economy in disequilibrium, it is the monetary theory of interest that wins the day; but if
instead we examine the underlying tendencies of the economy, corresponding to dynamic equilibrium, it is the capital-based theory of the classical
economists that should be studied ever more deeply; but neither the one
nor the other can be considered as sufficient in itself. *In fact they are complementary rather than contradictory.*

3. Ubiquity of the interest rate (142)

The essential character of the phenomenon of interest is its ubiquity. *For there is no sector of the economy in which it does not act, explicitly or implicitly, playing a major role.*

Take value: the various prices in general are in fact nothing but the present values of future income streams and thus depend directly on the rate of interest.

If we take the income circuit, the distribution of individuals' expenditure at a given point in time is directly related to the rate of interest, which is the determining factor in the division between present and future consumption, between immediate expenditure and saving. In the same way, the distribution of the national income among the different stakeholders (workers, landowners, capitalists, entrepreneurs) depends directly on the level of the rate of interest.

Turning to the technical structure of production, its entire edifice depends, as we have seen, on the level of the rate of interest, which determines whether the production processes used are to be more or less roundabout.

And in the same way again, the determination of money balances in real terms, the adjustment of price levels to this real value, and the amount of money in existence are all directly related to the phenomenon of interest. The functioning of the entire monetary mechanism is built on the interplay of reciprocal disparities in the rate of interest.

Finally, these different interrelations play their respective roles both in the national and the international context.

Hence the phenomenon of interest is ubiquitous in the economy. It is met with everywhere, and the different roles it plays are closely interconnected. Obviously, they can be distinguished rationally and studied separately for ease of exposition, but this can be no more than a study aid: *for genuine comprehension there can be no substitute for considering the economic system as a whole.*

The fact is, however, that this is *an extremely demanding* task. We can have direct intuition only of those mechanisms that involve just one of these interconnected roles, while the others act only as corrective factors. The same applies, for example, to the gravitation of the earth around the sun. The principal action is that of the sun. The action of the moon or the stars is exerted only as a corrective factor. It is thereupon possible to obtain an idea that is both simple and correct by studying these different actions successively and separately. But this would no longer be the case, of course, if the sun, the earth, and the moon were of comparable mass. In that case, the problem would become much more complicated, and intuition could play only a secondary role.

Now it so happens that in almost the whole field of the phenomena studied in physics this division of complex phenomena into simple, elementary phenomena is possible. In general, a single dominant phenomenon is found that is comparatively easy to analyze. This fact, although seldom stated explicitly, hugely facilitates our understanding of physical phenomena.

In economics too it is usually possible to subdivide complex phenomena into simpler elements in order to study them. Whether it is the market for a particular good that must be studied or the action of an individual or firm, it is safe to regard the rest of the economy as given and study in isolation how the small sector in question adjusts to equilibrium. The overall equilibrium may be taken, as a sufficient approximation, to result from the combination of the former general equilibrium and of the partial equilibrium studied separately.

I have described this method of reasoning as *additive reasoning*.[1] It basically consists in considering an economy in equilibrium and examining what would occur if a new component was introduced. For instance, if a given area of new land is added, there will be little effect on overall prices if the area involved is small; price levels may be taken to be unchanged, and the ground rent of the new land will emerge as determined by the difference between the preexisting market price and the production cost corresponding to the land.

This additive reasoning, applicable as it is to every category of goods or services, is no longer applicable when the phenomenon of interest is being considered. An economic equilibrium involving time cannot be deduced by simply modifying an economic equilibrium from which time is absent. This is the key to the exceptional difficulty of interest theory.

This difficulty is of the *same nature* as that displayed by the theory of social efficiency,[2] for there too no one part of the economy can be considered in isolation: only the overall structure matters. The interdependences are essential. But the difficulty of the theory of interest is *far greater in degree*. For although it is perhaps less difficult in purely mathematical terms, interest theory is economically far more complex.

1. See my *À la recherche d'une discipline économique*, no. 223.
2. No. 55.

The reason for this is that the theory of social efficiency can be grasped in a single thought, whereas interest theory, though simpler in each of its component parts, requires thought to progress through several successive stages and cannot be grasped as a whole except via the intuitive idea—clear in its overall conception, but relatively vague and imprecise in its specific applications—that can be had of the mutual interdependence of parameters connected by simultaneous conditions.

This difference may fittingly be compared to two views of the same landscape, one capturing abundant fine detail in a single view, the other encompassing the entire horizon in a much less detailed circular panorama, the individual parts of which have to be viewed one by one in a successive process. Each part of the circular panorama is simpler in its detail than the snapshot with its greater detail but narrower field, but because of its greater scope and the sheer physical impossibility of viewing all its parts at once, the mind can only obtain an overview of the circular panorama at the cost of a much greater effort.[3]

In real economic life, all the mechanisms directly connected to the rate of interest are so interconnected in their diversity that it is impossible to isolate any of them. Interest theory must take this state of affairs into account. Granted it cannot avoid the need to examine one after the other, chapter by chapter, the various interdependent roles involved, but it cannot claim that any of these studies is complete in itself. Such a division is impossible. It is in the nature of things that each separate study should leave unexplained certain facts the explanation of which must be found in another chapter.

This is why it is so exceptionally difficult to treat the interest mechanism as a whole. The interest rate is an omnipresent parameter that plays a key role in *all* the markets at once. The least of its variations immediately sends tremors through a whole range of sensitive and closely interdependent sub-mechanisms.

Moreover, while costs and risks play roles in the markets for goods other than capital and money, which can safely be disregarded in first approximation, it so happens that in the case of the interest mechanism, which is already so difficult on account of its ubiquity, these costs and risks play a role that is absolutely fundamental and cannot be disregarded without

3. On a personal level, I may say that finalizing my presentation of the theory of restricted social efficiency (no. 60) took me less than a month, whereas finalizing my presentation of the theory of interest took me more than 50 months of continuous, sustained reflection.

gravely distorting reality. Hence a multitude of premiums must be introduced, and instead of differential reasoning, arithmetical reasoning that is far more complex must be substituted.

These difficulties explain the obstacles that economists have hitherto met in constructing a satisfactory general theory of interest.[4] In reality the entire economy would need to be remade for such a goal to be attained.

In this context it cannot be too strongly emphasized that any theory of interest necessarily coincides with the theory of the overall economic mechanism, including the study of the main interconnections between the principal economic sectors. The phenomenon of interest cannot be understood without a clear view of the overall economic mechanism, and vice versa.[5]

My own study is therefore in fact no more than a general theory of the fundamental interconnected economic sub-mechanisms in which the accent is systematically placed on the phenomenon of interest; it is and can be no more than a broad outline, depicting an extraordinarily complex mechanism.[6]

It has been pointed out,[7] for good reason, that the construction of a theory such as interest theory is an exceedingly delicate undertaking in which perfection, no doubt, will never be attained. I trust that the theory set out herein, though doubtless far from what it may one day become, nevertheless represents significant new progress toward clarity.

---

4. To these purely scientific difficulties must of course be added those due to all the ethical, social, or political prejudices, conscious or otherwise, that are constantly met with in the different theories of interest (see no. 116) and that tend to deflect the arguments in the direction of some position already held for other reasons, and those due to long habits of thought, never submitted to honest examination, such as that which inclines our mind *at the outset* to refuse to accept the notion of negative interest.

5. I personally arrived at overall understanding of the economy only by detailed study of the problem of interest. Indeed, it was this study, to which I was led by reading Irving Fisher's seminal *The Theory of Interest*, that was the *fons et origo* of all my work.

6. One effect of these different facts is that the reader will only be able to achieve an accurate understanding of the phenomenon of interest by undertaking to read the work twice. For only after obtaining an overview by an initial perusal will he be enabled to grasp in their entirety the different parts of this work. Here more than anywhere, the mind needs to alternate continually between the particular and the general, between analysis and synthesis. But the goal to be attained is well worth the effort demanded!

7. A. Landry, "La théorie de l'intérêt d'après Irving Fisher," *Revue d'économie politique*, 1934.

4. Need for mathematical logic and of abstraction (143)

Need for mathematical logic

Study of the close interdependence between the various economic mechanisms involving the theory of interest indispensably demands recourse to the part of general logic that we call mathematics.

Everyday modes of logic are in fact quite inadequate for analyzing relationships of interdependence and studying the effects of their simultaneous interplay. To attain an overall grasp of the phenomenon of interest it is therefore imperative to resort to a more sophisticated process than everyday logic. "*Now there is only one way to encompass the various components of a complex phenomenon in a single argument, viz. to translate the interreactions of these various components into a series of simultaneous equations.*"[1]

Note that, notwithstanding an opinion sometimes met with, there is no opposition between everyday logic and mathematical logic. The latter simply extends and perfects our everyday reasoning process, thereby substantially increasing both our deductive powers and the range of subjects to which they may be applied.

Mathematical analysis is simply a *specialized* reasoning-machine — one that can only operate with a special category of concepts: those that represent magnitudes and are condensed into the form of symbols by means of a definition. This machine *automatically* yields "the result of complex intellectual operations by applying purely formal rules to the initial symbols."[2]

Whenever relatively complex interdependences are involved, as is usually the case when more than two simultaneous conditions apply, this is *the only* approach that enables the effects of their collective interplay to be determined.[3]

Even in the exceptional, simpler cases in which the solutions to the problems being studied could be arrived at by the rules of common logic, the mental effort needed to explain or understand the demonstrations by this

---

1. J. Moret, *L'emploi des mathématiques en économie politique* (Paris: Giard, 1915), 25. Emphasis mine.

2. J. Rueff, *Des sciences physiques aux sciences morales* (Paris: Alcan, 1922), 25.

3. The examples studied in the appendixes (nos. 171 to 221) show how *childish and presumptuous* it is to claim to be able to deduce by simple verbal reasoning the resultant effects of simultaneous interdependent mechanisms. Reality is far too complex for any such approach to work.

means alone would be far greater than is needed to assimilate once and for all the elements of the various branches of mathematics.

For instance, any attempt to provide rigorous proof of the theorem of social productivity[4] without recourse to mathematical logic would require—if such a thing were possible at all—a huge number of pages and would call for extraordinary efforts of attention and abstraction on the part of even the most talented reader. And such an effort would be quite futile as it can easily be avoided!

Indeed, not only is mathematical logic indispensable for studying the branch of economics concerned with equilibrium dynamics, i.e., relations of interdependence, but it also offers invaluable help in the context of disequilibrium dynamics, i.e., of cause-and-effect relations. For although everyday reasoning processes may suffice in the latter case, the guidance furnished by their labyrinthine deductions usually proves very imperfect, obscure, and superficial, whereas the systematic use of mathematical symbols, by condensing and simplifying the argument, makes our thought processes easier and more penetrating to an extent that the uninitiated would never suspect but that no one who has tried it would agree to give up.

The mathematical method has often been taxed with having no positive discovery to its credit. The facts alone suffice by way of reply. If the reader recognizes that the findings set out in the present study are of great importance and could not have been reached or even understood except by mathematical deduction, this work alone stands out as a vivid demonstration of the fruitfulness of the mathematical approach. The present writer, without venturing beyond the limits of his own personal experience, can declare that *not one* of the original conclusions set out herein could have been reached without this powerful analytical tool, *which no difficulty can resist* when the trouble is taken to use it appropriately.[5]

The phenomenon of interest offers an indisputable illustration of the absolute necessity for economics to make use of mathematical logic if it is not to become inextricably bogged down in the sort of verbiage that can strike even the most powerful minds irredeemably barren. *Experimental proof* of this has been provided by the centuries of debate during which the greatest endeavors of minds, some of them undoubtedly exceptional, were never able to construct a theory universally recognized as valid. This is a fact that will not be difficult to explain for anyone willing to reflect on *the*

4. No. 69.
5. Who would dare say as much of ordinary logic?

difficulty—in my view insuperable—that would be entailed by any attempt to give unassailable and convincing expression to the key findings of the present study using only the common logical processes, without failing either in rigor or in ease of assimilation.

Admittedly some thinkers[6] refuse to face the facts. In their view, there exists an entity called "mathematical economics," purely ideal and without any practical utility, that happens to appeal to a handful of thinkers in their ivory tower whom they refer to (in an unmistakably significant tone of voice!) as "theorists"—unhappy creatures who live utterly divorced from reality in the phantom world of their abstractions. They see no interest in mathematical economics except to satisfy curiosity. The more benevolent of them are ready to display their generosity to onlookers by accepting the newcomers into the family circle, but they take care to relegate them to the lower end of the table, reserved for poor relatives. The others, for whom no further problems remain to be solved, never stop deprecating the devotion of so much effort to such barren endeavors.

The sheer accumulation of so many declarations, imperturbably and tirelessly trotted out, might succeed in breeding disquiet among the host of the undecided if history were not there to provide us as often as needed with a salutary reminder of the stories of the reactionaries (they have always existed!) of yesteryear. To take only astronomy, did not Galileo's adversaries sneer at him for being a "theorist cut off from reality" who undertook—what a scandal!—to use mathematics for the advancement of astronomy?[7] However improbable such events may now seem, they are found in every age. The dawn of every new science has invariably been decried by the metaphysicians of the day with the pompous verbiage of their counter-argumentation. But time is on the side of truth and often enough the very names of these gainsayers are only spared oblivion thanks to the immortality of the works they jeered at. I have no doubt that three centuries hence the incomprehension or even hostility (whether open or covert)

6. I say "some" because happily there are many others, including—I am happy to say— the most eminent authorities in our Faculties of Law [Economics was treated as a subsection of Law in French universities until 1959.—Trans.], who, though not formally trained in mathematics, have displayed highly praiseworthy perspicacity in recognizing the role that must be played by mathematical thought in economics to make it an exact science in the same way as physics or mechanics.

I wish prompt success to their efforts to modernize the spirit prevailing in certain quarters and to reform the teaching of economics in France.

7. V. Pareto, *Les systèmes socialistes*, vol. 1 (Paris: Giard, 1926), 285.

that some of our "literary" economists continue to display toward mathematical logic will appear to philosopher-historians quite as incomprehensible as the attitude of Galileo's adversaries appears to us today.

There are clear signs that progress in this direction is already underway. Is it not symptomatic that we are seeing young law professors plunge into the study of mathematics? Indeed, have we not recently seen provision made in the context of our faculties of law for the teaching of mathematics as a preparation for the study of economics?

This progress can only continue. Indeed, *"it seems perfectly clear that economy, if it is to be a science at all, must be a mathematical science,"*[8] because the magnitudes it treats of do not cease to be magnitudes because of their economic character, and the study of the relations between magnitudes pertains essentially to mathematical logic. *Indeed, even those who refuse to use it explicitly cannot refrain from frequent implicit recourse to it,* and thereby "continually betray in their language the quantitative character of their reasonings,"[9] but *hoping to make quantitative deductions without explicit recourse to mathematical logic is condemning oneself to impotence.* The facts speak for themselves. There is no instance of an economist having received a mathematical education who has not felt, to a greater or lesser degree, the need to call upon it in the study of economic problems and who, having once tried this approach, has not continued to use it. Every day new converts subscribe, and *the day is not far off when the study of economics will begin with compulsory study of general mathematics.*

Need for abstraction

Some will no doubt find fault with this study for being too theoretical and abstract. My answer, once again, is (a) that *theory is simply a condensation of reality into a simple, outline form,* and (b) that amid the diversity and sheer quantity of the relevant facts, there is no way of unravelling the broad outline of the basics except by disregarding all that is secondary—at least in first approximation.

Such is the aim of the present study with regard to the phenomenon of interest. I am the first to recognize that it is imperfect and incomplete. *It is no more than a first approximation. My overriding ambition is simply for*

8. S. Jevons, *The Theory of Political Economy*, preface to the second edition. Emphasis mine.

9. Jevons, preface to the second edition.

the present study to be, of all first approximations currently possible, the one that will seem most satisfying to the reader and will best clarify in his mind the basic interconnections of the economic machine.

The fact is, and it cannot be too strongly emphasized, that

> *we do not know and never shall know any concrete phenomenon in all its details; we can only know ideal phenomena which correspond ever more closely to the concrete phenomenon.*

Let us take a very simple example. Suppose we are studying the shape of the earth. It is already of the highest importance to know that the earth resembles a spheroid in form, but it is only a first approximation. Astronomy does not press its inquiries beyond the study of this basic shape. Geography provides us with a second approximation: upon the spheroid representing the earth, it sketches in the seas, continents and islands and depicts the mountain ranges, rivers and the abysses of the oceans. Topography offers a third approximation: it takes account of hills, knolls and streams. But no description of the surface of the globe will ever be able to do justice to every tiny molehill and pebble.[10]

In the same way, the study of pure economics tells us the general form of the phenomenon; the study of the real economy provides a second approximation, but no theory will ever contrive to include an account of the economic life of each individual and of every enterprise.

Besides, what matters for us is not to reach a sort of all-embracing knowledge that would drown us in documents and render us powerless to act; we need a usable synthesis to enable us to act effectively. Moreover, "*Anyone who embarks on practical experimentation without first seeking the light of understanding by serene reflection on the level of speculation and theory is exposing himself to the setbacks to which empiricism is liable.* I do not deny that it may often enough be preferable to run the risk of such disappointments rather than to remain inactive, indeed I think it is a necessity of the human condition, but this necessity is no excuse for overlooking the fundamental practical importance of rational research."[11]

10. V. Pareto, *Cours d'économie politique*, vol. 1 (Lausanne: Rougé, 1896), 16. Emphasis mine.

11. F. Divisia, *L'épargne et la richesse collective* (Paris: Sirey, 1928), introduction, iv. Emphasis mine.

Need for precise terminology

I may also be reproached for introducing a whole new terminology, and one that (like every terminology) is ultimately arbitrary. But however the problem of terminology may be resolved, the solution selected in the present work deserves to be welcomed by all those who are tired of the babel currently prevailing in economics, for, whatever its drawbacks, it has the overriding advantage of being precise and therefore does not lend itself to confusion.

For in reality, "*it does not so greatly matter what name we select by which to call a concept. The important matter is to select for consideration those concepts which are fruitful in scientific analysis.*"[12]

Indeed the gravest errors to have gained currency in economics have been due to the obscurity that too often continues to enshroud the basic concepts. And study of the problem of interest has suffered especially from the habit of reasoning about concepts that have been insufficiently analyzed and of drawing dialectical conclusions from words whose meaning has been only vaguely or obscurely grasped: this has led to confused and sterile debates that have simply suffocated the finest minds.

Future of mathematical thinking

There has been much debate about the best method to use in economics and doubtless much more is still to come. My own view is that "a *good method*, like a *good workman*, is recognized by its results."[13] With regard to this study, the only question is whether it could be expounded and made comprehensible with equal clarity and rigor using everyday logic alone.

Whatever directions the science of economics may take in the future, one thing seems to me certain already. Economists, their critical spirit once aroused, will declare themselves increasingly dissatisfied with solutions that do not respect the most rigorous demands of science, and an irresistible tide will carry us each day farther from "the danger that rest may be found in one of those shallow solutions which are easily embodied in convenient catchwords but cannot be systematically thought out to the end."[14]

---

12. Fisher, *The Nature of Capital and Income*, ch. 4, § 7. Emphasis mine.

13. Pareto, *Cours d'économie politique*, vol. 1, preface, iii. Emphasis mine.

14. Eugen von Böhm-Bawerk, *Geschichte und Kritik der Kapitalzins-Theorien* [History and critique of interest theories], end of the appendix to the second edition (1900). Translated into English as *Recent Literature on Interest* by Dr. William Scott (London: Macmillan, 1903).

So if the vicissitudes and obscurity of the world we live in allow the future to be predicted, it can only be the imminent and definitive triumph of mathematical methodology in economic theory, for there is no example of ramparts powerful enough to arrest the progress of an advancing truth.

Indeed many obstacles have already been successfully overcome since the publication of my first work. Opposition arose, of course, to the method of which I made systematic use, *some of it the harder to combat for its refusal to express itself publicly in writing.*[15] But the opposition is rattled. Every day sees new minds rally to the method I have championed, and these conquests are *definitive. The movement is slow but sure, in one direction only and irreversible: in the near future it will succeed in winning over all thinkers.*

The slowness of its current advance is proportionate to the prejudices it must overcome. It is a sign of the general backwardness of economic thought in France, but while the resistance I have encountered has been greater than I initially anticipated, it has also been much weaker than I feared.

The mathematical thought process is a marvelous tool that liberates the mind from the darkness, confusion, and impotence of the word, and enables it gradually to overcome every difficulty, without undue effort, in an incomparable blaze of light and clarity. Only those who have no experience of it can persist in doing without it. They do not realize what they are missing! As for those who undertake the voyage of Initiation, they will never again dream of returning to the earth of verbal metaphysics, and they will pursue an ever-richer path in ever-brighter light.[16,17]

15. Intellectual courage is not a dominant characteristic of the decadent period in which we live.

16. In case anyone is still in doubt as to the benefits of the mathematical approach, allow me to cite a personal example.

The systematic use of mathematical thinking enabled me *in six years* of study, entirely self-taught (and hence under far from ideal conditions), not only to assimilate the fundamentals of economics but also to produce several personal studies. Indeed, when I began to study economics in July 1940 I had practically no relevant knowledge, and during these six years, as a senior civil servant in the Corps of Mining Engineers, I was responsible for administrative work *that was often very demanding and on average took up more than half of my time.*

Nor should it be supposed that my case is exceptional. For some months now I have been monitoring the progress of young mathematics graduates embarking on the study of economics using the methods I advocate. It has proved extraordinarily rapid and effective.

17. Readers wishing to study these methodological issues in greater detail will find some complementary information in the introduction to my general study *À la recherche d'une discipline économique,* nos. 13–16.

B. Interest and Social Efficiency

1. Interest, social efficiency, and production (144)

The rate of interest is specifically the price paid for the use of a good available in limited quantity: reproducible capital. Its role, like that of every price, is precisely to ensure that the best use is made of this scarce capital, i.e., to bring about maximum social efficiency. *This means ensuring optimal distribution of the scarce means of production over the whole range of needs to be satisfied.*

The theory of social efficiency shows that the highest technical interest rates correspond to the most pressing needs.[1] Thus, under a single interest rate, all techniques whose efficiency rate is lower than the market rate are eliminated so that the existing capital can be allocated to the productions in greatest demand.

Without this fine-tuning of the demand for capital, the economy would inevitably come up against inextricable difficulties. For instance, in the wake of a scientific breakthrough such as the electric tram, all the world's cities naturally want to acquire this new convenience as soon as possible. However, any attempt to give immediate satisfaction to all of these demands at once, even reduced to a given degree, would monopolize productive power out of all proportion to other needs and hence plunge the whole economy into disarray. It is precisely the role of interest, in a competitive exchange economy, to redress the situation by an increase in its rate.

And it should be borne in mind that this adjustment occurs quite irrespective of what the interest rate is at the time, be it positive, zero, or even negative.

For example, if the interest rate were zero, the adjustment would be obtained by the need to pay off in full, by sufficient receipts, the primary costs of production. And this would automatically rule out any combination corresponding to negative technical interest rates, which are in fact the most numerous.

This mechanism of eliminating less urgent demands for capital in order to give priority to satisfying more urgent ones requires *a single technical interest rate to be constantly in force throughout the production sector.* And this can only in fact be the case if there is a competitive capital market

1. Since the value created is then greatest (nos. 44 and 62).

subject to the supply-and-demand mechanism,[2] which is therefore a fundamental prerequisite of the maximization of social efficiency.

Thus the basic role of the rate of interest in the production sector is to limit the demand for capital to the level of the available supply. This limitation takes place, either directly, by restricting the directly consumed services of durable goods,[3] or indirectly by elimination of unduly roundabout production processes that call for too much capital, achieved via a rise in the price of directly consumable services proportionate to the capital investment required for their production.[4] In this light, the rate of interest is seen to constitute a yardstick by which all may identify the minimum technical interest rate that any new investment must meet if it is to be profitable; it is a price paid on account of the scarcity of capital goods at a given moment.

Thus the purpose of economic calculation based on consideration of the technical interest rates and of the market interest rate is to ensure that quantitatively limited means of production are distributed among all the needs to be satisfied in the way most conducive to the general interest.[5]

The *inescapable necessity* of a rate of interest[6] for every economy[7] in which a given quantity of capital is available and that wishes to maximize its social efficiency lies in fact in the scarcity, i.e., the quantitative limitation, of the capital available and it is by keeping demand for capital constantly adjusted to the quantity that in fact exists that the rate of interest represents the fundamental regulatory parameter of every system of production.

Whether it is an ineluctable condition that capital must be so scarce that the rate of interest is always positive is a quite different question, which must be carefully distinguished. My own opinion is that this is a field in which the State could and should intervene to good purpose, either indirectly by modifying the institutional framework in which the competitive economy functions, or directly by acting on the capital market.[8] But

---

2. Only the "demand for capital" aspect is considered here. For the supply side, see the explanations below (no. 145).

3. Private cars or refrigerators, for instance.

4. Thus an increase in the rate of interest affects rental prices much more than the price of clothes (note 7 to no. 71).

5. I.e., to which there corresponds no dead loss.

6. Whether positive, zero, or negative.

7. Whether collectivized or not (note 1 to no. 55).

8. No. 164.

whatever one's conviction may be on this subject, there is one *scientifically* established fact, *viz.* that in any economic state in which capital is available in limited quantity, the manner of using it that best promotes the general interest is that which best agrees with the principle of profitability established by economic calculation.[9] This is why the whole of the present study has been conducted on the assumption of a competitive context.[10]

A quite different question is how the interest yielded by the limited capital available to the economy as a whole should in fact be distributed. This is a question concerning distribution, the solution to which is theoretically independent of the problem of what sort of management is most conducive to the public interest.[11]

9. No. 44.
10. Note 3 to no. 2 and no. 55.
11. No. 56.

2. Interest, social efficiency, and consumption (145)

While a unique interest rate is absolutely necessary for maximizing social efficiency in the production sector, this is by no means the case in the consumption sector. The only role played by the rate of interest in this sector is to modify the distribution of national income between the generations and how individuals choose to distribute their income between present and future, i.e., their preference respectively for present or future satisfaction; how the conditions of this double distribution are determined can only depend on data of an ethical or political nature; from the point of view of economic theory the matter is entirely arbitrary.[1]

It was, and still is, one of the *fundamental* errors of the traditional liberals to think that *only* the maximization (in the meaning of Pareto[2]) of *present* satisfactions must be retained and hence to maintain that a unique rate of interest throughout the economy is a necessary condition of maximization of social efficiency and that the competitive mechanism of the supply and demand of capital operating under our present institutional conditions of structure brings about an inherently optimal situation.

It is actually quite true that competitive uniqueness of the rate of interest throughout the economy is a sufficient condition for social efficiency, but it is by no means a necessary condition. The spontaneous competitive mechanism operating under our present structural conditions simply ushers in one of the multiple positions of maximum social efficiency. But *this position can by no means be regarded as an intrinsic optimum. Its management is indeed optimal, but its distribution may or may not be.*

It cannot be too often stated that economic theory alone cannot, in terms of capitalization, provide us with any basis on which to determine a distribution optimum. Only considerations of an ethical or political nature can be relevant here.[3]

In reality there are an infinity of possible income distributions over time that satisfy the condition of maximum social efficiency and the State alone can bring about any conceivable distribution, by acting indirectly

1. No. 63.

2. No. 54.

3. On the independence of management issues and distribution issues, see what is said at the end of no. 56.

(institutional framework of the economy) or directly (on the savings or capital markets).

In the context of our present institutions and in the absence of any direct State intervention, the spontaneous equilibrium that arises merely brings about one specific way of distributing disposable income over time. *From an exclusively economic point of view this distribution cannot be considered to be more or less desirable than any other.*

Indeed it is perfectly conceivable that by appropriate action, psychological interest rates might be held at levels different from the technical interest rate used in the production sector without preventing social efficiency from remaining maximal.

In this way *a collectivist State* might apply a rate of interest in the consumption sector such that the various individuals would spontaneously realize the volume of savings that would enable them to make provision for their old age.[4] Similarly, if it judged the saver's psychological rent unethical, it could perfectly well maintain in the consumption sector a zero interest rate while still using in the production sector the positive interest rate corresponding to the stock of equipment available to the economy. In this case it could satisfy the needs of old age by a compulsory pension scheme. Such a scheme would in fact be equivalent to using psychological interest rates different from zero, but the influence of the rates would be implicit, and they would not explicitly appear at all, so that appearances would be saved.[5]

The question may arise whether, in a collectivist economy, it is more beneficial in terms of social efficiency to bring in the funds needed to finance the economy via spontaneous savings or via taxation. It is clear that, contrary to what established theory claims, both procedures are equivalent in terms of social efficiency, always provided, of course, that

---

4. This policy of course depends on obtaining, via taxation, the sums needed to pay the interest to whatever extent the rate yielded to savers exceeds the rate of interest used in the production sector.

5. No. 63, § "Savings policy," and no. 77, § "Possible modes of State intervention."

Note that such a system would enable different psychological rates to be implemented ensuring the same level of old-age pensions whereas, in the first policy considered, all psychological rates are equal and each individual fixes the scale of his future income in a different way depending on the market's single rate of interest.

the taxation involved does not in itself constitute an obstacle to the maximization of social efficiency.[6,7]

It goes without saying that in *a non-collectivist economy* in which private ownership of production goods is allowed, it is impossible to hold psychological interest rates *rigidly* below the technological interest rate used in the production sector, for individuals have the option of investing their funds in private enterprises.[8] And in the same way, if it were deemed desirable to keep psychological interest rates higher than the common level of technical interest rates, this could only be achieved if the State were to take over both the management of savings and the financing of the whole economy, which would practically amount to wholesale collectivization of the means of production.

So the practice of multiple rates can be rigorously shown to be unrealizable in the context of a non-collectivist economy, but considerable options remain at the State's disposal in such an economy, as it can still, by appropriate policies, fix the common level of the different interest rates at the value chosen,[9] act on the individual distribution of income over time by compulsory pension schemes,[10] and bring about a measure of differentiation between technical and psychological interest rates over a broad sector by an appropriate taxation scheme.[11] *These options suffice in my opinion to ensure that the State's legitimate desire to bring about a certain distribution of incomes between present and future does not require it to adopt any particular stand concerning the system of ownership of the means of production.*[12]

6. No. 56 *in fine*.

7. And that, as we have seen (note 16 to no. 77), a degree of organization is provided for the risk market.

8. However, if only land ownership were public, the State would in theory be able to confiscate via taxation the pure interest received and thereby maintain *over a broad sector* the rate differentiation it deemed desirable.

9. Nos. 77 and 138.

10. No. 77.

11. See note 8 above.

12. See what has already been said on this subject in no. 77. A decisive answer to this question of great social importance can in fact only be made on the basis of other criteria (see notes 6 to no. 159 and 1 to no. 169).

C. Interest and Social Productivity

1. Social efficiency and social productivity (146)

We have seen that *for a given equipment stock* every optimal position[1] of the economy implies a price system equivalent to the system that would prevail in a perfect competition economy, at least in those economic sectors in which competition is possible. Such a situation, which generally goes with a non-zero interest rate in the production sector, corresponds to what I have called *the maximization of social efficiency*.

However, this management optimum is only defined in relation to a specific stock of equipment, and we have still to learn what happens when this equipment stock is no longer a datum, but varies, for instance, as a result of State policy.

As a first approximation the real economy may be compared to a stationary model. For when structural conditions are stable, as is usually the case, the different consumptions and productions vary relatively little from one year to the next.[2]

So if such stationary models are studied from the theoretical standpoint, we may inquire which of them—their social efficiency being already maximal—are the most socially advantageous, i.e., have maximum output for a given labor input.

Theoretical argument shows that *the most advantageous stationary state of maximum social efficiency is precisely that in which the rate of interest is zero*.[3] This rate itself assumes a certain equipment stock.

---

1. We have seen that there are an infinity of such positions depending on the methods of distribution deemed preferable (no. 56).

2. See note 9 to no. 77.

3. It is easy to see the underlying reason why this is so.

Let us assume a stationary model in which 100 million man-hours of labor of a given quality are devoted annually to the production of electrical energy, 90 million of which constitute the labor input for the various stages that precede final production (dams, transport networks, machinery, etc.) and 10 million for the final stage itself.

It is only possible for the production of electrical energy for a given total annual input of 100 million man-hours to be maximal if the output on the margin corresponding to one further hour's input in the pre-final stages of production is equal to the output on the margin corresponding to one further hour's input during the final stage of production.

But in economic reality, what is maximized is *not the output produced for a given input in man-hours but the output produced for a given wage-expenditure*. Hence the division be-

Under such stationary conditions, once the corresponding equipment stock is in place, the productivity of labor is maximal. In other words, for a given labor input, output quantities are maximal. This is what I have termed *the maximization of social productivity*.

Thus the maximization of social productivity constitutes a *maximum maximorum*, and there is by no means any incompatibility between the simultaneous pursuit of maximum social efficiency and of maximum social productivity.[4]

Social productivity is of course proportionately greater as the capital stock approaches its optimal value and this emphasizes the fundamental role played by the use of capital in the production cycle, by increasing the output obtained for a given labor input.

Indeed, the constant efforts made to ensure continuous increase in investment are the key to the development of modern civilization. Which in turn shows that the propensity to save, as manifested by such investments, is one of the pillars of our civilization.

---

tween direct and indirect labor input is arranged so as to achieve the same output for the same marginal wage-expenditure during the final stage as during the various previous stages. And since, when the rate of interest is positive, the same labor input has a higher value in the cost price when it occurs at an earlier stage than during the final stage of production, it is clear that output maximization means a division of direct and indirect labor input such that the marginal output corresponding to one further hour's input in the indirect stages is higher than the marginal output corresponding to an extra hour's input during the final stage. Hence production cannot be maximized for a labor input of a given number of hours.

Marginal output could be equal for direct and indirect labor input—i.e., social productivity could be maximized— only *if direct and indirect man-hours were counted at the same unit value in the final cost price, i.e., if the rate of interest were zero.* (This proof simply explains in everyday language the mathematical analysis found in the first demonstration of no. 69.)

4. In fact for an economic state considered at a given point in time, when social productivity is not maximal, the only incompatibility is between maximization of restricted social efficiency (no. 60) and maximization of [generalized] social productivity, but we have seen that the maximization of restricted social efficiency simply brings about among all possible states of maximum social efficiency those that correspond to a certain distribution of incomes over time. Thus there is no contradiction between maximized social productivity and maximized social efficiency, but only between maximized social productivity and certain income distributions over time.

The difference is due to the fact that the concept of restricted social efficiency corresponds exclusively to the interests of one generation considered *at a given point in time*, whereas generalized social efficiency takes into account the interests of the same generation *at each of the different points in its life* as well as the interests of future generations.

However, new investments can of course only be considered beneficial if they occur in an economy in which capital is still rare enough for the rate of interest to be still greater than zero.

From this angle, an economy's equipment stock may be considered optimal if its industrial equipment is such that the marginal technical interest rate is zero for every increase in this stock and if the economy would be respectively undercapitalized or overcapitalized depending on whether its capital equipment stock was less than or greater than the optimal stock.

From these definitions it is clear that *our present economies are undercapitalized* as the rate of interest corresponding to competitive equilibrium in production is far from being zero. It is also clear that the widespread opinion that savings are excessive and liable to give rise to excessive capital is very far from the truth. In reality, as long as the technical interest rate for new investments is not zero, capital accumulation cannot be considered to be excessive.

However, while a country cannot be over-equipped, in absolute terms, as long as the marginal technical interest rate is positive, it may yet be relatively over-equipped in the sense that this marginal rate, although greater than zero, may yet be less than the rate of interest corresponding to the stationary equilibrium that would spontaneously arise, under the relevant structural conditions, especially regarding land ownership and the monetary system.[5] In this case a decrease in the national equipment stock would be necessary in order to attain equilibrium, even though the economy was undercapitalized.

Contrary to an idea that has gained widespread acceptance at least implicitly, *the equipment stock whose technical interest rate is zero would not be infinite and could certainly be reached in a relatively short time.*[6]

Once this optimum was attained, the pure interest rate would be zero. That would not, of course, mean that the use of capital equipment would no longer cost anything, but simply that the income derived from it would cover only depreciation due to wear and tear and obsolescence together with remuneration for risk.

It is crucial to emphasize that under stationary conditions the new savings needed to maximize social productivity *once achieved* would, provided only that their level was maintained, enable aggregate real income

5. It is normal for such situations to occur at the end of all periods of prosperity during economic cycles (no. 109).

6. No. 121b and note 10 to no. 70.

to increase *indefinitely* for all following generations. For, assuming equal labor input, the output obtained under stationary conditions is proportionately greater as the capital equipment initially available increases. This is an essential fact if the advantages of zero marginal productivity of capital are to be fairly evaluated.

We have seen that from the point at which the competitive equilibrium interest rate was on the order of 5%, this advantage may be taken to be on the order of 20% of national income and that the situation of the workers would be improved by about 50%.[7]

7. No. 72.

2. Social productivity and classical theory (147)

According to classical theory, spontaneous competitive equilibrium coincides with the inherent optimum, in other words, the situation that arises under current structural conditions through the competitive mechanism based on the law of supply and demand is deemed preferable to any other.

We have already seen how unjustified this thesis turns out to be just from the viewpoint of social efficiency theory, since optimal management is by no means synonymous with optimal distribution. In the first place, taking only the satisfactions of a given point in time, other distributions are possible than those corresponding to the current ownership structure, and that fulfill equally well the condition of maximization of social efficiency.[1] Moreover, for a present distribution of property deemed to be the best, the competitive mechanism is based exclusively on the present satisfactions of present generations and takes account neither (a) of their future satisfactions, since they are involved in present satisfactions only through the idea individuals now have of their future psychology,[2] nor (b) of the future satisfactions of future generations.

From both of these points of view the spontaneous competitive equilibrium that tends to arise in the absence of all State intervention does indeed correspond to a management optimum, but certainly cannot be regarded as optimal in terms of distribution, as would be necessary for an inherent optimum.

The theory of social productivity brings to light a further inadequacy in the thesis that spontaneous competitive equilibrium represents an inherent optimum. For even if we assume that the distribution of consumable services among individuals, the distribution over time of the income of each individual, and the distribution of the national income between present and future generations brought about by spontaneous competition are deemed preferable, the equilibrium so obtained only corresponds to an optimum for the stock of capital equipment then existing. But the theory of social productivity precisely shows that, *among all the possible models having maximum social efficiency corresponding to a given distribution, there is one for which consumable output is maximum.*[3] And this *maxi-*

---

1. No. 56.

2. No. 60.

3. In the meaning of no. 69, i.e., where no virtual modification of the equipment stock could, if present and future satisfactions (satisfactions S_0 and S_1) are constant, bring about any available production surplus.

mum maximorum model corresponds in the production sector to the use of a single pure interest rate equal to zero.

Since under present structural conditions it is absolutely impossible to obtain a zero pure interest rate in a competitive equilibrium,[4] it is clear that the theory of social productivity highlights a new flaw in the classical theory identifying spontaneous equilibrium with inherent optimum.

Of course, assuming that a single rate of interest applies throughout the economy and that a zero pure rate of interest is achieved via suitable changes to structural conditions[5] and policy, a different distribution over time of the income of individuals would arise, but *in terms of economic theory this new distribution would be neither more nor less desirable* than the one that would have arisen under the rate of interest corresponding to the spontaneous competitive mechanism[6] acting under present structural conditions.

Moreover, in the event that this distribution of individuals' incomes over time was not judged preferable, for instance, on social grounds, the State would always have the option of modifying the distribution in the direction chosen, without compromising the maximization of social productivity.[7]

In fact, from a situation in which the equilibrium interest rate was on the order of 4% to 5%, maximization of social productivity could be attained only at the cost of restricting present consumption over a certain period, but this restriction should not be exaggerated.[8]

4. No. 137.

5. Collectivization of land and continuous depreciation of money (no. 139).

6. I.e., with no direct State intervention on the savings market.

7. By using either (a) a double interest rate under collectivist conditions (psychological interest rates being maintained at the desired level in the consumption sector while technical interest rates are held at zero in the production sector) or (b) a compulsory savings system in an economy having private ownership of capital and using a single interest rate (no. 77, § "Possible modes of State intervention," and nos. 144 and 145).

8. It would be much less than the consumption restriction currently needed for war-devastated countries to restore their 1939 capital levels over five or six years. Thus in 1939, France's national capital was on the order of five times its national income. Estimating capital losses at twice national income, to restore the previous capital levels over six years entails a net annual saving of a third of the national income. By comparison, the amount of capital needed to pass from the 1939 situation to a position of maximum social productivity can be estimated at a value on the order of three or four times the national income (note 10 to no. 70), showing that to pass from a situation comparable to that prevailing in 1939 to a maximum situation implies net annual savings E_1 of only half as much as E_0 corresponding to a return to the 1939 situation in five or six years.

It should be stressed that savings of half the amount correspond to a much slighter restriction of consumption, for as we have seen (note 10 to no. 70), although savings E_1 could

The simple circumstance of permanent full employment would enable social productivity to be maximized in 20 or 30 years without significant detriment to our standard of living.

It may be added that continuous depreciation of money, by reducing balances to their minimum levels, would inevitably tend to ensure that the propensity for ownership was satisfied by wider recourse to financial investment, thereby reducing the equilibrium interest rate. And in the same way, once all land was publicly owned, the aggregate capital owned by individuals would be restricted to reproducible capital and would thus be, on aggregate, for an unchanged rate of interest, far below its present level. This would naturally lead to a fall in expected future incomes. Thereupon, these two motives (lower satisfaction of the desire to own and lower satisfaction of future needs) would inevitably lead, in a competitive environment, to a considerable increase in the inducement to invest and hence to a substantial fall in the rate of interest. Under these conditions, *it is by no means unbelievable that maximization of social productivity would tend to arise spontaneously in the event of land collectivization and continuous depreciation of money.*[9]

This shows that *the current insufficiency of savings is much less due to an insufficient propensity to save,* which could only be overcome by major sacrifices, *than to our current institutions,*[10] *which, far from favoring the expansion of reproducible capital to its optimal levels, actually connive at its scarcity and thereby undeniably obstruct the general welfare.*

And finally, it shows that the claims of the classical theory that the rate of interest automatically settles at the level best adapted to the good of society and that the spontaneous competitive equilibrium corresponding to current conditions of structure constitute an inherent optimum cannot be accepted as justified.[11]

---

be obtained simply by ensuring full employment with no decline in the average standard of living, savings $E_0 = 2E_1$ would require, even on the most favorable hypothesis of full employment, a restriction in the consumption of national income equal to E_1.

9. See what has already been said in no. 139.

10. Private land ownership and a fixed link between the circulating currency and the accounting currency.

11. The classical authors were led astray here by their dogmatism. With hindsight it is now clear how hasty they were in dismissing as puerile the opinion that the rate of interest does not tend of itself to take on the most desirable level, an opinion that for centuries if not millennia enlightened judgment had regarded as certain and evident.

There are in fact two entirely different kinds of issue, and they must be carefully distinguished: the first fall exclusively within the scope of economic theory while the second involve economically arbitrary data of an ethical, social, or political nature.

Economic theory can only provide us with definitive conclusions for the first kind of issue. These conclusions include the theorems of social efficiency and social productivity that consist of *factual data* of which *every* economic policy must take account.[12]

For *the existence of a maximum for social productivity does not necessarily imply that the policy of systematically pursuing this maximum by suitable policies*[13] *corresponds to an inherent optimum.* From a purely economic point of view such a policy is neither better nor worse than the policy of simply maintaining the present status quo. Only considerations relating to distribution and of a social or political nature can provide criteria by which to decide.

Hence it is important to distinguish between the theory of social productivity considered in itself and the practical politics to be adopted in its light in such and such circumstances. These two kinds of issues are sharply distinct, and it would be dangerous to confuse them. But whatever policy may be deemed preferable, the importance of social productivity theory

---

No doubt today we are equipped to spot the errors committed by the scholastics as well as those of the mercantilist school, but neither should we be blind to the huge advantage the classical school would have derived from more thorough study of their theories.

At every period of history minds have tended to react by rejecting *en bloc* as erroneous the opinions of the period preceding their own; while this tendency has on balance proved beneficial to scientific progress, it has nonetheless in individual cases hampered that progress by confining opinions to extreme positions.

It is certain that the present enthusiasm for jettisoning wholesale the tenets of the classical school is an example of the same excess that led the members of that school themselves to disregard the opinions of the mercantilists. Let us hope that this trend will not succeed in imprisoning minds for three or four generations in formulae as rigid and dogmatic — and hence just as harmful and dangerous — as were those of the classical authors. For in reality it is just as erroneous to deny, with the current trend, the usefulness and necessity of the competitive price mechanism for every economy aiming to be efficient, as to assert, with no further proof (as did the "enlightened" opinion of a century ago), that laissez-faire spontaneously leads to the structure of production and distribution most beneficial to all.

There is no worse attitude in any period than systematically to dismiss one's predecessors as unintelligent if not utterly blinded by prejudice.

12. Whether that of the USSR, the United States, or any of our West European nations.
13. No. 77.

for any efficient economic policy[14,15] is clear, *and in any event, the situation deemed optimal may differ considerably from the spontaneous competitive equilibrium corresponding to current structural conditions.*

14. Irrespective of the political and social standpoints chosen, it is important for the legislator to be aware of

1. the effects on production of increasing equipment and the fact that a maximum is attained for a zero pure interest rate;
2. the obstacles that currently prevent reduction of the rate of interest to zero;
3. the changes that would spontaneously occur in the overall equipment stock if these hindrances were eliminated.

The theory of social productivity, in association with the theory of the rationale of interest (chapter 9), sheds essential light on these topics.

15. The example of Soviet Russia provides an excellent illustration of why the theory of social productivity is crucial for any State that does not consider the level of its stock of industrial equipment to have been irrevocably fixed by destiny.

D. Interest and Money

1. The rate of interest: the price paid for the use of money (148)

The foregoing explanations highlight the critical role played by the rate of interest in monetary mechanisms.

Money is an intermediate good that is advantageous to hold on account of the costs that would be involved in buying and selling assets, realizing securities, or borrowing as one's needs varied. Hence its use has a value that may be termed the liquidity premium of money.[1]

Under disequilibrium dynamics, the study of which corresponds to the cause-and-effect relationships prevailing in economic development, the disparities between the liquidity premiums corresponding to money balances and the technical interest rates corresponding to financial investments determine the direction of monetary flows toward either cash or securities. In the first case, prices tend downward and in the second upward. This is the fundamental principle that governs all economic development.[2]

Under equilibrium dynamics, the study of which corresponds to the relationships of interdependence that tend to arise beyond the contingent appearances of causal relationships, the rate of interest emerges as the key regulatory factor balancing savings and investment. *As a first approximation*, it can be taken to be independent of monetary conditions, and *the degree of liquidity preference determines not the interest rate but the price level*. Prices are proportionately higher as the total quantity of money is greater and as liquidity preference is weaker.[3]

Interest theory and monetary theory are thus seen to be closely connected and cannot be dissociated without grave prejudice to the understanding of reality.

Contrary to what first appearances may suggest, *there is no real opposition between capital-based and monetary theories of interest*. Each stresses one aspect of the subject and the real task of the economist is not to take sides between them but to delineate their respective fields of application and clarify their underlying interconnections.

---

1. No. 82.
2. Nos. 98 and 100.
3. Nos. 97 and 99.

The capital-based theory sheds light on the economy's deep underlying tendencies, and its comprehension is indispensable to determining any overall economic policy. It is our guiding light for long-term action, whereas monetary theory, which sheds light on each day's events, is indispensable to prevent our action from running aground on the shoals of contingency and to make a long-term interest rate policy both possible and effective.[4]

4. No. 141.

2. Rates of interest and economic cycles (149)

While in a neutral-money economy having no inflation, deflation, or hoarding of cash or of demand deposits, theory shows with a high degree of probability that the economic mechanism leads to a stable equilibrium,[1] it is clear that no stable equilibrium can exist in an economy whose money is not neutral.

In particular it can be shown that *for a constant quantity of ready cash the possibility of issuing unbacked demand deposits and the hoardability of money*[2] *comprise two factors favoring disequilibrium, either of which alone would suffice to explain why economic cycles occur, and in the absence of both of which no overall cyclical fluctuation would be conceivable.* So the presence of at least one of these factors is a necessary and sufficient condition of the existence of cycles. And thus the explanation of economic cycles is complete.[3]

The observed disturbances of the economy, delicate though its operation undoubtedly is, should not be attributed to innate necessity. The regulatory mechanism of the rate of interest, on which economic development as a whole must depend, would work perfectly well if only monetary neutrality could be maintained.

It follows from what we have seen that such a situation could not in fact be brought about unless the banks' demand deposit accounts were 100% backed by an equivalent amount of ready cash and unless the hoardability of money was rendered impossible by continuous depreciation. *Failing these conditions, no stable equilibrium is conceivable.*

The importance of these conclusions is inescapable. They enable economic policy to be provided with the means of avoiding cyclical fluctuations and hence of correcting the fundamental defect of the classical competitive system.

1. No. 98.
2. Whether in the form of cash or demand deposits.
3. Nos. 100 and 112.

3. Money and social efficiency (150)

The theory shows that the use of money hinders the maximization of social efficiency, which can only be achieved in a monetary economy in the specific case in which the price paid for the use of money is zero.[1]

While practically speaking this circumstance is of only slight importance, as the relevant losses in social efficiency can only be slight, it is nevertheless of *major theoretical importance*, for it demonstrates that *the classical thesis according to which the competitive mechanism automatically leads to optimal management of the economy is not true as a generality*. It is verified only with a degree of approximation, which makes it impossible to accept as rigorous and satisfying the intuitive demonstrations offered in favor of that thesis, since they do not differentiate between the cases in which the theory is true and those in which it cannot be applied except with a degree of error.

This identifies a new lacuna in the classical theory and shows the *absolute necessity* for economics, if it seeks to be effective, to extricate itself from purely verbal pseudo-demonstrations that can only lead to confusion and to stay firmly within the limits of rigor. *Intuition is and can only ever be a research approach. Never can it be used as a tool of demonstration, on pain of risking errors of the utmost gravity.*

---

1. As we saw at the end of no. 136, reduction of the liquidity premium l_m of money, and hence of the price m paid for the use of money (no. 82, equation [10]), to zero must be deemed quite *impossible to achieve*.

E. The Rationale of Interest

Rationale of interest (151)

Examination of the rationale of interest gives rise to two questions: (a) Why is there a rate of interest? (b) Why is this rate positive?

(a) Why there is a rate of interest

1. Necessity of interest (152)

It is imperative to understand that, whether its level be positive, negative, or zero,[1] the existence of a rate of interest is an inescapable phenomenon.

No matter how society may be organized, any good that only becomes available at some point in the future will always constitute a distinct good from the same article available at once, just as wine is a distinct good from oil. It follows that interest rates will always exist just as there is in general a difference between the price of wine and the price of oil.

If the structure is competitive, these various rates will have the same value. But of course, the necessary existence of a single interest rate in a competitive economy of itself implies no condition concerning its level, which may equally well be positive, zero, or even negative, depending on the structural conditions of the economy in question.

---

1. Of course, the existence of negative interest rates would imply, in light of the foregoing, that the structural conditions were different from those currently prevailing (see § b, "Why the rate of interest is always positive," below).

2. The collectivist economy and the rate of interest (153)

The need for a rate of interest is an intrinsic necessity, applicable to all economies, of whatever kind, if they wish to be efficient and to avoid useless waste.

It is possible that the existence of a positive interest rate in a competitive economy is connected with certain structural conditions, but it is not true that the phenomenon of interest in principle owes its existence to acceptance of the institution of private property as was asserted by the socialist disciples of Marx, Lassalle, and Rodbertus.

Quite irrespective of structural conditions, the use of capital, like any other service, will always have a price, whatever it may be,[1] because capital must always exist in a certain quantity[2] relative to human needs and wishes.[3] This price cannot but subsist, either explicitly as such, or else implicitly as a coefficient of equivalence whenever public ownership replaces private ownership, as in Russia. So the phenomenon of interest has an intrinsic existence, quite independent of prevailing structural conditions.

Indeed the only effect of the institution of private property, relative to the existence of a rate of interest, is to ensure that its costs are met by and its profits reaped[4] by private persons rather than by the State; it is simply not, and can never be accepted as being, in any way, the basis of its existence.

1. Positive or negative depending on whether or not the equipment stock is insufficient (no. 146).

2. Insufficient or superabundant.

3. While it may seem to be a peculiarity of the use of capital that under certain structural conditions this price can become negative, the reason for this is that under these conditions the service sought after is not the *use* of capital but its *conservation*.

The same might also apply to an everyday commodity such as the consumption of bread, if structural conditions were such that some economic agents might have their satisfaction increased by the consumption of the commodity by other agents.

In this case their desire may well be strong enough for them not only to offer the commodity free of charge but even to accompany it with a supplementary premium; this would make the price of the commodity involved negative. This is no different from what happens in the context of the family economy when some parents offer their children pocket money to encourage them to eat.

4. Whether positive of negative: it must be remembered that in a competitive economy having private ownership of capital but public ownership of land and continuous depreciation of money, the equilibrium interest rate might be negative.

Willingly or otherwise, a collectivist economy is bound to have recourse to some adjustment of the capitalistic structure of its production.

And there is only one way to achieve this adjustment conveniently and efficiently, *viz.* to establish a uniform price for the use of capital and only to carry out the projects that yield technical interest rates superior to this price. Thus recourse to a rate of interest is shown to be necessary.

And in the same way, any collectivist economy must necessarily establish a certain balance (a) between the present and the future consumptions of the present generation and (b) between the (present and future) consumptions of present generations and the (future) consumptions of future generations. Such a policy necessarily implies the explicit or implicit use of an interest rate in the consumption sector.

So, whether or not it uses a single rate to govern its economic action, any collectivist economy, by the simple fact of implementing a certain policy, turns out to be using coefficients of equivalence, i.e., using interest rates under another name, which shows that the existence of these rates is indeed an intrinsic and inescapable phenomenon.

However, a distinction must naturally be made between the abolition of interest and a zero interest rate. These two things are entirely distinct, and while the former is absolutely impossible, the latter by no means appears to be outside the realm of possibility under certain conditions.[5]

5. No. 138 and no. 157 below.

(b) Why the rate of interest is always positive

1. Necessity of an invariably positive interest rate under present structural conditions (154)

The explanations given above[1] have shown that in exchange economies, based on freedom, the universal and permanent existence of a positive interest rate in every time and place is due to the twin circumstances of private land ownership and the identification of circulating currency with the accounting currency.

These structural conditions necessarily give rise to an invariably positive rate of interest, irrespective of what the other structural conditions — notably the level of the propensity to save — may be. For this reason, *any attempt under current structural conditions to bring the rate of interest down to zero, whether initiated by the spontaneous desire of individuals or by a concerted State policy, can only prove utterly vain.*

The fact that a positive interest rate is necessarily found, under the prevailing conditions of the economy, means that under these conditions, for reasons already expounded, individuals have, on the margin, a preference for present goods relative to future goods, but it by no means implies that this preference is due to intrinsic data inherent in the psychological dispositions of individuals or in the technical characteristics of production.

In reality, if the two structural conditions that currently hinder the rate of interest from descending to zero were abolished, the spontaneous interest rate that would arise would certainly be lower and might even be negative, even for identical psychological and technical structures.[2]

Hence the fact that the rate of interest is never zero or negative certainly cannot be regarded as intrinsically necessary. It is simply a contingent phenomenon due to the conditions of economic structure specific to our own times.

Given that the existence of an invariably positive interest rate must be attributed at the same time to private ownership of land and to the identification of the circulating currency with the currency of account, it is plain that there is no justification for the complaints of social reformers who attribute the maintenance of a positive rate that "paralyses their

1. Chapter 9, particularly no. 137.
2. No. 147.

efforts to improve the well-being of the people" to "the monopolistic requirements of capitalists who levy by constraint a heavy tribute on the
national income" and call on them to be content with, if not a zero rate,
at least a much lower one. Although the capitalists undeniably benefit, via
the saver's rent,[3] from the maintenance of this rate, it remains completely
independent of their will and in no way due to any concerted action; indeed capitalists are the only economic group in contemporary society *not
to be organized for the defense of their collective interests.*[4] *It is not in
their power to make this invariably positive interest rate disappear.* It is exclusively due to specific structural conditions the true effects of which are
quite as unknown to capitalists as to public opinion in general.

Of course, these observations by no means exclude the possibility that
in an economy having public land ownership and circulating money that
undergoes progressive depreciation the rate of interest that would spontaneously arise might yet remain positive, but under these conditions, the
maintenance of a positive rate of interest would be due not to intrinsic
reasons but to an insufficient propensity to save that could easily be corrected by appropriate State intervention on the savings market.

3. No. 41.

4. In reality, to the (fairly slight) extent that an increase in the propensity to save is liable, under present structural conditions, to lead to a fall in the rate of interest, "those who
advocate lower interest should, consequently, really direct their zeal not against the savers,
but against those who do not save, against unnecessary consumption on the part of the individual or the State" (G. Cassel, *Traité d'économie politique*, vol. 1 [Paris: Giard, 1929], 354
[bk. 2, ch. 26]).

2. Collectivist economy and positive rate of interest (155)

In a collectivist economy organized on a competitive footing,[1] having no private land ownership and in which money depreciated over time, it is perfectly possible that the rate of interest might yet be maintained, explicitly or implicitly, at a positive level on account of scarcity of capital.

In such an economy the prevailing positive rate of interest maintained would have the role of sifting demands for available capital. If the capital stock was below its optimal level, only the most important ones[2] could be satisfied and the others would have to be eliminated.

These observations bring out the regulatory role played by the interest rate — *a regulatory role that remains necessary in a collectivist economy*, and show how unjustified are the present complaints of businessmen who accuse the banks' interest rate policy of stifling the spirit of enterprise and curbing economic development since, as capital remains necessarily limited on account of current structural conditions, the demand for it must necessarily be adjusted to the quantity that exists. The unavoidable necessity of the rate of interest is due to the scarcity of available capital.

The only genuinely essential difference there would be between (a) a competitive collectivist economy in which a positive interest rate was maintained and (b) a private ownership economy having the same psychological and technical structure as the former is that in the former all or some of the interest would be received by the State, whereas in the latter the interest would be received only by certain consumers.

But in any event a collectivist economy would be unable, in the case in question, to suppress what has been inexactly described as exploitation of the worker.[3] For it would be unable, for instance, to pay 300 francs to have a tree planted that would only be worth 300 francs in 25 years' time, if elsewhere only 100 francs would be paid for the same labor input; under such conditions everyone would want to work in forestry and no one would want to exercise the trade of tailor or baker any longer. As long as production processes take time and the aggregate capital stock is below its optimum level it will be quite impossible, except by means of an arbitrary and unjust redistribution, to grant as wages to the various laborers

---

1. I.e., the only efficient kind of economy, as pointed out in no. 55.
2. I.e., those having the highest technical interest rate.
3. No. 120.

the value of the finished consumable product obtained once the production process is over. Under one form or another the interest levy will have
to be maintained.[4]

4. Neither could a collectivist society, should it wish to increase its aggregate capital, give
up distributing in wages a lesser value than the value produced if wages once distributed were
to be immediately spent, in their entirety, on consumption goods. The effort of saving can no
more be avoided than the levying of interest.

3. Legal limitations of the rate of interest (156)

We have now seen that under present structural conditions the existence of a positive rate of interest is absolutely necessary. Given these structural conditions, no legislative measure could prevent people from preferring, in light of their available resources, one particular distribution of their consumption over time to another,[1] or one specific form of financial investment to another,[2] any more than it could convince one particular individual of the gastronomic superiority of roast chicken over a leg of lamb. Under such conditions there is no more sense in protesting against the interest rate than in waxing indignant at the fact that a pound of meat is worth more than a pound of bread. This fact must be constantly borne in mind if gross errors are to be avoided.

Hence it is an entirely vain undertaking, under present structural conditions, to seek to limit the interest rate level by legal measures, or to bring in legislation against usury.

The law seems to presume that the money-lender, dealing with necessitous persons, can take advantage of their necessities, and exact conditions limited only by his own pleasure. It might be so if there were only one money-lender within reach. But when there is the whole money-capital of a wealthy community to resort to, no borrower is placed under any disadvantage in the market merely by the urgency of his need. If he cannot borrow at the interest paid by other people, it must be because he cannot give such good security: and competition will limit the extra demand to a fair equivalent for the risk of his proving insolvent.

Though the law intends favor to the borrower, it is to him above all that injustice is, in this case, done by it. What can be more unjust than that a person who cannot give perfectly good security, should be prevented from borrowing of persons who are willing to lend money to him, because they are not permitted to receive the rate of interest which would be a just equivalent for their risk? Through the mistaken kindness of the law, he must either go without the money

---

1. Note that when the rate of interest falls, the total capital at the disposal of consumers increases on account of the increase in land-capital; consumers then tend to spend more and thus at the same time diminish the volume of reproducible capital (no. 135).

2. Reminder: when the rate of interest falls, financial investment in the form of holding money becomes more worthwhile and this tends to bring about a decrease in the volume of reproducible capital (no. 139).

which is perhaps necessary to save him from much greater losses, or be driven
to expedients of a far more ruinous description, which the law either has not
found it possible, or has not happened, to interdict.[3]

In other words, under present structural conditions, *the limitation or
suppression of interest can only relieve borrowers of the weight of interest
by depriving them of the advantages of being able to borrow at all.*

And in any event, the existence of a positive rate of interest cannot "be
prevented by prohibiting loan contracts. To forbid the particular form of
sale called a loan contract would leave possible other forms of sale, and ...
*the mere act of valuation of every property right involves an implicit rate of
interest.*[4] ... Indeed, as long as buying and selling of any kind were permitted, the virtual effect of lending and borrowing would be retained;"[5] there
is a rate of interest that, though not explicit, is nonetheless real.

It was in this way, "for instance by rent purchase, that the medieval pro-
hibitions of usury were rendered nugatory. Practically, *the effect of such restrictive laws is little more than to hamper and make difficult the finer adjustments of the income stream*, compelling would-be borrowers to sell wealth
yielding distant returns instead of mortgaging them, and would-be lenders
to buy such wealth instead of lending to the present owners."[6]

No doubt the explicit rate of interest may disappear under such conditions, but certainly not the implicit rate of interest hidden in every contract, which is in reality the only one that really matters.

*The phenomenon of interest is far too ubiquitous for it to be possible to
conjure it away merely by attacking haphazardly one of its forms: no one who
has grasped its real nature and* raison d'être *under present structural conditions could seriously attempt to abolish it.*

Indeed, *far from bringing down its effective rate, no policy of limiting or
prohibiting interest has ever done other than to raise it, on account of the
greater risks involved for those inclined to lend.* And social productivity has
thereby been lessened, resulting in substantial losses for the community as
a whole that could have been avoided.

---

3. John Stuart Mill, *Principles of Political Economy*, bk. 5, ch. 10, § 2. Emphasis mine.
4. Since it amounts to assigning a value to future income streams.
5. Fisher, *The Theory of Interest*, ch. 5, § 6. Emphasis mine.
6. Fisher, ch. 5, § 6. Emphasis mine.

4. Present justification of interest (157)

Under present structural conditions two cases must be distinguished depending on whether the maximum supply of capital corresponds to a positive or a negative level of the rate of interest (fig. 10.2).

In the first, and most likely case, as we have seen,[1] the existence of a positive rate of interest has the effect of raising the amount of capital saved to a level higher than it would have in the absence of such interest. As this increase in capital is useful to the community, since it increases social productivity, there can be no doubt that, under the economy's present structural conditions, service is rendered. However, as we have seen, only marginal interest[2] can really be considered as the reward for an actual service and as far as can be judged its amount is far lower than the amount[3] of the interest that the increase $C_e - C_o$ in capital costs the community, the difference being a genuine rent.

In the second case, the capital saved would be even greater if savers received no interest or even if the rate of interest were negative. In that case interest received could by no means be regarded as the reward for the effort of saving and should rather be considered to be in its totality a true rent.[4]

Thus in *both cases savers enjoy as a result of their saving a true rent*, greater or less according to the case,[5] but which on average seems, as far as can be judged, to be of an order close to the totality of the interest received.

However, *under current structural conditions this rent is neither more nor less justified than the rent received by the consumer in the consumption of any good whatever, the corresponding psychological satisfaction being in general far greater than its cost.*

Interest is in fact absolutely necessary to raise capital to a sufficient amount, for experience shows that, *under the conditions currently prevailing,* people are no fonder of waiting than of working. It is therefore quite as necessary to pay the saver for waiting as it is to pay the laborer for

1. No. 40.
2. Represented by the area $C_o C_e M_e$ of figure 10.2.
3. Equal to the product $I_e C_e$.
4. In fact, maintaining the market interest rate at value I instead of zero allows savers to enjoy a rent represented by the area $O C_o M_e I_e$, which is greater than the product $I_e C_e$ representing the sum of the interest payments received.
5. Note 2 to no. 41.

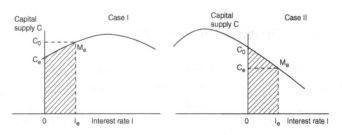

FIGURE 10.2

working and whether or not there is a rent *the economic justification of interest seems complete.*

At the margin, there is absolute equivalence between the supplementary saving effort made and the interest received. The interest represents the exact price of the service rendered and the very fact that the borrower agrees to pay the agreed rate of interest shows that he benefits from the transaction.

The fact that this equivalence means at the margin for the saver a rent corresponding to the rest of his savings is not a characteristic peculiar to the phenomenon of interest. The rent received by savers apart from the remuneration of marginal savings is of the same nature as the rent received by the worker when he consumes his food, which gives him much greater satisfaction than the effort he had to exert in order to earn the corresponding value.[6] These rents are absolutely parallel, and it is hard to see why one ought to be abolished and not the other. Moreover even if there were good reasons for abolishing it, it would be practically impossible to do so in view of the insuperable obstacles that would be involved in determining the saver's rent.

However, and the point is a crucial one, *these observations are only valid under the present structural conditions of our economic society.* For the scarcity of reproducible capital that is at the origin of the saver's rent is exclusively due to conditions that are specific to our present economy. Indeed it follows from what has already been set out that if land ownership were public and if money depreciated continuously in real terms, the rate of interest that would spontaneously arise in the absence of State intervention would be, if not actually zero, at the very least much lower than the rates

6. No. 41.

currently observed.[7] And in any event, the State could always, sooner or later, build up the supplementary savings needed for a zero market rate.[7] Under these conditions, the real income of current savers would fall, but the income of the community as a whole (comprising present and future individuals) would increase, since the production processes employed would become more productive.

Hence present owners of capital are obtaining entirely unmerited profits at the expense of the community as a whole (present and future generations) from the regrettable situation (the scarcity of capital) due to our current land ownership and monetary systems.

In fact the owner of capital currently collects interest only because capital is scarce, just as the landowner can collect a rent because land is scarce. But, *whereas the scarcity of land is explained by an intrinsic reason, there is no intrinsic reason justifying the scarcity of capital.*

Society currently pays a very high price for a service that it could easily have more abundantly at no expense at all.

Under these conditions, the rent represented by area $OC_eM_eI_e$ displays all the features of *excess profit* in the strictest sense. For the scarcity of capital that is the source of this rent is exclusively due to legal characteristics specific to our present economy and for which there is no intrinsic necessity.

Of interest actually received,[8] only marginal interest[9] can, in the case in which savings increase with the rate of interest (case 1) be socially justified on the grounds that it strictly compensates the sacrifice of abstinence savers make by raising the level of their savings from C_o to C_e, while the difference[10] emerges as representing excess profit, pure and simple, with no possible justification, as *it depends on circumstances that may safely be deemed socially harmful.*[11]

As has been shown, the amount of this *"excess profit from capital accumulation"* ought not to be very different from the aggregate value of interest received, since, as far as can be judged, the level of marginal interest[9] is negligible.

---

7. Nos. 139 and 147.

8. Represented by the area of the curvilinear quadrilateral $OC_oM_eI_e$.

9. Represented by the area of the curvilinear triangle $C_oC_eM_e$.

10. Represented by the area of the curvilinear quadrilateral $OI_eM_eC_e$.

11. Because it hinders the maximization of social productivity.

Naturally in case II, where in the usual range of interest rates savings would decrease with the rate of interest, the whole of the interest received should be deemed to be excess profit from capital accumulation.

Thus we find that *interest, under current structural conditions, is simply the payment made for a useful service rendered to the community, but that this service is only useful as a result of these very conditions — conditions that are in fact very unfavorable for society and necessarily lead to a certain scarcity of capital.* In short, the service rendered and its remuneration only exist as a result of the continuance of this untoward situation.

This means that there is a fundamental difference between the saver's rent and the consumer's rent, for while the latter cannot be eliminated, the former is not due to any intrinsic necessity.

The community as a whole is currently paying some of its members a high price for a service that, under different structural conditions, could be supplied at a much lower price if not gratis, and in greater quantity.

F. Economic and Social Dimensions of the General Theory of Interest

Theory of interest: general conclusions (158)

Thanks to the foregoing analysis we are now in a position to clarify the general conclusions that flow from detailed study of the rate of interest. These conclusions chiefly concern the problems of economic management, savings and investment, money, and the rationale of interest.

From the viewpoint of management, we have seen that for a given stock of capital equipment there exists an intrinsic optimum corresponding to use in the production sector of a single interest rate enabling investment projects worthy of pursuit to be distinguished from less profitable ones. This intrinsic management optimum can be attained only by universal application of the profitability principle in a competitive exchange economy based on the free play of the law of supply and demand among free, independent economic agents.[1]

From the savings and investment perspective, we have seen that in the consumption sector a single interest rate is not necessary for maximization of social efficiency and that, when it occurs, it succeeds only in bringing about, of the many possible distributions, one particular distribution of each individual's disposable income over time and one particular distribution of the national revenue between the different generations, but that this distribution cannot be considered in purely economic terms to be preferable to any other.[2]

In the production sector, the theory has shown us that there is an optimal stock of capital equipment that corresponds in a competitive context to a zero interest rate, that this equipment level can be achieved only by initially curtailing national consumable income but that, once this restriction has been accomplished, the supplementary consumable output obtained can be maintained indefinitely with no further effort.[3]

From the monetary angle, we have seen that the rate of interest is the basic regulatory parameter of the whole economy, constantly adjusting to

1. Chapter 6 (no. 62 in particular) and no. 144 above.
2. Chapter 6 (no. 63 in particular) and no. 145 above.
3. Chapter 7 (nos. 69, 71, 74, and 77 in particular) and nos. 146 and 147 above.

one another the two elements, real and monetary, of which the economy is composed.[4]

In equilibrium, as a first approximation, the rate of interest is due only to the relative propensities to save and to invest, so that the equalization of the price paid for the use of money and the rate of interest simply determines the real value of money balances and hence—in light of the overall money stock—the price level.[5]

In economic development under disequilibrium, the disparities between marginal technical interest rates and between the liquidity premiums of money balances determine variations in investment and price fluctuations. We have seen that this mechanism leads—for a constant money stock and in the absence of hoarding—to a stable equilibrium, but that (a) banks' ability to issue unbacked deposit money and (b) the hoardability of money lead the economy into a state of permanent instability characterized by cyclical movements in which phases of prosperity alternate with phases of depression.[6]

Finally, *with regard to the rationale of interest itself*, we have seen that whereas the existence of a rate of interest is a necessary phenomenon that it is quite impossible to eliminate, the fact that this rate is always positive is purely contingent, being exclusively due to present structural conditions of private land ownership and the fact that money can be hoarded at no appreciable cost. We have seen that if these conditions were eliminated, the rate of interest would fall, in equilibrium and in the absence of State intervention, to a far lower level than it has at present, perhaps even reaching zero or negative values. Under these conditions, our present institutions, far from promoting capital abundance, appear rather to be the reason for its scarcity, and interest received emerges not as an inevitable and necessary reward, but an excess profit caused by a shortage that itself results from essentially contingent circumstances.[7]

These conclusions, which have been set out in the preceding pages with all the nuances and distinctions they call for, *evoke the possibility of a coherent economic policy involving radical changes in our view of the economic and social issues of the day.*

4. Chapter 8 in its entirety and no. 148 above.

5. Chapter 8 (nos. 97 and 99 in particular) and no. 148 above.

6. Chapter 8 (nos. 98 and 100 in particular) and no. 149 above.

7. Chapter 9 (nos. 135, 136, 137, and 139 in particular) and nos. 151–57 above.

In view of the importance of what is at stake, and notwithstanding my intention to devote a special study to the subject including all needful explanations in a forthcoming work,[8] I feel bound here and now, by way of epilogue to the present study, to sketch out the broad outlines of such a policy.

Notwithstanding the evident drawbacks of abridged presentations concerning a topic that so closely affects human lives, I have taken the view that the reader who has read the explanations and distinctions set out in the foregoing pages[9] can, without danger of confusion or misunderstanding, be presented at once with the basic practical suggestions that are the fruit of a dispassionate examination, using all the resources of up-to-date science, of the theoretical problems posed by interest.

Even if this step seems premature in some quarters, it has in its favor the crucial advantage of avoiding further delay in offering a new contribution to the distressing debate, so momentous for the future of mankind,[10] between the proponents of "laissez-faire" and those of "authoritarian planning"—a contribution capable of bringing to light hitherto unperceived options, equally distant from the opposing extreme and simplistic solutions we are offered and asked to choose between.

For events are moving so swiftly that I do not think it right to delay publication of the basic economic principles of this "competitive democracy" that both my theoretical studies and my personal contacts with economy policy making led me to six years ago and in which I see the true solution that all contemporary societies are groping toward, notwithstanding their apparent divergences, *but at the price of so many errors and so much unnecessary suffering!*[10]

---

8. This work, which I intend to publish under the title *The Philosophy of the Economy of Tomorrow: Competitive Socialism*, will develop the summary indications given above in as much detail as could be wished for while insisting on the opportuneness, the possibility, and the ways and means of implementing the proposed policy.

9. As well as those provided in my earlier works *À la recherche d'une discipline économique* (published by the author); "Économie pure et rendement social" [Pure economics and social efficiency], *Annales des mines et des carburants*, no. 15 (January 1945); *Prolégomènes à la reconstruction économique du monde* [Prolegomena to world economic reconstruction] (Paris: Sirey, 1945); "Organisation concurrentielle ou Planisme central" [Competitive organization or central planning], *Bulletin des transports*, July 1946; *Abondance ou misère* [Abundance or misery] (Paris: Librairie de Médicis, 1946); "Quelques réflexions sur l'inégalité, les classes et la promotion sociale" [Inequality, class and social promotion: Some reflections], *Économie et humanisme*, July–September 1946.

10. See my pamphlet *Prolégomènes à la reconstruction économique du monde*.

(a) Proposals for reform

1. Systematic organization of competition (159)

Study of the specific phenomenon of interest merely confirms the general findings of the study of economic equilibrium. It shows that competitive equilibrium, and hence *optimal management*, is automatically achieved when a competitive economy pursues maximum satisfaction for individuals and maximum income for firms.[1] And indeed the conditions that characterize any state of optimal management form a system that no central organism could ever directly adopt, because

1. hardly any of the satisfaction and production functions involved have yet been determined and
2. the conditions involved are too numerous[2] to be capable of resolution by calculation.

Hence only an experimental solution using the price mechanism in a competitive economy of independent agents can be envisaged.

The competitive organization of the economy is thus shown to be both a necessary and a sufficient condition for the maximization of social efficiency *for a given technology*.

And this competitive organization also emerges as the organizational method the most conducive to technological progress.[3]

This means that the main issue confronting every aware economy is how to organize competition in the labor market, the capital market, and the goods and services market.

The requisite organization should address the definition of services and products, official recognition of professional qualifications and aptitudes, product rationalization, diffusion, and information; and the struggle

---

1. At least as a first approximation (see note 2 to no. 55). Readers wishing to study this subject in greater detail will find all necessary information in my pamphlet *Économie pure et rendement social* (Paris: Sirey, 1945), nos. 13 and 31.

2. For a community of 10 million individuals consuming only 1,000 different goods, all handmade, there would be 10 billion equations.

3. This brings out a second aspect of the theory of social efficiency corresponding to a dynamic structure, whereas its first aspect concerns a static structure.

against monopolistic tendencies of every sort (monopolies, trusts, employers' syndicates, trade unions, etc.).[4,5,6]

4. I note here simply that competitive organization of the labor market implies that for
each labor category *a price is paid that equates supply and demand*. Such market organization
by no means implies the return of laissez-faire, but *simply recourse to a non-arbitrary criterion
for fixing wage levels*. Of course no such organization can be conceived without considerable
improvement of the conditions for qualification and information and without strong input
from trade unions. Neither is it in any way exclusive of direct grants at the expense of the
community (not of businesses) to all those whose competitive wages are judged insufficient
(see no. 56).

5. Such a competitive organization of the economy would naturally call for major efforts
to perfect the competitive capital market. At this point, I will simply outline their nature.

The market would have to be fully informed as to the opportunities for employing capital.
To this end, firms would be required to declare their operating results as per their books, and
their bookkeeping could itself be subject to a specific accounting system for each profession.
The authorities would be committed to ensuring that these obligations were in fact respected.

The practice of setting aside reserves or even totally replacing production equipment by
drawing directly on profits might also be prohibited. It could be stipulated that income be
distributed to shareholders who would thus be able to use it according to the opportunities
available in the market (see what has been set out in no. 41).

From this point of view it seems eminently desirable that financial investment companies
comparable to the British *Investment Trusts* should become widespread, as the shareholder is
usually ill-placed to verify the optimal use of the funds he has available.

Economic forecast centers could be established whose main duty would be to examine
investment issues.

Firms could be obliged to make their investment programs public as soon as they are
launched, although of course nothing could prevent them from planning their projects in secret.

These suggestions are not a comprehensive list; they are simply intended to show the reader
how easily the present economic system could be improved to make it more competitive.

*In this area huge improvements are possible. It is for us to identify them and put them into
practice.*

6. It should be most strongly emphasized that this organization of competition does not
necessarily imply an economy of private ownership.

*In reality, State ownership of the means of production and economic management by au-
thoritarian planning need not always go together*: either is perfectly conceivable without the
other (on this topic the reader may fruitfully consult my article "Organisation concurrentielle
ou Planisme central," *Bulletin des transports*, July 1946); but what is possible is not always
easy to implement, and the competitive organization of a totally collectivized economy would
inevitably raise *considerable* difficulties of a political nature, such that *in the present state of
popular political education they may well be deemed insurmountable.*

For it is difficult to imagine the political authorities leaving to business managers in an
entirely collectivized economy the considerable freedom of action that the realization of a
competitive economy entails.

As will be shown, this organization is perfectly compatible with *structural planning* in any direction deemed desirable, notably in the sphere of money and credit, land ownership, savings and investment, etc.

This competitive organization, in conjunction with structural planning could fittingly be termed *competitive planning* [planisme concurrentiel].[7]

For example, in order to ensure an allocation of collectivized capital equivalent to that which the competitive mechanism would give rise to in the context of private business ownership, it would be necessary to set up national financial investment companies, comparable to the English "Investment Trusts"; the capital at the State's disposal after the levies intrinsically necessary to the State sector, would then be distributed equally among them and they would be in competition with one another in the capital market, their management remuneration depending on results obtained. Thus the executives of these national companies would have freedom to manage the hundreds of billions entrusted to them *in total independence of any political authority.* Such power could not fail to appear excessive in present-day France, for instance.

However, subject to this *crucial* reserve, it must also be stated that, *from the exclusive viewpoint of economic methodology, a politically developed collectivist society would probably succeed better and more swiftly in realizing the economic conditions of maximum social efficiency than our present capitalist society even after reform.*

In reality, *only a genuine trial* could show whether, in the present state of our political education, a regime of public ownership of the means of production is, or is not, more favorable to the operation of a competitive economy than a regime of private business ownership. Such a trial *ought therefore to be made,* but to avoid running the risk of jumping out of the frying-pan into the fire and hastening toward a failure that would not only affect our own generation but might even jeopardize the advance of civilization, we ought only to undertake small-scale trials, *limited* to a few carefully selected and investigated test-firms. Only in the event that these small-scale experiments proved decisively that our political development is sufficient for a competitive economy (in the full sense of this word) to be able to function effectively in a collective context, could and should more extensive experiments be conducted. *Until this is so,* any structural modifications tending to bring about—explicitly or implicitly, sooner or later—the large-scale transformation of private business ownership into collective ownership would amount to an inhuman *gamble,* for even on the most favorable hypothesis, assuming competitive economic techniques suitable to the collective ownership context were available, the scale of the gains that could be expected in terms of possible improvement in income distribution would bear no proportion to the scale of the risks run, which would include a considerable decrease in average income and the perhaps irrevocable loss of the priceless advantages associated with the freedom of the individual and our civilization under its twofold, material and spiritual, dimensions. (On this subject, readers are referred to my study "Le problème de la planification dans une économie collectiviste," *Kyklos: International Review for Social Sciences,* July 1947.)

7. Readers who have been following the progress of my work may at first be surprised by this change of *terminology,* but it is in fact quite normal and has been forced on me by the fact that the terminology I used in the past risked giving rise to dangerous confusion in many minds.

It combines the main advantages of a market economy with those of deliberate State action in conformity with a clear plan aimed at bringing about an economy that is at once both fairer and more efficient.[8]

In the absence of such an organization, i.e., in any system of authoritarian planning[9] having no competition-based price mechanism, in which the

---

Hitherto, since the publication of my *Prolégomènes à la reconstruction économique du monde*, (cf. note 4 to this pamphlet), for the sake of terminological convenience I had used [the French word] *planisme* to denote central planning, i.e., a regime under which the various economic parameters are fixed by the authorities, which is in fact just one specific manifestation of economic planning in general. Experience has shown that this terminology runs the risk of giving public opinion the impression that I am a disciple of the laissez-faire school, opposed to all concerted, coherent action aimed at making the economy more efficient and fairer, whereas the reality is quite the opposite: *all my constructive proposals are based on such initiatives*.

Moreover, in the course of many discussions I have had in recent months, I have been surprised at how many thinkers, in principle opposed to competitiveness, were prompt to be won over to *it as soon as they realized that it was not incompatible with rational State intervention and indeed made such intervention easier*.

Finally, upon reflection, I think that the concept of planning is in itself a *key idea* that it would be absurd to discard, as it can lend invaluable help in disseminating the ideas I am defending.

This being so, I shall henceforth use the term *competitive planning* to denote the competitive management approach that I advocate. With regard to the expression *central planning*, which I formerly used to denote any system tending to replace competitive determination of prices and quantities by a system in which they are fixed by the authoritative action of a central organism, it now seems to me more in keeping with the facts and thus more suggestive, to replace it by the term *authoritarian planning*.

8. Such a Plan may underpin very effective blind economic faith, by acting as a catalyst for mobilizing energies with a view to bringing about the desired economy.

But note that *the efficacy of such a Plan remains fundamentally due to its economic coherence*, i.e., it is effective because it observes the principles of the market economy. Failure to comply with this basic condition will expose any Plan to grave illusions.

9. Note that the economies here referred to as being subject to authoritarian planning are those in which all the functions of economic life tend to be authoritatively directed by a central organism.

Such economies are quite distinct from economies planned in accordance with the competitive principle.

Competitive planning is based on planned structures (money, credit and exchange, information, general investment policy, urban and rural planning, public health and welfare system, etc.), *but within this framework, it is distinguished by the fact that the various economic agents are left independent and entirely free in their decisions*. Each good is traded in a market in which the supply and demand mechanism operates. Each seller endeavors to sell for the highest possible price and each buyer to buy for the lowest possible price. The principle is for each firm to seek to realize the maximum monetary return.

various economic agents, both individuals and firms, are not at all times able to pursue the highest satisfaction and highest incomes possible *by independent and free initiatives*, and in which the various economic activities (production and consumption) are, to a greater or lesser extent, governed by a *central organism*, all goodwill, all zeal, all effort, all knowledge are *inescapably* condemned to diminished efficiency, far from their possible maximum. This is an irrefutable scientific finding the failure of which to recognize is for every informed observer as tragic as its *absolute certainty* is manifest.[10,11]

In an economy subject to authoritarian planning, by contrast, economic management is itself planned. Prices and outputs are no longer determined by the action of the competitive mechanism operating in the context of supply and demand, but by the authoritarian decisions of central administrative organisms. For instance, how many cars are to be built or how many tons of cast iron are to be used is decided in this way.

Thus authoritarian planning is essentially a system that substitutes for the competitive determination of prices and quantities their authoritarian determination by central organisms.

By this definition, *any method of organizing the economy that refuses to make use of the competitive price principle* must be deemed to fall under authoritarian planning.

Authoritarian planning, in which the entire system of production and consumption is regulated by central planning, is opposed to competitive planning, which organizes economic freedom in a legal framework, which the present writer supports, and which the following analyses illustrate (see my articles "Organisation concurrentielle ou Planisme central" and "Deux conditions fondamentales d'un jeu efficace de la concurrence: La suppression du laisser faire et la stabilité monétaire" [Two fundamental conditions for the efficient action of competition: The elimination of laissez-faire and monetary stability], *Bulletin des transports et du commerce*, July and August 1946).

10. No one who has ever been closely involved in business management and has witnessed the *miracles* constantly wrought by the free play of personal interest and initiative and who has *at the same time* had the opportunity to watch how high-ranking civil servants work and to observe their laxity in calculations relative to the maximization of social efficiency could ever have *any practical doubt* about this issue: the findings of theoretical economics will simply confirm their own personal experience.

It is not that the men we see trying to centrally plan the economy are wanting in talent or goodwill. On the contrary, if we disregard careerists, they are generally people of outstanding ability, moved by a noble desire to promote the public interest, but who find themselves utterly unable to produce serious work on account of the sheer quantity of their daily tasks.

Economic calculation, it must be emphasized, if it is to be carried out correctly, requires *a division of intellectual labor*, operating in the competitive framework of the price mechanism. When it is no longer possible to have such a division of labor, those who direct the economy are *inevitably overwhelmed by a colossal task, surpassing the strength of any human being no matter how great his talents.*

11. I stress here that in my view there can be no worse fallacy than to consider the competitive economy as a right-wing doctrine, opposed to left-wing authoritarian planning.

The choice between a competitive economy and authoritarian planning is purely a matter of *technical economics*, quite distinct from the choice between capitalism and collectivism, i.e., between an economy based on private ownership and one based on collective ownership, a choice that fundamentally belongs to the political domain.

The best proof of this is that authoritarian planning finds convinced defenders in the right-wing parties in every country while the current Russian system has been gradually led, under the pressure of experience, to adopt a large measure of competitively based organization.

Authoritarian planning is not a left-wing doctrine any more than competition is a specifically right-wing doctrine.

For instance, there is no reason why an informed Communist government should not have recourse to the competitive technique just as in fact the Soviet government has increasingly done.

In fact, to my knowledge, the majority of executives in the French business world were or are convinced disciples of authoritarian planning. In this respect, they differ from most trade unionists only in emphasizing the need for private ownership and for central planning to be organized by business leaders rather than by the State or by trade unions. But such differences of opinion are irrelevant to the fundamental issue of the choice between competitive planning and authoritarian planning.

In reality, there are as many, if not more, supporters of authoritarian planning among the parties known as right-wing than among those known as left-wing.

Political parties are fundamentally classified according to their attitude to ownership, i.e., to distribution issues, whereas the choice between authoritarian planning and competitive organization is a management issue.

And there are in fact very many supporters of private ownership of the means of production who favor authoritarian planning just as there are supporters (still small in number but becoming daily more numerous) of collective ownership who at the same time favor competitive organization.

The outworn notion that private ownership and competitive organization go together on one side while collective ownership and authoritarian planning go together on the other are in full retreat, and this very development has helped focus attention increasingly on the real issues.

2. Selection of a stable unit of account (160)

The preceding analysis has underlined the importance of having available, for economic calculation, a unit of account that remains the same over time, and of engineering an economy in which nominal prices are sufficiently stable for comparisons to be made between them and to exclude serious disturbance to production or distribution.

Some economists have advocated gold as the standard, but experience has now shown that the gold prices of commodities can be subject to major fluctuations over time because of the inevitable variations in structural conditions (monetary needs, existing gold seams, methods of extracting and refining ore deposits, etc.) so that gold can no longer be accepted as a satisfactory unit.

Others have recommended as the unit of account a value nominally equal to the price index, i.e., a reference to the price index and the use of indexed contracts.

Undoubtedly a unit of this sort is much more satisfactory than gold; but precisely what index ought to be selected? The index of the general price level, the cost-of-living index, or the wholesale price index? For example, if the cost-of-living index is selected, what goods and services should be taken into account, and how?[1] The question is clearly more complex than it might seem at first sight.[2]

Indeed it is legitimate to wonder whether such a unit would ever be really satisfactory, no matter how it was defined. For between one period and another, tastes vary, product quality alters, and amounts consumed change. So it hardly seems an acceptable solution to select as unit of value the value of a particular group of goods defined once and for all and assigning once and for all to each of these goods its relative importance.

---

1. I.e., how should they be weighted relative to one another?

2. In any event indexation ought not to be limited only to the sums stipulated; it ought also to extend to the rates of interest. In fact interest rates ought to be continuously corrected to take account of price variations between the time of the agreement and the time when the interest payments are made (see note 13 to no. 111).

Much more satisfactory, in my view, would be to choose as unit of account the value of the unit of unskilled labor in a given locality.[3,4] As the basic role of the unskilled worker is to accomplish rough tasks in which physical strength is paramount, this kind of labor represents an economic good that remains *largely identical over time*. Whereas there can be no legitimate comparison between the oxcarts used by the Merovingian kings and a 20th-century limousine, and even for gold a basic difference is obvious between its weight-for-weight economic role in ancient Greece and in the modern world, unskilled labor emerges as a practically invariable economic datum, so that there is scarcely any difference, for instance, between the work done by a laborer under the pharaohs and that done by his modern-day counterpart on any of our building sites.

Granted *such a unit of account is arbitrary, as indeed every other unit must be; but of all possible units, this one seems to me to be, in human terms, the least arbitrary and the most satisfactory*.

Adopting this unit would amount to maintaining a fixed nominal value for the basic wage.[5] Under this system, nominal prices and interest levels would be *wage* prices and *wage* interest levels.[6] In terms of wages, prices would gradually fall owing to technical progress, and the purchasing power of all social classes would thereby be slowly but continually increased.

In an economy of this sort, the price system would be protected from the present monetary disturbances and the monetary system could be taken to be "*neutral*."

3. Paris in the case of France.

4. As the labor market may develop in a non-homogenous way in the different occupations, *this basic wage could be taken as equal to the average weighted value (depending on the size of the workforce) of the unit wages of the unskilled worker in each field of activity.*

5. It is beyond the scope of the present study to analyze the policy to be implemented to ensure the stability of this value in a competitive system or to assess its psychological possibility. However, a few remarks of a technical nature will be found in note 5 to no. 161 below.

6. Nos. 5 and 19.

3. Monetary depreciation (161)

As has already been remarked, the scarcity of capital is fundamentally attributable to present structural conditions (private land ownership and the fixed relationship of the circulating currency to the accounting currency). As this scarcity is undesirable, since it leads to lower social productivity, it is advisable to modify the structural conditions that prevent the equipment stock from reaching its optimal level. From the monetary angle this undertaking *necessarily* implies depreciation of money in real terms.[1]

Now, it so happens that this depreciation of money also comprises one of the *necessary* conditions of the elimination of economic cycles,[2] as it is the only effective way to prevent money hoarding.

For these reasons, depreciation of money is in my view imperative. But, as we have seen, the existence of a unit of account that remains constant over time is an equally indispensable condition for a properly functioning economy. *These two contradictory conditions can only be satisfied by separating the functions of money so that the circulating currency is distinct from the accounting currency*, as has been the case at different periods of history.[3]

While the unit of account would bear a constant ratio to the basic wage of unskilled labor, circulating money itself[4] would continuously depreciate at a rate depending on the economic situation assessed in light of experience.[5,6]

1. No. 139.
2. Nos. 100, 112, 113, and 149.
3. Note 1 to no. 6.
4. Comprising both cash and demand deposits.
5. As various proposals have already been put forward for the depreciation of money that, in my opinion, are either inapplicable or subject to major disadvantages, I think it appropriate to state here how such a policy could in fact be implemented.

The functions of unit of account and circulating medium would be fulfilled by two distinct kinds of currency: the accounting currency and the circulating currency.

The accounting currency, the unit of which could be called [for France] the "account franc" or more simply the *franc*, would bear a fixed ratio to the value of the unit of unskilled labor and would fulfill the function of unit of account over space at any given time and over time.

Prices would be set and contracts expressed in francs. The use of any other unit would be expressly prohibited and contracts directly or indirectly referring to one (for instance, in the form of indexed contracts) would be deemed null and void.

The unit of circulating money could be called the "circulating franc," or more simply the *circul*; at every point in time there would be an exchange rate in force expressing its value in relation to the account franc and it would have a physical form, like our present money, in the shape of notes or coins for small sums. The circul would be legal tender to settle any purchase or any debt expressed in francs, regardless of the amount.

The wage value of the circulating money would be progressively diminished in accordance with a rate established in light of experience. The nominal rate of this devaluation may be estimated at about 5% per annum.

For substantial payments (greater than 100,000 francs), the wage value of circulating money would be adjusted daily; for medium-sized payments (1,000 to 100,000 francs), it would only be modified once a week and for day-to-day payments (less than 1,000 francs) the exchange rate would be changed only once every month.

Tables would be regularly issued giving conversion formulae depending on the transaction date, and dedicated calculating devices of a simple model would be used in trade to facilitate their application.

In view of its continuous depreciation, circulating money would be periodically renewed to prevent the circul from becoming too low in value. For instance, whenever the value of the circul had fallen to 0.10 francs, all the old circuls would be withdrawn from circulation and replaced by circuls whose value was once more equal to 1 franc. Each circul would bear its respective date of issue. (For a 10% rate of depreciation this operation would occur every 23 years, a period that would increase to 46 years for a 5% rate.)

No doubt such a system would be in some respects difficult to apply and less simple than the present system, but in my opinion the following points are crucial:

1. This system is certainly much less complex than it seems at first sight.

People have long since become accustomed to the idea of currency exchange: it is easy to understand, and its application is not beyond anyone who has mastered the rule of three.

It is quite certain that the system proposed would be a source of many technical problems for accountants, but these problems would be easy to resolve and do not in my view raise any fundamental difficulties.

2. A comparable system worked in practice throughout the Middle Ages, although at that time education was much less widespread than it is today and the material facilities available were incomparably weaker.

3. The proposed system is the only one possible that reconciles the simultaneous need for an accounting currency whose value remains stable and circulating money that undergoes continuous depreciation.

As the rate of depreciation of circulating money is fixed, the amount of money in circulation could not be arbitrary. For *in equilibrium*, for a given nominal value of money, the level of nominal prices and hence the nominal value of the basic wage would be well determined as a function of the quantity of circulating medium. Hence, for the nominal value of this wage to remain precisely constant, i.e., for money to be neutral in the meaning of no. 160, the quantity of money would need to have a well-determined value. This value could only be determined by trial and error.

In theory, of course, the quantity of money actually in circulation would be constantly increased by regular issues of circuls so that the aggregate value of the circulation would remain constant in wage terms.

It would therefore in theory be regularly increased according to a rate equal to the annual depreciation rate d of the circulating currency. This would provide the State with annual resources equal to the fraction d of the wage-value of its circulating currency. On the basis of a 5% rate, these resources may be reckoned at some 3 to 4% of national income.

However, as structural changes could occur (in technology or in individual psychologies), the conditions for monetary neutrality would be only imperfectly realized: indispensable adjustments would have to be made in light of trends observed on the labor market.

For instance, if an upward trend in the nominal value (i.e., the value in account francs) of the basic wage at Paris (as defined in note 4 to no. 160 above) became apparent, it ought to be interpreted as meaning that the wage-value of the quantity of circulating money was higher than its neutral value and should therefore be diminished by issuing less circulating money. Needless to say, experience would be the safest guide to how this decrease ought to be applied in practice.

6. Comparable suggestions have already been made, among which special mention is due to those of Irving Fisher in his work *Stamp Scrip* and those of Silvio Gesell in his *The Natural Economic Order* (see note 34 to no. 164), although I have unfortunately not yet been able to take cognizance of either work.

4. 100% backing of demand deposits (162)

Since the fact that banks can issue unbacked deposit money comprises, as we have seen, one of the two basic destabilizing factors behind economic cycles, it is surely *indispensable* to forbid them to do so by obliging them to have 100% backing for their demand deposits.[1]

Banks would still be able to conduct discount operations, but they would have to do so using funds specially provided for this purpose.[2,3,4]

Under these conditions the role of the banks would be reduced to (a) the simplification of payments and (b) the concentration of savings with a view to their investment in production.

1. Nos. 100, 112, 113, and 149.

2. For this purpose, deposits could be divided into two categories: demand deposits and term deposits.

All demand deposits would be *denominated in circuls* since deposit money would have to depreciate at the same rate as money in the form of cash (note 4 to no. 161) and their value at the day's rate would have to be backed in its entirety by an equal amount of circulating money. The banks would debit from these accounts a corresponding conservation fee.

Term deposits, on which the banks would pay interest, would operate as under the present system.

The only difference would be that capital loaned by depositors to the banks would be loaned for a fixed period and would not be withdrawable on demand, while the banks would have to find the resources needed for their loans not in their demand deposits but in the capital loaned to them, for a short or long term, for this purpose.

In this way the disadvantages of the present system could be avoided while keeping the advantages.

3. To avoid any deflationary effect of the implementation of the reform it would be necessary for the Central Bank to deliver to the commercial banks, upon implementation, the circulating money needed to back their demand deposits in their entirety. In return for this the banks could deposit with the State either their own bonds or government or private securities for an equal amount, these securities being valued at the going rate (see what was said in note 23 to no. 108).

4. Similar proposals have already been made by a certain number of economists, including once again Irving Fisher (in his *100% Money*) as well as by very well-informed banking technicians such as M. Cauboue (in his *Philosophie de la banque* [Paris: Éditions de Banque, 1937], 97). To my regret I have not yet had the opportunity of becoming acquainted with Irving Fisher's work.

5. Collectivization of land ownership (163)

Since the private appropriation of land necessarily leads to an artificial scarcity of capital[1] and hence to a substantial loss of social productivity, I consider that the collectivization of land ownership[2] is imperative[3] for any economy wishing to adopt a rational organization.

It is important to note that land collectivization, far from being incompatible with the operations of a competitive economy in which reproducible capital is privately owned,[4] could only improve and facilitate them.[5,6,7]

1. No. 157.

2. N.B. ownership of the land itself (note 1 to no. 30).

3. See in particular note 5 to no. 139.

4. Of course all the following remarks remain a fortiori valid for an economy in which ownership of *all* production goods is collective. See notes 6 to no. 159 and 1 to no. 169.

5. Especially in terms of consolidation.

There would be no reason why the land could not be periodically let by the administration to the highest bidder.

The land system would be absolutely parallel to the general system in England except that the landowners would here be replaced by the community.

Lessees' obligations would be contractually specified. These would stipulate that at the end of the lease the land would revert to the State together with all improvements made to it of whatever nature and the lessee's duty to keep land and facilities in good working order throughout the period immediately preceding the end of the lease. The length of the lease would depend mainly on the use the land was put to; it could range from 5 to 100 years according to the case. The minimum lease would be for pastureland and the maximum for mines, electrical concessions, railways, etc., whenever the relevant reproducible capital was not already nationalized. At the expiry of one lease, when offers are being tendered for the next, the outgoing lessee would have right of first refusal.

It is all the harder to contest the possibility of such a system given that a very similar one has operated in England for centuries.

For "there is no evidence that a tenant-farmer would farm his holding less well simply because its owner was a public institution rather than a private individual; indeed the former would be more likely to have civil servants and agents equipped and empowered to check the tenant-farmer's work." (Roberto A. Murray, *Leçons d'économie politique suivant la doctrine de l'école de Lausanne* [Paris: Payot, 1920], 432.)

On the contrary, the substitution of public ownership for private ownership would enable certain enhancements to be made to the English system: systematic experimental studies of the various tenant-farming systems, standardization of contracts, specialization of inspectors, general rural development programs, general urban development programs, etc.

Note too that in terms of urban and rural planning an unlimited right of private land ownership is quite unjustifiable. It is unacceptable to let private whims and pretentions spoil whole areas by crowding them with disparate and disorderly buildings, each more absurd and

It cannot be too strongly emphasized that the reason why land collectivization is vital has nothing to do with the desire to bring about better social

---

ugly than the last. Indeed land collectivization seems to be the fundamental prerequisite of
any efficient urban and rural planning policy.

6. No doubt the objection will be made that depriving the farmer of the ownership of his
land amounts to cutting off his roots and would jeopardize development of agricultural life
and hence the very future of the whole country.

I am second to none, however, in my conviction of the farmer's mission: the farmer is the
very source of the Nation in terms of health of body and vigor of mind; he it is who ensures the
continuity and stability of national life, but I am no less firmly convinced that the land reform
here put forward, *far from compromising the future of the farming community, would provide
it with solid foundations for a better life and more effective techniques that it currently lacks and
without which its future may indeed be in danger.*

7. Detailed examination of the *possibility of a land buy-up* is beyond the scope of the present study. I note simply that two approaches are possible: either voluntary buy-up through the
mechanism of a Capital Accumulation Fund (no. 138 and in particular note 14), or compulsory
purchase against fair compensation.

In the latter case, theory shows (see my *À la recherche d'une discipline économique*,
no. 163) that, provided the rate of interest was systematically lowered, it would be possible for
the State to buy up land from its owners without their undergoing any financial loss whatever,
while the operation would be in the interests of the State.

For these two conditions to be simultaneously respected implies (a) that the buy-up price
be equal to the market price and (b) that the market price be lower than the real value of
the land.

Obviously the prices in question must be expressed in wage terms. For if land were bought
up at its nominal price and a general price rise unforeseen by the market ensued (whether or
not deliberately provoked by the State), it would amount to actual spoliation.

But both conditions would in fact be fulfilled if the wage-denominated interest rate was
systematically lowered by the State. For this fall would lead to an unforeseen increase in the
capitalized value of future land income expressed in wage terms, so that, *to reimburse the capitalized value of the land at the initial wage-denominated interest rate it would suffice, with the
new rates of interest, to leave the land at the disposal of the parties concerned for a finite number
of years, a number all the lower as the fall in the wage-denominated rate of interest was sharper.*

From the psychological point of view it could be stipulated that the buy-up terms would
under no circumstances deprive an owner of the free use of his land for the rest of his life—
a provision that could be extended to the next generation in the case of directly farmed
smallholdings.

Doubtless the objection will be made that the farming community would be sure to react
violently at the very idea of a measure that would at first sight appear to be to its disadvantage
by depriving it of the perpetual ownership of the land.

However, it should first be noted that the land reform proposed above would in fact leave
land-derived wealth unchanged in terms of wage value. It would simply appropriate to the
State any *unforeseen* excess profits derived from the land. So owners would be fully compensated for their expropriation and hence could not consider themselves wronged.

justice by public appropriation of capital gains from land on the grounds
of unjust enrichment, nor with the desire to provide the State with new resources, but is simply due to the fact that private land ownership necessarily brings about an artificial scarcity of capital, which is harmful to all.[8]

This remark is particularly applicable to landlords who do not farm their own land: they
would be *fully* maintained in their financial rights, the legitimacy of which might in other
circumstances have been contested.

On the other hand, the proposed suspension of the effect of the expropriation until the
death of the current owners, or of their children in the case of smallholders, would postpone
it until so distant a date that the present owners, not feeling themselves directly concerned,
would probably offer no more than weak opposition. Whereas immediate expropriation
would indeed run the risk of triggering major difficulties, deferred expropriation would certainly be accepted without too many protests. Once the principle was admitted, minds would
gradually become accustomed to the idea of a reform whose advantages would become apparent with experience.

Really serious resistance could only be expected from those farming or otherwise exploiting their own land, but their expropriation would occur at different dates depending on
individual deaths, which would make it much easier, for at any given point in time there would
be too few owners affected by dispossession and too many farmers interested in competing
for the lease of the newly available lands for the resistance to be really effective.

In fact, especially bearing in mind that in France active farmers own less than 35% of the
total land surface, they would soon realize that the land reform would in fact make the land
available to them under much fairer and more advantageous conditions (long-term leases, con-
solidated lands, the possibility of rational farming programs, and hence increased income, etc.).

Long-term land leasing by the community with first refusal on renewal would not be a
hindrance for the farmer. On the contrary, it would enable him to obtain full ownership of the
fruits of his own labor whereas at present he is in constant danger of being exposed to the
exorbitant demands of a greedy landlord. (Nor should the present Fédération Française [a
French farmers' union—Trans.], which is purely temporary, deceive anyone.)

Thus the land reform here proposed, *far from being opposed to the real interests of the
farming community, would strengthen its social position* and more than any other would enable farmers to recover their rightful place in the countryside—the first place—by eliminating
the feudal land rights of landlords who do not cultivate their own land. After appropriate psychological preparation and provided it was implemented gradually, accompanied by judicious
and convincing trials (consolidation, rational mechanization, etc.), this reform could thus be
realized, I am sure, *with the agreement of almost all the interested parties.*

These brief points make no claim to provide an exhaustive answer to a question fraught
with so many major problems calling for delicate handling. Their purpose is simply to show
right now that land collectivization, even in an economy of private ownership of capital, is a
measure that would be much easier to implement than might at first be supposed.

8. If land ownership were public and the rate of interest were lowered, the value of the
land owned by the State would increase indefinitely, but this would be of no consequence, as
land would be neither valued nor bought and sold. Only the services of land would have a
regular market.

Thus the fundamental motive for collectivization of land ownership is technical, not ethical, in nature. There might also be ethical grounds for taking the same step (in order to appropriate capital gains derived from land, for instance), but in this writer's opinion this is a purely subsidiary aspect that would not suffice on its own to justify the measure: land collectivization is not based on political or financial expediency; it is a *strictly technical measure*, imposed by the innate structure of the competitive economy under a regime of private property.

6. Realization of a zero rate of interest (164)

It follows from the foregoing analysis that *maximization of social produc-tivity would have the considerable advantage of raising disposable national income to a level well above that achieved under current structural condi-tions and that if these conditions were suitably modified, we may take it that for equal propensities to save and to own, the long-term equilibrium that would spontaneously tend to arise would lead to a situation little different from this maximization.*

However, even under conditions so modified, it is certain that rigorous maximization of social productivity could not come about spontaneously, and it would be highly surprising for the spontaneous equilibrium that would tend to arise to correspond exactly to a zero rate of interest. *State intervention must therefore be envisaged.*

I have stated that this intervention could only be made on social grounds, quite independent of pure economics, since such a policy would necessar-ily lead to a different distribution of national consumable income, either between the generations or, for a single generation, between the different periods of its life, whereas from the exclusively economic standpoint all possible distributions must be regarded as equivalent.

From the social standpoint, however, there is no doubt in my mind as to the choice to be made. At a time when so much misery is still found, surely the substantial, *permanent* increase in consumable national income that would result from an increased investment effort over a *limited* period ought not to be neglected. The more so since the reduced consumption that the present generation would have to bear—assuming that maximum social productivity had not been achieved, or even surpassed,[1] spontaneously— could be offset, via suitable policies, by an increase in its *own* consumption in the future.[2]

Such a policy would be no different in principle from the policy of a State that prevents inconsiderate exploitation of mineral deposits designed to increase output for equal labor input at the cost of compromising their

---

1. The latter possibility is *practically* excluded on account of the impossibility, in equi-librium, of stationary competitive conditions with a significant negative rate of interest—an impossibility that is due to the existence of goods, such as metals, capable of being stored at no appreciable expense (no. 136).

2. Nos. 74 and 77.

future exploitation. No one denies that it may be appropriate for the State to regulate the exploitation of natural resources so as to safeguard the interests of future generations or the future interests of present generations who may not at present be sufficiently heedful of their own future.

This shows that there are cases when the common good requires the spontaneous equilibrium generated by the free play of competition to be discarded, *precisely because competition takes account only of the individual aspirations of the individual members of a given generation at a given time and not of the interests of other generations, or even of the interests of the present generation at a later time.*

By implementing a policy of this kind the State is simply endeavoring to bring about a distribution of consumer goods different from that which would tend to occur spontaneously; inasmuch as it enables production to be increased and the social atmosphere to be improved, to the advantage of each individual considered separately, such a policy seems to me entirely justified.

In the case we are considering I have no doubt that the policy would be absolutely justified, provided that the sacrifices[3] of the currently active generation were compensated, as would be quite possible, by increasing its future consumption to match the whole increase in disposable national income obtained by this policy.[4] On the one hand, the increase in consumable national income, and on the other, a more provident distribution of individual incomes over time could not fail to bring about conditions more favorable both to increased production and to social order and harmony.

The State seems to me to be ideally suited to the role of arbiter of income distribution both between generations and between the different stages in the life of a particular generation. The State exists beyond time, or rather time does not count for it. Only the State can be objective in taking account of the interests of future generations and of the future interests of present generations. It alone can validly, in light of experience, deem socially preferable an income distribution different from the one that would emerge from spontaneous economic equilibrium, since it has in its *simultaneous* purview the individuals of every age and can thus infer by extrapolation from its observations of the psychology of the elderly, what the

3. Note, once again, that these sacrifices would only be needed if, even after suitable changes to present structural conditions, spontaneous savings remained insufficient to ensure the maximization of social productivity.

4. No. 74.

psychology of today's youth[5] is destined to become when they are old. And only the State can fairly evaluate the advantages that temporary restriction of consumption may bring in the future thanks to the increase in social productivity—advantages that will pass unnoticed by the solitary individual on the marketplace, since the only prices he can take account of in order to assess the future are present prices, whereas these prices would fall sharply if social productivity were increased.

Hence it is clear that *when a State increases savings by means of taxation in order to maximize social productivity, it is in large measure simply bringing about the equilibrium position that would arise spontaneously—by the free play of competition—if individuals had a clear and objective perception of their future psychologies and of the advantages that maximized social productivity would bring.*

If then it is recognized that the maximization of social productivity in the shorter or longer term is a desirable goal for every enlightened economic community,[6] a twofold problem arises:

1. *At what speed* should the volume of investment be raised to the level corresponding to maximization of social productivity, i.e., how quickly should the rate of interest[7] be gradually lowered[8] by appropriate State intervention on the Capital market?[9]
2. *How*, in light of this policy, should consumable output be *allocated* between the generations at each point in time?

With regard to the first question, a reasonable policy for France in 1938 would in my opinion[10] have been to aim to maximize social productivity over some 20 years, without decreasing consumable national income, while devoting to investment the increase in national output resulting from (a) stable full employment[11] and (b) technical progress.

---

5. See no. 63.

6. Irrespective of whether or not the ownership of production goods is collective.

7. Which, in the event that the unit of account is pegged to the basic wage of unskilled labor, is a *wage* interest rate.

8. After eliminating whatever may currently prevent it from being lowered (nos. 135 and 136).

9. Needless to say, for such a policy to be effective the conditions of the maximization of social efficiency must first be in place (no. 159).

10. These remarks are of course applicable to the United States in 1946.

11. Made possible by the monetary policy set out above (nos. 161 and 162) and based on the conclusions of nos. 100, 112, and 113.

The solution of the problem for France is at present rendered much more difficult on account of the destruction of a proportion of our capital, which can be estimated as roughly equivalent to two years' national income.[12] It is imperative for this capital to be *swiftly* restored (a) because such a reduced equipment stock corresponds in equilibrium to a greatly diminished national income[13] and, much more importantly, (b) because as the destruction affected unequally an equipment stock adapted to a specific interest rate level, the decrease in the national income that would follow from failure to rebuild our capital equipment levels would be *far greater* than if the undestroyed equipment stock had corresponded to a stable equilibrium.[14]

This rapid restoration of our 1938 capital is therefore necessary, and plainly it can be achieved only at the cost of substantially reducing our 1938 standard of living for several years. Obviously, this could be achieved under the best possible conditions if we were able to borrow the sums needed from the United States at a rate of interest close to their marginal technical interest rate. *Costly though this policy might at first appear, it would in due course mean a gain for us corresponding to the current difference between our own very high marginal technical interest rate[15] and the much lower rate prevailing in the United States.*[16]

Only a policy of this kind would enable our generation to avoid the suffering entailed in restoring our national capital on our own suffering of which the Russian predicament during the five-year plans can give us some idea.

Our 1938 equipment stock once restored, the easier-to-apply policy outlined above could of course be adopted.[17]

---

12. This destruction is in fact aggravated by the more or less visible destruction of capital that took place between 1930 and 1938 on account of the insufficient restoration of our equipment owing to consumption of part of our capital depreciation.

13. Diminished by about 20% (note 13 to no. 71).

14. From the twofold perspective of no. 73 of (a) the adjustment of the total equipment stock to the level of general economic activity and (b) its optimal distribution between the various branches of production.

For instance, it is clear that the failure to reconstitute the transport network would lead to a much greater loss in national income than the loss corresponding in equilibrium to a fall in the stock of equipment for equal value.

15. In my opinion on the order of at least 8%.

16. Unless of course some adventurous general policy of the French government should lead American lenders to require a particularly high risk premium (no. 99, § "The case of international equilibrium").

17. The delicacy of the *sociological issues* raised by any investment policy finally becomes clear, together with the fact that, although the results obtained by the theory of social

With regard to the second question, the easiest policy to implement in our economy of private ownership of capital,[18] is for the consumption sector to adopt the same rate of interest as prevails in the production sector, even if this means making up for the insufficiency of some forms of saving by compulsory savings[19] and compensating the present generation for its exceptional investment efforts by retirement pensions to be financed by coming generations.[20,21]

There ought to be no major difficulty in *implementing* such a policy.

The capital market would remain free, but the State would intervene in it to bring about the desired pure rate of interest in the event of its being lower than the pure rate of interest corresponding to spontaneous equilibrium.[22,23] It would do this by unlimited lending of risk-free capital[24] at the desired rate.[25]

---

productivity emerge as fundamental data that every government must take into account in fixing its policy, *maximum does not mean optimum*—the decision may very well be made to give up short-term maximization of social productivity in order not to crush the present generation.

For if realized too rapidly, the maximization might in fact be in the interests only of future generations, leaving present generations unable to derive any advantage from the operation beyond a surfeit of burdens that would be exceedingly hard to bear.

Thus it seems that the basic policy of the USSR from 1925 onward has been to pursue the maximization of social productivity, more or less by instinct, no matter how great the consequent sufferings of the present generation may be—and they have in fact proved to be enormous.

18. Which can remain in force, as has already been observed, in the context of collective land appropriation (no. 163).

19. In the form of social security contributions, for instance (no. 77).

20. Enabling the present generation to receive all or part of the increased output made possible by the present restriction of consumption (see the text preceding note 4 above and nos. 74 and 145).

21. Of course, in the case of the USSR, a double interest rate could be contemplated.

22. Taking account of the intended structural modifications (public land ownership and depreciation of money).

23. It would in fact be advisable for the State to make known *in advance* its program of lowering the rate of interest so that firms could take it into account in their profitability calculations. In this way, for instance, in the production of electrical energy, where investments are particularly long term, firms would be induced to implement almost at once the investments corresponding to a zero interest rate.

It is in such fields that "Planning" is highly desirable, but *the plan involved relates to structure rather than to action*, the latter being the very essence of Central Economic Planning (see note 8 to no. 159).

24. I.e., loans whose reimbursement in nominal value—in the present case in wage terms (no. 160)—is certain.

25. Obtaining the necessary resources via taxation.

Once a zero pure interest rate was in place, a similar policy could be pursued in the event that spontaneous savings remained or became insufficient.[26]

If, on the other hand, spontaneous savings became superabundant, in order to hold the pure interest rate at zero, the State would have to borrow unlimitedly at this rate all the capital on offer that could not be absorbed in the form of real investments.[27,28]

Of course, in any event, the State would only ever intervene in the risk-free capital market, so that other markets would all remain free and their rates of interest would settle at whatever level the competitive mechanism led to.[29]

The effect of a zero rate of interest is not that the use of capital goods would no longer cost anything, but that the income derived from them would have to cover at most the depreciation due to wear and tear and to obsolescence plus a certain margin corresponding to the reward for risks assumed and the reward for using skill and sound judgment. In other words, in the course of their existence durable goods would provide overall income covering at most the cost of the labor needed to produce them

26. Once again, I note that the timeliness of such a policy is a question of fact, depending fundamentally on weighing up the difficulty of implementing it against the advantages to be expected.

Thus technical progress might be so fast that it would become extremely difficult to achieve swiftly enough the volume of investment needed to bring the marginal technical rate of interest on capital down to zero. In this case, it would be puerile to insist on keeping the rate of interest at zero at any cost, thereby imposing on the present generation a crushing, if not utterly unbearable, savings effort. All that can be said, in my view, is that a zero rate of interest remains desirable and is a goal to be aimed at insofar as possible.

27. The funds received in this way would increase the resources of the State, which could at once re-inject them into the economy (civil engineering projects, reimbursement of funds previously received, etc.).

In this last case, in order to prevent public debt from exceeding whatever level is deemed desirable, an inheritance tax could be levied on those classes of the population presumed to be saving too much. The amount of this tax would be determined by trial and error with the aim of ensuring that spontaneous savings in equilibrium did not exceed the level needed to keep the rate of interest at zero. The State would use these resources to diminish its other taxes.

28. Note that a spontaneous equilibrium could not include a significantly negative rate of interest on account of the possibility of storing certain goods at no significant cost (see note 1 above), but as the permanent investment of capital in the form of stored goods might become a cause of potential price disequilibrium, it would be preferable to discourage the building up of such stores by holding the pure interest rate at zero.

29. When the pure interest rate was held at zero, each rate of interest would be equal to the sum of the various corresponding premiums considered in no. 84.

plus the costs of skill and watchfulness and a fraction corresponding to risk, in accordance with the same principles that currently govern the price of consumer goods, where capital costs account for only an insignificant proportion.[30]

Such a state of affairs would be perfectly compatible with the principle of the autonomy of action of economic agents, i.e., freedom of choice for individuals and freedom of management for firms. *Its only consequence would be the gradual disappearance of capitalists' excess profits derived from the value that the use of capital acquires as a result of its artificial scarcity.*

This effect ought to be counted a thoroughly favorable point in social terms. For, as I have emphasized, the rate of interest as the price of a service rendered continues to exist only as the result of unfavorable structural conditions. *This price constitutes an income essentially related to the preservation of the laissez-faire regime in a field from which it ought to be eliminated.*[31] For capital accumulation is too important to be left to the hazard of personal actions quite indifferent to the common interest[32] operating in a purely contingent context that is itself due to the randomness of history. Thus the task of the public authorities is to bring about structural

---

30. Some might argue that under a zero interest rate all incentive to real investment would disappear and progress would thus be shackled.

This idea is due to confusion. In reality, technical and economic progress are not due to a specific market interest rate but to the differences between this rate and the expected technical interest rates on capital in the intended investments. In fact these differences are the sole factors of progress. So the lower the market rate, the higher the returns production is able to offer: hence if a zero interest rate was successfully put in place in the market without infringement of freedom of choice for the individual or of freedom of management for firms, far from ultimately discouraging the spirit of enterprise, it would stimulate it. As for the supply of savings by individuals investing in capital, under such conditions, as has been shown, it could only be increased (nos. 147 and 154).

31. On this subject my conclusions concur with those of J. M. Keynes in his general theory, although they have been reached by an intellectual process far different from that followed by the great English economist.

32. Itself identical with the particular interest of *each individual*, properly understood.

conditions enabling capital to be expanded until it ceases to be scarce, and to intervene, if necessary, to ensure that this in fact happens.[33,34,35]

33. Reminder: a zero interest rate in the production sector leaves the State free elsewhere to follow whatever policy it deems preferable as to the distribution of the income of each generation between present and future consumption, irrespective of whether production goods are publicly or privately owned (see nos. 77 and 145).

34. As far as I am able to judge, general economic conclusions very close to my own, both as to the need for competitive organization and as to the advantages of collectivized land ownership, a zero interest rate and the ongoing depreciation of money have already been presented, *though using reasoning by and large very different from mine*, by Silvio Gesell in his work *Die natürliche Wirtschaftsordnung durch Freiland und Freigeld* [The natural economic order through free land and free money] (published by the author, 1906, 1911, 1916), translated into English from the sixth German edition under the title *The Natural Economic Order* (San Antonio, TX: Free-Economy Publishing Co.), of which I have unfortunately not yet been able to take direct cognizance (see in particular J. M. Keynes, *General Theory of Employment, Money and Interest*, bk. 6, ch. 23, § 6). Note that for Keynes, "the future will learn more from the spirit of Gesell than from that of Marx." It would certainly be an exceedingly useful undertaking to translate this work from German into French.

35. These proposals are of course limited to the national context of individual States—overall examination of international economic problems exceeds the scope of the present study. I note only at this point that the only reasonable solution to present international problems, alone able *at once* to banish all threat of war while enabling standards of living to be raised throughout the world, is *the organization of a Federal World Government based on the free circulation of goods, capital, people, and information*. Note that while at present substantial difficulties lie in the way of the realization of this global State, there is no real obstacle to the immediate (i.e., in the space of a few months) establishment, within the framework of a constitution such as that of the United States, of a *Western European Federation* that would comprise its *inevitable and necessary* first stage. For the great mass of public opinion in the various countries of Western Europe is already won over, really or virtually, we may say, to the underlying principles of such a Federation.

(b) General advantages of the proposed economic policy

1. Fundamental defects of the laissez-faire system (165)

Economic organization raises three problems:

1. How to organize production;
2. How to adjust the various sectors of the economy to one another;
3. How to distribute the disposable income produced.

In reality, *the laissez-faire capitalist economy has only partially succeeded in resolving the first question (how to organize production) and has entirely failed in respect of the other two.*

With regard to the organization of production, the laissez-faire economy has only partially brought about the competitive conditions implied by optimal management. For a long time the highly effective stimulant of competition was considered, under the influence of the liberal doctrines, to be essentially connected to the action of personal interest under a laissez-faire regime. But there is no basis for asserting such a connection. In reality, competition is not a necessary outcome of personal interest acting under a laissez-faire regime, and *while interest is the rule, spontaneous competition is not*. The doctrine of laissez-faire, which depends on one of the two, while presuming that it necessarily leads to the other, is therefore fundamentally unsound.

In reality, interest, economic freedom, and competition are not the three harmonious ingredients of an economic and social force that would automatically lead the economy to optimal management and absolve legislators of the need to resolve the difficult problem of economic order.

Fundamentally beneficial as it is, competition is possible, but it is neither spontaneous nor automatic, and it can only exist within the framework of the law.[1]

All the same, it must be stated that the unorganized character, or even absence, of competition, which has so often characterized the laissez-faire economy, is but a slight defect compared with *the artificial scarcity of capi-*

---

1. Naturally these criticisms in no way diminish the immensity of what has been achieved in a century by laissez-faire economics. They are intended to stress that much more still could have been achieved if the conditions of competition had always been realized.

tal that its economic ignorance and its systematic prejudice against intervention have fostered in the production sector. Whereas the State, with a few structural changes and at most a few relatively minor interventions in the capital market, could certainly have brought about maximization of the social productivity of land and labor more or less continuously, *its failure to do so has systematically checked our society's progress toward well-being, and the civilization that depends on it.*

As to the adaptation of the various sectors of the economy to one another, the laissez-faire regime has been able neither to prevent, nor even forecast, the cyclical depressions that have regularly wrought havoc with the economy and brought about so much misery, the last of which must be deemed to lie at the direct origin of the second world conflict. *Its resounding failure in this field has been especially disastrous,* for it has contributed more than any other to leading the economies of the various civilized countries, in an apparently inevitable way, toward forms of centralized authoritarian planning that can lead only to misery and to the disappearance of a philosophy of life gradually elucidated by centuries upon centuries of laborious effort.[2]

Finally, *with regard to distribution, laissez-faire economics has constantly led to a situation that is scandalous and intolerable to every unbiased observer* by enabling some parties to take advantage of monopolistic situations at the expense of the entire community, by leaving the victims of unemployment long unaided, by allowing working conditions to jeopardize workers' health and lives, by demoralizing society via unethical excess profits derived from inflation, and by allowing some parties to take advantage of an entirely factitious scarcity of capital. *There can be no denying that these conditions have truly given rise to "the exploitation of man by man" and, by their flagrant immorality, have brought personal interest into disrepute, whereas, properly used, it alone is able to bring about economic progress toward ever-higher levels of well-being.*

No doubt many initiatives have been undertaken in recent years with a view to alleviating the inadequacies of laissez-faire, but no matter how well-intentioned the legislator has been, *his measures have more often than not proved counterproductive and in any event have never tackled the real problems.*

Instead of organizing and perfecting competition, he has gradually eliminated the conditions needed for it to function; the problem of optimal

2. On this subject, see my pamphlet *Prolégomènes à la reconstruction économique du monde.*

management of the economy has never been clearly formulated,[3] and the issue of ownership has been constantly confused with that of management. The issue of optimal economic equipment has practically never been addressed.[3] The problem of economic cycles has remained unresolved. The practical solutions offered thereto have remained fragmentary and, overall, ineffective. As for distribution conditions, it is quite clear that no satisfactory policy could be put in place so long as the boom continued to alternate with depression and interest charges continued to allocate to some parties a share of the national income out of proportion to their savings effort.

By contrast, on these three issues of the organization of production, the adjustment of the various sectors to one another and distribution, the economic policy here proposed is capable of providing satisfactory solutions and hence of completely changing the appearance of economic and social problems, even internationally.[4]

---

3. Save by a very small number of economists.

4. The following observations are simply intended to sketch a broad outline of the economic and social advantages of the principles of political economy that I have presented.

2. Advantages of the proposed policy in terms of the organization of production (166)

With respect to management, my proposals *relate basically to organizing competition* and creating the most suitable framework for the *spontaneous* interaction of economic forces to bring about of itself all the possibilities that are within our reach.[1] Based as they are on structural reforms that in no way compromise the principles of the competitive mechanism, my proposals safeguard individual responsibility in its entirety as well as the decentralization of decision-making—the role of which is undoubtedly even greater than was suspected by even the most fanatical of 19th-century economic liberals. Hence they make it possible not only to maintain but even to improve a system that has already proved itself.

In respect of social productivity, keeping the economy close to the optimum would make possible a considerable increase in well-being, and the productive capacities of the economy once enhanced would themselves generate new progress.[2,3]

Finally, the proposed policy, by bringing about the simultaneous maximization of social efficiency and social productivity, would enable the community, *without effort or constraint*, to make maximum use of *all the production opportunities within its reach* and hence to achieve the highest conceivable degree of efficiency.[4]

In a world in which so much poverty and destitution still prevail, surely such advantages are priceless.

1. In particular by making the economy money neutral and using a unit of account that remains constant over time.

2. The advantages of maximization of social productivity have been sufficiently analyzed in chapter 7 (particularly in no. 71); there is no need to embark on a further detailed analysis.

3. It is worth stressing at this point that the maximization of social productivity would provide the world, and particularly the United States, with such investment opportunities as to rule out any possibility of over-production in the equipment industries in the coming decade.

4. Reminder: it has been shown above that this policy is the *only* one that enables these goals to be achieved.

3. Advantages of the proposed policy with regard to economic cycles (167)

Applying the proposed policy would enable the economy to be stabilized or at least to considerably reduce its oscillations away from equilibrium, as the fundamental factors of general disequilibrium of the economy—credit margins and the hoardability of cash—would be eliminated.

No doubt there would still remain in the economy much friction, much disequilibrium, and many troublesome adjustments to be made, but at least there would remain only those factors of disequilibrium that are by nature irreducible and incapable of being affected to any extent. And anyway, these disequilibria could only have a limited effect and could under no circumstances lead to deep, widespread economic disturbances.

Hence it is safe to conclude that in the context of this policy the economy would no longer undergo the large-scale oscillations that currently characterize it. *Each mechanism therein would include its own self-regulatory factor, coming into play immediately, and disequilibrium would no longer generate disequilibrium but equilibrium.*

Indeed *the disappearance of economic cycles, without any attendant threat to freedom or efficiency, would have an immense impact.*[1] A vital step on our path toward a better life might be taken.[2]

1. Thus, for instance, on the international level, "if nations can learn to provide themselves with full employment by their domestic policy (and, we must add, if they can also attain equilibrium in the trend of their population), *there need be no important economic forces calculated to set the interest of one country against that of its neighbors.* There would still be room for the international division of labor and for international lending in appropriate conditions. *But there would no longer be a pressing motive why one country need force its wares on another or repulse the offerings of its neighbor,* not because this was necessary to enable it to pay for what it wished to purchase, but *with the express object of upsetting the equilibrium of payments so as to develop a balance of trade in its own favor.* International trade would cease to be what it is, namely, a desperate expedient to maintain employment at home by forcing sales in foreign markets and restricting purchases, *which, if successful, will merely shift the problem of unemployment to the neighbor which is worsted in the struggle,* but a willing and unimpeded exchange of goods and services in conditions of mutual advantage" (Keynes, *General Theory of Employment, Money and Interest,* bk. 6, ch. 24, § 4.). Emphasis mine.

2. It seems to me crucial to emphasize that these advantages relative to balancing the various sectors of the economy *remain valid irrespective of our conception of the causes of economic cycles.* The existence of a standard of value that remains constant over time, 100% backing of loans, money unsuited to being hoarded, the adjustment of the rate of interest, to mention but these few measures, constitute, in any theory of cycles whatever, so many strong stabilizing factors by which to counter any major imbalance.

4. Advantages of the proposed policy with regard to distribution (168)

With regard to distribution, the proposed policy displays advantages that are absolutely fundamental.

Pure interest

The policy I am advocating makes it possible to realize *an aspiration that has been common to all social reformers of every period*—a zero pure interest rate—but that, despite so many attempts, has so far never in fact been achieved—and for good reason,[1] since the legislator's efforts have always borne on the symptoms of the phenomenon of interest and not on its underlying causes.[2]

The elimination of the rentier, which the proposed policy would make possible, would thus put an end to an abuse that has *bedeviled the action of the competitive mechanism*, especially over the last century and a half. By doing so it would signal the opening of a new era in the development of society.

The great advantage of this policy is that the rentier, the capitalist without a profession, could become extinct without any revolution, gradually and imperceptibly.[3]

---

1. No. 156.

2. Note that in our own days both National Socialism and Communism adopted the zero rate of interest as one of their basic goals, but both in Soviet Russia and in Nazi Germany a positive rate of interest had to be maintained.

3. Of course, the social advantages of a zero pure interest rate would only be fully achieved in the context of an economy having private ownership of capital and therefore, necessarily, a single rate of interest (nos. 77 and 145 and note 33 to no. 164) when the capital equipment stock had been sufficiently expanded for its marginal productivity to be zero.

Meanwhile there would be nothing to prevent—indeed quite the contrary—pure interest from being confiscated for the benefit of the community by an annual tax on capital owned, irrespective of actual income yielded by it (since this income includes, in addition to pure interest, components such as reward for risks run or for the specific qualities of the enterprises that, when the interests of the community are properly understood, ought never to be taxed). (See, on this topic, my *Abondance ou misère*, ch. 3, § 6, and ch. 4, § 7.)

Risk premiums

Of course, as the zero interest rate policy concerns only the pure interest rate, apart from any risk premium, and not the gross rate of interest on capital, which includes a risk premium,[4] judicious business investments part of whose return depends on chance would continue to yield positive interest rates.[5]

But as the risks due to the uncertainty of the future must be borne by someone in every economic society and maximization of social efficiency calls for them to be borne by those with a pronounced propensity for gambling, the social justification of this kind of interest in terms of risk premiums is sound.

Profits

In a neutral-money competitive economy business profits can only be technical profits (due to a decrease in cost price), competitive profits (due to judicious choice of activity and strategy by the firm), or random profits (corresponding to the reward for bearing risks).[6] *Like wages, therefore, profits are indispensable, because they are necessary for the maximization of social efficiency, and fair, since they correspond to the reward for a service that is eminently useful to the community, each firm being so much the more useful as it realizes greater profits.*

Moreover, under neutral monetary competitive conditions, *the sum of the gains and losses realized by firms is strictly zero;*[7] *whatever one firm gains, another has lost, so, on aggregate, businesses subtract nothing whatsoever from the national income.*

Finally, within the framework of the proposed policy, *all profit must be deemed to be due to an activity favorable to the public interest and costing*

4. Disregarding in first approximation the other premiums that go to make up the rate of interest (no. 84), concerning which similar remarks apply.

5. Unless the risk-taking propensity is exceptionally great, in which case the cost-of-risk premiums could indeed have negative values so significant as to offset the positive estimated-risk premiums, such that the aggregate risk premiums would become negative (no. 29). In this event, the economic organization here envisaged would be especially advantageous (since the upshot of the passion for gambling would be to disburden the community of the cost of risks).

6. Readers wishing to study these different circumstances in greater detail will derive profit from my *À la recherche d'une discipline économique*, nos. 157–62.

7. A crucial finding that remains very little known (see note 3 to no. 107).

the community on average nothing at all. These two motives complete the moral and social justification of profit.[8]

Savings

Within the framework of the proposals here put forward, every individual would remain free to save the income earned by his labor in order to be able to spend it at a later date, *but the wealth thus accumulated would not increase.* He would receive, in the future, a capital sum equal, in terms of work hours, to that which he saved. Thus all capital would strictly correspond to prior labor input.

Although each person would thus be deprived of the advantage of receiving a nominal interest rate—*illusory* as it is on account of successive waves of monetary depreciation—his purchasing power, on the other hand, would be preserved and *even increased*, as its value in wage terms would remain unchanged and prices would regularly fall, in terms of wages, owing to technical progress.

Inequalities

In the present economy pronounced inequalities are liable to be maintained and increased as a result of the fact that capital can yield pure interest. A zero pure interest rate would thus help *to restrict social inequalities to those corresponding to unequal services rendered to the community— inequalities that are both just and impossible to eliminate.*

Indeed, it seems likely that distribution of labor incomes in accordance with the competitive principle would bring about a much broader spread of wages than prevails in the present economy, and overall inequality comparable to that which is found at present.[9]

---

8. In an economy such as this no honors could be too great, no distinctions too high, to reward the entrepreneurs whose technical knowledge or intuition of the community's needs enabled them to realize substantial profits.

Naturally this wish, which remains just as valid whether capital is privately or publicly owned, *expressly* assumes as realized conditions such that excess profit is practically eliminated. *By the same token, it by no means applies to our present economy, in which unwarranted and unethical profits have become a veritable institution.*

9. Note that pure interest and land rents would no longer play any role as they do at present.

So inequality would not vanish, but it would be differently based: the hierarchy of ownership would be replaced by that of merit. This would enable *inequality to be rationally organized.*

Excess profits

Within the framework of the proposed economy, all excess profits would be practically eliminated.[10]

The abolition of excess profit from land would follow from land collectivization; excess profit from capital accumulation would be eliminated by a zero pure interest rate; monopoly profits would be eradicated by the competitive organization of the economy; and windfall profits by price stability and the elimination of economic cycles.

This would put an end to the utter immorality that characterizes our present economy.

Labor: the only source of income

Finally, in the economy I advocate, every income would be a present or deferred wage:[11] no unearned income would exist.[12,13]

Riches and poverty would then be what they ought to be: riches being the reward for labor and savings, and poverty the consequence and punishment of sloth and dissipation.

In this way it would be possible to bring about a social climate favorable both to efficiency in production and to social harmony.

10. Reminder: in accordance with my stated terminology I use the term "excess profit" [French *profit*] to designate any income that does not correspond to the reward for a service rendered to the community as a whole, so that "excess profit" is a notion that must be carefully distinguished from that of "profit" [French *bénéfice*] as such. (See note 4 to no. 107.)

11. Note that the simple elimination of pure interest and of land rent, together with the maximization of social productivity, would suffice to raise current wages in real terms by a factor that can be expected to be on the order of 50% (no. 72).

12. As noted above (note 4 to no. 107), the term "excess profit" in the terminology used herein designates that part of a firm's earnings that cannot be taken to correspond to the reward for a *service rendered* to the economy as a whole.

13. All income being now no more than the *fair reward for a socially useful activity*, all current taxes on industrial and commercial profits, wages and salaries, income, financial assets, and inheritance could be and ought to be abolished. (As I am unfortunately unable to enlarge on this subject within the scope of the present study, interested readers are invited to consult for further information my study *Abondance ou misère.*)

(c) Social aspects of the proposed reforms (169)

So a new form of economy is both desirable and possible: one that is equally far removed from the formulae of liberalism as from totalitarian principles.

Such an economy is characterized by the organization, within the framework of law, of economic freedom, essentially characterized by the systematic implementation of competition, the establishment of a standard of value remaining constant over time, the separation of the functions of money, ongoing depreciation of circulating money, 100% backing of demand deposits, regularization of the interest mechanism, and reduction of the rate of interest to zero together with public land ownership.[1]

---

1. Note that these statements are just as valid whether production goods (in the meaning of no. 42) are privately or publicly owned and that, on this question, *in the present state of science, it is absolutely impossible, in all conscience, to take a stand either for or against the collectivization of the means of production.*

For (a) collectivization would have considerable advantages on the social and psychological level in terms of distribution. And (b) scientific proof that it cannot be effectively accomplished is wholly lacking. The example of the Russian economy, grossly inefficient as it is in very many respects, cannot be accepted as decisive evidence, for the political conditions under which Russia has evolved have often been such that economic technique has played but a minor role.

Moreover, it must be admitted, only in very recent years has economics made progress enough for some facts to have been established with certainty.

Finally, *faithful to the lamentable custom of revolutionaries of every era*, the Russian rulers began by taking a stand diametrically opposed to the economic organization existing in capitalist countries. Needless to say, under the pressure of the facts, this simplistic position has had to be gradually abandoned, in part, but its effects remain no less with us.

For my own part I think that *in the present state of our political development, the operation of a competitive economy within the framework of complete collectivization is not possible, as it would call for political independence on the part of economic agents that is certainly not attainable under present conditions.* But I also think that there is no reason to reject all experimentation merely because these essentially contingent conditions might jeopardize the effective operation of a collectivist economy. As theory shows that the same economic techniques are needed whether production goods are privately or publicly owned, it is surely possible to undertake a gradual experiment of a new model of ownership, using collectivized control-enterprises set within the overall competitive context of private ownership. Just as the complex capitalist economy was not made or perfected in a day, *so it is not inconceivable that total collectivization of the means of production, though it would certainly be most unfavorable to general living standards if adopted in the immediate future, might yet tomorrow be perfectly realizable.*

Although, considered separately, most of these reforms are not new, considered as a whole they have not yet been debated. I hope I have shown how coherent this whole in fact is and how well it responds both to technical needs and to the aspirations of social ethics. It is particularly fortunate that these two factors should coincide, for it was by no means evident in advance—indeed observation of the facts made it appear doubtful—that a formula could be found that would reconcile both productive efficiency and equitable distribution in an economy in constant progress.

Yet the economy here proposed leads to *formulae that, from the viewpoint of distribution and social justice, fully respond to the aspirations and conclusions of the great social reformers of every epoch, from the Fathers of the Church to Marx and Lenin.* Public land ownership, zero interest, labor the sole source of income: such are the measures characterizing this economy in terms of income distribution. But the foundations they are

---

Moreover, it is quite certain that the collectivization of the means of production represents for a great mass of workers *an immense hope*, likely to introduce a considerable improvement in the economic and social atmosphere they live in. Hence, in my view, it would be just as disastrous systematically to oppose experimentation in a field in which, it must be stressed, science affords us no certainty and facts alone can bring us decisive evidence, as to hasten to enforce, as some wish or are inclined to advocate, wholesale collectivization.

These extreme positions would be equally unjustified from the scientific viewpoint since science does not allow us to decide between private and public ownership of the means of production, while *from the social point of view*, since, on the one hand, the refusal of any experimentation could only be a source of serious demoralization to a great many workers, in a way they would find *very hard to understand*, and on the other, the immediate realization of a full-scale experiment would run the risk of gravely prejudicing even our present standard of living, which is already exceptionally low.

In reality, there is no proof that the supporters of a collectivist regime could not be converted to competitivism, with all it means for human freedom, both economically and politically.

The experience of the USSR seems rather to point in the opposite direction, weakly enough, I admit, in some fields, but much more strongly in others.

Finally, note that if all income were labor-derived, as would be the case in the economy I am advocating, the ethical problem of ownership *would practically cease to exist*, as all property would simply become deferred wages, having constant real purchasing power.

Under these conditions, the only issue would be to find out what system of delegation of the rights of ownership would be best able to bring about the most efficient organization of production. *Only trial and error can furnish a decisive answer to this question* (see the remarks made in note 6 to no. 159). The reader could also profitably consult my study "Le problème de la planification dans une économie collectiviste," in *Kyklos: International Review for Social Sciences*, July 1947.

built on are not only ethical, but they are also, and indeed principally, the necessary conditions of all efficient production.

Special tribute is due at this point to forerunners such as Proudhon, Walras, and Silvio Gesell, who presaged the great reconciliation of individual and collective interests offered by the economy here put forward.

One of the most remarkable features of this economy is the fact that it satisfies not only my own conclusions but also those of economists (both French and from other countries) whose beliefs are far different from mine. For instance, the requirement for 100% backing for demand deposits responds to the critiques everywhere leveled at the present system of credit distribution, while nonetheless preserving the flexibility that is vital to its functioning.

*   *   *

This economy offers invaluable advantages.

On the material level, maximization of social efficiency and productivity with ongoing adjustment of production conditions to distribution conditions, leading to the elimination of economic cycles and to continuous full employment, could not fail to bring about a major improvement in our material well-being.

And *on the spiritual level*, the impact of the recommended reforms would be incalculable and the reconciliation of individual and collective interests that they would bring about would certainly enable an atmosphere of social peace to be attained that today belongs to the realm of dreams and utopia.

Granted, not all economic disequilibrium would be eliminated: weather conditions, technical progress, etc. would still cause many disturbances, but these are all irreducible phenomena that will subsist under any conceivable economy.

Moreover, the implementation of the proposed economy would be sure to raise new technical problems, some of them no doubt exceptionally intricate ones, especially in the monetary field; but the immense advantages that could be derived from it would far outweigh the undeniable difficulties involved.

In any event, it cannot be too strongly emphasized that *the reforms I am advocating are the necessary preconditions of any efficient and well-adjusted economy. There is no alternative, nor any scope for compromise.*

Admittedly an economic organization driven by personal interest has aroused many ethically based criticisms. Here I would simply stress that in the present state of individual psychologies most human activities need the stimulus of gain if they are to bear all their fruit.

> Moreover, *dangerous human proclivities can be canalized into comparatively harmless channels* by the existence of opportunities for money-making and private wealth, which, if they cannot be satisfied in this way, may find their outlet in cruelty, the reckless pursuit of personal power and authority, and other forms of self-aggrandisement. *It is better that a man should tyrannize over his bank balance than over his fellow-citizens*; and whilst the former is sometimes denounced as being but a means to the latter, sometimes at least it is an alternative.[2]

It may be conceivable that men will one day be inclined, habituated, or trained to have no interest in gain. But "*The task of transmuting human nature must not be confused with the task of managing it*,"[3] and so long as the average man or even a significant part of the community is strongly inclined to the pursuit of gain, wisdom and prudence will compel statesmen not only to authorize this pursuit, subject to certain rules and within certain limits, but even to use it in the best interests of all.

In any event, even if such a transformation took place, for instance, if man became disinterested enough to prefer an absolutely equal distribution of consumer goods, *the rule of competitive free play would still be no less necessary on the management level* so that everyone's equal share was raised to its maximum possible level. Prices, wages, land rents and rates of interest would all still be necessary. There would have to be markets in which the supply-and-demand mechanism operated. There would still have to be entrepreneurs sanctioned by the results of their profit and loss accounts, workers seeking to obtain the highest wages, financiers striving to identify the most lucrative investments, even if the various members of this utterly communist society ended by paying the incomes they received (*unequal on the level of production*) into a common fund so as to bring about *ultimate equality in the incomes they consumed, in terms of distribution*. This shows that even in this ideal situation, which no doubt will never be attained, society would still have to be organized on a competitive basis—the only basis able to make the best use of the talents of each

2. Keynes, *The General Theory of Employment, Interest, and Money*, bk. 6, ch. 24, § 1. Emphasis mine.

3. Keynes, bk. 6, ch. 24, § 1. Emphasis mine.

individual, as well as of natural resources, in order to maximize the equal income of everyone.[4]

In reality, by reducing the role of the State to its minimum possible and developing individual initiative to the maximum compatible with the common interest and by maintaining individual responsibility and decentralized decision-making, my proposals display, in pursuit of an ever-broader Humanism, the fundamental advantage of preserving individualism in its principle.

For individualism, once

purged of its defects and its abuses, is *the best safeguard of personal liberty in the sense that, compared with any other system, it greatly widens the field for the exercise of personal choice.* It is also the best safeguard of *the variety of life*, which emerges precisely from this extended field of personal choice, and the loss of which is the greatest of all the losses of the homogeneous or totalitarian state. For this variety preserves the traditions which embody the most secure and successful choices of former generations; it colors the present with the

---

4. It must be strongly emphasized that the generality of the theory of social efficiency is such that it would apply *even in a society of religious, occupied exclusively by disinterested labors.*

Whatever may be the ends pursued by these monks, if they wanted to pursue them efficiently (and how could they not, given that this efficiency would be the condition of their having enough time to devote to meditation and to prayer?) they would have to organize themselves on a competitive basis.

To this end they would have to attribute wages to their different capacities and labors, a rate of interest to the capital they employed, and land rents to the land they made use of. All their economic calculations would have to be made in conformity with the rules of free play of a competitive economy having private ownership.

Thus, of two monks, the one who must have the highest salary would be the one whose work was most difficult to obtain and most in demand. Each monk would have to donate his labor to the firm that offered him the highest wage, and each firm ought, for equal quality of services rendered, to seek as workers the monks disposed to accept the lowest wages.

This granted, the members of this vast religious association would still be free to repay their various incomes (wages, land rents, interest, profits) into the common fund of their community, which would then distribute the income according to the goals pursued.

This example clearly brings out

1. the absolute necessity of the free play of economic competition for every community, whatever its nature, if its economic organization is to be efficient; and
2. the arbitrary character of distribution, which can always be adjusted to this or that particular objective (see the explanations given in no. 56).

diversification of its fancy; and, being the handmaid of experiment as well as of tradition and of fancy, it is the most powerful instrument to better the future.[5,6]

Finally only such a competitive organization of the economy can resolve *the difficult problem of how to ensure the continuous and spontaneous emergence of elites from among the people in a classless world and how to ensure government by the most excellent.* Thus it provides *the only genuine way* to ensure both social peace and the economic, intellectual, artistic, and moral progress of societies.[7]

*   *   *

Indeed, *the principle of such organization is to make maximum use of the spontaneous impulses of individuals in order to realize its goals.* In place of the inefficiency to which the anarchy of laissez-faire or the omnipotence of authoritarian planning unfailingly gives rise, it substitutes the high yield that can only be achieved within the minimum constraint scenario that it embodies.

5. Keynes, *The General Theory of Employment, Interest, and Money,* bk. 6, ch. 24, § 3. Emphasis mine.

6. There still exists today a country, the United States, that remains as a whole firmly attached to the competitive principle. *But this attachment is unfortunately due in great measure to belief in the efficiency of the laissez-faire principle, and it is unable of itself to offer any solution to the problem of cyclical unemployment or to that of distribution* (unearned income from land rent, capital accumulation, or inflation).

For my part I am convinced that if the United States does not adopt in some form or another the measures here advocated they will be unable to avoid, in two to four years' time, *a major new economic crisis, more terrible still than that of 1929, that would this time be accompanied by a grave social crisis and would inevitably sound the death knell of competitive economic organization founded on individual freedom throughout the world, and with it of the democratic organization of society.*

The stakes involved are therefore vitally important for the future of the world and go far beyond the context of mere economics.

7. On this topic the reader may usefully refer to my study "Quelques réflexions sur l'inégalité, les classes et la promotion sociale," *Économie et humanisme,* July–September 1946.

This study endeavors to show that the notion of class is absolutely distinct from the notion of inequality and that the existence of classes is due to the correlation—resulting in turn from a monopolistic situation—between the situation of parents and that of their children.

Only a truly competitive order could reduce this correlation to its biological (and therefore irreducible) minimum.

In reality the world is not limited to choosing between unlimited freedom or no freedom at all. Between laissez-faire, which sees a panacea in the universal pursuit of spontaneous free development of individual activities without regulation and in the systematic absence of State intervention, *and authoritarian planning,* whose great ideal is to supervise and control every aspect of every activity by professional or public regulations, there lies *a third path—competitive planning,* distinguished by the organization of freedom within the rule of law and, at the same time, embodying minimum constraint and maximum efficiency.

A striking image, now classic, readily gives concrete shape to the fundamental differences between such a regime and laissez-faire or authoritarian planning.

Laissez-faire liberalism may "be compared to allowing motor vehicles to drive at whim without any highway code: there would be no end to the congestion, traffic jams and accidents that would ensue, unless the bigger cars demanded that the smaller ones yield them the right of way, which would be the law of the jungle,"[8] while the economy of authoritarian planning "would be like a traffic regime in which a central authority told everyone when to get out his car, where to drive to and by what route."[9] The consequences are easy to imagine.

Competitive planning, by contrast, is the system under which drivers are free to go where they will, provided only that they obey the Highway Code.

Planning of this sort is basically *structural planning*—quite different from the *action planning* that is the mark of authoritarian planning.[10]

It is the only regime that allows maximum efficiency to be combined with minimum recourse to constraint.

*   *   *

There is no denying that the realization of the economy I am advocating would inevitably conflict with a great many interests protected or tolerated by today's laws and the effect of which is to prevent the optimal functioning of the economy.

Indeed selfishness and want of intelligence are so widespread in our day that there may well be no social class that would not fear that such

8. L. Rougier, *Les mystiques économiques* (Paris: Librairie de Médicis, 1938), 88.
9. Rougier, 88.
10. Note 9 to no. 159.

reforms compromised or threatened its interests, but this may be the best evidence of the impartiality of the reforms themselves and of the fact that they indeed provide a fair reconciliation of hitherto divergent interests.[11] Moreover, as the foregoing explanations show, everyone would soon real-

11. It is fairly *symptomatic* in this respect to note that the liberals tend to categorize me as a socialist while the socialists are no less given to calling me a liberal.

Both are equally mistaken; their attention focuses on what divides us rather than on what unites us.

It is perfectly true that I am convinced of the fundamental primacy of individual life over the abstract concept of the State, and of the manifest superiority of the price mechanism based on the free play of supply and demand in a competitive framework over any authoritarian organization, but it is no less certain that I am a convinced adversary of laissez-faire, convinced that the State can and should intervene *systematically* to organize the institutional framework in which competition is to operate.

It is also perfectly true that any situation of monopoly or privilege operating for the exclusive benefit of a few seems to me utterly intolerable, and that I am an *ardent supporter* of land collectivization and zero interest rates, but for all that I am no less convinced that any economy that aspires to efficiency needs the competitive mechanism based on the profitability principle and the free action of gains and losses for firms, and I firmly believe that this mechanism *alone* can bring about, *automatically and without arbitrariness*, both the highest level of economic efficiency and the selection and social promotion of the best.

It may be that this position, which corresponds both to liberal socialism and to the social liberalism that Walras dreamed of, is exceptionally hard to champion at a time when minds tend to be divided into irremediably opposed camps, but whatever risks may be run by those who are not satisfied with ready-made opinions and obstinately refuse to sign up to any of the ruling factions, for my part I refuse and will always most strenuously refuse to allow myself to be locked into any system of ideas crystallized once and for all, none of which is wholly true or wholly false.

For I am convinced that the real solution is to be found in neither of the two opposing camps, nor in a compromise between them, but rather in a harmonious combination of the two based on the most recent data of theory and experience accessible to all those of either side who are ready in good faith to reexamine their beliefs in light of the latest scientific progress.

The gap that has gradually widened between liberals and socialists is the result of a long series of mistakes and misunderstandings; it ought not to be regarded as an unavoidable decree of fate.

My hope is to convince all thoughtful people, both on the left and on the right, of the following:

1. Authoritarian planning is a *particularly pernicious* economic system, whether in the context of a system of public ownership or of private ownership.
2. The only efficient management system is the competitive one.
3. Within the context of this system it is possible, without loss of efficiency and even increasing it, to establish conditions of distribution that satisfy the social aspira-

ize, by introspection and by observing the results obtained, that within the context of the proposed reforms his own personal interests, properly understood, were inseparable from the welfare of the community as a whole.

It may be that the organization of the competitive economy I am proposing would be less spectacular in its implementation than the imposition, by umpteen rules and regulations, of an economy of authoritarian planning. It would involve a gradual series of minor improvements rather than abrupt alterations and tactless transitions; hence it would require careful implementation and above all a constant attention extending down to the smallest details. But thanks to its theoretical and practical consistency and to the fact that it can be applied in a way that automatically excludes arbitrariness, it would be incomparably more effective.

It would of course require a general agreement to its principles and a shared commitment of all the parties involved loyally to pursue its implementation. Competitive democracy could not be organized in an atmosphere of conflict and violence, but this condition, belonging to the ethical and psychological sphere, depends only on us and *can by no means be dismissed as unrealizable* given that the solutions proposed would make it possible to overcome all the fundamental difficulties and to eliminate the underlying defects of the laissez-faire system while retaining whatever it contains of efficiency and human validity.

Nor should the very scale of the reforms being advocated be taken to be an obstacle to their fulfillment. History tells us of economic reforms that were brought off even though the interests involved were of comparable economic significance. One such case was the emancipation of the serfs in the Middle Ages and another, more recent, the abolition of slavery. Yet some of these reforms were successfully implemented without a break and without spoliation.[12]

Last but not least, the economy being proposed is just as far from laissez-faire as from authoritarian planning.[13]

---

tions of every age, i.e., the elimination of all unearned income and all unjust enrichment.

4. In this way it would be possible to lay the foundations of a harmonization in which the most authentically human aspects of both liberalism and Marxism could be reconciled, thus ending the sterile hostility of equally rigid and erroneous standpoints that threatens the world with catastrophe.

12. E.g., the abolition of slavery in Brazil in 1871 (see P. Lafitte, *Le grand malaise des sociétés modernes* [Paris: Éditions de la Sirène, 1922]).

13. See note 9 to no. 159.

It is not a laissez-faire regime leading to anarchy, but a regime of systematic State intervention, organizing individual freedom in the manner most favorable to the common interest. It endeavors to achieve the continuous realization of the conditions of free competition and free choice that it implies.

But although this economy includes substantial state intervention, *it is nonetheless at the opposite pole to any form of authoritarian planning.* The measures it remits to the State are all inspired by the overriding concern for economic freedom and not for its replacement by authoritarian organization. The corresponding economic mechanism is both efficient and automatic, whereas centralized economic planning can only ever be imperfect and calls for the despotic intervention of an all-powerful sovereign.

Indeed this economy replaces the wastefulness, inconsistencies, disorder, and injustice of laissez-faire with a "Plan" whose action is effective, systematic, coordinated, and equitable; but, within the framework of a market economy, a planning mechanism of this sort leaves intact the principle that prices and quantities are determined by the free play of the law of supply and demand. *At root it is the structures that are to be planned rather than the actions of individuals*, as envisaged by authoritarian planning, whose core principle is to replace the division of labor that results from the free action of independent economic agents with the *necessarily* imperfect, authoritarian, and arbitrary decisions of a central administration.

In its principles it contradicts neither socialist nor liberal aspirations in the profoundly human values of both systems.

The broadening of the functions of the State, which is necessary if full employment is to be maintained and optimum investment levels to be achieved, may be seen as a dreadful infringement of individualistic principles in the eyes of the surviving disciples of an Yves Guyot or even a Colson, *but such a broadening, on the contrary, is the necessary condition of preserving the happy exercise of individual initiative* as well as the profoundly human values enshrined in the individualistic aspirations of the 19th century.

It is also possible that preserving the principles of the competitive system may appear to loyal disciples of Marx as utterly incompatible with the passionate desire for social justice that spurs them on and their intense ethically motivated anxiety to deliver man from exploitation by his fellows, *but such a system in reality, far from opposing such aspirations, is in fact the only effective means available to fulfill them, completely, without constraint, and with the cooperation of all concerned.*

In their most authentically human values true liberalism and true socialism are much less irreconcilable than appears at first sight; I would even venture to assert that they are the same; after all, is there really so much difference between the social aspirations of Karl Marx and of John Stuart Mill?

By enabling a satisfactory distribution to be achieved without sacrificing either freedom or efficiency, it seems to me that the "Competitive Socialism" I am advocating is able to satisfy the chief demands of all schools of thought and goes beyond both liberalism and Marxism by completing them, clarifying them, renewing them, and harmonizing them, thus ending the barren strife, fueled by mutual misunderstanding, that is the drama of the present day. *Hence it seems to me to be the path that will be followed—sooner or later, but without fail—in the future that awaits us.*[14]

14. As I have stressed in my *Prolégomènes à la reconstruction économique du monde,* the possibility of such a harmonization receives support from observation of how various contemporary societies, whether authoritarian or liberal in type, have spontaneously evolved in recent years. For these economies do in fact appear to have gradually drawn closer, feeling their way at every step, by very different paths and *by force of circumstance,* to the structure that the theory recognizes as optimal, the essence of which lies in economic freedom organized within the framework of very extensive regulations and of partly collectivized ownership.

For instance, in a private ownership context, the National Socialist economy, despite complete central planning, strove increasingly to benefit from the advantages of free economic action in the context of highly developed legislation and regulation. In the same way, though in a collectivist context, the Soviet economy has gradually evolved toward a market economy, admitting wage differentiation and independent accountancy for firms. Indeed it has only been successful to the quite large extent that it has applied the principles of the competitive economy. Finally, the liberal Anglo-Saxon economy, realizing that laissez-faire on its own could only lead to anarchy, has continued to distance itself from Manchester Liberalism, to transform its ownership regime, and to regulate the free play of economic freedom while yet preserving it in principle.

Is it not a highly significant fact that systems thought to be utterly opposed and incompatible in the realm of ideas should gradually, by force of circumstances, find expression on the practical level *in achievements tending toward a single type? Should this not be accepted as evidence that overall agreement remains possible, despite so many disappointing appearances?*

Under such conditions, the only problem is to advance as swiftly as possible, without inflicting further pain by useless delay, toward this harmonization that safeguards all that is profoundly true in liberal thought while at the same time ensuring the social order and justice of the Socialist dream, and avoiding the errors, potentially fatal to civilization as a whole, of laissez-faire and of authoritarian planning.

By clarifying and defining the principles of this harmonization, the economy I advocate provides the very means needed to implement it swiftly and smoothly while respecting both order and social justice.

The competitive organization of the economy, public land ownership, a zero interest rate, the elimination of excess profit, exclusivity of labor as a source of income, the creation of a classless society by competitive selection of the best, the organization of a global federal State founded on the free circulation of goods, capital, people, and information:[15] *such in my view must be the essential scientific bases of tomorrow's economy.*[16]

For in reality what at present most deeply separates Marxist parties from the other parties is clearly not so much the objectives pursued as the methods advocated.

For Marxists, the old order can only be overthrown, and the society of the future combining efficiency with justice can only be ushered in, via an intermediate period of dictatorship of the proletariat, which alone, in their view, can give society a fresh start.

However, it seems clear that the vast majority of generous and dynamic thinkers, the only ones whose influence matters in a country's governance, could currently agree on such vital issues as the establishment of a classless world, the distinction between inequality of merit and inequality of class, the preservation of inequality of merit, and the suppression of unearned income, whatever its source (profits due to the receipt of interest on capital, profits due to increase in land values, inflationary profits due to expansion of the means of payment, etc.).

If this is in fact so, the main underlying source of disagreement, namely as to the method of implementation, could only disappear. If there is agreement as to fundamental goals, there can be no need for an intervening period of dictatorship, the drawbacks of which do not need to be spelled out; political and economic democracy can be maintained and the transition to a fairer and more efficient society can be carried out without any violent transition.

15. I mention the last two items on this list on account of their fundamental importance, notwithstanding the absence of any direct link between them and the overall case made in the present book.

16. The foregoing observations chiefly concern the outlines of the main principles of an efficient and equitable economic policy.

Readers wishing to explore how they could be applied in today's concrete reality will find a statement and discussion of the precise measures to be implemented in my *Abondance ou misère.*

At the End of a Study (170)

The ideas presented and developed in the present work are for the most part new and are often opposed to views believed in some quarters to have been rigorously established.

They will therefore meet with resistance. The sway held by the classical school and by certain contemporary schools are irresistibly reminiscent of that of some religions. The influence and attraction of mystery and the supernatural are so strong that it is a greater challenge to convince human minds to welcome simple, clear, and coherent ideas than to disseminate obscure notions open to countless interpretations and easily adapted to every taste.

The present study strives essentially for clarity and positive truth. I might have followed the advice strongly impressed on me in some quarters to take advantage of the foregoing explanations to criticize and systematically refute the opinions of my predecessors as I went along, but I take the view that in economics time devoted to refutation is generally wasted. What is left of so many objections raised by so many economists against one another? Little or nothing. "What matters and what lasts is the input of positive truth: *the true statement displaces the falsehood by virtue of its intrinsic power, and thus the best of refutations is the one that does not set out to refute anyone.*"[1]

Circumstances have delayed the drafting of this study for two years, but the delay has certainly had the advantage of enabling me to think through the same basic and intractable problems several times, at intervals of several months. And each time I have made an important new step forward. I believe therefore that *this study is itself but a stage* and that major refinements remain possible.

---

1. H. Bergson, *L'énergie spirituelle* (Paris: Presses Universitaires de France, 1940), 63. Emphasis mine.

I venture to hope that the general theory of interest herein set out will be received not so much as a destruction of previous theories as their harmonization and as a contribution to making the chain of reasoning complete, homogeneous, and solid.

It has been an immense comfort and encouragement to me to observe that *on every essential issue my thinking did no more than follow in the footsteps of the most penetrating theories of the classical and modern writers, not contradicting them but rather developing and harmonizing them.*

This observation shows that there exists a Truth the knowledge of which advances gradually, despite the innate difficulties of any new science, multiplied in the present case by the prejudices that always attend questions so closely involving so many interests.

Though readers may have found my explanations arduous and off-putting to read, I hope and trust that, now that their perusal is completed, they will judge the effort worthwhile. Never mind those who reflect on few or no problems, or who are attracted by the siren-song of sweet-sounding words rather than by the real effort needed to advance toward genuine knowledge; the lengthy, difficult, and arduous solutions; and the steep and thorny paths toward Truth. *What the young science of economics needs most at present* is not easily digested studies, however brilliant, that leave the mind unsatisfied and fretful, *but solid and unshakable footholds by which to rise above the mists of so much verbal confusion.*

There is no doubt in my mind that our youth is anxious to attain such knowledge. Many clear signs announce that the advent of positive economic science is not far off and that soon economics in its turn will abandon the whirligig of abstruse speculation in order to take its definitive place alongside the mathematical and physical sciences.

It will be the task of the youth of today to emancipate economics definitively from its wretched status of handmaid to bourgeois conservatism and financial feudalism as well as to the barren and destructive authoritarian planning advocated by certain revolutionary thinkers.

If our epoch is a time of revolution in the material world, the revolution we are experiencing in the realm of economic thought is a yet greater one; *the full extent of its effects will become apparent some 20 years hence.*

In the path I have embarked on, every day brings some new adherent, some stronger encouragement, some more substantial aid,[2] some firmer

---

2. Let me take this opportunity to extend my most sincere thanks to some of my friends, who, notwithstanding the modesty of their means, have not hesitated to place substantial sums at my disposal in order to disseminate my writings among students.

friendship. *I have no doubt that my point of view will gradually spread and in due course win the adherence of every mind.*

At the term of such a journey there lies not only an exact and profound knowledge of the problems we face, but also concrete solutions. I am convinced that science is able to lead us toward *an economic and social ideal capable of reconciling men, over and above their particular temporary interests, in a single Faith.* From the rubble of the economy of yesteryear, a new economy can arise. The hope of the present study is to contribute to building it.

Is it too fanciful to hope that my proposals will in fact be adopted? Are they too foreign to the influences that govern the development of organized societies? Are the interests they challenge more powerful and more conspicuous than those they favor?

I shall not be replying to these questions here. Even to sketch the broad outline of the measures that could be progressively adopted on the basis of these ideas would require a work far different from the present one.[3]

But if these ideas are correct — and I find it hard to suppose otherwise — *it would be unwise, I predict, to underestimate their long-term influence.*

As Keynes has admirably stressed at the end of his latest work:

> *At the present moment people are unusually expectant of a more fundamental diagnosis*; more particularly ready to receive it; eager to try it out, if it should be even plausible. But *apart from this contemporary mood, the ideas of economists and political philosophers, both when they are right and when they are wrong, are more powerful than is commonly understood. Indeed the world is ruled by little else.* Practical men, who believe themselves to be quite exempt from any intellectual influences, are usually the slaves of some defunct economist. Madmen in authority, who hear voices in the air, are distilling their frenzy from some academic scribbler of a few years back. *I am sure that the power of vested*

I have been all the more moved by this help given that selfish old Europe (alas, France appears to be in this respect in the front rank!) cares little for its youth. Whereas in generous young America there is hardly a successful man to be found who is not intensely conscious of the vital duty of aiding the young to overcome the obstacles he has himself come up against, in general we see nothing of the same sort over here. Those who become rich or settled accumulate and conserve their wealth for themselves and their near and dear alone.

It is clear where such class selfishness will lead us. (On this subject, see my study "Quelques réflexions sur l'inégalité, les classes et la promotion sociale," in *Économie et humanisme*, July–September 1946.)

3. Which I intend to publish in a few months' time under the title "Philosophie de l'économie de demain."

interests is vastly exaggerated compared with the gradual encroachment of ideas. Not, indeed, immediately, but after a certain interval; for in the field of economic and political philosophy there are not many who are influenced by new theories after they are twenty-five or thirty years of age, so that the ideas which civil servants and politicians and even agitators apply to current events are not likely to be the newest.[4]

But it is ideas, and not vested interests, which ultimately prove more powerful and carry the day in the evolution of societies.

Saint-Cloud, 1 May 1946

4. Keynes, *The General Theory of Employment, Interest, and Money*, bk. 6, ch. 24, § 5. Emphasis mine.

Illustration of the General Theory of Interest by the Study of Simplified Models

Generalities (171)

The preceding general study has made it possible to elicit the main features of the phenomenon of interest and to clarify the general links of interdependence that characterize it.

However, the various demonstrations so far furnished have only ever been partial ones, relating exclusively to some specific aspect of the phenomenon of interest considered in isolation.

Such an approach is necessary and inevitable but remains insufficient to attain certainty, for the piecemeal examination of the different components of a mechanism can never suffice to grasp their simultaneous interaction. If we are to study the economic mechanism as a whole, together with all its interacting parts, it can only be by using simplified models in which each of the numerous relations that characterize each mode of interdependence can in fact be isolated. Such is the aim of the three appendixes that now follow.

It is worth emphasizing their value. The great advantage of such models is to enhance concentration by forcing the mind to seek a simplified representation of the basic interrelated economic mechanisms—one reduced to the basics—and to enable it to examine and interpret the results obtained from analytical transformations of the starting conditions.

This double effort is *richly rewarded*. For my own part I can bear witness that it is what enabled me to clarify results already obtained but that remained in some respects obscure, to elicit various results not yet discovered, and eventually to attain certainty.

Take questions such as the influence of physical productivity, of production processes, of land ownership, or of the use of circulating money on interest rate levels, whether there is an optimal capital equipment stock or whether a positive, or negative, rate of interest is possible under stationary conditions: it is *quite impossible* for any serious researcher to give a definitive answer on such matters without first verifying by the use of specific cases, in which the general economic interdependences can be studied in concrete form, the conclusions that can be obtained by a sequence of inferential arguments.[1]

Needless to say *the study of such simplified models is not a method by which results are capable of being strictly proved* since it is not possible to reason from the particular to the general, *but it does allow certain deductions to be eliminated in all safety and the inanity of some inferences to be exposed without the slightest doubt*, since what is true in general must remain true in the particular instance.

For instance, it enables us to reject as devoid of any value the arguments put forward by economists who claim that under stationary conditions no interest rate is possible since *by taking the same general assumptions*, we can offer specific examples in which such conditions apply.

The method involved consists essentially in comparing the results obtained by general economic argumentation with the data yielded by studying simple models that satisfy *the same general premises*, merely adding case specifics. While it has no positive value in the sense that it cannot furnish proof of this or that property, it has an extremely high negative value in the sense that it enables us to eliminate without further examination certain arguments and certain theses. Hence, while having no intrinsic probative force concerning certain properties, it can raise the probability of their accuracy by putting them in the spotlight during the study of specific cases.

Finally, *no matter how abstract or difficult the following analyses may be, how remote from reality they may at first sight appear, or how much their novelty may disconcert*, I am convinced that readers willing to embark on a thoughtful, in-depth study of them will be prompt to admit these points:

1. *The use of simple abstract models is of high methodological value for verifying economic argumentation.* As in mechanics or physics, so too in economics, they

---

1. See the remarks made in no. 3 *in fine*.

can refute certain general inferences whenever, from identical premises, they reach different results for specific cases.

2. *It is imperative for economists to agree to study abstract models* in which their premises and the reasoning they have built on those premises are embodied and their compatibility with reality and their exactitude can be easily verified.

    Without precise and rigorous studies there can be no science, and mere intuition cannot replace study, which, albeit dry, is always both necessary and fruitful. What value, after all, had the intuition and common sense of Harvey's adversaries when they denied the circulation of the blood? The present author's view is that in the present state of economics it is in fact highly dangerous to appeal to intuition. *On the contrary, our days are more than ever in imperative need of the effort of rigor and penetration*, no matter how dry and demanding it may appear.

3. As a rule, *systematic recourse in abstract applications to the part of logic known as mathematics cannot fail to prove outstandingly fruitful in economics.* It would be a grave error to reject it on the pretext that the theoretical aspect of its deductions seems at first sight to distance them from the real world.

Indeed the distinction between theory and practice is invariably unfounded and often perilous; in reality both are twin aspects of a single endeavor to comprehend the facts.[2]

2. I take this opportunity to extend special thanks to M. Debreu, holder of the *agrégation* in mathematics, for kindly verifying in detail all the calculations contained in these appendixes.

Illustration of the Theory of Social Productivity[1]

1. Conditions assumed (172)

L et us take a complex economy and assume that one of the goods produced, $(\bar{A})$, is obtained from labor (X), from the services (H) of indirect good $(\bar{H})$ used exclusively in production $(\bar{A})$, and from the services (U) of land $(\bar{U})$ in accordance with production function

(1) $$\bar{A} = f(X_A, H_A, U_A),$$

where $\bar{A}$ denotes the quantity of good $(\bar{A})$ obtained from quantities (X_A), (H_A), and (U_A) of services (X), (H), and (U) and it is assumed that indirect good $(\bar{H})$ is itself obtained from labor (X) in accordance with the production function

(2) $$H_A = g(X_{II}),$$

where H_A denotes the quantity of good $(\bar{H})$ obtained from quantity (X_{II}) of service (X) and it is assumed that this good $(\bar{H})$ ceases to exist after a single use and *cannot therefore be used in any other production*.

Let us further assume that stationary conditions prevail in the economy we are considering. On these assumptions, each period T_q is identical to the preceding period T_{q-1}. Hence productions, consumptions and prices remain constant over time.

---

1. Expounded in chapter 7.

APPENDIX TABLE I.I **Table representing this production over period *T***

	Factors of Production Utilized			Productions	
Industries	Labor	Land	Capital	Capital goods	Consumer goods
Equipment industry	X_H			H_A	
Consumption industry	X_A	U_A	H_A		A
Total	X	U_A			A

In this equilibrium the production process of good $(\overline{A})$ is as follows. Over a given period of time a certain quantity X of labor (X) is devoted by the economy to producing good $(\overline{A})$. One part, X_A, of this labor input goes directly toward this production, together with fraction U_A of land services (U) and quantity H of good $(\overline{H})$ produced during the previous period. The other part, X_H, goes indirectly toward the production of a quantity H_A of good $(\overline{H})$ to be used during the following period.

Finally we assume that social efficiency is maximal[2]—a hypothesis that implies, notably, that the price of every good or service is equal to its marginal cost.[3]

Now let x, u, and h be respectively the prices of the services (X), (U), and (H) and let $\bar{a}$ and $\bar{h}$ be the sale prices of goods $(\overline{A})$ and $(\overline{H})$.

As the factors of production (X), (H), and (U) are used in industries $(\overline{A})$ and $(\overline{H})$ until their marginal products in real terms $\bar{a}f'_X$, $\bar{h}g'_X$, $\bar{a}f'_H$, and $\bar{a}f_U$ are equal to their costs x, h, and u, we have

$$(3) \qquad \frac{1}{\bar{a}} = \frac{\dfrac{\partial f}{\partial X_A}}{x} = \frac{\dfrac{\partial f}{\partial H_A}}{h} = \frac{\dfrac{\partial f}{\partial U_A}}{u}$$

and

2. Reminder: the theory of social productivity is meaningful only in an economy already assumed to have maximum social efficiency (no. 67).

3. This is because the theory of social efficiency shows that a necessary condition for an economy's social efficiency to be maximum is that it should use, explicitly or implicitly, a price system such that the price of every good or service is equal to its marginal cost.

In this form the statement of the theorem of social efficiency calls for no distinction between the "differentiated sector" and the "undifferentiated sector" (see note 2 to no. 55) and this, as the reader will observe, is an advantage, since it enables us to show that the theorem of social efficiency is of general application, just as valid for the undifferentiated as for the differentiated sectors.

(4)
$$\frac{1}{h} = \frac{\dfrac{dg}{dX_H}}{x}.$$

As the output $\overline{H}$ produced during a given period is not used until the following period, and ceases to exist after a single use, once again if we take (H) as the unit of service rendered by a unit of good $(\overline{H})$ during period T, we obtain

(5)
$$h = (1 + I)\overline{h},$$

where I is the rate of interest corresponding to the period in question. This equation states that the value of service (H) is equal to the sum of its depreciation $\overline{h}$ and of the interest $I\overline{h}$ on its value.

2. Condition of maximization of social productivity (173)

As each year the community uses the quantities

$$X = X_A + X_H \tag{6}$$

[1]

of labor ($\overline{X}$) and U_A of land service (U) in order to produce good ($\overline{A}$), it is reasonable to inquire upon what condition output $\overline{A}$ obtained from quantities X and U_A assumed to be given will be maximal. This amounts to investigating whether there exists an optimal division of the total labor input X devoted to production ($\overline{A}$) between direct labor X_A and indirect labor X_H.

As we have

$$\overline{A} = f[X_A, g(X - X_A), U_A], \tag{7}$$

it is clear that for X and U_A assumed to be given, $\overline{A}$ can only be maximal if

$$\frac{d\overline{A}}{dX_A} = 0 \tag{8}$$

or, in other words, if

$$\frac{\partial f}{\partial X_A} - \frac{\partial f}{\partial H_A}\frac{dg}{dX_H} = 0. \tag{9}$$

However, in light of equations (3) and (4), this condition implies that

$$h = \overline{h} \tag{10}$$

and indeed, taking equation (5) into account, that

$$I = 0. \tag{11}$$

---

1. To facilitate cross-reference, the equations of the appendix are continuously numbered throughout, irrespective of the numbered section in which they appear.

Obviously, this means that if output $\overline{A}$ is to be maximal, the rate of interest I prevailing in the stationary process we are considering must be zero.

And it is easy to see that if the economy being studied has maximum social efficiency, this condition is also sufficient.

For if conditions (3), (4), (5), and (11) are verified, condition (9) must also be so, and production $\overline{A}$ is stationary.

Moreover, in order for production $\overline{A}$ actually to be maximal, it is sufficient that

(12)
$$\frac{d^2\overline{A}}{dX_A^2} < 0,$$

i.e., that

(13)
$$\frac{\partial^2 f}{\partial X_A^2} + 2\frac{\partial^2 f}{\partial X_A \partial H_A}\frac{dH_A}{dX_A} + \frac{\partial^2 f}{\partial H_A^2}\left(\frac{dH_A}{dX_A}\right)^2 + \frac{\partial f}{\partial H_A}\frac{d^2 H_A}{dX_A^2} < 0.$$

Now the theory shows that for social efficiency to be maximal it must be impossible to produce any surplus value in any virtual displacement *when prices are assumed to be given*. And this means that in the present case we have

(14)
$$\bar{a}\delta\overline{A} + \bar{h}\delta\overline{H} - x(\delta X_A + \delta X_H) - h\delta H_A - u\delta U_A \le 0$$

for every displacement compatible with the constraints

(15)
$$\overline{A} = f(X_A, H_A, U_A), \qquad\qquad H_A = g(X_H),$$

$\bar{a}, \bar{h}, x, h$, and u being the prices of goods $(\overline{A}), (\overline{H}), (X), (H)$, and (U), and corresponding to maximum social efficiency.

Since we have

(16)
$$\delta\overline{A} = d\overline{A} + \frac{d^2\overline{A}}{2}, \qquad\qquad \delta\overline{H} = d\overline{H} + \frac{d^2\overline{H}}{2},$$

and, according to conditions (3), (4), and (5),

(17)
$$\bar{a}\,d\overline{A} + \bar{h}\,d\overline{H} = 0,$$

while the variables X_A, X_H, H_A, and U_A may be taken as independent variables so that in consequence,

(17') $d^2X_A = d^2X_H = d^2H_A = d^2U_A = 0,$

condition (14) translates into

(18) $\bar{a}\,d^2\bar{A} + \bar{h}\,d^2\bar{H} \le 0.$

As for $I = 0$ we have

(19) $\dfrac{\bar{h}}{\bar{a}} = \dfrac{h}{a} = \dfrac{\partial f}{\partial H_A},$

it follows that condition (18), for displacements such as

(19') $dU_A = 0,$ $dX_A + dX_H = 0,$

yields, notably

(20) $\dfrac{\partial^2 f}{\partial X_A^2}\,dX_A^2 + 2\dfrac{\partial^2 f}{\partial X_A\,\partial H_A}\,dX_A\,dH_A + \dfrac{\partial^2 f}{\partial H_A^2}\,dH_A^2 + \dfrac{\partial f}{\partial H_A}\dfrac{d^2 H}{dX_A^2}\,dX_A^2 \le 0,$

a condition that is the same as equation (13).

In conclusion, it can be seen that where social efficiency is maximal and the quantities of the primary factors of production (X) *and* (U) *devoted to production* $\bar{A}$ *are given, the necessary and sufficient condition for maximization of production* $\bar{A}$ *is that the rate of interest be zero.*

N.B. 1. The case of other productions

Similar deductions could also be made in respect of the various other productions of indirect goods $(\bar{A})$, $(\bar{B})$, ..., $(\bar{Z})$ in the economy in question.

It would emerge that when the rate of interest is zero, the division of labor between direct and indirect use is optimal for *each* production.

N.B. 2. The case of other primary factors of production

It is important to note that if production $(\bar{H})$ also required use of land service (U), so that the quantity used U was divided between direct use U_A and indirect use U_H, the condition of maximization of production A for a given quantity of land services

(21) $$U = U_A + U_H$$

would still give

(22) $$I = 0,$$

for the calculations would proceed in exactly the same way.

It is thus clear that when the rate of interest is zero, the division of all the primary factors of production (different qualities of labor and different land services) between direct use and indirect use corresponds to the maximization of the various productions.

3. Application to a specific case (174)

It is easy to verify the foregoing conclusions using a specific case.
For instance, let us assume that

(1')
$$\overline{A} = \sqrt{X_A(KH_A + K'U_A)},$$

(2')
$$H_A = K''X_H,$$ [1]

where K, K', and K'' are constants.
Equations (3) and (4) can be written

(3')
$$\frac{1}{a} = \frac{KH_A + K'U_A}{2x\sqrt{X_A(KH_A + K'U_A)}} = \frac{KX_A}{2h\sqrt{X_A(KH_A + K'U_A)}}$$

$$= \frac{K'X_A}{2u\sqrt{X_A(KH_A + K'U_A)}},$$

(4')
$$\frac{1}{h} = \frac{K''}{x}.$$

In light of equation (5) a simple computation reveals that

(23)
$$\overline{A} = \frac{KK''X + K'U_A}{\sqrt{KK''}} \frac{\sqrt{1-I}}{2+I}.$$

Now *physically* we have

(24)
$$\overline{A} = \frac{\sqrt{KK''X_A[KK''(X - X_A) + K'U_A]}}{\sqrt{KK''}}.$$

---

1. To facilitate comparison of the results obtained here with those to be obtained in appendix II, the same production functions are used here as will be used there (see no. 176); they are homogeneous and first order in relation to the factors of production. However, verification would also be possible, as readers may easily confirm, using any functions, provided only, of course, that the economic state was one of maximum social efficiency.

$\overline{A}$ is thus revealed to be an increasing function of a product of two terms the sum of which is constant. Its maximum for a given X is attained when these two terms are equal, i.e., when

$$(25) \qquad X_A = \frac{KK''X + K'U_A}{2KK''}.$$

And we then obtain

$$(26) \qquad \overline{A}_m = \frac{KK''X + K'U_A}{2\sqrt{KK''}},$$

and it is immediately verified, from equation (23), that this maximum value is indeed attained in the economic state of maximum social efficiency under consideration when the rate of interest is zero.

Illustration of General Economic Interdependences

Generalities (175)

*T*he following studies are intended to illustrate, using a single general plan, the influence of the basic elements of the theory of interest* (physical productivity of capital, preference for present goods, private or collective land ownership, liquidity preference, propensity to own).

As the reader will realize, the studies are, from the exclusively economic angle, relatively complex, but *this complexity is due to the nature of the problem being examined.*

To the purely economic difficulties must be added others of an analytical nature due to the fact that the different representative functions of competitive equilibrium display an algebraic form requiring extensive explanation in order to be fully understood. Hence the reader is liable to be distracted from the strictly economic questions by irrelevant technical details, which would be a pity.

However, despite my best efforts, I have not always been able to avoid this danger. Numerous trials established that the example chosen, notwithstanding its relative complexity in algebraic terms, is nevertheless *the simplest* study model that could be found.[1] While it cannot be ruled out that

---

1. I.e. the simplest of all possible systems of equations (a) involving the *simultaneous* action of all the variable factors indicated above and (b) *capable of being fully resolved* by analytical methods.

easier models may one day be identified without detriment to the power of illustrating the theory, I personally doubt whether this will ever happen.

To avoid laborious algebraic calculations, which would have considerably lengthened the text, I have limited myself to outlining the various calculations and the final formulae they would reach.

A. The Case of an Economy without Money or Propensity to Own

1. The economy studied (176)

The economy we shall be studying is an account-based economy, in which there is no money that actually circulates; *stationary competitive conditions and perfect foresight* are assumed, while time is divided into equal successive periods of duration T.

Demographic structure

This economy is assumed to contain only *one category of individuals, whose life extends over two periods* Θ_0 and Θ_1, each equal in duration to T.

During each period T_i, therefore, two generations are both alive: the one composed of the young (J), whose age is inferior to T, and the other of the elderly (V), whose age lies between T and $2T$. As stationary conditions are assumed, the population of the young is equal to that of the elderly and will be denoted by n. Thus the total population is equal to $2n$.

APPENDIX TABLE 2.1 **Table of the succession of the generations**

Generations	Periods			
	T_{n-1}	T_n	T_{n+1}	T_{n+2}
G^{n-1}	Θ_0^{n-1}	Θ_1^{n-1}		
G^n		Θ_0^n	Θ_1^n	
G^{n+1}			Θ_0^{n+1}	Θ_1^{n+1}
Total population	$2n$	$2n$	$2n$	$2n$

General conditions of labor, consumption, and ownership

Each individual works only in his youth (Θ_0) and consumes only one service (A), in quantity $A_0^i = \dfrac{A_0}{n}$ during his youth (Θ_0) and $A_1^i = \dfrac{A_1}{n}$ in his old age (Θ_1); the parameters A_0 and A_1, respectively, denote the consumptions of the young and the old during any period T.

It is assumed that *the duration of the labor period is fixed by law, that there is no inheritance, and that all land is privately owned.*

Psychological structure

The satisfaction S_0^i of each young individual is assumed to be of the form

(1) $$S_0^i = \ln A_0^i + \alpha \ln A_1^i,$$

where α is a positive coefficient. This function corresponds, as the reader may readily confirm, to the general data set out above.[1]

It can immediately be seen that in the plane of the A_0^i and A_1^i, the slope of the tangent along the straight line 0Δ of slope q passing through the origin is identical, and equal to $\dfrac{q}{\alpha}$ for all the lines of indifference. This shows that there is a *marginal preference for present goods* (in the meaning of no. 130) at all points of the plane located above line $0\Delta_1$ of slope equal to α.

It can also be seen that an *average preference for present goods* (in the meaning of note 4 to no. 130), characterized by a greater extension of the domain of possible consumptions where the relative desirability $\dfrac{S'_{A_0^i}}{S'_{A_1^i}}$ of present goods over future goods is greater than unity, corresponds to a value for coefficient α inferior to unity.

Under these conditions the average preference for present goods may be characterized by the coefficient

(2) $$p = 1 - \alpha,$$

1. Introspection makes it possible to show that the desirability of a service A_0 relative to a service A_1 is a decreasing function of the quantity consumed A_0 (see my *À la recherche d'une discipline économique*, no. 62, p. 123). In other words, we have

$$\frac{\partial}{\partial A_0^i} \frac{\frac{\partial S_0^i}{\partial A_0^i}}{\frac{\partial S_0^i}{\partial A_1^i}} < 0,$$

a condition that is in fact verified since it is now written

$$\frac{\partial}{\partial A_0^i} \frac{A_1^i}{\partial A_0^i} < 0.$$

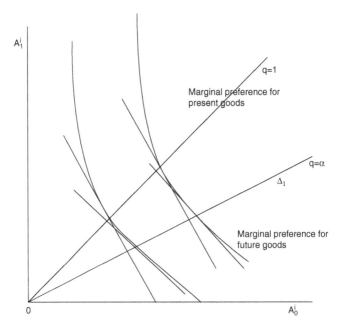

APPENDIX FIGURE 2.1

this preference being so much the greater as p has a higher positive value. Naturally an average preference for future goods would therefore be characterized by a negative value for coefficient p.[2]

During old age, the satisfaction S_1^i of each individual is assumed to take the form

(3) $S_1^i = \ln A_1^i$.   [3]

Finally, note that, whether old or young, the individuals are assumed to derive no satisfaction from either ownership or the act of bequeathing, since their satisfaction functions involve only their own consumptions.

---

2. Readers may easily confirm that if there is a preference for present goods ($\alpha < 1$), the function S_0^i fulfills condition (1) of note 4 to no. 130.

3. Once again, I have selected a logarithmic function, but of course it might equally well be any function, having no relation to the function S_0^i (see no. 60), subject only to the general condition of satisfying the data of the present psychological introspection.

624 APPENDIX II

Technical structure

Good $(\overline{A})$ is obtained from labor input (X), the services (H) of an indirect good $(\overline{H})$ and the services (U) of land $(\overline{U})$ in accordance with the production function

$$(4) \qquad \overline{A} = f(X_A, H, U),$$

where $\overline{A}$ denotes the quantity of good $(\overline{A})$ obtained during period (T) from quantities $X_A, H,$ and U of services $(X), (H),$ and (U).

The indirect good $(\overline{H})$ is assumed to cease to exist after a single use and to be itself obtained from labor input (X) in accordance with the production function

$$(5) \qquad \overline{H} = g(X_H),$$

where $\overline{H}$ represents the quantity of good $(\overline{H})$ obtained during period (T) from quantity X_H of service (X).

It will be assumed that the production techniques in industries $(\overline{A})$ and $(\overline{H})$ are such that the best production techniques corresponding to the output actually consumed are achieved by the juxtaposition of identical firms, i.e., that competition is possible.[4] Indeed, *for the sake of simplicity* it will be assumed that conditions of perfect competition apply, i.e., that the number of firms is infinite, meaning that every technique $(\overline{A}, X_A, H_A, U_A)$ or $(\overline{H}_A, X_H)$ is assumed to be constituted by the juxtaposition of an infinity of identical techniques. Under such conditions, it can be shown that functions f and g are necessarily homogeneous, their degree of homogeneity being equal to unity.[5]

To make it easier to grasp the nature of the calculations used, the following functions will be taken as the functions f and g

$$(6) \qquad \overline{A} = \sqrt{X_A(KH + K'U)},$$

$$(7) \qquad \overline{H} = K''X_H.$$ [6]

4. I have termed such industries *differentiated industries* (see note 2 to no. 55).
5. See my *À la recherche d'une discipline économique*, nos. 83 and 124.
6. Reminder: these production functions are the same as those already used in no. 174.

It can be seen that outputs indeed increase with the quantities of factors of production consumed, but that the yield from these factors is constant or decreasing, which accords with observation.[7]

Good $(\overline{A})$ will be assumed *not to be storable*, while good $\overline{H}$ will be assumed not to be storable for longer than period T so that it must be put to immediate use in the period following that of its production.

Stationary conditions

If X_i denotes the labor input of each young person, the total available labor is

(8)
$$X = nX_i,$$

which of course gives us

(9)
$$X = X_A + X_H.$$

As conditions are assumed to be stationary, each period T_q reproduces identically the preceding period T_{q-1}. Outputs, consumptions and prices remain constant over time.

The production process for good $(\overline{A})$ is as follows: in each period (T), quantity X of labor (X) is devoted by the economy to producing good $(\overline{A})$. A fraction of labor X, denoted X_A, is used directly for this production concurrently with the whole, U_A, of the land service (U) and a fraction, H, of service (H) rendered by good $(\overline{H})$ produced during the preceding period. The other labor fraction X_H goes indirectly toward the production of quantity $\overline{H}$ of good (H), which is used during the following period.

---

7. The yield of factor (X) in industry A, for instance, equal to

(1)
$$\frac{\overline{A}}{X_A} = \sqrt{\frac{KH + K'U}{X_A}},$$

is a decreasing function of X_A.

Prices

The symbols x, u, h, and a will denote the price of services $(X), (U), (H)$, and (A), while $\bar{a}, \bar{h}$, and $\bar{u}$ will denote the sale price of goods $(\bar{A}), (\bar{H})$, and $(\bar{U})$, and I the rate of interest.

State intervention

$\bar{H}_E$ will denote the quantity of capital $(\bar{H})$ owned by the State and D will denote the public debt. Under these conditions the net value of the wealth belonging to the State is

(10) $\Delta = \bar{h}\bar{H}_E - D.$

The interest on this capital *is assumed to be paid to the young.*[8]
The quantity $\bar{H}_I$ of capital $(\bar{H})$ owned by individuals is thus equal to

(11) $\bar{H}_I = \bar{H} - \bar{H}_E.$

Conduct of economic operations

It will be assumed for the sake of simplicity that all economic operations of a period occur *at the end of that period.*

Presentation of the discussion

The discussion of the model will comprise three parts. Part I (nos. 177–186) will be devoted to determining and discussing the analytical solutions to the conditions of equilibrium; part II (nos. 187–94) will provide a complete study of a specific case; and part III (nos. 195–99) will give the *economic interpretation of our findings.*

---

8. If Δ is negative, this assumption means that the State levies the interest for servicing its debt by taxation of the young.

(a) Analytic determination of the solutions

1. The conditions of competitive equilibrium (177)

Givens and unknowns

Quantities X, U, and A constitute the data characterizing the available national labor, land, and State intervention, while quantities $x, \bar{a}, a, \bar{h}, h, \bar{u}, u, I, X_A, X_H, \bar{H}, H, \bar{A}, A, A_0$, and A_1 are unknowns.

Consumption

During their youth, individuals work and earn wages. Further to this they receive a sum $I\Delta$ corresponding to the State's net income from capital.[1] These receipts are devoted to paying for consumptions A_0 and A_1 the prices of which at the initial instant[2] are respectively a and $\dfrac{a}{1+I}$. This means that for individuals in the aggregate

$$(12) \qquad\qquad xX + I\Delta = aA_0 + \frac{aA_1}{1+I}. \qquad\qquad [3]$$

For total receipts of $(xX + I\Delta)$ and prices a and I, which he takes as given, each young person distributes his expenditure between present consumption and future consumption A so as to maximize his satisfaction S_0^i.

When this is so, it must follow that

---

1. If Δ is positive, the sum $I\Delta$ may be regarded as paid by the State to the young in remuneration, for example, for the services of policing and national defense provided by the young.

If Δ is negative, the sum $I\Delta$ corresponds to a tax paid by the young to the State in order to enable it to service its debt.

2. Corresponding to the end of period (Θ_0).

3. For ease of cross-reference the equations are numbered continuously throughout this appendix, as in appendix I, instead of renumbering for each new numbered section.

$$\textbf{(13)} \qquad \frac{\dfrac{\partial S_0^i}{\partial A_0^i}}{a} = \frac{\dfrac{\partial S_0^i}{\partial A_1^i}}{\dfrac{a}{1+I}} \qquad\qquad {}^4$$

or, in light of equation (1),

$$\textbf{(14)} \qquad\qquad\qquad aA_1 = \alpha a A_0 (1 + I).$$

This equation in fact gives expression to the fundamental relationship on the basis of which young individuals distribute their present income

$$\textbf{(15)} \qquad\qquad\qquad R = xX + I\Delta$$

between their present expenditure aA_0 and their future expenditure aA_1. To their decision there corresponds a saving

$$\textbf{(16)} \qquad\qquad\qquad E = R - aA_0 \qquad\qquad {}^5$$

or, in other terms,

$$\textbf{(17)} \qquad\qquad\qquad E = xX + I\Delta - aA_0,$$

4. No. 130, equation (2).
Note that we must at the same time have

$$a\, dA_0^i + \frac{a}{1+I}\, dA_1^i = 0,$$

$$\frac{\partial S_0^i}{\partial A_0^i}\, dA_0^i + \frac{\partial S_0^i}{\partial A_1^i}\, dA_1^i = 0,$$

for every system of variation dA_0^i, dA_1^i satisfying one of these equations.
5. Readers may observe that in view of equations (12), (14), and (17) we have

$$\textbf{(1)} \qquad\qquad\qquad E = \frac{\alpha R}{1 + \alpha}.$$

This implies that *for a given income R* the capital saved by the young does not tend toward zero, as the rate of interest rises indefinitely. This finding may at first sight appear to contradict the statements made in no. 40, but in reality this is not so. It simply means that the psychological structure here considered does not, for very high levels of future consumption, match our psychological introspection, but this does not alter in the least the conclusions to be drawn from our analysis of the present model for finite values of the various parameters.

which they invest in land to a value of $\bar{u}\overline{U}$, in reproducible capital to a value of $\bar{h}\overline{H}_I$, and in government bonds to a value D. For this purpose they buy from the elderly such land $\bar{u}\overline{U}$ and government bonds D as they possess, and they invest funds $\bar{h}\overline{H}_I$ in industry. This gives us

$$(18) \qquad\qquad E = \bar{u}\overline{U} + D + \bar{h}\overline{H}_I.$$

Of course, the consumption A_1^i of each *old* person depends on economic decisions taken when young. Thus the elderly have no freedom of action and their consumption A_1 *results from earlier decisions*. The value aA_1 of this consumption is equal to their previous savings plus the interest thereon, which gives us

$$(19) \qquad\qquad aA_1 = (1 + I)E.$$

Let us now take account of the equation

$$(20) \qquad\qquad A = A_0 + A_1,$$

which states that output A is constantly equal to the aggregate consumption of young and old. In its light, equation (14) now gives us

$$(21) \qquad\qquad A_0 = \frac{A}{1+\alpha(1+I)},$$

$$(22) \qquad\qquad A_1 = \frac{\alpha(1+I)\,A}{1+\alpha(1+I)}.$$

And combining these conditions with equation (12), we obtain

$$(23) \qquad\qquad aA = \frac{1+\alpha(1+I)}{1+\alpha}(xX + I\Delta).$$

These three conditions (21), (22), and (23) are equivalent to equations (1), (4), and (10) and can be substituted for them.

Production

Once the competitive equilibrium is in place, the marginal products $\bar{a}A'_X$, $\bar{h}H'_X$, $\bar{a}A'_H$, and $\bar{a}A'_U$ of the factors of production (X), (H), and (U) used in industries $(\overline{A})$ and $(\overline{H})$ are equal, in real terms, to their costs x, h, and u. This gives us

(24)
$$\frac{1}{a} = \frac{\overline{A}'_X}{x} = \frac{\overline{A}'_H}{h} = \frac{\overline{A}'_U}{u},$$

(25)
$$\frac{1}{h} = \frac{\overline{H}'_X}{x}.$$

In light of equations (6) and (7), these equations immediately tell us that

(26)
$$\overline{a}A = 2xX_A = 2h\frac{(KH + K'U)}{K} = 2u\frac{(KH + K'U)}{K},$$

(27)
$$\overline{h} = \frac{x}{K''}.$$

As the output $\overline{H}$ produced during any period is used only in the following period and ceases to exist after a single use, we have

(28)
$$h = (1 + I)\overline{h}. \qquad \qquad \text{6}$$

And as output $\overline{A}$ is assumed to be consumed immediately and also ceases to exist after a single use, we have

(29)
$$a = \overline{a}.$$

Since the value of a parcel of land under stationary conditions is, for *all positive values of interest rate I*, equal to the product of the land rent by the inverse of the rate of interest,[7] we find that

(30)
$$\overline{u} = \frac{u}{I}.$$

Finally, if we take as the unit of services, the service rendered by the units of goods over a period T, we have

6. This equation is no more than a simple application of equation (1) of no. 29.
7. No. 30.

(31) $A = \bar{A},$ $H = \bar{H},$ $U = \bar{U}.$

And writing

(32) $$\beta = \frac{KK''}{K'},   \frac{X}{U},$$

we may immediately infer from equations (6), (7), (9), (26), (27), (28), and (31) the following equations:

(33) $$h = \frac{x}{K''}(1+I),$$

(34) $$u = \frac{xX}{\beta U}(1+I),   \bar{u} = \frac{xX}{\beta U}\left(1+\frac{1}{I}\right),$$

(35) $$H = \frac{K''X}{\beta}\frac{\beta-(1+I)}{2+I},$$

(36) $$A = \sqrt{KK''}\, X\left(1+\frac{1}{\beta}\right)\frac{\sqrt{1+I}}{2+I},$$

(37) $$a = 2\sqrt{\frac{1+I}{KK''}}x.$$

These six equations are equivalent to equations (6), (26), (28), and (30) *and may replace them.*[8]

The existence of one degree of freedom in general equilibrium

If we eliminate the unknowns $\bar{A}$, $\bar{H}$, $\bar{U}$, and $\bar{a}$ given by equations (29) and (31), it can be seen that 12 equations[9] are available to determine the

---

8. Note that in the model we are now studying the different parameters representing the production sector form a block that depends on consumer psychologies only through the agency of interest rate I.

9. Equations (7), (9), (21), (22), (23), (27), (33), (34), (35), (36), and (37).

13 unknowns $X_A, X_H, H, A, A_0, A_1, \dfrac{a}{x}, \dfrac{u}{x}, \dfrac{\bar{u}}{x}, \dfrac{h}{x}, \dfrac{\bar{h}}{x}, \dfrac{\Delta}{x}$, and $I.$[10] *This confirms that the stationary-state equilibrium we are studying allows one degree of freedom.*[11]

It can be seen that in the absence of State intervention ($\Delta = 0$), the equilibrium is well determined, whereas in the event of State intervention ($\Delta \neq 0$) the equilibrium includes an arbitrary parameter, which may be the State's net capital Δ, the rate of interest I, or any other parameter.

For ease of analytical discussion, and without prejudging either the cause-and-effect links found in economic evolution or the way in which such and such an equilibrium may be realized *in practice*, it will be best, as the reader may readily verify, to choose the rate of interest I as the arbitrary parameter.[12]

Consumptions, satisfactions, net capital of the State,
reproducible capital, land as capital, private capital,
national capital, and national income

In combination with our definition of coefficient β, equations (21), (22), and (36) give

(38)
$$A_0 = \sqrt{KK''}X\left(1+\frac{1}{\beta}\right)\frac{\sqrt{1+I}}{2+I}\frac{1}{1+\alpha(1+I)},$$

(39)
$$A_1 = \sqrt{KK''}X\left(1+\frac{1}{\beta}\right)\frac{(1+I)^{\frac{3}{2}}}{2+I}\frac{\alpha}{1+\alpha(1+I)},$$

(40) $\quad S_0^i = (1+\alpha)\ln\left[\dfrac{\sqrt{KK''}}{n}\,X\left(1+\dfrac{1}{\beta}\right)\right]+\alpha\ln\alpha+\dfrac{1+3\alpha}{2}\ln(1+I)$

$$- (1+\alpha)\ln(2+I)-(1+\alpha)\ln[1+\alpha(1+I)],$$

---

10. It may be noted that parameters $\overline{H}_E$ and D play a role in the conditions of economic equilibrium only by the quantity Δ, net value of the wealth owned by the State, defined by condition (10).

11. As indicated in no. 49.

12. But of course a quite different parameter could be chosen.

$$(41) \qquad S_1^i = \ln\left[\frac{\sqrt{KK''}X}{n}\left(1+\frac{1}{\beta}\right)\right] + \ln\alpha + \frac{3}{2}\ln(1+I) - \ln(2+I)$$
$$- \ln[1+\alpha(1+I)]$$

By introducing the values for α and A derived from equations (36) and (37) into equation (23), we obtain the following equation:

$$(42) \qquad \frac{1+\alpha(1+I)}{1+\alpha}\left(1+\frac{I\Delta}{xX}\right) = 2\left(1+\frac{1}{\beta}\right)\frac{1+I}{2+I}.$$

This equation determines the value, in wage terms, $\dfrac{\Delta}{x}$ of the State's net capital, as a function of I.

An easy calculation now gives us

$$(43) \qquad \Delta = -\frac{xX}{\beta}\frac{\alpha\beta I^2 + (\alpha\beta - 2\alpha - \beta - 2)I - 2 - 2\alpha}{I(2+I)[1+\alpha(1+I)]}.$$

For the discussion on which we are about to embark it is *convenient* to consider not the total wealth Δ possessed by the State, but the excess

$$(44) \qquad \delta = \Delta - \bar{u}\bar{U} = \bar{h}\bar{H}_E - D - \bar{u}\bar{U}$$

of this wealth over the value of the land.

In light of equations (32) and (34) we then have

$$(45) \qquad \Delta = \delta + \left(1+\frac{1}{I}\right)\frac{xX}{\beta},$$

so that, taking δ as unknown instead of Δ, equation (42) becomes

$$(46) \qquad \frac{1+\alpha(1+I)}{1+\alpha}\left(1+\frac{1+I}{\beta}+\frac{I\delta}{xX}\right) = 2\left(1+\frac{1}{\beta}\right)\frac{1+I}{2+I}.$$

This equation gives

$$(47) \qquad \delta = -\frac{xX}{\beta}\frac{\alpha I^2 + (\alpha\beta + 4\alpha + 1)I + 1 + 3\alpha - \beta + \alpha\beta}{(2+I)(1+\alpha+\alpha1)},$$

for all positive values of I.

Naturally, we have $C_\mu = \overline{h}\overline{H}$ for *reproducible capital*, in view of equations (27), (31), and (35),

(48)
$$C_\mu = \left(1 - \frac{1+I}{\beta}\right)\frac{xX}{2+I},$$

for *land* we have $C_\varphi = \overline{u}\overline{U}$, in view of equations (31) and (34),

(49)
$$C_\varphi = \left(1 + \frac{1}{I}\right)\frac{xX}{\beta},$$

for *private capital* $C = E$ defined by equation (18), in view of equation (10),

(50)
$$C = E = C_\mu + C_\varphi - \Delta,$$

or indeed, in light of equations (17), (21), and (23),

(51)
$$C = E = \frac{\alpha}{1+\alpha}(xX + I\Delta),$$

for *national capital*

(52)
$$C_N = C_\mu + C_\varphi,$$

for *national income* $R_N = aA$, in view of equations (36) and (37),

(53)
$$R_N = 2\left(1 + \frac{1}{\beta}\right)\frac{1+I}{2+I}xX,$$

and for the ratio of reproducible capital to the national income

(54)
$$\frac{C_\mu}{R_N} = \frac{1}{2(1+\beta)}\left(\frac{\beta}{1+I} - 1\right).$$

Primary national income and primary national capital

From our definition of primary national income, we have in wage terms[13]

---

13. Note 12 to no. 47.

(55)
$$R_{N\omega} = X + \frac{u}{x}U,$$

i.e., in combination with equation (34),

(56)
$$R_{N\omega} = X\left(1 + \frac{1+I}{\beta}\right).$$
[14]

For primary national capital, taking account of equation (7) we obtain, in wage terms,[13]

(57)
$$C_{\mu\omega} = X_H = \frac{\overline{H}}{K''} = \frac{C_\mu}{\hbar K''},$$

which in view of equation (27) is tantamount to

(58)
$$C_{\mu\omega} = \frac{C_\mu}{x}.$$

The value of primary national capital is therefore equal to the wage-denominated value of reproducible capital.[15]

---

14. According to this equation, primary income $R_{N\omega}$ appears in our model as a function of interest rate I, and its variations with interest rate I emerge as not negligible, even in first approximation. This finding might at first sight appear to contradict the working assumptions of no. 47, but it does not do so in reality. The interdependence of primary income and interest rate is so marked in our model only because, in light of production function (6) of no. 176, land and capital are now perfectly interchangeable, *a condition that is not verified in reality and that has been accepted only for the sake of simplifying calculations.* The reader will be able to verify with ease that this detail makes no change to the general significance of the example studied.

Moreover this peculiarity would have completely disappeared if we had chosen as production function the function

$$\overline{A} = \sqrt{H(KX_A + K'U)},$$

but on such an assumption there would no longer be the possibility of a direct process.

15. The value in wage terms of reproducible capital is here equal to the value of primary national capital only because of the peculiarity of the productive system, including as it does only two production periods. This of course is a circumstance that does not correspond to reality and has been assumed only in the interests of simplicity. It is easy to verify that it makes no change to the overall scope of the model studied.

Direct labor and indirect labor

Equations (7), (9), and (35) make it immediately possible to find, for indirect labor X_H and direct labor X_A,[16]

$$(59) \qquad X_H = \frac{X}{\beta}\frac{\beta-(1+I)}{2+I},$$

$$(60) \qquad X_A = X\left(1+\frac{1}{\beta}\right)\frac{1+I}{2+I}.$$

Production period

Our definition of the production period[17] here gives us

$$(61) \qquad \Theta_N = \frac{xX_H}{xX+uU},$$

i.e., in light of equations (34) and (59),

$$(62) \qquad \Theta_N = \frac{\beta-1-I}{(2+I)(\beta+1+I)}. \qquad [18]$$

Physical productivity of production processes

Since production, for zero recourse to capital (i.e., using only direct processes), is equal to

$$(63) \qquad A_d = \sqrt{K'XU},$$

it follows that the physical productivity of the indirect process of production used is, in accordance with our definition,[19]

$$(64) \qquad \pi = \frac{A_i - A_d}{A_d} = \left(\sqrt{\beta}+\frac{1}{\sqrt{\beta}}\right)\frac{\sqrt{1+I}}{2+I}-1.$$

16. In the meaning of no. 20.
17. No. 47, equation (3).
18. This verifies that the production period is indeed a decreasing function of the rate of interest (no. 47).
19. No. 68, equation (1).

2. The circuit of values (178)

It is interesting to note how the value flows characterizing a given period are divided.

The payments, assumed to occur at the end of the period, in fact take the following form:

Budget of the young

The *young* receive a wage of xX together with the interest $\bar{Ih}\bar{H}_E$ on the capital owned by the State. These receipts are devoted to immediate consumption of value aA_0, to payment of taxes to the amount of ID, and to savings. Since all land is owned by individuals, these savings include first the value $\bar{u}\bar{U}$ of the land that the young buy from the elderly; next it includes the amount D of the public debt, which they also buy from the elderly, and finally the value $\bar{h}\bar{H}_I$ of the fraction $\bar{H}_I$ of reproducible capital owned by individuals. Thus the budget of the young may be expressed by the equation

(65) $$xX + \bar{Ih}\bar{H}_E = aA_0 + ID + \bar{u}\bar{U} + D + \bar{h}\bar{H}_I.$$ [1]

Budget of the elderly

The resources available to the *elderly* are: first, the value $\bar{u}\bar{U} + D$ of the land and government bonds that they sell to the young, then the depreciation $\bar{h}\bar{H}_I$ and interest $\bar{Ih}\bar{H}$ on capital invested in industry during the previous period, and finally the rent uU on their land and the yield ID on their government bonds. These resources are used for consumption of value aA_I.

Thus the budget of the elderly can be expressed by the equation

(66) $$\bar{u}\bar{U} + uU + (D + \bar{h}\bar{H}_I)(1 + I) = aA_1.$$

1. This equation can of course be obtained by elimination of E between equations (17) and (18).

Budget of firms

Taken as a whole, *firms* pay wages of xX, depreciations of $\overline{hH}$, interest of $I\overline{hH}$, and rent of uU; they receive from individuals savings of $\overline{hH}_I$, and from the State savings of $\overline{hH}_E$, while they receive sums amounting to aA in payment for their products.

So the balanced budget of firms considered collectively is expressed by the equation

$$(67) \qquad xX + (1 + I)\overline{hH} + uU = aA + \overline{hH}_I + \overline{hH}_E.$$

Budget of the State

Finally, *State* receipts comprise, first, taxation to the amount ID levied on the young and, second, depreciation and interests $\overline{hH}_E(1 + I)$ on the sums invested in industry in the preceding period. This income provides the State with the resources needed for payment of the interest ID on its bonds, the interest $I\overline{hH}_E$ paid to the young on their reproducible capital, and finally investment in industry to the amount of $\overline{hH}_E$.

This means that the State's balanced budget may be stated as

$$(68) \qquad ID + \overline{hH}_E(1 + I) = ID + I\overline{hH}_E + \overline{hH}_E.$$

Value flow diagram

All value flows may be represented by appendix figure 2.2.

Budget equations and general conditions of the equilibrium

It can be seen that equation (68) reduces to an identity and that equations (65), (66), and (67) may, in light of equations (10) and (31), be written

$$(69) \qquad xX + \Delta(1 + I) = aA_0 + \overline{h}H + \overline{u}U,$$

$$(70) \qquad (\overline{u} + u)U + \overline{h}H(1 + I) = aA_1 + \Delta(1 + I),$$

$$(71) \qquad xX + I\overline{h}H + uU = a(A_0 + A_1).$$

It may then be observed that the member-by-member sum of equa-

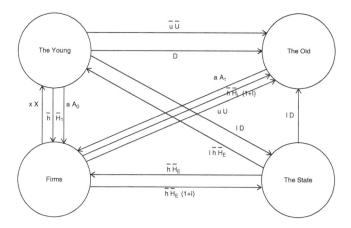

APPENDIX FIGURE 2.2 Value circuit under conditions of private land ownership

tions (69) and (70) gives equation (71) again, while equation (71) itself flows directly from equations

(72) $$xX_A + (1 + I)\bar{h}H + uU = aA$$

and

(73) $$xX_H = \bar{h}H,$$

which represent the operating accounts of industries $(\bar{A})$ and $(\bar{H})$ and themselves result from equations (26), (27), (28), and (29).

With regard to equation (69), it is at once apparent, in view of equation (30), that it results from the elimination of A_1 between equations (12) and (71).

This proves that *the circuit equations indeed follow from the general equilibrium equations found above.*

Supply and demand of capital

Naturally, the sum of land capital $C_\varphi(I)$ and reproducible capital $C_\mu(I)$ must be equal to the sum of capital E saved by young individuals—here equal to the capital offered by individuals $C_0(I)$ and—and the net wealth Δ owned by the State. This means that

(74)
$$C_\varphi(I) + C_\mu(I) = C_0(I) + \Delta.$$
[2,3]

Since equations (12), (15), and (16) have given us

(75)
$$C_0(I) = \frac{aA_1}{1+I},$$

i.e., in combination with equation (22),

(76)
$$C_0(I) = \frac{\alpha}{1+\alpha(1+I)} aA,$$

or again, in view of equations (36) and (37),

(77)
$$C_0(I) = 2\left(1+\frac{1}{\beta}\right)\frac{\alpha(1+I)}{[1+\alpha(1+I)](2+I)} xX,$$
[4]

it is clear that in light of equations (48) and (49), equation (74) translates into

(78)
$$\frac{1}{\beta}\left(1+\frac{1}{I}\right)xX + \frac{1}{2+I}\left(1-\frac{1+I}{\beta}\right)xX$$

$$= 2\alpha\left(1+\frac{1}{\beta}\right)\frac{1+I}{[1+\alpha(1+I)](2+I)}xX + \Delta.$$

It will be easy for the reader to verify that this equation is equivalent to equation (43) and may be substituted for it.

If we consider, instead of the State's net capital Δ, the excess $\delta = \Delta - C_\varphi$ of this capital over land wealth, equation (74) becomes

2. An equation similar to equation (2) of no. 97.

3. Readers may confirm this result immediately, in view of equations (31) and of the equality $C_0 = E$ from equations (12) and (69).

4. It is crucial to emphasize that the supply of capital here considered is the capital supply corresponding to dynamic equilibrium, not the capital supply corresponding to dynamic disequilibrium considered in note 5 to no. 177. (See the remarks already made about this distinction in notes 12 to no. 40, 46 to no. 47, 18 to no. 97, and 18 to no. 135.)

(79) $$C_\mu(I) = C_0(I) + \delta,$$

i.e.,

(80) $$\frac{1}{2+I}\left(1-\frac{1+I}{\beta}\right)xX = 2\alpha\left(1+\frac{1}{\beta}\right)\frac{1+I}{[1+\alpha(1+I)](2+I)}xX + \delta,$$

an equation equivalent to equation (47) and that can be substituted for it.

As will be seen, the interest of these two equations (78) and (80) is that they lend themselves to an easy geometric discussion of the link between interest rate I and capital Δ or δ.

3. Conditions of validity of solutions (179)

Taking interest rate I as independent parameter, let us seek the conditions it must satisfy for the analytical solution set out above to be acceptable.

a. As no capital can lose more than 100% of its value from one period to another, it is necessary that

(81) $1 + I > 0.$

b. *As the various consumptions and productions must necessarily have a positive value*, examination of the relations established above shows that this condition is certainly satisfied if

(82) $H > 0,$

i.e., from equation (35)

(83) $1 + I < \beta.$

c. Equation (30), which gives the value of land, is valid only if the second series of no. 30 is convergent, i.e., if interest rate I is positive. The point at issue will be meaningless *in the context of private land ownership* unless

(84) $I > 0.$

d. If reproducible capital $\overline{h}\overline{H}_E$ owned by the State is not zero, but the public debt D is greater than it, such that the State's net wealth

(85) $\Delta = \overline{h}\overline{H}_E - D$

is negative, *everything takes place as though* all reproducible capital $\overline{h}\overline{H}$ belonged to individuals. Adopting this hypothesis, we assume that if Δ is negative, $\overline{H}_E$ is zero.

On the other hand if Δ is positive while D is not zero, *everything takes place as though* individuals owned a fraction, of value D, of the State's reproducible capital $\overline{h}\overline{H}_E$. To simplify, it will be supposed that this fraction is included in $\overline{h}\overline{H}_I$. In other words, when Δ is positive, D is assumed to be zero.

If we then have

(86)
$$\Delta < \overline{h}\overline{H},$$

reproducible capital is owned in part by individuals and in part by the State. There is no public debt.

On the other hand, if we have

(87)
$$\Delta > \overline{h}\overline{H},$$

i.e., if the State's wealth is greater than the value of existing reproducible capital, its excess over this value necessarily corresponds to the total *indebtedness* of individuals. *Everything takes place as though* a fraction of the land owned by individuals in fact belonged to the State.

It follows from what has been said that *the hypothesis of private freehold, unmortgaged ownership of all land*, necessarily involves the assumption that

(88)
$$\Delta \leq \overline{h}\overline{H},$$

i.e., from the definition (43) of δ,

(89)
$$\delta \leq \overline{h}\overline{H} - \overline{u}\overline{U}.$$

The rate of interest *I* must therefore have a level such that the parameter δ determined by equation (47) satisfies condition (89).

Finally it is evident that the difference $(\Delta - \overline{h}\overline{H})$ cannot exceed the value of the land $\overline{u}\overline{U}$ owned by individuals since, if it did, the young, upon becoming old, could no longer obtain resources by selling their land holdings. Hence it is necessary that

(90)
$$\Delta - \overline{h}\overline{H} < \overline{u}\overline{U},$$

i.e., in light of equation (44),

(91)
$$\delta \leq \overline{h}\overline{H}.$$

It is easy to see that this condition is tantamount to the one already indicated,[1]

---

1. See § b above.

(92) $$A_1 \geq 0,$$

for a positive or zero value of consumption A_1.[2]

According to conditions (22) and (36), this condition will in fact be fulfilled if inequality (81) obtains. Condition (90) therefore leads to no new condition at this point for interest rate I.

---

2. It is immediately confirmed from equation (70) that in view of equalities (30) and (31) and of inequality (81), condition (89) is equivalent to the condition

$$\frac{aA_1}{1+I} = \overline{\hbar H} - \Delta + \frac{u+\overline{u}}{1+I}U = \overline{\hbar H} - \Delta + \overline{u}\overline{U} > 0.$$

4. The case of collective land ownership (180)

In this case, if a market for land existed and if the value of land were finite (which requires $I > 0$), the State would possess total wealth

(93) $$\Delta_1 = \bar{h}\bar{H}_E - D_1 + \bar{u}\bar{U},$$

where D_1 denotes State indebtedness and where the price $\bar{u}$ may be found from equation (30).

In fact, as land ownership cannot be transferred or negotiated, what should be considered is not this total wealth, which, for a zero or negative rate of interest is meaningless, *but the capital owned by the State to the exclusion of land,*

(94) $$\delta_1 = \bar{h}\bar{H}_E - D_1.$$

Adopting similar assumptions to those of the previous case, it will be assumed that the State distributes to the young land rent uU and the interest $I\delta_1$ on its capital δ_1,[1] and that D and $\bar{h}\bar{H}_E$ are respectively zero, depending on whether δ_1 is positive or negative.[2]

Naturally if δ_1 is negative and I is positive, i.e., if the formula

$$\bar{u}\bar{U} = \frac{uU}{I}$$

is meaningful, everything takes place as though the individuals owned, in addition to the reproducible capital and perhaps some government debt, all or a part of the land.[3]

---

1. If δ_1 is negative, the term $I\delta_1$ corresponds to a levy of value $I\delta_1$ on the young via taxation.
2. In other words it is assumed that if δ_1 is positive we have

$$\delta_1 = \bar{h}\bar{H}_E, \qquad\qquad D = 0,$$

whereas if δ_1 is negative we have

$$\delta_1 = -D, \qquad\qquad \bar{H}_E = 0.$$

3. See the similar points already made (no. 179, § d).

Conditions of competitive equilibrium[4]

Here, equation (12) becomes

(95) $$xX + uU + I\delta_1 = aA_0 + \frac{aA_1}{1+I},$$

while equation (23) becomes

(96) $$aA = \frac{1+\alpha(1+I)}{1+\alpha}(xX + uU + I\delta_1).$$

The other equations found all remain unchanged except, of course, equation (42), which becomes

(97) $$\frac{1+\alpha(1+I)}{1+\alpha}\left(1 + \frac{uU}{xX} + \frac{I\delta_1}{xX}\right) = 2\left(1+\frac{1}{\beta}\right)\frac{1+I}{2+I}$$

or, in view of equation (34) unchanged,

(98) $$\frac{1+\alpha(1+I)}{1+\alpha}\left(1 + \frac{1+I}{\beta} + \frac{I\delta_1}{xX}\right) = 2\left(1+\frac{1}{\beta}\right)\frac{1+I}{2+I}.$$

This equation gives

(99) $$\delta_1 = -\frac{xX}{\beta}\frac{\alpha I^2 + (\alpha\beta + 4\alpha + 1)I + 1 + 3\alpha - \beta + \alpha\beta}{(2+I)(1+\alpha + \alpha I)},$$

for any value of I except zero, in which case equation (98) reduces to an identity.[5]

The conditions that remain unchanged will be termed C conditions.

---

4. Note that State ownership of land by no means prevents the market for land-use from being competitive (no. 163).

The same applies, at least in theory, to the use of capital in the event that it is collectively owned (note 6 to no. 159).

5. The case of a zero interest rate will be examined later (no. 182).

The circuit of values

In this case the circuit of values becomes as shown in appendix figure 2.3 below.

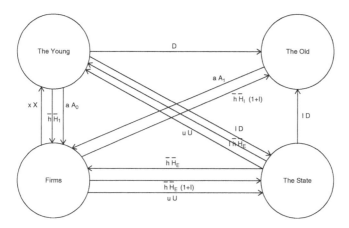

APPENDIX FIGURE 2.3 Circuit of values in case of collective land ownership

The supply and demand of capital

In case of collective land ownership, equation (74) of course becomes

(100) $$C_\mu(I) = C_0(I) + \delta_1,$$

i.e., given the fact that expressions (48) and (77) remain unchanged,

(101) $$\frac{1}{2+I}\left(1-\frac{1+I}{\beta}\right)xX = 2\alpha\left(1+\frac{1}{\beta}\right)\frac{(1+I)xX}{[1+\alpha(1+I)](2+I)}+\delta_1.$$

an equation equivalent to equation (99) and that can be substituted for it. It is noteworthy that this equation is valid even for a zero level of interest rate I and hence that the same applies to equation (99).

Conditions of the validity of solutions

Conditions (81) and (83) of course remain unchanged, but here conditions (84) and (90) disappear as land is assumed to be owned by the State and is no longer negotiable.

5. Private and collective land ownership (181)

If we note that condition (99) can be deduced from condition (47) by simply replacing δ by δ_1 and that the C conditions remain unchanged, it becomes apparent that discussion of the two cases before us, viz. private or collective ownership of land, reduces to discussion of either one or the other of them.

It can be seen that this fact was to be expected, since the case in which, on the assumption of private land ownership, the excess

$$\text{(102)} \qquad\qquad \delta = \overline{h}\,\overline{H}_E - D - u\overline{U}$$

of the capital owned by the State over the value of land has value v, is evidently *equivalent* to the case when, on the assumption of collective land ownership, the capital

$$\text{(103)} \qquad\qquad \delta_1 = \overline{h}\,\overline{H}_E - D_1$$

owned by the State *to the exclusion of land* has the same value, since in both cases competitive equilibrium obtains and the capital owned by the State in addition to land has the *same value* v. Transition from one analytic solution to the other therefore takes place by simple permutation of δ and δ_1.[1]

Thus δ_1 is a parameter characterizing the state of collective land ownership whereas δ is a parameter characterizing the state of private land ownership, and to any value of δ_1 in the first system of equations there corresponds a value *equal* to δ in the second.

If, when the equality $\overline{u} = \dfrac{u}{I}$ is meaningful, the totality of the State's wealth, in the case of collective land ownership, is denoted by Δ_1,

$$\text{(104)} \qquad\qquad \Delta_1 = \delta_1 + \overline{u}\,\overline{U},$$

---

1. Readers may immediately confirm that equations (95) and (96) are deduced from equations (12) and (23) by changing variable (44)

$$\Delta = \delta + \overline{u}\,\overline{U}$$

and by changing δ to δ_1.

APPENDIX TABLE 2.2

	Private Land Ownership	Collective Land Ownership
Total State wealth	$\Delta = h\overline{H}_E - D$	$\Delta_1 = h\overline{H}_E - D_1 + \overline{u}U$
Excess of total State wealth over land value	$\delta = h\overline{H}_E - D - \overline{u}U$	$\delta_1 = h\overline{H}_E - D_1$

it can also be seen that transition from one analytic solution to another is obtained by simple permutation of Δ and Δ_1.

In the event that the equality $\overline{u} = \dfrac{u}{I}$ is meaningful, i.e., in the case for which interest rate I is positive, these circumstances may be summarized as in appendix table 2.2.

Of course when

$$(105) \qquad\qquad D_1 = D + \overline{u}U,$$

we have

$$(106) \qquad\qquad \Delta_1 = \Delta, \qquad\qquad \delta_1 = \delta.$$

Hence the case of collective land ownership and the case of private land ownership both lead us to the *same system of equations*, but in the first case we can consider only interest rate levels that satisfy conditions (84) and (91), whereas this restriction ceases to apply in the second case, which is therefore *more general. For this reason, the discussion will be pursued on the assumption of collective land ownership*, replacing parameters δ_1 and Δ_1 in all equations, of course, by parameters δ and Δ, which are equal to them.

6. Noteworthy levels of interest rate *I* (182)

(i) Value of the limit inferior

The limit inferior of interest rate *I* corresponds, from condition (81), to

(107) $I = -1.$

For this level, equations (99) and (48) tell us that

(108) $\delta = xX,$ $C_\mu = xX.$

In this case, therefore, the State owns all land, and all reproducible capital and public debt is zero.[1]

Moreover, from conditions (36) and (59) we have

(109) $X_H = X,$ $A = 0.$

in other words, all labor is devoted to the production of capital goods, the output of consumer goods being zero.

As we know from equation (34) that $u = 0$, it is clear from equation (95) that all the resources of the young go to pay the State a sum $-I\delta_1 = xX$, corresponding to the negative interest on capital.

(ii) Limit value for recourse to roundabout processes

This limit corresponds to the condition $H = 0$, which, in combination with equation (35), gives

(110) $I = \beta - 1.$

For levels of *I* greater than $(\beta - 1)$ it is the direct production process corresponding to equation

---

1. Note that δ cannot exceed the value $C_\mu = \bar{h}H$, for if it did so, the young, upon becoming old, would have no available resources and could not service the debt amounting to $(\delta - C_\mu)$ that they would have contracted during their youth.

(111)
$$\overline{A} = \sqrt{K'XU},$$

which is used.[2] In which case we have, from equations (32), (34), and (37),[3]

(112)
$$u = \frac{X}{U}x, \qquad\qquad a = 2\sqrt{\frac{X}{K'U}}x.$$

(iii) Zero rate of interest

When the rate of interest is zero, equation (99) can no longer be derived from equation (98). However, it is easy to see that equation (99) is still valid.

This is because in the case being studied of collective land ownership, the equation of the budget of the young[4] translates into

(113)
$$xX + \overline{Ih}\overline{H}_E + uU = aA_0 + ID + D - \overline{h}\overline{H}_I,$$

i.e., from condition (94)

(114)
$$xX + uU = aA_0 + \overline{h}\overline{H} - I\delta - \delta.$$

For $I = 0$, this equation combined with equations (21), (27), (31), (34), (35), (36), and (37), gives

(115)
$$\delta(0) = -\frac{xX}{\beta}\,\frac{1+3\alpha-\beta+\alpha\beta}{2(1+\alpha)}.$$

The value of δ corresponding to a zero rate of interest is therefore simply the value given by equation (99), which therefore remains valid irrespective of the level of interest rate I.

Of course, all these computations assume that the general solution found is acceptable, i.e., that the zero level of the rate of interest here considered is in fact lower than the critical level $(\beta - 1)$, in other words that coefficient β is greater than 1.

---

2. This is because the analytical solution corresponding to the use of the roundabout process is no longer acceptable, as equation (35) would yield a negative value for H.

3. Taking $1 + I = \beta$.

4. Which for private land ownership conditions was expressed by (65).

Should this coefficient be *less* than 1, the rate of interest being zero, only the direct process would be used and parameter δ would be given by an equation different from equation (99).[5]

(iv) The level corresponding to spontaneous equilibrium[6] in the case of collective land ownership

This level corresponds to a zero value for capital δ, i.e., to the condition

(116) $\delta = 0.$

In this case, the State owns only the land, and its net capital to the exclusion of land is of zero value. It can be considered that the public debt D and reproducible capital $\overline{hH}_E$ belonging to the State are zero, or else (which amounts to the same), that public debt D is precisely equal to whatever reproducible capital may be owned by the State.

According to equation (99), the corresponding level of I must therefore be a root of the equation

(117) $\alpha I^2 + (\alpha\beta + 4\alpha + 1)I + 1 + 3\alpha - \beta + \alpha\beta = 0.$

As the first member is positive infinite for high values of I, whether positive or negative, and negative for $I = -1$ since it is equal to $-\beta$ for this value, and positive for $I = \beta - 1$ since it is equal to $2\alpha\beta(1 + \beta)$ for this value, there exists a root falling between -1 and $\beta - 1$ and there exists only one such root. There is therefore but *a single* spontaneous equilibrium for collective land ownership.

(v) Level corresponding to spontaneous equilibrium[7] in the case of private land ownership

This level corresponds to a zero value for total wealth Δ, i.e., from equation (44), to the condition

---

5. Equation (137) below.
6. I.e., corresponding to the absence of any State economic intervention apart from collective land ownership.
7. I.e., corresponding to the absence of any State economic intervention.

(118) $$\delta = -\bar{u}\bar{U}.$$

In this case the net wealth of the State is zero. It may be considered either that the State owns nothing at all, whether land or capital, and that the public debt is zero, or else that the public debt is exactly equal to the State's total wealth in land plus equipment.

From equation (43), the corresponding value of I must be a root of the equation

(119) $$\alpha\beta I^2 + (\alpha\beta - 2\alpha - \beta - 2)I - 2 - 2\alpha = 0.$$

As the first member is positive infinite for very high positive or negative values of I, and negative for $I = 0$, there can be only one positive root capable of corresponding to a state of equilibrium having private land ownership, since such a state necessarily implies a positive rate of interest.[8] However, for $I = \beta - 1$, since the first member, equal to the expression

(120) $$\beta[\alpha\beta^2 - (\alpha + 1)\beta - 2\alpha - 1] = \beta(\beta + 1)(\alpha\beta - 1 - 2\alpha),$$

is, for values of β greater than one (which alone are relevant, as equilibrium interest rate I must be both positive and lower than $[\beta - 1]$), positive or negative depending on whether

(121) $$\beta < \text{or} > 2 + \frac{1}{\alpha},$$

it follows that the root of equation (119) is less than or greater than $(\beta - 1)$, depending on the case. Only in the first eventuality does a spontaneous equilibrium obtain and a private land ownership rate using the indirect process (see appendix fig. 2.4).

(vi) The value corresponding to the limits of the states
realizable in case of private land ownership

According to condition (89), the states of private land ownership correspond to the condition

(122) $$\delta \leq \bar{h}\bar{H} - \bar{u}\bar{U},$$

8. No. 179, § c.

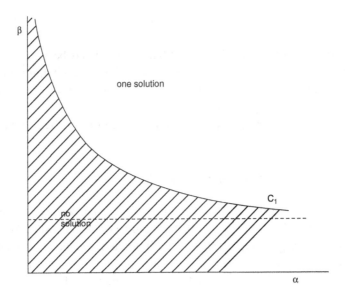

one solution

C_1

no solution

β

α

APPENDIX FIGURE 2.4

while the limit states correspond to the equality

(123) $\delta = \overline{h}\overline{H} - \overline{u}\overline{U}.$

When this is so, the total wealth of the State $\delta + \overline{u}\overline{U}$ is equal to total reproducible capital. It may then be considered that the State owns all capital goods, public debt is zero, and all land belongs to individuals.

From equations (27), (30), (31), (34), (35), and (99), condition (122) can be written[9] as

(124) $\alpha I^2 + (1 + \alpha - 2\alpha\beta)I + 2(1 + \alpha) \leq 0,$

while the equality

(125) $\alpha I^2 + (1 + \alpha - 2\alpha\beta)I + 2(1 + \alpha) = 0$

corresponds to the limit of states realizable under private land ownership.

___

9. After elimination of the binomial parasite $(1 + I)$.

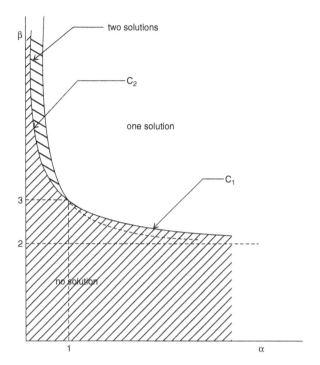

APPENDIX FIGURE 2.5

As the reader may easily verify, the discussion of the acceptable solutions to this equation, i.e., of solutions falling between 0 and $(\beta - 1)$, may be summarized as follows:

Let C_1 be the curve already met in section (v) above, representing the equation

(126)
$$\beta_1 = 2 + \frac{1}{\alpha},$$

for $\alpha > 0$, and let C_2 be the representative curve of $0 < \alpha < 1$ of the equation

(127)
$$\beta_2 = \frac{1}{2}\left(1 + \frac{1}{\alpha}\right) + \sqrt{2\left(1 + \frac{1}{\alpha}\right)}.$$

The C_2 curve is always located below the C_1 curve and is tangential to it at the point $\alpha = 1, \beta = 3$.

Equation (125) admits zero, two or one[10] acceptable solutions depending on whether point (α, β) is within the zone located below curves C_1 and C_2, between curves C_1 and C_2, or above curve C_1. A solution is possible only if $\beta > 2$, while if $2 < \beta < 3$, at most only one solution is possible.

Observe that when equation (119) admits an acceptable solution, equation (125) admits one and one only solution, and that when equation (125) admits two solutions, equation (119) admits none.

10. See no. 192 *in fine*.

7. Conditions of equilibrium in the case in which no roundabout processes are used (183)

As we have seen,[1] non-use of roundabout processes corresponds to the condition

(128) $$I > \beta - 1.$$

In this case it is easily verified that equations (6), (26), (34), (37), (38), (39), (40), and (41) respectively become

(129) $$\overline{A} = \sqrt{K'XU},$$

(130) $$\overline{a}\overline{A} = 2xX = 2uU,$$

(131) $$u = \frac{X}{U}x, \qquad \overline{u} = \frac{X}{U}\frac{x}{I},$$

(132) $$a = 2\sqrt{\frac{X}{K'U}}x,$$

(133) $$A_0 = \frac{\sqrt{K'XU}}{1+\alpha(1+I)},$$

(134) $$A_1 = \frac{\alpha\sqrt{K'XU}(1+I)}{1+\alpha(1+I)},$$

(135) $$S_0^i = (1+\alpha)\ln\frac{\sqrt{K'XU}}{n} + \alpha\ln\alpha + \alpha\ln(1+I) - (1+\alpha)\ln[1+\alpha(1+I)],$$

(136) $$S_1^i = \ln\frac{\sqrt{K'XU}}{n} + \ln\alpha + \ln(1+I) - \ln[1+\alpha(1+I)].$$

In view of these equations, equation (96) now gives

(137)
$$\delta = -\frac{2\alpha}{1+\alpha(1+I)}xX$$

and, in accordance with condition (104),

(138)
$$\Delta = \frac{1+\alpha-\alpha I}{I[1+\alpha(1+I)]}xX.$$

It is immediately verified that for $1 + I = \beta$, these equations indeed give for $\bar{a}$, $\overline{A}$, u, $\bar{u}$, a, A_0, A_1, S_0^i, S_1^i, δ, and Δ the same values as those already found.

Capital supply and demand

In view of the fact that capital is zero, the equilibrium of collective land ownership corresponds to the condition

(139)
$$C_0(I) + \delta = 0,$$

while the private ownership equilibrium corresponds to the condition

(140)
$$C_\varphi(I) = C_0(I) + \Delta,$$

where land capital $C_\varphi(I)$ and the supply $C_0(I)$ of capital by individuals are expressed as

(141)
$$C_\varphi(I) = \frac{xX}{I},$$

(142)
$$C_0(I) = \frac{aA_1}{1+I} = \frac{2\alpha}{1+\alpha(1+I)}xX.$$

Equations (139) and (140) are of course equivalent to conditions (137) and (138).

Noteworthy interest rate levels

In the present case, apart from the value $(\beta - 1)$, the noteworthy values for the rate of interest are the following:

(I) THE VALUE CORRESPONDING TO SPONTANEOUS EQUILIBRIUM[2] AND COL-
LECTIVE LAND OWNERSHIP.   This value, for which δ must be zero is, in view
of equation (137) infinite, so no acceptable solution corresponds to it.

(II) THE VALUE CORRESPONDING TO SPONTANEOUS EQUILIBRIUM[3] AND PRI-
VATE LAND OWNERSHIP.   In light of equation (138), it emerges that this
value, for which $\Delta = 0$ is necessary, is given by the condition

(143) $$I = \frac{1+\alpha}{\alpha}.$$

This is a decreasing function of coefficient α.

(III) THE VALUE CORRESPONDING TO THE LIMIT OF STATES REALIZABLE IN
THE CASE OF PRIVATE LAND OWNERSHIP.   Since $\overline{H}$ is zero under these conditions, this value is, by conditions (118) and (123), equal to the foregoing one.
    It can be seen that under conditions of private land ownership, with re-
course to the direct production process, the rate of interest cannot fall below
the value $\frac{1+\alpha}{\alpha}$.[4]

N.B. Comparison of cost prices of the direct and indirect processes

Assume an economic state in which the indirect process is not employed
and in which prices have values x, u, a, and I. For the indirect process not
to be used, it is necessary that for market prices the cost price that would
be obtained in the basic optimal firm using the indirect process should be

---

2. I.e., corresponding to the absence of any State economic intervention apart from collective land ownership.
    3. I.e., corresponding to the absence of any State economic intervention.
    4. Readers may easily verify that if the critical value $(\beta - 1)$ falls between the roots of
equation (124) corresponding to the limit of states realizable when land is privately owned
and roundabout processes are used (i.e., if there is one, and one only, acceptable root), this
critical value is necessarily greater than $\frac{1+\alpha}{\alpha}$. They may also verify that if the value $(\beta - 1)$
does not fall between the roots of equation (124), it must necessarily be less than the value
$\frac{1+\alpha}{\alpha}$, while if $\beta - 1 = \frac{1+\alpha}{\alpha}$, interest rate I, equal to this common value, must itself be a root of
equation (124) (see no. 182, § vi, and no. 192 *in fine*).

greater than α. Since all basic firms are identical,[5] this price is simply the price that corresponds to the use of the factors of production below. It is therefore given by condition (37). The condition of non-use of the indirect process can therefore be written as

$$(144) \qquad 2\sqrt{\frac{X}{K'U}}x < 2\sqrt{\frac{1+I}{KK''}}\,x,$$

i.e., from equation (32)'s definition of β

$$(145) \qquad \beta < 1 + I,$$

which is precisely condition (128).

The same condition could of course be obtained by writing that in an economic state using the indirect process, this process is in fact less costly than the direct process.

5. No. 176.

8. Specific study of the variations in the noteworthy values of the rate of interest and of the no-land case (184)

a. States of spontaneous equilibrium and collective land ownership

Such states are defined by the equation[1]

(146) $\alpha I^2 + (\alpha\beta + 4\alpha + 1)I + 1 + 3\alpha - \beta + \alpha\beta = 0.$

(I) THE RELATION BETWEEN I AND β FOR CONSTANT α.   We have

(147) $$\beta = \frac{\alpha I^2 + (1 + 4\alpha)I + 1 + 3\alpha}{-\alpha I + 1 - \alpha}.$$

Noting that the numerator has for root the value $I = -1$, this equation may be written

(148) $$\beta = (1 + I)\frac{\alpha(1 + I) + 2\alpha + 1}{-\alpha(1 + I) + 1}.$$

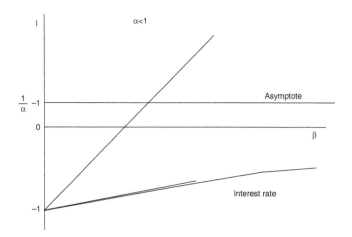

APPENDIX FIGURE 2.6

---

1. No. 182, equation (117).

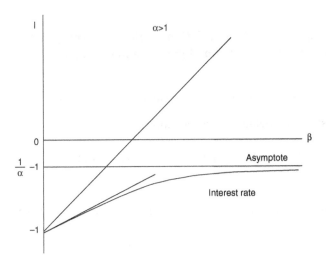

APPENDIX FIGURE 2.7

Given the conditions $(1 + I) > 0$ and $(1 + I) < \beta$, this equation shows that coefficient β is an increasing function of rate I and that the relation between interest rate I and coefficient β may be represented, depending on the value of the coefficient α, by appendix figures 2.6 and 2.7.

It is clear that in all cases the rate of interest increases with coefficient β and tends toward the value $\dfrac{1}{\alpha} - 1$ when coefficient β increases indefinitely.[2]

(II) THE RELATION BETWEEN I AND α FOR CONSTANT β. We have

$$\alpha = \frac{\beta - 1 - I}{(I + 1)(I + 3 + \beta)}.$$

(149)

It is easily verified that for values of I falling between -1 and $\beta - 1$, coefficient α is a constantly decreasing function of rate I.

The variation of the rate of interest with coefficient α may then be represented, depending on whether or not β is greater than unity, by appendix figures 2.8 and 2.9.

2. It can be seen that to each set of values (α, β) there corresponds a state of spontaneous equilibrium in which land ownership is collective.

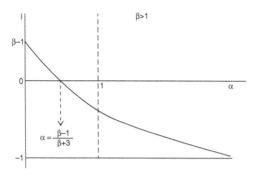

APPENDIX FIGURE 2.8

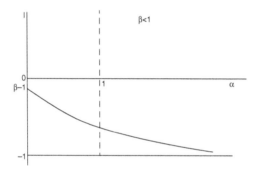

APPENDIX FIGURE 2.9

It can be seen that in all cases the rate of interest varies inversely with coefficient α, and tends toward −1 as coefficient α increases indefinitely.

It is noteworthy that the value of α for which rate I becomes zero equal to $\dfrac{\beta-1}{\beta+3}$ is always less than one.

b. States of spontaneous equilibrium and private land ownership

These states are defined by the equation[3]

(150) $\alpha\beta I^2 + (\alpha\beta - 2\alpha - \beta - 2)I - 2 - 2\alpha = 0.$

---

3. No. 182, equation (119).

(I) THE RELATION BETWEEN I AND β FOR CONSTANT α.   We have

(151)
$$\beta = \frac{2(\alpha + 1)(1 + I)}{I(\alpha I + \alpha - 1)}.$$

In light of the fact that coefficient β is positive, and of conditions (83) and (84),

(152)
$$1 + I < \beta, \qquad\qquad I > 0,$$

this equation enables us to show without difficulty that the relation be-tween interest rate I and coefficient β for a given value of coefficient α may be represented, depending on the value of coefficient α, by appendix fig-ures 2.10 and 2.11.

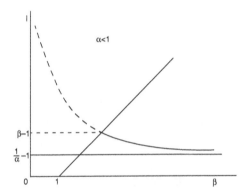

APPENDIX FIGURE 2.10

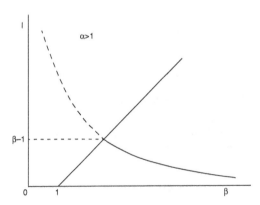

APPENDIX FIGURE 2.11

It can be seen that in every case the equilibrium interest rate varies inversely with coefficient β and tends respectively toward $\frac{1}{\alpha} - 1$ or toward zero as coefficient β increases indefinitely, depending on whether coefficient α is greater than or less than one.

(II) THE RELATION BETWEEN I AND α FOR CONSTANT β.   We have

(153)
$$\alpha = \frac{(\beta+2)I+2}{\beta I^2 + (\beta-2)I - 2}.$$

In light of the fact that coefficient α is positive and of conditions (152), this condition enables it to be shown without difficulty that the relation between equilibrium interest rate I and coefficient α for a given value of coefficient β can be represented by appendix figure 2.12.[4]

It can be seen that equilibrium interest rate I is a decreasing function of coefficient α and tends toward the value $\frac{2}{\beta}$ as coefficient α increases indefinitely.

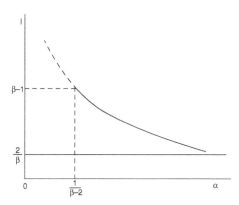

APPENDIX FIGURE 2.12

4. It is of course appropriate for coefficient β to be greater than 2. (See no. 182, § vi.)

c. Limits of the states realizable under private ownership of land

These limits are defined by the equation

(154) $\alpha I^2 + (1 + \alpha - 2\alpha\beta)I + 2(1 + \alpha) = 0.$

(I) THE RELATION BETWEEN I AND β FOR CONSTANT α.   We have

(155) $\beta = \dfrac{1}{2}\left(I + \dfrac{1}{\alpha}\right) + \dfrac{1}{2} + \dfrac{1+\alpha}{\alpha I}.$

In light of the fact that coefficients α and β are positive and of the conditions

(156) $0 < I < \beta - 1,$

this equation enables it to be shown without difficulty that the relation between the limit interest rate and coefficient β for a given value of coefficient α may be represented, depending on the value of coefficient α, by appendix figures 2.13 and 2.14.

It is clear that when there is only one solution I for given values of coefficients α and β, this solution is a decreasing function of coefficient β. When there are two solutions, I_1 and I_2, the lowest I_1 is a decreasing function, and the highest I_2 is an increasing function, of coefficient β.

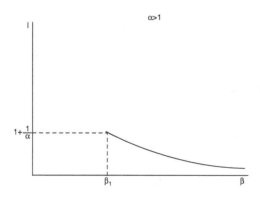

APPENDIX FIGURE 2.13

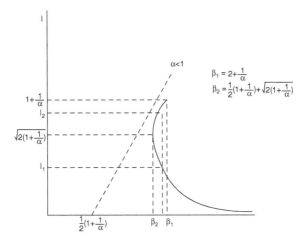

APPENDIX FIGURE 2.14

(II) THE RELATION BETWEEN I AND α FOR CONSTANT β. We have

(157)
$$\alpha = -\frac{I+2}{I^2 + (1-2\beta)I + 2}.$$

In view of the fact that coefficients α and β are positive and of the conditions

(158)
$$0 < I < \beta - 1,$$

this equation enables us to show without difficulty that the relation between the limit interest rate and coefficient α for a given value of coefficient β may be represented, depending on the value of coefficient β, by appendix figures 2.15 and 2.16, where α_1 and α_2, respectively, represent the inverse functions of functions

(159)
$$\beta_1 = 2 + \frac{1}{\alpha},$$

(160)
$$\beta_2 = \frac{1}{2}\left(1 + \frac{1}{\alpha}\right) + \sqrt{2\left(1 + \frac{1}{\alpha}\right)},$$

and I_m and I_M, respectively, represent the lowest and the highest roots of the equation

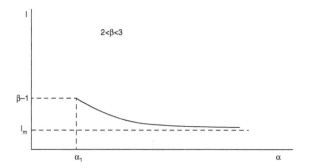

APPENDIX FIGURE 2.15

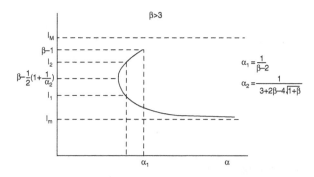

APPENDIX FIGURE 2.16

(161) $$I^2 + (1 - 2\beta)I + 2 = 0.$$

It is clear that when there is only one acceptable solution I for the given values of coefficients α and β, this solution is a decreasing function of coefficient α, and when there are two solutions, I_1 and I_2, the lower, I_1, is a decreasing function and the greater, I_2, is an increasing function of coefficient α.

d. The case in which there is no land

If there is no land,[5] we have $U = 0$ and coefficient β is infinite, which gives us

---

5. This case is of course identical to that in which land exists ($\overline{U} \neq 0$) but is unusable ($K' = 0$).

(162)
$$\overline{A} = \sqrt{KX_AH},$$

and direct processes can no longer be used. In this case we find

(163)
$$h = \frac{x}{K''}(1+I),$$

(164)
$$H = \frac{K''X}{2+I},$$

(165)
$$A = \sqrt{KK''} X \frac{\sqrt{1+I}}{2+I},$$

(166)
$$\Delta = \delta = -\frac{\alpha I + \alpha - 1}{(2+I)(1+\alpha+\alpha I)} xX,$$

and it is easily verified that the variation in the capital δ owned by the State is represented as a function of rate I by figures 2.17 and 2.18 depending on whether or not α is lower than unity.

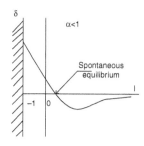

APPENDIX FIGURE 2.17

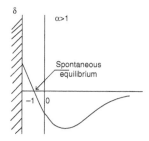

APPENDIX FIGURE 2.18

The spontaneous equilibrium position corresponds to the value

(167)
$$I = \frac{1}{\alpha} - 1.$$

And the corresponding rate of interest I is thus a decreasing function of coefficient α.

9. General discussion (185)

We have seen[1] that the equilibrium interest rate for collective land owner-ship is a solution to the equation

(168) $$C_\mu(I) = C_0(I) + \delta$$

and that the equilibrium rate of interest for conditions of private land own-ership is a solution to the equation

(169) $$C_\varphi(I) + C_\mu(I) = C_0(I) + \Delta,$$

where we have

(170) $$C_\varphi(I) = \begin{cases} \dfrac{1}{\beta}\left(1+\dfrac{1}{I}\right)xX & \text{for } I \le \beta - 1 \\[2ex] \dfrac{xX}{I} & \text{for } I \ge \beta - 1; \end{cases}$$

(171) $$C_\mu(I) = \begin{cases} \dfrac{1}{2+I}\left(1-\dfrac{1+I}{\beta}\right)xX & \text{for } I \le \beta - 1 \\[2ex] 0 & \text{for } I \ge \beta - 1; \end{cases}$$

(172) $$C_0(I) = \begin{cases} 2\alpha\left(1+\dfrac{1}{\beta}\right)\dfrac{1+I}{(2+I)[1+\alpha(1+I)]}xX & \text{for } I \le \beta - 1 \\[2ex] \dfrac{2\alpha}{1+\alpha(1+I)}xX & \text{for } I \ge \beta - 1. \end{cases}$$

These equations will make it easier for us to discuss the relation linking parameters I, δ, and Δ.

Let C_φ, C_μ, C_{TU}, and C_0 be the representative curves of the functions $C_\varphi(I), C_\mu(I), C_{TU}(I) = C_\varphi(I) + C_\mu(I),$ and $C_0(I)$ corresponding to land cap-ital, reproducible capital, total capital used, and capital supplied by indi-viduals. These curves appear as shown in appendix figure 2.19 below.

1. Nos. 178 and 183.

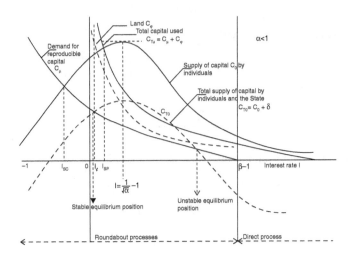

APPENDIX FIGURE 2.19

Function C_φ is constantly decreasing; the same applies to function C_μ in the interval $(-1, \beta - 1)$ and hence to function C_{TU}. Function $C_0(I)$ passes through a maximum for the value $I = \dfrac{1}{\sqrt{\alpha}} - 1$ when $\beta > \dfrac{1}{\sqrt{\alpha}}$. This value is negative or positive depending on whether coefficient α is greater or less than one.

(i) The case of collective land ownership

As the point of spontaneous equilibrium corresponds to the intersection of curves C_μ and C_0, it is at once evident that there exists one, and only one, point of spontaneous equilibrium ($\delta = 0$) for collective land ownership; it corresponds to value I_{SC} for the rate of interest. This value may be negative or positive depending on whether

(173) $C_0(0) <$ or $> C_\mu(0)$,

i.e., on whether we have

(174) $\alpha <$ or $> \dfrac{\beta - 1}{\beta + 3}$.

When the State, aside from land, owns capital δ, the new equilibrium value for the rate of interest corresponds to the intersection of curve C_μ and curve C deduced from curve C_0 by upward translation parallel to the y-axis of amplitude δ and representative of the total supply of capital from both individuals and the State. There is only one value of I for a positive value of δ. This value decreases as δ increases.

When capital δ is negative and low, it can be seen that there are two solutions: one close to I_{SC} corresponding to use of the indirect process and the other, positive and high, corresponding to use of the direct process.[2]

As capital δ increases by negative values, the lower of these solutions increases and the higher decreases. When capital δ exceeds in absolute value the value $C_0(\beta - 1)$ the production process corresponding to the greater of these values becomes indirect. A point occurs when curve C_{T0} becomes tangential to curve C_μ; there are then two equal solutions. For higher values of δ no solution exists.

The variation of capital δ as a function of interest rate I may then be represented as shown in appendix figure 2.20.

Note that the rate of interest may take any value within the range of variation $(-1, +\infty)$.

It can also be observed that for certain negative values of capital δ two equilibrium positions exist, but it is easy to see that the one corresponding to the higher level for the rate of interest is a *point of unstable equilibrium*. This is because for this value the net supply of capital $C_0 + \delta$ is greater than demand at values of rate I slightly lower than its equilibrium value, while it is lower than demand at values slightly higher. *Hence if capital δ is frozen*, the slightest movement in the rate of interest will dislodge the system from its point of equilibrium. For instance, if the rate of interest accidentally rises above its equilibrium value, the supply of capital falls below demand, and hence the rate of interest tends to rise, thus aggravating the initial gap.

By contrast, the equilibrium point corresponding to the lower of the two values for I corresponds to a stable equilibrium. This confirms that for a given capital δ (given structural conditions) there is only *one stable state of equilibrium*[3] and that the corresponding rate of interest is a decreasing function of this capital.

---

2. Given by the intersection of the curve C_{T0} with the x-axis.
3. No. 49.

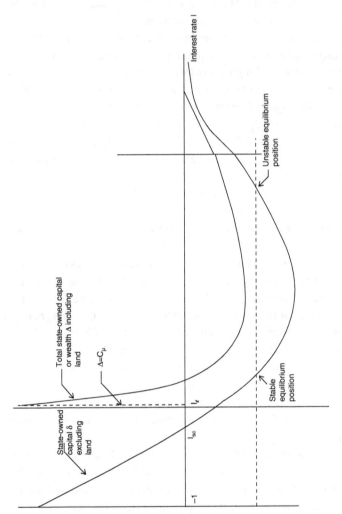

State-owned capital δ excluding land

Total state-owned capital or wealth Δ including land

$\Delta = C_\mu$

Interest rate I

Unstable equilibrium position

Stable equilibrium position

I_{sc}

I_ℓ

−1

APPENDIX FIGURE 2.20

The corresponding equilibrium point could in fact only be achieved if the State used suitable policies to hold interest rate I at a fixed level,[4] allowing capital δ to settle of itself at the corresponding value.

(ii) The case of private land ownership

As the point of spontaneous equilibrium ($\Delta = 0$) corresponds to the intersection of curves C_{TU} and C_0, it can be seen that if we have

(175) $$C_{TU}(\beta - 1) < C_0(\beta - 1),$$

i.e., if

(176) $$\beta > 2 + \frac{1}{\alpha},$$

there exists at least one point of equilibrium in the range $(0, \beta - 1)$. The analysis conducted in no. 182 further shows that *only* one is to be found in this range. Moreover, it is a point of stable equilibrium.

In this case, the analysis presented in no. 183 shows that there exists no spontaneous equilibrium under conditions of private land ownership and direct production process.

On the other hand, if

(177) $$\beta < 2 + \frac{1}{\alpha},$$

the same analyses show that there still exists only one point of spontaneous equilibrium with private land ownership, but that this equilibrium point corresponds to an interest rate greater than the value $(\beta - 1)$, i.e., to the use of the direct production process, the corresponding equilibrium is stable.

Ultimately, it is clear that curves C_{TU} and C_{T0} have only one point of intersection, yielding for rate I a value I_{SP}, less than or greater than $(\beta - 1)$ depending on whether

(178) $$\beta > \text{or} < 2 + \frac{1}{\alpha}.$$

---

4. We saw in no. 164 how such a policy could be carried out.

This is the point to which stable equilibrium corresponds.

When the State owns capital Δ, the new equilibrium value of the rate of interest corresponding to the intersection of curve C_{TU} and curve C_{T0} is deduced from curve C_0 by an upward translation parallel to the y-axis of amplitude Δ. Hence there is only one value for I when capital Δ has a positive value. This value decreases as Δ increases. However, if land is privately owned, Δ is upwardly limited by the value C of reproducible capital. Hence rate I has a limit inferior, below which it cannot fall, which corresponds to the condition

(179) $$C_\varphi(I) = C_0(I).$$

When capital Δ is negative and low, it can be seen that there are two solutions, one close to I_{SP} and the other, very high and positive, corresponding to the use of the direct process.

As capital Δ increases through negative values, i.e., when there is a public debt that is increasing, the lower of these solutions increases and the higher decreases. A point occurs at which curve C_{T0} becomes tangential to curve C_{TU}; there are then two equal solutions. For lower values of capital Δ no solution exists.

The variation in capital Δ as a function of interest rate I may then be represented as shown in figure 2.20.

The minimum value of capital Δ is reached for a value of rate I less, or greater, depending on the case, than the value $(\beta - 1)$.

It can be seen that for certain negative values of capital Δ there are two equilibrium points, but only one of these equilibrium points is stable and the corresponding interest rate level is a decreasing function of capital Δ.

Figure 2.19 shows (i) that there is at least one point of intersection of curves C_0 and C_φ, (ii) that there can only be two within the range $(0, \beta - 1)$ if curves C_{T0} and C_{TU} have no point of intersection within the same range,[5] i.e., if no spontaneous equilibrium exists for conditions of private land ownership and use of the indirect process, and hence (iii) that when two points of intersection of curves C_{T0} and C_φ fall within the range $(0, \beta - 1)$ there necessarily exists a third in the range $(\beta - 1, +\infty)$, since in that case there is a point of intersection of curves C_{T0} and C_{TU}, and hence of

5. For if they had, appendix figure 2.19 shows that the fact of a double intersection for curves C_{T0} and C_φ in the interval considered would also lead to a double intersection in the same interval of curves C_{T0} and C_{TU}, which we know to be impossible (no. 182, § v).

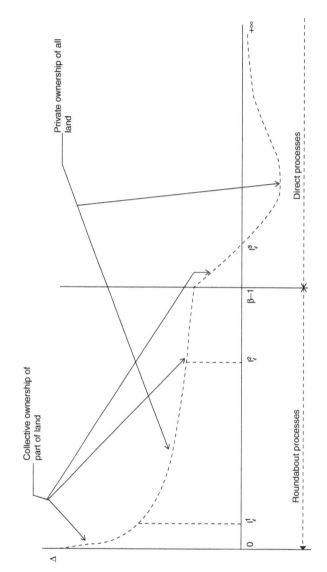

curves C_{T0} and C_φ within the same range, as C_{T0} and C_φ become indistinguishable in that range.

We then have the shape as shown in appendix figure 2.21 for the representative curve of capital Δ as a function of interest rate I.

It can be seen that there can be only one, three, or zero values of interest rate I that satisfy the condition $C_\varphi(I) = C_0(I)$.

In all these cases it is confirmed that when all land is privately owned, only certain rates of interest are possible.

VARIATION OF NOTEWORTHY VALUES OF THE RATE OF INTEREST WITH COEFFICIENT α.   As function $C_0(I)$ is an increasing function of α, it can be geometrically confirmed that the rates of interest corresponding to spontaneous equilibria under both public and private land ownership are indeed decreasing functions of coefficient α. The same applies to the single solution, or to the lowest I_l^1 and the highest I_l^3 of the three solutions to the equation $C_\varphi(I) = C_0(I)$. In the case in which there are three solutions, the middle solution is an increasing function of coefficient α.

10. The case of use of a double rate of interest[1] (186)

It is interesting to inquire what happens to the foregoing findings *in the case of a collectivist economy*[2] using a double interest rate: a technical interest rate I_T in the production sector and a psychological interest rate I_P in the individual savings sector.[3]

In this event, from equations (21) and (22), we have

(180)
$$A_0 = \frac{A}{1 + \alpha(1 + I_P)},$$

(181)
$$A_1 = \frac{\alpha(1 + I_P)A}{1 + \alpha(1 + I_P)},$$

and from equations (36), (37), and (48), we have

(182)
$$A = \sqrt{KK''}X\left(1 + \frac{1}{\beta}\right)\frac{\sqrt{1 + I_T}}{2 + I_T},$$

(183)
$$a = 2\sqrt{\frac{1 + I_T}{KK''}}x,$$

(184)
$$C_\mu = \overline{hH} = \left(1 - \frac{1 + I_T}{\beta}\right)\frac{xX}{2 + I_T}.$$

The circuit of values

In such an economy, as interest rates I_P and I_T are different, the financing of industry is entirely provided by the State, which consequently owns all reproducible capital. The circuit of values then looks as shown in appendix figure 2.22.

---

1. As readers will readily appreciate, careful consideration of this case, to be clarified using a specific example in no. 194, is crucial for the understanding of economic theory.

2. I.e., one in which all tangible capital (land and industrial equipment) is owned by the State.

3. Nos. 63 and 77.

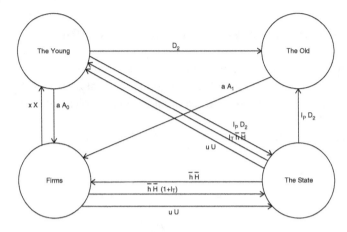

APPENDIX FIGURE 2.22

If in this case we use the term D_2 to denote State debt,[4] the budget of the elderly is expressed by

(185) $$D_2(1 + I_p) = aA_1,$$

i.e., in light of conditions (134) and (135) above,

(186) $$D_2 = \frac{2\alpha}{1+\alpha(1+I_P)} \frac{1+I_T}{2+I_T}\left(1+\frac{1}{\beta}\right)xX.$$

4. Of course we now have for the State's aggregate capital to the exclusion of land

$$\delta = \bar{h}\bar{H} - D_2,$$

so that in combination with equation (94) of no. 180 we have

$$D_2 = D_1 + \bar{h}\bar{H}_1,$$

from which in light of equation (105) we obtain

$$D_2 = D + \bar{u}\bar{U} + \bar{h}\bar{H}_1.$$

For capital owned by the State, *to the exclusion of land* $\delta_1 = \overline{h}\overline{H} - D_2$, this equation gives

$$(187) \qquad \delta = \left(1 - \frac{1 + I_T}{\beta}\right)\frac{xX}{2 + I_T} - \frac{2\alpha}{1 + \alpha(1 + I_P)}\left(1 + \frac{1}{\beta}\right)\frac{1 + I_T}{2 + I_T}xX.$$

The reader will easily be able to satisfy himself that for $I_P = I_T = I$ this condition is in fact the same as expression (89) already found.

Determination of equilibrium

He will also be able to confirm that in this case the equilibrium under stationary conditions depends on two arbitrary parameters for which it is convenient to take rates I_P and I_T.[5]

To each group of these values there corresponds a public debt D_2 the expression for which as a function of these rates is given by equation (186).

---

5. Naturally, the domain of variation to be considered for rates I_T and I ranges from -1 to $+\infty$.

(b) Complete study of a specific case

1. Characteristics considered (187)

As full discussion of the model studied requires, in the most general case, relatively extensive explanations without offering any special interest from the point of view of economics, I shall confine myself at this point to the study of one specific case.

The case to be studied in detail is that which corresponds to the following characteristics

(188) $K = K' = K'' = 1,$ $\alpha = 1.5,$ $X = 4,$ $U = 1,$ $x = 1,$

and hence to the value

$$\beta = 4,$$

for the constant β defined by condition (32).

The satisfaction and production functions we shall be making use of are the functions

(189) $$S_0^i = \ln A_0^i + 1.5 \ln A_1^i,$$

(190) $$S_1^i = \ln A_1^i,$$

(191) $$\overline{A} = \sqrt{X_A(H + U)},$$

(192) $$H = X_H.$$

2. Interpretation of the conditions (188)

Thus defined, the characteristics of the model we are to study may be interpreted as follows.

First, as has been remarked in no. 176, the value 1.5 of coefficient α corresponds to a psychological structure such that on average there is a preference for future goods.

The value 1 for x means that the unit of account is defined as equal to the value of the labor unit.

The value 4 for X means that we take as unit of quantity of labor one-quarter of the actual labor input of n individuals during their youth (Θ_0).

So too, the value 1 for U must be understood to mean that we are taking as unit of area the total area of land available.

The value 1 for coefficient K'' must be understood to mean that as unit of capital equipment ($\overline{H}$) we are taking the output produced during period T for a labor input equal to unity, i.e., one-quarter of the labor input of the set of young individuals during period (T).

The value 1 for the ratio of K' to K means that in accordance with condition (6) the units of labor input and of land as defined above play the same role as in the production of good ($\overline{A}$).

The value of the ratio of K' to K being thus understood, the absolute values equal to unity of coefficients K and K' mean that the unit of good ($\overline{A}$) is chosen so as to be equal to the product output per unit labor input in combination with the unit of area.

Illustration by a concrete example

To fix our ideas, the case being studied may be specified in concrete terms as follows.

Let us assume that the community studied forms a group of 100,000 young individuals growing cereals, each working for 2,000 hours per annum.

Let us assume that the duration of each period (T) is 20 years. Thus, during each period (T) the labor input amounts to 4 billion man-hours. From what has been said above this means that the unit of labor quantity is 1 billion man-hours while the unit of value is taken in the model as equal to the value of 1 billion man-hours.

Let us assume that the community cultivates 100,000 hectares of land. It follows from the foregoing that the unit of area is 100,000 hectares.

As the unit of land service is the service rendered per unit of area per unit of time (period T), it is clear that the unit of land service is 2 million year-hectares.

Let us assume that the capital good in question comprises a certain sort of agricultural machine of which the unit takes 20 years to produce and the useful life is also 20 years, while the per unit labor input for its production is 100,000 hours. As the unit of quantity of the machine is defined as the quantity produced per unit of labor input, the unit of quantity of machines is 10,000 machines.

And since the unit of service of the machines is the service rendered per unit of quantity per period T, it can be seen that the unit of machine-service is 200,000 machine-years.

If we assume that for the combined use of one individual, two hectares of land, and 2/10 of the annual service of one machine a yield of 4,000 kg per hectare is obtained, it can be seen that an output over 20 years of $4,000 \times 2 \times 20 = 160,000$ kg must correspond to

$$(193) \qquad \overline{A} = \sqrt{X(H+U)} = \sqrt{\frac{4}{10^5}\left(\frac{2}{10^5}+\frac{2}{10^5}\right)} = \frac{4}{10^5}$$

units of quantity of good $(\overline{A})$, given that A, X, H, and U represent the production and consumption per unit of time, i.e., for a period of 20 years, since the use by one individual of 2 hectares and of 2/10 of machines over 20 years corresponds to values, expressed in the same units used above, of

$$(194) \qquad X = \frac{20 \times 2,000}{10^9} = \frac{4}{10^5}, \qquad H = 20 \times \frac{2}{10} \times \frac{1}{200,000} = \frac{2}{10^5},$$

$$U = \frac{20 \times 2}{2 \times 10^6} = \frac{2}{10^5},$$

from which we conclude that the unit of good A is equal to

$$\frac{1,600 \times 10^5}{10 \times 4} = 4 \text{ million tons.}$$

If we assume that the community in question uses the franc as its monetary unit and that one man-hour of labor is worth 10 francs, it can be seen from what has been said that the value unit of the operation outlined is taken to be equal to 10 billion francs.

The psychology studied

Condition (189), which represents the individual psychologies of the young, may be interpreted in the concrete by assigning specific values to consumptions A_0^i and A_1^i.

For instance, the reader may verify[1] that each young person deems the *daily cereal consumptions* given in appendix table 2.3 to be equivalent.

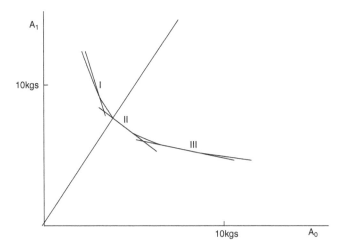

APPENDIX FIGURE 2.23

APPENDIX TABLE 2.3

I	3 kg in the first period and	10 kg in the second
II	5 kg in the first period and	7.5 kg in the second
III	8.5 kg in the first period and	5 kg in the second

In these three solutions their *equivalences at the margin* between his present consumption and his future consumptions are respectively given in appendix table 2.4.

1. Using the equations

$$S_0^i = \ln\left(A_0^i A_1^{i\frac{3}{2}}\right), \qquad \frac{dA_1^i}{dA_0^i} = -\frac{2}{3}\frac{A_1^i}{A_0^i}.$$

APPENDIX TABLE 2.4

I	1 kg in the first period and	2.2 kg in the second
II	1 kg in the first period and	1 kg in the second
III	1 kg in the first period and	0.4 kg in the second

There is thus a preference for present goods in situation I, a preference for future goods in situation III, and equivalence between present and future goods in situation II, while on average, as has been said, the preference is for future goods.

3. Conditions of equilibrium in the case of use of the indirect process (189)

Under these conditions and in light of what has been said above, the economic equilibrium for the case in which indirect production processes are used is as follows:

$$\bar{h} = x + 1,$$
$$h = u = 1 + I,$$
$$\bar{u} = 1 + \frac{1}{I},$$
$$a = \bar{a} = 2\sqrt{1 + I},$$
$$H = \frac{3 - I}{2 + I},$$
$$\bar{A} = A = 5\frac{\sqrt{1 + I}}{2 + I},$$

(195)
$$A_0 = \frac{10}{5 + 3I}\frac{\sqrt{1 + I}}{2 + I},$$

$$A_1 = \frac{15}{5 + 3I}\frac{(1 + I)^{\frac{3}{2}}}{2 + I},$$

$$S_0^i = \frac{5}{2}\ln\frac{5}{n} + \frac{3}{2}\ln\frac{3}{2} + \frac{11}{4}\ln(1 + I) - \frac{5}{2}\ln(2 + I) - \frac{5}{2}\ln\frac{5 + 3I}{2},$$

$$S_1^i = \ln\frac{15}{n} + \frac{3}{2}\ln(1 + I) - \ln(2 + I) - \ln(5 + 3I),$$

$$\delta = -\frac{3I^2 + 26I + 15}{(2 + I)(5 + 3I)},$$

$$\Delta = 2\frac{-6I^2 + 3I + 5}{I(2 + I)(5 + 3I)}.$$

Reproducible capital C_μ has the value

(196)
$$\bar{h}\bar{H} = \frac{3 - I}{2 + I},$$

and land capital C_φ has

(197)
$$\overline{u}\overline{U} = 1 + \frac{1}{I}.$$

National income

(198)
$$R_N = aA = 10\frac{1+I}{2+I}$$

includes *wages* to the amount

(199)
$$xX = 4,$$

land rent to the amount

(200)
$$uU = 1 + I,$$

and interest to the amount

(201)
$$\overline{Ih}\overline{H} = I\frac{3-I}{2+I}.$$

That still leaves

(202)
$$X_H = \frac{3-I}{2+I},$$

(203)
$$X_A = 5\frac{1+I}{2+I},$$

(204)
$$\frac{C_\mu}{R_N} = \frac{3-I}{10(1+I)},$$

(205)
$$\Theta_N = \frac{3-I}{(2+I)(5+I)},$$

and finally

(206)
$$\pi = \frac{A_i - A_d}{A_d} = \frac{5}{2}\frac{\sqrt{1+I}}{2+I} - I.$$

4. Conditions of equilibrium in the case of use of direct process (190)

When the economy uses only direct processes, these equations respectively become[1]

$$x = 1,$$
$$a = \bar{a} = u = 4,$$
$$\bar{u} = \frac{4}{I},$$
$$\bar{A} = A = 2,$$
$$A_0 = \frac{4}{5+3I},$$

(207)
$$A_1 = \frac{6(1+I)}{5+3I},$$

$$S_0^i = \frac{5}{2}\ln\frac{2}{n} + \frac{3}{2}\ln\frac{3}{2} + \frac{3}{2}\ln(1+I) - \frac{5}{2}\ln\frac{5+3I}{2},$$

$$S_1^i = \ln\frac{6}{n} + \ln(1+I) - \ln(5+3I),$$

$$\delta = \frac{-24}{5+3I},$$

$$\Delta = 4\frac{5-3I}{(5+3I)I}.$$

Here we have

(208)
$$C_\mu = 0,$$
$$C_\varphi = \frac{4}{I},$$
$$R_N = 8.$$

This national income includes wages to the amount of $xX = 4$ and land rents to the amount of $uU = 4$.

---

1. No. 183.

5. Noteworthy values of the rate of interest (191)

The noteworthy values of interest rate I are the following:

(i) The limit value of the use of indirect processes

From equation (110), this value is in the present case

(209) $$I = 3.$$

(ii) The value corresponding to spontaneous equilibrium where land ownership is collective and indirect processes are used

This value, which corresponds to the equation $\delta = 0$, is, according to equation (195), which gives δ, a root of the equation

(210) $$3I^2 + 26I + 15 = 0.$$

This equation has only one root greater than -1, which answers the question, its value being

(211) $$I \sim -0.62.$$

(iii) The value corresponding to spontaneous equilibrium where land ownership is private and indirect processes are used

From equation (119), this value, corresponding to the equation $\delta = -\bar{u}\bar{U}$, is a root of the equation

(212) $$-6I^2 + 3I + 5 = 0.$$

Once again, this equation has only one positive root that answers the question, and its value is

(213) $$I \sim 1.20.$$

*(iv) The value corresponding to the limit of economic states
capable of realization under conditions of private
land ownership and use of the indirect process*

From equation (124), this value, which corresponds to equation $\delta = \overline{h}\overline{H} - \overline{u}\overline{U}$, is a root of the equation

(214)
$$3I^2 - 19I + 10 = 0.$$

This equation too has only one positive root that answers the question, i.e., is less than the value $\beta - 1 = 3$, and its value is

(215)
$$I \sim 0.58.$$

*(v) The value corresponding to spontaneous equilibrium in the case of
private land ownership with use of the direct process*

From equation (143), this value is

(216)
$$I = \frac{5}{3}.$$

As this value is less than the limit value where the direct process is used, no acceptable corresponding solution exists.

6. Discussion (192)

The discussion may then be summarized in appendix figures 2.24, 2.25, 2.26, and 2.27, which give the variation in the different magnitudes as interest rate I varies from -1 to $+\infty$.[1]

The main points of this discussion are as follows:

Ownership of land and capital and State debt

For rates of interest falling between -1 and 0, including zero itself, the ownership of all land is necessarily collective.

For the value $I = -0.62$ for the rate of interest, the net capital owned by the State to the exclusion of land is zero. The net fortune of individuals is equal to the value of the reproducible capital. This solution corresponds to the spontaneous equilibrium point under collective land ownership.

For interest rate levels lower than this, the State owns, besides land, net wealth equal to a fraction of the total reproducible capital, which is greater as the rate of interest is lower. For the limit value $I = -1$ the State's total capital to the exclusion of land is equal to the totality of existing reproducible capital.

For interest rate values falling in the range $(-0.62, 0)$ the State, already owner of the land, is indebted to a net amount that is greater as the rate of interest is higher. The fortune of individuals comprises (i) a fraction of the value of this debt, and (ii) the value of reproducible capital $\overline{h}\overline{H}$.

For positive interest rates lower than the value 0.58, a fraction of the land is necessarily owned by the State.[2] For these values the State's net wealth Δ is greater than the value of the reproducible capital.

For $I = 0.58$ the net wealth of the State is equal to the total value of reproducible capital. Hence if land is privately owned, individuals own only the land; to this level for the rate of interest corresponds the limit of economic states in which land is privately owned.

For interest rate values higher than $I = 0.58$, the State's *total* wealth Δ is less than the value of the reproducible capital, which means that the corresponding economic states are realizable under conditions of private land ownership.

---

1. For this representation, n has been taken to be equal to 1 in equations (195) and (207).

2. Directly or otherwise. For in the event that the individuals were indebted to the State, this debt would be a tantamount to a mortgage on their land to the same amount.

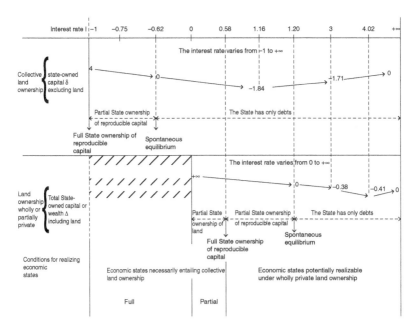

APPENDIX FIGURE 2.24 Model representing an account-based economy: *ownership regime*

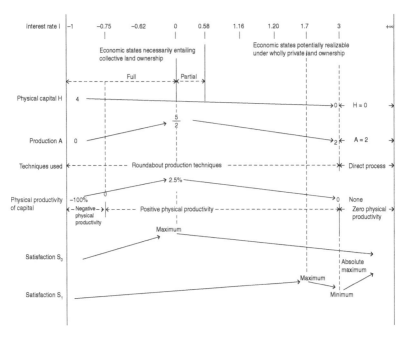

APPENDIX FIGURE 2.25 Model representing an account-based economy: *physical productivity of capital and satisfactions*

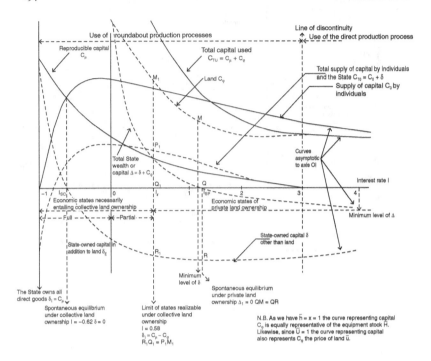

APPENDIX FIGURE 2.26 Model representing an account-based economy: *graph showing ownership regime*

For the value $I = 1.2$ the State's net wealth Δ is zero. From which we may conclude that individuals own all land and there is no State debt. This value corresponds to the spontaneous equilibrium point for private land ownership. For values of the rate of interest greater than $I = 1.2$ the State's net wealth Δ is negative. In which case the net wealth of individuals includes this net debt, together with the value of the land and the value of the capital.

Technology used

In the range $(-1, +3)$ of variation of the rate of interest, the indirect process is used, while above $I = +3$ the direct process is adopted.

For $I = -1$ all usable labor goes toward the production of capital goods and consumable production is nil. As the rate of interest rises from this level, labor devoted to the production of capital goods decreases constantly, reaching zero at $I = 3$.

Physical productivity of capital

The variation in physical productivity is here identified with the variation in production A.

As the rate of interest rises from the level (-1), physical productivity begins negative, reaches zero for $I = -0.75$, peaks at $I = 0$, then falls constantly, while remaining positive, until becoming zero at $I = 3$. From this point on, only the direct process of production is used, production remains stationary, and productivity remains nil.

The variation of satisfactions

Note that satisfaction S_0 peaks at the same point as production A, viz. at $I = 0$.

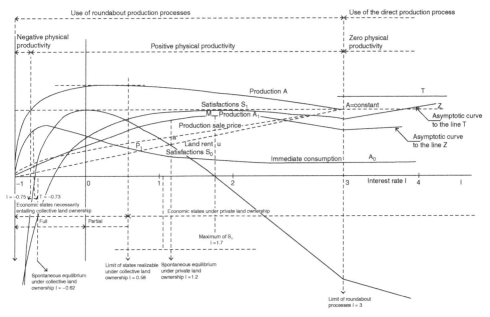

APPENDIX FIGURE 2.27 Model representing an account-based economy: *variations of productions and satisfactions*

As I rises from the -1 value, satisfaction S_1 begins by increasing, peaks for a value of I close to 1.5, decreases, reaches its lowest level for $I = 3$,[3] then increases anew.

It should be noted that in ranges $(-1,0)$ and $(1.5,3)$ satisfactions S_0 and S_1 vary in the same direction.

3. This minimum corresponds to a peak of the representative curve of satisfaction S_1 on account of the discontinuity corresponding to the transition from the indirect processes to the direct process.

7. Interpretation of the solutions (193)

It may be worthwhile to make some remarks, for purposes of illustration, in the context of the concrete example considered in no. 188, concerning the solution found for a determined value of the rate of interest, e.g., $I = 1$.

For this value of I the indirect process is the one used, and, *using the values of the model's different units indicated above*[1] and given that each period lasts for 20 years, we have:

$I = 1$, giving a rate of 5% per annum payable at 20-year intervals.[2]

$\bar{h} = 1$, giving a value of one million francs for each machine.[3]

$h = 2$, giving a value of 100,000 francs for the annual service rendered by each machine.

$\bar{u} = 2$, giving a value of 200,000 francs for each hectare of land.

$u = 2$, giving an annual ground rent of 10,000 francs for the service rendered by each hectare of land.

$a = \bar{a} \sim 2.8$, giving an approximate value of 7 francs per kg for each kg of cereal.

$H = \dfrac{2}{3}$, giving a capital equipment stock of about 6,600 machines for the whole economy.

$X_H = \dfrac{2}{3}$, giving a workforce of some 16,500 in the equipment industry.

$X_A = \dfrac{10}{3}$, giving a workforce of about 83,500 in the consumer goods industry.

1. No. 188.

2. This rate is broadly equivalent to an annual rate of 3.5% payable annually (no. 10), but this rate need not be taken into account at this point, as we are assuming that all payments are made at the end of each 20-year period (no. 176).

3. In view of the units used, the equation $\bar{h} = 1$ means that 10,000 machines are worth 10 billion francs (no. 188).

$\overline{A} = A \sim \dfrac{7}{3}$, giving a total annual output of about 470,000 tons of cereal.

$\dfrac{A_0}{A} = \dfrac{1}{4}$, giving a daily consumption of some 3.2 kg
of cereal for each young person.

$\dfrac{A_1}{A} = \dfrac{3}{4}$, giving a daily consumption of some 9.6 kg of cereal
for each elderly person.[4]

$\Delta_1 \sim 0.16$, giving a value of 1.6 billion francs for the total
wealth of the State.

$C_\mu = \dfrac{2}{3}$, giving total reproducible capital worth some 6.6 billion

francs, of which the State owns about 1.6 billion and individuals
about 5 billion.

$C_\varphi = 2$, giving land capital worth 20 billion francs entirely
owned by individuals.

$R_N = \dfrac{20}{3}, \quad xX = 4,$ giving annual national income of about
3.3 billion francs, of which 2 billion
$uU = 2, \quad Ih\overline{H} = \dfrac{2}{3},$ are wages, 1 billion land rents and
0.3 billion interest.

$\Theta_N = \dfrac{1}{9}$, giving an average production period of 2.2 years.

---

4. The greater consumption in old age is due to the fact that young individuals have a high average preference for future goods ($\alpha = 1.5$) (no. 188).

For a pronounced preference for present goods, for instance, $\alpha = 0.25$, for identical technology and for the same psychological rate of interest, from conditions (21) and (22) we should have

$$\frac{A_0}{A} = \frac{2}{3}, \qquad \frac{A_1}{A} = \frac{1}{3},$$

which would give a daily cereal consumption of 8.6 kg for the young and 4.3 kg for the elderly.

The annual budget of young and old emerges as follows:

Each young person earns 20,000 F per annum and also receives 800 F as his share of interest received by the State from firms for the 1.6 billion F of capital that it owns. Out of these 20,800 F, he devotes about 8,300 to consumption, 10,000 to land purchase and 2,500 to capital purchase.

Each elderly person receives annually 10,000 F of land rent, 2,500 F of interest on his capital, 10,000 F from the sale of his land and 2,500 F from the sale of his capital. He devotes the whole of the 25,000 F thus received to consumption.

N.B. In the case we are considering, land ownership is necessarily collective for all values of I inferior to 0.58, while private ownership is possible for all values greater than 0.58.

It may then be inquired whether this is a general rule, so that the fact that the equilibrium corresponding to a certain value of I corresponds to private ownership of all land necessarily implies that every equilibrium corresponding to a higher value of I can also correspond to private ownership of all land.

But it is easily proved from the general case we are studying that this is not so. For, as we have seen,[5] there are values of α such that both roots of equation (125) fall between 0 and $(\beta - 1)$.

This is particularly so when

(217)
$$\alpha = \frac{68}{139}, \qquad \beta = 4.$$

In this case, equation (125) has two acceptable roots:

(218)
$$I_1 = \frac{9}{4}, \qquad I_2 = \frac{46}{17}. \qquad \text{[6]}$$

The critical value $\dfrac{1+\alpha}{\alpha}$ corresponding both to the limit of states of private land ownership in the case of direct processes and to spontaneous equilibrium for private land ownership, which here has the value

---

5. Nos. 182 and 187.

6. Note that the recognition of two acceptable roots for equation (125) does not imply that there are two states of spontaneous equilibrium in which land is privately owned and the indirect process is used. Indeed, we have seen that there is still only one (no. 182).

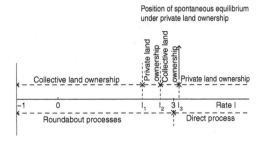

$I_3 = \dfrac{207}{68}$, is greater than 3, and the ownership situation may be summarized as in appendix figure 2.28.

The reader may readily verify that in the range (I_2, I_3) as in the range $(-1, I_1)$ at least part of the land is collectively owned.

8. The case of a double rate of interest (194)

For the values

(219) $K = K' = K'' = 1,$ $\alpha = 1.5,$ $X = 4,$ $U = 1,$ $x = 1,$

to which corresponds the value

$$\beta = 4,$$

equations (180), (181), and (182), corresponding to use of a double rate of psychological and technical interest,[1] become

(220)
$$A_0 = \frac{2A}{5 + 3I_P},$$

(221)
$$A_1 = \frac{3(1 + I_P)}{5 + 3I_P} A,$$

(222)
$$A = 5\frac{\sqrt{1 + I_T}}{2 + I_T}.$$

Curves of equal technical interest rate

Let C_T be the curve that is the locus of coordinates S_0 and S_1 for a given value of rate I_T and hence for total production A. The C_T curves are curves of *equiproduction*.

The parametric representation of these curves is given by the equations

(223) $S_0^i = \ln A_0^i + 1.5 \ln A_1^i,$ $S_1^i = \ln A_1^i,$ [2]

where parameters A_0^i and A_1^i are the quotients of the values given by equations (220) and (221) divided by the number n of individuals comprising each generation.[3]

1. See no. 186.
2. No. 187, equations (189) and (190).
3. For the geometric representation of appendix figure 2.27 n has been taken to be equal to 1 (see note 1 to no. 192).

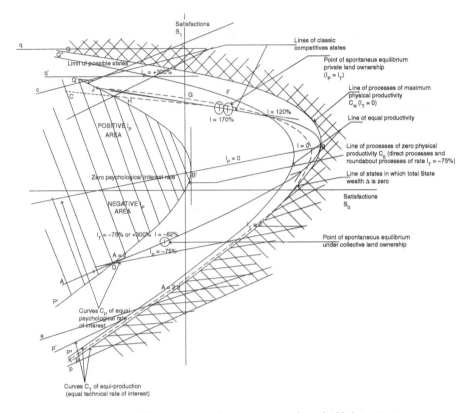

APPENDIX FIGURE 2.29 Diagram representing an economy using a double interest rate

All the C_T curves lie inside curve C_m corresponding to maximum production (zero technical interest rate).[4]

The zone of possible economic states inside curve C_m includes two areas enclosed by curve C_0 representing processes having zero physical productivity.[5]

Within the unshaded area lying between curves C_m and C_0 physical productivity is positive; to each of these points there correspond two different economic states having the same production and the same psychological interest rate but with two different technical interest rates, the one positive and the other negative.

In the single-shaded area, physical productivity is negative; to each

4. This curve includes two infinite branches asymptotic to straight lines q and p.
5. This curve includes two infinite branches asymptotic to straight lines q' and p'.

point there corresponds only one possible economic state of negative technical interest rate.

Curves of equal psychological interest rate

It is clear that the C_P curves, which are the loci of the points corresponding to an identical psychological rate of interest, but to different rates of technical interest, are parallel straight lines. For a given value of I, equations (220) and (221) give us

(224) $$A_1 = \lambda A_0,$$

where λ is a constant. It follows that the corresponding C_P curves have as their equation

(225) $$S_1 = \frac{2S_0}{5} + \frac{2}{5}\ln\lambda. \qquad {}^{6}$$

The reader will have verified at once that each C_T curve admits a vertical tangent at its point of intersection with whichever of the straight C_P lines corresponds to a zero psychological rate of interest. Each of its points corresponds to a maximum of satisfaction S_0^i for a given value of production A.

The curve of classic competitive equilibrium states

Classic competitive states of equilibrium are characterized by equality between rates I_P and I_T.

The reader may verify that their locus is tangential to curve C of maximum production ($I_T = 0$) at its point of intersection with the straight-line locus of points corresponding to a zero psychological interest rate.[7]

The states of spontaneous equilibrium under collective and private land ownership are respectively represented at E and F.

6. Resulting from the elimination of parameters A_0^i and A_1^i between equations (223) and (224).

7. The curve corresponding to the analytic equality of rates I_T and I_P includes two infinite branches asymptotic to the straight lines a and c, but the asymptotic branch c does not correspond to economically acceptable solutions as the interest rate for the indirect process cannot exceed 300%.

Beyond the corresponding point H the locus of classical competitive states is represented by the HQ' branch of line C_0, representing economic states using only direct processes.

Satisfactions S_0^i and S_1^i are respectively maxima at B and G for values 0 and 170% of interest rate I.

I have used H to designate the point at which the line of classic competitive states using indirect processes meets the line $P'B'Q'$ of direct processes, and J to designate the point on the line of direct processes from which satisfaction S_1^i becomes greater than its maximum value reached at G on the line of classic competitive states using the indirect processes.

Locus of points at which the net wealth of the State is zero

This locus corresponds to the equation

(226) $\Delta = 0$

or to the equation

(227) $\delta + \bar{u}\bar{U} = 0,$

where δ is given by equation (187) and where rate I_T is necessarily positive. Equation (227) then gives

(228) $\dfrac{5 + 3I_P}{15} = \dfrac{I_T(1 + I_T)}{1 + 3I_T},$

and hence, from equations (180) and (181)

(229) $A_0 = \dfrac{2}{3}\dfrac{1 + 3I_T}{I_T(2 + I_T)}\dfrac{1}{\sqrt{1 + I_T}},$ $A_1 = \dfrac{15I_T^2 + 9I_T - 2}{3I_T(2 + I_T)\sqrt{1 + I_T}}.$

Hence rate I_P can vary only within the range (0.17, 3) whereas rate I_T varies from -1 to $+4.33$.

Naturally the locus considered passes through point F of spontaneous equilibrium under private land ownership and as rate I_T falls as far as 0.17, the corresponding point recedes to infinity along branch FLK, very close to branch BP of the maximum social productivity curve.

When rate I_T increases beyond 120%, the locus ends naturally at its point M of contact with the curve of zero physical productivity ($I_T = +3$), since beyond that only the direct process is used and it is no longer possible to define a technical interest rate.

For all the economic states of the locus we are studying, the State's net wealth is zero ($\Delta = 0$) and State intervention is confined to bringing about the dissociation of the technical and psychological interest rates I_T and I_P.

(c) Economic discussion of the solutions

1. Generalities (195)

In the foregoing long analytical discussion[1] I have *deliberately* eschewed all economic interpretation. While this approach may be drier for the reader, it offers the crucial advantage of allowing him to devote his undivided attention to the *economic* discussion that now ensues. He will find the various commentaries therein grouped in logical sequence and clearly differentiated from the mass of calculations among which they would otherwise have inevitably been mingled in the text.

---

1. Nos. 177 to 194.

2. General conditions of equilibrium (196)

The findings that the foregoing discussion enables us to reach as to the general conditions of equilibrium are essentially the following:

(i) Possibility of a rate of interest under stationary conditions

Notwithstanding the allegations of certain authors,[1] the foregoing analysis proves beyond cavil that stationary conditions do not necessarily lead to a zero rate of interest.

This is a theoretical finding of considerable significance and that could not in fact have been regarded as evident a priori.[2]

(ii) Determination of the equilibrium

The foregoing discussion enables the general assertions that have been made concerning stationary equilibria to be confirmed with regard to a specific case.[3]

In the absence of State intervention (spontaneous equilibrium) we have seen that for given structural conditions, e.g., private land ownership, there exists only one stable stationary equilibrium and hence that the pure equilibrium interest rate is well determined by the general structural conditions.

When the State intervenes, a further degree of freedom arises and there are an infinity of stationary states corresponding to the psychological and technical structure being studied,[4] each of these states corresponding, for given State intervention, to a different capital equipment stock $\overline{H}$ and to a different interest rate I.

1. See no. 119.
2. While I readily grant that for anyone who has devoted serious thought to the question it is almost self-evident that there can be a rate of interest under stationary conditions, I am no less sure that for those who are not yet convinced of the fact there can be no substitute for a rigorous demonstration based on a specific case.
3. No. 49.
4. Defined in no. 176.

(iii) State intervention and the rate of interest

It can be seen that the rate of interest prevailing in the market depends essentially on State intervention.

In the specific case we are analyzing,[5] if the State owns no material wealth (land or capital), the rate of interest cannot fall below a critical level equal to 120%.

If, however, the State owns a fraction of the reproducible capital but no land, the interest rate cannot fall below a critical level of 58%.[6]

And if the State owns only a fraction of the land, the interest rate cannot be zero or negative.

This shows *the decisive role played by State intervention on the capital market*. Depending on the scale of such intervention, the range of variation of the rate of interest may expand or contract. The more the State owns,[7] the less easy it is to satisfy individuals' propensity to save, the more capital there is and the lower the rate of interest will be.[8,9]

(iv) Land collectivization and spontaneous savings

Whereas the spontaneous equilibrium rate of interest is +58% under conditions of private land ownership, it becomes −62% when *all land* is collectively owned. This proves *that collectivization of all land has the effect of increasing spontaneous investment* $\overline{H}$.[10]

It should be emphasized that in the general case the spontaneous equilibrium interest rate corresponding to collective land ownership is

5. Nos. 187 to 194.

6. I emphasize that this condition is much more restrictive for the rate of interest than equation (84) alone for the positiveness of the rate of interest and is evident a priori.

7. I.e., the greater the State's net wealth Δ.

8. It may also be said that the more the State is indebted, the more the propensity to save is satisfied by government securities, the less extensive are real investments and hence the higher the rate of interest since the rate of interest varies inversely with investment volume (no. 45 and no. 177, equation [35]). (Of course, this inference is no longer applicable when there are no longer any indirect production processes, and in fact it is immediately verified [no. 192, appendix fig. 2.24] that in this case the rate of interest may be proportionately greater as the State is less indebted.)

9. For we have seen that in the case of a stable equilibrium, the only case that is relevant at present, interest rate I, is a decreasing function of wealth Δ (no. 187).

10. Note that in equilibrium collective ownership of a fraction of the land does not necessarily correspond to an increase in the stock of capital equipment (see no. 193 *in fine*).

not necessarily negative; but it can be shown that it is always less than the spontaneous equilibrium interest rate corresponding to private land ownership.

(v) Modalities of State intervention

Practically speaking, the State can only fix the rate of interest at a given level by lending or borrowing capital at this rate without limit, depending on the market demand or supply at this rate. This suffices to justify the use of the rate of interest as an independent parameter in the plan analyzed.

The findings reached[11] show, however, that under private land ownership such a policy may turn out to be quite impossible for low interest rate levels. Which confirms the points made in no. 135.

(vi) Rate of interest and technical progress

In the general case, the rate of interest corresponding to spontaneous equilibrium under private land ownership[12] is in fact a function of the ratio

$$(230) \qquad\qquad \beta = \frac{KK''}{K'}\frac{X}{U}.$$

As β may equally well increase or decrease when technical progress occurs,[13] it is confirmed that *the equilibrium interest rate may likewise equally well rise or fall following technical progress.*

However, while in dynamic disequilibrium technical progress leads to a rise in the rate of interest,[14] no such conclusion follows when dynamic equilibrium prevails.

If the technical progress occurs in the production of capital goods[15] or in their utilization,[16] coefficient β increases, and from the findings of no. 184, the equilibrium interest rate rises. This result was foreseeable a priori, as an increase in the efficiency of the factors of production used in

11. Nos. 184 and 192.
12. Root of equation (119).
13. I.e., as coefficients K, K', and K'' increase.
14. No. 23.
15. Increase in K''.
16. Increase in K.

a roundabout way can only increase the demand for capital and hence, for a given supply, increase the rate of interest.

The reader may verify in the same way that if the technical progress occurs in the use of factors of production used directly,[17] it leads to a fall in the rate of interest.

(vii) Equipment and technical progress

For the same reason, the stock of capital equipment $\overline{H}$, a function of coefficient β,[18] may in consequence equally well increase or decrease with technical progress.

It is thus proved that, contrary to a very widespread opinion, technical progress does not necessarily lead to expansion of capital equipment.

(viii) Distributed income and national income

Our model notably enables us to confirm that income distributed to individuals cannot as a rule be identified with national income.[19]

For from no. 178 we have

(231) $$R_D = xX + \overline{Ih}\overline{H} + uU + ID + \overline{h}\overline{H}_I,$$

whereas equations (72) and (73) have established that

(232) $$R_N = aA = xX + IhH + uU.$$

17. Increase in K'.
18. Equation (35).
19. No. 37.

3. Social efficiency, social productivity, and satisfactions (197)

(i) Restricted social efficiency and stationary conditions

It must be stressed that the economic equilibrium under stationary conditions that we have been considering is entirely determined by the behavior of the young individuals who, in light of their incomes and of price levels, maximize their satisfaction by the way they behave in the market.[1]

The income and the consumptions of the elderly have in fact been entirely determined by their economic behavior when they were young and consideration of their satisfaction S_1^i is irrelevant to the determination of the equilibrium.[2]

Under these conditions, as has been observed, the spontaneous competitive mechanism only achieves the maximization of social efficiency in the restricted meaning.[3]

It is also crucial to stress that this maximization does not achieve the absolute maximization of satisfaction S^i, but its maximization subject to initial and final conditions.

This can easily be proved, for to any stationary process there corresponds an interest rate level, which in general is not zero, and a certain production A.

Now for the value of this production it is easily seen that the satisfaction

(233) $$S_0^i = \ln A_0 + \alpha \ln A_1 - (1 + \alpha) \ln n$$

of individuals is not the greatest possible. This is because, for the value

(234) $$A_0 + A_1 = A,$$

assumed to be given, the maximization of S_0 gives

(235) $$A_1 = \alpha A_0,$$

1. No. 177, equations (12) and (13).
2. No. 177.
3. No. 60.

a condition that, according to equation (14) of no. 177, is realized only when the rate of interest is zero.[4,5]

4. See the remarks already made in note 6 to no. 63.

5. I stress that there are no grounds for linking the *physical maximization* of satisfaction S, here envisaged for a given total production A, with the *maximization in the market* of satisfaction S^i for given incomes and prices, which leads to equation (14) of no. 177.

While the first of these maximizations is *absolute*, involving only *physical* elements, the second is only a *relative* maximization carried out in the context of a *market economy* using prices.

The issue is precisely to find out whether intrinsic maximization starting from physical elements alone is indeed obtained starting from economic maximization in the context of a market economy. The analysis presented in the text precisely demonstrates that this is not the case, at least not in general.

Two entirely distinct kinds of reasoning are involved and the only link I am seeking to establish between them consists in determining whether they lead to similar outcomes, which in fact, as a rule, they do not.

The issue here encountered bears a close parallel to Plato's cave allegory. It will be recalled that the prisoners held in the cave perceive external reality only by means of the shadows that appear on the walls, reflecting the events that take place outside the cave. For them, the only reality is the shadows, yet it is quite evident that these shadows are in fact no more than a *relative* reality, an epiphenomenon, as they comprise but a deformed image of the genuine outside reality that is the phenomenon in absolute terms. In our case, the economic maximization of satisfaction S_0^i in the market for given incomes and prices is no more than an epiphenomenon; the real question is how far this maximization may in fact be accepted as an absolute maximization of satisfaction S_0^i in light of the total production A available.

This situation can easily be represented geometrically. Let R be the total income of the young, and we have

(1) $$aA_0 + \frac{aA_1}{1+I} = R.$$

This condition means that point M of competitive equilibrium must necessarily be situated on the straight line Δ perpendicular to the vector $\overrightarrow{op}$ of coordinates a and $\frac{a}{1+I}$ passing through point H of vector $\overrightarrow{op}$ such that $OH = R$.

It is at once apparent that *economic* maximization of the satisfaction amounts to seeking the point M on straight line Δ such that the function S_0^i is as great as possible. This point M corresponds to competitive equilibrium.

The absolute maximization of satisfaction S_0^i, by contrast, amounts to seeking the *physical* maximization of the function S_0^i for a total quantity $A^i = A_0^i + A_1^i$ assumed to be given, i.e., seeking the point M' of the straight line Δ_1 perpendicular to the bisector of the x- and y-axes and that passes through point M for which function S_0^i is maximal. This point M' is generally distinct from point M and coincides with it only when the vector $\overrightarrow{op}$ bisects the x- and y-axes, i.e., when the interest rate is zero.

This might suggest that the theorem of social efficiency is thereby shown to be flawed, but this is not so at all. For the theorem is *only valid between two given points of time and under well-determined initial and final conditions.*[6] Now in the stationary-state case we are studying, these initial and final conditions are characterized by the existence of a consumption A_1 of the elderly at the initial instant and of a consumption A_0 on the part of the young at the final instant—parameters that must be deemed *to be given.*

A similar remark might be made concerning stationary processes displaying negative interest. Under such conditions, restriction of the output of equipment $\overline{H}$, starting from a given point in time, would enable production to be increased, indeed indefinitely increased. Which, once again, might suggest a flaw in the theorem of restricted social efficiency.

But, once again, this is not so, for reasons similar to those stated in the preceding case. For among the initial and final conditions of the present case figures is the existence of a certain capital equipment stock $\overline{H}$ that must therefore be counted *as a given.*

The model studied, once again, makes it possible to verify the difference between the maximization of restricted social efficiency and the maximization of generalized social efficiency. For instance, in appendix

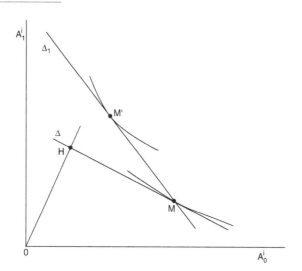

APPENDIX FIGURE 2.30 FOOTNOTE

6. Nos. 58 and 59.

figure 2.29 in no. 194, the *single* point F corresponds, for a given capital stock of $H\sim 5.6$, to the maximization of restricted social efficiency, whereas *all* the points on the line of equal social productivity passing through F correspond to the maximization of generalized social efficiency for the same equipment stock. Along the whole of this line the psychological rate of interest can in fact have any value.

(ii) Physical productivity of roundabout production processes

From equation (64) of no. 177, the physical productivity π of roundabout processes is a function on the one hand of coefficient β, i.e., of technical structure, and on the other hand of the interest rate I prevailing in the market, i.e., of the economic equilibrium. It is therefore due to the combination of these two elements.[7]

This at once confirms that, in conformity with the general theory, for a given technical structure (i.e., for a given value of coefficient β) the physical productivity π of roundabout processes is in fact maximal when the rate of interest is zero.[8,9]

---

7. Given that from equation (35) the rate of interest is seen to be a function of coefficient β and of equipment stock H, it may also be said that the physical productivity of indirect processes depends both on the coefficient β, i.e., on the technical structure, and on equipment stock H, i.e., on the capital intensiveness of the system of production.

As coefficient β may equally well increase or decrease with technical progress, it can be seen that *for a given equipment stock* H *the physical productivity of the indirect production processes may increase or decrease with technical progress.*

8. It may be worth emphasizing that the low relative variation in production A and in productivity π in our example as the interest rate varies in the vicinity of zero cannot be extrapolated to reality. The ratio of the relative variations of A or of π to I in fact depends essentially on the specific data characterizing each case studied.

9. Our example makes it possible to illustrate using a specific case the interconnection of the second demonstration I have given of the theorem of social productivity. (See note 15 to no. 69.)

For we now have

(1) $$(dR_N) = a\,dA,$$

i.e., from the equations numbered (195) in no. 189,

(2) $$(dR_N) = -\frac{5I\,dI}{(2+I)^2}.$$

But we now have

It is also verified that the representative curve of physical productivity π as a function of the rate of interest has exactly the same shape as that indicated in no. 70, which automatically confirms the various conclusions reached in that numbered section. It also confirms that the value productivity of capital represented by interest rate I is by no means the same thing as its physical productivity denoted by coefficient π, that there may be physical productivity ($\pi > 0$) without value productivity ($I > 0$), and that all that can be said is that *if* there is value productivity ($I > 0$), there must certainly be physical productivity ($\pi > 0$), while if there is physical unproductiveness ($\pi < 0$), there must certainly be value unproductiveness ($I < 0$).

(iii) Social productivity and labor intensiveness

The labor intensiveness[10] of production A has for expression, from equation (36),

$$(236) \qquad \frac{X}{A} = \frac{1}{\sqrt{KK''}\left(1 + \dfrac{K'U}{KK''X}\right)} \frac{2+I}{\sqrt{1+I}}.$$

This proves that for given values of K, K', K'', U, and X this labor intensiveness is indeed at its minimum when the rate of interest is zero, but,

---

$$(3) \qquad R_N = \int_0^{+\infty} e^{i\theta}\varphi(\theta)\,d\theta = xX_A + (1+I)xX_H + uU,$$

and hence, for given prices for the primary factors of production,

$$(4) \qquad di\int_0^{+\infty} e^{i\theta}\frac{d\varphi(\theta)}{di}\,d\theta = dI\left[x\frac{dX_A}{dI} + (1+I)x\frac{dX_H}{dI}\right],$$

i.e., bearing in mind the equalities $X_A + X_H = X$ and $x = 1$ and expression (202) from no. 189 for X_H,

$$(5) \qquad di\int_0^{+\infty} e^{i\theta}\frac{d\varphi(\theta)}{di}\,d\theta = Ix\frac{dX_H}{dI} = -\frac{5I\,dI}{(2+I)^2},$$

which confirms the exactness of the equality

$$(6) \qquad (dR_N) = di\int_0^{+\infty} e^{i\theta}\frac{d\varphi(\theta)}{di}\,d\theta.$$

10. No. 23.

as indicated in no. 69, the minimum in question is merely a relative minimum for a population X taken as given. It can be seen that the absolute
minimum labor intensiveness corresponds to zero population, a value that
corresponds in the model being studied, as the reader may readily check,
to the population optimum.[11]

(iv) Zero interest rate and satisfaction

We confirm that the satisfaction S_0^i of the young is indeed maximal when
the rate of interest is zero.

This is due to two facts: first, production A is maximal (in terms of
physical productivity) and, secondly, the distribution of production A between the consumption of the young and that of the old is optimal in
terms of the maximization of satisfaction S_0^i.[12]

(v) Transition from one stationary state to another

It is clear that exclusively *from the angle of production* A, *abstracting
entirely from any question of how this production is distributed between
young and old*, stationary conditions must be preferred to any other conditions if social productivity under stationary conditions is closer to its
maximum. Thus, in the case of the specific example studied, the stationary
conditions corresponding to collective land ownership and to State intervention such that the rate of interest is zero, are, in terms of production,
preferable to the spontaneous stationary conditions under private land
ownership corresponding to a 120% interest rate.

However, it goes without saying that transition from the second stationary state to the first would require a prior accumulation of capital ($\overline{H}$)
to make the increase in social productivity possible, and hence greater
savings would need to be made than those corresponding to spontaneous
competitive equilibrium under private land ownership.

This means that restriction of consumer production would have to occur at a given point in time, via diminution of direct labor X_A, together
with an increase in the production of equipment, via increase in indirect
labor X_H, but it is easy to see that no generation would necessarily be sac-

---

11. Optimal population is zero here because there is no undifferentiated sector in the
sense of note 2 to no. 55 (see my *À la recherche d'une discipline économique*, no. 322, § D).

12. See § i above.

rificed in the sense that the total consumption $A_0^i + A_1^i$ of one generation need necessarily be diminished in favor of the following generations.

This is because matters could be arranged so that during the first period T_0 of supplementary savings, the consumption of the elderly was left unchanged while only that of the young was cut back; then in the following period T_1, the surplus productivity obtained by increasing the stock of capital equipment could be used (a) to increase the consumption of the elderly, leaving the consumption of the young unchanged between the two periods, and (b) to diminish further the direct labor X_A in favor of indirect labor X_H. It is quite conceivable that such a policy should be pursued until maximum social productivity is attained.

This shows that *the transition to optimal conditions may be achieved by a simple modification of the distribution over time of the income of each generation*—a distribution of which the conventional and arbitrary nature has been emphasized.[13]

(vi) The use of a double rate of interest

Appendix figure 2.29 enables the conclusions of no. 73 to be confirmed[14] and provides a striking illustration of the link between the rate of interest, generalized social efficiency, and social productivity.

For a given stock of capital equipment, all representative points corresponding to maximum social efficiency are to be found on a curve C_T of equiproduction.[15] To each of the points on this curve corresponds a different psychological rate of interest and for a given stock of capital equipment there is only one point corresponding to equality between the rates of psychological interest and technical interest, i.e., to classical competitive equilibrium.

When physical productivity is positive, each point (S_0^i, S_1^i) may be obtained in two different ways, each corresponding to a given equipment stock and a given rate of technical interest. On the other hand, when physical productivity is negative, each point (S_0^i, S_1^i) can be obtained in only one way, corresponding to a negative rate of technical interest.

13. No. 63.

14. No. 73, fig. 7.7.

15. This curve should be compared with the curve of maximum social efficiency in figure 6.1 of no. 56.

Appendix figure 2.29 enables it to be immediately verified that for a given production A, satisfaction S is maximal when the psychological rate of interest is zero.[16]

For positive rates of technical interest, production reaches its minimum when indirect processes are no longer used (zero physical productivity). For negative rates of technical interest, production declines gradually as the rate of interest falls, reaching zero when the rate of interest touches (–1).

From the viewpoint of economic philosophy it can be seen that *while for given structural conditions there exists only one stationary state corresponding to a stable spontaneous equilibrium,[17] under private land ownership, it remains quite possible to bring about a double infinity of other economic states, on condition (a) of State intervention in the investment market and (b) of dissociation of the psychological and technical interest rates.*

In the event of State intervention in the investment market without separation of the psychological and technical interest rates, only a single infinity of economic states out of the double infinity available can be realized. It corresponds to the line of classical competitive states.[18]

In the same way, if the State does not modify the level of real investment corresponding to spontaneous equilibrium under private land ownership, limiting its intervention instead to dissociating the psychological and technical interest rates, only a single infinity of economic states out of this double infinity is in fact realizable. It is represented by the equiproduction curve passing through point F, which represents the spontaneous equilibrium under private land ownership.[19]

It is obvious that of two economic states, the one that must be preferred is the one that simultaneously realizes higher values for both satisfactions S_0^i and S_1^i.

It follows that for a given structure of production equipment (the technical rate of interest and the stock of capital equipment being given), only the branch of the equiproduction curve located above the straight line BB' representing a zero psychological rate of interest corresponds to economically preferable states. For on this branch, to an increase in satisfaction S_1^i there necessarily corresponds a decrease in satisfaction S_0^i, and vice versa, so that it is not possible for both satisfactions, S_0^i and S_1^i, to be

---

16. Which confirms the statements made in § iv above.
17. I.e., in the absence of any State intervention.
18. Line $ADEBFHQ'$ of appendix fig. 2.29 in no. 194.
19. Line $P''FQ''$ of appendix fig. 2.29 in no. 194.

increased or decreased at the same time. By contrast, on the equiproduction curve located below the straight line BB', both satisfactions S_0^i and S_1^i
vary in the same direction, so that for a given rate of technical interest *the
economic states corresponding to a negative psychological rate of interest
can never be considered advantageous.*

For a given ratio of S_1^i to S_0^i, as each of these satisfactions embodies a
certain distribution of psychological income over time, *the most advantageous economic state is the one located on branch* BQ (located above the
line BB' of zero psychological interest rates) *of the line of maximum physical productivity corresponding to a zero technical interest rate.* From the
economic point of view, all economic states corresponding to this branch
BQ must be deemed to yield equivalent advantages; only considerations
of an ethical or political nature can make such and such a ratio of S_1^i to
S_0^i (i.e., such and such a distribution of income between young and old)
preferable to another.

If the technical and psychological interest rates are not separated, i.e.,
if only a single rate of interest prevails in the economy and if no indirect
measure such as compulsory pension schemes undermines this situation,[20]
the corresponding economic states are all located on the line $ADBGHJQ'$
of classical competitive states. Evidently, not all the economic states corresponding to the ADB branch could be considered preferable, as at point
B satisfactions S_0^i and S_1^i have superior values at the same time. The same
applies to both of the GH and HJ branches since at point G satisfactions
S_0^i and S_1^i once again both have superior values at the same time.

If, however, point B on both of the other branches BG and JQ' corresponds to a maximum of production A, it could not be deemed to correspond to an economic optimum where a single rate of interest is assumed
to be given, for if production declines from B toward G until reaching a
minimum and remains at this minimum level on the JQ' branch, the decrease in satisfaction S_0^i is offset by an increase in S_1^i and there can be no
way, other than in terms of economically arbitrary conventions of an ethical or political nature, of comparing the decrease in the one satisfaction
with the increase in the other and deciding whether this displacement of
the economic equilibrium should be judged disadvantageous. From this
point of view, *since uniqueness of the psychological and technical interest rates is assumed to be given, it can be seen that the maximization of
social productivity need not constitute a rationally necessary goal; but if,*

20. See notes 9 to no. 63 and 17 to no. 77 and the related explanations in the text.

on the other hand, the uniqueness of the rates of interest is deemed to be
no more than a contingent fact, which might be avoidable, even if in fact
it was retained on the savings market by a system of compulsory pension
contributions,[21] *it can be seen that maximization of social productivity is*
indeed an intrinsically desirable objective.[22]

(vii) Social productivity and distribution

Between points G and B on the line of spontaneous competitive states,[23]
an increase in social productivity leads to variations in opposing directions of present and future satisfactions S_0^i and S_1^i. Only on the HG and
ADB branches an increase in social productivity lead to a simultaneous
increase in both satisfactions S_0^i and S_1^i.

This confirms that in the context of a classical competitive state characterized by a single rate of interest, the increase in social productivity does
not necessarily have the effect of simultaneously increasing the different
satisfactions of the same individual over the different periods.[23]

However, it also confirms[24] that starting from any initial state it is always possible to make a *simultaneous* increase in both satisfactions S_0^i
and S_1^i correspond to an increase in social productivity. It is enough to
separate the psychological and technical rates of interest.

21. Reminder: (a) direct dissociation of the psychological and technical interest rates does
not in all rigor seem to be realizable except in a collectivist economy (no. 77, § "Possible
modes of State intervention," and no. 145 *in fine*), and (b) public ownership of firms cannot in
the present state of economics be deemed necessarily preferable to their private ownership
(note 8 to no. 159).

22. Subject, of course, to the savings effort to be made during the transition period
(nos. 74, 77, and § v above).

23. Thus, in the case being studied, while the maximization of social productivity, which
moves the economic equilibrium from F to B, increases satisfaction S_0^i, on the other hand it
diminishes satisfaction S_1^i.

24. No. 194, appendix fig. 2.29.

4. The rationale of interest (198)

(i) Rationale of interest and the preference for present goods

The model studied enables us, in the first place, to clarify the fundamental distinction between the preference at the margin for present goods in a given situation (slope of the tangent to the line of indifference greater than unity) and the average preference for present goods (positive value of the coefficient $p = 1 - \alpha$).

Moreover the results obtained show that *an average preference for future goods in a given situation may very well prevail without any necessity for a marginal preference for future goods, i.e., a negative interest rate.* The case studied offers an example of this, for where coefficient p is negative and equal to $-\frac{1}{2}$, i.e., where there is an average preference for future goods, the spontaneous equilibrium interest rate under private land ownership is equal to +120%.

In the same way, the analysis set out in no. 184 shows that for values of coefficient β greater than one, *an average preference for present goods* $(\alpha < 1)$ *does not, in an economy of collective land ownership,*[1] *necessarily lead to a positive rate of interest,* the rate of interest being in fact positive or negative depending on whether coefficient α, which is less than 1, is or is not lower than coefficient $\dfrac{\beta - 1}{\beta + 3}$ (appendix fig. 2.8 of no. 184).[2,3]

1. Economies of collective land ownership are suitably considered here because we have seen, and the following analysis will confirm, that private land ownership necessarily entails a positive value for the rate of interest. Hence to study the specific effect of average preference for present goods it is necessary to exclude private land ownership from the structural conditions.

2. The results obtained in no. 184 (appendix fig. 2.6) showed that even if the preference for present goods is on average a strong one (i.e., the value of coefficient α is very low), it always remains possible under collective land ownership conditions for the rate of interest to be negative. It suffices for coefficient β to be low enough. This confirms the analysis found in no. 137 preceding footnote reference 4.

3. From the equation

$$\frac{A_1}{A_0} = \alpha(1 + I),$$

It may be deduced that the theory of Böhm-Bawerk, being false in particular cases, cannot be true for the general case.

By contrast, the model studied shows that, all other things being equal, *the different equilibrium interest rates*, together with the limit inferior below which the interest rate cannot fall when land ownership is in private hands, *are proportionately greater* as coefficient α is lower, i.e., as *the average preference for present goods is greater* (no. 183 and appendix figs. 2.8, 2.9, 2.15, and 2.16 to no. 184).

In this sense, but *only in this sense*, Böhm-Bawerk's theory of the link between the interest rate level and preference for present goods is confirmed.

(ii) Rationale of interest and the physical productivity of indirect production processes

I have used coefficient π, denoting physical productivity,[4] to characterize the productivity of a production process, but this productivity depends (a) on the interest rate I actually prevailing, i.e., on both individual psychologies and on the extent of State intervention, and (b) on the structural conditions of the productive system, i.e., on the productive capacity of the stock of capital equipment.

It will be worthwhile for us to characterize this capacity by a coefficient to be called the *coefficient of productive capacity*, and to determine how the different equilibrium interest rates vary with this coefficient.

In the case of the model studied, it emerges that the use of the indirect process is, all other things being equal, proportionately more advantageous as coefficient K', characterizing the efficiency of labor using the direct process is lower and as coefficients K and K'' to which the efficiency of indirect labor is directly proportional are higher. From which it can

---

resulting from equations (38) and (39) of no. 177 it further follows, as readers may verify, that an average preference for present goods ($α < 1$) does not necessarily lead to a greater value for present consumption A_0. In fact everything depends on the rate of interest prevailing in the market.

In the same way an average preference for future goods ($α > 1$) does not necessarily lead to a value for future consumption A_1 greater than present consumption A_0. For instance, in the example we have been studying ($α = \frac{3}{2}$) this applies to the case of spontaneous equilibrium under collective land ownership ($I = -0.62$).

4. Defined by equation (64) of no. 177.

be seen that the productive system's capacity can be characterized by coefficient β.[5]

In light of the findings of no. 184, it can be seen that although the spontaneous equilibrium interest rate under collective land ownership is an increasing function of productive capacity β, when land is privately owned it is a *decreasing* function of the same capacity.

From section (c) of that numbered section it follows that the rate of interest corresponding to the inferior limit of economic states feasible under private land ownership is a decreasing function of productive capacity β.

Note too that introduction of the possibility of indirect processes, i.e., of productive capacity, lowers the spontaneous equilibrium interest rate under private land ownership from the value 5/3 corresponding to the direct process alone[6] to the value 1.2 corresponding to the possibility of indirect processes (no. 192).

From this it is clear *not only that it is an error to attribute the existence of a positive rate of interest to the use of physically productive processes*, since under collective land ownership[7] the spontaneous equilibrium rate of interest may be negative even if physical productivity π is not,[8] *but also that*

---

5. The same conclusion may also be reached by using π_m to denote the maximum productive capacity attainable by the system. Given the fact that this maximum productivity is realized for a zero interest rate, it becomes clear in light of equation (64) of no. 177 that we have

(1)
$$\pi_m = \left(\sqrt{\beta} + \frac{1}{\sqrt{\beta}} \right) - 1.$$

And since, from condition (83) of no. 179,

(2)
$$1 + I < \beta,$$

the only values for coefficient β to be considered for a zero interest rate are values greater than unity, it is clear that productivity π_m is an increasing function of coefficient β and hence that the productive capacity of the productive system may be represented by this coefficient.

6. The value corresponding to zero for Δ in equation (207) of no. 190 giving Δ.

7. The standpoint of collective land ownership is here adopted because private land ownership suffices alone to ensure a positive interest rate (see note 1 above).

8. As is the case, for instance, in the example studied in no. 192 in which physical productivity is positive for the value –0.62 for the rate of interest. See too figure 7.2 of no. 70, confirmed by § ii of no. 197.

it is equally erroneous to claim, as did Irving Fisher,[9] *that the productive capacity of nature* (so much the greater in the present case as coefficient β is greater) *displays a tendency to increase the level of the equilibrium interest rate.*

(iii) Rationale of interest and private land ownership

The foregoing analysis shows that while under collective land ownership all values of the rate of interest from –1 to +∞[10] may be observed,[11] *when land ownership is private not only is it impossible for the rate of interest to become negative, but in fact it has a limit inferior,[12] irrespective of the level of State intervention,[13] comprising a positive minimum that is a function of structural data.*[14] This establishes that private land ownership alone constitutes a sufficient condition for the rate of interest to remain at every point in time greater than a certain positive minimum, irrespective of government policy.[15]

9. "Nature's productivity," he tells us in *The Theory of Interest*, pt. 2, ch. 8, § 6, "has a strong tendency to keep up the rate of interest."

10. See no. 14, § "Range of variation of interest rates."

11. Either because, for a given psychological and technical structure, i.e., for given values of coefficients α and β, the wage-denominated capital (excluding land) owned by the State $\frac{\delta}{x}$ varies or because, for a given value of this wage-capital, e.g., zero (spontaneous equilibria), coefficients α and β vary (nos. 184 and 185).

12. No. 192, appendix fig. 2.24.

13. Represented by the value Δ of the net wealth owned by the State.

14. I.e., in the model we are studying, of coefficients α and β.

15. It is interesting to wonder for what analytic reason the rates of interest constituting solutions to the system of equations defining the equilibria under private land ownership continue to have a limit inferior.

To answer this question, note that from equation (43) of no. 177, we have for low values of I

$$\Delta \sim \frac{xX}{\beta I}.$$

This equation shows precisely that interest rate I could have very low values only if the State's net wealth Δ increased indefinitely—which would be impossible under private land ownership since the State's net wealth could not exceed the value of the reproducible capital C_μ, which, from equation (48), remains finite as the interest rate tends towards zero. From equation (34) it can be seen that for low values of I we have

It also establishes that in the absence of State intervention on the savings and investment market, *the effect of land collectivization is to lower the spontaneous equilibrium interest rate.* In the specific case studied, this interest rate even becomes negative.[16]

The results obtained also *seem* to show that for a given level of State intervention,[17] for instance, *no* intervention (spontaneous equilibrium),[18] there is a tendency for the rate of interest to be lower as the area of land is less.[19] This tendency could be intuitively explained by saying that the less the propensity to save can be satisfied by land ownership, the more it tends to seek an outlet by investing in reproducible capital and hence the lower the rate of interest.[20]

This intuition finds support in the observation that the greater the area of the lands involved, the higher is the minimum beneath which the rate of interest cannot fall as long as lands are privately owned, irrespective of the level of State intervention.[21]

$$\Delta \sim \frac{uU}{I}.$$

This equation shows that a very low interest rate under conditions of private land ownership is only conceivable if the State in fact owns nearly all the land.

Needless to say, all these properties are geometrically evident (see no. 185).

16. In fact its value passes from +120% to –62% (no. 192).

17. Represented by a given value for its net wealth Δ.

18. For which $\Delta = 0$.

19. For we have seen in no. 184 that the spontaneous equilibrium interest rate for private land ownership is a decreasing function of coefficient β, in other words, an increasing function of the land area U since we have $\beta = KK'' \frac{X}{K'U}$ (equation [32]).

20. I stress that the points made here are intended merely as a stimulant to further research. What satisfies the propensity to save is not so much land considered in itself as the *value* of the land, i.e., the product of its quantity by its unit price. Thus the way in which this price varies with the quantity of land inevitably constitutes an important factor.

Of course this reasoning is no longer applicable when there is no longer any indirect process (for in that case the link between the interest rate and the capital equipment stock no longer exists—see the points already made in note 8 to no. 196). This appears to explain the fact that the equilibrium interest rate $\frac{1+\alpha}{\alpha}$ under private land ownership where indirect processes are not used (no. 183), a quantity independent of coefficient β, is not a decreasing function of this coefficient.

21. This minimum is in fact a decreasing function of coefficient β and hence an increasing function of the quantity of land (no. 184).

And further support is provided by equation (124), showing that as land area tends toward zero[22] the limit inferior of the rate of interest also tends toward zero.

(iv) Rationale of interest, preference for present goods, and private land ownership

In the specific case studied[23] the spontaneous equilibrium under collective land ownership corresponds to a negative level of the rate of interest, but as has already been pointed out, it is obvious that this is only so because of the specific conditions considered[24] and as a matter of fact other values for the constants characterizing the general model we have been analyzing might correspond to a positive value for the spontaneous equilibrium interest rate under collective land ownership.[25]

In this way we establish that *private land ownership is a sufficient, but not a necessary, condition for the rate of interest to be positive; in other words, needless to say, conditions of economic structure may be such that the strong preference of individuals for present goods alone*[26] *explains why a positive rate of interest prevails.*[27]

(v) Rationale of interest and storage

It must be stressed that in the model studied the only reason why the rate of interest cannot in fact become negative under conditions of collective land ownership is the assumption excluding the storage of either consumer goods or capital goods.[28]

If, for instance, no-cost storage was possible, the current price $\dfrac{a}{1+I}$ at any point of time of good A available in the following period could not become higher than price a itself, for if it did so, it would become advantageous to store it, giving us necessarily

---

22. I.e., as coefficient β tends toward infinity.
23. No. 187.
24. No. 187, conditions (188).
25. As shown by appendix figures 2.6 and 2.8 of no. 184.
26. I.e., under conditions of collective land ownership.
27. These results confirm the remarks made in the fourth paragraph of no. 137.
28. No. 176.

(237)
$$\frac{a}{1+I} \leq a,$$

i.e.,

(238)
$$I \geq 0,$$

equality being attained in the case of storage. Thus the rate of interest would necessarily be positive or zero.[29]

(vi) Superior limitation of the rate of interest under private land ownership

The points made at the end of no. 192 bring out *the possibility of a limit superior to the rate of interest under conditions of private ownership of land, irrespective of State intervention on the capital market.*

This is basically because as the rate of interest rises, capital demand[30] is enabled to fall more rapidly than land wealth[31] and to fall below it, so that for certain interest rate levels it can become impossible for individuals to own all the land.

Perhaps this theoretical circumstance offers a possible explanation of why observed pure interest rates have always been normally less than 15%? The question deserves further study.

(vii) Social productivity and private land ownership

The model studied makes it possible to establish that maximization of social productivity is not feasible when land is privately owned.

From which it evidently follows that *absolute* Pareto-maximization of satisfactions can be achieved only if the technical interest rate is zero and hence land ownership is collective.

29. These points confirm the general analysis of no. 136.
30. Equal to the total supply of capital in the meaning of no. 39.
31. No. 177, equation (49).

5. State intervention (199)

(i) The nature of State intervention

The State can intervene in two different ways.

First, in the classical single-interest-rate context it can act on the equilibrium interest rate via its intervention on the capital market.[1]

Secondly, without itself owning or owing anything, it can still intervene at any point as intermediary between the savings sector and the production sector so as to bring about distinct rates of psychological and technical interest.[2]

The State policy most commonly met with embodies a combination of these two kinds of intervention.

In both cases the State intervenes neither as consumer nor as producer. *Its only role is to allow, at every point in time, certain flows of income either between the current generations or between the savings sector and the production sector.*

Its role is therefore neither more nor less than that of a catalyst enabling the realization of certain economic states such as those corresponding to the maximization of social productivity or those corresponding, for given social productivity, to a certain distribution of income between the young and the old, which without its intervention would not be possible.[3,4]

---

1. This is the action examined in no. 192.

2. This kind of intervention corresponds to the locus of the points for which the State's net wealth Δ is zero, i.e., to the equation

$$\Delta = \delta = \overline{u}\overline{U} = 0,$$

where δ has the value corresponding to equation (187) of no. 186.

3. Comparing the economic state of spontaneous equilibrium under private land ownership with one of the economic states corresponding to a certain State intervention, it is noticeable that in both cases the goods circuits are self-completing without State involvement whereas in the second case the value circuits are only completed thanks to State intervention. We may therefore conclude that in case of no State intervention the need for the value circuits to be complete excludes certain states, such as those of maximum social productivity, from coming about.

4. This role of catalyst is exceptionally well brought out by appendix figure 2.19 of no. 185 in which the State's action simply leads to a displacement, one relative to the other, of the curves C_0 and C_μ.

An economic regime of spontaneous competitive equilibrium with private land ownership, by the fact of fulfilling the double condition of a single interest rate and equal income flows between young and old, corresponds to only one of the two infinities of situations that can be realized for the psychological and technical structures considered.

It is noticeable from the example given[5] that there are in fact no grounds for preferring the stationary conditions corresponding to spontaneous equilibrium under private land ownership[6]—indeed far from it. Such a stationary state is seen to be just one of the numerous possible equilibrium states, and the only objective factor by which it is in reality possible to distinguish between them emerges as being (a) the social productivity level and (b) the distribution of income between young and old that each respectively makes possible.

(ii) State policy

These findings show that *the State[7] may have a twofold objective, seeking either to increase social productivity or to modify the distribution of income effected by each generation between its young and its old.*

It can be seen at once, in view of the discussion of no. 194, that whatever the State's point of view as to the optimal distribution of aggregate output of A consumed by a generation between consumption A_0 of its youth and consumption A_1 of its elderly, the best solution can be obtained only if social productivity is first maximized and if the rate or rates of psychological interest are positive.[8]

Thus the only economically arbitrary element is the distribution of total consumption A, previously maximized, of each generation, between consumption A_0 of the young and consumption A_1 of the elderly, always supposing, of course, that psychological interest rates remain positive. Indeed this distribution can be determined only by criteria of an ethical or political nature.

5. No. 194, appendix fig. 2.29.

6. Corresponding to the absence of all State intervention, i.e., to laissez-faire.

7. Represented by its leaders.

8. Branch BQ of the curve of maximum physical productivity of appendix figure 2.29 in no. 194.

Practically speaking, the State's wish to bring about optimal social euphoria will lead it to effect a certain equivalence between satisfactions S_0^i and S_1^i, i.e., to maximize a certain function

(239) $$\Sigma = \sum (S_0^i, S_1^i) = \sum (A_0^i, A_1^i).$$ 9

Now as has been seen,[10] when a classical competitive economic regime is in force, with a single interest rate, and the State intervenes on the capital markets with a view to maximizing social productivity, it is not Σ that is maximized but satisfaction S_0^i.[11]

This makes it clear that maximization of function Σ requires further intervention on the part of the State, without prejudice either to social efficiency or to social productivity and tending to displace the economic equilibrium on the line of maximum social productivity by simple modification of the distribution of the income of each generation between its youth and its old age.

This intervention, which theoretically requires separation of the technical and psychological rates of interest, may in practical terms be envisaged, as has already been noted,[12] under two widely divergent forms.

The first would consist in maintaining in the spontaneous savings sector a psychological rate of interest differing from the zero rate of technical interest in place in the production sector.

In the case of the model studied, this assumption would give[13]

(240) $$A_1 = \alpha A_0 (1 + I_p),$$

and maximization of Σ for a given total consumption A corresponds to the conditions

(241) $\Sigma'_{A_0} = \Sigma'_{A_1}$, $A_0 + A_1 = A.$

9. It cannot be too strongly emphasized that any State whatever in practice tends by its action to maximize a certain function Σ. This is because simply adopting a certain pensions policy, for instance, already implicitly seeks to maximize a certain function Σ.

10. Nos. 192, 194, and 197, § i.

11. For in this case the economic state realized corresponds to point B on appendix figure 2.29, no. 194.

12. No. 77.

13. No. 186, equations (180) and (181).

This shows that it is possible to choose the psychological rate of interest I_p so that consumptions A_0 and A_1 satisfy equations (241), i.e., so that Σ is maximum. However, as has been pointed out,[14] to maintain a different rate of interest in the savings sector and in the production sector does not seem to be *rigorously* feasible except in an economy having collective ownership of the means of production.[15]

The second conceivable policy would consist in compulsory savings of a minimum amount levied by taxation. In our model this would be the case of a tax on the income of the young enabling the old to be guaranteed a consumption A_1 greater than under free savings. In this case the young, knowing without doubt that they will have this value available in their old age, would devote the whole of their income to present consumption. As has been noted, this solution is compatible with maintaining a single market interest rate throughout the economy and it is in fact practiced in the Western economies in the form of pension contributions.

In fact, it would amount to using for each individual a psychological interest rate I_p^i different from the technical interest rate, be it zero or otherwise, prevailing in the production system. This rate could not be other than the rate that, under conditions of free savings, would induce the individual in question to effect spontaneous savings equal to the compulsory savings. Naturally, this rate differs from one person to another.

14. No. 77, § "Possible modes of State intervention," and note 8 to no. 145, in particular.

15. Note, however, that the separation of the psychological and technical interest rates over a wide sector is only possible in an economy of private ownership, via a suitable tax on pure interest, whereas under collective land ownership the respective rates may be fixed at any level (note 8 to no. 145).

B. The Case of a Monetary Economy with No Propensity to Own

(a) Cash not depreciated over time

1. The economy studied (200)

For the sake of simplicity the foregoing study adopted the perspective of an account-based economy having no money. Let us now see *how its analysis must be modified for a case in which physical money circulates in the form of cash*.

Our analysis requires us once again to assume *collective land ownership*.

As conditions are assumed to be stationary, the account value of the unit of circulating money remains constant: we shall take it to be equal to 1.

We shall further assume that firms hold no money balances but that to balance their accounts, given that their different receipts and expenditures are not concomitant, the young need a money balance M^i and that the marginal liquidity premium, i.e., the marginal use-value of this balance, relative to a period T is for them

$$(242) \qquad\qquad l_M^i = \frac{\gamma x X^i}{M^i},$$

where $x X^i$ denotes the wages received and γ is a constant.[1]

Under these conditions the desired money balances M^i of each young person for an interest rate I are[2]

$$(243) \qquad\qquad M^i = \frac{\gamma x X^i}{I}.$$

This demand is thus proportional to wages $x X^i$ and inversely proportional to interest rate I. It therefore increases indefinitely as the rate of

---

1. It would be more in keeping with reality to assume that the liquidity premium is inversely proportional to the square of the money balance (note 12 to no. 82), but to simplify the calculations I have simply assumed inverse proportionality to the balance itself.
2. No. 82.

interest tends toward zero. This assumption agrees with the general analysis of demand for money.[3]

Hence the community's total desired money balance $M = \sum M^i$ is

(244)
$$M = \frac{\gamma x X}{I}.$$

The total money stock

(245)
$$M = \sum M^i$$

is assumed to be given.

---

3. An equation that is the counterpart to equation (3) of note 12 to no. 82. The specific function considered has been selected exclusively with a view to simplifying the calculations.

2. The conditions of competitive equilibrium (201)

Here equation (95) becomes

(246)
$$xX + uU + I\delta + \frac{M}{1+I} = aA_0 + \frac{aA_1}{1+I} + M,$$

since the young, *ex hypothesi*, obtain a total money balance M that is naturally available to them in their old age. This equation translates into

(247)
$$xX + uU + I\delta = aA_0 + \frac{aA_1}{1+I} + \frac{IM}{1+I},$$

[1]

which, in combination with equation (244) becomes

(248)
$$xX\left(1 - \frac{\gamma}{1+I}\right) + uU + I\delta = aA_0 + \frac{aA_1}{1+I},$$

while equation (96) becomes

(249)
$$aA = \frac{1+\alpha(1+I)}{1+\alpha}\left[xX\left(1 - \frac{\gamma}{1+I}\right) + uU + I\delta\right].$$

All the other equations already established remain unchanged[2] except of course equation (98), which becomes[3]

(250)
$$\frac{1+\alpha(1+I)}{1+\alpha}\left[1 + \frac{1+I}{\beta} + \left(\frac{I\delta}{xX} - \frac{\gamma}{1+I}\right)\right] = 2\left(1 + \frac{1}{\beta}\right)\frac{1+I}{2+I}.$$

---

1. This equation is simply the application to the specific case considered of equation (4), no. 82.

2. The equations numbered (6) in no. 82 in fact now become identical to those numbered (8) in the same numbered section. The liquidity premium in fact depends only on the labor input X^i; satisfaction S^i has been assumed to be entirely independent of it (no. 176).

3. This means that the representative curves (no. 192, appendix figs. 2.26 and 2.27) of functions $\overline{uU}, \overline{hH}, A_0, A_1, A, a, u, S_0,$ and S_1 of interest rate I remain unchanged. Only the representative curves of functions δ and Δ and the noteworthy values of the rate of interest are changed.

3. The circuit of values (202)

The circuit of values now becomes as shown in appendix figure 2.31.

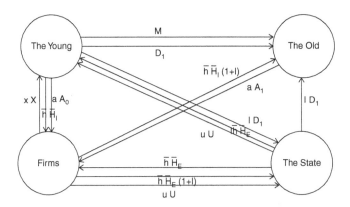

APPENDIX FIGURE 2.31 Circuit of values under collective land ownership and use of money

Supply and demand of capital

If we note that the total supply of capital by individuals remains equal to

(251)
$$C_0(I) = \frac{aA_1}{1+I},$$

but that their net supply to the market is only

$$C_0(I) - C_M(I) = C_0(I) - \frac{M}{1+I},$$

since they have available during their old age purchasing power nominally equal to M in the form of a money balance, the present value of which is $C_M(I) = \frac{M}{1+I}$,[1] equations (74) and (100) of nos. 178 and 180 defining equilibria under private and collective land ownership now become

---

1. Monetary capital is here equal to $\frac{M}{1+I}$ and not to M as in no. 97 on account of the particular division of time into periods (T) here considered.

(252) $$C_\varphi(I) + C_\mu(I) = C_0(I) - C_M(I) + \Delta$$ [2]

and

(253) $$C_\mu(I) = C_0(I) - C_M(I) + \delta$$

or indeed

(254) $$C_\varphi(I) + C_\mu(I) = C_0(I) - \frac{\gamma x X}{I(1+I)} + \Delta$$

and

(255) $$C_\mu(I) = C_0(I) - \frac{\gamma x X}{I(1+I)} + \delta,$$

where functions $C_\varphi(I)$, $C_\mu(I)$, and $C_0(I)$ have the same values as before.[3] Needless to say, as can be easily confirmed, equation (253) is equivalent to equation (250) and can be substituted for it.

---

2. An equation comparable to equation (1) of no. 97 corresponding to a zero value for Δ.
3. No. 185.

4. Conditions of validity of the solutions (203)

Conditions (81) and (83) of no. 179 of course remain unchanged,[1] but we now necessarily have

(256) $$I > 0.$$

For it is inconceivable that the equilibrium interest rate should be negative given that at equilibrium the various financial investments must have equal value-yields and from equation (242) of no. 200 investment in money enables a positive rate of interest to be guaranteed.

Moreover, as the capital owned by individuals cannot fall below the value M of their total money balances,[2] the total capital (to the exclusion of land) δ owned by the State, cannot, *while land is collectively owned*, become greater than the value $C_\mu = \overline{h}\overline{H}$ of total reproducible capital, so that the equilibrium interest rate must satisfy the condition

(257) $$\delta \leq \overline{h}\overline{H}$$

or, in other terms, the condition

(258) $$C_M(I) \leq C_0(I),$$

an equation corresponding to the limit of feasible states for cases where money is used and land ownership is collective.

When land is privately owned, this condition becomes

(259) $$\delta \leq \overline{h}\overline{H} - \overline{u}\overline{U},$$

i.e.,

(260) $$C_\varphi + C_M \leq C_0,$$

an equation corresponding to the limit of feasible states for cases where money is used and land ownership is private.

---

1. See nos. 179 and 186.
2. No. 136, § 2.

5. General discussion (204)

The general discussion is exactly identical to that set out for moneyless conditions,[1] function $C_0(I)$ being now replaced by the net supply of capital

(261)
$$C_{on}(I) = C_0(I) - \frac{\gamma x X}{I(1+I)}.$$

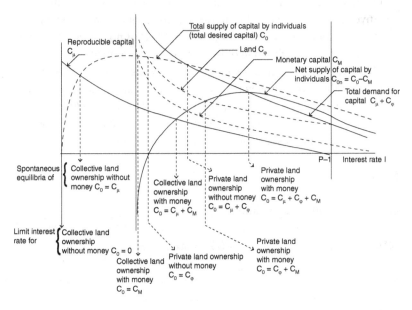

APPENDIX FIGURE 2.32

It is clear that, whatever the values of parameters δ and Δ may be, *the use of money has the effect of raising all interest rate levels corresponding to stable equilibria* as well as the limit inferior beneath which the interest rate cannot fall under private land ownership.[2] The rise is greater as the propensity for liquidity[3] is greater.

1. No. 185.

2. These results confirm in particular what is said in no. 97 and the arrangement of the figure 8.13 in that numbered section.

3. Represented by the coefficient γ.

The case of low values of coefficient γ

As coefficient γ tends toward zero, the level of the equilibrium interest rate corresponding to spontaneous equilibrium and private land ownership, and the level of the interest rate corresponding to the limit of states realizable under private land ownership tend through superior values toward the values found above for moneyless conditions.

The same applies to the rate corresponding to spontaneous equilibrium and collective land ownership when there is no money and the rate is positive. Should it be negative, however, the equilibrium rate tends towards zero.[4]

Finally, as coefficient γ tends toward zero, the level of the rate of interest corresponding to the limit of states realizable under collective land ownership tends toward zero through positive values.

4. It is noteworthy that in the case of the specific structure defined in no. 187, the value toward which the spontaneous equilibrium interest rate tends, under collective land ownership when money is used, as the coefficient γ tends toward zero, is not equal to the value –0.62 of the spontaneous equilibrium interest rate under collective land ownership and moneyless conditions.

6. Study of a specific case (205)

Greater clarity may be obtained by studying a specific case, for instance, one in which

(262) $\alpha = 1.5,$ $\beta = 4,$ $\gamma = 1,$

where α and β have the same values as in the specific case already examined for the general moneyless hypothesis.[1]

The noteworthy values of the rate of interest are as follows:

(i) The value corresponding to spontaneous equilibrium[2]
under collective land ownership

This value corresponds to a zero value for capital δ, i.e., from equation (250), to the condition

(263) $$\frac{1+\alpha(1+I)}{1+\alpha}\left(1-\frac{\gamma}{1+I}+\frac{1+I}{\beta}\right)=2\left(1+\frac{1}{\beta}\right)\frac{1+I}{2+I}.$$

For the (262) values above for coefficients α, β, and γ this condition is expressed as

(264) $3I^4 + 29I^3 + 29I^2 - 29I - 40 = 0.$

This equation admits only one positive root that answers the question, and its value is

(265) $I \sim 1.$

---

1. No. 187.

2. I.e., corresponding to the absence of any State economic intervention apart from collective land ownership.

(ii) The value corresponding to the limit of states realizable under collective land ownership

From the conclusions of no. 203 this limit corresponds to the equation

(266)
$$\delta = \bar{h}\bar{H},$$

i.e., in combinations with conditions (48) and (250), to the equation

(267)
$$\frac{1+\alpha(1+I)}{1+\alpha}\left[1-\frac{\gamma}{1+I}+\frac{1+I}{\beta}+\left(1-\frac{1+I}{\beta}\right)\frac{1}{2+I}\right]=2\left(1+\frac{1}{\beta}\right)\frac{1+I}{2+I},$$

i.e.,

(268)
$$\frac{1+\alpha(1+I)}{1+\alpha}\left[\frac{1}{\beta}-\frac{1}{\beta(2+I)}+\frac{2}{2+I}\right]-2\left(1+\frac{1}{\beta}\right)\frac{1+I}{2+I}$$

$$-\frac{1+\alpha(1+I)}{1+\alpha}\frac{\gamma}{(1+I)^2}=0$$

or again

(269)
$$2\alpha\left(1+\frac{1}{\beta}\right)I(1+I)^2-\gamma(2+I)[1+\alpha(1+I)]=0$$

or, finally, for the (262) values of α, β, and γ,

(270)
$$15I^3+24I^2-7I-20=0.$$

As the reader may readily verify, this equation admits only one positive root, little different from 0.8, and condition (257) is equivalent to the condition

$$I \geq 0.8.$$

*(iii) The value corresponding to spontaneous equilibrium under
private land ownership*

This value corresponds, as has been seen, to a zero value for net State
wealth Δ, i.e., from condition (44) to the condition $\delta = -\bar{u}\bar{U}$. In combination with equations (49) and (250) this condition gives

(271)
$$\frac{1+\alpha(1+I)}{1+\alpha}\left(1-\frac{\gamma}{1+I}\right)=2\left(1+\frac{1}{\beta}\right)\frac{1+I}{2+I}$$

or, for the (262) values of coefficients α, β, and γ,

(272)
$$12I^3 - 6I^2 - 60I - 50 = 0.$$

This equation has only one positive root that answers the question, and
its value is

(273)
$$I \sim 2.7.$$

*(iv) The value corresponding to the limit of states realizable under
private land ownership*

In light of condition (259) this value corresponds to the condition $\delta = \bar{h}\bar{H} - \bar{u}\bar{U}$, in other terms, from equations (48), (49), and (250) to condition

(274)
$$\frac{1+\alpha(1+I)}{1+\alpha}\left[1-\frac{\gamma}{1+I}+\left(1-\frac{1+I}{\beta}\right)\frac{I}{2+I}\right]=2\left(1+\frac{1}{\beta}\right)\frac{1+I}{2+I},$$

i.e., finally, for the (262) values of coefficients α, β, and γ,

(275)
$$3I^4 + 29I^3 + 23I^2 - 45I - 50 = 0.$$

Readers will have no difficulty in verifying that this equation has only
one positive root that answers the question and that its value is

(276)
$$I \sim 1.25,$$

while condition (259) is equivalent to the condition

$$I \geq 1.25.$$

7. The price level (206)

For a state of equilibrium defined by a given value of the rate of interest I to which there corresponds, from equation (250), a certain value of the State's capital (excluding land), the price level is determined by the relation

(277)
$$x = \frac{MI}{\gamma X},$$
[1]

which fixes the level x of the unitary wage.

---

1. Equation (244) above.

8. Social efficiency (207)

Equations (13), (24), (25), and (28) of no. 177 remain unchanged in the present case, so there is no loss in social efficiency. Only the distribution of consumable income is modified owing to the use of circulating money.

It must be stressed, however, that this is *exclusively* due to the assumptions made as to the liquidity functions (no money held by firms and specific forms of the liquidity function [242] and the satisfaction functions).[1,2]

---

1. See what was said above in note 2 to no. 201.
2. See no. 104.

9. Economic interpretation of the results obtained (208)

The foregoing analysis has enabled us to establish that

(i) Whether land ownership be collective or private, the stationary equilibrium conditions corresponding to the absence of State intervention ($\delta = 0$ or $\Delta = 0$ depending on the case) are well determined; when the State intervenes, a further degree of freedom is introduced and there are an infinity of possible stationary states corresponding to the psychological and technical structure in question, each of these states corresponding to a different capital equipment stock and a different rate of interest.

(ii) When the propensity for liquidity[1] remains relatively weak, the equilibrium interest rate of an economy having private land ownership may *as a first approximation* be regarded as independent of monetary conditions — prices settling at a level such that the sum of individual desired money balances, itself a function of the rate of interest and proportional to the general price level, is precisely equal to the total volume of money.[2]

(iii) *As a second approximation* the equilibrium interest rate under private land ownership depends on the propensity for liquidity and it is so much the higher as this propensity is greater, but in any event the interest rate is independent of money stock M.

(iv) When land is collectively owned, the use of cash whose value remains constant in wage terms prevents the equilibrium interest rate not only from falling to zero, but even from falling — irrespective of State intervention — below a certain floor value, meaning that the use of money of constant wage-denominated value constitutes a sufficient condition for the rate of interest not to have low positive values.[3]

(v) As a general rule the use of money that does not depreciate over time has the effect of moving (a) the interest rate levels corresponding to stable equilibria and (b) the limit inferior beneath which the interest rate cannot fall when land is privately owned to higher values than they would have in the absence of such money — this circumstance being explained by

---

1. Here represented by the coefficient γ.
2. No. 97.
3. No. 136, § 2.

the fact that owning money partially satisfies the propensity to save and to that extent diminishes real investment $\overline{H}$.[4]

(vi) In an economy in which land is in private hands and money is used that does not lose value over time, the fact that the rate of interest is not only always positive but indeed always superior, irrespective of State intervention, to a certain minimum, is due to the combination of private land ownership and the use of circulating money of constant wage value.[5]

4. See note 20 to no. 198 concerning private land ownership.
5. It may be worth mentioning that the increase in the rate of interest arising from these circumstances in combination is less than the sum of the increases arising from each factor considered in isolation. The results obtained are summarized in appendix table 2.5.

These circumstances are connected with the stability of the equilibrium.

APPENDIX TABLE 2.5 FOOTNOTE

Economic Conditions	Variation of the Rate of Interest	
	Limit	Spontaneous Equilibrium
Private land ownership	$0.58 - (-1) = 1.58$	$1.2 - (-0.62) = 1.82$
Use of money of constant value in wage terms	$0.8 - (-1) = 1.8$	$1 - (-0.62) = 1.62$
Combination of the above	$1.25 - (-1) = 2.25$	$2.7 - (-0.62) = 3.32$

(b) Circulating money depreciated over time

1. Conditions of equilibrium (209)

Let N be the number of cash units in circulation at point t, and $\overline{m}_t$ their unit value. Their aggregate value is

(278) $$M_t = N_t \overline{m}_t.$$

Let us assume that from one period (T) to another each unit loses a fraction d of its value, giving us

(279) $$\overline{m}_{t+T} = (1 - d)\overline{m}_t.$$

Assuming next that the nominal value M of the money stock is held constant, we obtain

(280) $$N_{t+T}\overline{m}_{t+T} = N_t \overline{m}_t.$$

In view of equation (279) this equation shows that the State must issue during each period T a quantity

(281) $$N_{t+T} - N_t = dN_{t+T}$$

of circulating money of value

(282) $$(N_{t+T} - N_t)\overline{m}_{t+T} = dM.$$

The consequence for the State is therefore a net receipt dM that we assume to be paid to the young by way of land rent. Under these conditions, equation (246) of no. 201 now becomes

(283) $$xX + uU + I\delta + \frac{N_t \overline{m}_t (1-d)}{1+I} + dM = aA_0 + \frac{aA_1}{1+I} + N_t \overline{m}_t,$$

since the N currency units obtained by individuals in their youth at price $\overline{m}_t$ are worth only $(1 - d)\overline{m}_t$ in their old age.

This equation is written

(284) $$xX + uU + I\delta = aA_0 + \frac{aA_1}{1+I} + (1-d)\frac{IM}{1+I}.$$

Let us now suppose once again that

(285) $$l_M = \frac{\gamma x X}{M}.$$ 1

As we have

(286) $$l_M = \frac{m}{\overline{m}}$$ 2

and

(287) $$\overline{m}_t = \frac{m_{t+T}}{1+I} + \frac{\overline{m}_{t+T}}{1+I},$$ 3

from equation (231) we have

(288) $$\frac{1}{1-d} = \frac{l_M}{1+I} + \frac{1}{1+I},$$

i.e.,

(289) $$l_M = \frac{I+d}{1-d},$$

which gives us for the total demand for money balances

(290) $$M = \gamma x X \frac{1-d}{I+d},$$

1. Since all the young behave identically, we have

$$\frac{X^i}{M^i} = \frac{X}{M}.$$

2. No. 82, equation (10).
3. No. 33, equation (0).

an equation that reduces to equation (244) for $d = 0$.

Under these conditions equation (283) is written

$$(291) \qquad xX + uU + I\delta = aA_0 + \frac{aA_1}{1+I} + \frac{(1-d)^2}{I+d}\frac{I}{1+I}\gamma xX,$$

and equation (250) now becomes

$$(292) \qquad \frac{1+\alpha(1+I)}{1+\alpha}\left[1 - \frac{\gamma(1-d)^2 I}{(I+d)(1+I)} + \frac{1+I}{\beta} + \frac{I\delta}{xX}\right] = 2\left(1+\frac{1}{\beta}\right)\frac{1+I}{2+I},$$

i.e., eliminating the erroneous solution $I = 0$

$$(293) \qquad \frac{1+\alpha(1+I)}{1+\alpha}\left[\frac{\delta}{xX} - \frac{\gamma(1-d)^2}{(I+d)(1+I)}\right] + \frac{\alpha}{1+\alpha}\left(1+\frac{1+I}{\beta}\right) + \frac{1}{\beta} - \frac{I+\frac{1}{\beta}}{2+I} = 0,$$

an equation that defines the link between the rate of interest and the capital δ owned by the State, to the exclusion of land, for every value of rate d of money devaluation. All the other equations remain unchanged.

Supply and demand of capital

If we observe that the value of the money holding of the elderly is

$$(294) \qquad \frac{M(1-d)}{1+I} = \frac{\gamma(1-d)^2}{(1+I)(I+d)},$$

equations (254) and (255) now become

$$(295) \qquad C_\varphi(I) + C_\mu(I) = C_0(I) - \frac{\gamma(1-d)^2}{(1+I)(I+d)} + \Delta$$

and

$$(296) \qquad C_\mu(I) = C_0(I) - \frac{\gamma(1-d)^2}{(1+I)(I+d)} + \delta.$$

This last equation is equivalent to equation (293).

Discussion

Curve $C_M(I)$ instead of admitting the line of the ordinates as asymptote, admits instead the vertical of the abscissa

$$I = -d.$$

Readers will have no difficulty in verifying that all values of the rate of interest corresponding to stable equilibria as well as the limit beneath which the rate of interest cannot fall, being identical to those already found[4] for $d = 0$, are decreasing functions of rate d.[5]

Condition (256) now translates into

(297) $I \geq -d,$

but condition (257) under conditions of collective land ownership has the effect of maintaining the rate of interest at levels that, irrespective of State policy, are greater than a certain minimum, which is itself greater than $-d$.

As the rate of depreciation tends toward unity, readers will have no difficulty in verifying that all values of the rate of interest corresponding to stable equilibria as well as its floor value tend either toward $-d$ or toward the values that would correspond to moneyless conditions, depending on whether or not these values are lower than $-d$.

The case of a continuous price increase

The final example to be studied corresponds to the case in which nominal prices are wage-denominated prices and money is depreciated in wage terms, the circulating currency being dissociated from the accounting currency.

No difficulty will be found in verifying that the equations obtained remain identical under quasi-stationary conditions[6] such that the unit of account being taken as equal to the unit of circulating money, nominal prices increase by $d\%$ per unit of time, provided that prices $a, \bar{h}, h, \bar{u}$, and u are

4. No. 205.
5. This is particularly evident from the geometric standpoint, curve C_M being lowered and curve C_{0n} being raised.
6. Nos. 69 and 97.

wage-denominated prices and that interest rate I is the rate of interest expressed in wage terms.[7]

It then becomes clear that the various noteworthy values of the rate of interest are lowered or raised under semi-stationary conditions depending on whether prices are moving upward or downward. The case of a very swift price increase naturally corresponds to the case in which the preceding rate d is very close to unity.

---

7. Equal to the various real rates of interest under quasi-stationary conditions.

2. Economic interpretation of the results obtained (210)

The results obtained enable us to verify that

(i) the depreciation of money lowers levels of the interest rate corresponding to stable equilibria as well as the limit inferior beneath which the rate of interest cannot fall;

(ii) under quasi-stationary conditions the various noteworthy values of the rate of interest are decreasing functions of the relative rate of price rise.[1]

1. No. 97.

(c) Simultaneous use of cash and deposit money

1. Conditions assumed (211)

Let us now assume that conditions are still stationary but that individuals make use not only of cash but also of deposit money.

It will be assumed, in conformity with the general analysis, that cash and demand deposit money are *practically substitutable one for the other*, yet not quite so.[1] Reprising the notations of nos. 94, 95, and 99[2] this means that the liquidity premiums l_{MA}^i and l_S^i of cash and deposit money for a given individual depend mainly on the sum $M^i = M_{MA}^i + M_S^i$ of his cash and deposit money, and relatively little on the quantities M_{MA}^i and M_S^i. To simplify our calculations we shall take it that

$$(298) \qquad l_{MA}^i = \frac{\gamma x X^i}{(M^i)^{1-u}(M_{MA}^i)^u},$$

$$(299) \qquad l_S^i = \frac{\varphi x X^i}{(M^i)^{1-u}(M_S^i)^u},$$

where γ and φ are constants and exponent u has a low value.

---

1. Note 1 to no. 91.

2. It is indispensable for the reader to review those numbered sections if he is to grasp the succinct analysis presented in the present number.

2. Conditions of the equilibrium (212)

In view of what has been said in no. 94, we have in equilibrium

(300)
$$\frac{\gamma x X}{M^{1-u} M_{MA}^{u}} = I,$$

(301)
$$\frac{\varphi x X}{M^{1-u} M_{S}^{u}} = \kappa I.$$

For the ratio ρ between deposit money and cash[1] we therefore have

(302)
$$\rho = \frac{M_S}{M_{MA}} = \left(\frac{\varphi}{\kappa\gamma}\right)^{\frac{1}{u}},$$

which is thus constant[2] and for total money holdings we have

(303)
$$M = M_{MA} + M_S = \gamma(1+\rho)^u \frac{xX}{I}.$$

It is thus evident that for each value of rate I total money demand is greater than it would be if there were no deposit money ($M_S = 0$).

In view of the low value assumed for u, a simple discussion shows that total money balances can only be significantly independent[3] of the propensity to hold deposit money[4] if

(304)
$$\frac{\varphi}{\kappa\gamma} \sim 1. \qquad\qquad\qquad\qquad 5$$

1. I am using ρ here to designate this ratio, rather than α as in no. 99, in order to avoid any confusion with the coefficient α as used elsewhere in this appendix.

2. This is the assumption of no. 99, equation (14).

3. Note 10 to no. 99. Of course, in reality this independence is due, as we have seen, to reasons entirely different from those of this equation (304), but the reasons for which total money holdings are substantially independent of whether or not deposit money is used have no relevance to what follows.

4. Represented by the coefficient φ and hence by the coefficient o, for given values of coefficients γ and κ.

5. I stress that in view of the low value for coefficient u this condition does not imply that coefficient o is close to unity.

The young leave on deposit in the banks an overall sum of $M_S = M_{MB} + (M_S - M_{MB})$ composed of (a) a sum M_{MB} of cash and (b) a sum $(M_S - M_{MB})$ corresponding to bills presented for discount.[6]

For their deposits, the young receive from the banks interest payments amounting to

$$\textbf{(305)} \qquad\qquad M_S i_D = (1 - \kappa)I M_S,$$

but they pay into the banks by way of discount a sum amounting to

$$\textbf{(306)} \qquad\qquad (M_S - M_{MB})I,$$

which is equal to it, since we have[7]

$$\textbf{(307)} \qquad\qquad M_{MB} = \kappa M_S.$$

From this it is clear that young individuals need to obtain a total sum

$$\textbf{(308)} \qquad\qquad M_M = M_{MA} + M_{MB}$$

of cash devoted (a) to building their cash holding M_{MA} and (b) to contributing in the amount M_{MB} to the total M_S of their deposits.[8] This total sum M_M will come back to them in the shape of receipts when they are old and in their turn cede their cash reserves to the young. The equation representing their budget is thus written

$$\textbf{(309)} \qquad xX + uU + I\delta + \frac{M_M}{1+I} = aA_0 + \frac{aA_1}{1+I} + M_M.$$

In view of the equation

$$\textbf{(310)} \qquad\qquad M_M = \frac{1+\kappa\rho}{1+\rho}M$$

obtained by eliminating M_M, M_{MA}, and M_{MB} from equations (302), (303), (307), and (308), equation (250) now becomes

---

6. No. 95.

7. No. 99, equation (6).

8. The other part of M being composed of an amount $(M_S - M_{ML})$ of discounted bills.

(311) $$\frac{1+\alpha(1+I)}{1+\alpha}\left(1-\frac{\gamma_1}{1+I}+\frac{1+I}{\beta}+\frac{I\delta}{xX}\right)=2\left(1+\frac{1}{\beta}\right)\frac{1+I}{2+I},$$

when we write that

(312) $$\gamma_1=\frac{1+\kappa\rho}{1+\rho}(1+\rho)^u\gamma.$$

Supply and demand of capital

Of course, equations (254) and (255) now become

(313) $$C_\varphi(I)+C_\mu(I)=C_0(I)-\gamma_1\frac{xX}{I(1+I)}+\Delta$$

and

(314) $$C_\mu(I)=C_0(I)-\gamma_1\frac{xX}{I(1+I)}+\delta,$$

since we now have

(315) $$C_M=\frac{M_M}{1+I}=\frac{1+\kappa\rho}{1+\rho}\frac{M}{1+I}=\frac{1+\kappa\rho}{1+\rho}(1+\rho)^u\frac{\gamma xX}{I(1+I)}.$$

Equation (314) is of course equivalent to equation (311) and can be substituted for it.

Discussion

If we note that for low values of coefficient u and for values of the ratio $\frac{1+\kappa\rho}{1+\rho}$ similar to those commonly observed,[9] coefficient γ_1 is certainly less than coefficient γ, it is clear that for a given value of coefficient γ it is possible to pass from the use of cash alone to the case we are considering in which cash and deposit money are both found, by replacing coefficient γ in equation (250) by the *lower* coefficient γ_1. As interest rate levels corresponding to stable equilibria as well as the limit inferior beneath which

9. I.e., lying between 4/5 and 1/8 (note 11 to no. 99).

the interest rate cannot fall are, in the cash-only model increasing functions of coefficient γ,[10] it is verified that introducing credit has the effect of lowering these values.

It is also verified that, in view of our assumptions regarding coefficients u, κ, and φ,[11] extensive use of deposit money (significant value for ρ) in combination with a low value for liquidity ratio κ,[12] leads, for stable equilibrium interest rate levels and for the interest rate's limit inferior, to values that differ little from those that would prevail in an account-based (moneyless) economy, or to zero, depending on whether these values are positive or negative.[13]

Price level

The price level is given, in view of equations (303), (310), and (312) by the equation

$$(316) \qquad\qquad x_1 = \frac{I_1 M_M}{\gamma_1 X},$$

where I_1 satisfies condition (311), whereas in the absence of deposit money it would be given by the equation

$$(317) \qquad\qquad x = \frac{I M_M}{\gamma X},$$

where I satisfies condition (250).

This gives us

$$(318) \qquad\qquad \frac{x_1}{x} = \frac{\gamma I_1}{\gamma_1 I}.$$

---

10. No. 204.

11. Which are necessarily implied by the general properties of cash and deposit money (nos. 91 and 99).

12. A combination to which there corresponds a low value of γ_1.

13. No. 204, § "The case of low values of coefficient γ."

Now, in view of condition (250), it is easy to show that as coefficient γ decreases, the ratio $\dfrac{I}{\gamma}$ increases,[14] so that we have

(319) $x_1 > x.$

Thus the effect of using deposit money is to raise the price level to a value greater than it would have if only cash were used.[15]

---

14. Suffice it to verify for the moment that for $\alpha = \dfrac{3}{2}$, $\beta = 4$, $\delta = 0$, and $\gamma = 1$, we have $I \sim 1$ (no. 205, equation [265]), i.e., $\dfrac{I}{\gamma} \sim 1$, whereas for $\alpha = \dfrac{3}{2}$, $\beta = 4$, $\delta = 0$, and I and γ very low, we have $\dfrac{I}{\gamma} \sim \dfrac{8}{3}$ (no. 201, equation [250]).

15. It is important to emphasize that the fall in the interest rate and the rise in the price level brought about in our model by the use of money are basically due to the assumptions made of the almost perfect substitutability between cash and deposit money and of the almost perfect independence of the total demand for money balances in relation to the propensity φ to hold deposit money. Hence readers may easily verify that if we had

$$l^i_{MA} = \frac{\gamma x X^i}{M^i_{MA}}, \qquad l^i_S = \varphi \frac{x X^i}{M^i_S},$$

i.e., if cash and deposit money were *independent* goods, it would be necessary to replace the coefficient γ_1 in the above results by the coefficient

$$\gamma_2 = \gamma + \varphi$$

greater than coefficient γ.

In which case the interest rate and the price level would be respectively raised and lowered instead of lowered and raised.

This demonstrates the importance of the general properties of cash and deposit money relative to the deductions reached concerning the influence of credit on the rate of interest and the price level.

3. The case of rediscount by a central bank (213)

Let E be the amount of bills rediscounted by the Central Bank.[1] Young individuals need now obtain only the amount $(M_M - E)$ of cash, since the sum E of cash is guaranteed by the agency of rediscount without any need for individuals to own it.

It follows that equation (309) is now written

(320) $$xX + uU + I\delta + \frac{M_M - E}{1+I} = aA_0 + \frac{aA_1}{1+I} M_M - E,$$

the other equations remaining unchanged.

It is notable that we now also have

(321) $$M_M = \frac{1+\kappa\rho}{1+\rho} M$$
$$= \frac{1+\kappa\rho}{1+\rho}(1+\rho)^u \gamma \frac{xX}{I}$$
$$= \gamma_1 \frac{xX}{I},$$

so that equation (311) of no. 212 now becomes

(322) $$\frac{1+\alpha(1+I)}{1+\alpha}\left(1 - \frac{\gamma_1}{1+I} + \frac{I}{1+I}\frac{E}{xX} + \frac{1+I}{\beta} + \frac{I\delta}{xX}\right) = 2\left(1 + \frac{1}{\beta}\right)\frac{1+I}{2+I}.$$

The circuit of values

The circuit of values remains as shown in appendix figure 2.31 of no. 202 with the single exception that for flow M of that figure flow $(M_M - E)$ must be substituted, while the following circuits should be added, corresponding to discount carried out both by the banks and by the Central Bank, and to the interest payments made by the banks to their depositors.

---

1. I shall be using the notations of nos. 95 and 99 of which readers are invited to refresh their memory to ensure that they clearly grasp the following analysis.

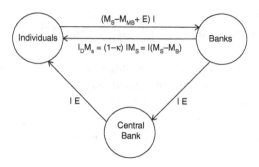

These new flows are self-contained and call for no modification to equation (320) expressing the budget of the individuals.

Supply and demand of capital

As pointed out in no. 95,[2] the equation expressing the equality of demands and supplies of capital now becomes

$$(323) \qquad C_\varphi(I) + C_\mu(I) = C_0(I) - \frac{(M_M - E)}{1+I} + \Delta$$

or

$$(324) \qquad C_\mu(I) = C_0(I) - \frac{(M_M - E)}{1+I} + \delta,$$

depending on whether land is privately or collectively owned.

In light of equations (321), these conditions are now expressed as

$$(325) \qquad C_\varphi(I) + C_\mu(I) = C_0(I) - \gamma_1 \frac{xX}{I(1+I)} + \frac{E}{1+I} + \Delta$$

and

2. Equation (1).

$$(326) \quad C_\mu(I) = C_0(I) - \frac{\gamma_1 xX}{I(1+I)} + \frac{E}{1+I} + \delta.$$

Of course, readers can readily verify that this last equation is equivalent to equation (322).

Price level

From equations (321), we naturally have

$$(327) \quad x = \frac{IM_M}{\gamma_1 X}$$

or, if we continue to use A to denote the amount of cash ($M_M - E$) *in existence (excluding all rediscount)*,

$$(328) \quad x = \frac{A+E}{\gamma_1 X} I.$$

Effects of rediscount

It is clear that as the volume of rediscount increases the price level rises, becoming infinite for an infinite rediscount volume.

In light of equation (327), equations (325) and (326) now become

$$(329) \quad C_\varphi(I) + C_\mu(I) = C_0(I) - \frac{A\gamma}{A+E} \frac{xX}{I(1+I)} + \Delta$$

and

$$(330) \quad C_\mu(I) = C_0(I) - \frac{A\gamma_1}{A+E} \frac{xX}{I(1+I)} + \delta.$$

This reveals that the introduction of discount has the effect of lowering the value of coefficient γ_1 and hence is equivalent to a decrease in the propensity for liquidity.

An implication worthy of note is that as the volume of rediscount increases indefinitely, the stable equilibrium values of the interest rate and the limit inferior of the interest rate tend either toward the values they would have under moneyless conditions when these values are positive,[3] or toward zero when they are negative.[4]

Stabilizing effect of the rate of discount

It is clear that if coefficients γ or φ vary, i.e., if coefficient γ_1 varies, it is possible to maintain the rate of interest at its previous level by varying the volume of rediscount so that the ratio $\dfrac{\gamma}{A+E}$ remains constant in value. Condition (327) shows that in this case the same policy also stabilizes the price level.

3. This is especially applicable to private land ownership.
4. No. 204, § "The case of low values of coefficient γ."

4. Economic interpretation of the results obtained (214)

In summary, the results obtained enable us to verify that, in light of the general properties of cash and deposit balances,

1. the use of deposit money has the effect of bringing stable equilibrium interest rate levels, and the limit inferior of the interest rate, to values closer to those that would prevail in the absence of any circulating money, or to zero, depending on whether these values are positive or negative, and of raising the price level to a higher value than it would have in a cash-only economy;
2. rediscount on the part of the Central Bank acts in the same direction as the extension of credit by the banks and accentuates its effects;
3. the greater or lesser extent of rediscounting by the Central Bank may provide a means, in the event of variation in the preference for liquidity, either as cash or as deposit money,[1] of stabilizing both the equilibrium interest rate and the price level.

---

1. Represented by coefficients γ and φ as before.

C. The Case of a Propensity to Own and to Bequeath

1. The economy studied (215)

Hitherto we have been assuming that the satisfaction functions depended only on consumptions and that inheritance did not exist.

It is worth determining what modifications need to be made to the results we have obtained when the satisfaction function involves owned goods, i.e., when we add to the satisfaction procured by consumption the satisfaction procured by ownership and when it becomes possible to bequeath.

The economy studied, *which we shall assume to be moneyless*, will be the same as that studied before except as to the following points:

It will be assumed that at the end of his old age Θ_1 each old person leaves each young person, by way of *legacy*, capital to the value C_1^i and it will be assumed that the satisfaction s_0^i of each young person takes the form

$$(331) \qquad s_0^i = \ln A_0^i + \alpha \ln A_1^i + \mu \ln \frac{C_1^i}{x},$$

where $\dfrac{C_1^i}{x}$ denotes the wage-denominated value of capital C_1^i and μ denotes a positive coefficient.

On these assumptions, the propensity to own is, strictly speaking, a propensity to bequeath, but readers will observe that all the following analysis can readily be extended to the case involving, for instance, the capital owned by the young at the end of period Θ_0.

With regard to the satisfaction s_1^i of the elderly, we shall assume that it takes the form

$$(332) \qquad s_1^i = \ln A_1^i + v \ln \frac{C_1^i}{x}.$$

As perfect foresight is assumed, the psychological link between consumption A_1^i and legacy C_1^i must be the same at point t_0 as at point t_1,[1] in other terms we must have

$$(333) \qquad\qquad \frac{\mu}{\alpha} = v.$$

As before, the discussion will address the case of *collective land ownership*.

---

1. A more detailed analysis of the necessary links between the different satisfactions of a single individual considered at different points in time under perfect foresight will be made further on (no. 219).

2. Conditions of competitive equilibrium (216)

If we use $\dfrac{C_0^i}{n}$ to denote the capital received by each young person at the end of his youth (Θ_0) and $\dfrac{C_1^i}{n}$ to denote the capital he bequeaths at the end of his old age, equation (95) now translates into

$$(334) \qquad C_0 + xX + uU + I\delta = aA_0 + \frac{aA_1}{1+I} + \frac{C_1}{1+I},$$

using C_0 and C_1 to denote the sums $\sum C_0^i$ and $\sum C_1^i$.

For total receipts of $\dfrac{C_0 + xX + uU + I\delta}{n}$ and prices a and I, which he takes as given, each young person divides his expenditure between his present consumption $\dfrac{A_0}{n}$, his future consumption $\dfrac{A_1}{n}$, and the legacy $C_1^i = \dfrac{C_1}{n}$ that he can bequeath to his legatee in such a way as to maximize his satisfaction s_0^i.

This being so, we must have

$$(335) \qquad \frac{\dfrac{\partial s_0^i}{\partial A_0^i}}{a} = \frac{\dfrac{\partial s_0^i}{\partial A_1^i}}{\dfrac{a}{1+I}} = \frac{\dfrac{\partial s_0^i}{\partial C_1^i}}{\dfrac{1}{1+I}},$$

equations that imply

$$(336) \qquad aA_1 = \alpha a A_0(1 + I),$$

$$(337) \qquad C_1 = \mu a A_0(1 + I).$$

As stationary conditions are assumed, equations (334) and (337) become

$$(338) \qquad xX + uU + I\delta + \frac{IC}{1+I} = aA_0 + \frac{aA_1}{1+I},$$

$$(339) \qquad C = \mu a A_0(1+I).$$

In combination with equation (20), equations (336), (338), and (339) now become

(340)
$$aA = \frac{1+\alpha(1+I)}{1+\alpha-\mu I}(xX + uU + I\delta),$$

(341)
$$C = \frac{\mu(1+I)aA}{1+\alpha(1+I)}.$$

At point T_1 the resources of the elderly are equal to

(342)
$$(1 + I)(C_0 + xX + uU + I\delta - aA_0),$$

and they divide them between their consumption A_1 and the bequeathed capital C_1, so as to maximize their satisfaction s_0^i in light of the condition

(343)
$$(1 + I)(C_0 + xX + uU + I\delta - aA_0) = aA_1 + C_1,$$

where the first member is assumed to be given. This condition yields

(344)
$$\frac{\dfrac{\partial s_1^i}{\partial A_1^i}}{a} = \frac{\dfrac{\partial s_1^i}{\partial C_1^i}}{1},$$

an equation that translates into

(345)
$$C_1 = vaA_1,$$

but this equation, already obtainable by combining conditions (336) and (337) with condition (333), introduces no new condition.

All the other equations hitherto found remain unchanged, except of course equation (98), which becomes

(346)
$$\frac{1+\alpha(1+I)}{1+\alpha-\mu I}\left(1+\beta+I+\frac{\beta\delta}{xX}I\right) = 2(1+\beta)\frac{1+I}{2+I},$$

from which

(347) $\delta = -\dfrac{xX}{\beta} \cdot \dfrac{\alpha I^2 + (1+4\alpha+\alpha\beta+2\mu+2\mu\beta)I + 1+3\alpha-\beta+\alpha\beta+2\mu+2\mu\beta}{(2+I)(1+\alpha+\alpha I)}.$

In light of equation (36), equation (341) becomes

(348)
$$\frac{c}{x} = 2\mu\left(1+\frac{1}{\beta}\right)X\frac{(1+I)^2}{[1+\alpha(1+I)](2+I)},$$

which finally gives us

(349)
$$s_0^i = S_0^i + \mu L\frac{C}{nx}$$

and

(350)
$$s_1^i = S_1^i + \frac{\mu}{\alpha}L\frac{C}{nx},$$

where S_0^i, S_1^i, and $\frac{C}{x}$ respectively have the values given by equations (40), (41), and (348).[1]

The circuit of values

The circuit of values now becomes as shown in appendix figure 2.34.

Supply and demand of capital

If we note that the supply of capital by individuals is now

(351)
$$C_0^I(I) = \frac{aA_1}{1+I} + \frac{C}{1+I},$$

i.e., in light of the equation $A_0 + A_1 = A$ and of conditions (336) and (341),

1. As we have

$$\frac{C}{x} = \frac{2\mu\left(1+\frac{1}{\beta}\right)X}{\left(1+\frac{1}{1+I}\right)\left(\alpha+\frac{1}{1+I}\right)},$$

it is clear that $\frac{C}{x}$ is a constantly increasing function of interest rate I, and that the maximum for function s_0^i, when it still exists, is reached for a positive interest rate I level greater than zero, for which function S_0^i was maximal.

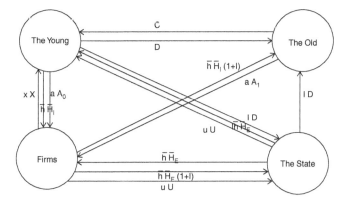

APPENDIX FIGURE 2.34

(352)
$$C_0^I(I) = \frac{\alpha a A}{1 + \alpha(1 + I)} + \mu \frac{aA}{1 + \alpha(1 + I)},$$

i.e., finally, in combination with equation (76),

(353)
$$C_0^I(I) = \left(1 + \frac{\mu}{\alpha}\right) C_0(I),$$

equations (74) and (79) of no. 178 defining the equilibria for private and collective land ownership are now written

(354)
$$C_\varphi(I) + C_\mu(I) = \left(1 + \frac{\mu}{\alpha}\right) C_0(I) + \Delta$$

and

(355)
$$C_\mu(I) = \left(1 + \frac{\mu}{\alpha}\right) C_0(I) + \delta,$$

where functions $C_\varphi(I)$, $C_\mu(I)$, and $C_0(I)$ have the same values as before.[2] Equation (355) is of course equivalent to equation (346), as it is easy to confirm, and can be substituted for it.

---

2. No. 185.

Conditions of validity of the solutions

Legacy C must be positive, but this condition is necessarily filled for all the envisaged values of I satisfying the condition that $1 + I > 0$.

Thus the conditions of validity of the solutions remain the same as in the previous case studied under collective land ownership.[3]

Discussion

The general discussion is absolutely identical to that carried out in the case with no money and no propensity to own or bequeath, the function $C_0(I)$ being simply replaced by the function

(356) $$C_0^I(I) = \left(1 + \frac{\mu}{\alpha}\right) C_0(I).$$

It is evident that the presence of a propensity to bequeath has the effect of lowering all levels of the interest rate corresponding to stable equilibria, as well as the limit inferior beneath which the interest rate cannot fall under conditions of private land ownership.

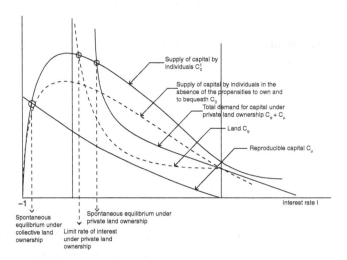

APPENDIX FIGURE 2.35

3. Appendix II, § A, "The Case of an Economy without Money or Propensity to Own."

3. The case of a double interest rate (217)

In this case, equations (340) and (341) become

(357) $$aA = \frac{1+\alpha(1+I_P)}{1+\alpha-\mu I_P}(xX +uU + I_P\delta),$$

(358) $$C = \frac{\mu(1+I_P)}{1+\alpha(1+I_P)}aA,$$

and equation (346) becomes

(359) $$\frac{1+\alpha(1+I_P)}{1+\alpha-\mu I_P}\left(1+\beta +I_T +\frac{\beta\delta I_P}{xX}\right)= 2(1+\beta)\frac{1+I_T}{2+I_T}.$$

Once again, we have two independent parameters that may be taken to be equal to I_P and I_T and to each set of values for these parameters there corresponds a determined value of capital (excluding land) δ owned by the State.

From equations (21), (22), (36), (37), and (358), we then have

(360) $$A_0 = \sqrt{KK''}\left(1+\frac{1}{\beta}\right)X\frac{1}{1+\alpha(1+I_P)}\frac{\sqrt{1+I_T}}{2+I_T},$$

(361) $$A_1 = \alpha\sqrt{KK''}\left(1+\frac{1}{\beta}\right)X\frac{1+I_P}{1+\alpha(1+I_P)}\frac{\sqrt{1+I_T}}{2+I_T},$$

(362) $$\frac{C}{x} = 2\mu\left(1+\frac{1}{\beta}\right)X\frac{1+I_P}{1+\alpha(1+I_P)}\frac{1+I_T}{2+I_T}.$$

It is then possible to define in the plane of (s_0^i, s_1^i), as in nos. 186 and 194, curves of equal rate of technical interest (equal productivity) and curves of equal psychological rate of interest.

Social efficiency and social productivity

Here once again there is a double infinity of (s_0^i, s_1^i) points, but as is easily confirmed, the curve limiting the double infinity of possible points no longer corresponds to the condition $I_T = 0$, in other words this condition is, in general, neither necessary nor sufficient for the satisfactions to be Pareto-maximal.

But this does not imply the detection of a flaw in the theorem of social productivity, for *the quest for a scenario representing an intrinsic physical optimum, independently of recourse to a price system, no longer has any meaning* given that the wage-denominated capital $\dfrac{C}{x}$ involved in the satisfactions is *not a physical concept* and can be defined only *in relation to a specific price system*. In other words, the theorem of social productivity is not at fault because the question it answers is no longer applicable to the case.

To seek a *physical* maximum of social productivity independently of any price system would make sense only if the functions s_0^i and s_1^i depended not on the value C of the capital bequeathed but, for instance, on the quantity $\overline{H}_l$ of the good $(\overline{H})$ bequeathed. This would be the case if we had

$$(363) \qquad s_0^i = \ln A_0^i + \alpha \ln A_1^i + \mu \ln \overline{H}^i,$$

$$(364) \qquad s_1^i = \ln A_1^i + v \ln \overline{H}^i.$$

Under these circumstances, it is evident that the satisfactions could only be physically Pareto-maximal if the quantity $\overline{H}^i$ bequeathed of good $\overline{H}$ was equal to its physically possible maximum $\dfrac{\overline{H}}{n}$ where $\overline{H}$ represents the total quantity of good $\overline{H}$ in existence in the economy. This would give us

$$(365) \qquad s_0^i = \ln A_0^i + \alpha \ln A_1^i + \mu \ln \dfrac{\overline{H}}{n},$$

$$(366) \qquad s_1^i = \ln A_1^i + v \ln \dfrac{\overline{H}}{n}.$$

It is clear that on this assumption Pareto-maximization of the satisfactions may correspond to a negative technical interest rate. This would be so if coefficients μ and v were great enough for the increment of satisfaction procured by using a capital $\overline{H}$ that was greater than the capital corresponding to the maximization of the physical productivity π of capital were greater than the decrease in satisfaction resulting from the corresponding decrease in consumable output $A_0 + A_1 = A$. All that could be said is that the technical interest rate now corresponding to the Pareto-maximization of the satisfactions would necessarily be negative, since as long as it is positive its decrease *enables* a parallel increase in capital used $\overline{H}$ and in consumable output $\overline{A}$ and hence a *simultaneous* increase in satisfactions s_0^i and s_1^i.

However, it is obvious that if storage is physically possible, the Pareto-maximization of the satisfactions would once again correspond to a zero rate of technical interest, the quantity of $\overline{H}$ stored becoming equal to the value at which its desirability becomes zero.

Finally, it can be seen that *in the case of a propensity to own and to bequeath, the theory of social productivity must be clarified and completed. In fact it only makes sense if the propensity to own or to bequeath involves physical quantities, not values, and insofar as it remains meaningful it subsists only if storage is possible. In this last case it remains desirable, for the sake of maximizing satisfactions in the meaning of Pareto, for the physical productivity of production processes to be maximal, i.e., for the technical interest rate to be zero.*

Illustration of the Generalized Theory of Social Efficiency

1. Illustration of the generalized theory of social efficiency by the study of a specific example (218)

The complete and rigorous demonstration of the theorem of generalized social efficiency calls for lengthy argumentation quite beyond the limited scope of the present study.

However, as the theorem cannot truly be understood without grasping the demonstration it is based on, I think it necessary at this point to set out that demonstration, such as it is, for the very elementary case of a *highly simplified economic model.*

2. The economy studied (219)

The economy we shall be studying is assumed to consist of two individuals α and β during two periods, T_1 and T_2, limited by the points t_0, t_1, and t_2.

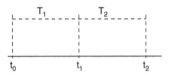

APPENDIX FIGURE 3.1

All economic operations are assumed to be concentrated at the ends of the periods and perfect foresight is assumed.

There are only two consumable services, A and B, obtained from fungible goods $\overline{A}$ and $\overline{B}$. The unit of service for each of them is taken to be equal to the quantity of service rendered per unit of time, which gives us

(1) $\qquad A_1 = \overline{A}_1, \qquad B_1 = \overline{B}_1, \qquad A_2 = \overline{A}_2, \qquad B_2 = \overline{B}_2,$

using $A_1, B_1, A_2, B_2, \overline{A}_1, \overline{B}_1, \overline{A}_2, \overline{B}_2$ to denote the quantities consumed and produced of services A and B and of goods $\overline{A}$ and $\overline{B}$ during periods T_1 and T_2.

Psychological structure

At points t_1 and t_2, the satisfactions S_1^α, S_1^β, S_2^α, and S_2^β of individuals α and β are assumed to take the form

(2) $\qquad\qquad\qquad S_1^\alpha = S_1^\alpha\,(A_1^\alpha, B_1^\alpha, A_2^\alpha, B_2^\alpha),$

(3) $\qquad\qquad\qquad S_1^\beta = S_1^\beta\,(A_1^\beta, B_1^\beta, A_2^\beta, B_2^\beta),$

(4) $\qquad\qquad\qquad S_2^\alpha = S_2^\alpha\,(A_1^\alpha, B_1^\alpha, A_2^\alpha, B_2^\alpha),$

(5) $\qquad\qquad\qquad S_2^\beta = S_2^\beta\,(A_1^\beta, B_1^\beta, A_2^\beta, B_2^\beta);$

in other terms, the shape of the lines of indifference during the old age of individuals is assumed to depend, as is in fact generally the case, on their memory of their patterns of consumption during youth.[1]

It is easy to show that, with *foresight assumed to be perfect*, functions S_1 and S_2 are not independent. Let us consider, for example, functions S_1^α and S_2^α relative to individual α.

First, for given values of consumptions A_1^α and B_1^α, it is clear that if a combination $(A_2^\alpha B_2^\alpha)$ is preferred to a combination $(A_2^{\alpha'} B_2^{\alpha'})$ at point t_2 (satisfaction S_2^α) it will also be so preferred, in view of the perfect foresight, at point t_1 (satisfaction S_1^α). I.e., if for given consumptions A_1^α and B_1^α satisfaction S_2^α remains constant, the same applies to satisfaction S_1^α, and hence satisfaction S_1^α must be of the form

(6) $$S_1^\alpha = \sum\nolimits_1 (A_1^\alpha, B_1^\alpha, S_2^\alpha).$$

In the same way for given values of consumptions A_2^α and B_2^α it is clear that if a combination $(A_1^\alpha B_1^\alpha)$ is preferred at point t_1 (satisfaction S_1^α) to a combination $(A_1^{\alpha'} B_1^{\alpha'})$, the same combination will enable a higher level of satisfaction to be attained at point t_2 (satisfaction S_2^α).[2]

Which means that if for given values of consumptions A_2^α and B_2^α satisfaction S_1^α remains constant, the same must apply to satisfaction S_2^α, and hence satisfaction S_2^α must take the form

(7) $$S_2^\alpha = \sum\nolimits_2 (A_2^\alpha, B_2^\alpha, S_1^\alpha).$$

These conditions respectively give

(8) $$\frac{\dfrac{\partial S_1^\alpha}{\partial A_2^\alpha}}{\dfrac{\partial S_1^\alpha}{\partial B_2^\alpha}} = \frac{\dfrac{\partial S_2^\alpha}{\partial A_2^\alpha}}{\dfrac{\partial S_2^\alpha}{\partial B_2^\alpha}}$$

---

1. I am deliberately selecting here a structure somewhat more complicated than that considered in no. 60.

2. Thus if I know that next year I shall not be going on a skiing holiday but spending a fortnight at the seaside, and in the light of this knowledge I choose a fortnight's skiing this year instead of the seaside because I enjoy a change, it is certain that next year my seaside holiday will bring me a higher level of satisfaction for having chosen skiing this year instead.

The same factors that make me prefer one situation to another in the first year leave this scale of preference unchanged the second year.

and

$$(9) \qquad \frac{\dfrac{\partial S_1^\alpha}{\partial A_1^\alpha}}{\dfrac{\partial S_1^\alpha}{\partial B_1^\alpha}} = \frac{\dfrac{\partial S_2^\alpha}{\partial A_1^\alpha}}{\dfrac{\partial S_2^\alpha}{\partial B_1^\alpha}}.$$

These equations state that for a given present consumption the relative desirability of future consumptions is the same whether considered at point t_1 or t_2 and that for a given future consumption the relative desirability of present consumptions is the same whether considered at point t_1 or t_2. Moreover these properties may be considered to be directly derived from our introspection in the context of perfect foresight.[3,4]

These equations give

$$(10) \qquad \frac{\dfrac{\partial S_2^\alpha}{\partial A_2^\alpha}}{\dfrac{\partial S_1^\alpha}{\partial A_2^\alpha}} = \frac{\dfrac{\partial S_2^\alpha}{\partial B_2^\alpha}}{\dfrac{\partial S_1^\alpha}{\partial B_2^\alpha}} = \lambda^\alpha \, (A_1^\alpha, \, B_1^\alpha, \, A_2^\alpha, \, B_2^\alpha)$$

and

3. Of course conditions (6) and (7) or (8) and (9) do not imply that the functions S_1^α and S_2^α are identical or even that they depend on A_1^α, B_1^α, A_2^α, and B_2^α only by the intermediary of two functions $\varphi\,(A_1^\alpha, B_1^\alpha)$ and $\psi\,(A_2^\alpha, B_2^\alpha)$. For example, it may easily be verified that the functions

$$(1) \qquad S_1^\alpha = \frac{\sqrt{A_1^\alpha} + B_1^\alpha \sqrt{B_2^\alpha}}{1 - A_2^\alpha B_1^\alpha}, \qquad\qquad S_2^\alpha = \frac{A_2^\alpha \sqrt{A_1^\alpha} + \sqrt{B_2^\alpha}}{1 - A_2^\alpha B_1^\alpha}$$

satisfy the conditions

$$(2) \qquad\qquad\qquad S_1^\alpha = B_1^\alpha S_2^\alpha + \sqrt{A_1^\alpha},$$

$$(3) \qquad\qquad\qquad S_2^\alpha = A_2^\alpha S_1^\alpha + \sqrt{B_2^\alpha},$$

which are in fact of type (6) and (7).

4. Moreover, it would be a grave error to think that under perfect foresight the areas of indifference corresponding to the functions S_1 and S_2 must be absolutely identical.

Just because at time t_1 the individual has perfect knowledge of the psychology he will have at time t_2 and hence of the importance he will then attach to the consumptions of time t_1 relative to those of time t_2, it does not follow that he will adopt at time t_1 the same relative preference between present and future. Foreknowledge is not the same thing as fore-action.

$$
\textbf{(11)} \qquad \frac{\dfrac{\partial S_2^\alpha}{\partial A_1^\alpha}}{\dfrac{\partial S_1^\alpha}{\partial A_1^\alpha}} = \frac{\dfrac{\partial S_2^\alpha}{\partial B_1^\alpha}}{\dfrac{\partial S_1^\alpha}{\partial B_1^\alpha}} = \mu^\alpha \left(A_1^\alpha, B_1^\alpha, A_2^\alpha, B_2^\alpha \right).
$$

In the same way of course we also have

$$
\textbf{(12)} \qquad \frac{\dfrac{\partial S_2^\beta}{\partial A_2^\beta}}{\dfrac{\partial S_1^\beta}{\partial A_2^\beta}} = \frac{\dfrac{\partial S_2^\beta}{\partial B_2^\beta}}{\dfrac{\partial S_1^\beta}{\partial B_2^\beta}} = \lambda^\beta \left(A_1^\beta, B_1^\beta, A_2^\beta, B_2^\beta \right),
$$

$$
\textbf{(13)} \qquad \frac{\dfrac{\partial S_2^\beta}{\partial A_1^\beta}}{\dfrac{\partial S_1^\beta}{\partial A_1^\beta}} = \frac{\dfrac{\partial S_2^\beta}{\partial B_1^\beta}}{\dfrac{\partial S_1^\beta}{\partial B_1^\beta}} = \mu^\beta \left(A_1^\beta, B_1^\beta, A_2^\beta, B_2^\beta \right).
$$

Technical structure

The two individuals are assumed to supply, during periods T_1 and T_2, equal given inputs of labor determined by the legal labor duration over which they have no influence. This gives us

$$
\textbf{(14)} \qquad X_1 = 2X, \qquad\qquad X_2 = 2X,
$$

where X_1 and X_2 denote the total labor inputs and X is the legally compulsory labor input.

Goods $\overline{A}$ and $\overline{B}$ are assumed to be produced during the two periods under consideration using labor from the individuals and the services H and K of two indirect goods $\overline{H}$ and $\overline{K}$ in accordance with the production functions

$$
\textbf{(15)} \qquad
\begin{aligned}
\overline{A}_1 &= f(X_1^A, H_1), & \overline{A}_2 &= f(X_2^A, H_2) \\
\overline{B}_1 &= g(X_1^B, K_1), & \overline{B}_2 &= g(X_2^B, K_2),
\end{aligned}
$$

while goods $\overline{H}$ and $\overline{K}$ are themselves produced during period T_1 in accordance with the production functions

$$
\textbf{(16)} \qquad \overline{H}_1 = l(X_1^H), \qquad\qquad \overline{K}_1 = m(X_1^K).
$$

It is assumed as before, for the sake of simplicity,[5] that functions f, g, l, and m are homogeneous and first order.

We assume that at the initial point there exist quantities $\overline{H}_0$ and $\overline{K}_0$ of goods $\overline{H}$ and $\overline{K}$, giving us

(17) $H_1 = \overline{H}_0, \qquad K_1 = \overline{K}_0, \qquad H_2 = \overline{H}_1, \qquad K_2 = \overline{K}_1,$

taking as unit of service the service rendered per unit of good over one period.

Of course, as economic life is assumed to end at point t_2 there is no reason for the production of goods $\overline{H}$ and $\overline{K}$ to continue during period T_2.

(18)
$$X_1^A + X_1^B + X_1^H + X_1^K = 2X,$$
$$X_2^A + X_2^B = 2X.$$

And of course we also have

(19)
$$\begin{array}{ll} A_1^\alpha + A_1^\beta = A_1, & A_2^\alpha + A_2^\beta = A_2, \\ B_1^\alpha + B_1^\beta = B_1, & B_2^\alpha + B_2^\beta = B_2. \end{array}$$

5. No. 176, § "Technical structure."

3. Conditions of competitive equilibrium (220)

I shall be using $x, \bar{a}, \bar{b}, \bar{h}, \bar{k}, a, b, h,$ and k to denote the prices of goods X, $(\bar{A}), (\bar{B}), (\bar{H}), (\bar{K}), (A), (B), (H),$ and (K).

It will be assumed that there is no money and that price levels at points t_1 and t_2 are determined by the given unitary wage levels x_1 and x_2.

Consumption

We shall assume that State action enables the same rate of technical interest I_T to prevail throughout the production sector, but that two different rates of psychological interest, I_α and I_β, apply to the two individuals α and β. This assumes that the two individuals α and β have no options other than State investments and that the State supplies and demands the use of capital at rate I_α for individual α and I_β for individual β.

We shall further assume that the individuals must pay taxes $J_1^\alpha, J_1^\beta, J_2^\alpha$, and J_2^β at points t_1 and t_2. For the sake of broader applicability, it will be assumed that these taxes can have negative values, a negative tax being the payment by the State of a subsidy equal in value to the absolute value of the tax.

Then let us consider, for example, individual α at the end of period T_1; he loans the State the sum of

$$\textbf{(20)} \qquad \Delta_1^\alpha = x_1 X - a_1 A_1^\alpha - b_1 B_1^\alpha - J_1^\alpha.$$

Of course, at point t_2 the State repays him the same principal plus its interest, i.e.,

$$(1+I_\alpha)\Delta_1^\alpha,$$

so that at point t_2 we have

$$\textbf{(21)} \qquad x_2 X + (1+I_\alpha)\Delta_1^\alpha = a_2 A_2^\alpha + b_2 B_2^\alpha + J_2^\alpha.$$

Ultimately, it can be seen that the budget of individual α at point t_2 for the whole of his existence emerges as follows:

$$\textbf{(22)} \qquad x_1 X + \frac{x_2 X}{1+I_\alpha} = a_1 A_1^\alpha + b_1 B_1^\alpha + J_1^\alpha + \frac{a_2 A_2^\alpha}{1+I_\alpha} + \frac{b_2 B_2^\alpha}{1+I_\alpha} + \frac{J_2^\alpha}{1+I_\alpha}.$$

This equation may be substituted for equation (21).

At point t_1, prices a_1, b_1, a_2, b_2, interest rate I_α, and taxes J_1^α and J_2^α comprise his *data*, and he seeks to maximize his satisfaction S_1^α in light of condition (22), so that we have

(23)
$$\frac{\dfrac{\partial S_1^\alpha}{\partial A_1^\alpha}}{a_1} = \frac{\dfrac{\partial S_1^\alpha}{\partial B_1^\alpha}}{b_1} = \frac{\dfrac{\partial S_1^\alpha}{\partial A_2^\alpha}}{\dfrac{a_2}{1+I_\alpha}} = \frac{\dfrac{\partial S_1^\alpha}{\partial B_2^\alpha}}{\dfrac{b_2}{1+I_\alpha}}.$$

The budget of individual α at instant t_2 is no different from equation (21) where quantities $x_2, X, (1+I_\alpha), \Delta_1^\alpha, J_2^\alpha$ and prices a_2 and b_2 comprise his data, and he determines his consumptions A_2^α and B_2^α in such a way that his satisfaction S_2^α shall reach as high a level as possible, giving us

(24)
$$\frac{\dfrac{\partial S_2^\alpha}{\partial A_2^\alpha}}{a_2} = \frac{\dfrac{\partial S_2^\alpha}{\partial B_2^\alpha}}{b_2},$$

but in view of condition (8) this condition is tantamount to the preceding condition (23). So it does not in fact introduce any new condition.[1]

Of course, similar conditions could be written for individual β and in particular we have

(25)
$$x_1 X + \frac{x_2 X}{1+I_\beta} = a_1 A_1^\beta + b_1 B_1^\beta + J_1^\beta + \frac{a_2 A_2^\beta}{1+I_\beta} + \frac{b_2 B_2^\beta}{1+I_\beta} + \frac{J_2^\beta}{1+I_\beta},$$

(26)
$$\frac{\dfrac{\partial S_1^\beta}{\partial A_1^\beta}}{a_1} = \frac{\dfrac{\partial S_1^\beta}{\partial B_1^\beta}}{b_1} = \frac{\dfrac{\partial S_1^\beta}{\partial A_2^\beta}}{\dfrac{a_2}{1+I_\beta}} = \frac{\dfrac{\partial S_1^\beta}{\partial B_2^\beta}}{\dfrac{b_2}{1+I_\beta}},$$

(27)
$$\Delta_1^\beta = x_1 X - a_1 A_1^\beta - b_1 B_1^\beta - J_1^\beta.$$

1. It can thus be seen that if condition (8) was not satisfied, no economic process of perfect foresight would be possible. As such an impossibility is patently inconceivable, we may deduce from it a new proof of condition (8).

Production

When competitive equilibrium prevails, we have

$$\frac{1}{\bar{a}_1} = \frac{\dfrac{\partial f}{\partial X_1^A}}{x_1} = \frac{\dfrac{\partial f}{\partial H_1}}{h_1}, \qquad\qquad \frac{1}{\bar{a}_2} = \frac{\dfrac{\partial f}{\partial X_2^A}}{x_2} = \frac{\dfrac{\partial f}{\partial H_2}}{h_2},$$

(28)
$$\frac{1}{\bar{b}_1} = \frac{\dfrac{\partial g}{\partial X_1^B}}{x_1} = \frac{\dfrac{\partial g}{\partial K_1}}{k_1}, \qquad\qquad \frac{1}{\bar{b}_2} = \frac{\dfrac{\partial g}{\partial X_2^B}}{x_2} = \frac{\dfrac{\partial g}{\partial K_2}}{k_2},$$

$$\frac{1}{\bar{h}_1} = \frac{\dfrac{\partial l}{\partial X_1^H}}{x_1}, \qquad\qquad \frac{1}{\bar{k}_1} = \frac{\dfrac{\partial m}{\partial X_1^K}}{x_1};$$

(29) $\qquad h_2 = (1 + I_T)\bar{h}_1, \qquad\qquad k_2 = (1 + I_T)\bar{k}_1;$

(30) $\qquad a_1 = \bar{a}_1, \qquad b_1 = \bar{b}_1, \qquad a_2 = \bar{a}_2, \qquad b_2 = \bar{b}_2.$

As functions $f, g, l,$ and m are homogeneous and first order, we have[2]

$$\bar{a}_1 A_1 = x_1 X_1^A + h_1 H_1, \qquad\qquad \bar{a}_2 A_2 = x_2 X_2^A + h_2 H_2,$$

(31) $\qquad \bar{b}_1 B_1 = x_1 X_1^B + k_1 K_1, \qquad\qquad \bar{b}_2 B_2 = x_2 X_2^B + k_2 K_2,$

$$\bar{h}_1 H_1 = x_1 X_1^H, \qquad\qquad \bar{k}_1 K_1 = x_1 X_1^K.$$

equations that express that in equilibrium the prices of the various productions are equal to their costs.

2. The homogeneity of the first order of the production functions in fact means that we have

$$f(X_1^A H_1) = X_1^A \frac{\partial f}{\partial X_1^A} + H_1 \frac{\partial f}{\partial H_1}$$

and similar conditions.

Budgets of the State

As the State is assumed to own goods $\overline{H}_0$ and $\overline{K}_0$ and finances the entire machinery of production, its budget at instants t_1 and t_2 is written respectively as

(32)
$$h_1 H_1 + k_1 K_1 + \Delta_1^{\alpha} + \Delta_1^{\beta} + J_1^{\alpha} + J_1^{\beta} = \overline{h}_1 \overline{H}_1 + \overline{k}_1 \overline{K}_1$$

and

(33)
$$h_2 H_2 + k_2 K_2 + J_2^{\alpha} + J_2^{\beta} = (1 + I_{\alpha}) \Delta_1^{\alpha} + (1 + I_{\beta}) \Delta_1^{\beta},$$

but it is easy to see that both of these equations are already implied by the foregoing equations.[3]

3. Thus equation (20) and (27) give

$$\Delta_1^{\alpha} + \Delta_1^{\beta} + J_1^{\alpha} + J_1^{\beta} = 2x_1 X - a_1 A_1 - b_1 B_1,$$

i.e., from equations (18), (30), and (31),

$$\Delta_1^{\alpha} + \Delta_1^{\beta} + J_1^{\alpha} + J_1^{\beta} = x_1 X_1^H + x_1 X_1^K - h_1 H_1 - k_1 K_1 = \overline{h}_1 \overline{H}_1 + \overline{k}_1 \overline{K}_1 - h_1 H_1 - k_1 K_1,$$

in which equation (32) is obtained again.

In the same way, equation (21), which itself results from equations (20) and (22), and the parallel equation for individual β give

$$x_2 X_2 + (1 + I_{\alpha}) \Delta_1^{\alpha} + (1 + I_{\beta}) \Delta_1^{\beta} = a_2 A_2 + b_2 B_2 + J_2^{\alpha} + J_2^{\beta},$$

i.e., from equations (18), (30), and (31),

$$(1 + I_{\alpha}) \Delta_1^{\alpha} + (1 + I_{\beta}) \Delta_1^{\beta} = h_2 H_2 + k_2 K_2 + J_2^{\alpha} + J_2^{\beta},$$

by which equation (33) is obtained again.

Determination of the equilibrium

Finally, it can be seen that for quantities of labor X and price levels x_1 and x_2 assumed to be given, we have 51 parameters[4] linked by 46 conditions.[5] There are therefore five arbitrary parameters that may be taken to be equal to the ratios $\dfrac{J_1^\alpha}{J_1^\beta}$ and $\dfrac{J_2^\alpha}{J_2^\beta}$, which characterize the distribution of taxes and subsidies, i.e., the distribution of income, and to the rates of technical and psychological interest I_T, I_α, and I_β, which may thus be fixed at arbitrary levels.

4. Viz. parameters

$$A_1^\alpha B_1^\alpha A_2^\alpha B_2^\alpha A_1^\beta B_1^\beta A_2^\beta B_2^\beta A_1 B_1 A_2 B_2 \overline{A}_1 \overline{B}_1 \overline{A}_2 \overline{B}_2 H_1 K_1 H_2 K_2 \overline{H}_1 \overline{K}_1,$$
$$a_1 b_1 h_1 k_1 \overline{a}_1 \overline{b}_1 \overline{h}_1 \overline{k}_1 a_2 b_2 h_2 k_2 \overline{a}_2 \overline{b}_2,$$
$$X_1^A X_1^B X_1^H X_1^K X_2^K X_2^A X_2^B J_1^\alpha J_1^\beta J_2^\alpha J_2^\beta \Delta_1^\alpha \Delta_1^\beta,$$
$$I_T I_\alpha I_\beta.$$

5. Conditions (1), (15) to (20), (22), (23), and (25) to (30).

4. Demonstration of generalized social efficiency (221)

Let E be an economic state characterized by *given* values for the following *physical* consumptions and productions

$$A_1^\alpha, B_1^\alpha, A_2^\alpha, B_2^\alpha, A_1^\beta, B_1^\beta, A_2^\beta, B_2^\beta, A_1, B_1, A_2, B_2, \overline{A}_1, \overline{B}_1, \overline{A}_2, \overline{B}_2,$$
$$H_1, K_1, H_2, K_2, \overline{H}_1, \overline{K}_1$$

and assumed to be of maximum generalized social efficiency.

We know that under such conditions a satisfaction S_1^α, for example, must be regarded as maximal when satisfactions S_2^α, S_1^β, and S_2^β are held constant.

Hence the statement that generalized social efficiency is maximal is tantamount to saying that function S_1^α is maximal, in view of the physical constraints

$$S_2^\alpha (A_1^\alpha, B_1^\alpha, A_2^\alpha, B_2^\alpha) = \text{constant},$$

$$S_1^\beta (A_1^\beta, B_1^\beta, A_2^\beta, B_2^\beta) = \text{constant},$$

$$S_2^\beta (A_1^\beta, B_1^\beta, A_2^\beta, B_2^\beta) = \text{constant},$$

$$R_1 \equiv \overline{A}_1 - A_1 = 0, \qquad\qquad R_2 \equiv \overline{B}_1 - B_1 = 0,$$

$$R_3 \equiv \overline{A}_2 - A_2 = 0, \qquad\qquad R_4 \equiv \overline{B}_2 - B_2 = 0,$$

$$R_5 \equiv f(X_1^A H_1) - \overline{A}_1 = 0, \qquad R_6 \equiv g(X_1^B K_1) - \overline{B}_1 = 0,$$

(34) $\quad R_7 \equiv f(X_2^A H_2) - \overline{A}_2 = 0, \qquad R_8 \equiv g(X_2^B K_2) - \overline{B}_2 = 0,$

$$R_9 \equiv l(X_1^H) - \overline{H}_1 = 0, \qquad\quad R_{10} \equiv m(X_1^K) - \overline{K}_1 = 0,$$

$$R_{11} \equiv \overline{H}_0 - H_1 = 0, \qquad\qquad R_{12} \equiv \overline{K}_0 - K_1 = 0,$$

$$R_{13} \equiv \overline{H}_1 - H_2 = 0, \qquad\qquad R_{14} \equiv \overline{K}_1 - K_2 = 0,$$

$$R_{15} \equiv 2X - X_1^A - X_1^B - X_1^H - X_1^K = 0,$$

$$R_{16} \equiv 2X - X_2^A - X_2^B = 0,$$

$$R_{17} \equiv A_1 - A_1^\alpha - A_1^\beta = 0, \qquad\qquad R_{18} \equiv B_1 - B_1^\alpha - B_1^\beta = 0,$$

$$R_{19} \equiv A_2 - A_2^\alpha - A_2^\beta = 0, \qquad\qquad R_{20} \equiv B_2 - B_2^\alpha - B_2^\beta = 0.$$

Under these conditions, according to the theory of constrained maxima, the Lagrange differential

$$s_\alpha \, dS_1^\alpha + \frac{s_\alpha(I_T' - I_\alpha')}{\mu^\alpha(1 + I_\alpha') - \lambda^\alpha(1 + I_T')} \, dS_2^\alpha + s_\beta \, dS_1^\beta$$

$$+ \frac{s_\beta(I_T' - I_\beta')}{\mu^\beta(1 + I_\beta') - \lambda^\beta(1 + I_T')} \, dS_2^\beta + \bar{a}_1' \, dR_1$$

$$+ \bar{b}_1' \, dR_2 + \frac{\bar{a}_2'}{1 + I_T'} \, dR_3 + \frac{\bar{b}_2'}{1 + I_T'} \, dR_4 + \bar{a}_1'' \, dR_5$$

(35) $\qquad + \bar{b}_1'' \, dR_6 + \dfrac{\bar{a}_2''}{1 + I_T'} \, dR_7 + \dfrac{\bar{b}_2''}{1 + I_T'} \, dR_8 + \bar{h}_1' \, dR_9$

$$+ \bar{k}_1' \, dR_{10} + h_1' \, dR_{11} + k_1' \, dR_{12} + \frac{h_2'}{1 + I_T'} \, dR_{13}$$

$$+ \frac{k_2'}{1 + I_T'} \, dR_{14} + x_1' \, dR_{15} + \frac{x_2'}{1 + I_T'} \, dR_{16} + a_1' \, dR_{17}$$

$$+ b_1' \, dR_{18} + \frac{a_2'}{1 + I_T'} \, dR_{19} + \frac{b_2'}{1 + I_T'} \, dR_{20},$$

where the parameters λ^α, μ^α, λ^β, and μ^β have the values yielded by equations (10) to (13) and where the indeterminate coefficients

$$S_\alpha, \frac{s_\alpha(I_T' - I_\alpha')}{\mu^\alpha(1 + I_\alpha') - \lambda^\alpha(1 + I_T')}, S_\beta, \frac{s_\beta(I_T' - I_\beta')}{\mu^\beta(1 + I_\beta') - \lambda^\beta(1 + I_T')}, \bar{a}_1', \bar{b}_1', \frac{\bar{a}_2'}{1 + I_T'}, \frac{\bar{b}_2'}{1 + I_T'},$$

$$\bar{a}_1'', \bar{b}_1'', \frac{\bar{a}_2''}{1 + I_T'}, \frac{\bar{b}_2''}{1 + I_T'}, \bar{h}_1', \bar{k}_1', h_1', k_1', \frac{h_2'}{1 + I_T'}, \frac{k_2'}{1 + I_T'}, x_1', \frac{x_2'}{1 + I_T'},$$

$$a_1', b_1', \frac{a_2'}{1 + I_T'}, \text{ and } \frac{b_2'}{1 + I_T'}$$

known as Lagrange multipliers[1] are regarded as constants, must be uniformly zero, whatever the variations

$$dA_1^\alpha, dB_1^\alpha, dA_2^\alpha, dB_2^\alpha, dA_1^\beta, dB_1^\beta, dA_2^\beta, dB_2^\beta, dA_1, dB_1, dA_2, dB_2, d\overline{A}_1,$$
$$d\overline{B}_1, d\overline{A}_2, d\overline{B}_2, dH_1, dK_1, dH_2, dK_2, d\overline{H}_1, d\overline{K}_1, dX_1^A, dX_1^B, dX_1^H, dX_1^K,$$
$$dX_2^A, dX_2^B$$

of the parameters.

This condition requires the coefficient of each of the variations in the Lagrange differential to be zero, from which, in combination with conditions (10) to (13), we obtain the following conditions:[2]

Variations	Conditions
dA_1^α	$\dfrac{s_\alpha(\mu^\alpha - \lambda^\alpha)(1+I_T')}{\mu^\alpha(1+I_\alpha') - \lambda^\alpha(1+I_T')} \dfrac{\partial S_1^\alpha}{\partial A_1^\alpha} - a_1' = 0;$
dB_1^α	$\dfrac{s_\alpha(\mu^\alpha - \lambda^\alpha)(1+I_T')}{\mu^\alpha(1+I_\alpha') - \lambda^\alpha(1+I_T')} \dfrac{\partial S_1^\alpha}{\partial B_1^\alpha} - b_1' = 0;$
(36) dA_2^α	$\dfrac{s_\alpha(\mu^\alpha - \lambda^\alpha)(1+I_\alpha')}{\mu^\alpha(1+I_\alpha') - \lambda^\alpha(1+I_T')} \dfrac{\partial S_1^\alpha}{\partial A_2^\alpha} - \dfrac{a_2'}{1+I_T'} = 0;$
dB_2^α	$\dfrac{s_\alpha(\mu^\alpha - \lambda^\alpha)(1+I_\alpha')}{\mu^\alpha(1+I_\alpha') - \lambda^\alpha(1+I_T')} \dfrac{\partial S_1^\alpha}{\partial B_2^\alpha} - \dfrac{b_2'}{1+I_T'} = 0;$
dA_1^β	$\dfrac{s_\beta(\mu^\beta - \lambda^\beta)(1+I_T')}{\mu^\beta(1+I_\beta') - \lambda^\beta(1+I_T')} \dfrac{\partial S_1^\beta}{\partial A_1^\beta} - a_1' = 0;$

1. The indeterminate Lagrange multipliers appear in this unconventional form so that the results of the computation may be more readily apparent.

2. The coefficient of dA_1^α has for its expression

$$s_\alpha \frac{\partial S_1^\alpha}{\partial A_1^\alpha} + \frac{s_\alpha(I_T' - I_\alpha')}{\mu^\alpha(1+I_\alpha') - \lambda^\alpha(1+I_T')} \frac{\partial S_2^\alpha}{\partial A_1^\alpha} - a_1',$$

i.e., in view of condition (11),

$$s_\alpha \left[1 + \frac{\mu^\alpha(I_T' - I_\alpha')}{\mu^\alpha(1+I_\alpha') - \lambda^\alpha(1+I_T')}\right] \frac{\partial S_1^\alpha}{\partial A_1^\alpha} - a_1'.$$

$$dB_1^\beta \qquad \frac{s_\beta(\mu^\beta-\lambda^\beta)(1+I'_T)}{\mu^\beta(1+I'_\beta)-\lambda^\beta(1+I'_T)}\frac{\partial S_1^\beta}{\partial B_1^\beta}-b'_1=0;$$

$$dA_2^\beta \qquad \frac{s_\beta(\mu^\beta-\lambda^\beta)(1+I'_\beta)}{\mu^\beta(1+I'_\beta)-\lambda^\beta(1+I'_T)}\frac{\partial S_1^\beta}{\partial A_2^\beta}-\frac{a'_2}{1+I'_T}=0;$$

$$dB_2^\beta \qquad \frac{s_\beta(\mu^\beta-\lambda^\beta)(1+I'_\beta)}{\mu^\beta(1+I'_\beta)-\lambda^\beta(1+I'_T)}\frac{\partial S_1^\beta}{\partial B_2^\beta}-\frac{b'_2}{1+I'_T}=0;$$

Variations	Conditions	Variations	Conditions
dA_1	$-\bar a'_1+a'_1=0;$	dA_2	$-\dfrac{\bar a'_2}{1+I'_T}+\dfrac{a'_2}{1+I'_T}=0;$
dB_1	$-\bar b'_1+b'_1=0;$	dB_2	$-\dfrac{\bar b'_2}{1+I'_T}+\dfrac{b'_2}{1+I'_T}=0;$
$d\bar A_1$	$\bar a'_1-\bar a''_1=0;$	$d\bar A_2$	$\dfrac{\bar a'_2}{1+I'_T}-\dfrac{\bar a''_2}{1+I'_T}=0;$
$d\bar B_1$	$\bar b'_1-\bar b''_1=0;$	$d\bar B_2$	$\dfrac{\bar b'_2}{1+I'_T}-\dfrac{\bar b''_2}{1+I'_T}=0;$
dH_1	$\bar a''_1\dfrac{\partial f}{\partial H_1}-h'_1=0;$	dH_2	$\dfrac{\bar a''_2}{(1+I'_T)}\dfrac{\partial f}{\partial H_2}-\dfrac{h_2}{1+I'_T}=0;$
dK_1	$\bar b''_1\dfrac{\partial g}{\partial K_1}-k'_1=0$	dK_2	$\dfrac{\bar b''_2}{(1+I'_T)}\dfrac{\partial g}{\partial K_2}-\dfrac{k'_2}{1+I'_T}=0$
$d\bar H_1$	$-\bar h'_1+\dfrac{h'_2}{1+I'_T}=0;$	$d\bar K_1$	$-\bar k'_1+\dfrac{k'_2}{1+I'_T}=0;$
dX_1^A	$\bar a''_1\dfrac{\partial f}{\partial X_1^A}-x'_1=0;$	dX_2^A	$\dfrac{\bar a''_2}{(1+I'_T)}\dfrac{\partial f}{\partial X_2^A}-\dfrac{x_2}{1+I'_T}=0;$
dX_1^B	$\bar b''_1\dfrac{\partial g}{\partial X_1^B}-x'_1=0;$	dX_2^B	$\dfrac{\bar b''_2}{(1+I'_T)}\dfrac{\partial g}{\partial X_2^B}-\dfrac{x'_2}{1+I'_T}=0;$
dX_1^H	$\bar h'_1\dfrac{\partial l}{\partial X_1^H}-x'_1=0;$	dX_1^K	$\bar k'_1+\dfrac{\partial m}{\partial X_1^K}-x'_1=0.$

These equations show that there exist coefficients x_1', x_2', a_1', b_1', h_1', k_1', $\bar{a}_1'$, $\bar{b}_1'$, $\bar{h}_1'$, $\bar{k}_1'$, a_2', b_2', h_2', k_2', $\bar{a}_2'$, $\bar{b}_2'$, I_T', I_α', and I_β' such that we have

(37)

$$\frac{\dfrac{\partial S_1^\alpha}{\partial A_1^\alpha}}{a_1'} = \frac{\dfrac{\partial S_1^\alpha}{\partial B_1^\alpha}}{b_1'} = \frac{\dfrac{\partial S_1^\alpha}{\partial A_2^\alpha}}{\dfrac{a_2'}{1+I_\alpha'}} = \frac{\dfrac{\partial S_1^\alpha}{\partial B_2^\alpha}}{\dfrac{b_2'}{1+I_\alpha'}},$$

$$\frac{\dfrac{\partial S_1^\beta}{\partial A_1^\beta}}{a_1'} = \frac{\dfrac{\partial S_1^\beta}{\partial B_1^\beta}}{b_1'} = \frac{\dfrac{\partial S_1^\beta}{\partial A_2^\beta}}{\dfrac{a_2'}{1+I_\beta'}} = \frac{\dfrac{\partial S_1^\beta}{\partial B_2^\beta}}{\dfrac{b_2'}{1+I_\beta'}},$$

$$\frac{1}{\bar{a}_1'} = \frac{\dfrac{\partial f}{\partial X_1^A}}{x_1'} = \frac{\dfrac{\partial f}{\partial H_1}}{h_1'}, \qquad \frac{1}{\bar{a}_2'} = \frac{\dfrac{\partial f}{\partial X_2^A}}{x_2'} = \frac{\dfrac{\partial f}{\partial H_2}}{h_2'},$$

$$\frac{1}{\bar{b}_1'} = \frac{\dfrac{\partial g}{\partial X_1^B}}{x_1'} = \frac{\dfrac{\partial g}{\partial K_1}}{k_1'}, \qquad \frac{1}{\bar{b}_2'} = \frac{\dfrac{\partial g}{\partial X_2^B}}{x_2'} = \frac{\dfrac{\partial g}{\partial K_2}}{k_2'},$$

$$\frac{1}{\bar{h}_1'} = \frac{\dfrac{\partial l}{\partial X_1^H}}{x_1'}, \qquad \frac{1}{\bar{k}_1'} = \frac{\dfrac{\partial m}{\partial X_1^K}}{x_1'},$$

$$h_2' = (1+I_T')\bar{h}_1', \qquad k_2' = (1+I_T')\bar{k}_1',$$

$$a_1' = \bar{a}_1', \qquad b_1' = \bar{b}_1', \qquad a_2' = \bar{a}_2', \qquad b_2' = \bar{b}_2'.$$

Now it is possible to determine parameters

$$(J_1^\alpha)', (J_1^\beta)', (J_2^\alpha)', (J_2^\beta)', (\Delta_1^\alpha)', \text{ and } (\Delta_1^\beta)', \qquad \text{[3]}$$

such as to give us

(38) $$x_1'X + \frac{x_2'X}{1+I_\alpha'} = a_1'A_1^\alpha + b_1'B_1^\alpha + (J_1^\alpha)' + \frac{a_2'A_2^\alpha}{1+I_\alpha'} + \frac{b_2'B_2^\alpha}{1+I_\alpha'} + \frac{(J_2^\alpha)'}{1+I_\alpha'},$$

3. Indeed, it is possible so to define them in a double infinity of ways.

$$(\Delta_1^\alpha)' = x_1'X - a_1'A_1^\alpha - b_1'B_1^\alpha - (J_1^\alpha)',$$

$$x_1'X + \frac{x_2'X}{1+I_\beta'} = a_1'A_1^\beta + b_1'B_1^\beta + (J_1^\beta)' + \frac{a_2'A_2^\beta}{1+I_\beta'} + \frac{b_2'B_2^\beta}{1+I_\beta'} + \frac{(J_2^\beta)'}{1+I_\beta'},$$

$$(\Delta_1^\beta)' = x_1'X - a_1'A_1^\beta - b_1'B_1^\beta - (J_1^\beta)'.$$

It can therefore be seen that if state (E) is considered to display maximum generalized social efficiency, it is possible to determine coefficients

$$x_1', x_2', a_1', b_1', h_1', k_1', \bar{a}_1', \bar{b}_1', \bar{h}_1', \bar{k}_1', a_2', b_2', h_2', k_2', \bar{a}_2', \bar{b}_2', I_T', I_\alpha', I_\beta',$$
$$(J_1^\alpha)', (J_2^\alpha)', (J_1^\beta)', (J_2^\beta)', (\Delta_1^\alpha)', \text{ and } (\Delta_2^\alpha)',$$

such that all the foregoing equations for the competitive equilibrium corresponding to price levels x_1' and x_2', to interest rate levels $I_T', I_\alpha',$ and I_β' and to a tax distribution $\dfrac{(J_1^\alpha)'}{(J_1^\beta)'}$ and $\dfrac{(J_2^\alpha)'}{(J_2^\beta)'}$ are verified.

The foregoing simply assumes that generalized social efficiency is stationary. It could be shown that if it is in fact maximal, the competitive equilibrium thus defined is stable.[4]

It is thus clear that if an economic state E displays maximum social efficiency a stable competitive equilibrium can be made to correspond to it which is *physically* identical to it and in which the technical and psychological interest rates are separated.

By way of corollary, the foregoing analysis shows that the generalized social efficiency of every competitive equilibrium in which the technical and psychological interest rates are separated is stationary, and it could be demonstrated that if this equilibrium is stable its generalized social efficiency is indeed maximal.[4]

Finally, it is confirmed that in the context of the structure studied, the necessary and sufficient condition for the generalized social efficiency of a given economic state to be maximal is that it be possible to make a physically identical competitive equilibrium correspond to it in which there exists throughout the production sector a single rate of technical interest, although there may prevail in the savings sector as many rates of psychological interest as there are individuals, having different technical interest rate levels.

---

4. The relevant argumentation is beyond the scope of the present study. Interested readers may find its fundamentals in my *À la recherche d'une discipline économique*, ch. 4, § E.

This confirms that although the maximization of generalized social efficiency requires a unique rate of technical interest, it does not imply general uniqueness of the technical and psychological interest rates, or even uniqueness of the psychological interest rates considered separately.

Separation of the rates of interest and State intervention in the savings market

It is noteworthy that the rates of interest can be separated only if the State intervenes in the savings market to modify the spontaneous savings level that would otherwise have obtained, and vice versa.

For if we had

(39) $$I_\alpha = I_\beta = I_T = I$$

from equations (14), (29), and (31), this would give us

(40) $$a_1 A_1 + b_1 B_1 = x_1 X_1 + h_1 H_1 + k_1 K_1 - \overline{h}_1 \overline{H}_1 - \overline{k}_1 \overline{K}_1,$$

(41) $$a_2 A_2 + b_2 B_2 = x_2 X_2 + (1 + I)(\overline{h}_1 \overline{H}_1 + \overline{k}_1 \overline{K}_1),$$

equations that are precisely those that would correspond to a competitive equilibrium with private ownership of capital and no State intervention on the savings market. In such an equilibrium the State could intervene, but only to modify the initial distribution between individuals α and β of the value $(h_1 H_1 + k_1 K_1)$ of the capital existing at the start.

This confirms that uniqueness of the rates of interest is equivalent to non-intervention on the part of the State on the savings market, or, if preferred, to intervention the outcome of which changes nothing as to the total savings of the community.

Moreover, it is easy to confirm that if, when single rate conditions prevail *in the market*, State intervention had the effect of raising the community's savings to a value greater than they would have in the absence of intervention, at least one of the spontaneous savings Δ_1^α and Δ_1^β would become zero and the equilibrium equations would no longer be the same. Thus, for a zero value for saving Δ_1^α the three equations numbered (23) would be replaced by the three following:

(42) $$\Delta_1^\alpha = 0,$$

$$(43) \qquad \frac{\dfrac{\partial S_1^\alpha}{\partial A_1^\alpha}}{a_1} = \frac{\dfrac{\partial S_1^\alpha}{\partial B_1^\alpha}}{b_1},$$

$$(44) \qquad \frac{\dfrac{\partial S_1^\alpha}{\partial A_2^\alpha}}{\dfrac{a_2}{1+I}} = \frac{\dfrac{\partial S_1^\alpha}{\partial B_2^\alpha}}{\dfrac{b_2}{1+I}}.$$

and a psychological interest rate I_α different from the market rate *would reappear outside the market.* This is what happens in the case of compulsory savings corresponding to pensions schemes (no. 77). In this case, despite the single market interest rate, the different interest rates are in fact separate.

Finally readers will be able to verify without difficulty that if the only goal were the Pareto-maximization of the S_1 satisfactions without reference to the S_2 satisfactions, the equations obtained would be those of the competitive equilibrium corresponding to unique market interest rates and no State intervention to modify the spontaneous savings equilibrium.[5] They will thus see that maximization of social efficiency in the restricted meaning, i.e., the classical meaning, in fact implies the absence of State intervention (in the above meaning) in the savings market, whereas generalized social efficiency is not incompatible with such action.

<hr />

5. Note that the market's spontaneous equilibrium in the absence of State intervention, while requiring uniqueness of interest rates in the market, does not necessarily imply actual uniqueness of interest rates. This is the case of a given individual when, in light of the market rate, he makes no savings. We are then in the situation of equations (42) to (44). In such a situation, State intervention on the savings market of course leads for this individual to no modification in the conditions of the equilibrium.

Index

Page numbers in italics refer to figures and tables.

abstinence, 8; account-based economy and, 97, 100–102, 152; equilibrium and, 97, 100–102, 152; Fable of the Fishermen and, 46; general theory of interest and, 551; problem of interest and, 446, 448

abstraction, 59n1, 514–17

account-based economy: abstinence and, 97, 100–102, 152; capital and, 77, 80n8, 93–94, 98–99, 127–28; capital market and, 146–55; consumer goods and, 103; disequilibrium dynamics and, 146–55; duration of production process and, 120–21; economic interdependences and, 621, *693*, *694*, *695*, 732, 757; equilibrium and, 89–145; general theory of interest and, 2, 506; hoarding and, 96n11; income distribution and, 93–94, 127–28; indirect processes of production and waiting, 107; investment forecasts and, 119; monetary capital and, 104; money and, 231–32, 305–8, 313n34, 330n19, 352, 370; motives for saving and, 92–99; national production period and, 126–28, *129*, 133, 134n37, *137*, 498n3; primary national capital and, 132–41; primary national income and, 123–29, 133, 136n39, 140; problem of interest and, 469, 472n13, 478n26, 480; production function and, 123n11, 124n16, 125–26, 130; production period and, 107, 120–45, 153; production stages and, 103–6; psychological interest rates and, 98–99, 110n6, 152;

reproducible capital and, 104; savings and, 98–99; social efficiency and, 159, 169; supply and demand and, 89–145; supply of capital and, 90–102; technical interest rate and, 108–15, 116nn1–2, 119, 153

additive reasoning, 510

administrative costs: capital and, 52; general theory of interest and, 19; money and, 257n6, 284, 287, 297; perfect foresight and, 25

agio theory, 444n5, 450–55

À la recherche d'une discipline économique (In quest of an economic discipline) (Allais): equilibrium and, 120n3, 136n39; general theory of interest and, xxvi, 1n2, 3n2, 10n1, 26n3, 37n3, 519n17, 555n9, 569n7; mimeographing of, xxin1; money and, 263n17, 297n27, 308n15, 330nn18–19, 334n29, 335n32, 366n2, 386n4; problem of interest and, 449n6, 496n14; rigor of, xxi; social efficiency and, 156n1, 157n4, 169n1, 170n9; social productivity and, 192n13, 199n36

Allais, Maurice: background of, xx; disequilibrium and, xxvi; economic policy and, xxvii–xxxi; general equilibrium theory and, xxvii; impact of, xix–xxi; multi-agent modeling and, xxii–xxiii; Pareto and, xxiv; social efficiency and, xxiv

"Allais paradox," xxix

Anglo-Saxon school, 6n7, 322, 599n14